SOCIALIST

REGIST

THE SOCIALIST REGISTER

Founded in 1964

EDITORS:
LEO PANITCH
COLIN LEYS

FOUNDING EDITORS
RALPH MILIBAND (1924-1994)
JOHN SAVILLE

Visit our website at:

http://www.yorku.ca/org/socreg/
for a detailed list of all our issues, order forms and an online selection of
past prefaces and essays,

...and join our listserv by contacting
socreg@yorku.ca
for a discussion of the essays from this volume and issues relevant to socialists.

SOCIALIST REGISTER 2003

FIGHTING IDENTITIES:
RACE, RELIGION AND ETHNO-NATIONALISM

Edited by LEO PANITCH and COLIN LEYS

MERLIN PRESS
FERNWOOD PUBLISHING
MONTHLY REVIEW PRESS

First published in 2002
by The Merlin Press Ltd.
PO Box 30705
London
WC2E 8QD

British Library Cataloguing in Publication Data is available from the British Library

Canadian Cataloguing in Publication Data
National Library of Canada Cataloguing in Publication Data
Main entry under title:
Socialist register 2003 : fighting identities : race, religion and ethno-nationalism /
edited by Leo Panitch and Colin Leys.
Includes bibliographical references.
ISBN 1-55266-087-7
1. Ethnic relations–Political aspects. 2. Race relations–Political aspects. 3.
Nationalism. 4. Political violence. 5. Religion and politics. 6. World politics–1989–
I. Panitch, Leo, 1945- II. Leys, Colin, 1931-
HX44.5.S62 2002   320.9'049   C2002-902251-7

ISSN: 0081-0606

Published in Europe by The Merlin Press
0850365 08 2 Paperback
0850365 07 4 Hardback

Published in the USA by Monthly Review Press
1 58367 085 8 Paperback

Published in Canada by Fernwood Publishing
1 55266 087 7 Paperback

Typeset by Jon Carpenter

Printed in the UK by CPI Bookcraft

CONTENTS

PREFACE

We decided to devote this, the 39th volume of the *Socialist Register*, to the theme of 'fighting identities' in mid-2000, a year before September 11, 2001. The volume is thus not about terrorism, or the 'war on terrorism', but it is about the conflicts and contradictions of which the attacks on New York and Washington DC were epiphanic. It is surely clear that the dangerous possibilities that flow from those terrible events can only be averted if the underlying relationships that gave rise to them are first fore-grounded and understood.

The 'fighting identities' we are concerned with reflect two closely linked global realities. One is the dual role of the American state as both the manager of a world capitalist order (a role it alone can play) and as the embodiment of the American national interest – and an all too often chauvinist identity. The other reality is the way particularist and exclusivist identities are so often a response to something universal, i.e. the pain felt by victims of oppression and exploitation everywhere. Even reactionary fundamentalist identities may be seen as distorted and perverse responses of this kind, in the vacuum created by the defeat of rational and progressive alternatives.

It is for these reasons that the volume begins with an essay on 'the American campaign for global sovereignty' by Peter Gowan, based on his 2001 Isaac Deutscher Memorial Lecture. Deutscher himself contributed the lead essay to the first volume of the Register in 1964, and given what we have just said about the nature of today's 'fighting identities', it is worth recalling that in his essay, which was on Mao's Chinese revolution, Deutscher argued that 'ever since the middle of the nineteenth century... China had been seething with anti-imperialism and agrarian revolt; but the movements and secret societies involved in the risings and revolts were all traditional in character and based on ancient religious cults'.

We chose to focus on race, religion, ethnicity and nationalism because they are still at the centre of so many major conflicts at the beginning of the twenty-first century. Our initial aim was to highlight the centrality of race, but like all identities when they are used in political mobilizations, race is almost always linked to others, and especially to religion, ethnicity and nationalism. Unlike the extensive recent literature that discusses the articulation of such identities in the abstract, however, the essays in this volume seek to take race, religion, ethnicity and nationalism seriously by setting them in their widely varying historical and geographical contexts, from the Indian subcontinent to the Middle East, Africa, the former communist countries and, finally, the 'West' – where, in the context of the forced migration of economic and political refugees from these regions, xenophobia fuels right-wing 'identity politics' in Europe, and in the USA over-laps with, and complicates, the unresolved issues of race and racism in working-class politics.

In every case three key themes emerge: a) racial, religious and national iden-tities are anything but epiphenomenal; b) there are historical reasons why these identities have such purchase on the lives of so many people – and for several centuries now these reasons have been more or less closely bound up with the evolution of capitalism; and c) it is therefore necessary to articulate the struggle against capitalism with these 'actually existing' identities.

Intellectuals have a particular responsibility to try to get this right. Race, in particular, has always been implicated in the discourse of the natural sciences. There is a long history of claims that race is genetically imprinted, and these claims have again been at issue in recent research into the human genome: hence the inclusion of a critical review of 'science and race' by Nancy Stepan. The social sciences and humanities have also long been preoccupied with the iden-tities focused on in this volume; in the last decade, in fact, academe has been rife with claims for the primacy of 'identity politics', claims closely associated with a 'post-modern' repudiation of the 'grand narrative' of history as class struggle, which allegedly prioritized the male, western working class as the agent of history, at the expense of the interests of women, people of colour, oppressed nationalities, etc. The need today is, by contrast, to take political identities seri-ously: not seeing them as 'natural', but also not consigning their significance to mere 'difference', disconnected from any historical and materialist analysis. In the wide-ranging essay that concludes this volume John Saul argues that we must support the legitimate aspirations and demands associated with these identities, and that class needs to be integrated with them in ways that will change the terms of class struggle – based on an awareness of the evolving shape of the global capi-talist order, and the strategies needed to challenge it.

Are contemporary left politics equal to this task? Our choice of a cover photo-graph of Zapatista women represents perhaps the most famous contemporary example of a progressive 'fighting identity', an indigenous group which has represented its struggle as being conducted in the name of all oppressed identi-ties, and which has particularly inspired the worldwide anti-globalization movement. Two of the essays included in the volume, however, ask whether that movement, which was the subject of two much-discussed essays by Naomi Klein and André Drainville in *Socialist Register 2002*, has overcome the problem of unifying multiple identities in a single struggle. Amory Starr questions the charge that the North American anti-globalization movement is itself racist, while Stephanie Ross critiques the undemocratic character of a politics that strings together, but does not unify or make accountable, a plurality of diverse oppositional identities. And a third essay focuses on a political practice which anti-globalization activists particularly admire, and which has clearly opened up participation in local government to a wide range of popular interests and iden- tities – the Participatory Budget in Porto Alegre, one of the defining features of the new kind of class politics championed by the Brazilian Workers Party. Sergio Baierle's timely analysis argues that the Participatory Budget now faces a 'Thermidor', and highlights a series of critical problems that will have to be over- come if the principles of the Participatory Budget are to survive and be carried forward into other spheres of government. The prospects for this depend on the kind of sober probing of left strategy and practice that Baierle undertakes, and which most activists who attended the World Social Forum in Porto Allegre in January 2002 have still to do. We are always in greatest danger when the left's theory and practice is divorced from careful, self-critical strategic thinking.

Among our contributors, Peter Gowan is Professor of International Relations at London Metropolitan University. Aziz Al-Azmeh teaches Islamic and Middle East Studies at the American University of Beirut; and Avishai Ehrlich teaches political sociology at Tel Aviv University and at Tel Aviv-Jaffa Academic College. Susan Woodward is Professor of Political Science at the Graduate Center, City University of New York; and Georgi Derluguian teaches sociology at Northwestern University. Pratyush Chandra is a labour activist in New Delhi; and Mahmood Mamdani is Herbert Lehman Professor of Government and Director of the Institute of African Studies at Columbia University, and President of the Council for the Development of Social Research in Dakar. Hugh Roberts is a Senior Research Fellow of the Development Studies Institute at the London School of Economics and Political Science, and currently Visiting Research Scholar in the Department of Political Science, American University in Cairo. Stephen Castles is Director of the Refugee Studies Centre at the University of Oxford; and Hans-Georg Betz is Associate Professor of Political Science at York University, Toronto. Jörg Flecker is scientific director of FORBA, the working life research centre at Vienna, where he also teaches sociology. Huw Beynon is Director of the School of Social Sciences at Cardiff University; and Lou Kushnick is Director of the Ahmed Iqbal Ullah Race Relations Archive at the University of Manchester. Bill Fletcher, Jr. is Executive Director of the Trans-Africa Forum in Washington DC, and Fernando Gapasin is President of a local union in Los Angeles and teaches at the Cesar E. Chavez Center for Interdisciplinary Studies in Chicana/o Studies at UCLA. Amory Starr teaches sociology at Colorado State University; and Stephanie Ross, who has been teaching labour studies at McMaster University, is completing a doctorate at York University, Toronto. Sérgio Baierle is a member of the board of direc- tors of Cidade (Centro de Assessoria e Estudos Urbanos), a Brazilian NGO, an analyst at the Central Bank of Brazil, and teaches history at the Department of

Education of Porto Alegre. Nancy Stepan teaches the history of science and medicine at Columbia University; and John Saul teaches political science at York University, Toronto.

We want to thank all our contributors, while reminding readers that neither they nor the editors necessarily agree with everything in the volume – our usual caveat. We also want to thank Marina Biasutti for her help with the translation of Sergio Baierle's essay, PA Photos for the cover photograph, Louis Mackay for the cover design, and Jan de Jong and the Foundation for Middle East Peace for permission to reproduce the map on page 69. We are especially indebted to Martijn Konings, the Register's editorial assistant at York University, and to Tony Zurbrugg and Adrian Howe at the Merlin Press in London, for their skilled and dedicated work in the production of this volume.

L.P C.L.

July 2002

THE AMERICAN CAMPAIGN FOR GLOBAL SOVEREIGNTY

PETER GOWAN

INTRODUCTION

The main feature of world politics since the collapse of the Soviet Bloc has been the American state's campaign to rebuild and expand the protectorate systems that formed the basis of American global political dominance during the Cold War. This campaign has, of course, been linked to parallel expansionist efforts by the West European states, and partly cooperative and partly conflictual attempts by the Atlantic powers to organize a new global set of political–legal regimes for reorganizing international economic relationships in ways favourable to the international dominance of American and European business. The purpose of this essay is to explore this campaign for a new protectorate system, though it will also make reference to the connection between this project and the other changes being pushed forward in the international political economy.[1]

I: ORIGINS AND EVOLUTION IN THE COLD WAR

When the Soviet system of military alliances and protectorates collapsed at the start of the 1990s, the American system of protectorates did not follow suit. Instead successive US administrations have sought to revivify and enlarge the American-centred systems into a framework for the structural consolidation of American global power in the twenty-first century. Many, particularly within the American security zones, had imagined that the US protectorates existed only as defensive mechanisms against Communism and Soviet power. But the Soviet collapse showed that, at least as far as the American state was concerned, this was not the case. The origins of the US protectorate system lay in the defeats of Germany and Japan and in the US-led alliance systems to 'contain' Eurasian

Communism. But although the protectorate system began as a means for addressing those issues, it became an end in itself for the American state. Indeed, by the 1980s American anti-Sovietism had itself become in large measure a means for preserving and reorganizing the protectorate system itself.

The Origins and Character of the US Protectorate System

The US protectorate system has covered the capitalist core: not only North America, but also the two Eurasian 'rimlands' of Western Europe and East Asia (Japan, Taiwan, South Korea, Australia and New Zealand). Of course, it has extended beyond these zones, but these zones were decisive. It was established in the 1950s as a set of security alliances between the United States and other states under which the US provided external and, to some extent, internal security to the target state, while the latter gave the US the right to establish bases and gain entry for other of its organizations into the jurisdiction of the state. The US was also given effective control over many aspects of the external policies (and some internal policies) of the states concerned.[2]

One important aspect of the system was its 'hub-and-spokes' character which applied also in the West European NATO states: each protectorate's primary military-political relationship had to be with the United States. Attempts by the West European members of NATO, for example, to construct West European caucuses within NATO were slapped down by the United States.[3] This rule against intra-protectorate regional caucusing did not apply to economic politics – hence the institutions of West European integration – but it did apply in military-political affairs.

The protectorate system imposed strict limits on the external orientations of the subordinate states: they could not polarize against the main thrusts of US global policy vis-à-vis the Soviet Bloc and they were expected to respect limits laid down by the United States on their relations with Soviet Bloc countries and Soviet Bloc allies. The US could not only define the enemies of the core. It could also decide when the protectorate zone faced a state of emergency and when it did not: Korea 1950, yes; Hungary 1956, no; Cuba 1962, yes; Czechoslovakia 1968, no; Afghanistan 1979, yes; Poland 1981, yes, and so on.

At the same time, the leadership of the US over its protectorate systems gave it the right to lay down rules for each system without itself being bound by those rules: it claimed the right to invade states deemed hostile, to use covert actions to overthrow governments, to wage proxy wars, mount economic blockades, etc. etc. This right to unilateral action in breach of rules deemed harmful to important US interests applied also in the field of international political economy.[4]

This, then, was a system of US political domination that approached political sovereignty over the way the protectorates related to their external environment in the sense of that term used by Carl Schmitt: sovereign is the power which can define the community's friends and enemies and can thus give the community its social substance (in this case, American-style capitalism); sovereign is the power which can define a state of emergency; and the community's norms apply to the sovereign only in a situation judged normal by the sovereign.[5] Such US political sovereignty over the capitalist core was never total or absolute and at times it was gravely weakened, as during the Vietnam defeat. But it amounted to a qualitatively new type of political order for the core capitalist states.

At the same time, the protectorate system gave the US varying degrees of *direct access* to the *social systems* of the protectorates.[6] US agencies could operate within the protectorate societies to track communist subversion in trade unions, political parties and the media or intelligentsia, and US media and entertainment sectors also gained large openings.[7] And, of course, US firms won wide degrees of access for their exports to and, often, their investments in the protectorates, whose markets were successfully opened by the US during the 1950s.[8]

No less important was the fact that the internal political institutions of the protectorates were harmonized with their external orientations: in those that were liberal democracies the officially acceptable governing parties and mass media organizations were aligned with anti-Communist and anti-Soviet ideology and politics. This gave the US a capacity for mass mobilization on a transnational scale behind its main international political campaigns. Brzezinski has rightly likened this institutionalized anti-Communist political culture to quasi-religious belief systems.[9]

It is very important to note that the protectorate system was never in any sense a juridical empire or principally dependent upon international legal or institutional arrangements. The very fact that it was not, and that states retained their juridical sovereignty as full subjects of international law, was both a key way in which the protectorate system was legitimated *and* a very real source of the ability of the protectorates to continue to be organizing centres of national capitalism.[10]

Coercion and Consent in the Protectorate System

The protectorate system could not, of course, have been established without the coercive occupation of West Germany and Japan at the end of World War II. But at the same time it would be a fundamental mistake to view this system, as it emerged in the 1950s, as the result of coercive diktat produced by US military superiority. The builders of the system – above all Dean Acheson in the last phase of the Truman administration – offered the key states in the system very substantial advantages. The defeated German and Japanese capitalist classes were offered the chance to rebuild their economies as regional capitalist hubs as they had been before 1945, along with re-integration into the state system, though under rather tight US political controls. France and Britain had to accept this US line but were offered other advantages of their own. Britain was allowed to try to hang on to its Empire and given important US support (in the monetary and financial field) for doing so, and was prepared to accept US European dominance in exchange. France and Italy were offered strong support against domestic Communist challenges and France was also offered the role of leading 'European integration' and thus influencing the revival of German capitalism, as well as support in Indo-China. Most of the elites of the dominant classes in these states accepted the US protectorate offers readily and the system remained predominantly consensual during the 1950s and 1960s, apart from the Suez crisis and de Gaulle's withdrawal from the NATO military structure. Serious inter-state tensions pitting groups of protectorates against the US arose only in the 1970s.

And not only did the system offer acceptable national political strategies to the main protectorate states: it was combined with a protectorate-wide political economy regime which offered viable national accumulation strategies to match. At the same time, and very importantly, the protectorate system gained a substantial mass political basis within the protectorates, winning support not only on the centre-right but also within the social democratic movement and large parts of the trade union movements. Gaining and institutionally consolidating this base was partly the result of covert activity in some countries but it was mainly the result of the substantial economic and social gains achieved by labour under the system during the post-war boom. Such gains were undoubtedly an indirect result of the social challenge from Communism after the war. But the American economic paradigm made substantial social concessions to labour viable.

We thus have a paradox: an international political order which qualitatively weakened the foreign policy autonomy of the non-US core states and seriously compromised the internal political autonomy of some of them; but one which at the same time produced widespread consent, either active or passive, amongst a very broad and disparate range of classes in these countries. In this connection, the link between the protectorates' external orientation and the central mechanisms of domestic political domination is particularly noteworthy. The anti-Soviet external orientation proved a very potent mechanism for combating the left internally. The parties of the right, which were the main political mechanisms for confronting working-class movements, were time and again able to use the supposed Soviet threat as their trump card against the left, and by doing so they re-enforced the structure of American dominance. These domestic political structures could also be used by the US against centre-left or centre-right state leaderships on occasion (Willi Brandt 1974, Aldo Moro 1978, etc). The domestic political structure made any kind of direct challenge to US international power difficult to manage domestically: De Gaulle could be considered one, perhaps singular, exception.

Yet the protectorate system also rested upon the American state's coercive military capacities. Indeed this coercive dimension became increasingly important as time passed, and the capitalisms of the protectorates revived and inter-capitalist tensions increased in the 1970s. But these US coercive capacities were exerted on the protectorates *indirectly*: through structuring the state security *environment* of the states concerned, and not at all through threatening the application of US military force against any protectorate. This use of military force to shape the environment of the rest of the core has, indeed, been the secret of American statecraft since 1947. It came into operation once the states concerned had entered a political alliance with the USA against the USSR. Given that political orientation, these states quickly found their entire national military security dependent upon the military political relationship between the USA and the USSR (and/or China). A US-Soviet war, wherever it started, could engulf their region, and if it did it could spell the annihilation of their society. They thus found the security of their state and their population lay entirely outside their own hands.

At times they feared that in a military confrontation with the Soviets the US would allow their annihilation in order to avoid a generalized nuclear war that would destroy the USA. At other times they feared that the USA's brinkmanship might plunge them needlessly into a devastating war. And at yet other times, they feared that the US might strike deals with the enemy which would disadvantage them in some other way. But in all these scenarios the effect of US coercive power on their environment made them cleave to the USA and seek to influence it as their number one priority, and the precondition for influence was that they should be loyal and useful allies.

A second use of US military-political capacity for brigading the protectorates lay in US efforts to gain and maintain control over certain key inputs for the economies of the protectorates, above all oil, but also other strategic minerals. This involved making US political dominance in the Gulf a national security priority of successive US administrations, along with control over sea routes. This was linked to a more general protectorate dependence on the USA's preponderant military influence over the periphery and over the routes to it, for both key economic inputs and for protecting investments and other economic links with the South.

The International Capitalism of the Protectorate System

The protectorate system profoundly altered the character of the capitalist core. In the first place, it ended the possibility of great power wars between core capitalist states. After the Suez debacle, the protectorates' military capacities, still large in world terms, were confined to operations tolerated by the United States. This transformation allowed much more secure exchanges to develop between core capitalisms. And the internal transformation of social relations within the protectorates in the direction of the American 'fordist' system of accumulation opened up the possibility of a vast expansion of their *internal markets*, with the working class not only as the source of expanded surplus value but also as an increasingly important consumption centre for *realizing* surplus value. The centrality of the old imperial patterns of European and Japanese accumulation thus withered.

At the same time, after the war the American state did not try to turn the protectorates into its own capitalist socio-economic empire: it did not make a grab for the key centres of property of the defeated powers or prostrate capitalisms of Europe; and it did not destroy the capacity of other core states to act as *autonomous organizing centres* of capital accumulation. It merely *limited the scope* of this autonomy in Europe, as it sought a range of 'national rights' for its capitals to enter the jurisdictions of European states.[11] The protectorates could still plan and organize their accumulation strategies domestically and internationally.

National systems of accumulation were organized through spinal cords of state-financial sector–industrial systems, with commercial banks (often nationalized) playing a central role as transmission belts. And they could use an array of instruments for projecting their capitals abroad.

Where the US proved sensitive and assertive in the economic field proper was in assuring its own control over the international monetary system and in preserving US dominance in what are usually called 'high tech' fields. That included two areas: first, key military technologies – the US has fiercely defended its own military technological dominance over its protectorate allies; secondly, control of the new leading sector technologies – those of what seem to be the new 'infrastructure' (capital goods) industries of the future. Signs of a Japanese edge in some of these areas in the 1980s, for example, provoked fierce hostility from Washington.[12] Linked to this aim to control the high tech sectors has been a determination to drive the high tech sectors it controls through the whole protectorate system to ensure as far as possible that they do form the basis for the new wave of economic transformation across the core. The protectorate status – political dependence – of the rest of the core ensured that the US had great political leverage for precisely ensuring the dominance of its own capitalism in critical areas.[13]

The US protectorate system as it grew up and consolidated itself during the Cold War was the basis for a new type of dominant global power, qualitatively different from British hegemony in the nineteenth century. The US was not the most powerful among a dispersed set of the core capitalist states: it was political master of a core 'brigaded' by it, and it was this relationship with the rest of the core which gave the US extraordinary global power. The basing arrangements, logistics and intelligence facilities supplied by its protectorates, and the institutionalized political alignments of the protectorates internally as well as externally, gave the US truly gigantic capacities for mobilizing massive political force, both ideational and material.

The Reaganite Turn of the 1980s

The great challenge to this system came with the economic and political crisis of the 1970s. The catastrophic defeat and disintegration of American military power in Vietnam was combined with a fierce competitive crisis between the main centres of the triad – the US, Germany and Japan. The US responded to the crisis with big unilateral moves to favour US capitalism against its competitors, such as destroying the Bretton Woods system and imposing a dollar system on the world. The European states attempted to establish a regional political caucus and the US broke it up; and so on.

The Reagan administration attempted a radical reorganization of socio-economic relations within the core and between it and the countries of the South, using the political structures of the protectorate system. The essence of the Reaganite programme was to encourage an offensive against labour and social rights both in the core and in the periphery, so as to strengthen the rights and power of capital in ways that would simultaneously encourage the revival of

American capitalism. The earlier post-war development models – the social democratic welfare state, the import-substitution models – were all to be scrapped. So too were the social alliances underpinning these models. Capitalist classes were offered the prospect of enriching themselves domestically through this turn, as rentiers cashing in on the privatization or pillage of state assets and as employers cracking down on trade unions, etc. And the restrictions on the international movement of capitalist property – the systems of capital controls – would also be scrapped, giving capital the power to exit from national jurisdictions, thus strengthening further their domestic social power over labour.

At the same time as these old Cold War restrictions on capitalist property rights were dismantled, capitalist states were expected to make major concessions to American capitalism. They were to support a dollar-centred international monetary system in which the US was free to manipulate exchange rates to suit its exclusive national economic strategy; they were to support the dominance of the American financial system internationally, weakening or preferably breaking the old national spinal cords of state-finance-industry linkages driving national capitalisms; and they were to open up their consumer markets, labour markets and assets to American capitals in the key areas where American capitalism was seeking to build its global dominance: finance, other 'service' sectors, electronics, defence industries etc. – the new 'Uruguay Round' agenda pushed by the Reagan administration from 1981 onwards.

This entire Reaganite turn in US national accumulation strategy was driven forward by a powerful international political campaign, which re-articulated anti-Communism. The USSR was no longer so much an expansionist state: it was an evil empire of controls on 'freedom', controls which also existed in 'socialistic' state structures in the West including social-democratic and development state structures. All such arrangements restricted the freedom of markets and crushed free enterprise with crippling taxation and other restrictions such as 'rigid' labour markets and the like.

But at the same time the Reaganite programme also involved strong elements of inter-state coercion on the part of the US against other core states: fierce coercive pressures on Japan using economic statecraft – driving the dollar down against the yen and brutal confrontations on trade issues; threats of theatre nuclear war in Europe, and threats of aggressive trade war there too.

The Reaganite drive was only a partial success within the core protectorate zones. It succeeded in rallying European elites to halt and start reversing the European social democratic model of capitalism; it gained free movement of capital in the core and in the early 1990s it eventually won a deal on the Uruguay Round, not least because of the new prospects for Atlantic capitals to expand outwards into East and South East Asia as well as the periphery through such a deal.

But it was also marked by failures. The American blandishments for a new rentier capitalism fell on deaf ears in East Asian bourgeoisies. And the Japanese responded to US economic warfare by both regionalizing their accumulation strategy and acquiring leverage over US policy through taking large holdings in the US debt market.[14] And Europe's response combined the shift against the social rights of labour with a new and increasingly political West European regionalism combining the Single Market Programme with a Deutschmark zone on the road to monetary union. These arrangements combined the Reaganite (now called 'neoliberal') turn against labour with a defensive shield against the US dollar system of international monetary relations. There were signs of a remarkable regional alliance of European capitalisms around a common capital accumulation strategy which sat uneasily with a political system requiring loyalty to the American centre.

It is worth noting also that the US activation of the protectorate political structure in the Second Cold War produced a shattering of that structure's mass base in Europe. In the late 1980s enormous peace movements swept Western Europe and popular opinion swung over massively towards the Gorbachev leadership of the USSR. The result was that the Bush administration lost control of European politics in 1989-90: the German government, linked to the Soviet government and riding on a huge popular wave in Western Europe, was able to forge German unification and raise the prospect of an entirely new European political system, replacing the protectorate structures altogether.

II: THE US DRIVE TO PRESERVE THE PROTECTORATE SYSTEM AFTER THE SOVIET BLOC COLLAPSE

With the collapse of the Soviet Bloc, the American policy establishment swiftly decided to struggle to preserve its protectorate system. This political decision has driven or strongly conditioned most of the major political conflicts of the last decade, from the Gulf War through the wars in the Western Balkans to the Bush campaign against 'the Axis of Evil'.

The most blunt evidence of the US decision was the (probably officially inspired) leak of the Defence Planning Guidance document of the Pentagon and National Security Council in early 1992.[15] This indicated that maintaining the protectorate system was the US's *most fundamental strategic goal*. It declared that the 'dominant consideration' in US national strategy would be 'to prevent any hostile power from dominating a region whose resources would, under consolidated control, be sufficient to generate global power'. Those regions were specified as Western Europe, East Asia, the territory of the former Soviet Union and Southwest Asia.[16] This could only mean one thing: stamping out autonomous regionalist challenges to the US protectorate system from the West Europeans and from Japanese or Japanese-Chinese regionalist projects. Put positively, the US was striving to preserve its protectorate systems and to expand them in a new global Pax Americana.

At the time of its appearance the document, written by Lewis Libby and Paul Wolfowitz, drew criticism from some Democrats. As Wolfowitz later explained, Senator Biden, Chair of the Senate Foreign Relations Committee, ridiculed the proposed strategy as 'literally a Pax Americana. ... It won't work'. But Wolfowitz adds:

> Just seven years later, many of these same critics seem quite comfortable with the idea of a Pax Americana ....Today the criticism of Pax Americana comes mainly from the isolationist right, from Patrick Buchanan, who complains that 'containment, a defensive strategy, had given way to a breathtakingly ambitious offensive strategy – to 'establish and protect a new order.[17]

And Wolfowitz continues:

> One would like to think that this new consensus – Buchanan apart – reflects a recognition that the United States cannot afford to allow a hostile power to dominate Europe or Asia or the Persian Gulf; that the safest, and in the long run the cheapest, way to prevent this is to preserve the US-led alliances that have been so successful .... But in reality today's consensus is facile and complacent .... Still, one should not look a gift horse in the mouth. There is today a remarkable degree of agreement on a number of central points of foreign policy. No one is lobbying to with-draw troops from Korea, as was the case as recently as the late 1980s. No one is arguing that we should withdraw from Europe. American forces under President Clinton's command have been bombing Iraq with some regularity for months now, without a whimper of opposition in the Congress and barely a mention in the press. Even on ballistic missile defence there is today an emerging consensus that something needs to be done – although no agreement on precisely what.[18]

Wolfowitz's claim in 2000 that his central strategic goal of 1991 became the central goal of the Clinton administration cannot seriously be doubted. Anthony Lake, Clinton's first National Security adviser, also stressed the bipartisan nature of core US strategy, declaring that 'Political leaders may change with elections, but American interests do not'.[19] In his first major keynote speech on US grand strategy Lake stressed that the fundamental 'feature of this era is that we are its dominant power. Those who say otherwise sell America short. ... Around the world, America's power, authority and example provide unparalleled opportu-nities to lead ... our interests and ideals compel us not only to be engaged, but to lead'. (The word 'lead' here is code for protectoratism.) And he continued: 'The successor to a doctrine of containment must be a strategy of enlargement – enlargement of the world's free community of market democracies'.[20]

Lake recognized that in the early 1990s the 'community' of 'market democ-racies' faced two problems: internal tensions over economics; and a so-called 'military problem', which turned out not to be a military problem at all but the following: 'If NATO is to remain an anchor for European and Atlantic stability, as the President believes it must, its members must commit themselves to updating NATO's role in this new era'.[21] In other words the protectorate system had to be revivified.

This theme of strengthening the US alliance systems was a constant in the speeches of the Clinton administration. In 1996 Lake was still stressing 'acts of construction on the core security issues' and by this he meant first and foremost 'to strengthen and broaden our core alliances as we lay the groundwork for peace in the 21st Century'.[22] And in laying this groundwork for tackling problems around the world, these speeches are striking for what they miss out: not a single word about the UN or any force other than US-led alliances with the US, acting, according to Lake, on the following watchwords: 'Diplomacy where we can; force where we must'.[23] Nothing in these core concepts differs one whit from the concepts of Wolfowitz. And the guiding concepts in Clinton's second term were no different, with Madeleine Albright from Brzezinski's kindergarten playing a central role.[24]

The US drive to revivify its protectorate system was, as Lake indicated in the speech quoted above, linked to a second strategic thrust: the drive for 'economic globalization'. This was an aggressive campaign to reshape international and transnational economic relations within the protectorates, and in the ten 'Big Emerging Markets', in line with the perceived interests of US capitalism. In pursuing this second strand of strategy the Clinton administration announced that economics would no longer be separated from politics within the capitalist core: for the USA, economics was now to be treated as a 'national security' issue. As Andrew Bacevich of Johns Hopkins puts it:

> At the very heart of the Clinton administration's approach to strategy is the concept of globalization. As a rationale for the role of the United States in the world, 'Globalization' today has become the functional equivalent of the phrase 'Free World' during the 1950s and 1960s. It contains an important truth, but vastly oversimplifies that truth. It implies mysteries grasped fully only in the most rarefied circles of government. It suggests the existence of obligations to which ordinary people must submit. It is a powerful instrument of persuasion, the rhetorical device of last resort, to which ... there is no counter.[25]

We will consider later what this second strand of strategy has been about.

No one can, of course, doubt the commitment of the Bush Junior administration to pursue more vigorously than ever the maintenance, strengthening and enlargement of the protectorate system. It entered office determined to give a more activist and coercive accent to this drive at both ends of Eurasia as well as in the Middle East. After a shaky start, these goals were given new focus and impetus by September 11, which was quickly understood by the Bush administration as an *opportunity*, an occasion for achieving precisely what they had wanted to achieve all along. Within four days of the attack Colin Powell and Bush were agreeing that it gave the American state an opportunity to recast global relations as a whole.

III: THE SOURCES OF THE PAX AMERICANA DRIVE

Before proceeding to consider the prospects for consolidating the new Pax Americana we must briefly try to assess what its political and/or social basis is: what combination of forces does it really represent?

Demand-led Supply of Global Order

Some realist American international relations theorists have tried to argue that only the coercive power supplied by a 'hegemon' maintains order within the core capitalist states: without the Leviathan's Pax Americana there will be a Hobbesian war of each against all. The Pax is thus an American burden with the US supplying the crucial 'public good' of order and cooperation to the system as a whole. The classic statement of this position was John Mearsheimer's famous essay on Europe, entitled 'Back to the Future',[26] arguing that only continued US dominance can prevent Europe from returning to pre-1914 style rivalries.[27]

Yet this interpretation, though having an important grain of truth in the 1950s, had become false by the 1990s, thanks to the transformation of both European inter-state and transatlantic relations. By then, the real problem was that the collapse of the Soviet Bloc had removed the security undergirding of Europe's protectorate status and the West European states were seriously banding together, overcoming the hub-and-spokes patterns of the Cold War security system. The fear of Wolfowitz and others was precisely that Western Europe was coming together dangerously and threatening to throw off the protectorate controls.

The core capitalist countries do indeed engage in constant rivalries to gain advantage in the struggle for shares in global capital accumulation. But they simultaneously engage in efforts to maintain cooperation to preserve arrange-ments that foster the accumulation interests of all. The idea that intra-core cooperation today depends principally upon protectorate structures policed by an intrusive Leviathan is propagandistic. A particular type of cooperation requires US hegemony, but there are other possible types as well.

American Political Culture

Others detect the source of the US drive for global dominance in the pecu-liarities of American political culture – the messianic strain in it – suggesting that the US is an exceptional (God given?) state with a manifest destiny to transform the world: the naive assumption that Americans have all the answers to all the world's problems and that resistance to American solutions derives from evil sources.[28]

This strand certainly does exist in American political culture. But so do many other strands that contradict these impulses to global activism, and during the 1990s these other strands have evidently been predominant within the American polity. Since 1989, American voters have been extremely reluctant to endorse any global activist agenda to consolidate a new Pax Americana. This has been a constant source of sorrow and frustration among US state elites. *Only since September 11* has the electorate swung over to support global activism and

political assertiveness, and this has been based on the belief that the Bush administration is defending America. The American electorate is not aware that the
Bush team is using their fear of terrorism to implement a quite different project
for a new global Pax Americana of protectorates.

The State Establishment as 'rent seekers'

David Calleo suggests an interest group source for the Pax Americana drive.
He says that 'America's large Cold War military, diplomatic, financial, industrial
and academic establishments naturally favoured a new age of triumphant global
hegemony. But the rest of the country was not necessarily for it'.[29] This fits with
conceptions of a military-industrial complex – industrial groups and the US military along with members of Congress whose constituencies benefit from their
operations.

This complex does of course exist. But so do lots of other 'complexes' whose
bottom lines or 'maximands' are not directly linked to the military budget. Such
groups might be expected to favour a downsizing of Big Military Government
and either allocating tax dollars to other fields or perhaps slashing taxes. At the
very least such a direct interest group explanation would suggest a big battle
within business over the Pax Americana project. Yet that has not been the
pattern: consolidating the Pax has become completely bipartisan and consensual
outside small nationalist-isolationist circles around Buchanan. Calleo's focus on
the various establishments with a direct stake in the Pax does not seem sufficient.
Why have the very broadest coalitions of internationally-oriented US business
backed this grand strategy?

The Relationship between International Politics and Economics

The general answer lies in the fact that the relationship between international
economics and politics is not, in fact, what it is widely supposed to be. There is
not, in fact, an *autonomous* and *general* set of norm-based market rules governing
international economic exchanges. The legal and institutional arrangements
governing international exchanges is extremely extensive but although it is legitimated as governed by clear liberal formulae such as 'multilateralism' and 'free
trade', such terms are pure ideological mystification and the rule networks are in
reality *thickets of policies* saturated in power relations between states. And these
power relations are not at all confined to relationships of economic power: all
kinds of political forces are brought into play by states in the shaping and
reshaping of international economic rules and regimes.

The ideology of globalization is, of course, geared to obliterating this fundamental fact. But nobody with any link to the international economic policy of
the United States could be fooled by such ideology for a minute. In reality, it
'stands to reason' for all sections of US business with international interests that
a political protectorate system must be good for the US if the costs to US business of maintaining it are not cripplingly high.

The Structure of Contemporary US capitalism Depends upon the Protectorate System

But this general argument dovetails with a much more specific one: a consensus within the broad US business class and state policy-making elites that *the real existing structure of US capitalism* depends upon the preservation and extension of the Cold War protectorate systems in the post–Cold War world.[30] A glance at this specific structure of accumulation indicates why:[31]

> ★ the dominance of the dollar rests upon US military-political power. This dollar dominance favours US importers and US exporters. It enables the US to open its markets to imports from the South almost without trade deficit limit, thus ensuring that the US financial sector gains its debt repayments. The same opportunity for huge trade deficits (equivalent to over *1% of world GDP* in 2000) gives the US great leverage over the economies of East and South East Asia to get them to reciprocally open their jurisdictions to US capitals.
>
> ★ the dominance of Wall Street in the financial sector also rests on both dollar dominance and the fact that the US is the world's dominant military power. This gives the US the benefit of huge flows of funds from all over the world into the US financial market and into the satellite London market dominated by US operators. In the year 2000 the IMF's global accounts showed that the world had an export surplus with itself (sic!) of over 180 billion dollars: this represents just one part of the huge capital flight mainly into the US financial market in a single year. This brings down US interest rates, boosting the whole US economy.
>
> ★ the IMF/World Bank system and the UN system operate largely as instruments of US state policy because of the USA's role as the world's dominant military power. These structures bring a whole host of great benefits to US capitalism, creating new proletarians for US businesses, opening a whole range of markets and doing so very heavily through lending non-American money from other core states.
>
> ★ the protectorate structure gives the American state leverage to protect US ascendancy in a whole range of potentially very important areas from high tech/capital goods to energy resources and prices. It would, in principle, be possible for the other core states to launch a new high tech set of sectors on a world scale focused upon, say, new energy conservation and environmental protection industries. Such a strategic move could produce new waves of capital accumulation across the planet. But insofar as that kind of initiative does not fit with the current structure of US capitalism, US dominance over the security systems of other capitalist powers can block such bold initiatives.

If we take all these features together we can see that their loss would transform social relations within the United States. It would involve the US having to tackle its current account deficits, having to tackle its debt problems, and ending a situation where it relies for its own investment upon sucking in finance from the rest of the world. Tackling such problems would bring American capital face to face with its own working population in a confrontation that would almost certainly result in American workers demanding the kinds of welfare protections and social rights that would make up for the impact of the down-sizing of the economic perks of US power.

While interest group pressures, trends in political culture and transnational linkages between capitalist groups across the core all play some part, the current structural relationship between US capitalism and the rest of the world's social systems is surely a critical causal factor behind the broad consensus among US elites for a revival and extension of the protectorate structures.

IV: THE GEOPOLITICAL CHALLENGES FOR A NEW PAX AMERICANA

The Problems for US Grand Strategy

The key military-political problem facing the revived protectorate project lay in Europe. The collapse of the Soviet Union meant that Western Europe was no longer dependent on the US-Soviet military relationship. That freed Western Europe from the underpinnings of protectorate status. It also opened the way for each of the main West European 'spokes' to link up with each other in primary security relationships rather than with the US, creating a West European caucus. The US had to try to re-impose strategic dependency on Europe, re-impose official dominance over military-political issues in Europe and re-impose hub-and-spokes structures. These tasks were far from simple given the fact that Europe might not perceive itself to be remotely threatened either from Russia (especially if its switch to capitalism was combined with strong political and economic linkages with Europe) or from the Middle East. The military-political problem was less acute in East Asia because of the US's ability to play off rivals in the region: China-Japan-South Korea.

The second problem for the US lay in the fact that the whole structure of domestic class political relations within the protectorates tended to re-enforce US hegemony during the Cold War but did not necessarily do so after the Soviet Bloc collapse. During the Cold War, Centre-Right parties fought the Left on the basis of anti-Sovietism and anti-Communism and thus mobilized their domestic social constituencies in ways that fitted in with the overall leadership role of the United States. A large middle-class constituency in the protectorates and their peripheries was thus predisposed to accept US international campaigns articulated through anti-Soviet and anti-Communist themes. With the Soviet collapse, the US lost a powerful undercurrent of transnational socio-political support for its international military-political manoeuvres. US actions violating its own declared rules of international order, which had been tolerated by large transnational constituencies during the cold war, could face serious legitimation problems in the new situation. And this was, indeed, a problem within the USA too until September 11, 2001: there was no readiness on the part of the US electorate to support a sustained global military-political assertion of power by the US state, and this restricted the scope for large-scale US power-plays.

The third general problem for the US lay in the economic field: if the US was trying to rebuild its protectorate system in the context of economic tensions and rivalries within the capitalist core, the erstwhile protectorates could view the attempt to re-establish the protectorate arrangements as part of an attempt to impose new form of exploitative domination over the core. Or to make the same point the other way around, the other core states would desire to throw off protectorate status, or at least to attenuate it, in order to be able to assert themselves more strongly in the field of economic rivalry. In this area of relations the USA was fortunate in facing few acute economic conflicts with Europe, especially once the 'Uruguay round' deal was achieved. Its really big economic target was East and South East Asia where there was a very serious economic problem for the USA: the great economic growth there was occurring in political economies whose assets and markets were very difficult for US capitals to dominate. Clinton's 'globalization' strategy was principally targeted at opening up these economies to US capitals and opening their financial systems to the US. If this problem was not addressed it could lead to another: growing regionalizing tendencies there, with the nightmare scenario lying in China and Japan creating a single regional economic zone. The US thus chose to begin with an aggressive, assertive push to reduce Europe once more to protectorate status, while focusing on the economic problem in East Asia, downplaying the military-political dimension of operations there until after the East Asian crisis of 1997.

The point about US military-political statecraft is fundamental. When the US uses military action it always has political goals. But it is a fundamental error to assume that the main political goals behind the action are concerned with reshaping political relations with the manifest military enemy. Indeed, that part of the political goals may be trivial compared to the way the military action reshapes political relations with protectorate 'allies'. The failure of political analysts to grasp this basic point has often blinded them to what has been going on in contemporary world politics.

Western Eurasia and US Statecraft

The collapse of the Soviet Bloc created one immediate overwhelming political beneficiary: the uniting Federal Republic of Germany. In 1989-90 this caused something close to panic in Washington. The Bush administration toyed with trying to keep the Soviet Bloc in place. There were fears that the Kohl government would go for a German-Soviet redevelopment of East Central Europe – the so-called Herrhausen Plan, although the assassination of Herrhausen (and the attempted assassination of one of the plan's supporters, Lafontaine) led Kohl to abandon the project. There was also the threat of 'Genscherism' – the construction of a pan-European peace and collective security order including the Soviets which would end Washington's political dominance over Europe. But Gorbachev was too focused on the Soviet-US 'partnership' to consolidate this concept, and the Gulf War followed by the Soviet disintegration buried it.

The danger for Germany lay in its West European neighbours ganging up against it in a common front with Washington – the line urged in 1990 by the Thatcher government in Britain. But President Mitterrand took a different course, judging that French power in Europe and internationally could be maximized only as Germany's partner. This choice (challenged by some sectors of French elites) was reinforced by the crucial fact that France and other continental states had already chosen to harmonize their capital accumulation strategies with Germany's through both the construction of a Deutschmark zone and the Single Market programme – the combination forming a neoliberal path: anti-inflation, welfare state downsizing, and restructuring through unemployment. All these elements were combined with a revived political Europeanism. This emergent EU as a *political concert of European capitalisms* was in place when the Soviet Bloc collapsed. (Britain was at this time in limbo and confronting a crisis of national strategy which has really continued throughout the 1990s.) Mitterrand believed that France's role on the UNSC and its military intervention capacity could give it a leading political role as a regional power in alliance with a Germany which led the European concert in the political-economy field. And this approach was necessary for Germany to prevent its European neighbours ganging up against it after unification and to ensure that the East Central European states bordering Germany and Austria were drawn towards Germany (through EU mechanisms of course) in secure ways. For Germany the key to all this was the link with France.

Thus, the Franco-German-led EU concert held together and sought both to strengthen the political dimension of the EU and to project its political (as well as its economic) influence eastwards. Put another way, France, Germany and other EU states *sought to make their political relations with each other at least as important as the relations of each with the United States*. They were moving to replace the Cold War protectorate system of hub-and-spokes subordination to the US with a West European political caucus and to give that a relatively autonomous role in power projection eastwards.

None of this was, of course, remotely motivated by a desire to mount a direct challenge to US economic interests: the EU has continued to be rather accommodating to these. Even more important, the West European capitalist leaderships shared and valued the general, transnational class line of the US international business coalition: 'globalization', downsizing social rights, flexible labour markets, states can't control capital, etc. The European concert only wanted more collectivity, more autonomy, more autonomous political influence eastwards, along with a currency zone and a political definition to match.

But it was, in fact, a very grave threat to the entire US protectorate system for Europe, threatening to wither away NATO and US military-political dominance over Europe. The result is that since 1991 European international politics has been largely dominated by the USA's efforts to reassert its military-political control over Western Eurasia and to reimpose a hub-and-spokes protectorate system, and by West European states' counter-manoeuvres.

We have not the space to survey these battles in detail here. They have been fought out mainly in the Western Balkans.[32] In 1991 the Bush administration thought the EU would split down the middle on the Croatian war. Instead Mitterrand and even Major rallied behind the German position in December 1991. The Bush administration fought back by encouraging the start of the Bosnian war and then by sabotaging the efforts of the EU to lead the process of restoring peace. Finally the French capitulated to the Clinton administration and thus to the idea that the US should lead through NATO on European military-political affairs. The French then sought entry into NATO's military structures on the basis that the European states should be allowed to coordinate their military activities in the Mediterranean and should have a political caucus within NATO. The idea of such a caucus was backed by other West European powers including even the British in 1996. The Clinton administration repudiated such ideas. This led to the Franco-British St Malo declaration involving a direct EU military political role parallel to (though in some kind of relationship with) NATO. The US responded by successfully manoeuvring the West European states into the NATO war against Yugoslavia. The war was very nearly a debacle for NATO and the USA. And immediately after it, the West Europeans feverishly set in place the European Security and Defence Policy involving EU military planning by the general staffs of the West European armed forces and a range of other military-political caucus activities.

In short, ten years of US manoeuvring had not re-imposed the hub-and-spokes protectorate system on Europe. NATO had acquired, in effect a, European caucus, presenting the US with common views on a range of issues. The US response, under Bush Junior, would be to try to sideline NATO as an institutional structure for the War Against Evil, forcing each West European state into a bilateral hub-and-spokes relationship with the US for what the Bush administration hoped would be the new campaigning form of its global protectorate politics.

At the same time, during the 1990s the US achieved what seemed to be one great victory in Europe: it benefited from its Bosnian victory to expand NATO aggressively eastwards towards Russia, thus polarizing Europe versus Russia, notably over the NATO war against Yugoslavia. It simultaneously made NATO the dominant military-political institution of Europe as a whole, excluding Russia. And this exclusion of Russia, turning it potentially hostile, made a future confrontation with it seem possible. This in turn raised the possibility that Europe would once again feel threatened by Russia and thus in need of US military capacity. In short, Europe could return to its Cold War condition of being dependent on the US-Russian strategic relationship.

Or could it? What if Russia remained on the capitalist road, maintained and developed its liberal democratic system and revived economically with a strong political orientation toward Europe (Germany) as against the United States? Paradoxically, German acquiescence in NATO enlargement and in the US war against Yugoslavia could result in a Russian-European linkage. And what political substance could NATO have as an instrument of US power over Europe if Russia could not be 'enemy-ized'?

The US-Russian Relationship

Until 1998 Washington was the dominant influence within Russia and the Clinton administration's policy of a 'strategic partnership with Russian reform' gained victory after victory, successfully urging Yeltsin into confrontation with the Russian parliament in 1993 and working to defeat (through electoral fraud) the still powerful Russian Communist Party. Within this political alliance, the US Treasury established an extremely close linkage with the Chubais clan to do no less than redesign the social relations of Russian economic life and build the new social oligarchy of Russian capitalism, in a close umbilical relationship with US capitalism.[33]

This extraordinary political success not only had devastating effects on the lives of the Russian people and precipitated a collapse in the power of the Russian state: it also enriched Western financial operators with the shift of tens of billions of dollars' worth of property into London and New York. And it was combined with the Clinton administration's ability even to gain the Yeltsin government's acceptance of NATO expansion into Poland in 1997, and to pursue an evidently anti-Russian policy in the Caucasus – a remarkable political achievement.

Yet the Clinton administration proved incapable of following through on these extraordinary triumphs. In the midst of the global financial panic of 1998, the US government was unable to prevent both the collapse of the rouble and the Russian government's repudiation of its government bond debt. The small, economically fragile and pro-Western emergent Russian middle classes faced crippling economic losses. The NATO war against Yugoslavia of 1999 then produced a strong and deep swing of all sections of Russian public opinion against the United States.

Thus, by the time that Bush Junior entered the White House, the US had been unable to find a stable basis for either making itself the key partner of Russia or for polarizing Europe against Russia. Instead, if has found itself in a competition with Europe for Putin's support. Putin's endorsement of Bush's 'war against terrorism' has been combined with a Russian drive to gain effective membership rights within NATO, a bid backed not only by Germany but by a Blair government proposal that would have given Russia membership rights on some areas of NATO policy. The Bush administration blocked this and the May 2002 NATO-Russia agreement still essentially keeps Russia an outsider in European politics. And the Bush administration's attempt to offer Russia a national strategy which would privilege its relationship with the USA remains fraught with difficulties and obstacles in the energy field, in Eastern Europe and over the Caspian.

The East Asian Theatre

It is difficult to exaggerate the stakes in the US battle to reshape political and thus socio-economic relations in East Asia. These societies, in European terms ranging from large in the case of South Korea to huge in the case of others, have the potential to become the central region of the world economy. The task of

US strategy is to prevent China from becoming the centre of a cohesive regional political economy while simultaneously attempting to transform China in ways that will make it structurally dependent upon the USA. All the resources of the American state – economic statecraft, military statecraft and ideological instruments – will be mobilized for this battle in the coming years.

One strand of US strategy must be to foster the internal destabilization of the Chinese state in order to produce a regime change. The terms of China's entry into the WTO may be viewed in this context, particularly the requirement that China open its agricultural market to foreign competition. This could place huge pressure on the Chinese peasantry and generate sharp internal social conflicts. A second thrust will, of course, be directed against China's state enterprises and the working class within them, and a third thrust will involve trying to open China for financial/exchange rate warfare on the model of the hedge fund strikes during the East Asian financial crisis.

At a regional level the US is attempting to push Japan into strong regional competition with China, with Japan doing the work of pulling much of South East Asia away from Chinese influence. But it remains far from clear that the Japanese state will accept these US buck-passing efforts. The possibility of Japanese capitalism developing an increasingly strong linkage with China, and the two states reaching agreements on regional preferential trade arrangements, cannot be ruled out. The Japanese social system is thus drifting in both internal and external gridlock and presents both the US and the region with one enormous question mark. Meanwhile the Chinese government pushes forward its regional integration strategy, gaining strong support not only in ASEAN but also, for example, in South Korea, whose Chaebols, fighting for their existence after the US strikes of 1997, could view links with China as a path to their salvation.

US coercive military pressure on China will supplement these thrusts, pushing the Chinese state towards an arms race which imposes strong budgetary strains on the state, decreasing its room for manoeuvre on the domestic social front. The Bush administration evidently wants to supplement this military pressure with confrontational brinkmanship over Taiwan and North Korea. But for a 'contain China' policy on the part of the US to work, Washington would have to be able to swing not only the rest of East Asia but also Russia and Western Europe behind such a drive. And this remains to be achieved. No one can safely predict what the outcome of these confrontations will be, but they will undoubtedly leave a huge mark on world politics in the first part of the twenty-first century.

The Middle East

Control of the energy belt from the Middle East through to the Caspian is a cardinal task for the construction of a new Pax Americana. In this context it is important to stress that such US military-political control is an exclusivist project: it entails the exclusion of strong West European, Russian or East Asian influence in the region. At the same time US control over the energy belt gives it an enormously powerful lever for resubordinating both Europe and East Asia.

Washington has not, up to now, considered that its control in this region is best secured by resolving the conflicts in the Middle East. Quite the contrary: US ascendancy has been secured on the basis of *manipulating* the Israeli-Palestinian and Israeli-Arab conflicts as well as by manipulating other conflicts within the Arab world. By maintaining and buttressing Israeli power, it has made Israel a threat to other Arab states and has thus been able to act as what might be called a 'hegemonic broker'. Only the US has the military-political capacity to restrain Israel. The West Europeans and others are marginalized. And the US has also been able to act as the guardian state over Saudi Arabia and the Gulf in the face of threats to these states from Iran and Iraq.

But since the mid-1990s its Machiavellianism has led the US into a strategic morass. It was outmanoeuvred by the Iraqi government, was unable to gain an international political base broad enough to launch a new war to crush the Iraqi state, lost control of the Israel-Palestinian conflict, and produced mass popular hatred in the Arab world over its support for Israel and its exterminist blockade of Iraq, involving the killing of hundreds of thousands of women and children. And the political base of the US in Saudi Arabia has been steadily undermined both by these policies and by the Saudi regime's own extremist Wahabi ideology.

Thus by September 11, 2001 US policy in the region was adrift and almost entirely isolated internationally. The Bush administration has been attempting to use September 11 to launch a new military-political offensive to regain a more secure position in the Middle East. To achieve this it has set its sights on a war to overthrow the Baathist regime in Iraq. This is a perilous undertaking: the US risks an explosive upheaval in the region involving uncontrollable conflicts. Such an eventuality could set back the drive for a global Pax Americana in a decisive way. And a US military victory over Iraq would risk sucking the US into protracted manoeuvres within the area to restore stability.

Where the US campaign since September 11 has achieved remarkable break-throughs is in Central Asia and in Georgia. With new bases in Uzbekistan, Tajikistan and Kyrgyzstan, and with the introduction of US military forces in Georgia, the US has dramatically strengthened its efforts to gain predominant influence over the Caspian vis-à-vis Russia and Iran. It has also acquired new bases on China's Western flank, thus greatly strengthening its geostrategic capacity vis-à-vis China. But the costs of these advances may also be heavy: the Bush administration has failed as yet to stabilize a new state in Afghanistan, it faces a dangerously unstable Pakistan and has contributed substantially to the sharpening of tensions between Pakistan and India.

Thus the whole vast region from the Eastern Mediterranean to India and China has become a fluid and explosive zone in which the US is being continually challenged to demonstrate its power, to try to manage inter-state tensions or conflicts and to maintain a whole series of often shaky political regimes allied to US interests. And it has to handle all these problems without risking direct engagement in attempting to control populations on the ground militarily – an operation which risks the US getting bogged down in the type of military–political conflict it cannot win.

V: THE US CAMPAIGN AND CAPITALIST WORLD ORDER

For all the American ideological stress on free market capitalism and 'economic globalization', then, we find that the American state, backed by its business class elites, has been engaged during the 1990s in increasingly feverish and increasingly militaristic geopolitical manoeuvres to reconstruct the inter-state system as a means to anchor the dominance of US capitalism in the twenty-first century. And its preoccupation with re-engineering patterns of inter-state relations clashes with other fundamental realities of contemporary world politics. Two of these realities need stressing: (1) the fact that world politics in the modern world is transnational mass politics as never before, and that consequently the legitimation of power politics matters; (2) the fact that there are urgent objective issues on the agenda of world society which any political force aspiring to global political leadership needs to address.

On all these fronts, the United States is facing one defeat after another. Paradoxically it is the West Europeans who have hit upon a serious set of ideas for managing these problems, but their ideas clash with the US protectorate project.

Mass Politics and American Military Power

Every military thrust or threat by Washington in its geopolitical manoeuvring attracts the political attention of hundreds of millions of people around the world. Movements of opinion and action at a popular level and with a wide geographical reach have now stretched to unprecedented scope; in the last hundred years the problems of maintaining order and control over populations have become very much more complicated, even if the resources of states for managing their populations have also become more sophisticated.

American military power is incapable of directly controlling populations in the countries of the South, never mind anywhere else. The US must rely upon other states to control their populations. And for these states to carry out that task they have to find political bases for doing so, involving the organization of loyalty rather than naked force. But each American campaign throws these mass loyalty structures at a state level into turmoil. Sometimes this turmoil is pro-American, as was the case in much of Western Europe during the Kosovo war. Sometimes it is anti-American, as in the Muslim and Arab worlds over the Bush–Sharon axis against the Palestinians in 2001 and the first quarter of 2002. But each American campaign is legitimated in different ways from the previous one and seeks different kinds of appeals to different global political constituencies. Principles invoked for one campaign are flagrantly contradicted in the next. Time and again, the efforts of states to gain popular support for one US campaign are undermined by the next US campaign.

Thus in the 1990s US geopolitics has rapidly undermined its own global mass base all over the world, and at this level it has sharply diminishing returns. And this affects not only popular attitudes but the state security concerns of many states, given the fact that their state security is centrally concerned with retaining bases of popular loyalty. The mass mobilizations in the Arab world against the Bush-Sharon axis had exactly this effect, shifting the policies of the Arab states, and this in turn threw the Bush campaign against Iraq onto the defensive, at least momentarily. The American use of a war crimes tribunal as a tactic in its Bosnian manoeuvres, and its legitimation of its war against Yugoslavia in 1999 as a 'humanitarian war' for human rights, was used by the West European states to push forward their idea for a International Criminal Court, an initiative viewed by Washington as a threat to its own military statecraft.

The response of US leaders to these 'blow-back' effects, and to the rapid shrinkage of its global mass political base has, under the Bush regime, been to attempt aggressive gestures of defiance. At the same time it increases pressures on the US to lash out with further military thrusts to prove that it is not intimidated by popular hostility.

All the various aspects of the centrality of mass politics come together in the way in which the US has been relating to international institutions, such as the UN Security Council, the international financial institutions, the WTO and bodies such as NATO, as well as a host of international treaty regimes. Time and again it has simply flouted the institutional norms and rules of these bodies in order to impose its will. This undermines the legitimacy not only of the United States but also of these institutions themselves. And given that these institutions are overwhelmingly designed for protecting the interests of the major capitalist states and their economic operators, US policies are tending to conflict with the collective interests of major capitalist centres.

The Transnational Political Agenda and the US Campaign

The US's military-political campaign has also been combined with an increasingly prominent tendency to oppose, weaken or largely ignore a whole range of global political and policy issues of varying degrees of importance or urgency for other states and for transnational social coalitions. It has been systematically undermining or seeking to weaken a whole network of arms control agreements from the Test Ban Treaty to the ABM treaty, conventions on chemical warfare, landmines, small arms and so on. In the field of international monetary and financial relations it has resisted efforts by the other main capitalist states to stabilize the main exchange rates or to reform the financial architecture to reduce the threat posed by large movements of hot money. Despite its own evident gains from the existence of the WTO, it has made little effort to play an international leadership role within that body, using it instead for short-term and often rather narrow domestic constituency interests. And on issues such as the environment, global poverty and debt, as well as AIDS and the fight against racism, the US has been quite incapable of presenting itself as a global leadership force. Instead it has been increasingly inclined to treat international conference diplomacy on these issues with hostility, or as damage limitation exercises.

The only rationale for this approach to international political management would seem to be that US administrations believe that by using their coercive instruments to pull other major states under their influence they can undermine the social forces taking up these kinds of political issues.

The European Concept of Ultra-Imperialist Hegemony and the US Response

Washington has found itself confronting a fairly coherent set of concepts put forward by the West European states for consolidating a new form of Atlantic/OECD hegemony over the populations and states of the world. The big European idea involves using the structural forms of law that have evolved in the capitalist era as the central instrument of a new hegemony.

Capitalist legal forms have had a binary character, involving a division between municipal (domestic) law and international public law. International law recognizes the juridical sovereignty of states. This implies that states cannot be bound by any legal rules which they have not voluntarily accepted through signing and ratifying international treaties or through ratifying their membership of treaty-based international organizations. At the same time, sovereign states are free to design their municipal domestic legal frameworks as they wish. But these legal forms also contain the idea that when a state does subscribe to an international treaty, its obligations under that treaty trump its own municipal law.

It is this rule which the EU states have picked up and have used as a powerful instrument for socio-political engineering within the EU zone itself. In the past states confronted with this rule had typically been very careful to ensure that their adhesion to international treaties would not restrict their domestic freedom of action to redesign municipal law as they wished in line with changing domestic social balances and requirements. But the Treaty of Rome that founded the EEC in 1958 was highly unusual in taking the form of an international treaty whose substance focused heavily on the regulation of domestic socio-economic legal and institutional arrangements. Inter-governmental negotiations by the executives of EEC member states could produce laws about domestic matters which trumped existing domestic law and which could not be overturned by domestic parliaments. For almost thirty years, the EEC member states did not actually make very much use of this mechanism. But in the 1980s, as they turned towards neoliberalism, the member states began to use it very aggressively and in its strongest form – that of new laws with *domestic* application created by inter-governmental treaty revision conferences of the member states: the Single European Act, the Treaty of European Union (Maastricht), Amsterdam and Nice. The substance of this regulatory effort was directed mainly at class relations within each member state in the field of economic and social policy: anchoring neoliberal policy and institutional frameworks and dynamics within each member state in ways that could not be overturned by parliamentary majorities in any of them.

This principle was then offered by the EU states to the US administration in the Uruguay Round: constructing the WTO as a treaty-based regime which would then trump the municipal law of states adhering to the WTO – locking them in, so to speak, to the open door provisions of the WTO on services as well as trade issues, monopoly rents on intellectual property rights, etc. But this mechanism can be extended far more widely and can be used to lock in states and social formations across a whole range of issues for the kinds of open door regimes that favour the penetration of Atlantic capitals. And the mechanism can be extended beyond political economy issues. Indeed, from the start of the 1990s, the EU has used the mechanism to push forward the reorganization of state political institutions with its Human Rights, Democracy and Good Governance diplomacy. Presented as a juridical method, rooted in a set of ethical norms, this form of diplomacy has actually proved a potent form of power politics. When target states resist EU economic policy goals they can be hit by HRDGG diplomacy, while target states compliant with EC economic objectives can be treated gently in the HRDGG field. This diplomacy thus buttresses EU economic imperialism and legitimates the EU domestically, and at the same time can be used to strengthen the juridical systems of target states so as to provide predictable environments for EU capitals. Last but not least it helps the EU overcome the fact that it is not a democratic structure by making itself an instrument for imposing and invigilating democracy elsewhere!

At the same time, the EU backs such diplomatic instruments with an array of instruments of economic statecraft (above all the granting or denial of market access, a ladder of economic sanctions and aid programmes, sponsorship in the IFIs, etc). And for the EU the ultimate sanction could be the military one, in which the US would play a leading role. Of course this repertoire of instruments is efficacious not only as a means of coercively imposing relations of dominance over target states: it also offers ways for the capitalist classes of the target states to strengthen their own domestic positions in various ways. But the power relation is nevertheless crucial, and it enables the metropolitan centres to expel all kinds of internal problems outwards.

This repertoire of instruments is then offered by the EU to the rest of the OECD world as the kernel of a collective world order project, anchoring the dominance of the richest capitalist countries over the globe for the twenty-first century. But for the EU states such a project would have to be based upon collegial global bodies within which the leading capitalist states would haggle over the precise positive law content of the various legal regimes to be imposed upon other countries. And while the social substance of the regimes would be that of a G7 world order, the main West European states want the (American) use of aggressive military force to be under the discipline of the UNSC. They have carefully ensured that the International Criminal Court does not consider aggressive war against sovereign states to be a war crime or a crime against humanity of any sort. Indeed the EU states support aggression against states whose internal arrangements the EU opposes. But they want such aggression to be sanctioned politically by the UNSC.

Thus the West European concept of a new world order would be a potently coercive one directed to transforming domestic jurisdictions, polities and economies throughout the world. But all the coercive instruments would be legitimated by law.

CONCLUSION

For the American state, this EU project is perceived as a major threat to American global dominance. The entire regime offered by the EU is acceptable only as a sub-system above which stands the American eagle untrammelled by the regimes beneath it to which others may be chained. Under Clinton and Bush Junior the US has therefore exerted increasingly intensive efforts to pressurize or even threaten West European security interests to bring the region back to protectorate status.

The conflicts around these issues are now intensifying. As they do so, various parts of the left, both social liberal and socialist, are beginning to draw together to build a new road forward towards a different kind of world order. The anti-capitalist globalization movement has thrown down a very significant challenge to the ultra-imperialist project of West Europe and, with its added super-imperialist twist, of Washington. The intervention of young peace activists challenging Israeli guns and breaking the siege of the Church of the Nativity with food packages was an inspiring demonstration of real political force. The capacity of gigantic state military force to reshape international politics through terrorizing populations is often underestimated by the Left. But the capacity of popular mass movements to resist and defeat such bureaucratic-technological terror is often underestimated by the Right. It seems that this is a lesson which the American state will yet again have to learn, hopefully before it has plunged, by blustering blunder or by design, millions into the horror of further wars.

NOTES

This is a rewritten version of my Deutscher Memorial Lecture in November 2001.

1   On the political economy side of US protectorate relations see the important article by Leo Panitch, 'The New Imperial State', *New Left Review,* 2 (March–April), 2000. See also Peter Gowan, *The Global Gamble,* London: Verso,1999.

2   The classic analysis of this process is Samuel Huntington, 'Transnational Organisations in World Politics', *World Politics,* XXV (April), 1973.

3   Geir Lundestsad, *'Empire' by Integration,* Oxford: Oxford University Press, 1998.

4   The US was never, for example, formally a member of the GATT: the Senate never ratified US adhesion.

5   See Carl Schmitt, *The Concept of the Political,* New Brunswick, N.J.: Rutgers University Press, 1976, and Carl Schmitt, *Political Theology: Four Chapters on the Concept of Sovereignty* (Studies in Contemporary German Social Thought), Cambridge, Mass.: MIT Press, 1985). See also Peter Gowan,

'The Return of Carl Schmitt', *Debatte: Review of Contemporary German Affairs*, 2(1) (Spring), 1994.

6   See Barbara Haskel, 'Access to Society: A Neglected Dimension of Power', *International Organisation*, 34(1) (Winter), 1980.

7   Frances Stonor Saunders, *Who Paid the Piper? The CIA and the Cultural Cold War*, London: Granta Books, 1999.

8   Comparative research on the differentiated extents of US penetration in different protectorate societies still remains to be done but it seems likely that the degrees of penetration varied greatly.

9   Zbigniew Brzezinski, *The Grand Chessboard*, New York: Basic Books, 1997.

10   Failure to appreciate this point and its continued relevance vitiates important parts of the argument in Antonio Negri and Michael Hardt, *Empire*, Cambridge, Mass.: Harvard University Press, 2000.

11   'National Rights' in this context means that US economic operators gain exactly the same legal rights to operate within a national jurisdiction as the national operators within that state.

12   On such concerns see Jeffrey E. Garten, *A Cold Peace: America, Japan, Germany and the Struggle for Supremacy*, New York: Times Books, 1992, and Lester Thurow, *Head to Head: the Coming Economic Battle among Japan, Europe and America*, New York: Wm. Morrow & Co, 1992.

13   As Robert Gilpin has pointed out, West German dependence on US political and military support in the 1960s was crucial in enabling the US to ensure that its businesses were able to establish operations in the Federal Republic in order thereby to become a major force within the European Economic Community (Robert Gilpin, *The Political Economy of International Relations*, Princeton: Princeton University Press,1987).

14   See Miles Kahler, *International Institutions and The Political Economy of Integration*, The Brookings Institution, 1995, and Miles Kahler and Jeffrey Frankel, eds., *Regionalism and Rivalry: Japan and the U.S. in Pacific Asia*, Chicago: University of Chicago Press, 1993.

15   The obvious motive for the leak was to warn the Europeans of the strength of the US will as Washington drove forward its campaign for an independent unitary Bosnia and thus for a Bosnian civil war just after the triumph of German diplomacy in gaining EU backing for an independent Croatia and Slovenia. On these issues see Peter Gowan 'The Western Powers and the Yugoslav Tragedy', *New Left Review* 234 (May-June), 1999. On the general debate in US elite circles on grand strategy after the Cold War and on the dominance of the groups advocating US 'primacy', see Barry R. Posen and Andrew L. Ross, 'Competing Visions for U.S. Grand Strategy', *International Security*, 21(3) (Winter), 1996/97.

16   Paul Wolfowitz, 'Remembering the Future', *The National Interest*, 59 (Spring), 2000.

17   Wolfowitz, 'Remembering the Future'.

18   Ibid.

19 Anthony Lake, 'Laying the Foundation for a Post-Cold War World. National Security in the 21st Century', *Speech to the Chicago Council on Foreign Relations*, 24 May 1996.

20 Anthony Lake 'From Containment to Enlargement', School of Advanced International Studies, Johns Hopkins University, Washington DC, 21 September 1993.

21 Lake 'From Containment to Enlargement'.

22 Ibid.

23 Ibid.

24 As Warren Christopher declared after his retirement, 'by the end of the [first Clinton] term, "should the United States lead?" was no longer a serious question': Warren Christopher, *In the Stream of History: Shaping Foreign Policy for a New Era*, Stanford: Stanford University Press, 1998.

25 Andrew Bacevich, *The National Interest,* 56 (Summer), 1999.

26 John Mearsheimer, 'Back to the Future: Instability in Europe after the Cold War', *International Security*, 15(1) (Summer), 1990.

27 John Harper of the Paul Nitze School of International Studies makes essentially the same point: 'Stripped to its bare essentials, the post–World War II transatlantic relationship has been an American protectorate, invited and to an extent shaped by the Europeans themselves. The protectorate has served a double purpose: promoting peace and harmony among the Europeans as well as counterbalancing Russian power' (John L.Harper, 'Bush and the Europeans', *SAISPHERE,* Paul Nitze School of Advanced International Studies, John Hopkins University, 2001).

28 For a sophisticated culturalist/constructivist interpretation, see David Campbell, *Writing Security: United States Foreign Policy and the Politics of Identity*, Manchester: Manchester University Press, 1998.

29 David Calleo, *Rethinking Europe's Future*, Princeton: Princeton University Press, 2001, p. 176.

30 For an interesting analysis of shifting opinion in US business coalitions see Ronald W. Cox and Daniel Skidmore-Hess, *US Politics and the Global Economy. Corporate Power, Conservative Shift*, Boulder: Lynne Rienner,1999.

31 These issues are treated at greater length in Gowan, *The Global Gamble*, and also in Peter Gowan, 'Explaining the American Boom: The Roles of Globalisation and US Global Power', *New Political Economy*, 6(3), 2001.

32 This was stressed in the famous 1991 national security document written for the Bush administration by Paul Wolfowitz and Lewis Libby. For more on these issues see Peter Gowan, 'The Twisted Road to Kosovo', *Labour Focus on Eastern Europe*, 62, 1999. See also Paul Cornish, *Partnership in Crisis. The US, Europe and the Fall and Rise of NATO*, Royal Institute for International Affairs and Pinter, 1997.

33 Janine Wedel, *Collision and Collusion: The Strange Case of Western Aid to Eastern Europe 1989-1998*, New York: St. Martin's Press, 1998.

POSTMODERN OBSCURANTISM AND 'THE MUSLIM QUESTION'[1]

AZIZ AL-AZMEH

'...ihm doch schien, als ob irgendwo inmitten zwischen den strittigen Unleidlichkeit, zwischen rednerischem Humanismus und analphabetischer Barbarei das gelegen sein müsse, was man als das Menschliche oder Humane ... ansprechen durfte' – Thomas Mann*

'Je voulais, moi, occuper les Français à la gloire ... les mener à la réalité par les mensonges' – Chateaubriand**

Let me start by stating that by the 'Muslim Question' – the name is derived from an analogy with the 'Eastern Question', which bedevilled statesmen of the Great Powers in the nineteenth century, and has several elements in common with it – I mean that bundle of things concerning political Islamism on which minds have been universally concentrated since September 11, 2001: the existence of movements that pursue relentlessly the quest for an unattainable absolute, regarded by them as a divinely-commanded Shangri-La. In other words, it refers to treating a particular inflection of political Islamism, which might be compared to the Anabaptists and other radical Protestant groups in their relation to mainstream Lutheranism, or the Russian Raskolniki in the

---

*   It appeared to him as if, somewhere amidst this contentious incongruity, between chattering humanism and illiterate barbarity, should lie what might express the human or the humane.

** As for me, I wanted the French to be preoccupied with glory, ... to lead them to truth with lies.

seventeenth century relative to Orthdoxy, as characteristic of not just political Islamism generally, but of Islam *tout court*.[2] This is of course a standard mechanism of stereotyping, in which an ethnological fragment is seen as a total ethnological type, much like regarding all Germans as either skinheads or Bavarian rustics, every Hungarian male a melancholy Atilla or Arpad, every US person a cowboy or noble Indian. In order to understand this 'Muslim Question', then, it must be made to stand on its feet rather than on its head, as it does in the common imagination at present, and for this to be done the name 'Islam' must be taken apart, and what it refers to reconstituted.

But how can one conceivably disassociate the constituent elements of an entity which has for years now been reiterating its ubiquity, its exotic vastness, its singularity of pride and prejudice, its massive presence? A presence constantly displaying an elemental force, claiming an authentic atavism, enforcing this claim with a spectacular display of sheer energy and senseless violence – all the while asserting its inevitability as the post-colonial destiny (albeit also the 'original' condition) of an entire host of nations, of territories, almost of entire continents, termed Islamic?

Let me first of all dispose quickly of the easiest of relevant issues, that of the 'war of civilizations', the common cant expressed in Dr. Strangelove scenarios proposed most famously by Professor Huntington – and by his double, Mr. Bin Laden, the two locked in a fevered mutual demonization, unmitigated by the primitive political language of President Bush and much of his constituency: quite simply because civilizations do not go to war. What go to war are societies, armies, institutions. Civilizations are not societies, though some societal forms may in certain instances be symbolically sustained by appeal to fictitious genealogies which might be called civilizations; civilizations are rather hyper-social systems. They are not entities but performative categories, now active, now not. And in any case, speaking of entities, though there are indeed many Muslims in the world and Muslim religious sub-cultures, there is no longer in existence something that might remotely be called an 'Islamic civilization' – like Hellenism and Romanity, this is now no more than a bookish memory, no matter how much its spectral presence might inflame the political imagination of interested parties, partisan (revivalists of all hues: nationalist, populist, subalternist) and hostile alike, in ways some of which will become clear in the following paragraphs.

We have to curb our fascination with the imposing visibility of things Islamic and the political stakes associated with them. Fascination is none other than beholding an object as if it were a marvel, and the spectacle of marvels suspends the normal operation of human understanding. It is precisely this suspension of the understanding for which Paul Valéry was the spokesman: he relished the intoxicating Orient of the mind, this reverie of 'least exact knowledge', this 'disorder of names and imaginable things', in which neither logic nor chronology kept the elements from falling together into 'their natural combinations'.[3] But history, and recent memory, will tell us that the imposing visibility and amplitude of political and social Islamism is a new phenomenon, which dates back a mere thirty or so years, however beguiling it may be to its detractors, its adherents, and its admirers alike. Yet the all-too-human proclivity to short-sightedness colludes with the political perspectives of the moment to project a fragmentary image of the present as the essence of eternity, and to postulate 'Islam' as the trans-historical protoplasm of the life of all Muslims.

A vast culture, and indeed a vast industry of misrecognition, has been put in place, all the more firmly since September 11, as much by advocates of Islamism as by western opinion, expert and inexpert, purporting to find, over and above the complex and multiple histories and present conditions of Muslim peoples, a homogeneous and timeless Islam, construed as a culture beyond society and history, a repository of 'meaning'. This, it is maintained, informs all significant thoughts and actions of real or putative Muslims at all times and places (any contrary evidence being treated as an anomaly). Thus these super-Islamized beings are supposed to create Islamic economies unlike all economies; Islamic political systems with bizarre and irrational principles; Islamic forms of knowledge whose anachronism makes them either charming or repellent, according to taste; Islamic sensibilities of a pronounced distemper; Islamic dress and coiffure; Islamic law as clear, univocal, and barbarous as it is Levitically strict[4] – in short, a total and totalizing culture which overrides the inconvenient complexity of economy, society and history.

Islam thus becomes fully a 'culture' in the most inchoate, yet most comprehensive and determinative of senses: entirely *sui generis*, and in need of recognition on its own terms and in need, too, of empowerment. This Islam becomes impenetrable by anything but its own unreason, utterly exotic, thoroughly exceptional, fully outside, frightfully different – or, alternatively, it becomes an affective subject with prodigious internal coherence. In this construction, the religion of Islam becomes something that at once fully describes and adequately explains peoples, histories and countries.

In everyday discourse such notions take the form of the proposition that, in some way, Muslims have in the past three decades been *returning* to the things that constitute them *essentially*; that they are reverting to type, rejoining their transhistorical nature; and that fundamentalist Islam is a strident and bloody but adequate expression of this inherent nature. Impenetrable by the normal equipment of the human and social sciences, the phenomena Islamica – 'the Muslim Question' since September 11 – thus come to acquire a more than radical exoticism (and I am here using the term 'exoticism' in a fairly rigorous etymological sense). This means that to study them we are supposed to make a special effort of distanciation and estrangement, in the name of achieving a sympathetic understanding: a hermeneutical procedure whereby the observer is spiritually translocated and in a sense trans-substantiated into the recesses of this Muslim other; or whereby the two meet at a conversational site (a 'dialogue of civilizations'), that ethereal in-between so beloved by postmodern anthropologists, and by perplexed politicians and strategists in Non-Governmental Organizations, and increasingly by office-bearers of many states and international organizations, including the United Nations. This largely accounts for the recent tendency towards a radical relativism regarding the study of matters Islamic, under the banner of respect for 'cultural specificity' – which, like other forms of exoticism, I take to be a grid of misrecognition.

I am truly galled by this extraordinary revival of nineteenth century procedures of ethnological classification in the guise of social-scientific innovation, after all the fertile debates on orientalism in the past two decades, and after history and professional ethnography had seriously – albeit unevenly – contested its conceptual equipment. We need to remember that whereas ethnography carries no necessary classificatory agendas or loyalties, ethnology is above all a theory of racial and cultural types, and is in practice never free from an implicit or explicit normative ranking. It is apt at this juncture to indicate an unfortunate by-product of the use now ordinarily made of Edward Said's critique of orientalism. While this use, under the rather grandiose title of post-colonial discourse, tapped a certain libertarian impulse, its excess of zeal – most characteristically in the United States – has led to a *reverse orientalism*.

The late capitalist, postmodern emphasis on self-referentiality and self-representation, the drift towards conceiving difference as incommensurability, the cognitive nihilism associated with postmodernism, the dissolution of objects of ethnographic study into 'voices' – all this, to my mind, leads to rejecting the tools of the historical and social sciences implicitly, even if in most cases inadvertently and unreflectively, in favour of an irrationalist and anti-historicist sympathetic sociology of singularity, and of an instinctivist theory of culture which tends, with its vitalist metaphysics, to collapse knowledge into being by relating it not to cognition, but to recognition, and particularly recognition of the collective self. The result is that what mediates being and representation is life as Will, and that social knowledge, represented as 'culture', becomes but a moment of Being itself. All this is undertaken in the name of giving voice to marginalized subjects and restoring their histories. Such a sociology of meaning, such valorization of 'the voice', degenerates in practice into substituting associative prolixity, self-referentiality, and political posturing for scientific practice. And such advocacy of singularity invariably results in essentializing identity through declaring the irreducibility of difference, and consequently in being limited to uttering unassailable clichés (the recent vogue of the theme of 'memory' is premised in this context on obscuring the fact that collective memory itself has a history).

Thus emerges a vicious circle, in which anti-orientalism leads directly, in its claims for authenticity and singularity, to the re-orientalization of orientals – however much this is denied. And thus arose a traffic in mirror-images between re-orientalizing orientals speaking for authenticity, and orientalizing neo-orientalists, now working with social rather than philological materials, speaking for difference. This takes on particularly deleterious forms in the social sciences, when the claim is made that categories of ostensibly western provenance, like religion and class, are intransitive, incommensurable, entirely collapsible into their origins as if ontologically so fated, and therefore inapplicable to Muslim peoples as either descriptive or explanatory categories.

I will leave this matter for the time being, and will simply propose that this construal of Islam *as a culture* which in itself explains the affairs of Muslim collectivities and over-determines their economies, societies, and non-religious cultures, is the fundamental element in the misrecognition that I am addressing. It has two main protagonists, who provide mirror-images of one another: one is the Islamist revivalist and politician, the other is the western writer or actor who shares the essentialist culturalism of the former, and who elevates an obscurantist discourse on the present, past and future of Muslims to the status of indisputable knowledge: i.e., the all-too-common procedure by which the essentialist reading of the past, present, and future propounded by Islamist political (or otherwise apologetic) discourse is taken as an adequate reading of the past, a diagnosis of the present, and a blueprint for the future of all Muslims.

This reading is, of course, summed up in a number of basic propositions ceaselessly repeated and formulaically reiterated: that the history of Muslims is constituted essentially by religion; that the past two centuries are a story of usurpation and denaturing by 'westernizing elites', unrepresentative of 'civil society'; that the future must be a restoration, with minor adjustments, of a prelapsarian condition of cultural innocence which modernity has not altered, but only held, somewhat ravaged, in abeyance.

But if the 'Muslim Question', if phenomena termed Islamic, or laying claim to this or that interpretation of Islamism, are really to be understood, the first step must be critically to decompose the notion of Islam, and to look at the conditions of its recent emergence: social forces, historical mutations and developments, political conflicts, intellectual and ideological realities, devotional and theological styles and institutions, in addition to local ethnographic detail – it being clearly understood that ethnographic detail is to be regarded for what it is, and not simply as an instance or merely a concrete figure of a pervasive Islamism of life. Without this decomposition, the totalizing category of 'Islam' will continue to perform its phantasmatic role of calling things into being simply by naming them. Once this decomposition has been performed, however, once the reality of history has been disengaged from wanton fancy, we may be able properly to understand what is meant by Islam and by the appeal to this name.

It is useful to begin by considering the *timing* of the extraordinary visibility of what today appears as the 'Muslim Question'. The conjunctural element is crucially important, and the trope of a 'return' to a pristine past cannot be understood without it. I will confine my comments largely to the Arab World. There, Muslim political phenomena developed out of marginal pietistic and proto-fascist youth militias and sporting club movements in the 1920s and 1930s; some in brown shirts, others in grey shirts, mainly active in Egypt, but also in Syria broadly conceived. In the 1950s and 1960s these movements were nurtured and provided with extraordinary financial largesse, mainly by petro-islamic agencies and their obscurantist systems of public education (of which

Mr. Bin Laden and his cavemen are sterling, unalloyed later products). By these means they built cultural, educational, and organizational structures, international as well as local, animated by hostility to Arab nationalism and a conception of Muslim extra-territorialism that corresponded to conditions in countries with sub-national, communal and pre-civic political structures such as Saudi Arabia and Pakistan. This took place, initially, in the context of an international climate dominated by the Truman Doctrine. The policy of containing Communism had a spectacular career, and in the Arab World developed into a policy of countering secular Arab nationalist, socialist and arguably pro-Soviet regimes. Anyone who reads expert works on Arab politics published in the 1950s and 1960s will find very clear statements of the theory of Islam as a bulwark against Communism, and see that the main cultural and ideological theme of the Cold War in the Arab World (and also in Indonesia and Malaysia) was the encouragement of social conservatism and political Islamism. Later, in Afghanistan, this same policy was to have messier, bloodier, and more immediately dramatic effects, well illustrated by Rambo III, American champion of the leonine tribesmen of Afghanistan, initiating the danse macabre of the months following September 11.

Yet these movements had little initial success, especially in the Arab World (though more in South East Asia), and only came conspicuously and strongly to the fore in the mid- and late 1970s, in a specific conjuncture, marked by two elements. The first of these elements was the continuing trend towards minimizing state action in the economy and society, under the impact of new international structural conditions, characterized by deregulation and the ascendancy of finance and complemented by a natural theology of the free market. In social terms, this entailed the break-down of the post-Second-World-War Keynesian consensus, with its emphasis on social and cultural no less than on economic progress. This breakdown led, in the west, to structural unemployment and attendant results, like the rise in the influence of extreme right-wing ideologies, and the counter-racism of various brown European and North American groups, some of which defined themselves as Muslim. And attendant upon these trends was the growing incidence of cult phenomena, with bizarre cosmic beliefs. At the same time, the unremitting structural disorientation and various forms of deracination caused by globalization in some Muslim areas led to a virulent xenophobia as an antidote to anomie and national frustration, and produced nihilistic political phenomena such as the so-called 'Arab Afghans' who, with the support of certain Islamist political forces, pursued an apocalyptic 'war of civilizations', waged against a spectral enemy. And please note here that although I am speaking of a general mood permeating Islamist movements, I will also be speaking of a specific sub-culture within them, represented by Bin Laden, arising from very specific circumstances. Networks that go determinedly about waging a war of civilizations are marked by meta-political rather than political calculation, in which the criteria of efficacy are extra-mundane, even when they are not declared to be eschatological.

In the Arab World as elsewhere in the South, these new global conditions, including 'structural adjustment', have been exacting a very heavy social price, and a breakdown of both the will and the capacity to carry out policies of development. States have been increasingly reduced to pure administration and merely policing the effects of global deregulation. With economic deregulation came also social and cultural deregulation, exemplified by the communalist, anti-state paternalism adopted by western Non-Governmental Organizations and their local analogues, which became not only distributors of aid, but also loci for the production of culturalist knowledge and social practice in the name of Difference – a sort of gentrification of backwardness.

Mass social and economic marginalization in the South also led to results analogous to those in the North. Among these is the strong appeal of the ultra-conservative, hyper-nationalist populism with a chiliastic flavour which we call radical Islamism, or which in India is associated with movements like the RSS (Rashtriya Swayamsevak Sangh). Both political Islam and the RSS – and indeed also the Revisionist Zionism so powerful in Israel today – followed the rhythm of modern world history. They emerged at the same time as Fascism in the 1920s and 1930s under al-Banna, Golwalkar and Jabotinsky, and revived at the time of the retreat of modernism and the spurning and denigration of the Enlightenment in the 1970s and 1980s, and the accompanying revival in the west of conservative ideologies, religious and secular. Political Islam and the RSS both had benign as well as malignant forms, xenophilic as well as xenophobic; both were premised on a culturalist differentialism which has recently become hegemonic, and both speak of that 'cultural specificity' which, towards the end of the twentieth century, came to perform the same conceptual functions as 'race' had performed earlier.[5] Racial, national and religious 'profiling', as practised since September 11, most hysterically in the United States, would be unthinkable without this differentialism.

So much for the singular rhythm of political Islam. But let me add this, before I widen my purview: the Islam of militant Islamism repudiates the lived Islam of its milieu, in its attempt to 'return' to the utopian Islam presumed to have been out there before the Fall, and imagined to be still seething below the surface of falsehood and inauthenticity. This accounts for the extraordinary violence it has always needed to deploy in the quest for authenticity. It constructs an imagined Muslim past, using symbolic materials derived from Muslim canonical and quasi-canonical texts, but cast in ideological moulds common throughout the international history of conservative populism, as well as anti-Enlightenment motifs (along with an aggressive posture of subalternity such movements become, somehow, adorably postmodern). These moulds and motifs use vitalist and fiercely social-Darwinist conceptions of history and of society, a romantic notion of politics as restorative Will and direct action, an organismic conception of culture and of law, all of them reminiscent not of Muhammad and the Koran, but rather of Herder, Savigny and Spengler; of de Bonald, Gobineau and Le Bon; and perhaps most pertinently in present circumstances, of Nechaev, Osinsky and

Morozov. Two of the most influential works of revolutionary Islamism in Arabic and Persian (by Sayyid Qutb and `Ali Shariati) both specifically esteem most enthusiastically the work of Alexis Carrel, a Frenchman who started his highly distinguished medical career in New York, where he developed highly elaborate social-eugenic theories that were crowned with a Nobel Prize, and then went on to become the cultural and scientific oracle of Maréchal Pétain at Vichy. His works are now standard reading material in youth summer camps run by the Front National in France.

Carrel's emphasis on the creative salvational minority, his strictures against cultural and racial degeneration, were of course not as systematic, broad, or sophisticated as those of German thinkers such as Nordau, Klages, Nietzsche and Jünger.[6] But the point is that this notion of degeneration and decadence, sometimes hankering after a precapitalist arcadia, has generic ideological and conceptual affinities with the Islamist critique of contemporary society: both are products of times of considerable commotion and disorientation, and both are anchored in a vitalist conception of society. But whereas the Germans (and Americans like Albert Freeman and Henry Ford) blamed the proletariat and the massification of society and polity for this degeneration, Muslim thinkers like Mawdudi and Qutb blamed what they termed *jahiliyya*, un-islamity pure and simple, or 'Occidentosis' or 'Westtoxification', according to the English translators of the Iranian Magus of authenticity, Jalal Al-i Ahmad.

I might add that all the European figures I have mentioned are of prime importance for political life and thought in modern European history. The fact that they are not so very well-known today, or that they have until recently been relegated to minor positions in textbooks of political and social theory, can only be read as a rather optimistic collective amnesia organized on the part of liberal regimes after the Second World War. The postmodernist adulation of 'difference' is not often enough aware of its own ideological and conceptual provenance.

And to round out the picture I must also add that between Islamists and representatives of European political irrationalism there is also a far more than subliminally elective affinity, regarding the mystique of death and sacrifice as the morbid edges of life, and as antidotes to a vision of decay; and a glorification of blood and fire and steel as direct forms of political action. One might mention here by way of example the similarities between Ernst Jünger's memoir of the First World War, and the notion of *jihad* according to radical Muslims.[7] Just as pertinently, the Russian Narodnovoltsy and certain fringes of European anarchism, particularly in Russia and Spain, might be cited: Morozov's immortalization of the revolutionary, Nechaev's Cathechism; more generally the metaphysical rather than immediately functional status given to the insurrectionary act of terror, the cult of self-sacrifice including death, regardless of by whose hand it might come; the 'absolute present' (Karl Mannheim's term[8]) which sees insurrection as but an immediately present instance of an indistinct eternity.[9] I am not suggesting that Mr. Bin Laden may have heard of Mikhailovsky or Morozov or have read Carl Schmitt, but rather that all of these and many others were possessed by an apocalyptic language of ultimate war and death as the ultimate affirmation of life, and that all of them belong to a modern world in which the distinctiveness of political violence, unlike the Middle Ages, is correlated with the emergence of a notion of 'the people' who might be made to rise up by acts of exemplary violence, in order to precipitate a predetermined outcome.[10] They all belong equally to a modern world, in which it was possible to think of war in vitalist terms as the ultimate manifestation of collective energy, an antidote to decadence and degeneration, and to believe that the world will again rise from the ashes of the *Götzendämmerung* they intend to precipitate.[11] All this is believed and thought with an *amor fati*, in a spirit of Dionysian nihilism, the nihilism of an Absolute Subject in which life and death are seen to be interchangeable and where the latter is indeed proof of the former and the supreme testimony of it; the nihilism of a transcendental Narcissus which in its defiant reversal of degenerate values generates the heady sense of freedom that I believe energized the perpetrators of the acts of September 11 (who also clearly possessed a keen sense of the postmodern mediatic aesthetic of the Absolute Event in real time).

It is however crucial to resist the habit of looking at these acts as being entirely inspired by the promise of a tumescent Paradise, for what we have here is a cult of martyrdom and of war in which self-sacrifice is a rite of passage and an act of intense socialization; and radical Islamic political movements do subject their members to intense re-socialization.[12] It may be recalled that Goebbels declared that war was the most elementary form of love for life,[13] an attitude which to my mind also provides the fundamental affective element in Carl Schmitt's theory of the state. Bin Laden's warning to what he termed Jews and Crusaders that he and his people loved death more than their enemies loved life, belongs to the same trope of militaristic nihilism, and we may try to render this apparently nonsensical fact intelligible in terms of anthropological theories of sacrifice and the feast.[14]

Such analogies as I am drawing may appear to some people as improbable and indeed gross. But they are very suggestive, and the analogy I am making between religious zealotry and romantic anarchism and nihilism, imperfect as its definition might be, is premised on a shared repertoire of vitalist notions that were not available before the era of modernity; or, to put it better, both emerge from the same conditions of possibility, which allows for convergence and comparability. Thus I would also add that radical Islamists use much the same political language and make similar use of archaic political iconography as vitalist romantics everywhere, for all atavism harbours a primitivist aesthetic which appeals to a concrete image of a prelapsarian, arcadian nature that must be restored. This was evident in the Balkans recently, among other places. The penultimate televisual appearance of Mr. Bin Laden took place before a cave, recalling the Cave of Harra`, where Muhammad first received his divine inspiration. All this is not too dissimilar to certain colourful fringe phenomena in the Vienna of Hitler's youth, such as the revaluation of racial purity and of ancient Germanic myths by Guido von

List, who adopted the swastika as the emblem for his Aryan fraternities, and is particularly reminiscent of the 'folkishness' of Georg Schönerer.[15] Likewise Bin Laden and his associates adopted a medievalizing coiffure and manners of dress and holy relics, as well as ways of private behaviour and affected turns of phrase not very unlike the lurid and exhibitionistic culture of bad taste of analogous cult groups, in a sort of dandyism in reverse. They acted according to a notion of authenticity which is analogous to the Hindutva of the communalist Right in India, and they also combined a political mysticism of the kind adopted by the secular Zionist Right with a mild form of the doctrine of divine election, such as that propounded by Jewish fundamentalism.

It is important to note that the rhetoric of authenticity and the trope of return in religio-political revivalism are not the unmediated voice of the natural history of a culture or of a race, but a rather recherché self-representation of a particular social force seeking normative hegemony. It is precisely such a process that people commonly call an *identity*, a word much overused and abused in current public debate. Authenticity, in this perspective, is highly *in*authentic, indeed, a counterfeit identity, for identity is a performative, not an indicative category; it presents, as described by Adorno in another context, a *für-Andere* masquerading as an *an-sich*. This is true of the wholesale invention of vestimentary and intellectual traditions by Islamist movements, and the simultaneous assertion that these correspond to social practice; it is also true of the deification of the Buddha in the atheistic religion of Buddhism, and of the elevation to divine of primacy of Ram by Hindu communalists, in what has been termed the Semitization of Hinduism.

In all these and other cases we witness a *traditionalization* as distinct from traditionalism; we witness the folklorization of classicism, in which elements from the remote past are presumed to constitute the lived present, which often results in a more or less Disneyfied self-parody. One may most appropriately be reminded here of a great anthropologist, little read today, Edward Tyler, who asserted that 'the serious business of ancient society may be seen to sink into the sport of later generations, and its serious belief to linger on in folk tales'.[16] In this way tangible tokens or icons of authenticity are produced, such as a particular manner of dress or of punishment, and thus also are 'virtual' collective memories exhumed from old books and made into elements of populist rhetoric, by asserting them to be actual memories. Through these virtual memories a historical romance is constructed which is then put forward as a utopian social programme, whose purpose is to construct a finalist and definitive Shangri-La where everyone and everything will be authentic, be this called an Islamic state, a thousand-year Reich, life in the Ramrajya according to the Sanskritik dharma, or indeed the arrival of the Messianic age once the perfect red heifer has been genetically engineered by Jewish Ayatollahs in the occupied territories: the perfect red heifer whose presence presages the coming of the millennium, and as a consequences renders legitimate, indeed imperative, the construction of a Jewish temple on the site of the al-Aqsa mosque. Under such conditions, life most often degenerates into performance, the performance of a socially and politically disembodied psychodrama, which may indeed gather social momentum and come to constitute a facet of social reality. But this constructed facet is a measure of the distance between the actual past and its iconographic monumentalization, or bloody memorialization.

I might add that although this primitivism has become standard fare in Islamist movements, the radical primitivism that came to the fore in the figure of Bin Laden goes further, and relentlessly abstracts itself from both its conditions of genesis and its present condition and lodges itself in a perpetual psychodramatic performance, determined by the tropes of extraterritoriality and exile made possible by the social and physical topographies of provincial parts of Saudi Arabia and Yemen, from where many members of al-Qaeda came, and Afghanistan, to which they moved; or indeed by the self-alienation that can be experienced in a country like the United States, or by the multicultural placelessness experienced by people living in the ethnic cantons of various European countries, countries – not unlike the Hasidic cantonement at Borough Park, Brooklyn, for instance, or at Finsbury Park in London, where the Hasidim coexist with an equally insular Muslim community, with whom they cooperate over matters concerning public morals and multicultural educational demands. It is from such conditions that al-Qaeda and the Jewish Defence League recruit their membership.

But not, of course, the suicide bombers active in Palestine in past months. There we witness acts within a very specific political situation, with discernible and specific antagonists, acts perpetrated in a situation of almost absolute national disempowerment. The embryonic structures of Palestinian self determination were being systematically destroyed by acts that go radically counter to all norms except those of a primitive tribalism – the confiscation of land, the destruction of civil service records, of educational and cultural institutions (much as in Sarajevo), of security forces, of medical and health infrastructures, of water and power resources, of houses and entire residential quarters, of businesses and banks; and the physical liquidation of children and the bulk of political cadres. All this according to a savage political doctrine, echoing some of those we have discussed earlier, and eloquently expressed by Ariel Sharon when he stated that it was an 'iron law' of history that 'he who won't kill will be destroyed by others', and 'better a live Judeo-Nazi than a dead saint'.[17]

In the same interview Sharon stated: 'We shall start another war, kill and destroy more and more, until they have had enough. And do you know why it is worth it? Because it seems that this war has made us more unpopular among the so-called civilized nations.' Quite apart from the psychopathological condition underlying the need to be feared rather than admired, this unfinished 'dirty work of Zionism' takes on the aspect of a sub-political, biological, vitalist predation (comparable to the notion of *Lebensraum*). The unspeakably savage (the word is used deliberately, to convey the sub-political and sub-civil character of this political genocide) reduction of politics to war, and of contestation to annihilation, provokes responses in kind, themselves equally captive to the impotence of language and reason. Thus the young woman who exploded herself in Jerusalem on 12 April, 2002, declared on video that she was intending to 'state with her body' what the Arabs had not said with words: in a situation where the means of resistance and of national self-determination have been rendered bereft of politics and transformed into Darwinist predation, a vitalist counterpoint appears eminently purposive. This is particularly reinforced by the ambience of complicity and indifference surrounding the Israeli invasion: the robotic surrealism of US statements, betokening complicit malevolence and diplomatic cover, the aimless and ineffectual pirouetting of Arab countries, and the hesitations of the European Union, politically and morally adrift.

In these circumstances martyrdom becomes not an apocalyptic cult, as with al-Qaeda, but a nationalist act of resistance, akin in its mechanisms and conceptions to Sorel's myth of the national strike. In past months (these lines are being written towards the end of April, 2002), the religious character of the discourse surrounding suicide bombers has gradually receded in favour of (and has become blended with) a more decidedly, and sometimes very distinctive, Palestinian nationalism, not only on the part of suicide bombers belonging to the secular al-Aqsa Brigades (al-Aqsa mosque being a national symbol), but also of bombers belonging to Hamas. This pattern is not too dissimilar to that of the suicide bombers in South Lebanon in the 1990s who belonged to the Communist Party and the Syrian Nationalist Party, and whose actions had more consequential effects.

Having identified and highlighted a very specific and important distinction, I will return to the mainstream of this essay, and state that I conclude from all this that, over and above iconography, there is precious little that is generically distinctive about Muslim fundamentalism, beyond the specific ways in which the tissue of each of its different times and places is given by its various conjunctural and structural elements. The 'return' to 'Islam' is in fact to a place newly created. Its different components are generated from romantic and vitalist ideological elements in the repertoire of universally available political ideas, no matter how much the rhetoric of 'identity' and of authenticity may deny this; they are crafted out of a social material which requires for its understanding not an ethnology of pre-colonial Arcadia but a sociology of structural marginality and of elite competition, a social psychology of middle- and upper-class youthful radicals in situations of normative schizophrenia and structural closure, and last but not least, a sociology of subcultures and cults. In short the understanding of Islamic political phenomena requires the normal equipment of the social and human sciences, not their denial.[18] And let us not forget a new feature that has supervened in the international legal order since the collapse of the Socialist Bloc and forms an extremely important part of this context: the fact that the indeterminate fluidity typical of extra-legal and extra-territorial regimes has given rise to a novel legal norm, the 'power of exception',[19] celebrated in the US and its affiliated states and international organizations as a conjunction of virtue and limitless muscularity, and overdetermined by hegemonic military capacity – rendering previous modes of legality, including notions of national sovereignty, virtually irrelevant. The best examples of this are the embargo against Iraq, and Israeli state-terroristic depradations in the Occupied Territories. In such a situation of normative legal fluidity it is hardly surprising that lawlessness is seen as legitimate: a lawlessness both in international relations and in economies structurally beset by illegal transactions. This requires precise analysis and cannot be understood through moral condemnation.

And contemporary Muslim revivalism is not generically specific. Construing the desired utopia as a re-enactment of supposed origins or beginnings, the trope of return to authentic beginnings, is a constant feature of all religious discourse, and of nationalist and indeed much conservative discourse too. In the Christian religious tradition it is called 'typology': putative origins and the present are understood as 'type' and re-enactment, as beginning and manifestation, original and figure, and Reformation as simple fidelity to origins. Thus many Christian kings were described as a New David and as *typus Christi*, Byzantine emperors were likewise regarded as instances of *Christomimesis*, and their capital was regarded as the New Jerusalem. All this forms a standard component of a broad sweep of *Heilsgeschichte* (salvation history) found in every monotheistic religion. That it also occurs in Islam is entirely unremarkable, and is a matter to be investigated in the context, not of an unreconstructed ethnology of *homo Islamicus*, but of the history of religions, which has much to say about beginnings as types and mythological charters, of stereotypical reproduction, of mythopraxis (in Sahlins' expression), and of the relation of these to ritual.

It may perhaps surprise some readers to be told that Islamism is an offspring of modernity rather than of tradition. But we need to remind ourselves that from the mid-nineteenth century onwards the Arab world, like all parts of the globe, was variously and unevenly incorporated into an international order of ideology and culture, in which circulated discursive forms and ideas which, albeit of western European origin, were to become universal. These ideas were then produced and reproduced locally, becoming rooted in the cultural, legal and educational apparatus of Bonapartist states – that is, states that made it their business to become hegemonic in the cultural and legal spheres. These states were spread throughout the world from the early nineteenth century onwards: by Napoleon himself in Spain, Italy, and Poland; and by others following Napoleon's example, such as the states created in Latin America by Simon Bolívar and his imitators; and the Ottoman Reformed state, which is the one particularly relevant to the Arab World. This was a state of extraordinary innovativeness, which incorporated into its reforms some of the most advanced ideas of the age, such as non-sectarian education, ideas which in their countries of origin were thought to be dangerously avant-garde. The reformed Ottoman state of the mid-nineteenth century was almost a veritable laboratory for Comtean ideas and of positivist social engineering – Comte himself was quite aware of this, and his delight was evident in the open letter to Reshid Pasha that he included at the beginning of the first volume of his *Système de politique positive*. We could even say that the history of the Arab world in the past century and a half is an accelerated history of acculturation, in which major changes occurred very rapidly, much like the cultural history of England in the seventeenth century – including the absorption of irrationalist ideological motifs and concepts.

Among the new cultural forms were the journalistic article, the pamphlet, and evolving forms of the novel, all of which utilized a new form of Arabic, generated in the mid-nineteenth century, which incorporated some syntactic developments, and substantial lexical and stylistic ones. Among the ideas one might cite those of the nation, the economy – which was in any case born as a determinate conceptual field only in the eighteenth century – and of society itself, which in the early nineteenth century superseded the notion of estates: the 'body-social' as an assembly of individuals, that we get most particularly from English philosophy, and the related idea of an abstract assembly of rights that we find in natural right theories. Likewise ideas of progress, of popular will, no less than romantic notions of the organic continuity of history and the homogeneity of society, and many others.

All of these ideas belong to the universal regime of modernity, which in one of its aspects constituted an exclusive repertoire of the conceptual apparatus by means of which peoples world-wide thought and wrote on public affairs – what an influential book on nationalism calls 'modules'.[20] None of them has a precedent in Muslim traditions. And what I wish to insist upon is that what constitutes the specificity of Islamist groups – their appeal to a particular historical experience and its symbols, construed as a foundational myth – is not some explosion of ethnological force long repressed, but a very recherché primitivism, deliberately crafted out of these universal modules of modern ideologies; and that the discourse of inwardness, of authenticity, of particularity, expresses a political sentimentalism, formulated in a language and by means of concepts that are entirely heteronomous.

Sentiments, however – feelings of 'identity' – are not immediately translatable into politics. They must first be sensualized in emblematic or iconographic forms, which act as 'nodes' of ideological interpellation and can then be translated into ideological propositions. The broader current in which religious sentimentalism was thus articulated ideologically was not the work of theologians, but of a group that emerged from the new public educational system. The education system marginalized the public role of the Muslim priestly establishment (and I am not here speaking of the peculiar conditions of Saudi Arabia),[21] and was analogous in its purpose and some of its effects to the role played by the *lycée* system in France and the *Gymnasium* system in Germany. A new class of intellectuals arose, analogous to that which some German scholars, with reference to their own history, refer to (with some dread) as the *Bildungsbürgertum* – or rather, in the case of the Arab world, *Bildungskleinbürgertum* – the stratum of intellectuals fulfilling the historic role of a bourgeoisie, so important in refashioning culture and society alike.[22] It is this same intelligentsia that sustained secular ideologies, in concert with the state. But it was the subaltern components of this intelligentsia that produced Islamism: reformist Islamism at the end of the nineteenth century, and political revivalism at the end of the twentieth. In both cases, it was secularization that led to the defining of religion separately from the social realities in which it had previously been embedded, and giving it the internal homogeneity, coherence and consistency of a total social and political programme.[23]

None of the things I have highlighted is particularly mysterious. The socio-economic conditions, the birth of Islamism in the interstices of universal modernity, the virtual reality of particularity which uses universal modules to construct itself, the multiple causalities that work to produce – amongst some Muslims as well as other social groups – projects of involution and interioriza-tion: all these, and many other collateral matters, are well-documented, and in some instances well studied in published work, and they alone, unlike the post-modern mood, can help us clarify the 'Muslim Question'. What is particularly striking is that there is so much resistance to perceiving the realities of the situ-ation, so much insistence upon misrecognition.

I do not intend all over again to review the debates about orientalism, nor to dwell in the fetid alleyways of collective European memories of historical antag-onisms, clearly but not always articulately evident in Bosnia, Iraq, and Palestine in the last few years. Nor do I wish to mention, except in passing, and by way of reminder, the systematic and fevered demonization, under the title of terrorism, of various Muslim peoples, or the never-ending story of political inter-ests, including those of arms manufacturers.[24]

What I do intend to do is to return to the present point in time, and to try and understand why it is that misrecognition is so passionately willed; to probe the conditions for the attribution of exceptionalism to Muslim peoples, which places them outside historical and sociological understanding and relegates them to ethno-logical folklore; in short, to consider why it is that I – like many others – have to waste so much of everyone's time on matters that ought to be taken for granted.

To a considerable extent this has to do with the social and political organiza-tion of knowledge about Islam in western countries, the production and circulation of this knowledge, its criteria of public validation, and the status of rigorous research as distinct from what is publicly claimed as expertise. It is mani-festly the case that expert knowledge on these matters – institutionally known as orientalism and area studies – is marginal; it has no social authority to arbitrate knowledge on Islam. Members of the public, and persons in positions of authority, seem free to make all manner of whimsical or irresponsible statements and assumptions concerning matters Islamic without serious fear of disgrace or even of definitive correction. There is hardly a body of exact knowledge concerning Islam which is publicly authoritative and self-perpetuating, and this also applies, grosso modo, to the organization of university faculties, in which studies of Islam occupy a marginal and rather slight position (which some scholars of Islam regard as a seraphic blessing). This largely explains not only the mani-fest conceptual backwardness of this field, and its vulnerability to common cant, but also the virtual absence of Islamic materials in the context of other disciplines, including the history of religions.

This marginality is evident in many other ways too: for example, the fact that the substantial though scattered advances in the study of Muslim societies in the past two decades have failed to get into general circulation; that the excellent products of contemporary research published in Arabic are not read, for lack of linguistic competence on the part of western experts as much as because of their contempt for Arabic scholarship; and above all that public primacy is generally given to forms of expression and of discourse that are more essentially ideological, and have wider appeal, than orientalist or area expertise. (This is not new, of course. Perhaps most glaringly, the public authority on matters Islamic in nineteenth century Germany, for instance, was no other than Otto von Ranke. Ranke wrote what was then regarded as the definitive history of the Ottoman and Spanish empires in the sixteenth and seventeenth centuries, in which he paid scant attention to orientalist scholarship or Ottoman sources and preferred to rely instead on Venetian archives.)

At present, such authority is assumed most specifically by mediatic forms of representation and their pre-literate techniques of semiosis, to whose conditions and categories university experts frequently succumb – not necessarily out of dishonesty, but rather because of conceptual vulnerability and disorientation, rendered all the more acute by the constraints of the televisual media. This general situation applies also to books in general public circulation which enjoy a public credibility far exceeding that of more careful research. I would cite as an example here the work of the late Ernest Gellner, which theorizes the demotic notions of Islam in common currency and shares with this demotic notion one of its constitutive features, that of overinterpreting an ethnographic fragment (or, more traditionally, textual fragment) as a total ethnological type. Gellner studied a village in the Moroccan Atlas in the 1950s and concluded that the bird's-eye view from these panoptical heights revealed an apparition, indeed an epiphany, of Islam, in its full integrality as history, society and culture – a view which at once exemplifies it and sums it up. In this totalizing vision the general and the particular correspond absolutely, in the same way that concrete and abstract classifiers are mutually convertible in myth.[25] Thus Islam is fully representative of Muslims, and can indeed be substituted for them.

In short, public discourse on matters Islamic at present is characterized by what we might call *neo-Renanism* – referring to Ernest Renan's famous theories about the congenital incapacity of the Semitic mind to produce science and philosophy, but to excel nevertheless in the realm of poetry – i.e. a discourse based on taxonomic antitheses. We thus have a political neo-Renanism which speaks, among other things, of the essential inappropriateness of democracy for countries characterized as Muslim because democracy goes against the grain of Muslims as Muslims (alternatively we have the proposition propounded in many circles that democracy for such countries would be best achieved if they were to be ruled by groups which most correspond to the authentic nature of these societies, which is Islam). We also have a neo-Renanist pseudo-sociology, which takes the populist declamations of authenticity as accurate descriptions of social reality and which denies the secular realities of Arab life and holds that Arabs are congenitally incapable of secular life, and calls for a 'revival' through a 'return' to the past. This discourse has as its leitmotif a culturalist ethnology which supposes 'cultural meaning', including the trope of return, to be determinant both of action and the interpretation of action. This is a matter to which I have given considerable thought, and I have concluded not only that culturalism uses the same figures and tropes that were previously employed in racialist discourses, but that like racialism it operates in a rather simple manner, which consists of selecting visible tokens of ethnographic distinctiveness, such as skin colour, a certain mode of dress, or certain propositions concerning the organization of gender relations, and then proceeding to give these the status of iconic markers or stigmata of otherness – or of inwardness – as nodes of ideological interpellation, as I indicated earlier. These are finally served up as totalizing criteria of ethnological classification, constituting Muslims by analogy with ethnotypes, or what older American anthropology referred to as 'patterns of culture'. This is like regarding Lederhosen and skinheads as the iconic markers of Germanity, or cowboys and mobsters as markers of the North American identity, corresponding to the inner nature and constituting the cultural genetic capital of these societies, and then proceeding to construct an ethnic type based on the associations of these images.

Clearly, this procedure has all the characteristics of polemical rather than scientific discourse, notwithstanding copious footnotes. It would be highly instructive to compare the narrative features of this commonplace discourse on Islam with the tropes of polemical discourse generally, including anti-Masonic, anti-Arab, anti-Communist, anti-Semitic, and other forms of propaganda based on antagonism. One might well compare, for example, in terms of structure, imagery, and argumentation, Muslim history conceived in this fashion with left-wing histories of the Society of Jesus written in nineteenth-century France, in which the record of Jesuit history was read as a symptomatology of the Jesuit spirit, and in which links between events were seen as having mythical rather than causal significance.[26] All polemical discourse, like religious discourse, is typological: a history of beginnings and re-enactments, in which change is illusory and where every particular is a mere illustration of the dark general, and in which the primacy of mythical signification is undisputed.

Yet in the recent past all this has been expressed in terms of a disarming condition of innocence, often represented as a postmodern concern for diversity, individuality, the empowerment of the marginal, and a whole host of other propositions on which there is a convergence between xenophobes and liberals, third world communalists and fundamentalists, all of whom adopt the rhetoric of diversity, of difference, of particularity – a rhetoric which conflates the banal realities of diversity and particularity with analytic categories of culturalist and ethnographic classification. All in all, the kitsch and the spectacular are taken for the authentic and invariant, and this procedure is often freely encouraged not only by spokesmen for authenticity, but also by various other native informants, some of them professional, who play to an eager gallery – although this is not often noticed by anthropologists, journalists, and other experts.[27]

This postmodernist delight in the premodernity of others is all the rage; what really underlies it is a vigorous and triumphalist postmodernism, premised on post-Communism, and bereft of the normative, aesthetic and cognitive attributes of modernism. It is hence captive to the relativistic drift inherent in the use, by history and sociology, of the metaphor of the organism to describe identities as absolute subjects – which is, to repeat, a standard component of European irrationalism and political romanticism.

It is therefore particularly disturbing to me that Gellner – and I refer to him specifically because he captured with particular eloquence and limpidity, and in an increasingly firm demotic mood, things that others prefer to state more guardedly, and carried them with authority, and considerable ideological fervour, beyond the field of area studies into general circulation – it disturbs me particularly that Gellner, the anti-relativist par excellence, should state that 'in Islam, it is all different'[28] (which once again reminds me of an anti-Jesuit polemic of 1880, by a forgotten novelist, Jules Durantin, who wrote: '[e]verything progresses, except the Company of Jesus').[29] Gellner liberates himself from the burden of proof – but equally, and most saliently, he liberates himself from the discipline of his trade of sociologist, anthropologist, and theorist of history. He proceeds to state and restate an entire interpretation of Muslim histories and of present-day Islam, which he reduces to an invariant model, supposedly emanating from his rustic observatory in the Atlas Mountains, whose schematism is breathtakingly peremptory, and empirical objections to which he simply ignores. Briefly stated, his notorious 'pendulum-swing' theory of Islam postulates two forms of religiosity, the enthusiastic-rural and the puritanical-urban, in a primordial conflict and cyclical alternation which fundamentally constitutes Muslim history – so fundamentally, indeed, that the present condition of the Muslims can be conceived in no other terms, and can have no other outcome than the triumph of urban puritanism. Correlative with this religious characterization of a history reduced to religious culture is the proposition that for Muslims modernism is inconceivable in any terms but those of the puritanical version of Muslim doctrine and its corollaries.

Gellner's Moroccan village is an ethnological fragment construed in terms of an ethnological theory which he read into the work of, first, David Hume and, second, of Ibn Khaldûn (whom he had to read in the poor standard English translation), who in turn based his own theories on a particular reading of the history of North African Muslim dynasties; in fact, Ibn Khaldûn is less a guide to the interpretation of North African history than himself a Maghribi phenomenon, in need of historical interpretation. Yet this theoretical genealogy appears largely fictitious when one looks at the actual origins of this theory in French colonialist historiography of North Africa, which had a substantial input from the deterministic German social geography of Ratzel, and which is best exemplified in the work of Emile-Félix Gautier and Robert Montagne[30] – the latter is much praised by Gellner overall. And if it were assumed – and this would be a very dubious assumption – that this model was applicable to certain moments of North African history, the fact remains that it is still utterly foreign to Ottoman history. Gellner seems simply to regard the 500 years of Ottoman statehood over central Muslim lands as having been anomalous and uncharacteristic: he never said so explicitly, but it is inherent in the logic of excision and abridgment he deployed in the various versions and editions of his theory.

What this procedure displays, in fact, is a certain will to conceptual arbitrariness – arbitrariness with regard to facts of history and society, one which construes central facts as anomalous, and partial or local phenomena as norms; a conceptual arbitrariness which allows indiscipline to flourish under the title of exceptionalism. There is an objective correlation between this arbitrariness and its historical conditions of possibility in the world outside the university, for this intellectual unaccountability is matched only by the presumption of public unaccountability that underlies an article published by Gellner in *The New Republic* which opens with the following statement: '[m]uslims are a nuisance. As a matter of fact, they always were a nuisance'[31] – I shudder to think what would have happened to the author (and to the *New Republic*) had he said the same, not necessarily with his usual irony, about Afro-Americans, for instance, or Jews. But what is of particular salience in this statement is that it was simply a preface to reducing to a unity, in Islamic exceptionalism, Moroccan corsairs off the coast of Newfoundland in the eighteenth century, Khomeini, and the Organization of Petroleum Exporting Countries. Clearly, the will to conceptual arbitrariness goes with a will to a certain form of combat which is bound by no rules. Societies, countries, territories, histories – all are reduced to one specific aspect that makes them manageable for purposes of confrontation or containment. The connection with, and anticipation of, the theses of Samuel Huntington is manifest; both repeat commonplace prejudices with equal banality.

This will to violence (which since September 11 is no longer merely symbolic): this will to conceptual indiscipline, this will to reduce complexity to simplicity, wantonly to ignore reality, to contradict both history and ethnography[32] – what this will leads to in scholarship is precisely what I started out with: the over-islamization of Muslims, endowing them with a superhuman capacity for perpetual piety, reducing their history and their present life to a drama about the recovery of religious motifs, and hence the denial of their actual history and their actual present. It would be wrong to suppose that Gellner's theories always amount to mere vulgar Islamophobia, or reflect some immediately political position. Yet these theories, such as his last theory about the impossibility of secularization in Muslim lands (the very secularization that is so evident in the fundamental thrust of modern Arab history),[33] are based on an imperious will to deny: a will, at a time in global history when 'outsiders' are being barbarized – treated as barbarians, barbarically – to deny their cultural capacity, their capacity for economic, social, political, and cognitive development, and to assert that they are predisposed to violence, factionalism, overpopulation, and even famine.[34]

NOTES

Parts of this paper were delivered in a variety of forms over recent years as lectures in a variety of fora, and have benefited much from keen and diverse audiences, at the universities of Georgetown, Columbia, Harvard, California (Berkeley), and Lund; at The Central European University, Budapest, the Nehru Memorial Museum and Library, New Delhi, and the Institutes of Advanced Study in Berlin and Uppsala. An early version was published as a pamphlet under the title *Reconstituting Islam* by The Center for Muslim–Christian Understanding, Georgetown University, in 1995 (Swedish translation as 'Att rekonstituera islam', in *Tidskrift för mellanösternstudier*, n. 2, 1998).

1 For the term 'postmodern obscurantism' I am indebted to a conversation in Beirut with Aijaz Ahmad, to whom this essay is dedicated.
2 For a clear statement of the radical position, see William E. Shepard, *Sayyid Qutb and Islamic Activism*, Leiden: Brill, 1996; Gilles Kepel, *The Prophet and the Pharaoh*, translated by Jon Rothschild, London: Al-Saqi Books, 1985.
3 Paul Valéry, 'Orientem Versus', in idem., *History and Politics* (*Works*, Vol. 10, *Bollingen Series*, Vol. 45), New York: Pantheon Books, 1962, pp. 380-381.
4 We also have now an 'Islamic archaeology': Timothy Insoll (*The Archaeology of Islam*, Oxford: Blackwell, 1999), proposes that there are 'islamic' archaeological traces which find their unifying principle in the Muslim religion as a total and ineradicable 'way of life'. That the empirical evidence sketched in the book (on the domestic environment, dress, war, visual imagery, and much else) indicates conclusions that are almost wholly directly in contradiction to the basic proposition of the book does not dent the spirited enthusiasm with which this proposition is repeated.
5 Aziz Al-Azmeh, 'Culturalism, Grand Narrative of Capitalism Exultant', in idem., *Islams and Modernities*, 2nd ed., London: Verso, 1996, ch. 1.
6 Various facets of the relation between Islamism and universal irrationalism in politics are explored in Al-Azmeh, *Islams and Modernities*, passim. Let me say parenthetically that it is too early to predict how the postmodern reclamation of obscurantism and its predilection for the backward in the name of post-coloniality will react to September 11, and whether it will feel the waves of disorientation, dislocation, and terminal menace that have started seriously to beset Islamist political movements of all shades. What is certain is that I have not yet seen descriptions of the destruction of the World Trade Center as quite simply a performative speech-act, nor anything comparable to Lyotard's playful characterization of the Second Gulf War as an unreal, virtual happening – although, I must say, feminist descriptions of the events as an act of supreme phallicism have indeed been voiced (see Sascha Lehnarzt, 'Auch Muslime müssen müssen', *Frankfurter Allgemeine Zeitung*, 23 September 2001; and Christopher Norris, *Uncritical Theory: Postmodernism, Intellectuals and the Gulf War*, Amherst: University of

Massachusetts Press, 1992).

7   Much uninformed writing has been devoted to this historically very complex notion by Islamist as well as by western authors. See the exemplary historical account of Mahmud al-Rahmuni, *al-Jihad. Min al-Hijra ila'-d-da`wa ila'd-dawla* [*Jihad: Emigration, Proselytism, State*], Beirut: Dar at-Tali`a, 2002.

8   Karl Mannheim, *Ideology and Utopia*, London: Routledge and Kegan Paul, 1966, pp. 215, 225 ff.

9   Cf. Richard D. Sonn, *Anarchism and Cultural Politics in Fin de Siècle France*, Lincoln and London: University of Nebraska Press, 1989, pp. 263 ff.; Mark Juergenmeister, ed., *Violence and the Sacred in the Modern World*, London: Frank Cass, 1992, pp. 106 ff. and passim.

10   Franklin L. Ford, 'Reflections on Political Murder: Europe in the Nineteenth and Twentieth Centuries', in Wolfgang Mommsen and Gerhard Hirschfeld, eds., *Social Protest, Violence and Terror in Nineteenth- and Twentieth-Century Europe*, London: The German Historical Institute in association with Berg Publishers Ltd., 1982, pp. 182 and passim. See in general MarcJuergenmeister, *Terror in the Mind of God*, Berkeley and Los Angeles: University of California Press, 2000, and Richard D. Burton, *Blood in the City. Violence and Revelation in Paris*, Ithaca: Cornell University Press, 2001.

11   Cf. Sonn, *Anarchism and Cultural Politics*, p. 299.

12   For instance, the memoir of a former member of one such group: Khaled al-Birri, *al-Dunya ajmal min al-janna* [*The World is Preferable to Paradise*], Beirut: Dar an-Nahar, 2001.

13   Cf. Roger Caillois, *L'homme et le sacré*, Paris: Gallimard, 1950, pp. 223, 231 ff.

14   For instance, Roger Caillois, 'Guerre et sacré', in idem., *L'homme et le sacré*, Appendix III; Juergenmeister, ed., *Violence and the Sacred*, passim.

15   See Brigitte Hamann, *Hitler's Vienna. A Dictator's Apprenticeship*, translated by Thomas Thornton, New York and Oxford: Oxford University Press, 1999, pp. 206 ff., 236 ff.

16   E. B. Tylor, *The Origins of Culture*, Gloucester, Mass.: Peter Smith, 1970, p. 16.

17   Interview with Amos Oz in *Davar*, December 17, 1982 - English translation: http://www.counterpunch.org/pipermail/counterpunch-list/2001-September/01.

18   For an exemplary analysis of a comparable phenomenon, see Aijaz Ahmad, 'Fascism and National Culture: Reading Gramsci in the Days of *Hindutva*', in idem, *Lineages of the Present: Ideology and Politics in Contemporary South Asia*, London: Verso, 2000, ch. 5.

19   Antonio Negri and Michael Hardt, *Empire*, Cambridge, Mass.: Harvard University Press, pp. 13 ff.

20   Benedict Anderson, *Imagined Communities*, London: Verso, 1991.

21 On the character of religious radicalism in Saudi Arabia, see Ali E. Hillal Dessouki, *Islamic Resurgence in the Arab World*, New York: Praeger, 1982, ch. 9; Al-Azmeh, *Islams and Modernities*, ch. 7; Mahmud A. Fakhash, *The Future of Islam in the Middle East*, Westport and London: Praeger, 1997, ch. 5. The best study of this and other aspects of Saudi Arabia remains Waddah Sharara, *Al-Ahl wa'l-ghanima: Muqawwimat as-siyasa fi'l-mamlaka al-`Arabiya al-Su`udiya* [*Clansmen and Booty: The Pillars of Politics in the Kingdom of Saudi Arabia*], Beirut: Dar at-Tali`a, 1981.

22 *Bildungs(klein)bürgertum* refers to the (petty) bourgeoisie by education, that is to say, by virtue of access to education, specifically Gymnasium and university education, the bedrock of the German bureaucracy and intelligentsia.

23 Cf. Serif Mardin, *Religion and Social Change in Modern Turkey*, Albany: State University of New York Press, 1989, p. 118. A similar development took place in modern Buddhism and Judaism, and in other religions as well; see Gideon Aran, 'From Religious Zionism to Zionist Religion', in Peter Pedding, ed., *Studies in Contemporary Jewry, II*, Bloomington: Indiana University Press, 1986, p. 122 and passim; and Donald K. Swearer, 'Fundamentalistic Movements in Theravada Buddhism', in Martin E. Marty and R. Scott Appleby, eds., *Fundamentalisms Observed*, Chicago: Chicago University Press, 1991, pp. 649 f.

24 On this theme, see Aziz Al-Azmeh, 'The Middle East and Islam: a Ventriloqual Terrorism', in *Third World Affairs 1988*, London: Third World Foundation, 1988, pp. 23-34; Annemarie Oliverio, *The State of Terror*, Albany: State University of New York Press, 1998, and Louis Pinto, 'La croisade antiterroriste du professeur Walzer', *Le Monde Diplomatique*, May 2002, p.36.

25 Claude Lévi-Strauss, *The Savage Mind*, London: Weidenfeld and Nicolson, 1966, ch. 5, passim.

26 See particularly Geoffrey Cubitt, *The Jesuit Myth. Conspiracy Theory and Politics in Nineteenth-Century France*, Oxford: Oxford University Press, 1993, ch. 5, pp. 192-3 and passim.

27 This is perhaps most poignantly apparent in the cultural determinism of Margaret Mead, which has had a truly structuring impact on cultural anthropology – a cultural determinism empirically built on an 'aberrant' construction of the object of her field-work in Samoa, a construction based upon the credulous acceptance as serious of a prank played upon her by local adolescent girls, which 'produced such a spectacular result in centers of higher learning throughout the western world': This 'wonderfully comic' matter is traced in detail by Derek Freeman, *Margaret Mead and the Heretic*, Harmondsworth: Penguin Books, 1996, pp. xiii, 107, and passim.

28 Ernest Gellner, *Muslim Society*, Cambridge: Cambridge University Press, 1981, p. 62.

29 Quoted in Cubitt, *The Jesuit Myth*, p. 193.

30 On this constellation of topics, see Aziz Al-Azmeh, *Ibn Khaldun in Modern Scholarship*, London: Third World Centre for Research and Publishing, 1981, ch. 5.

31 5 December 1983, p. 22.

32 For ethnography, see particularly Martha Mundy, *Domestic Government*, London: I. B. Tauris, 1995, especially pp. 52-54.

33 Aziz Al-'Azma, *Al-'Ilmaniyya min manzur mukhtalif* [*Secularism from a New Perspective*], Beirut: Markaz Dirasat al-Wahda al-'Arabiyya, 1992.

34 Aziz Al-Azmeh, 'Civilization, Culture and the New Barbarians', *International Sociology*, vol.16, no. 1, 2001.

PALESTINE, GLOBAL POLITICS AND ISRAELI JUDAISM

Avishai Ehrlich

Recent events in the Middle East have to be seen in light of the contradictions of the politics of globalization. With the demise of the Soviet Union many national conflicts which had been subsumed into the Cold War rivalry now served no purpose in the new world architecture. The continuation of some of them became dangerously disruptive to the 'new world order' and had to be defused, although others, which presented less of a threat to the capitalist world system, were left to linger on. The Israeli-Arab conflict, especially since it is played out in an area that fulfills a major role in the world economy and is close to Europe, fell into the first category. The Oslo peace process was viewed by many observers as the route to an historic compromise agreement and the end of the Israeli–Palestinian conflict; and, in its wake, to the end of the Israeli–Arab conflict too.

Yet the interplay of the multi-layered contradictions that compose the Israeli-Arab conflict has produced a very different outcome. While writing this essay, in mid-April 2002, the world is watching with shock and horror the death, devastation and deliberate chaos caused by the Israeli invasion of the Palestinian Authority. The situation has been set back many years. Not only has the rectitude of the Jewish State again become an issue for world debate, but the situation in the Middle East has contributed to interrupting the triumphal march of globalization and shattering the naïve belief in its ideological message of peace, progress, democracy and improved human rights under capitalism. The change of political course in the USA after September 11 has transformed the globalization agenda, and opened up a much more gruesome perspective. Public fear created the acquiescence necessary to push through, without much resistance, 'anti-terrorist acts', first in the USA and later in many other countries. These laws have curtailed human rights and political freedoms and empowered state exec-utives. A global war on terrorism has been declared. Military force against 'rogue states' was implemented in Afghanistan and is being prepared against Iraq and other, as yet unspecified, states. An ideological justification for a 'new liberal imperialism' is being prepared by various think tanks.[1]

In this context, the Middle East and many of its regimes are again in the eye of the storm. The USA has declared more 'rogue states' in this region than in any other part of the world. The cutting down to size and subordination of nation-alist and religious regimes in the 'new world order' raises many questions about a possible redrawing of the map of the Middle East, as was the case after World War I. How it will be handled by the USA – the global power – will be deter-mined by the way the US resolves its disagreements with the European powers and with its client states in the Middle East, and on how all this intertwines with the opening up to world markets of alternative oil reserves in Central Asia.

But if the Israeli–Arab conflict is again enmeshed in major global contradictions, the inter-communal struggle between Palestinians and Israelis still remains at the core of the conflict. Indeed, the central argument of this essay is that the contra-dictions of what I shall call Israeli Judaism are increasingly determining the nature of the conflict, and impinging directly on the form the global contradictions take in the region. The concept of Israeli Judaism is employed here as a way of revealing the central dilemmas of the articulation of the Jewish project in Palestine, especially in relation to the major ideological currents of labour, liberal and reli-gious Zionism. But it is a concept that goes beyond ideology to the realm of culture and to mental constructs, beliefs and ethos prevalent among Jews in Israel.

As with other world religions like Islam and Christianity, Judaism today is many things to different people.[2] Judaism in modernity has a great many artic-ulations. Jews come in different colours, live in many countries – today mainly in the developed world – and belong to different classes. They do not share a common creed or political values. Many accept as fellow Jews only those who have a Jewish mother; others – as in the case of citizenship law in Israel and the definition adopted by the Nazis – include those whose Jewish descent is more remote. Many Jews have, with modernity, become secular or atheists – 'non-Jewish Jews', in Deutscher's famous phrase. Others have reacted to modernity and its threat of assimilation by becoming more observant – the ultra orthodox. Others still have modified their religious observance to fit their modern lifestyle – conservative or reform. The majority of Jews define Judaism as a world reli-gion and see themselves as nationals of their countries of domicile. Others view themselves as a nation defined by its religion, somewhat like the Serbs, Armenians and Greeks. Some view Judaism as a nationality sharing language, culture and tradition, as the Labour Bund did in Central and Eastern Europe. Others define Jews as a world nation united by a common history of exclusion and persecution.

It was the latter definition, of course, that originally motivated Zionism. Zionism was established in Europe at the turn of the twentieth century and those who adopted it strove towards the establishment of a state that would be a home to, and an ingathering of, all the Jews. But it was divided, shortly after its inception, into three broadly defined creeds: liberal Zionism, labour Zionism and religious Zionism. Jews who came to Palestine out of conviction, Zionist or Orthodox, or because they had no choice, were faced with dilemmas specific to Palestine, different from those facing Jews in other places. They brought with them their worldviews and responded to new situations accordingly. Zionism is an oddity among modern nationalisms – it did not just call for self-determination in the place where its 'nationals' resided, but shifted its imagined community to a different place. Zionism is thus a colonizing ideology and project. The contradictions of Judaism in modernity have thus been superimposed onto another set of contradictions – the realities of the Middle East, where, after the end of World War I, the Zionist project entered into conflict with emerging Pan-Arab and Palestinian nationalism.

This essay attempts to link the global and the local in relation to Palestine by showing how the changing architecture of the world system has continually changed the modalities of the local and regional conflict; and how the continuation of the colonizing project under changing world conditions has determined, in turn, the shifts of hegemonic political ideology within Israel, first from labour Zionism to liberal Zionism and then to today's form of religious Zionism closely associated with orthodox Judaism, which may properly be called 'political Judaism'.

THE ISRAELI-ARAB CONFLICT IN GLOBAL-HISTORICAL PERSPECTIVE

The Israeli–Arab conflict has evolved in several stages.[3] The initial *colonial stage*, lasting from 1920 to 1948, was characterized by the conflict that had emerged between the Jewish settlers and their nascent society and the native Arabs in Palestine under the British mandate after World War One. The conflict was expressed mainly through the Jews' creation of a separate, exclusive, economic and political community. The conflict was confined by the rule of the British government which maintained law and order and prevented the possibility of a decisive war. The limits on power that stemmed from a lack of sovereignty on either side meant that Jews had to purchase land rather than take it by force, and that Arabs could not wage war against the Jews or legislate against their immigration and settlement. British policy first encountered the antagonism of the Arabs in Palestine as it favoured the Jews, and then of the Jews when, prior to the Second World War, the British tried to balance their policy and restrict Jewish state building – a policy determined by changing international circumstances and growing Arab nationalism. This stage ended when the British decided to return their mandate to the UN and leave Palestine. Following the UN decision to partition Palestine, growing hostilities between irregular forces of Jews and Arabs resulted in the defeat of the Palestinians and the declaration of a Jewish state. The resolution was not accepted by the Arab states, who declared war on

Israel, the first Israeli-Arab war, which ended with Israel holding 78 per cent of Palestine (instead of 55 per cent as stated in the UN resolution on partition) and most of the Palestinians becoming refugees – remaining either inside Israel or expelled from it. The Palestinian state never came into being; its territory was annexed by Israel and Jordan (the West Bank) and by Egypt (which administered but did not annex the Gaza Strip).

In the subsequent *inter-state stage* from 1948 to 1969, the conflict was mainly between Israel and surrounding Arab states and thus assumed new forms. As well as full scale wars in 1948, 1956 and 1967, there were border skirmishes and infiltrations by state armies and irregulars, attendant growing expenditure on militarization, and economic warfare through direct boycotts by Arab countries and secondary boycotts imposed by appeal or pressure on non-Arab countries to ban all ties with Israel. The conflict also took the form of ideological warfare – a concerted effort by each side to denigrate and isolate the other in international organizations and the world media and thereby to fortify their international alliances. During most of this period, the Palestinians played a secondary role. Various Arab states used instrumentally the Palestinian issue in inter-Arab politics; at the same time, they confiscated much Jewish property and most Jews in the Arab countries felt insecure and emigrated. Inside Israel, the Palestinians who remained after much of their land and property was expropriated obtained a status of second class citizens. The Middle East was still influenced during this stage by the declining colonial powers, Britain and France, but after 1956, the pro-colonial regimes were replaced by revolutionary nationalist governments in several Arab countries, and the superpowers – the Soviet Union and the USA – began the process of penetration and competition in the region.

The beginning of what might best be called the *bipolar superpower stage* of the conflict is marked by the War of Attrition between Israel and the Arab states following June 1967. In this war Israel completed the conquest of Mandatory Palestine (the West Bank and Gaza) and took over Sinai from Egypt and the Golan from Syria. The superpowers supplied their clients with arms and new technologies, thus subsuming this conflict – as happened elsewhere – into the Cold War and their own global contest. Consequently, the Israeli-Arab conflict became a war by proxy between the superpowers who fought indirectly via their clients (e.g. in 1973). The military build-up at this stage reached proportions far beyond the economic and scientific capabilities of the warring sides. As a result, the opponents become economically and militarily dependent on their patrons and received from them a much higher level of foreign military and economic aid. After 1967, diplomatic and economic ties between Israel and the Soviet bloc were severed. This increased Israel's isolation and denied it access to significant world markets both in the Warsaw Pact bloc and in the non-aligned countries. The Israeli-Arab conflict also became central in the ideological war between the superpowers. Zionism was equated with racism in a UN resolution backed by the Soviet bloc and Arab and Islamic states. On the other hand, the US demanded the right of Soviet Jews to emigrate and made it a condition for economic transactions with the USSR. The Palestinians were brought back to the forefront of the conflict when, with Soviet and Egyptian support, they formed the PLO in 1969. It was during this stage that the economic aspect of the conflict began to significantly affect the global economy. The use of oil and petro-dollar power by OPEC countries in solidarity with the Arabs following the 1973 war is usually cited as a major factor in the economic crisis of the 1970s and the slowdown in Western economic growth. The US stepped in to fight the secondary boycott against Israel and break up OPEC's power.

The beginning of a new stage, defined in terms of American global hegemony, is best marked by the Stockholm Conference (1988) where Arafat announced his willingness to recognize Israel, cease the armed struggle and enter negotiations. This was a pre-condition set by the US and the Europeans to end Arafat's isolation in Tunis and afford him recognition as the leader of the restive Palestinians in the impending Middle East peace talks. But in fact this new stage was already presaged when Anwar Saddat decided to break Egypt's alliance with the Soviet Union – a development brought about through disappointment with the Soviets' inability to force an Israeli withdrawal from Egyptian soil or supply Egypt with superior military technology.

Even before the end of the 1980s it became clear that the ailing Soviet bloc was no longer able to aid and arm its Middle Eastern clients. The new affiliation between Egypt and the US heralded a new era in the Middle East's place in the Pax Americana, even before the demise of the Soviet bloc. The peace treaty between Egypt and Israel was a triangular peace: between the US and Egypt, and between Egypt and Israel. Egypt received annual economic and military aid ; in return, it had to recognize Israel and sign a formal peace treaty. Israel had to return all occupied Egyptian territory, as stipulated by UN resolution 242; in return, Israel received a large aid package as compensation for redeployment. Since then both sides have also received annual economic and military aid. This pattern of triangular peace agreements became the model for future US-brokered accords with Israel. The logic of the US-brokered peace lies in the fact that conflict between two allies of the same superpower weakens that power and it must act to reduce tension and increase solidarity within its camp. But the peace agreement was also the first measure that removed the threat of a major war that could endanger the very existence of the Jewish state. The peace agreement entailed the fixing of borders. Establishing mutually and internationally recognized borders between two sovereignties is a sine qua non condition to any peace agreement.

The agreement with Egypt was a breakthrough in the long-term principled refusal of the Arabs to recognize Israel in any form. Israel's military might and Egypt's commitment to stay out of a military coalition against Israel also considerably reduced the chances of any other Arab country going to war with Israel. As a result, Israel could reduce its security budget and divert funds to other uses. The first peace was, therefore, the most valuable, and the price paid for it was deemed worthwhile by the Israeli leadership. Notably, however, it was not followed by more agreements until the demise of the Warsaw Pact. Nor did the agreement prevent another war by Israel against Lebanon in 1982 (the first war where an Arab capital city was captured by Israel), and large tracts of south Lebanon remained under Israeli control until 1999. Following closely on the return of Sinai, the Lebanon war severely tested the peace treaty with Egypt, and relations between Israel and Egypt remain cold and formal to this day. Social and economic relations are limited to official channels. Egypt is also hostile to Israel in international forums. Hostility to Israel is popular and is maintained in the media and in education curricula in schools.

For the United States in the post-Soviet world, the Middle East has presented a particularly important but difficult area: the 'dual containment' policy against Iraq and Iran did not prove particularly successful, and as already noted more 'rogue states' have been identified by the US in this region than anywhere else (Iraq, Iran, Libya, Sudan, Syria). The Islamic belt stretching from Pakistan and Afghanistan to the Muslim ex-Soviet republics of Central Asia and up to the former Yugoslavia threatened the globalization process with an apparent 'clash of civilizations'. It was in this arena that the US chose to demonstrate, for the first time, its new role as 'Globocop' in the 1990 'Desert Storm' against its former ally in the war against Iran – Saddam Hussein.[4] The invasion of Kuwait by Saddam and the Arab coalition against Iraq also contributed to the break-up of Arab solidarity; following the war Arab nationalism was at its nadir. It is against this background that the Madrid and Oslo initiatives took place.

Peace with Jordan was, in the Middle East, the first result of American global hegemony, and was made possible by the weakening of Arab solidarity following the Gulf War. It was worthwhile for Jordan to atone for its previous (profitable) sin of being the inroad and the outlet for Sadam's Iraq. In the wake of the Gulf War, Jordan's policy took a U-turn to appease the USA. The borders and other issues outstanding between Israel and Jordan were not difficult to resolve as there had long been understanding and cooperation between them. As a result of the Gulf War and this second peace agreement, other Arab states – mainly in the Gulf and North Africa – relaxed their attitudes and established open contacts with Israel; and other Islamic states like Indonesia, or those with a large Muslim population like India, followed suit.

ISRAELI POLITICS IN THE 1990s

The overall effect of this process was the breakdown of the international and economic isolation of Israel and the opening of new markets for its exports. However, although important, all these were secondary effects; the main factor in the rapid economic growth of Israel in the 1990s, was the collapse of the Soviet Union. Israel was one of the main beneficiaries of the fall of the Soviet bloc. Because of Soviet support of the Arabs during the conflict, Eastern bloc countries severed diplomatic and economic relations with Israel. Soviet influence was also responsible for many non-aligned states refusing to establish relations with Israel. The collapse of the Soviet Union brought Israel's isolation to an end.

Diplomatic relations were renewed or established for the first time and, in their wake, major new markets in Central and Eastern Europe and in Asia were opened to Israel.

A second advantage gained by Israel from the collapse of the Soviet Union, and the attendant growing economic and political instability across its territories, was a major wave of immigration from the former USSR. To date the total number of immigrants has been more than one million. Besides the impact on the demography of Israel, and the reversal of the declining birth rate, the immigration brought Israel a huge amount of human capital. The immigrants included a much larger proportion of highly educated people than had the Israeli population, with a particularly high percentage of scientists. The timing of the immigration was opportune as it coincided with the burgeoning revolution in communications, computing and biological, genetic and medical research. Due to its previous military-industrial complex, Israel had already developed these areas; with the influx of the immigrants Israel was ideally positioned to benefit from this revolution. Moreover, the aid promised by the US for absorbing the Soviet immigrants, in the form of US loan guarantees of $10 billion, gave Israel access to funds at cheap rates of interest.

The coalescence of all these factors – opening markets, immigration of an expert labour force, fortunate timing and cheap loans – brought to Israel the economic boom which it enjoyed during the first five years following the peace process. The trading partners responsible for the major expansion of exports by Israel were not Arab countries but new markets in Europe, Asia and America. The renewal of diplomatic and economic relations with many countries also enabled Israel to improve its terms of trade and to replace expensive home-produced goods with much cheaper imports, increasing the purchasing power of Israeli consumers. Thus, most of the economic benefits of the 1990s came to Israel from the fall of the Soviet Union and not from direct economic relations with the Arab countries. Shimon Peres's idea of a new Middle East with Israel as its hub immediately met with negative responses from the Arab countries which saw it as a neo-colonial conspiracy. The economic benefits for Israel were not in the surrounding Arab world but rather with the normalization of the status of Israel in the family of nations, and the end of its status as outcast. From the beginning, Zionism created a total separation between the Jewish economy and the surrounding Arab economies. Due to the Arab boycott after 1948, Israel's areas of specialization and its trading partners were mostly far away in the West. The secondary boycott managed to isolate Israel in other parts of the world, some of which are now burgeoning economies demanding products from Israeli military industries, telecommunications, agribusiness, pharmaceuticals and electronics. It is these markets that Israel covets. The poor developing countries in the Middle East have neither the money nor the need for what Israel sells. They can only be exploited for their cheap labour. The interests of Israeli industrialists were not necessarily as well-served by ending the conflict as by its containment and management.

The Oslo peace process was, in fact, imposed on Israel from outside. The American economic aid mentioned above was part of a deal to bring Israel – under the premiership of Shamir, the 'peace opponent' – to the negotiating table in Madrid. Inside Israel, the debate among Israel's power elite was about timing; whether time plays against Israel or for it, and about the inevitability, or not, of the need to cede most of the occupied territories and finalize the borders of the state. One position, represented by Rabin, Peres and Barak, accepted the 'inevitable' and concurred with the US and Europe's wish to contain and stabilize the conflict, and tried to maximize the benefits for the concessions made. The other approach, represented by Shamir, Netanyahu and Sharon, was to try to delay and prevaricate in order to gain time: to continue a massive programme of settlements in the hope that these will create a new irreversible reality, and that external conditions pressing Israel to get out of the occupied territories would change. The changing attitudes towards peace in public opinion polls and voting did not so much represent a change in the economic interests of Israel, but rather reflected a slow realization of the inevitable, which had been hidden from Israelis by an internally-centred, jingoistic public discourse. This discourse was slowly breaking up under the pressure of global events, the missile attacks on Israel during 'Desert Storm' and the opening up of Israel to the world's media.

The Oslo process was an attempt, initiated by Europe and brokered by the USA, to try to gain a period of calm after the first Intifada (1987-93). This Intifada was mainly an unarmed popular insurrection led by the grass roots organizations of the PLO in the occupied territories, without the national leadership which had been in exile in Tunisia since the debacle in Lebanon in 1982. The idea of Oslo was an exercise in cooptation. It entailed the creation, in the occupied territories, of a representative Palestinian self-rule (Authority) which would gradually take over from the Israeli military government and work obediently with the USA and Israel to impose order. Arafat was chosen to do the job. At the time he was desperate enough after losing his backing in the Gulf States and Saudi Arabia following his support of Saddam. The carrot was the chance to be readmitted among his constituency from which he had been expelled three times in the past: in 1967, when he had to flee from the West Bank; in 1970, after Black September when the PLO was evicted from Jordan, and 1982, when he was forcefully separated by Sharon from the Palestinian diaspora in Lebanon. The creation of a semi-state (the Palestinian Authority) also offered Arafat the spoils of government and the symbols of a head of state as well as much foreign aid (mainly European). The stick, however, was total economic dependency on Israel and a gradual approach that linked further withdrawals by Israel to Palestinian willingness to cooperate in stopping the violence.

The Oslo agreement stipulated three stages over six years of Israeli handover of territory in the West Bank and Gaza to the Palestinian Authority, whose main obligation was to assume effective control over the territories and prevent terrorist acts. At the end of the period, and after trust had been established, the hard questions of Jerusalem and the Palestinian refugees would be dealt with. A

Palestinian state would be established and recognized and the two states would sign an agreement ending the conflict between them. The Oslo process linked willingness to eventually end the conflict with Israeli withdrawal. It depended on both sides' willingness to accept UN Resolution 242. That meant a new partition of Palestine – around 80 per cent to Israel and 20 per cent to the Palestinians. To Israelis this also meant that the implementation of other UN resolutions – such as Resolution 194 regarding the return of refugees – no longer pertained within this framework. Many believed at the time that the agreement could work, but there was strong opposition to it on both sides.

Rabin's Labour-based coalition government, which signed the Oslo agreement, had a slim majority and relied on the support of the Arab parties. The nationalist-religious opposition (whose growing influence and power we shall examine in the next section) contested the legitimacy of any decision regarding the future of Israel made by a majority that included non-Jews. This opposition was further strengthened by Rabin's resolve to reach a simultaneous agreement with Syria that entailed withdrawal from the Golan and an end to the occupation of South Lebanon. This raised the opposition of the security hardliners. The inability or unwillingness of the Palestinians to curb the terrorist activities added to the mistrust. The campaign against Oslo developed into a campaign of civil disobedience and open incitement threatening violence and civil war. It led, in November 1995, to the assassination of Rabin. Shimon Peres, who headed a caretaker government before early elections, lost the support of the Israeli Arabs. This was due to Israel's assassination of a Hamas master-terrorist which escalated into a wave of terrorist retaliations against Israel just before the elections. In addition, a military campaign against Hizbollah in South Lebanon misfired and resulted in the death of more than 100 Lebanese civilians. Having lost the Arab vote, Peres lost the elections.

Benjamin Nethanyahu won by less than a one per cent majority. He formed a narrow Likud-based coalition which relied on the growing religious bloc. His government was characterized by a fundamental contradiction: it was against the Oslo agreement, yet it was expected to respect the obligations undertaken by the previous government and proceed with their implementation. Nethanyahu was not able to start open negotiations with the Syrians and could not stop the low intensity war with Hizbollah which continued to exact casualties. He tried to navigate between opposing pressures by yielding to religious demands in internal matters, and to the settlers by starting new settlements, and by endless prevarications and manipulations. One such incident, in September 1996, involved the provocative opening of a tunnel to the Temple Mount which resulted in a flare-up with the Palestinians and scores of casualties. By means of such diversions Nethanyahu managed to postpone the second Israeli withdrawal in the West Bank for more than a year beyond the schedule agreed at Oslo. Nethanyahu's coalition lasted for only two and a half years; it collapsed after he was forced by Clinton (at the Wye Plantation Conference) to agree to a second, smaller, withdrawal. The letter of Oslo was saved, but its spirit was long dead.

The religious bloc and the extreme right quit the coalition. In despair Nethanyahu asked Labour to form a unity coalition but Labour's new leader, Ehud Barak, declined.

Barak came to power by a margin of 12 per cent in the early elections of May 1999. His coalition, like Nethanyahu's, was based on the support of the religious bloc, which had further increased its power in Parliament. He started negotiations with the Syrians but balked at the prospect of allowing a Syrian foothold in the waters of the Sea of Galilee. Barak's main achievement in his first year in office was a unilateral pull-back from South Lebanon. Thus, in May 2000, he ended Israel's occupation which had lasted since 1982. This pull-back earned him the trust of the left which believed he was honestly striving for peace; they overlooked the fact that during this time the Jewish settlements in the West Bank had been growing at a faster rate than under Nethanyahu.

The third pull-back stipulated by the Oslo agreement was by now overdue. In the third instalment Israel was supposed to hand over areas that included many settlements. Barak was not willing to risk, as Rabin had, a clash and civil strife with the right and with the religious bloc. Besides, his coalition differed from Rabin's in that it depended on the religious bloc. From this constraint the idea was born to skip Oslo's overdue third stage and move instead speedily into a final settlement. With hindsight it is clear that by taking this approach Barak forced a high-risk situation that, had it failed, would have exploded. He had no alternative as, with the coalition he had, he could not execute the third stage withdrawal.

Barak managed to convince Clinton to accept his approach. In turn Clinton forced Arafat, via Egypt's President Mubarak, to attend the Camp David conference in July 2000. At Camp David, Barak refused to meet Arafat directly. What Clinton suggested as an outline agreement was not what Barak actually offered at Camp David, and what he did offer exactly is still debated. Some claim it was 91 per cent of the West Bank and Gaza and agreement to the division of Jerusalem, but even if this is so, it is clear that he insisted on absorbing most of the post-1967 settlements into Israel, and that their geographic location would have divided the Palestinian state into enclaves economically and strategically dependent on Israel (hence their designation by critics as Bantustans). In any case, Barak had not prepared Israeli public opinion for significant concessions, even if he did intend to make them. On the contrary, he had vowed never to divide Jerusalem. All the public opinion polls at the time showed that a large majority would have rejected these agreements – and Barak was well aware of the polls. The question of the Temple Mount (Haram Al-Sharif) was not resolved; neither was the question of the refugees.[5]

Clinton put a lot of pressure on Arafat and not as much on Barak. Arafat was not willing to compromise on territory or on full sovereignty over Haram Al-Sharif. On this last issue he was encouraged to stand fast by Egypt, Jordan and Saudi Arabia. Arafat also refused to commit himself to ending the conflict. Camp David broke up without an agreement and Clinton put the blame on Arafat.

Barak had succeeded in subverting the last stage of the Oslo process and put the blame on the Palestinians. But his success was also his downfall and his coalition broke up. In the few months before the elections in Israel and before Clinton left office there were several attempts to resume the negotiations. The talks in Taba, hosted by Mubarak, lead to some understandings but these came too late. Barak was a lame prime minister, and there was a change of the guard in the White House. Early in September Ariel Sharon, Likud's candidate for the premiership, seized the opportunity to visit the Temple Mount. This act and its timing was perceived by the Palestinians as a provocation, a gesture of legitimate claim to the place. It was the last straw which set the second Intifada aflame, roughly when the Oslo period was supposed to come to its end.

What we have tried to show in this brief outline is that internal Israeli politics are deadlocked on the issue of withdrawal from the West Bank and Gaza. Three prime ministers – Rabin, Nethanyahu and Barak – have failed to proceed with the Oslo agreements. Rabin, who committed himself to the process, was murdered; Nethanyahu, who opposed the process, delayed the second stage withdrawal as much as he could, thus contributing to the bad faith between Israelis and Palestinians; Barak found a way out of the process. In Rabin's case it was because he relied on Israeli Arabs against the religious–nationalist opposition; in the case of Barak and Nethanyahu it was because they relied on the religious bloc. In all three cases governments fell in mid-term. In all three cases the religious bloc was pivotal. We must therefore turn to a closer look at the political power and the attitudes of the religious bloc in contemporary Israeli politics.[6]

THE RELIGIOUS BLOC AND THE UNANSWERED QUESTIONS OF ISRAELI JUDAISM

The religious bloc in Israel comprises three streams: Nationalist Religious, Occidental Ultra Orthodox and Oriental Religious. Of late they have gained about 21 per cent of the vote; their power has been on the rise since the mid-1980s. The main factor in this increase was the meteoric rise of the Oriental Religious party (Shas), which has managed to channel the social grievances of the Oriental Jewish lower classes and articulate them within a religious discourse. This party is now the third largest in Parliament with 13 per cent of the vote. The rise of the religious bloc can be best understood in relation to the decline of the two main parties Labour and Likud, which have always headed Israeli governments. While in the mid-1980s these two parties together marshalled 95 out of 120 Members of Parliament, by 1999 their total had fallen to only 45. In any case, so long as Labour and Likud cannot agree on the issue of a peace programme, the religious bloc holds the key to the formation and dissolution of any government.

What has especially characterized the rise of this bloc is the convergence between religiosity and chauvinism. The National Religious Party (NRP), a Zionist party which tried to combine modernism and religion, had, until 1977, always been a partner in Labour's coalitions. Since the early 1970s the NRP has undergone a profound transformation: it perceives Israel's occupation of the whole of Palestine in Messianic terms, as a divine act heralding redemption. This party has become the main political and ideological arm of the settlers. NRP supporters have also become more pious and observant, even though, unlike the Ultra Orthodox Jews, they are involved in the economy and society and serve in the army.

Meanwhile, the Ultra-Orthodox have become more nationalistic even as the National Religious have become more Orthodox. The Ultra-Orthodox Occidentals (Ashkenazi) are traditionally non-Zionists. They oppose secular Zionism as a secular rebellion against religion, threatening the spiritual annihilation of Judaism. Though they vote in elections, and sit in the Parliament and in the government, they do so for instrumental reasons, for material and legislative benefits. They do not acknowledge the legitimacy of democratic principles and institutions, and they maintain that a Jewish state should be ruled by religious law (Halacha). The Ultra-Orthodox behave like an elitist sect, led by sages. Unlike Ultra-Orthodox Jews in other countries, many men willingly refrain from gainful economic activity and live poorly on state national security and donations from abroad. They also enjoy cultural autonomy within the state: they live in separate quarters, maintain a separate educational system (which today includes about 20 per cent of all pupils) and have their own civil society. They refuse to serve in the army and the state exempts most of them from military service. In the past they kept a deliberate distance from key national issues. However, their growth in numbers and the need for financial support from the state has moved them closer to national politics. Their Jewish creed sets them firmly against equal citizenship for non-Jews in a Jewish state. The Ultra-Orthodox have also moved to live in the occupied territories and they see the whole of Palestine as God's patrimony to the Jews.

The Oriental Religious party (Shas) split from the Ultra-Orthodox following accusations of discrimination and the tendency of the Occidental Orthodox establishment to regard Oriental Judaism as inferior. Shas also expresses Oriental Jews' (mostly immigrants from Arab countries) feelings of resentment against their absorption into Israel under Labour rule during the 1950s and 1960s, and against socio-economic inequalities. Shas articulated this resentment into the accusation that Labour secular Zionism deliberately tried to abolish their traditional religious way of life. Unlike Occidental Orthodoxy, Shas is populist and open. Most Shas followers serve in the army and do not seclude themselves from the rest of Israeli society; on the contrary, they do much missionary work to bring secular Jews back to the fold. But like the Ultra-Orthodox, Shas does not regard itself as Zionist and strives towards a religious state ruled by religious law. In terms of its attitude to non-Jews and to the occupied territories, Shas voters stand to the right of the Likud.

The rising importance of the religious bloc as a key factor in Israeli politics has, somewhat paradoxically, coincided with the effects on Israeli politics of the Russian-Israelis' search for a political identity. Immigrants from the former Soviet Union now number more than one million out of Israel's 6.5 million (a figure which includes one million Israeli-Palestinian citizens). Economically they have integrated well; culturally they tend to maintain their Russian language and culture – there are currently more than sixty Russian-language newspapers and journals in Israel. There are also Russian-language schools and radio stations, and most Russian-Israelis are linked by cable TV to Russian-language (and Turkish) TV stations. Politically there are two 'Russian' parties which are now in government. A fair proportion (some say 20 per cent, some say more) of Russian-Israelis are not Jewish by religious definition (i.e. not born to a Jewish mother). They achieved Israeli citizenship through the secular 'Law of Return' which defines 'Jewish' in wider terms of descent. Though the large majority of the Russian-Israelis are secular, the majority incline towards the right and are strongly nationalistic. Most have imported Soviet conceptions of nationality: they view Jews as a nation (not as a religion) and see Israel as the homeland of the Jewish nation. In Israel, therefore, they believe that only Jews should have full citizenship rights. Non-Jews, such as Israeli-Palestinians, should only have minority rights such as existed for minorities in the various Soviet republics. Liberal conceptions of equal rights for all citizens regardless of religion or ethnicity are alien to the majority of Russian-Israelis.[7] Russian-Israelis also tend to be hard-liners on questions of security and see, as in the former Soviet view, the necessity of maintaining buffer territories against possible military invasion (Golan, and the Jordan Valley). Since the 1990s many Russian-Israelis also settled in the West Bank, some for ideological reasons, though mostly for reasons of cheap housing. There is also a trend among Russian-Israelis to return to religion and much missionary work is directed towards them by some Ultra Orthodox sects, especially the Chassidic Chabad, which is also ultra-nationalistic.

These developments have highlighted more than ever the conflict between Israeli Judaism and the modern concept of nationhood and statehood, a conflict which expresses itself in many forms in Israel:

* Israeli Jews waver between a secular conception of territory (Patria) and a Jewish religious conception (Sanctum). Is 'The Place' – 'The Land of Israel' – a place that one belongs to by birth, language, local culture and personal memories; or is it God's dwelling place? Is it 'The Place' where His third Temple must be built in place of the Muslim Haram al-Sharif? Is it a 'this worldly' place where each inhabitant chooses his own lifestyle and creed; or is it a Jewish sanctuary where only Jews can live on condition they maintain a Jewish religious code? Who decides what this code is?
* What is the status of non-Jews in 'The Place'? Can they be equal citizens or must they have an eternally inferior status (garim)? How can non-Jewish natives or immigrants become citizens? Is the place kept forever as an exclusive place for Jews worldwide, and for them alone? In any case what is a Jew, and who decides?
* What is an Israeli Jew? Can one be simply an Israeli Jew without having further divisory categories imposed on one: Ashkenazi (Occidental) Sephardi (Oriental), Ethiopian, Yemenite, etc? Categories which are carried over from

the divided history of Judaism worldwide and which now reproduce divisions in a place where they want to be one society? What is the Jewish religious customary law applicable to all (observant) Jews in Israel? Even observant Jews cannot eat at each others' homes. Is there one Israeli Judaism in Israel or many? Can there be freedom of religion, even for observant Jews in Israel (e.g. Reform Jews)? Is there freedom from religion in Israel?

★   What is a 'Jewish society'? Is it just a Jewish community writ large? Can it be a society which evolves voluntarily without legal impositions by the state?

★   What should the relation be between state and religion in a Jewish state? Can a Jewish state be a state that maintains full human rights for all its citizens (e.g. can a Jew and a non-Jew marry)? Can one be a secular Jew in Israel without recourse to religion?

These questions, and the contradictions they expose, are now the hub of Jewish Israeli internal politics. When Israel was founded in 1948 (with only 650,000 Jews) its Labour Zionist leaders made a conscious decision not to decide any of the above questions and deferred them to later generations in the hope that a larger proportion of world Jewry living in Israel would resolve them. This is not what happened. Strangely enough, it was during the first days of the Jewish state that Israel was most cohesive. Since then, with more Jews, with a stronger economy and a mightier army, but also with more non-Jews and with more territories, it seems to be less able to resolve these contradictions; they have become more pressing and exact a heavier toll on Israel.

The late Itzhak Rabin understood these dilemmas well when he entered the Oslo process. He explicated them in a speech he made in 1994:

> These days we are in the middle of a battle without guns, in a battle without fire, that will probably be one of the most important and decisive in the history of the Jewish people in the last generations: The battle for the character of the state of Israel. We shall have to choose: between the road of fanaticism, tendencies to dreams of grandeur, corruption of moral values and Judaism as a result of domination of another people, blind faith, arrogance – 'me and nobody but me' – and the road of maintaining democratic liberal Jewish life which takes into consideration the beliefs of others, amongst us, alongside us, where each lives according to their creed. The battle for the character of the Jewish state in the 21st century has begun. In this battle we return to the graveyards, this time in order to bury old concepts, to bury a lifestyle of a state under siege. We are saying farewell to the world of the albums of victory in wars. The coming years will be shadowed by essential questions: Who are we? Where are we striving to get to? What is our new character? What kind of a nation do we want to be? How are we going to live with those around us? Are we going to be 'a light to the nations' or are we going to be a nation 'like all nations'? Will it be religion that will continue to conserve Judaism? 'Chosen people'? What is the place of secularism? Will there be a new Jew, a new Zionist, a new Israeli?[8]

Alas, Rabin was lost in the battle, or rather, the battle was lost. In the 1970s hegemony shifted from Labour Zionism to Liberal Zionism. Labour's state capitalism no longer suited the development of Israel's economy and its secular Occidental worldview was not able to integrate the Orientals. In the Messianic nationalist fervour after 1967, hegemony passed to Liberal Nationalism: liberal in the economic sense and nationalist with regard to settlement of the newly-occupied territories. This hegemonic phase seems presently to be at its end, Rabin was its last representative. It is being replaced by Political Judaism.

At present Judaism in Israel serves as a political ideology which provides cohesion, justification and legitimacy to a social structure full of unresolved contradictions. It serves the character of state and society under the growing struggle of the Palestinians, both inside Israel within the pre-1967 territories and in the West Bank and Gaza. Judaism (rather than anti-Semitism) has become the main justification for the right to be in 'The Place'; Judaism is the internal integrative mechanism and the uniting factor both among Israeli Jews and between them and world Jewry. Judaism, not Zionism, has become the reason for western emigration to Israel.

It is not that the majority of Israeli Jews have become more observant, far from it; lifestyles in Israel have never been less observant. What I refer to is the widespread yearning, in various strata of Israeli society, for unity through a closer association with Judaism. It is the feeling of loss of meaning in secular existence. It appears in many forms: in the attachment to progressive (Reform) Judaism by the Zionist left; in the feeling of secular Jewish intellectuals regarding the lack of knowledge of Jewish thinking and tradition, and the Jewish study groups established; in the spread of Jewish mysticism and spiritualism; in projects undertaken by the Center for the Commemoration of Rabin to find a mutually accepted program with the settlers. It is demonstrated in the recent social agreement (the Kinneret Document) produced by prominent Labour members together with Orthodox Rabbis; in the flocking to Nethanyahu of many Ultra Orthodox Jews;[9] the innocent *bon ton* blessing 'with God's help' that has become standard fare; or the apology among secular Jews when they telephone during the Sabbath. Judaism is converging with Zionism and replacing it. The political concomitant of this phenomenon is the convergence of Left and Right.[10]

THE NEW INFITADA

Sharon won the elections against Barak by a landslide: 62.3 per cent to 37.6 per cent. Most Israeli-Palestinian citizens did not cast their vote. Sharon formed a wide unity coalition that included Likud, Labour, the religious bloc and extreme right parties to fight the Intifada. To the world and to many Israelis the issue was – and still is – how to return to negotiations. However, Sharon and the majority of his right-wing government who oppose the peace process have a different agenda. They want to dissolve any possibility of an agreement that would entail dismantling the settlements. In order to achieve this they must destroy the Palestinian Authority – now the only possible partner to an agreement. Sharon had to shift the political agenda in Israel away from the peace process towards a mood of war for survival – and do it whilst maintaining political consensus. For this purpose Sharon needed Labour in the government, in order not to repeat the mass protests that followed the 1982 war in Lebanon. The deepening cycle of violence was also necessary in order to legitimize the use of Israel's full military might against an asymmetric opponent.

The bloody events of the Intifada served Sharon's purpose. He did not try to reduce the violence; indeed he fanned its flames. The mounting death toll, cruelties on both sides, erosion of security, economic crisis in Israel and disaster in the occupied territories serve constantly as a self-fulfilling prophecy to both sides that there is no partner for peace. Under these conditions the extremists thrive.

On the Palestinian side, Hamas and Islamic Jihad are rejectionist organizations. They oppose any peace settlement and call for armed struggle to liberate the whole of Palestine, return the 1948 refugees, destroy the 'Zionist entity', and establish an Islamic republic in its place. Arafat, on the other hand, has accepted the existence of Israel since 1988 and calls for a two-state solution. Hamas and Jihad's indiscriminate attacks on civilians are consistent and follow logically from their ideological position. Indiscriminate killings of civilians inside Israel (pre-1967) contradict Arafat's declared aims and cast doubt on his sincerity and real goals.

Arafat's indecision, his inability or unwillingness to curb Hamas and Jihad, was seized upon by Sharon's government. On the pretext that they were stopping 'ticking bombs', the Israelis implemented a policy of liquidating Palestinian activists and political leaders; in many cases they killed innocent civilians instead. A careful examination of the so-called 'targeted killings' shows that their timing was deliberate and aimed at retaliation and revenge and at forestalling any reduction of violence. The curfews and closures imposed on the West Bank and Gaza brought their economy to a halt and caused the entire population impossible hardship and suffering. Sharon's government sought and achieved a showdown with the Authority.

Since the beginning of 2002, Arafat's organizations have also been implicated in suicide attacks against civilians inside the Green Line. From a military viewpoint, the suicide bombers became the most effective weapon in the Palestinian arsenal. They were 'human guided delivery systems', the equivalent of smart bombs, they were cheap and they helped to improve, though not to turn around, the ratio of casualties between the two opponents.[11]

Politically however, indiscriminate suicide bombings and shootings have helped Sharon to convince the Israeli public that Arafat's real goal was the destruction of Israel – a claim always maintained by the Right. The bombers served Sharon's purpose of forging unity among Israelis; he could demonstrate the threat to everyone's personal security and undermine the argument that Arafat is still a partner to peace. The suicide bombings also succeeded in disrupting daily life in Israel and caused heavy losses to the economy, though not to the same degree as the Israelis caused in the West Bank and Gaza. Moderate voices among the Palestinians who called for a reconsideration of the right of return, and the brave voices criticizing the use of armed struggle or indiscriminate suicide bombings, have been muted. In Israel, too, the peace movement has been greatly weakened, though not silenced. Contacts between Palestinians and Israelis across the Green Line have been curtailed. Relations within Israel between Jews and Palestinian-Israeli citizens have reached a crisis-point. There is little will to listen to the other side's anguish. Under these conditions of fear, anger and hate, extreme ideas of ethnic cleansing have increased their popularity among Israeli Jews.[12] Similar calls for 'a fight to the bitter end' and agreement with suicide bombings have increased on the Palestinian side too.

The September 11 attack on the USA occurred when the Intifada had been raging for a year. It changed the world and put the events in Palestine/Israel in a different context. The anti-withdrawal right in Israel has always manoeuvred tactically to prevent the implementation of Resolution 242. Israel was much quicker to understand the long-term global implications of that event, and to readjust its tactics and strategy to fit the new Bush Manichean view of the state of the world in terms of for or against terrorism. The suicide bombings enabled Sharon to present Arafat internationally as one of the rejectionists; subsequently, many Palestinian organizations were added to the USA's list of world terrorist organizations – a move bolstered by the interception of the Karine A, a ship loaded with arms for the Palestinians from Iran – and the fight against the Palestinian Authority was portrayed as equivalent to, and part of, the global fight against El-Qaida and other terrorist organizations.

Since September 2001 the indiscriminate terrorist attacks have become, in my view, counterproductive for the Palestinians. Arafat, however, was unable to understand this and readjust his strategy. Unlike Arafat, other Arab countries did understand it and trod cautiously in their support of the Palestinians. In that respect, too, Arafat – who still thinks in pan-Arab terms – may have gained the support of the Arab masses but not the full support of Arab governments, apart from Iraq whose side he took in 1989. The Intifada, which started as a war about the settlements, was now repackaged by Israel and marketed internally and internationally as an alliance with the forces of darkness against the forces of light. It worked very well in Israel, reasonably well in America until now, and not so well elsewhere.

Is Arafat a terrorist or a freedom fighter? Posing the question as if it were an either/or situation is misleading. Freedom fighters often use terrorist methods. Those who know the history of the Jewish struggle against the British in Palestine between 1942 to 1947 know that the 'Fighters for the Freedom of Israel' (LEHI), better known by their British given name 'The Stern Gang', and the 'National Military Organisation' known also as the 'Irgun' (ETZEL), used terrorist methods against British and Arab civilians. Among many, most famous was the assassination in Cairo of Lord Moyne, Deputy Minister of State for Middle East Affairs and a close aid of Churchill, and the bombing of the King David Hotel in Jerusalem in which more than 80 people – British, Arabs and Jews – were killed. One side's terrorist is the other side's freedom fighter. After Israel's independence leaders of both these organizations became prime ministers: Menachem Begin and Itzhak Shamir.[13] Many similar examples can be added, Ireland and Algeria to name but two.

The Palestinians did not invent suicide missions. They were used by Japanese Kamikaze during the Second World War, and by militant non-state armed groups in Sri Lanka, Chechnya, Pakistan, Lebanon, Turkey, Egypt and in New York and Washington.[14] The attack by Baruch Goldstein, a fanatical religious Jewish settler and member of the racist Jewish Defense League, on Muslim worshipers during prayer in the Tomb of the Patriarchs in Hebron on January 25, 1994, killing twenty-nine Palestinians before he was killed, also falls into this category.

Sharon has no alternative peace plan. The occupation and expansion of settlements remains central to his thinking and that of all his coalition partners. Labour and Likud are both responsible for the colonization of the territories occupied in 1967 with a view to establishing Israeli control and preventing the establishment of a Palestinian state. Labour was in power from 1967 to 1977 and erected the infrastructure and institutions for the creation and expansion of the settlements. In this early period settlements were founded in an incremental way, ostensibly subordinated to 'security' considerations. However, security and settlement in Israeli thinking are existential concepts inextricable from sovereignty and Jewish state-building. Moshe Dayan once explained why Jewish settlements in the occupied territories are essential '…not because they can ensure security better than the army, but because without them we cannot keep the army in those territories. Without them the IDF would be a foreign army ruling a foreign population'.[15]

Likud came to power in 1977, and did away with the 'security' discourse of settlement. It justified the morality of wholesale settlement of Jews in all the areas of the 'Land of Israel'. Menchem Begin, Likud's leader, did not see any difference between the settlements founded before and after 1948 and the settlements built after 1967. In an address to the Knesset in May 1982 he said that the settlements are the expression of the enduring vitality of Zionism and its moral vision: 'Settlements – scores, almost one hundred years ago, in areas of the Land of Israel populated by Arabs and sometimes solely by Arabs – was it moral or immoral? Permitted or forbidden? One of the two. If it was moral – then settlement near Nablus is moral … There is no third way'.

In September 1977 Ariel Sharon, then minister of Agriculture in Begin's government, unveiled a plan to settle two million Jews in the occupied territories by the end of the century. In 1972 the number of settlers in the West Bank and the Gaza strip was only 1500; by 1992, on the eve of the Oslo process, it was 109,784; by the end of 2001 it was already 213,672. In East Jerusalem the number of settlers was 6,900 in 1972, 141,000 in 1992 and 170,400 in 2001. These numbers are in addition to the number of settlers in the West Bank. At the end of 2001 the number of settlements was 130 in the West Bank (on 5,640

The West Bank After Oslo: Control and Separation— June 2002

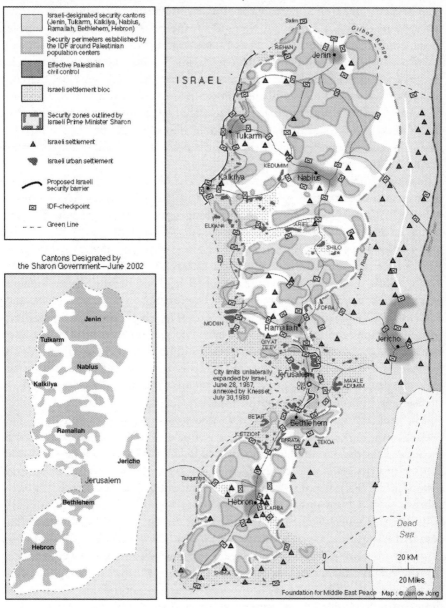

Cantons Designated by
the Sharon Government—June 2002

Foundation for Middle East Peace   Map : © Jan de Jong

sq. km.), 16 in the Gaza Strip (on 360sq. km.) and 11 in East Jerusalem area.

Sharon and his political partners are willing to pay an economic price, antagonize world opinion and sacrifice many casualties. Indeed, during the Israeli
invasion of the West Bank in April 2002 new settlements have been started in
East Jerusalem, Hebron and the West Bank. For many years, Sharon held the idea
that Jordan should be the Palestinian state. The struggle between Palestinians and

Israelis could easily deteriorate into a regional war. There are many internal and regional actors seeking to escalate the conflict. Messianic and nationalist extremists in Israel hope for a regional war and for the breakdown of peace between Israel, Jordan and Egypt. Only under such conditions of general war can the ethnic cleansing of Palestinian-Israeli citizens and Palestinians from the occupied territories to Jordan and Egypt take place. On the Arab/Islamic side, there are pan-Arab nationalists and fundamentalists who dream of doing away with the pro-American Arab regimes and creating Arab/Islamic unity, which will destroy the 'Zionist entity' and liberate the Middle East from American domination. These dangers are further exacerbated by the presence on both sides of weapons of mass destruction.

Is there a solution to the present impasse? The obvious answer is that violence must be reduced and the two sides must return to negotiations. Upon coming to power Sharon offered to negotiate a 'long term interim agreement' within which Israel will pull out of 53 per cent of the West Bank and Gaza. Coming after the long years of 'Oslo' and the bad blood that has since passed between Israelis and Palestinians this is a non-starter, just another prevarication. Negotiations must start where they stopped in Taba before Sharon came to power. This is easier said than done. The events in Palestine/Israel since September 2000 have set us back many years. They have confirmed each side's worst suspicions and fears about the other. The settlement project of the West Bank and Gaza has been Sharon's life work and he is unlikely to agree to withdrawal from the settlements. In any case his government will collapse the moment that negotiations appear on the agenda. Sharon would not even have the backing of his own party on this issue.

The problem, however, goes deeper. A newly-elected government could well make Sharon look moderate. The whole political map in Israel has shifted far to the right. Labour has ousted its Oslo leadership and has chosen hardliners instead. Despite this change of face, the polls show that were elections to be held in Israel now (April 2002) Labour, associated in the public memory with the Oslo process, would be decimated and reduced to a third of its present strength. Within the Likud, Nethanyahu marshals as much support as Sharon. The National Religious, the settlers' party, has chosen a new leader in a secular former general who turned religious and declares that he was chosen by God to lead Israel. He stands openly for war and ethnic cleansing. Further to the right of these are two parties which now have more than six per cent of the vote and who also support ethnic cleansing and, as the polls show, may double their vote.

I have painted a dark picture. I do not think that Israeli society is ripe, from within, for a resolution of the Israeli-Arab conflict. The problem goes much deeper than whether Arafat is a partner or not. Israelis cannot agree among themselves about what peace means in terms of their national aspirations and being part of the Middle East. Until Jews in Israel know what they are, until they decide on the extent of the territory on which they wish to build their state, they cannot agree on borders. Until they agree what kind of society and state they want, they cannot accommodate non-Jews whose territories they covet. They cannot even attract the majority of western Jewry as long as there is no religious pluralism in Israel. They cannot be secular until they separate state and religion.

Israeli Judaism is riddled with contradictions; Jews in Israel have not resolved the inner contradictions imposed on Judaism by modernity. Zionism, which proclaimed to have the solution, has only transplanted those problems to the Middle East, a region which, in itself, has not resolved its contradictions with modernity. This is a dangerous brew indeed in a context where the growing contradictions that attend global American hegemony seem increasingly to be coming to a head in this region of the world.

NOTES

1   See 'A new imperialism cooked up over a Texan barbecue', *The Guardian*, 2 April 2002; 'The new liberal imperialism', *The Observer*, 7 April 2002; R. Cooper, *The Postmodern State and the World Order*, Demos/Foreign Policy Centre, London, 2002; M. Leonard, ed., *Reordering the World: The long-term implications of September 11th*, The Foreign Policy Centre, London, 2002, which also contains an article by Ehud Barak.

2   At a conference on Islam, Judaism and the Political Role of Religions in the Middle East, which I attended last year, philosophers, theologians, Rabbis, Mullahs, historians and political scientists argued *ad nauseam* about 'essences' and 'right' and 'wrong' interpellations and interpretations of those religions. God may be one but there are many Christianities, Islams and Judaisms, and they vary and change in time and place.

3   See A. Ehrlich, 'A Society in War: The national Conflict and the Social Structure', in U. Ram, ed., *Israeli Society – Critical Perspectives*, Tel Aviv: Breirot Publishers,1993 [Hebrew].

4   See A. Ehrlich, 'The Gulf War and the New World Order', in R. Miliband and L. Panitch, eds., *Socialist Register 1992*, London: Merlin Press.

5   For further detail see R. Malley and H. Agha, 'Camp David: The Tragedy of Errors', in *N.Y. Review of Books,* 9 August 2001; R. Falk, 'Ending The Death Dance', *The Nation,* 29 April 2002; R. Wright, 'Understanding Arafat', www.msnbc.com/news741015.asp?0si=; G. Sher, *Just Beyond Reach,* Tel Aviv: Hemed Books, 2001 [Hebrew]; and Y. Beilin, *A Guide to a Wounded Dove,* Tel Aviv: Hemed Books, 2001 [Hebrew].

6   See A. Ehrlich, 'The Religious in Israel and the Failure of the Peace Process', *Monthly Review*, October 2001.

7   See D. Shumsky, 'Ethnicity and Citizenship in the Perception of Russian Israelis', in *Theory and Criticism,* 19 (Fall), 2001 [Hebrew].

8   Excerpt from a speech by Itzhak Rabin in the Levy Eshkol prize-giving ceremony, 6 October 1994.

9   See Tzvia Greenfeld, *They are Afraid*, Tel Aviv: Chemed Publishers, 2001 [Hebrew].

10 See Yoram Hazony, 'Israel's Right and Left Converge', *NY Times,* 26 April 2002.

11 www.idf.il/daily_statistics/english/6.gif.

12 See Asher Arian 'Israeli Public Opinion on National Security', *Jaffe Center for Strategic Studies Memoranda no. 60,* Tel Aviv University, August 2001. www.tau.ac.il/jcss/publications.html#memoranda, also: www.tau.ac.il/peace/peace_index/p_index.html

13 See C.D. Smith, *Palestine and the Israeli-Arab Conflict,* Boston: Bedford/St Martin's Press, 4th Ed., 2001, pp. 175-6, p.188.

14 See 'Suicide attacks – a tactical weapon system', International Institute of Strategic Studies, London, 24 April 2002, www.iiss.org/pub/tx/tx02007.asp.

15 The quotations and figures in this and the following two paragraphs are taken from *Israeli Settlements in the Occupied Territories: A Guide,* Foundation for Middle East Peace, Special Report 2002, www.fmep.org/reports/2002/sr0203.html. Another good source on the settlements is *Land Grab: Israel's Settlement Policy in the West Bank – A Comprehensive Report,* B'tselem, May 2002, http://www.btselem.org.

THE POLITICAL ECONOMY OF ETHNO-NATIONALISM IN YUGOSLAVIA

SUSAN L. WOODWARD

A longside the real wars that tore apart the Socialist Federal Republic of Yugoslavia there has been an ongoing battle of interpretation. Were the wars caused by ethnic hatreds between national communities in the Balkan peninsula that go back centuries, or were they caused by cynical politicians who politicized and manipulated ethnic and religious identities to gain or retain power? Whether one sides with the primordialists or the constructivists, however, the central role of ethno–nationalism is not in doubt. Their agreement on this point was heavily influenced, moreover, by the propaganda campaigns of the real wars. Aware that their chief obstacle might be the reigning civic pluralism of their primary audience in Western capitals, those who won the battle for separation intentionally skirted nationalist rhetoric. They chose to argue instead that Yugoslavia was an artificial state that had no legitimate basis to continue. National communities came together to form Yugoslavia in 1918 and again in 1945, they asserted, but the voluntary basis of this pact and its legitimation in the internationally recognized right to national self-determination had never been respected. Now that democracy was possible in the former Titoist dictatorship, Yugoslavia's respective nations had the right to dissolve that union and form separate nation-states. Their choice for independence was not nationalist; it was for a more *natural* and *modern* state.

The Yugoslav collapse is hardly the first or even the bloodiest instance of ethnic warfare in the post–Cold War international environment, but its location in Europe and the stories of atavistic brutality that dominated journalistic coverage of the ensuing wars sent shock waves through Western publics. The result was a sweeping reinterpretation of civil conflict worldwide, and its pre-eminent threat to international peace and security, based on generalizing this interpretation of the Yugoslav collapse. The post–Cold War era would be domi-nated by ethnic conflict. Wars during the Cold War came to be called ideological wars whereas those occurring since 1989-90 were labelled ethnic wars, or wars of identity.[1] In similar fashion to the influence that the first propa-ganda wars of the Yugoslav tragedy had on interpretations of subsequent developments there, no amount of scholarship demonstrating the minimal explanatory power of the ethnic–conflict label for contemporary civil violence,[2] or the unsubstantiated nature of the distinction between 'new' and 'old' wars,[3] has been able to penetrate this new world view of contemporary conflict, based largely on Western reactions to the Yugoslav case.

This framing is unfortunate. In the case of the Yugoslav successor states – five at this time of writing, but two more likely on the horizon – the creation of nation-states out of multinational Yugoslavia did nothing to resolve the causes of the Yugoslav break-up and subsequent wars. Not only are the new states facing the same challenges that led to break-up, but the mystification of the causes as ethnic conflict has prolonged the disintegration scenario and appeared to prevent alternatives that might facilitate a different, and better, future. The same concern applies to the global generalization of the Yugoslav case. The global shift from political-economic to cultural understandings of politics and civil violence has actually diverted attention away from possible remedies and narrowed the options for resolving such conflicts, leaving many areas of the world in situations of frozen conflict or at the mercy of private remedies, including those of religious organi-zations, for what are properly public issues. Despite the apparent attention such culturalist explanations give to cultural particularity and national distinctiveness, their use in fact denies the particular institutional, historical, political, social, or economic characteristics of countries that do explain why political conflict can become violent and result in war. Ethnic conflict becomes a gloss in need of no further examination. In the Yugoslav case, and by extension in its generalization globally, moreover, the demand for national rights was in fact an attack on the socialist character of the regime (as embodied in the federal institutions and economic policy). But by justifying those national rights on ethno–nationalist grounds, on the claim that the Yugoslav state was artificial or dictatorial, or both, the propagandists deprived socialists, social democrats, and other left forces of any grounds for debate. Left-wing alternatives to right-wing forces are silenced by the simple act of non-recognition. Globally, this leaves few if any secular ideologies available for protest and mobilization by those disadvantaged in the contempo-rary conjuncture.

I. AN ALTERNATIVE EXPLANATION OF THE YUGOSLAV COLLAPSE

The Yugoslav model of socialism was an attempt to combine socialist ideals and policies at home with openness to the world economy – above all to foreign trade, aid, and supplements to the capital needs of their strategy for industrial-ization and national sovereignty. Forged in the heat of the early Cold War period, first antagonizing the Americans, then the Soviet leadership, and after ex-communication from the Communist camp (the Communist Information Bureau) being embraced again by the Americans as a splendid propaganda oppor-tunity, the system depended throughout its forty years on this particular balancing act between East and West. Its reformist position was most notable in its leadership of the nonaligned movement and its periodic advocacy of a new international economic order between North and South, but the core of the balancing act was a strategic bargain struck with the West: it would maintain a strong military capacity independent of Moscow, including a critical role in defence of NATO's southern flank against possible Soviet movement west, in exchange for Western economic assistance and membership in global economic organizations such as the International Monetary Fund (IMF), with its access to World Bank loans, association with European trading blocs (the EFTA and the EC), and by 1965, the General Agreement on Tariffs and Trade (GATT).

This bargain was to support a liberal, sometimes called 'market', socialist approach to economic growth and development. The economic ideology guiding that development strategy, as with any economic ideology, required for its implementation particular social, political, and institutional relations, above all a social organization of labour (employment in production, exchange, and administration). For reasons I discuss elsewhere, the Yugoslav system alternated between two models and their respective development strategies and organiza-tional consequences, but the liberal model was preferred and its organizational requirements were the default institutions – economic management through regulation of money and prices, financial and operational autonomy for producers, and the incentive of economic interest (property rights and produc-tivity-based incomes) for achieving rising productivity.[4] Society would be organized around associations of producers (thus minimizing 'non-productive' employment such as in governmental bureaucracies or commercial firms), and social ownership would not only eliminate the antagonistic, irreconcilable conflicts between capital and labour, but allow labour to think like capital. As early as 1950, the primary principle of political organization was thus decentral-ization and the participation of direct producers (workers) in decisions about the allocation of net profit between wages and new investment (as an incentive to productivity and a long time horizon on wage increases).

Although this second principle, for which the Yugoslav system became partic-ularly renowned, was called 'workers' self-management' (and even 'workers' control'), its objective was to give workers the right to decide how to rationalize the cost of labour: for example, by cutting individual wage levels temporarily, by plowing more of proceeds into productivity-enhancing investments, or by cutting the actual number employed – particularly, as in 1949-52 when it was introduced, in times of foreign trade crisis and skilled labour shortage. Autonomous workplaces were actually managed by directors and the adminis-trative staff, although directors were formally elected by a workers' council; and the workers' councils – elected representatives of all those in production – tended to be dominated by the labour aristocracy, highly skilled workers, of each period; indeed, the original purpose of workers' councils was to hand power back to staff when a tight labour market had given workers increasing power to demand higher wages than the country could afford. The principle of representation, and the need to get approval by an annual assembly of all those employed in the workplace (whether a factory, a school, a hospital, a grocery, or a foreign trade firm) of the budget, economic plan, and rulebook on wages and salaries, certainly instilled a widespread belief in political rights over economic assets and decisions; but the goal of workers' self-management was in fact to avoid raising employment (and thus the aggregate wage bill) above economic sustainability at the level of the firm, locality, and country as a whole.

This system of economic rights, however, belonged only to the sector of socially-owned firms and associations, while a second property sector of individual and household labour (in essence, a private sector) was permitted in agriculture and small crafts and trades, so as to absorb excess labour that could not be employed efficiently in the socialized, or public, sector. To ensure the capacity of this sector to absorb surplus labour and guarantee means of subsistence, regulations maintained small holdings (defined in terms of land, number of employees, market profits, or other capital assets) and prevented consolidations and accumulation that might generate true proletarianization.

But the critical characteristic of this system was that employment status defined the identities, economic interests, social status, and political loyalty of Yugoslav citizens. One's place of work was the centre of one's social universe. Social status, income guarantees, social benefits, and political rights to participate in economic decisions and to be elected to legislative chambers for the economy varied according to the sector – social or individual – in which one was employed. Political rights and incomes also varied according to whether one was in managerial, administrative, and professional positions paid for out of budgets (people on 'guaranteed salary') according to a sliding scale tied to rates of change in workers' incomes or in production ('associated labour'), and, in turn, according to one's level of education (professional, skilled, semi-skilled, unskilled). The level of territorial decentralization also meant, *de facto*, that one's economic and social prospects depended on the economic base of one's locality and republic (including its capacity to finance education and social benefits, to invest in employment generation, and to keep tax levels low). The social organization of employment in Yugoslavia thus defined individuals' economic, social, and political position, rights, and prospects.

This reform model of socialism was eventually also chosen by Hungary, Poland, and China, and in 1985, by Gorbachev in the USSR. These countries' experimentation with the political principles of decentralization and workers' participation remained only that, and crucially, their choice did not depend on the strategic bargain made by the Yugoslavs and the extent of its international exposure. The vulnerabilities of this political-economic model in a globalized economy were thus expressed most intensely in the Yugoslav case.

The dynamic of public policy in this Yugoslav system, from the late 1940s until the late 1980s, was driven by the federal government's response to changes in its international conditions – both economic and security conditions. The continuing need to give priority to external conditions, moreover, introduced a high level of unpredictability in federal policy, making planning and policy consistency difficult, at best. The best explanation of changes in federal economic policy can be found in crises in the foreign sector of the economy when the authorities could no longer resist adjustment to changed international conditions or when external shocks were so great as to require an immediate response. What I have labelled the Yugoslav leaders' Faustian bargain,[5] gaining special access to foreign assistance and trade based on their international strategic position in the Cold War, led to an increasing dependence on Western capital and Western markets, and accompanying domestic policies of structural adjustment, to resolve balance-of-payments, foreign liquidity, or foreign debt crises. Yet the bargain also imposed limits on their methods of adjustment, because authorities could not alter their strategic choice, for example by cutting military expenditures or moving fully into one of the two Cold War camps.

A policy path driven largely by externally induced crises, moreover, is fiendishly difficult to manage domestically. For reasons I analyze extensively elsewhere, federal politics swung between a politics of economic redistribution among republican and local governments and one of competition for greater autonomy over social property, that is, the disposition of revenues, profits, and capital gains.[6] But because property rights in the socialized sector were shared – among autonomous enterprises and local, republican, and federal governments (depending on the economic sector) – these property claims generated intense competition among multiple claimants for more exclusive rights (jurisdictions). In effect, federal politics was a continual competition for and over financial capital (rights to retain profits and foreign exchange, revenues for social funds and public budgets, bank credits, federal transfers, foreign aid), which generated an insatiable demand for foreign credits as one way to keep domestic peace and the economy growing.

Labour rationalization and identity politics

Why is this relevant to fighting identities after 1990? The only real method of adjustment to economic downturns or crises in this system was to rationalize the use of labour – that is, to cut the cost of labour (wages, benefits, number employed) or to increase labour productivity. As socialists, it was critical for the leaders that rationalization avoid mass layoffs and not threaten subsistence – in the jargon of the system, that it not lead to capitalist unemployment. The primary solution chosen was to move 'less productive' labour (as defined primarily by skills, and somewhat by discipline) from better status and pay to lower status and less well-paid positions, and to fire first those who were assumed to have alternative means of subsistence – women and young people (whose families would provide), rural migrants (on the assumption they could 'return to the land'), and those who could claim a retirement pension – and even to encourage some to choose temporary work abroad. This solution required both detailed labour regulations and union approval of decisions on dismissal or transfer. A second method was to increase financial autonomy (and accountability, *khozrascët*) of economic units, such as firms, social services, or territorially circumscribed governments, so as to increase the directness of economic incentives to increase productivity.

The original social organization of employment to suit the leaders' development strategy thus became over time an entire society organized around labour rationalization – regulations on employment, reward, and reassignment. To improve one's prospects or protest one's disadvantage, individuals did not combine into associations to protest public policy, over which they would have little or no effect, given the orientation to foreign developments on the one hand, and the financial autonomy of workplaces on the other. Instead, they competed individually to improve their relative individual 'capital' (for example, increased schooling and certification, personal or political contacts and loyalties, or temporary migration for Western currency to invest in the individual sector of economic activity upon return home) as a means to a social sector job and the social status and benefits it conferred; or they appealed individually to the union or the courts against decisions to exclude them from such a position, or they combined to fight the individual criteria or collective categories of regulations on employment in the social sector.

Labour markets in this decentralized system of economic decision-making and reward, to the extent they existed at all, were local, or in a few instances, operated at the level of a republic (a unit in the federal system). Wage bargaining took place within the firm, with occasional input from local governmental or party authorities. Institutionally, therefore, there was no basis for a society-wide concept of collective interest as a counterweight to the social segmentation created by criteria for employment and income, or to the ongoing demands for greater autonomy over capital. Unemployment was high (and largely structural), but it was largely invisible. It consisted of persons shunted off to the individual and household sector of the economy, including women and retirees; young people who had no employment status into their late twenties because they could not find even a starting position; and in a huge temporary exodus for work abroad. And while the legitimacy of the League of Communists (as the Communist Party was known) seemed rooted in the rising standard of living (increasingly based on credit) of the overall population, its power depended on its international leverage.

The impact of neoliberalism

The 1980s were difficult times for the Yugoslav economy and its citizens. Foreign debt in 1979 was $19.3 billion, and the decade from 1979 to 1989 was preoccupied with policies aimed at reducing the debt and replenishing foreign reserves, and at structural change that would enable the country to service its debt over the long term (in other words, export orientation to Western markets). The federal government had to undertake macroeconomic stabilization policies, designed to meet the conditions of new IMF financing and cut domestic demand, and the refinancing of its commercial debt with private banks. This required a reversal of the policies of the 1970s which had handed such powers to the republics. Liberalization of foreign trade and the economy's orientation to price signals required a reintegration of the internal Yugoslav market and a recentralization of monetary, trade, foreign exchange, and incomes policies. Nonetheless, industrial (development) policy remained in the jurisdiction of the republics and thus the extent to which employment levels could be sustained (or their fall could be buffered, under the increasingly harsh austerity policies during the decade) depended on the economic policies of each republic. Within the harsh new constraints of federal policy, structural adjustment was the responsibility of the republics.

Political reaction to this change of economic policy and the institutional changes required to implement the change came primarily from those political and social groups who had the most to lose, and who also had economic and political resources to take initiative and gain attention. That is, reaction came from those now threatened with unemployment for the first time.[7] At the level of the republics and provinces, the reaction to the new federal policies was strongest and earliest in Slovenia, the only area in the country where full employment reigned. As the primary producer of exports to Western markets, its voice could not be ignored. Equally important in the long run, the fact of full employment for nearly the entire post-war period had generated a political system within Slovenia that is usually associated with market (bourgeois) economies – parliamentary responsiveness, competitive elections, and a burgeoning civil society – which gave the republican government enormous resources to wield in a fight over federal policy. Like the EU countries it would be first in line to join as a parliamentary democracy after 1991, moreover, its economic policies were also protectionist, and opposed to federal policies and regulations that threatened its full employment, standard of living (wage and salary levels), and capacity to import new technology to remain internationally competitive. The IMF-defined stabilization program (i.e. devaluation and an end to the foreign-exchange retention quotas, an independent central bank responsible for monetary policy, limits on wage increases) threatened all of those goals.

Equally consequential politically was the threat of unemployment from the decade-long policy-induced recession that now faced the last bastion of social privilege in the country – the administrative stratum and its university-educated children. While the Slovene government was mounting its attack on federal policies – from simple refusal to implement them in Slovenia, to organizing an anti-federal coalition in the debate on political reform and eventually denying any federal jurisdiction in the republic when Slovene and federal laws or regulations were in conflict – the middle class aimed their protest at the institutions responsible for employment allocation in white-collar, managerial, and administrative jobs. The League of Communists (at the federal level, especially) was accused of corruption. The rules of positive discrimination according to national identity (proportional quotas, called the 'national key') for any position of authority using federal funds or under federal regulations were declared in conflict with the meritocratic criteria necessary for economic growth. And the educational reforms being implemented during the 1980s that aimed to improve chances for social mobility for children of workers and peasants by eliminating the privileged *gimnazije* and its exclusive channel to university admission in favour of uniform secondary education were accused of the worst sort of levelling and political interference by socialist egalitarians.[8] Because employment and educational policy were within the jurisdiction of the republics, not the federal government, moreover, this middle-class revolt combined with that of their republican governments to protect republican control over economic assets and tax monies, on the one hand, and to mount a political campaign against federal transfers and expenditures (namely, the defence budget, federal government offices, and the welfare and development-assistance transfers to poorer communities), on the other. The argument was that they were diverting resources needed for new investment and jobs. Redistribution was seen generally as reducing incentives to investment and efficiency, while the transfers through the federal development fund, in particular, were seen as a gross waste on the part of politicians and directors in the south interested in prestige projects of little value and protecting padded work rolls.

The critical role of employment status and labour policy in defining political positions and protest during the economic crisis of the 1980s can also be seen by looking at the poorest part of the south, the opposite end of the socio-economic and political spectrum from Slovenia. In the autonomous province of Kosovo (in the Serbian republic) unemployment was so high that eighty per cent of the population earned their incomes in the individual (private) sector – in household agriculture and crafts, petty trades, family businesses, and temporary labour migration to Switzerland, Germany, and Italy, but also Slovenia. Just as full employment in Slovenia shaped its political system, so the employment profile of Kosovo generated a social and political organization based on family and ethnicity, including large extended families to support a household-based strategy of economic diversification, and an entire parallel society as the basis for mobilizing collective political action against the regime. At the same time, provincial autonomy during the 1970s had promoted local university education to the point where per capita, the proportion of the population with university education and expectations of managerial, professional positions in the social sector was the highest in the country. For these Kosovo students, in particular, the best solution to their meagre employment prospects was full republican status within the federation, and thus full control over local investment policy.

The turn to nationalism

To express a defence of republican rights against federal policy in anticommunist terms would have undermined the ideological basis of the property and employment rights that these governments and urban middle strata claimed. Moreover, most of those engaging in this campaign were themselves members of the League of Communists. The federal system, however, had been constructed to guarantee *equality* between the nations comprising Yugoslavia, independent of their numerical size. Each republic represented the right to self-determination of one of the six Slavic nations (Croats, Macedonians, Montenegrins, Serbs, Slovenes, and, eventually, Bosnian Muslims), and federal institutions required consensus and various proportional rules for representation, employment, and decision-making, on the grounds this would guarantee the cultural survival of even the smallest national communities.[9] Thus, claims for republic-level control over economic assets were difficult to refute if made in the language of national rights, while invoking the veto power of republics in federal forums was an effective way to prevent the emergence of alternative political formations and coalitions (worst of all, ones that might cross republican lines, such as labour organizations or social movements at the all-country level). In a global era promoting decentralization, in fact, their states' rights claims could be seen by outsiders, at least, as progressive, in relation to individual rights and freedoms, rather than anti-democratic.

In a period of prolonged severe recession it is difficult to contain peoples' search for scapegoats. By 1984 already the official unemployment rate was above 20 per cent in every republic except Slovenia and Croatia, and inflation was at 50 per cent and climbing. In 1985, 59.6 per cent of the registered unemployed were under the age of 25 (and 38.7 per cent of people under the age of 25 were unemployed), and 25 per cent of the population was living below the official poverty line. The use of the 'national card' as a legitimating principle in the contest over economic and political reform would inevitably be a resource in individual competition for jobs and status, despite constitutional prohibitions against speech likely to incite ethnic and racial intolerance. Because of the national quota in government jobs, people hoping for white collar jobs in poorer, ethnically mixed areas were likely to see the quotas, rather than their own qualifications, as the cause of their unemployment or unmet expectations. Similarly, a labour policy that moved people among jobs within a firm, or out of the social sector into the subsistence haven of the private sector, to keep labour costs down and labour productivity growing, also invited speculation that special connections, including ethnic affinity, were the real reason for losing (or not gaining) a particular job. It also encouraged young men to attack women's rights and urban residents to criticize recent migrants from rural areas. For the most part, people played the 'national card', not as an expression of individual identities but as a language justifying property rights and specific governmental jurisdictions as these issues became acute.

By the end of the 1980s, this began to change. As economic growth did not resume and the IMF requirements became increasingly radical and draconian, the politics of exclusion from public sector jobs in order to protect the incomes and status of those who remained came to focus on the very criteria of citizenship itself. When changes in the federal constitution to implement the economic reforms of 1988-89 required harmonizing republican constitutions with the federal amendments, the republican legislatures seized the opportunity. From a set of rights and governmental jurisdictions aimed at equality of all citizens regardless of national identity, national self-determination in the revised constitutional preambles appeared to be limited exclusively to the majority national group in each republic – Slovenia for the Slovenes, Croatia for the Croats, Macedonia for the Macedonians, Serbia for Serbs, Kosovo for Albanians, and so forth – and thus to protect the shrinking stratum of positions paid out of public budgets for people from the majority nation in each republic. The rhetoric of 'exploitation' was transferred from its Marxist origins to economic relations between nations in the federal system and began to be used by individuals to explain their declining fortunes.

Yet the social basis of this continuing revolt remains indisputable if one compares the almost total silence that accompanied simultaneous legislation aimed at attracting foreign investment to Yugoslav firms. In an enterprise law written by Slovene economic reformers and passed by the federal parliament in 1988, granting to foreigners not only ownership rights above 50 per cent (previously prohibited) but also the right of all managers to hire and fire workers freely, the core institution of Yugoslav socialism disappeared overnight. Moreover, the federal government was itself in line for demolition as the Slovene government launched multiparty competitive elections at the republican level in April 1990 and then reneged on its commitment to hold federal elections at the end of the year, once the round of the other republics' elections was complete. Perhaps the most defiant version of the election rhetoric, that of the presidential candidate in Croatia, Franjo Tudjman, illustrates the extent of the shift that had taken place in public employment criteria. According to Tudjman the goal of the election was 'de-communization', which was, he said, synonymous with 'de-Serbianization'.[10]

Democratic elections and civil wars, unfortunately, are games of numbers, not rights. Such nationalist rhetoric could appeal to those who had never been included in the socialized sector of the economy, or who had been excluded in the labour rationalizing policies on the argument that they were insufficiently 'productive'. Resentments at their second class citizenship had led many during the 1960s to do whatever they could (move to the city, get a university education, join the party) to gain access to a socialized sector job. While this was rarely successful, by the 1980s prospects were so dim and numbers were so large that there was a large pool of people ready to find hope in national preferences. Public opinion polls in the middle of 1990, at the time of the republican elections, showed that 70 per cent of the population were still in favour of Yugoslav integrity, and also showed that the reform prime minister, Ante Marković, was the most popular politician. But by the time that republican parliaments and public referendums voted for independence (first Slovenia, then Croatia, both of which labelled it 'dissociation', then Kosovo, and so forth), it is not surprising that ethnically mixed communities would begin to witness 'ethnic cleansing' – physical expulsion of the minority group in a particular locality – or that accompanying violence would occur in areas of Croatia, Bosnia-Herzegovina,

Kosovo, and Macedonia which were nationally mixed. Rank-and-file recruits for the militias attached to political parties, the paramilitary gangs, and the new 'national' armies that terrorized areas of contested territory during each war came largely from the ranks of unemployed young men and urban unskilled workers, resentful at being excluded from the benefits of a system ideologically legitimated as workers' control, and resentful of the rhetoric justifying their exclusion on grounds of lesser social worth. Wars of secession and national independence, moreover, are eventually not about jobs but about territory. Land for those left in the individual (private) sector was a family's insurance policy, even if it pursued a household economic strategy of diversification, sending some children to relatives in urban areas for secondary and university education and others to work abroad and send back remittances. No ethnic identity is needed to provoke subsistence farmers to take up guns to defend their land.

II. NATIONAL INDEPENDENCE

The republican leaders who chose independence and war remained in power from their election in 1990 until elections in 2000 (except for Macedonia, where the change took place in November 1998). Despite the claims that national independence would provide an escape from the Yugoslav economic crisis because it would end the federal fiscal drain on the republics, prevent 'exploitation' by the other nations in multinational Yugoslavia, and remove the power of the communist party and the federal army to oppose democratic rule, except in Slovenia the opposite occurred. Elected politicians used their power and the cover of war to capture economic resources for their party coffers and their personal gain. Privatization of social property was preceded by nationalization and centralization, and then a process of deeply corrupt insider privatization. By 2000-1 all the governments except Slovenia were on the verge of bankruptcy, and all the states were hostage to the particular interests of the nationalist parties which had conducted the war and their coalitions of socialist-era economic managers with an economic agenda of rent-seeking, not investment-promotion. As with former Yugoslavia, all of the new states were financially unsustainable without foreign aid and remittances from the diaspora and refugees. Foreign aid was channelled through political parties and distributed for political patronage, not economic growth. As in the 1980s, external donors used all the economic and political levers they had at their disposal (including, in some cases, even to remove from office leaders chosen in free, competitive elections) to support politicians they called 'reformers', who would introduce liberalizing economic reform and cut public expenditures. And even more than in the 1980s, all the countries in the region had unsustainable current account deficits and growing foreign debt.[11] They remain vulnerable to unpredictable external factors beyond their control, generating as before high levels of uncertainty that work against business investment (whether domestic or foreign).

Moreover, public preferences regarding the role of the state had not changed. Citizens still wanted protective (some might say, paternalistic) states providing public goods, welfare, services, and job security. Private (or market) provision was still viewed as supplemental – fees to private tutors, moonlighting, or bribes – and those who proposed private provision, for example of tertiary education or of health insurance, found the greatest and most effective opposition came from those employed in those public services, such as teachers or doctors. For the most part, the socialist-era legal regulations protecting employment and wage scales remain on the books, and their priority is to protect the breadwinner, that is, the male head of household who will be able to support the (unemployed) female and younger members of the family. The employment structure reflected a frozen age structure, while unemployment skyrocketed further and continued to grow, averaging in 2001, 22 per cent in Croatia, 32 per cent in Macedonia and around 50 per cent in Bosnia-Herzegovina and Kosovo.[12] As before, this unemployment fell disproportionately on new entrants to the labour force so that in the 1990s the high levels of youth unemployment of the 1970s and 1980s had more than doubled. While external donors and creditors pressed for the privatization of socialized sector enterprises, the primary distinction in labour markets was now between those working in the formal sector of the economy (paying taxes, subject to labour regulations, and so forth) and those working in the informal sector (including criminal activities) for lack of opportunities in the formal sector. Continuity also prevailed in the large proportion of unemployment that was long-term, and the predominance among the unemployed of those with low skills and educational qualifications.[13]

Although the constant theme in the constitutional quarrels of the 1980s was the size of the federal budget and its financing, public expenditures in the new states are far higher than in the socialist period, averaging 50 per cent of GDP. Moreover, these expenditures are for the two main categories under attack in the 1980s – the defence and internal security budget, now huge, and expenditures for public employment (now averaging about 50 per cent of the total) and for social redistribution such as pensions, unemployment compensation, and subsidies to heating, medicines, and social welfare. But in contrast to the socialist period, this fiscal redistribution has become increasingly regressive, protecting the jobs and incomes of those people who were employed in the social sector in 1990.[14] Nor did this still-extensive redistribution and protective legislation ameliorate the economic hardships of continuing austerity, war, and economic sanctions in the case of Serbia, Montenegro, and, by extension, Macedonia; the greatest source of inequality was the income differentials that existed within the working population so that poverty was very acute, especially among the 'working poor'. And while the World Bank, as the largest creditor, refrained from criticizing the new governments for their defence budgets (this being considered too political by the Bank's lawyers), they did make loans contingent on cuts in social expenditures which meant – for example in Bosnia and Herzegovina – the rationalization of and sharp cuts in veterans' benefits, along the lines demanded of the federal government by the Slovenes in the 1980s. Similarly, citizens attributed their poor economic conditions and poor public services to political corruption and, in particular instances, to political favouritism from which they did not benefit.

III. THE GLOBAL REFORM AGENDA

The end of the Cold War should have provided Yugoslavia a way out of its crisis. The primary slogan and rallying cry of all of the anti-communist revolutions in Eastern Europe was 'return to Europe' and 'Europe Now!' (the latter was even the slogan of the League of Communists of Slovenia in 1989). Removing the constraints on trade, foreign aid, foreign investment, and travel imposed by the division of Europe was equated with an end to isolation, to second-class citizenship in Europe, and to exclusion from the prosperity associated with bourgeois society. For Yugoslav reformers, it would also eliminate the conditions of its Faustian bargain and the growing costs of military self-reliance and neutrality between the blocs, including the need to protect strategic supplies and defence industries regardless of the requirements of liberalization. Indeed, the Slovene campaign against the federal government was most vocally waged against the federal army and its fiscal drain.

Most stories of the Yugoslav collapse remain at the level of domestic politics and, at most, include various national adjustments to international conditions. Nonetheless, the extent to which the Yugoslav conflict has defined interpretations of any number of state failures, civil wars, and 'ethnic' violence in the post-Cold War period makes it irresponsible to ignore the role of common international conditions in these calamities. Moreover, while the Yugoslav collapse can be explained by internal politics, the ethno-nationalist path that it subsequently took cannot be explained in those terms. A number of alternative paths were possible, including those presented by associations of left intellectuals (the first new political parties to emerge) and advanced by workers (and expressed in country-wide demonstrations) and a range of interests organized along economic lines. Why ethno-nationalism won out can only be explained once international conditions are taken into account.

Three elements are particularly important. First, as discussed above, the entire socio-economic and political order of socialist Yugoslavia was designed in response to the particular conditions of international recognition of its national sovereignty (including the socialist regime), in 1949-50, and the ongoing policies necessary for foreign assistance and support. States are organizations governing territories and populations, and are embedded in a state *system*, including institutionalized relations with neighbours and membership in economic and security alliances and organizations. For all the constraints of its Faustian bargain, Yugoslavia's survival was not in doubt – until its stability and territorial integrity were no longer of strategic interest to the United States and NATO's southern flank. Despite the clear success of Prime Minister Marković's economic reform and his personal popularity in the country, neither the US nor the European Community states were willing to loan the instalment necessary in the spring of 1991 to pay the interest on the Yugoslav foreign debt and keep economic reform on track. The contrast at the same time with Western aid to central Europe – Poland, Hungary, and then the Czech Republic – is striking.[15]

Simultaneously, Cold War constraints no longer stopped European states such as Austria, Germany, Switzerland, and eventually Italy, from encouraging the break-up by supporting the independence of Slovenia and Croatia and accusing the army and the Serbian government of aggression. The historical echoes of 1878, 1908-14, and 1939-45 in West European foreign policies were enough for some to accuse European powers themselves of 'ancient ethnic hatreds' and revenge. In contrast with central Europe, moreover, neither West Europeans nor Americans saw any reason to fill the security vacuum they had created in relation to Yugoslavia with something else.[16]

Their apparently negligent attitude can be understood once the second international factor we need to consider is introduced. The economic and political reforms that caused such contention during the 1980s, and led to the eventual break-up, were part of a global agenda, pushed by the US government and the multilateral institutions it controlled, promoting liberalization, privatization, stabilization, human rights, and democratization. Yugoslavia was only one of many countries that received bilateral aid, IMF and World Bank loans, and arms agreements in exchange for such domestic reforms. Nor was it alone in feeling the corrosive effects that these reforms had on the institutional arrangements and social commitments that underpinned social peace in most countries during the Cold War. With the end of the Cold War, however, this neoliberal agenda became a security policy as well. International peace and security were no longer to be achieved by international alliances among sovereign states and the obligations of membership in international organizations, such as the United Nations, and signatures on international treaties, but by extensive reform of domestic orders. Security communities as a constraint on the use of violence[17] were now supposed to result from like-minded states and isomorphism in internal orders. A particularly striking example of this trend is the difference between the first EU enlargements in 1975-86 (for Portugal, Greece, and Spain) and 1989-95 (for Austria, Finland, and Sweden) and the strict conditionality toward applicant states from the east in the 1990s, which, in order to be considered for membership, are required to adopt nearly the entire *acquis communitaire*, consisting of thousands of laws in 30 Chapters, and be subjected to annual, public reviews of their progress toward market economies, democracy, human rights, peaceful relations with neighbours, and so forth.

This Western security agenda was applied with particular intensity, however, to the Yugoslav successor states. The wars and their refugee flows were seen as a direct threat to peace and stability in Europe. The failure of the Western powers, including the EU and NATO, to act early to end the violence became by 1995-98 a matter of organizational credibility. What happened in the Balkans would reflect directly on the reputation of transatlantic and European security and foreign policy. In June 1999 the EU and partners (including the US, Canada, Russia, Norway, and many international organizations) inaugurated the Stability

Pact for Southeastern Europe, promising eventual membership in the EU to the states in the region on condition of demonstrated cross-border and regional (Balkan) cooperation. This was followed by a new instrument of association with the EU, the Stabilization and Association Agreement (SAA), designed specifically for the countries of southeastern Europe, in which an additional layer of conditions was added to the already heavy conditionality addressed to central European candidates.[18]

At the same time, the attitude of the major powers toward the parties at war had led to substantial variation in treatment and status within the region. Slovenia escaped surgically from the region and from judgment, winning early admission in the first round of candidates for EU membership and, by 2001, an offer of early admission to NATO. Viewing Croatia as a victim of Serbian aggression and a partner in the strategy to end the war in Bosnia-Herzegovina, the US and Germany supported Croatia in the form of a strategic alliance (including American military assistance) and special access to World Bank aid.[19] Economic assistance to Bosnia-Herzegovina in the first three years after the signing of the Dayton peace framework went solely (98 per cent) to the Bosnian-Croat entity (the Federation), while aid was withheld from the Bosnian-Serb entity until political demands (such as arresting and extraditing indicted war criminals to the Hague Tribunal on former Yugoslavia and allowing refugees to return home in the Republic) were met, with long-term consequences for sharply uneven development within the country. Economic sanctions and diplomatic isolation were imposed on Serbia from November 1991 until the electoral defeat of the Milošević government in late 2000 as a means of leverage to obtain political cooperation (the US continued to withhold most aid into 2002, with a renewal in June 2002 for another year of 'extraordinary measures' against Yugoslav firms), while direct budgetary support, development aid, and security assistance began to arrive in Montenegro in 1998 as a means of pressuring the Belgrade authorities (with direct consequences for the Montenegrin government's decision to seek independence and further Western support). Even Macedonia and Albania were rewarded with NATO assistance and small steps toward association with the EU as part of the policy to isolate Serbia, although economic assistance centred largely on border control and police training (to address the networks of drug and human trafficking into Western Europe), not the dire economic consequences (especially for Macedonia) of the policy of economic sanctions on its main trading partner, Serbia.

Despite this variation, all countries in the region had to meet the conditions of membership in the IMF – policies to settle foreign debt arrears that are nearly identical to those guiding economic and institutional reform in Yugoslavia during the 1980s – in order to gain access to World Bank loans, negotiate with their foreign creditors in the Paris and London Clubs, and participate in world trade and capital markets. All economic aid was in support of the same package of neoliberal, domestic economic and political reforms. Ignoring their negative experience with the same 'reforms' in the 1980s, and more nuanced programs for the transition advanced by many economists and political associations, all the governments have acceded to these conditions and given priority to macroeconomic stabilization, rapid privatization of the banking sector and socialist sector enterprises, and foreign trade liberalization.[20] As in 1988-90 under Yugoslav prime minister Marković, priority is being given to economic reform, not political development, with the aim of enticing foreign investment for their long struggle for recovery and reconstruction.[21]

This clear re-emergence of what I labelled the Faustian bargain for socialist Yugoslavia – i.e., the fact that all the current states in the region are being required to trade a particular role in Western security (defined by outsiders) for economic assistance, and that all of them are already dependent on foreign aid and its conditions for the long haul – may help to explain the lack of change in crucial political characteristics discussed above: we continue to witness a protectionist, even paternalist role of the state for selected groups, capture of the state for personal and party political aggrandizement, and a lack of domestic policy instruments to manage the economy. The absence of an autonomous domestic politics more than a decade after the break-up attracts increasing commentary and worried concern.

This is most poignant when we consider the third element of international influence that cannot be ignored – the role of external mediators (primarily the EU and the US) in negotiating frameworks for resolving the ongoing process of disintegration and the international protectorates used to ensure their implementation. The development of a new security architecture for Europe and the Western alliance after the Cold War has been driven largely by response to the Yugoslav conflicts. Having accepted the accusation of failure toward Bosnia-Herzegovina (and perhaps Croatia), the US, EU, and NATO began to intervene in the midst of conflicts over statehood and national rights in order to restore their credibility and develop mechanisms for the new challenges they face. In August-November 1995, the US and NATO forces intervened to end the war in Bosnia-Herzegovina, to impose a peace agreement, and to begin an international mission composed of 55,000 NATO troops (declining to 12,000 by October 2002) and a complex civilian administration set up to implement that agreement and to transform Bosnia-Herzegovina into a market economy and a multi-ethnic, liberal democracy. In March 1999, NATO powers chose to intervene in the conflict between Albanian secessionists in Kosovo and the Belgrade government with a 78-day bombing campaign against the Federal Republic of Yugoslavia to force the Yugoslav army and internal security forces out of the province and replace it with an international protectorate established by UN Security Council resolution 1244. In 2000, the EU and the US intervened to prevent incidents of violence between the Macedonian government and Albanian nationalists from escalating into full-scale war by imposing the Ohrid framework agreement (and its adoption by the Macedonian parliament) and to send a NATO-led security force to help implement its security provisions. In 2001-2, the EU intervened with another imposed agreement to end the constitutional dispute between Serbia and Montenegro.

Each of these agreements takes as its working premise that the war-threatening conflicts are ethno-national, and that the only way to peace is to design constitutional rights and protections according to ethnonational identity. Power-sharing principles, such as proportional distribution of government ministries to national groups, guaranteed seats for minorities in parliaments, extensive decentralization (including fiscal powers) to give minorities local autonomy, and complex electoral and decision-making rules to provide group protection (such as concurrent vetoes on matters deemed of 'vital interest' to national groups) characterize all of the third-party negotiated agreements – for eastern Slavonia in Croatia, Bosnia and Herzegovina, Kosovo, Macedonia, and Serbia/Montenegro. In effect, each agreement institutionalizes the power balances and group demands of those able and willing to use violence at the moment of outside intervention to negotiate a settlement. Some are intentionally temporary, such as the framework for Kosovo, while others freeze a particular situation and thus are *de facto* temporary.

At the same time, the international administrations tasked with implementing these framework agreements are under instructions to defeat the nationalists and restore commitment to multi-ethnicity, including the reversal of 'ethnic cleansing' with the return of refugees and displaced persons to their prewar homes. The tension between those institutionally empowered by the peace frameworks and this additional international agenda means not only that the agreements are not self-enforcing but that they have required ever increasing dictate by outsiders and a prolongation into the distant future of the international military and civilian governing presence. Their constitutional provisions (such as group rights, fiscal decentralization, and decision rules) appear to be both financially unsustainable without long-term foreign assistance and in conflict with the required economic and political reforms of the neoliberal consensus.

IV. CONCLUSION

The Yugoslav wars of the 1990s had a profound influence on people's general perceptions of the new world environment after 1989. Ethnic conflict, tribal atavisms, civilizational clash, identity politics – these would replace the ideological confrontation of the Cold War. What is so striking about the actual Yugoslav wars and post-Yugoslav outcomes, however, is how much the fights were actually about the same issues of economic security and insecurity of individuals and families, waged between the propertied and dispossessed, the relatively better off and worse off, over public expenditures and redistribution under conditions of growing economic austerity and adjustment to the global economy. The fight is still over state power and political rights, but now based on ethno-nationalist claims, not alternative ideologies and parties.

Nor does there seem to be any change over the long period 1979-2002 in the US-led global reform agenda. What have changed are the instruments and agents of this neoliberal, anti-social justice project. Economic and political 'reform' in the 1970s–80s was accomplished largely by economic conditionality, on terms negotiated with government officials behind closed doors, whereas since 1990 it was increasingly dictated by diplomats negotiating political deals, and by military and civilian officials administering international protectorates or conditions for membership in organizations such as NATO and the EU. While IMF-type conditionality continues to be used to force liberalization, economic assistance and trade relations are also increasingly used as political leverage to secure governments' compliance with political demands from major powers. And although the goal is said to be democracy as well as free markets, when governments do not move at an appropriate pace to meet such demands, the general consensus is that outsiders have not been sufficiently interventionist and assertive.

The convergence of economic and security interests among the major powers, banks, and investors takes a different form than during the Cold War, but its outcome – at least in the ex-Yugoslav cases – is eerily the same. Authoritarian socialism has been replaced by parliamentary democracy and private property, but the three constraints on socialist Yugoslavia that can be said to have brought about its ruin – foreign economic aid, trade and investment dependent on particular security relations, political institutions defined by ethnonational rights, and government policy driven by the demands of major powers and creditors – continue to characterize its successor states, with no alternative in sight.

NOTES

1   Particularly influential has been Chaim Kaufman, 'Possible and Impossible Solutions to Ethnic Conflict', *International Security*, 20(4) (Spring), 1996.
2   Two representative examples are Paul Brass, *Theft of an Idol,* Princeton, New Jersey: Princeton University Press, 1997, and Nicholas Sambanis, 'Partition as a Solution to Ethnic War: An Empirical Critique of the Theoretical Literature', *World Politics*, 52(4) (July), 2000.
3   See the very useful criticism of this distinction by Stathis Kalyvas, '"New" and "Old" Civil Wars: A Valid Distinction?' *World Politics*, 54(1) (October), 2001.
4   *Socialist Unemployment: The Political Economy of Yugoslavia, 1945-1990,* Princeton, New Jersey: Princeton University Press, 1995.
5   Woodward, *Socialist Unemployment*, in particular chapter 7 (pp. 222-59).
6   Ibid., in particular chapter 8 (pp. 260-309).
7   Poorer areas of the country and the disadvantaged (such as the private sector, the unemployed, and the producers of goods no longer in demand such as primary commodities, import-substituting and other heavy manufactures, goods produced for the Eastern market) were only in a position to ask for federal credits, exemptions, and transfer payments to buy the time they needed for adjustment.
8   Yugoslav parents reacted to this reform as if it were another plot by the communist party to limit individual merit, but the reform was actually initiated in the early 1970s after an OECD pilot project for all

Mediterranean countries in the 1960s, patterned after trends taking place in Western Europe at the time.

9 These protections were actually under attack by the efficiency-oriented reforms and IMF conditionality program, which only reinforced opposition to the program from those who wanted to protect republican rights.

10 Minority Serbs in Croatia, comprising 12.2 per cent of the Republic's population at the time, referred in turn to their situation as having been 'erased from the Constitution'. And in a sense, they were, for they comprised less than 4 per cent by the census of 2001.

11 For figures through 2000, see Vladimir Gligorov, 'The Role of the State in the Balkans', Vienna: Vienna Institute for International Economic Studies, 2002, pp. 4–5.

12 Figures for Bosnia-Herzegovina and Kosovo are estimates and may actually be even higher.

13 Researchers at the European Stability Initiative have demonstrated that the economic differences between rural and urban, private and public sectors of the Macedonian economy, with ethnic (Albanian, ethnic Macedonian) correlates, have not only remained high in the 1990s and of the same character as trends beginning in the early 1950s, but that these characteristics far better explain the current 'national' conflict within Macedonia that threatens the very integrity of that state and reveal 'underlying structural problems [that] must be addressed if Macedonia is to have any lasting prospect of stability' (executive summary) (ESI, 'The Other Macedonian Conflict', *ESI Discussion Paper*, 20 February 2002).

14 I depend for these labour market data and evaluations on the empirical research done by Milan Vodopivec. His research has focused most intensively on Bosnia-Herzegovina, but the generalizations apply broadly. Vladimir Gligorov refers to the regressivity and the unusually large share of the population still employed in the public sector, in relation to their contribution to GDP, as 'selective paternalism'; so one could argue that 'concern for social justice has in many cases all but disappeared'. ('The Role of the State in the Balkans', pp. 15–6).

15 See Laza Kekić, 'Aid to the Balkans: Addicts and Pushers', *Journal of Southeast European and Black Sea Studies*, 1(1) (January), 2001, for the facts and an analysis of the consequences.

16 In fact, already in the mid-1980s, Austria and Italy created structures (first Alpe-Adria and then Pentagonale) to embed Slovenia and Croatia in their western neighbourhood, thus reassuring the two republics that they could survive independently and that there would not be a power vacuum of the kind that still exists for the other successor states.

17 In the original Karl Deutsch sense (*Political Community and the North Atlantic Area; international organization in the light of historical experience*, Princeton, New Jersey: Princeton University Press, 1957).

18 By 2001, the EU did introduce an asymmetric trade agreement for those

with an SAA (Croatia, Macedonia, Albania in 2001) which removed most tariffs. The difficulty with this favourable agreement was that economic and institutional conditions in these countries made it very difficult to produce the competitive exports meeting EU standards to take advantage of this gesture.

19 According to World Bank criteria, Croatia is too wealthy to qualify for its loans, but US representation on the Executive Board of the World Bank was used to override this qualification and even to urge a substantial lending program, despite its large military budget (50 per cent of government expenditures, not including reputedly large off-budget expenditures as well) and its painfully slow compliance with the terms of loans for financial sector reform during the late 1990s.

20 Slovenia, which had the most elbow room, has conceded least. By contrast, Serbia, despite a careful program for the transition having been prepared by the G-17 group of reform economists in opposition to the Milošević regime, has largely conceded (in large part because of what donors were willing to finance) to the standard model.

21 Donors appear to think the two are the same (see the conclusions of the Peace Implementation Council in May 2000 for policy toward Bosnia-Herzegovina, for example, where rapid economic reform is explicitly labelled 'state-building'). For a lucid criticism of this path, see the special report commissioned by the UN Development Programme on human security in southeastern Europe written by a team of Balkan sociologists and economists under the leadership of Ivan Krastev of the Centre for Liberal Strategies, Sofia, for the UN's annual Human Development Report of 2000: Ivan Krastev, et al. *Human Security in South-East Europe*, August 1999. On the misplaced priority to security over development of the World Bank regional program for the western Balkans, see Vladimir Gligorov, *The West and Economic Stabilisation of Western Balkans*, Vienna, 6 May 2000.

HOW SOVIET BUREAUCRACY PRODUCED NATIONALISM, AND WHAT CAME OF IT IN AZERBAIJAN

Georgi Derluguian

In 1989-91, the Soviet Union experienced a revolutionary process – not unlike that of Russia in 1905, or indeed February 1917 – in which the old bureaucratic despotism was shaken, and for millions of people genuine emancipation seemed close. Their hopes were bitterly disappointed. The failure of revolutions to bring about their hoped-for outcomes is, of course, familiar; but the failure of this particular revolution to deliver what it had promised was more then usually painful, and this seemed to call for a more persuasive explanation than the mere logic of global neoliberalism. Something, it was presumed, had to be wrong with the peoples of the USSR, especially those in its peripheries. With the partial exception of the Baltic states, which are small, and close enough to the European Union to expect to be invited to join it, the peoples of the Soviet peripheries had failed to understand liberalism and had corrupted the transition to the market. An explanation was found – in the deep flaws of local ethnic cultures (or more grandly still, in the 'clash of civilizations') – and it looked superficially convincing, given the almost universal evidence of ethnically-channelled corruption and ethnically-organized crime, and the widespread incidence of ethnic wars in the former USSR, as well as in the former Yugoslavia. And indeed ethnicity, and ethnic leaderships, did play a key role in the revolutions of 1989-91.

But if we are serious about the analysis of contemporary history, we need to answer the following questions: What processes created these revolutionary situations? Who were the leaders? Why did they uniformly choose the same strategy of national democratic reform? And what conditions and constraints drove these movements to often bloody failure? Answering these questions requires us, in my opinion, to conduct an analysis on three different levels simultaneously: the micro-level of the events and personages of 1989-91; the level of national histories, and especially the past formative moments of 1905 and 1917, from which the revolutionaries of 1989 drew their symbols and scripts; and, finally, the global level of the modern world-system which provided the main reference point for all nationalist movements in the former USSR.

The analysis focuses on the trajectory of Azerbaijan over the last two decades. Azerbaijan not only provides a good empirical summary of the depressing trend in a large set of countries, from the Balkans to the Caucasus and Central Asia – political contestation leading to ethnic conflict, state breakdown, and an apparent return to Third World backwardness. It also happens that the Azerbaijan revolution, intertwined with an ethnic uprising in Nagorno Karabagh, an autonomous Armenian province inside the Azerbaijan SSR, signalled the final crisis of Soviet power. The manifest powerlessness of Gorbachev's administration in face of the escalating violence in the Caucasus started a chain reaction of national uprisings which in 1991 resulted in the disintegration of the USSR. But if we focus on Azerbaijan alone, we may succumb to the usual pitfall of attributing Soviet disintegration to nationalism alone. Therefore let us first undertake a compressed analytical description which should allow us to see more clearly something central to all the uprisings that precipitated the Soviet collapse – the position of national intelligentsias under state socialism.

For the pre-eminence of intellectuals in East European politics in 1989-91 seems universal. This observation holds for the entire region and thus the usual explanation in terms of national tradition obviously does not hold. Take the roster of the top post-communist leaders: in Lithuania it was a musicologist (Vitautas Landsbergis), in Estonia a visual anthropologist and documentary filmmaker (Edgar Savisaar), in Czechoslovakia a playwright (Havel), in Poland a whole host of philologists, medieval historians and social scientists. In the former Yugoslavia we find educators, historians, novelists (Serbia's Vuk Draskovic is just one example), and a former psychologist turned poet and then a warlord (Bosnia's Radovan Karadzic). In a totally different region, predominantly Muslim Central Asia, we encounter a physicist (Askar Akayev) turned president of Kyrgyzstan, an extremely gifted poet (Muhammed Salih) in the leadership of Uzbekistan's democratic opposition, and a young film director (Dovlat Hudonazarov) inspiring the rebellious masses in Tadjikistan. In Georgia in the early 1990s a typically bitter joke ran like this: God, save us from another civil war between the Shakespearean scholar (i.e. President Zviad Gamsakhurdia), the sculptor (the rogue commander of Georgia's National Guards, Tenghiz Kitovani), and the professor of cinema history (the self-styled warlord Prof. Djaba Ioseliani).

In the immediate neighbourhood of Azerbaijan, in the Caucasus, the same trend seems even more pronounced. In 1990-97 not just the political but even the military elite of Armenia was composed of former historians, musicians, school teachers, journalists, computer scientists and nuclear physicists. The vile chief of Armenia's police after 1990, Vano Siradeghian, previously earned a living by writing short stories for children, and the first President of Armenia, Levon Ter-Petrosian, at the height of the Karabagh war proudly continued his work on the Biblical translations from the medieval Syriac sources which he considered imperative for national spiritual revival. In the case of Azerbaijan, the post-Soviet elite was heavily populated not just by intellectuals but by orientalists, graduates of the Faculty of Oriental Studies at Azerbaijan State University. Foreign journalists and other observers noticed how puzzlingly numerous were these specialists in classical Arabic or Persian among the post-Soviet Azeri political elite.[1] Azeri intellectuals took this fact for granted, with an occasional chuckle: being native, they knew the reason. For us, explaining the reason will prove a useful way of grasping the social environment of Azerbaijan on the eve of the 1989 revolution.

But to go back for a minute to the phenomenon in its most general form: from Estonia to Tadjikistan, these are historically very different countries and their revolutions led to quite different political outcomes. So what could they have had in common to produce such an impressive uniformity of leadership at the peak of all their revolutions? The immediate reason for the unusual political role of what I will call cultural intellectuals is the common social structure created by state socialism throughout the USSR. After the revolution of 1905 Lenin famously said that Leo Tolstoi was the mirror of its contradictions.[2] The cultural intelligentsia of the USSR were likewise a mirror of the contradictions of the revolutions of 1989-91. These contradictions were created by the bureaucratic Fordism adopted by the Bolshevik leadership after 1917.

SOCIALIST BUREAUCRATIC FORDISM

In the initial phases of Bolshevik state-building the old social structures were drastically reduced and simplified. From the Civil War to the great purges the inchoate multiplicity of old social statuses, ranks, class and religious identities was uprooted and deliberately destroyed. The policy was initially spontaneous, but very soon – indeed before Stalin gave his name to the strategy – the destruction of actual and potential sources of political opposition became standard Bolshevik policy. From the Red Terror of August 1918, and Trotsky's infamous campaign of 'de-Cossackization' in the course of Russia's Civil War, the strategy was pursued through the collectivization of the peasantry (and its lesser-known analogy in Central Asia, the brutal sedentarization of nomadic tribes) until its culmination in the purges of 1936-38 and the ethnic deportations of the 1940s. The result of all this violence was that potentially oppositional social groups were simply eliminated: there were no landowners, no bourgeoisie or petty bourgeoisie, no liberal professions, no autonomous clergy, indeed no peasants. The social hierarchy was reduced, in theory at least, to the semi-closed caste of cadre bureaucrats (the nomenklatura) and the newly-created mass of proletarians – proletarians in the most fundamental sense of a social class whose livelihood depends on wage employment in the absence of alternative income. Whether they worked in towns, or on state farms, is not important; within a generation the whole Soviet Union was recast as a gigantic industrial enterprise which was a self-conscious emulation of the Fordist factory, the symbol of technological and organizational progress of its age. Extremely rapid proletarianization, carried out by despotic methods, was both the biggest tragedy and the biggest achievement of Soviet development.

The new Soviet proletarians faced formidable barriers to collective action. Under Stalin the secret police and informers were omnipresent and strikes were put down with machine guns. Later the Soviet rulers switched to less crude methods – the rituals of 'unanimous popular politics' (to pre-empt any actual politics) and, at the level of socio-economic structures, the cultivation of pater-nalistic dependency. The distribution of goods and welfare benefits was tied to the workplace and controlled by factory administrators and the official trade unions. The infamously shoddy quality of Soviet-made goods was not a mani-festation of the cultural inferiority of East Europeans but a triumph of the perverted class struggle waged by Soviet proletarians. Unable to bargain for higher wages, workers tacitly decreased their work effort – as the wry joke put it, 'they pretend to pay us and we pretend to work'. In the aftermath of Stalinism workers won a far better deal, though it remained unevenly shared between economic sectors and regions; the overall effect was to disperse and tame poten-tial industrial protest. Protests still occurred, and sometimes reached spectacular proportions, like the 1962 strike of the locomotive-builders in Novocherkassk (it was put down with extreme brutality but it was in the wake of Novocherkassk that Moscow resolved to begin importing food from America). The huge indus-trial investments of the previous generations began to pay off in the 1950s and1960s. Later, in the 1970s, as the smokestack heavy industries stagnated, while consumer expectations continued to rise, mass consumption was subsidized with the proceeds of oil and other mineral exports. This, in its barest bones, was the mechanism of internal peace under Khruschev and Brezhnev.

THE NATIONAL CULTURAL INTELLIGENTSIAS

According to 'scientific communism', fully developed socialist society had only two 'non-antagonistic' and increasingly merged classes, industrial workers and collective farmers. Bureaucratic office-holders were just a cadre of able and professionally competent managers advancing from the ranks of the people. This fuzzy and rosy picture of the ruling elite could be extended to include highly trained technicians without administrative powers, like engineers or medical doctors; and indeed the bureaucratic ladder of social mobility continued to operate throughout Soviet history, though at a rapidly decreasing rate. Once Brezhnev's famous 'stability of cadres' arrived, managerial openings in the top echelon grew scarce and careers slowed down considerably. A typical character under late socialism was the disenchanted low-paid engineer, stranded in the lower echelons of some sprawling bureaucratic organization, or in the unenvi-able position of a petty shop-floor manager, squeezed between a demanding boss and half-heartedly compliant workers. The social frustrations of this technically-trained intelligentsia, however, rarely found any political expression. Technicians were part of the same industrial compact, well-policed and at least satisfactorily fed. In addition, unlike ordinary workers, technicians remained the reserve pool for recruits into industrial management. The prospect of career advancement offered some hope.

What is notably lacking among all the classes and strata, including the intelligentsia, mentioned so far, is any ethnic character. The reason for this is the impact of proletarianization itself. It is not generally appreciated that the national dynamics of the Soviet Union, that gigantic example of bureaucratically-built Fordism under the banner of socialism, resembled contemporary America more than it resembled the old tsarist empire. The old empire was the infamous 'prison-house of the nations', whereas the Soviet Union, like the USA, was a melting pot – or more precisely, the USSR's big industrial towns, the all-Union bureaucracies, the armed forces – and the GULAG – were melting pots, fired by rapid proletarianization. So it seems a keen historical irony that Soviet developmentalism, having produced tens of millions of ethnically homogenized proletarians, should have ended in a concerted series of nationalist revolutions. To understand how this could happen we must first look at a different segment of the Soviet intelligentsia – the cultural intelligentsia.

By a necessary process of analytical elimination we have finally arrived at the social group that led the revolutionary assaults against state socialism in 1998 – the national cultural intelligentsias. The connection between 'national' and 'cultural' is not coincidental. Technological skills are not national. It would be ridiculous to speak of Azeri engineering or Ukrainian mathematics (not that such attempts are entirely unknown, but still they are considered extreme even by most nationalists). History, however, the humanities, and artistic expression draw their material from cultures that are often defined in ethnic terms, and in the Soviet Union this relationship was officially recognized and institutionalized in bureaucratically isomorphic forms: each republic (with the notable exception of Russia) had its own academy of sciences, its own university, its own teacher training colleges, national museums and art galleries, national theatres, a national publishing house, a film studio, national dance companies, etc.[3]

The policy of promoting ethnic cultures – indeed creating them almost from scratch – has no precedent in classical Marxism and seems not only unnecessary but actually contrary to the core tenets of the Soviet ideological program, which called for the maximum concentration of material assets and labour resources under the supposedly rational control of a central bureaucratic agency. Besides, industrial efficiency required the social homogenization of the newly-made proletariat. Soviet nationality policy therefore looks superfluous, and even contradictory, and has to be explained. It was in fact a set of complicated and mostly ad hoc compromises dating back to the very beginning of Soviet state, to the Russian Civil War, which the Bolsheviks won in large part by gaining the active support of – or at least dividing and placating – various nationalist forces.

The social make-up of the nationalists of 1917-20 betrayed the agrarian-bureau-cratic nature of the old Russian empire. Precious few consolidated national bourgeoisies existed. The people who created and governed the putative national states of this period were overwhelmingly the local intelligentsias, above all teachers and journalists. Their ideas were a mixture of socialist populism and enlightenment directed towards their (idealized) national peasantries, whom they saw as communities of egalitarian, but somewhat backward, rustics, whom they intended to enlighten and educate so that the nation could join the world of progressive Western nations.

In reality the peasant masses proved far less ideal. The defunct empire exploded in a series of agrarian revolts that were fuelled by the juxtaposition of tremendous demographic growth (between the abolition of serfdom in 1861 and the revolution of 1917 the population of the empire had nearly trebled), the pattern of land tenure, which resulted in desperate land shortages, and the spread of guns and military skills among peasants who had been recruited as soldiers in the First World War. Much of the grass-roots violence during the period, espe-cially in the Caucasus but also in Ukraine or Central Asia, appeared ethnically motivated, as the different ethnic peasant communities engaged in myriad local revolts and fights. But on closer inspection we discover everywhere confronta-tions over land rights. The fledgling national governments faced a choice of being swept away by spontaneous agrarian violence or trying to direct it in defence of their own peasant masses.

An additional catalyst, which is often forgotten today, was provided by the liberal conditions dictated by the Great Powers gathered at Versailles. In 1919 the new states emerging from the Russian empire were given twelve months to meet three requirements for diplomatic recognition: historical and cultural rights to territory, the will of the local population (to be determined in plebiscites), and what the international law of the colonial epoch called the right of effective occupation. Sure enough, committees of national scholars immediately got busy discovering the historical and cultural 'facts' regarding territorial rights; the rudi-mentary national armed forces and armed volunteers were sent into the problematic borderlands to suppress or expel separatist populations; and since these forces were insufficient, they often recruited and armed the local militias of their own ethnic kind against neighbouring communities that were now considered alien. The expression 'ethnic cleansing' had not yet been invented but the extent of these massacres far exceeded anything we have witnessed in the last decade: in the Karabagh war of 1990-94 the Azeri and Armenian casualties together are estimated at 10-15,000, but in 1919, in the same Karabagh, in just one episode lasting three days and nights nearly 20,000 people were slaughtered. This helps us to understand why in so many places the 1920 advance of the victo-rious Red Army was greeted with resignation or even hailed as a return to order.

The Bolsheviks promptly shut down ethnic and agrarian violence by using the dictatorial means forged in the Russian Civil War. But Lenin, Trotsky, and Stalin were also realist and very inventive politicians. They tried to remove the immediate causes of conflict by forcefully resolving territorial disputes, carrying out land reform and then collectivization, inviting the acceptable leadership among the nationalists (mostly artists and educators) to pursue their projects in the framework of the Soviet multi-national state, and, most inventively of all, not abolishing the national states. This tactical shift went against the expectations of both nationalists and orthodox Marxists, but it worked. Strategically the Leninists hoped, not wholly unreasonably, that with the impending industrialization the nationality question would evaporate. Later, in the 1930s, Stalin decided to speed up the extinction of the nationalists with the help of police terror. The remnants of the old intelligentsia were eliminated wholesale. This removed the potential danger of national rebellions. The new, Soviet-made national intelligentsias were perfectly docile and, having been produced in the paranoid isolationism of the Stalinist regime, possessed a very limited world-view.

The Stalinist nationality institutions were often dismissed as being artificial, intrinsically provincial, and mere ornaments on the Soviet imperial facade. To some extent they were. In a state as rigidly centralized as the USSR the big academy conducting 'real' scientific research was the mighty Soviet Academy of Sciences, and the leading film studios and publishing houses were in Moscow and Leningrad. But as time passes all institutions tend to acquire lives of their own. Even though the quality of research, education and the arts in the national republics might often seem mediocre (though marvellous exceptions occurred, especially in film-making and literature), the institutions of national culture did create numerous professional positions for the national intelligentsias. These jobs were respectable, relatively well-paid and not too demanding, which made them attractive. Moreover the institutions catering to national cultures fostered tightly-knit professional communities of educated men and women who normally lived their entire lives in the same town, the capital of their republic, since their credentials did not travel beyond the republic's borders. An engineer with a diploma from Siberia or Kazakhstan could find a job anywhere there was a factory, but a specialist in Azerbaijani poetry was hardly transferable to Estonia or Russia. Yet Soviet centralization, and the festivals of nationality cultures, regularly brought the artistic intelligentsias of the different nationalities together. Moscow's aim was to foster internationalism, but unofficially this allowed these cultural nationalists to exchange ideas and dreams. Little wonder then that the documents of Azeri nationalism in 1989 appear to be literal copies of the more advanced Estonian nationalist programmes – they were in fact copies, widely circulated through the national intelligentsias' network. The common dream was independence from Moscow, which promised to make the lesser national academies, universities, museums, etc. into institutions of sovereign states with direct access to the world arena. As long as the power of the Soviet Union looked rock-solid, this remained a pipe-dream. But things changed in 1988 with the events that took place in Nagorno Karabagh. And here, let us turn to the specific case of the Azeri orientalists.

AZERBAIJAN

Because of its easily accessible and rich deposits of oil, Azerbaijan became the site of industrial growth early on, in the late nineteenth century. Industrialization, however, was highly concentrated around Baku, the town on the coast of the Caspian Sea which allowed for the bulk export of Azerbaijan's main commodity. Fed by the oil boom of the 1880s–1900s, Baku rapidly evolved into a cosmopolitan town with a picturesque blend of cultures brought by western European investors, like the prominent Russo-Swedish Nobel family; by Russian colonial administrators and skilled professionals (of whom perhaps a majority were Russian subjects of other nationalities including Poles, Jews and Germans); and most importantly by Armenians, who were both native to the area and had the cultural advantage of being Christians, and hence being favoured by foreign employers. The Muslim natives (which is how they were perceived at the time – as just Muslims) occupied a typically ambiguous position. At the top of Baku society one could find quite a few Muslim merchants and landowners who had invested their wealth and social skills in the new oil business with great success. At the bottom of the social hierarchy were the numerous unskilled Muslim labourers and urban lumpens who had recently come to town. There were some Muslim intellectuals in the middle, but they were vastly outnumbered by Russians, Armenians, Jews, and Poles. This ethnic mosaic persisted in Baku throughout the entire Soviet period. The Western nationals were gone, the native bourgeoisie was undone, the old intelligentsia perished almost wholesale in the purges of 1936-38, and Soviet nationality policies had promoted many Azeris into official positions at the top. But the town remained a prosperous cosmopolitan enclave centred on its oil industry and the administration of the hinterland.

Outside Baku the hinterland remained another country altogether. The main native group of the region were Azeris whose ethnic identity was even more diffuse than elsewhere. Linguistically they were Turks, but before the arrival of Russians in the early 1800s the area had for many centuries been a province of Iran, so that the dominant culture was Persian and the prevalent religion was the Shiite brand of Islam practised in Iran. The very terms 'Azeri' and 'Azerbaijan' were invented by the nationalizing native intelligentsia in the early 1900s–1910s, and became official under the Soviet regime only after 1936. The rural population had no national identity. They knew that they belonged to the larger community of Shiite Muslims, and this identity was regularly exercised in religious rituals and codes of behaviour. They also belonged to local networks of extended families and village communities centred on the rural market towns that were controlled by quasi-feudal 'counties' – the khanates of Nuha, Shemaha, Gyandja, etc. These were small and fairly closed societies that rarely interacted with each other and maintained contact with Baku only via the export trade and the state administrative apparatus.

The traditional division of the area into 'counties' had been perpetuated de facto by the Russian colonial administration, and was continued by the Soviet state under the rubric of 'districts'. The main reason was purely administrative. On the one hand, the pre-existing territorial networks centred on small towns offered a logical basis for local government. On the other hand, there was no political need to disband the traditional 'counties' because they never served as a base for any organized resistance. The usual explanation offered for this is ethnic character – the idea, presumably, that Azeri peasants were particularly docile or devoid of civic spirit – and as usual it is a deceptively superficial stereotype. The political history of the region in the centuries before the Russian conquest was extremely volatile and violent. The Iranian shahs never firmly controlled this borderland area. The tiny khanates were fertile grounds for various mobile rack-eteers, predominantly Turkic nomadic chieftains; and in the mountainous Karabagh, for the last surviving dynasties of Armenian Christian lords, who competed fiercely among themselves for the right to exact rents from the peas-antry and the artisans in the towns. These petty despots used to come and go, unseating each other in perennial violent feuds, while the Iranian shahs were only concerned that they provided auxiliary troops and supplies for their endless impe-rial campaigns against Ottoman Turkey. In this environment the defenceless peasants developed an aloof resignation towards political power, hoping only that the next local ruler would not be too predatory. From this perspective the Russian colonial administrators, though infidels, seemed acceptable, because they prevented runaway violence and did not exact very much in taxes, since their revenues were largely provided by the oil industry of Baku.

The same traditional attitude continued throughout the Soviet period. The local administrators became native Azeris and were ostensibly communist, but the rural districts continued to be seen as a source of revenue and private enrichment. We have no reliable data whatever on the actual operations of local power in Soviet Azerbaijan (or any republic of Soviet Transcaucasia and Central Asia), but the extensive anecdotal evidence suggests that the position of district party secre-tary was *as a rule* sold to prospective office holders. We even know the price-tag – around 100,000 rubles during the Brezhnev period, which could be higher in particularly lucrative districts. Generally speaking, it worked in the following way. First, a locally prominent family accumulated money that was then lent to an ambitious career-oriented relative who was seeking office. By itself money was not enough; one also needed connections in Baku and an opportunity to present the bribe. Those who had been educated in the big town thus had a better chance, while the proper education credentials were themselves obtained with the obligatory bribes paid to professors during the admission process and in all the successive examinations up to the university diploma. Ironically, if one judges on the basis of Soviet statistics, by the mid-1960s the Azerbaijani nomen-klatura appeared exceptionally well-educated: nearly half of them had doctorates – which was, of course, a fictitious overstatement, since these were doctorates acquired through bribes. Higher education and the career it opened up was the way to develop the necessary contacts and the opportunity to join the patronage networks of the bigger bosses, all the way up to the First Secretary of the

Republic. Once the desired position in the party apparatus had been purchased the new office holder would begin to repay his debts by appointing his relatives and clients to locally lucrative subordinate positions: the chief of financial inspection, the head of the local police force, managers of cooperative shops, chairmen of collective farms, directors of building materials factories, etc. In turn these lesser officials would establish various illicit operations under their control so as to skim off funds with which they enriched themselves and paid regular bribes to their superiors for patronage and protection.

From the normative standpoint of rational bureaucracy this system looks thoroughly corrupt and deviant, an astonishing inner failure of the Soviet state that remained disguised and ignored by outsiders. Yet soberly speaking, the pattern of social power in Azerbaijan's countryside was not substantially different from the situation in other republics of Transcaucasia and Central Asia. The Soviet state simply failed to penetrate these areas, and Moscow eventually contended itself with the formal compliance dutifully exhibited by the various national *nomenklaturas*. It was essentially the continuation of an ancient prebendal system that worked like a siphon, taxing the local economy and funnelling the proceeds upwards, all the way to Baku which in turn paid off inspectors from Moscow and lobbied the Soviet central planning agencies for higher levels of investment in Azerbaijan.

This systematic corruption was unstable, because internecine bureaucratic feuding over the coveted positions was inherent in it, and Moscow periodically lashed out by removing the upper echelons of officials in the national republics. In 1969, for example, with the help of the KGB chief Yuri Andropov, the entire government of Azerbaijan was sacked and the reputedly honest and capable young chief of Azerbaijan's KGB, Gen. Heidar Aliev, was appointed to lead the purge. Incidentally, four years later in a similar move in neighbouring Georgia the KGB brought to power another police general, Eduard Shevardnadze. Both these young leaders conducted massive purges of corrupt officials and appointed their own clients, who proved even more corrupt. The problem was institutional and cultural, not one of wicked personalities. Both Aliev and Shevardnadze, arguably excellent politicians in the Machiavellian mould, clearly realized that their key role was to placate Moscow while consolidating their local power base by appointing loyal clients who, in order to rule and deliver, would have to indulge in the deeply entrenched practice of corruption. Any official who denied appointments to his relatives would lose the support of his family and hence would be eaten alive by competing families. Besides, the ethnic cultures of the region, not unlike those of the Mediterranean, required conspicuous consumption as proof of social status. An officeholder who could not provide the 'proper' level of entertainment and gifts for his relatives and guests would be judged a miserable failure.

It must be noted, however, that though the peasants had no hope of ever changing this corrupt system, they did not entirely give up hope of earning a better life for themselves and their families. The industrialization of the Soviet

Union and its growing prosperity in the 1960s-1970s translated into two major opportunities: labour migration and long-distance market trade. Many thousands of Azeri oilmen could be found as far away from home as the Soviet Arctic where they assiduously accumulated the hefty 'northern bonuses' before returning to their villages to get married and build sometimes ostentatious houses. Meantime many more Azeri peasant traders appeared in the markets of large Russian towns, where they specialized in selling produce from their sub-tropical native republic, mostly fruit and fresh flowers. Once again we know precious little about the actual organization of these market networks because from the standpoint of Soviet law code they bordered on crime. Yet it is clear that the peasants alone could not have managed the massive takeover of the arable land that was ostensibly under the control of collective farms, and the subsequent switching of the main crops away from industrial raw materials like cotton, whose cultivation was dictated by Moscow's central planners, to lucrative fruit and flowers. The local officials in Azerbaijan, Armenia, Georgia, and the other predominantly agrarian republics in the southern tier of the USSR, actively connived in this tacit de-collectivization and marketization in which they obviously had a pecuniary interest – for as the peasants grew richer they could afford bigger bribes, so long as their semi-legal enterprise continued to depend critically on an official cover-up.

The economic autarchy practised by the Soviet government, which excluded the frivolous expenditure of hard currency on imports of fresh produce, in effect ensured a steady monopolistic rent to domestic suppliers like the Azeris. The profits, of course, were redistributed by the endemic, highly inegalitarian, networks of corruption. Tremendous social inequalities and pervasive servility were thus glaring features of Soviet Azerbaijan society, but they remained mostly unnoticed by outsiders, and even by visitors to Baku. The city preserved its composite Oriental-Westernized charm and the oddities of local social patterns were presumed to be just the exoticism of the East.

Indeed on the eve of 1989 revolution Soviet Azerbaijan looked like a lesser version of the latter-day Ottoman empire. Big, prosperous, cosmopolitan Baku dominated the rural districts populated by unwashed ethnic peasants and petty despots. Like the Constantinople of yesteryear, the mixed population of Baku was ethnically and socially distinct from the countryside. The difference was very noticeable and strictly enforced by the urbanites. The latter had evolved into a composite pan-ethnic urban population of urbanized Azeris and Armenians, locally rooted Russians and Germans, Jews, Persians, and a myriad lesser minorities like the Tat, Lezgi, and Talysh, who all preferred to call themselves 'Bakintsy'. Their lingua franca was Russian, spoken in the colourful local Baku accent. Just as the inhabitants of Ottoman Istanbul, the Stambuli, did not regard themselves as Turks, and used the appellation 'Turks' only as a pejorative term for unwashed semi-nomadic people from the interior deserts of Eastern Anatolia, the Bakintsy invented a variety of pejorative words for rural Azeris. But the worst ridicule was reserved for recent arrivals in town who had to settle in the dusty and overcrowded suburbs – the much-ridiculed Mashtaga and other exploding slums, situated outside the town proper, in the former villages of the Apsheron peninsula. All jokes about homosexuals, gullible husbands, or fat, stupid and greedy wives were about the dwellers of those indeed fabulously corny places, the middle ground between village and town that had already lost the traditional norms of the village but had not yet acquired the cosmopolitan norms and codes of behaviour of the city. The jokes kept the 'Mashtagintsy' and their ilk in their proper place.

For the same reason in 1990-93 the semi-rural suburbs of Baku saw a brief (as it turned out), but probably not the last, flowering of Islamist fervour, whose seeds were supplied from Iran. Fundamentalism emerges in marginal spaces, in those urban margins that lack a proper name in English (where 'suburb' is associated with a middle-class lifestyle). Traditional peasants are comfortable with their religious rituals; they need not prove to anyone, least of all to themselves, that they are true Muslims, while true urbanites scorn religion for which they have little use except on such purely ritual occasions as the funeral of an old grandma who used to pray. Mashtaga, by contrast, yearned in its own clumsy way to fill the gaping void in its culture with something huge and respectable, like the newly assertive Islam.

The language of Baku was colonial Russian, and therefore the immediately obvious measure of social status was one's Russian accent. It varied from the thicker, sweet, Persianized vernacular of the Baku bazaris to the impeccable aristocratic smoothness cultivated in 'good' families. It must be appreciated that the Russian spoken by Heidar Aliev, the only Muslim ever to become member of the Politburo, was far more elegant and grammatically correct than that of Brezhnev or Gorbachev, who both spoke with bluntly southern Russo-Ukrainian peasant accents.

As anyone who has been to places like Oxbridge knows, you either acquire the right accent in your family, or you send the children to the right school – and you had better do both. Thus a meeting of two Bakintsy in the corridors of Moscow State University (where I observed them at length) always started with Masonic-sounding cryptic exchanges:

— Twenty-fourth. And you?
— Seventeenth.
— In Armenikent?
— And you, not by any chance on Darwin Street?

The numbers are the 'good' schools; and a 'good' street, like Hagani St., right behind the Government building, was the tell-tale address of several of my old friends in Baku.

But what happens after the good high school? In many countries it used to be the elite military academies, in modern France it has to be one of the *grandes Écoles* that train the bureaucrats, while the US ruling elite comes from the law schools. The ruling elite of Soviet Azerbaijan, to nobody's surprise, came mostly from the State Oil Polytechnical Institute. Its diploma allowed one not to become a grimy *neftchi* (oilman) on a platform out in the Caspian sea; it provided the best credentials for becoming a Party apparatchik who was supposed once to have been (if mostly on paper) an oilman – the 'true vanguard of Baku and the whole Transcaucasian working class'. Under the Soviet system of affirmative action, the party *nomenklatura* in the national republics had to be native, which made the Oil Institute a preserve of ethnic Azeris from Baku. In a social environment dominated by bureaucratic patronage and bribes the admission process, of course, was largely a charade, yet the competition was genuinely acute since the elite families had more sons than there were coveted freshman places. In a celebrated scandal of the late 1970s a young applicant was caught cheating: he stated on the admission forms that his father was a simple oil driller, a true Azeri proletarian, when in fact his parent was a prominent lawyer – since even such a lucrative position, when competing with the interests of other elite families, could not guarantee admission.

Slightly lower on the scale of prestige came the Medical Institute. Brecht's famous line in the *Caucasian Chalk Circle* about the merchant who sent his sons to medical school to teach them how to earn money was eminently true of Baku's medical establishment. The nickname of its Rector in the late 1980s was telling: 'Comrade Dollar'. Few *nomenklatura* officials were ever medical graduates but a medical diploma promised a comfortable and well-supplied life. Thanks to its relative political unimportance and profitability the profession was accessible and indeed favoured by Baku's ethnic Armenians, Jews, and Russians, as well as many Azeris. In the bribe-ridden society of Azerbaijan it was profitable because patients automatically expected to pay doctors something extra, hoping to get better and faster treatment in return. But best of all, the medical profession was the safest profession. Doctors, after all, were not running restaurants or shops where the state auditors were an unavoidable risk. The best doctors could not, after all, help receiving 'gifts' and other tokens of respect from grateful patients.

Still, what about those refined scions of high-status Azeri intelligentsia families who neither had the guts or the nerve to become apparatchiks, nor desired a medical career? Their choice was Azerbaijan State University. Inside the university there existed a scale of departmental prestige, directly translatable into the relative difficulty of admission. Chemistry and physics were considered relatively easy to get into because the curriculum was challenging and the job prospects not that great: half the graduates would end up teaching science in schools. The fact that genuine scientific credentials earned low pay (or led to jobs where bribes were only sporadic) caused feelings of injustice, and so we do find some scientists among the revolutionaries of 1989. Law, by contrast, was a status quo department. In the Soviet system court litigation was not very important, lawyers were few and by default disproportionately Jewish. The best career for someone with a degree in law was in the state prosecutors' agencies, the KGB and the police, all entrusted with fighting crime and corruption and thus wielding powerful tools for eliciting bribes. Soviet jurists thus tended be politically conservative. The radicals were found in the departments of history and philology.

They were the custodians of the nation's past, its national language and culture. Admittedly it was a local past and a local culture, preserved in museums and academic research institutes – respectable but low-paying institutions. Their young custodians vaguely yearned for a better appreciation of their symbolic value but as long as nationalism remained a political taboo this remained merely a dream.

Nonetheless there remained one relatively small and exclusive 'cultural' department that combined high prestige with the prospect of diplomatic career – the Faculty of Oriental Studies, or 'Vostfak' in its Russian abbreviation. Since Azerbaijan was historically an Islamic country, some limited training of native specialists was undertaken mostly with a view to placing a few Muslim non-Russians in the Soviet embassies in the Middle East. Vostfak offered training in real foreign languages like Arabic and Persian and, most importantly, foreign service assignments paid very hefty salaries in hard currency. All perfectly legal, very prestigious, very diplomatic. Moreover this was as close to a professional political training as one could get, not counting the KGB academy. In reality only a chosen few among the graduates of Vostfak, primarily those who had been recruited into the KGB, would ever get permanent jobs abroad. The Soviet foreign service was controlled from Moscow and even the best Baku families could not help their children there. Most Vostfak graduates ended up in academic research institutes and museums spending their lives studying, at a leisurely pace, old oriental manuscripts. If only Azerbaijan had had its own ministry of foreign affairs!

This description does not exhaust the actual pyramid of higher education. Below the Oil and the Medical institute, below the National University, there were the worthless pedagogical institutes (teachers colleges) that ranked very low because their diplomas assured postings in the least prestigious schools. In Azerbaijan, as in all Soviet republics, teacher training was divided into streams offering education in either Russian or native languages. The latter were the lowest of the low. The native language schools were predominantly situated in villages. Teaching in them commanded no prestige, the jobs were low paid, and there was little prospect of ever leaving this dead-end career. The students for teacher training in native languages were therefore drawn from the villages, many of them could speak only some broken Russian, they were poor and felt deeply alienated from Baku's urban life. No urban girl would ever give them a second glance. These students produced the most radical nationalist fringe in 1989 when it suddenly turned out that they actually spoke the native language of the angry masses.

The social dynamic of the Armenian-Azeri conflict now begins to look more comprehensible. Back in the 1920s the Bolsheviks had no alternative but to staff the new state apparatus, including the dreaded secret police, with the better-educated and more urbanized Armenians. Until the late 1930s there were almost no Azeris in the positions of leadership. But a generation later, thanks to Soviet nationality policy, the ethnic Azeris began to catch up. After 1956 they were helped by de-Stalinization, which rotated the cadres, and most of all by the tremendous expansion of the state apparatus in the prosperous and hopeful age of Khruschev. By the mid-1960s a great many Azeris had made it into the elite, but in the process they assimilated the lifestyle and the norms of Baku and effectively ceased to be like Azeris from the villages. The new elite assiduously prevented their children from learning the native vernacular, so that they would avoid having an uncultured 'bazari' accent and bazari manners. The same, incidentally, happened with the Baku Armenians who detached themselves from both the Armenian church and their rustic brethren in the backwaters of the Armenian enclave of Karabagh. In fact the great era of Baku's role as a melting pot was 1956-89. The new arrivals transformed themselves into members of the new urban society and effectively prevented further social mobility by establishing among themselves rigid hierarchies of official ranks, unofficial (yet ever more important) private networks, and general cultural statuses. The gates of the town were shut again.

As long as the USSR lasted the rural population were kept in their place, whether they were Azeris in the rural districts or Armenians in the god-forsaken distant province of Karabagh. The structural tensions were great, but up till the late 1980s they remained hidden. In February 1986, two years before the political eruption started, while travelling in Azerbaijan I got a few glimpses of the astonishing social hatred that lay just beneath the surface. First, in Baku, an Azeri driver, after his boss had left the car and entered the premises of Azerbaijan's Central Committee, spat in disgust and muttered in very coarse Russian (evidently learnt in the army): 'Bloodsuckers! The damn Party bloodsuckers! Look at their fat butts, they all eat caviar while we have to pay bribes for everything and my children eat bread and tea. How can I support a family on what they are paying me?!' Another incident happened not far from Karabagh. On a rural road the bus, with Baku licence plates, was stoned by a crowd of angry children. They were Armenians, an Azeri man sitting next to me explained. He felt appalled by this act of 'hooliganism', but not at all surprised, since such attacks happened routinely. The conflict was between two neighbouring villages, one Armenian, the other Azeri. The Armenians were protesting against the arrest of the accountant at a local fruit-processing plant. The accountant, an Armenian, had helped his boss, an Azeri, to cover up a typical embezzlement scheme. The accountant had received a death sentence, the Azeri boss walked free – because, it was widely assumed, he had bribed the entire police command and the court in Baku, all of them also Azeris.

As with many previous revolutions the triggering event in Azerbaijan was a convoluted intrigue. In February 1988 a clique of provincial officials in the capital of Karabagh, Stepanakert (pop. 40,000), decided to gain some additional leverage against their corrupt bosses in Baku, and incidentally to redistribute some local commodity flows that were then monopolized by the crafty bazaris and officials in the nearby Azeri market town of Agdam. The plan was to convince Moscow to allow the administrative transfer of Azerbaijan's autonomous province of Karabagh to the jurisdiction of neighbouring Armenia. To the conspirators it

seemed simple and straightforward: the population of Karabagh was predominantly Armenian, the Armenian homeland lay just a few kilometres away, and
Karabagh had ended up inside the borders of Azerbaijan by mistake, because back
in 1921 the evil Stalin had said so; and besides, two of Gorbachev's top advisors
were Armenians from Karabagh. It only remained, in the spirit of glasnost and
perestroika, to organize a demonstration of popular will. The organizers of the
campaign were provincially-minded bosses from a remote province. They
presented Gorbachev with a potentially utterly disruptive precedent, because the
Soviet apportionment of all 'national autonomous provinces' was no more logical
than the determination of any other colonial borders. In addition the proposal
gave Gorbachev's opponents in the Politburo a hefty counter-argument against
further democratization: 'look at what begins to happen once you allow the
freedom of expression'. Sensing Gorbachev's impasse, the leaders of Azerbaijan
branded the Karabagh campaign an affront to the republic's sovereignty. Although
most Azeris had been barely aware of Karabagh's existence (it was and still is an
insignificant borderland province, far removed from any economic centre), the
Armenian demands suddenly provoked a massive emotional response. The rest is
well known. In the ensuing war Agdam was seized by the Armenian insurgents
and now lies in ruins, Baku lost its power over Karabagh – and one of the original conspirators is now president of the internationally recognized Republic of
Armenia, so at least his bet paid off better than he could ever have expected.

This little provincial intrigue unexpectedly burst the dam. The first petition
campaign and rallies conducted in Karabagh by the Armenians provoked wildly
escalating counter-rallies in Azerbaijan. In the grimy industrial township of
Sumgait outside Baku an irate crowd of Azeri lumpens went on a rampage,
killing local Armenians on the pretext of clearing their apartments to make room
for Azeri refugees from Armenia. Despite the wildest rumours, the first pogrom
was almost certainly spontaneous. It is very hard to imagine that even the most
corrupt Soviet-era officials would dare to play with street violence. The social
environment of Sumgait was as bad as an inherently violent industrial suburb
could be. The township had been built by prison labour around the oil-
processing plants. It became the reservoir for Baku undesirables: all sorts of
hoodlums, former convicts and drug addicts, cleansed from the boulevards of
Baku. Sumgait had the highest crime rate in the entire USSR and witnessed
serious rioting even in the Brezhnev era. Little wonder that the first pogrom (in
February 1988) occurred there. Several weeks after Sumgait – and after the
whole country had witnessed the confused response from Gorbachev – street
rioting entered the repertoire of local collective action. Violence and counter-
violence escalated. In 1988-90 we see the spread of pre-emptive and retributive
strikes (sometimes in 'revenge' for massacres committed generations before) with
the attendant emergence of self-defence militias in every village, helped by
volunteer detachments arriving respectively from either Baku or Yerevan. On
both sides the fighters were either romantic students, inspired by nationalist ideas,
or just city street 'tough guys' who had suddenly acquired a cause.

Meantime, in the spring of 1988, a bunch of local elite intellectuals concentrated in Baku, who had known each other well since their university days, decided it was time to lead the Nation. Do not forget that in the previous years of glasnost they had been avidly watching the meteoric rise of the top Russian intellectuals in Moscow to the status of media celebrities and custodians of the national consciousness. Azerbaijan's bureaucratic elite was at loss. On the one hand, they had been disgraced by their inability to contain popular violence; on the other hand, they could no longer tell who their boss was in Moscow, or how to deal with Gorbachev, who talked endlessly without issuing any direct commands. Besides, most party apparatchiks showed dismal qualities as public speakers, quite unlike the literary intellectuals who delivered public speeches with gleeful panache. It was the hour of big speeches and thus the hour of oppositional orators: the liberal, Westernizing, high-status, patriotic intelligentsia.

And then the rioting worsens as the parading crowds get frustrated by their inability to achieve anything, and as the local elite and the KGB learn how to use the street violence in their intrigues. Unlike Sumgait, later pogroms and massacres seem pre-planned or at least channelled, although in the tumult it is impossible to determine by whom. In this mayhem a new force appears – those third-rate students from the Azeri-language teachers colleges and equally appalling places (the college of veterinarians, the association of village poets, etc.). This force had to be recklessly radical for they had no social status to lose and everything to gain. The pyramid of social symbols was now turned upside down. What previously was terribly uncool – speaking Azeri – became now the sign of true patriotism. Meanwhile, to no one's surprise, most of the Communist apparatchiks and even the elite national intelligentsia of Baku failed the test miserably. They proved in public their inability to speak the native language! (In Georgia and Armenia it was slightly different because high cultures existed in the native languages, with their ancient literary traditions and scripts. Nonetheless, the low-status radicals there simply used other symbols of native-ness and rurality – for instance, the Mingrel dialect in Georgia, associated with Zviad Gamsakhurdia.)

In Baku things got completely out of hand in the late autumn of 1989, as the Azeri revolutionaries saw on Soviet television – and even more, heard on foreign radio stations – what was happening in Eastern Europe. A group of Azeri insurgents from villages along the Iranian border led ecstatic crowds to demolish the Soviet border installations, apparently emulating the breaking down of the Berlin Wall. The revolutionary opposition was notionally united under an umbrella organization, the Azerbaijan Popular Front. The Popular Front was originally designed by the Vostfak elite intellectuals on the Estonian model, but in fact it became an assortment of very disparate groups spontaneously emerging all over Azerbaijan. It seems that in most districts the self-proclaimed cells of the Popular Front represented either big local families who were out of power at the moment, or teachers and other low-status rural intellectuals who finally saw a possibility of waging a class war against the corrupt local hierarchies. In any event, each district had its own version of the Popular Front with its own social composition and political agenda. In some places the local Party committee offices were sacked and burnt by peasant crowds, in other districts there emerged a sort of anarchistic local militias that rapidly evolved into warlord gangs, while in yet other districts 'alien' elements were expelled – but we have no information about who was expelling whom. By January 1990 Baku seemed on the verge of being taken over by the rural refugees and unenlightened crowds from suburbia. The Armenian population, nearly 120,000 people, were violently driven out of town, although according to all the evidence groups of Azeri intellectuals, the original core of Popular Front in Baku, seem to have done their best to calm the crowds and save the Armenians.

It was widely suggested that the pogroms in Baku were organized by Moscow to obtain a pretext for imposing martial law. Whether this was so remains anyone's guess, but in any case Moscow finally resolved to impose martial law and send the army into Baku. The Soviet troops, mostly ethnic Russian recruits who only vaguely knew that 'Muslim fanatics were on a killing spree', entered the city at night, shooting in all directions. The Azeris unanimously allege that this was a deliberate show of force, though it is much more likely to have been the opposite – that soldiers and officers were disoriented and scared out of their wits on entering the big unfamiliar town whose darkened streets were lit by burning tires.

The imposition of martial law in 1990 for two years introduced a weak regime of restoration. The 'new' old regime looked inept and pathetic, and ended when the USSR disintegrated. With the Soviet army gone, the conflict over Karabagh escalated into a full-scale war, which the shaky Azerbaijani state lost. Armenian forces not only took Karabagh but also occupied a buffer zone around it which they are still holding today as bargaining chip for a future settlement of the conflict. In Azerbaijan, in 1992-93, the Popular Front of Azerbaijan held power for a year. President Elchibey, a former dissident and a specialist in Arabic poetry, was by all accounts a decent man with lofty intentions who hoped to turn Azerbaijan into a secular and democratic state and to finance reforms with the country's oil revenues. But he had neither political leverage nor cadres capable of imposing his government on the country's feuding 'big families'. His short-lived regime barely controlled Baku, let alone the countryside. One of the rural rebellions (probably helped by the Russian military, worried at Azerbaijan's drift to the West) eventually forced Elchibey out of power. The period of 'revolutionary' rule ended ignominiously.

The epilogue followed the general lines of post-Soviet authoritarian stabilizations. The provincial warlord who ousted the Popular Front himself failed to hold onto the reins of power. Out from self-imposed exile re-emerged the grand old ruler, the seventy-five year old but still very vigorous Heydar Aliev, First Secretary of Azerbaijan in 1969-82 and a member of Andropov's Politburo. Like Shevardnadze in Georgia, Aliev allowed the border wars to continue. He could not stop them, so he allowed the dangerous warlords to confront the Armenian forces and get ground into pulp one after another. The rest of his potentially threatening opponents, and even over-powerful subordinates, were either forced into exile or imprisoned on charges of embezzlement (which was never implausible) or attempted coups (which looked less plausible.) The new/old ruler consolidated a tightly authoritarian regime, monopolized the oil industry by appointing his son as director of the State Oil Company, and placed his relatives and clients in other key positions. By 1995 a degree of peace had been re-estab-lished and a great many people, worn out by the traumatic events of the previous seven years, sincerely welcomed the restoration of minimal (for it was and is minimal) normality.

But the great communist padishahs of yesteryear, like Aliev and his colleague Shevardnadze, are very old, and the world around them is different now. They are superb Byzantine intriguers and benevolent despots, but how long will they hold power? Will they be able to create dynasties? Heydar Aliev certainly is grooming his son to become his successor. The web of corrupt patronage that he has woven is so complex yet at the same time so tenuous that Aliev and his closest courtiers simply cannot risk open elections and the possible transfer of power to a rival set of families. Yet it is impossible to avoid elections altogether because Azerbaijan is under too much Western pressure to follow that procedure in order to be recognized. Which is why today, as Aliev is aging, Azerbaijan witnesses a rise in oppositional sentiment among the intelligentsia that tasted poli-tics in 1988-93. It is a typical dilemma of weak authoritarianism that can be observed equally in Ukraine, Kazakhstan, or Russia itself. On the one hand, the rulers are constrained by the West from institutionalizing overt dictatorships. On the other hand, their power arrangements are too fragile to risk genuine elections and the regimes lack the resources to buy off all the opposition with comfort-able sinecures in business, embassies, universities and parliaments. And so it goes on, low-level repression and harassment along with mostly symbolic acts of opposition − for the oppositions are even weaker and less confident than the ruling regimes.

CHECHNYA

One last observation regarding the exceptional case of Chechnya. This small republic within the Russian Federation was not too different from Azerbaijan structurally. It too was a typically colonial combination of one big and cosmopolitan town, Grozny, that had also grown on oil, and the ethnic coun-tryside. Although the Chechens, unlike the Azeris, had waged a fierce resistance against the advancing empire in the nineteenth century, and again during the Stalinist collectivization and the purges, a loyal Soviet-made national intelligentsia developed in the late 1950s-1980s and dominated local politics during pere-stroika, pretty much like everywhere else. In 1988-91 the revolutionary sequence looked almost exactly the same as elsewhere.

But Chechnya was different in one crucial point − within the general sequence, the rural crowds succeeded in overpowering urban society and putting their idol, General Djohar Dudayev, on the throne. I have deliberately avoided using the word 'leader', for Dudayev did not lead; rather he symbolized the popular movement of the uneducated rural masses. In his endless pronouncements Dudayev expressed their deeply-felt grievances and confused aspirations – adding, of course, his own rather idiosyncratic twist. Yet despite the famous idiosyncrasies of Gen. Dudayev (much ridiculed by educated Chechens) he proved an adequate mobilizer of his warrior-peasant people. In a significant deviation from the general pattern, the embodiment of the Chechen revolution was not a 'soft' intellectual from the humanities like Elchibey. He was a military officer to the core, which his compatriots evidently found appealing. No less significantly, the second president of Chechnya, Colonel Aslan Maskhadov, was also a professional officer.

Unlike Azerbaijan or Georgia, Chechnya did not experience an authoritarian restoration with the return to power of the last Communist boss. Yeltsin's Moscow decided to correct history and obtain in Chechnya a more pliable counterpart, just as in Azerbaijan or Georgia where the Russian special forces almost certainly helped to organize the coups that took place there too. The Russian subversive operation against Dudayev in the summer of 1994 sought to facilitate precisely the same turn of events: to topple the perestroika-vintage 'demagogue' Dudayev and install a more predictable ruler, even if not entirely a puppet (yes, Moscow would have accepted someone like Azerbaijan's Aliyev, a tough partner but still a partner). But the Russian plotters proved to have insufficient resources and were simply inept. The operation's cover was blown when Dudayev's forces captured Russian servicemen fighting on the side of the anti-Dudayev opposition. Yeltsin now faced the choice of apologizing, or sanctioning an all-out invasion. Counting on silent approval from Washington, Yeltsin chose war, hoping that it would be a brief blitzkrieg and thus a good boost for his fortunes in the forthcoming elections. (Yeltsin and his circle, being admirers of Margaret Thatcher, were keenly aware of the role played in British politics by the Falklands war.)

Yeltsin's generals misjudged the degree of decay in Russia's own army, and the fighting spirit of the Chechens. The former is today well-known, the latter is over-mythologized and needs a brief clarification. The Chechen fighting spirit is not mythical, it is a collective protective reaction on the part of a people who, like the Armenians, live with the traumatic memory of recent genocide. From the popular Chechen standpoint, the Russian invasion was not a political game between Yeltsin and Dudayev but a threat to their very existence. The slow-moving and indecisive Russian military allowed the Chechen militias enough time to recover their wits, distribute the weapons that Dudayev had been stockpiling, and prepare the defences of Grozny under the able leadership of Col. Maskhadov. The rest was and, alas, remains an almost purely military dynamic.

The war destroyed Grozny, with its cosmopolitan culture and modern politics, and scattered its population as refugees. The remaining Chechen population were the resilient peasants and their village militias who sought political inspiration in a crude wartime form of nationalism, and actually won the first war on this wave. But the resulting national state, the second Chechen Republic of 1997-99, fell apart even faster than Dudayev's pre-war state. Most of the disappointed fighters,' and a sizable minority in the civilian Chechen population, subsequently turned their hopes towards radical Islam. The origins of the second Chechen war are shrouded in dirty secrets. It began in August 1999 with the inexplicable Chechen invasion of Daghestan, ostensibly to defend the Muslims of that neighbouring country from Russian oppression.[4]

This Islamist attack played the same role as Bin Laden's provocation against America two years later: it mightily consolidated the existing regimes on the platforms of military patriotism. First the unknown Vladimir Putin became the great president, then George W. Bush obtained his historic opportunity. The great game so far seems to go in their favour. But Afghanistan and Chechnya may soon be joined by Azerbaijan, Uzbekistan, and Allah knows what other states that are teetering on the brink of collapse. Their state structures are eroded by corruption of previously unheard-of proportions, their societies are demoralized by neo-sultanist regimes like the one Heydar Aliev has built in Azerbaijan, and their impoverished populations, both rural and urban, are seething with hatred. Whatever the future holds, one thing is clear. History did not end in 1989; it took a deep dive into the unknown.

NOTES

1   Thomas Goltz, *Azerbaijan Diary: A Rogue Reporter's Adventures in an Oil-Rich, War-Torn, Post-Soviet Republic*, Armonk, NY: M.E. Sharpe, 1998.
2   V.I. Lenin, 'Lev Tolstoi kak zerkalo russkoi revolutsii', *Izbrannye proizvedenia*, tom I., Moskva: Politizdat, 1974.
3   On Soviet bureaucratic isomorphism, see Victor Zaslavsky, *The Neo-Stalinist State*, Armonk, NY: M.E. Sharpe, 1982.
4   On the Chechen situation, see my 'Che Guevaras in Turbans', *New Left Review*, I/237, Sept-Oct 1999.

LINGUISTIC-COMMUNAL POLITICS AND CLASS CONFLICT IN INDIA

Pratyush Chandra

The commonplace view propagated in the media is that religious fundamentalism and militant identity assertion are incompatible with liberal–democratic capitalism, and represent a mediaeval revival. Innumerable arguments are advanced to prove their primordial nature. The theory of a 'clash of civilizations' is presented. The American-British 'war against terrorism' in Afghanistan, waged ideologically through the BBC, the CNN and their Third World franchisees, popularizes this myth and creates new symbols to characterize it. Religious and social identities are redefined.

The Indian sub-continent was already an arena of sharp identity clashes, and with right-wing majorities in power in each country it faces the natural outcome – an intensification of these clashes. In India, particularly, where conflicts are multifaceted, the repercussions are grave. The authoritarian measures taken by the Indian government in the form of the Prevention of Terrorism Act, and the characterization of every militant identity assertion as 'terroristic', are the immediate consequence. The Kashmiri question itself is labelled 'communal' and 'terrorist', along with militant Dalit and regional struggles against the caste structure and regional inequalities.[1] Some of the sufferings of Jewish communities at the hands of the Nazis have also befallen 'minorities' in India, especially Muslims. These 'minorities' are obviously not just contingent elements of society that happen to be assigned low status or are even excluded from the mainstream; their identities are *differentially included*, interwoven in the political structure from top to bottom.

Multiple identities exist, based on social, political, cultural and economic factors, and their mobilizations overlap. At different times and in different places we find different types of identity conflict at the centre of social relations – and the most prevalent mode of resolution of any given identity conflict is the posing of another. But the 'communal question' remains the most formidable; its volatile effects make it central to any political discourse in South Asia. Recent events have simply reasserted this on a global scale.

Approaches to the communal question tend to revolve around arbitrary enumerations of cultural facts. Rightists list the oppressive attitudes of others, and their own valorous heritage, while leftists enumerate which cultural heritage should be kept and which should be renounced. So we find left leaders writing pamphlets which preach a 'true', tolerant and 'secular' Hinduism. This is usually justified in the name of pragmatism, but what is seen as pragmatic never changes, because in this process the hegemonic discourse is never questioned; the rules of the game continue to be set by the hegemonic players.

The so-called 'secular' compromise, which has sealed the fate of any genuine non-communal practice, is starkly evident in relation to the question of India's national language. The language issue was manipulated to engineer political support for different elements of the elite. The 'secular' nationalists divided the options for a national language into three – Urdu, Hindi and Hindustani – which made the illiterate majority into pawns in the intra-class conflicts of the proper-tied class and its managers. Their talk of 'the national language' always concerned the written word and its script, which was really only of interest to those who knew the written word and script, in fact to those who could make a living from knowing them. Mobilizing mass support for this could be done only by attaching a popular identity to the language that was being championed – by Muslimizing or Hinduizing it.

At a time like the present, when emotions are running high, the only correct approach is to try to understand how identities are formed and what roles are defined for them in the present socio-economic formation. Any scientific analysis must be able to explain 'communal' and other social conflicts not as aberrations or deviations from some idealized politico-ideological practice, but as emanating from the very pores of the political-economic system. Seeking their causes in particular features of the religious and cultural heritage – such as the alleged degree of tolerance and intolerance inherent in this or that religion – is to surrender to 'cultural hereditarianism', leading, once again, to mere arbitrary recitations of facts.

A GENERAL THEORY OF IDENTITY FORMATION AND ITS ROLE UNDER CAPITALISM

The present socio-economic structure, rightly termed an 'acquisitive society', derives its dynamic energy from the competitive engine inherent in the logic of capital accumulation. Wherever it has penetrated, capitalism has appropriated the pre-existing social structures and metamorphosed them, radically transforming their basic character – converting them into ideological 'instruments', while more or less retaining their form. This process embeds the universal in the particular. On the one hand, competition becomes more and more general, as 'non-capitalist' structures are penetrated; on the other hand, greater competition increases social fragmentation, creating multiple new hierarchical identities within society. This is why globalization and post-modernity go hand in hand.

The whole history of capitalism is an empirical manifestation of this essential logic. The advent of the nation-state and colonization, the globalization of imperialist wars in the twentieth century, the birth of the United Nations and 'third world' nationalisms, can all be perceived as realizations of the same dialectical process. Its latest manifestations, coming from the advanced capitalist states, are a demand for stringent global legal structures, as economic boundaries everywhere are eroded by liberalization, combined in practice with continuing forms of protectionism.

Like any other class-based social system capitalism destroys primitive political and cultural institutions, but it builds new ones with the same bricks and mortar; it cannot abolish the context in which it is born. There is a long transition from the 'formal' to the 'real' subsumption of labour under capital, so old institutions persist with new meanings and roles. And throughout this process competition does the midwifery at every level: that is, in order to realize itself, 'capital in general' depends on the competitive struggles between individual capitals. Sociopolitical institutions and ideologies constitute the arena in which these battles are waged. Capitalists strengthen their positions by forming combinations, associations and cartels, and these formations and their tactics are legitimated through cultural identities (geographic, ethnic, religious, linguistic, communal, etc.). Such identities serve as effective mechanisms to obscure the real economic processes that are taking place. They structure the norms of power in markets, where the outcomes of intra-class rivalries are actually decided. They create political infrastructures through which individual capitals, or combinations of individual capitals, exert their influence.

But the most important point is that it is in this clash of identities that capitalism is reproduced. Through this means any decisive threat to its rule is neutralized. In the jargon of mainstream economics, it legitimates the segmentation of the labour market, which allows capital to 'add more value'. Through segmentation, competition among workers is increased, which is the foundation of wage slavery, the essential condition for capital accumulation. This social and economic segmentation fragments and ghettoizes the consciousness of the working class. It is politically subjugated by the sterilization of its capacity to question the conditions of its exploitation.

The fundamental reality of capitalist development – capital accumulation and the increasing exploitation of labour power, in which competition works as the essential midwife – is realized in necessarily fetishized social forms, relations and conflicts. The caste, race and religion of yesteryear become ideological realities, essential for reproducing and legitimizing the fundamental processes through which accumulation is occurring. Modern identity formation is a necessary representation of the capitalist race for acquisition, of unequal exchange.

THE SECULAR FOUNDATIONS OF COMMUNAL POLITICS

When we analyze communal conflict in the Indian sub-continent we must keep in mind that the centrality of this problem has historical causes, and that it polarizes the societies of the sub-continental in a far-reaching manner, more than other identity conflicts. The British, who spearheaded capitalist penetration in this region, discovered this truth and constructed a system of control based on it. But the persistence of communal conflict is not simply a colonial legacy, but an inevitable result of the penetration of capital's logic in a specific socio-cultural context. Liberal democracy only universalizes communal conflicts by frag-menting society still further, since the basic ideology of democracy, abstract individualism, makes citizens more prone to fundamentalist convictions: funda-mentalism comes to seem the only basis for stability in a fast-changing world. This paradox is just one of the numerous paradoxes of which capitalism is composed.

Communal Identities and Class Politics

The ironies we are concerned with here concern the 'secular' purpose of communal identities and their politics. If we look at the history of communal sentiment and communal conflict in the Indian sub-continent, we find that the modern forms of both arose with the installation of the competitive ethic at the time of the advent of the British. Reform and modernization movements within the various communities mediated the process of identity formation. Westernization, which connoted bourgeois culture, engendered two different tracks of socio-cultural development. First, a reaction, represented by revivalism, financed and led by the declining aristocracy; and second, a process of assimila-tion and adjustment by the protégés of the British. Both were complementary. Among the propertied strata, family structures accommodated both strands – modernity and ethnicity – and this gave birth to Indian nationalities and nation-alism. Western education generated a new sense of, and search for, identity, conditioned essentially by the question of who would get the 'scarce' material benefits that were available as rewards for the privilege of being educated. A new urban salariat[2] started expressing its demands and needs, and gave birth to modern Indian politics. The Indian National Congress was its most significant attempt to create a political lobby but numerous other associations, varying according to the specificities of India's diverse regions, began to be founded to voice the 'depri-vations' – caste, religious and regional – felt by the new salariat.

The newly-educated and the salariat among the Muslims in the Muslim minority regions also felt deprived of opportunities befitting their qualifications. The birth of the Muslim League epitomized this feeling, and was their attempt to associate for this purpose. Hamza Alavi points out that

> it is true that it was Muslim notables, so-called 'feudals', who presided over the birth of the Muslim League in December 1906 at Dacca. This has misled too many historians about the character of the Muslim League. The

fact of the matter is that the Muslim League, soon after its initiation by Muslim notables, was taken over by the Muslim Salariat .... Later, by 1910, the leadership and control of the Muslim League passed into the hands of men from a relatively more modest background who have been described as 'men of progressive tendencies' ... They pushed the Muslim League in a new direction and sought co-operation with the larger Indian nationalist movement and the Congress, provided Muslim Salariat rights were protected.[3]

The Muslim League did not display any fundamentalist tendency. Distrust of the 'secular' credentials of the Congress among the leaders of the Muslim League came only after the Congress chose to negotiate with the Deobandi Ulema as representatives of the Muslim community and to back their Khilafat – 'a bizarre movement of religious obscurantism that unleashed rabid and atavistic passions among Indian Muslims .... The movement promised to isolate the Muslim Salariat leadership from Muslim masses by arousing their fanatical passions behind a hopeless and anachronistic cause'.[4] Yet the 'secular' leaders of the Indian freedom struggle backed it! It was this fact that alienated the Muslim League from the Congress, since it clearly showed the opportunism of the majority within the leadership of the Congress. On the other hand, from its inception there was a growing influence of Hindu sectarianism within the Congress too, due to the character of its main social base. The development of Hindu sectarianism reflected the same competitive logic which drove the Muslim salariat towards Muslim sectarianism.

Communal sectarianism took an ugly turn when its proponents resorted to mass propaganda and mobilization for settling their intra-class dispute. But it would be wrong to attribute the communal conflict evident throughout the history of the freedom movement to the conscious deliberations of a few selfish bigots, or the tactical ploys of inconsistent 'secular' democrats. Inherent in it were the multifaceted dynamics of colonial capitalism. It was a birth-pang of a new society – the absorption of the vast subcontinent of India into the global machinery of capitalist accumulation as a 'late' capitalist society. At that time, as Sarkar says, 'one type of militancy could easily turn into another'.[5] Newly urbanized workers, recently impoverished peasants and artisans, powerless in the already saturated labour market, could only rely on their traditional loyalties and bonds – caste, religion and region – as political shields and initial ways to form 'combinations'. So, for example, Muslim and Hindu jute workers, both demanding holidays, rioted over when they should be – at Eid/Muharram, or Rathjatra. Significantly, 'the first relatively stable labour organization that we hear of in the Calcutta industrial area was the Muhammedan Association of Kankinara, founded in 1895'.[6] But then these associations took their own course – they would build temples and mosques, too. For a class response we must look to the action of the jute entrepreneurs, who demanded that the growth of these associations should be checked; which meant nothing less than repressing incipient working-class consciousness.

Although Islamic fundamentalism, like Hindu fundamentalism, was a response to the loss of the privileges and occupations that the 'organic intellectuals' (the clerks and the clergy) of yesteryear had formerly enjoyed, its mass base was provided by traditional artisans, guild-masters and petty traders, who were often lost in the new markets dominated by mass production, and relegated to the status of suppliers of raw materials. 'They became extremely bigoted and developed an uncompromising attitude towards the West. The Ulema's outlook reflected that also'.[7]

The Hindi-Urdu Conflict in Context

As indicated earlier, the elite origins of contemporary communal conflicts lie in the competition for supremacy between particular sections of the propertied interest and the professional political class which rules on their behalf. Skilled, educated workers are needed more and more in the production and service sectors, yet the production of 'human resources' always exceeds demand for them; in their desperate competition for privileged job opportunities they inevitably look for non-economic means to get them, and hence become first imbibers, and then agents and activists of the ideological abracadabra of fetishistic, homogenized socio-cultural identities. The Hindi-Urdu debate was a political artefact, which offered huge scope for dividing the ranks of the educated working class, since attaching a separate language to a social identity endows it with a sense of nationhood. In this particular case, however, the linguistic divide was itself false, rendering the whole concept of religious nationhood baseless and inconclusive, making the conflict between the 'nations' of Hindustan and Pakistan inherently irreconcilable.

For the Hindi/Urdu conflict was never about the legitimation of any popular language, but a struggle over a vocabulary and a script. Hindi and Urdu share an identical grammatical structure with somewhat different vocabularies and different scripts. With extra doses of Sanskrit words it becomes Hindi, and with extra doses of Persian and Arabic words it is Urdu; but Hindi-Urdu debaters conduct their arguments as if scripts and lexical borrowings were essential features of linguistic difference. It is worth remembering that most European languages use the same Roman script, while Japanese uses three different scripts. In terms of the way the proponents of Hindi versus Urdu conduct their debate, European languages would be considered all the same and Japanese would be considered three different languages; whereas from a European or Japanese standpoint, Hindi and Urdu are really two names for the same language. Yet by Muslimizing Urdu, and Hinduizing Hindi, the rivals in the competition for jobs for educated workers succeeded in making this false divide into a national one. Hindi would eventually become the official language of India, and Urdu of Pakistan.

The Hindi-Urdu issue was thus a vehicle of intra-class rivalry – between and among the rural and urban gentry. The 'Hindiwallahs', epitomizing the bid for power in the local state and other political institutions by rural and urban Hindu hegemonic interests, subordinated many rich popular languages, along with their speakers, the common majority. These languages were relegated to the status of rustic vernaculars – dialectal appendages of the sophisticated Savarna Hindi: Maithili, Bhojpuri, Magahi, Marwari – all were merged into the 'Hindi-belt'. This process gave the Hindu elite a homogeneous support base whose voice the newly arrived Hindiwallahs became – the organic intellectuals of the new propertied elements of the 'Hindi-belt'. Thus, the popular masses and their voices were 'subaltern'-ed. The vigour of Hindi imperialism was such that within a few decades local scripts such as Kaithi and Mahajani were completely forgotten. These successes inflated the hegemonic spirit of the Hindi elite, encouraging it to dub all attempts to counter it as divisive and insurgent. This created an unhappy situation after independence, especially for the non-Hindi 'nationalities'.

In the United Provinces one sees this conflict developing with the rise of rural elites who came mostly from families of Hindu landlords (Rajputs-Bhumihars), priests (Brahmins) and merchants (Baniyas), and their gradual urbanization; in the towns they found already existing and powerful Muslim and Kayastha elites. The new Hindu elites found allies in Bihar and the Central Provinces, where Sanskrit vocabulary was a major influence, while the Muslim elites found allies in the Western areas of the region, where Persian-Arabic influence was strong.

Differential treatment of these elites on regional and communal lines by the colonial rulers furthered the divide. Lieutenant-Governor Macdonnell decreed that 'The ratio of Muslims to Hindus should be reduced to three to five'. He wrote to the Governor-General, Lord Curzon: 'We are far more interested in [encouraging] a Hindu predominance than in [encouraging] a Mahomedan predominance, which, in the nature of things, must be hostile to us'.[8]

In general, the Hindi-Urdu conflict in the pre-independence era set the tone for all other linguistic and identity clashes in the region after independence. The failure to subjugate Urdu script, in which most of the progressive literature in the 'Hindi-belt' had been written in pre-partition days, forced the hegemonic forces to communalize the issue. They made the script debate an issue for communal mobilization. The marginalization of popular languages and scripts was an evident result of this process. The economic have-nots everywhere were culturally marginalized – they became cultural have-nots at the service of the haves. This ghettoization of 'the multitude' is an essential part of this process, through which 'the multitude' is disallowed as a political entity. Urdu – the diction and the script of the old nationalist consensus, which had been a popular radical instrument in the hands of non-institutional literates (like Nazir Akbarabadi, Jafar Zatalli and many others in the twentieth century), became a mere tool of clerical manipulation: Urdu became the Muslim language. Illiterate people, living in the same area and speaking in an identical way, but using no script, were divided into two 'linguistic' communities. This fact shows clearly that the Hindi-Urdu debate is not a linguistic debate, but a potent politico-ideological device.

Secular-Communal Politics and Class Struggle

In Muslim majority areas, west and east presented different pictures. On the whole, in none of these areas did the Muslim League and its community politics have any decisive influence before the late 1930s. Not even the slogan of

'Pakistan' could raise any support, except from a few utopian urban intellectuals and the salariat. In Punjab, for example, while the Muslim League existed, under the leadership of the great poet Iqbal, religious bigotry was not the basis of its politics; it simply wanted to unite the urban professionals and salariat in the Muslim community in defence of their interests. Even so it had a meagre presence in the political life of the region.

In the east, the dynamics of the polity were given by peasant struggles and landlord reaction, and this class struggle was by and large open and, hence, secular. The peasantry (both Hindus and Muslims) stood in solidarity with their brethren in Bihar and elsewhere, who were linked to the All India Kisan Sabha (AIKS) and the Bengal Provincial Kisan Sabha (BPKS) and their radical leaderships. Alongside this was a secular Krishak Proja Party, under the leadership of A.K. Fazlul Haq, in which power rested with a radical coalition of Muslims and Hindus united around the demand for the abolition of Zamindari. On the other side, to curb the menace of this peasant radicalism, the Hindu and Muslim Zamindars [tax-collecting landowners] of Bengal joined hands whenever they needed to, even if they belonged to different parties for their daily competitive purposes. The communal rift, in fact, became their single most important tactic for breaking up the unprecedented unity along class lines that was being displayed by the tenants and poor peasantry.

In the west, in Punjab, before the 1940s, the dominant ruling party was a secular landlord alliance – the Unionist Party, composed of Hindu-Muslim-Sikh landed magnates. Sir Fazli Hussain, with his right-hand man Sir Chhotu Ram, founded and dominated the party, and Sir Sundar Singh Majithia, the leader of the Sikh landed interest, completed the triumvirate. In Sindh, too, coalitions of Muslim and Hindu landlords dominated the politics of the province and formed the provincial government, their socio-political behaviour and legacy being similar to that of their counterparts in Punjab. So in these regions, too, communal politics was not dominant. On the other hand the Muslim peasantry, who predominated in the west, were unable to develop their own class politics as their counterparts did in the east, and the populist religious politics of religious leaders played an important role in keeping matters this way. These religious leaders, many themselves belonging to the landowning class or feeding off its patronage, anaesthetized and sublimated popular feelings of discontent, creating instead a mass base for their patrons. This religious influence proved lethal and potent for fundamentalist exploitation in later years.

It was only when the actual cultivators in the east raised a demand for tenancy rights, giving rise to fears of a pro-peasant tilt in the nationalist leadership throughout the country, that rent-squeezing landlords and the rural aristocracy started taking shelter under the cloaks of the Ulema and the Pundits, seeing this as the only way to protect their economic interests in what was still predominantly a rural society. As for the western regions, one may quote Hamza Alavi again:

> The politically more astute and, in terms of recognition of their class interests, far-sighted landlords, such as Mumtaz Daulatana and Nawab

Mamdot, saw the need to change horses earlier than many others. Ultimately, by that fateful year 1946, most of them accepted the change of tactics to preserve the long term interests of their class by joining the Muslim League and taking over the new state of Pakistan, which was to be the guarantee of their survival as a landlord class, which was threatened by the Congress commitment to land reform.[9]

I would add simply that the Congress' commitment to land reform turned out to be mainly tactical and verbal, as the whole history of the peasant movement in India attests.

As stated earlier, both the Congress and the Muslim League began as associations of the salariat, an auxiliary class whose natural attachment to the economically dominant class derives from their personal class 'origins' and career needs. This accounts for the opportunist and inconsistent stands taken by the Congress and the League throughout the history of the independence movement. They were always ready to compromise, however defiant they sounded. In the process they became vocal lobbyists for the indigenous fundamental classes, the rising bourgeoisie, landlords, moneylenders and others who wanted concessions from the state. Their apparent separateness from their protectors made them acceptable to the downtrodden fundamental classes whose grievances they also voiced – the peasantry, simple commodity producers and the proletariat. This made these associations powerful and effective agencies for controlling the lower classes for the benefit of their benefactors. Moreover this political structure revealed the crystallizing shape of the future post-colonial state.

The last decade of colonial rule in India saw massive unrest on class lines. When organized trade unionism and the peasant movement appeared on the political scene they terrified the established leadership of the nationalist movement. Although the propertied interests appreciated the value of mobilizations of the downtrodden when bargaining with the state in their own interests, they always tried to rein in the independent activities of these forces, aligning themselves for this purpose with the colonial regime. When the peasantry in Bihar stormed the Assembly in 1937, G.D. Birla, an industrialist and protégé-sponsor of Mahatma Gandhi, voiced the fears of the 'nationalists' when he warned that this could lead to an open assault on the bourgeois and petty bourgeois nationalist leadership: 'the rank and file', he said, 'seems to be confusing freedom with indiscipline'. Later, he complained that 'indiscipline' was leading to 'threats of a flight of capital from Congress ruled Bombay and UP to the princely states where labour laws hardly existed'.[10]

The Congress' willingness to serve the interests of its propertied trustees was reaffirmed in 1946 when independent working-class action 'infested' even the armed forces, and workers and peasants struck in unison throughout the whole country in a remarkable show of communal harmony – on the eve of the communal holocaust which was already being engineered in the plans for partitioning the subcontinent. An unprecedented situation arose when the nationalist leadership stood against the rising wave of revolutionary discontent, condemning as sinful the growing Hindu–Muslim unity at the grass roots. It was certain that if the British stayed any longer it would create a situation where the uprising would not be only against them, but also against the bourgeois leadership of the national movement. It was at this juncture that the national leadership abandoned every kind of mass initiative and started seeking administrative solutions to the 'national' question.

Partition was its inevitable result – a compromise between all the ruling-class forces in the region to thwart a bigger threat to established property relations. And post-colonial history confirms that partition provided a long-term formula for limiting any political fallout from the volatile path of bourgeois development. Indian and Pakistani 'nationality' became two ideologies by which nationalist-communal frenzy is fomented in each country to thwart any political 'instability' in the region. 'National security', 'foreign intrusion' and proxy wars constitute the post-colonial political lexicon in terms of which class-based unity among the exploited classes is routinely opposed.

PARADOXES OF 'SECULAR' AND DEMOCRATIC POLITICS – THE POST-COLONIAL MIASMA

The formation of the Constituent Assembly and the transfer of power in 1947 constituted a two-part compromise charted by the nationalists. First there was a purely legal-administrative gradual transfer of power in order to allow agitation to subside, to be isolated and managed, giving the hegemonic politico-economic interests enough time and space to take up their positions in the management of independence and the future government. The British aim was to develop the region as a future neo-colonial arena for business, direct colonialism having become redundant. They also sought to minimize the damage to foreign economic interests already established in the region. The influential presence of the Soviet Union naturally played an important part in determining the British formula for Indian independence.

The second dimension of the compromise proved decisive for the geo-polit-ical formation of the Indian State. It was a compromise between the rural feudal strata and small-scale capitalists, on the one hand, and the nationalists representing mainly the big bourgeoisie, on the other. The federal character of the Indian state represented this compromise. Landed interests and small-scale capitalists got a strong say in regional politics and mobilization, and a degree of relative autonomy, while 'national' planning, with its obvious tilt in favour of the big industrial interests (the Bombay Club), constituted the centre. The allocation of powers in the constitution via Centre, State and Concurrent lists confirmed this compromise: the passing and implementation of anti-zamindari laws became dependent on the regional ruling interests.

This compromise served to consolidate a peculiar kind of multi-party 'democracy' in which interests seem to be very fragmented, yet until recently were quite stable. A summary dating from the early 1970s remains apt, notwith-standing its Soviet provenance:

... a large number of organisations enjoying limited influence within the confines of a single state or even a single region within a state; a complex interweaving of revolutionary-democratic and bourgeois-nationalist ideology and politics; blurred distinctions between bourgeois and petty bourgeois interests; a significant role of religious, caste and regional interests behind the emergence and activities of political organisations, which provided a reliable reflection of the social and class structure of Indian society in the course of transition to capitalism, in which petty bourgeois strata and groups were predominant, but which also contained classes representing the now obsolescent feudal order. The political life of India had been affected by the specific character of the Indian bourgeoisie which was only just taking shape, the main groups in which consisted of small-scale entrepreneurs, often representing local, ethnic or regional interests, and also by the role of such traditional social institutions as caste and religion.[11]

In this context 'secularism' offered a political ideology to rationalize these compromises and the evolution of 'salad-bowl' democracy. In the wake of the mass *non*-communal upsurge of the rural and urban oppressed against their exploitation and oppression, 'secularism' was an engineered harmony between the rival communal leaderships, recognizing the communities represented by them as the negotiating units for independence. Throughout the years 1945-47, then, the issue of independence was negotiated as a communal problem. As mentioned above, the negotiators denounced the working-class and peasant struggles throughout the region which had hastened the departure of the British – and which, remarkably, had overcome the so-called 'communal problem' – as obstacles to the attainment of independence. This behaviour on the part of the nationalist leaders reflected their class allegiance, as events after independence proved. The Telangana Movement against landlordism led by Nizam, the Tebhaga struggle for tenancy rights, the Kashmiri uprising against Hindu landlords, the Warli uprising against the 'simple reproduction squeeze' of the moneylending merchants, were all crushed by the post-independence 'secular' government lest they call into question the 'composite' regime of exploitation negotiated during the transition.

The way the language issue was dealt with provides a glimpse of the India which the hegemonic forces sought to build. With the 'secular liberal' nationalist compromise between the bourgeoisie and the Hindu fundamentalist rural rent-squeezers, the former had to make considerable concessions to the latter. These compromises are evident in the constitution itself. Regarding the language issue, the Hindi/Urdu divide was constitutionalized, Urdu being reduced to the status of a communal language. Initially, it was not even included in the list of national languages, and when it was later included, at the behest of Nehru, Sanskrit accompanied it, as a 'modern' Indian language. The volatility of the issue was thus confirmed and ensured forever. The nationalist goal of a composite national language died with the advent of 'administered' freedom.

'Secularism' as practised in India thus represents not the defeat of communalist forces but a compromise between them. It is a screen behind which the bogey of communalism can safely rest, to be recalled from its slumbers whenever the 'fundamental' system requires. In recent years, however, the 'secular compromise' has been in crisis, reflecting politico-economic changes and realignments of class forces that have occurred since independence.

All this having been said, it is important to remind ourselves again that political engineering through identities and ideologies is not a mere 'legacy' of colonialism, as many would have us believe, but a necessary political realization of the competitive ethic inherent in the social relations of production in a 'late capitalist' country. It provides the necessary infrastructure for determining the pace and path of the constant reorientation of markets. In this regard, we may recall the complementary roles of baniyas (petty traders) and the Hinduization process in the tribal areas throughout the country. In the tribal regions they have been agents of both Hinduization and commercialization. The marginalized communities become part of the mainstream politico-economic processes – as potential consumers and recruits in the labour market. Maratha chauvinism and Ganapati utsavas in the Warli belt of Maharashtra destroy the simple isolated life of the tribal peoples at the same time that they monetize their social life by drawing them into costly Hindu festivities and giving them mainstream aspirations. The immediate effect of this process has been a tremendous growth in the plantation industry in this region, exploiting cheap female labour, while the male members of the community become 'lumpenproletarians' and are hired as agents of control by individual capitalists and merchants, and become enthusiastic activists and 'goons' for local political forces.

Another example is the way Hindu fundamentalism was the ideological weapon of choice of Hindu mercantile and financial interests facing tough competition from Muslim Bohras and Parsis on the western coast, while the power of the Hindu landlords-merchants in Muslim-majority areas was declining. After independence, the ousted feudal and rentier landlords joined the ranks of right-wing fundamentalism. Within the Congress itself there was a very powerful lobby of these classes. But productive capital and parasitic interests clashed frequently, leading to constant re-combinations of the latter as separate political forces – the Hindu Mahasabha, the Rashtriya Swayamsevak Sangh (RSS),[12] the Jan Sangh, the Swatantra Party, etc. The number of disaffected groups was further swelled by frequent crises in the federal structure, due to clashes between the general interest of the capitalist class, dominated by the monopolies, and the regional interests of the rising rich peasantry and petty bourgeoisie.

On the other hand, after Partition the Islamic community in India suffered an introversion; it became ever more suspicious of the intentions of the Hindu mainstream, as industrialization and the growth of the metropoles steadily impoverished the self-employed Muslim artisans and the Muslim lower middle class. This process created a mass base for Muslim politics, making the victims pawns of the hegemonic interests in the Muslim community – the traders, the clergy and the intelligentsia/salariat. Despite the absence of serious competition between Muslims and Hindu elites – or for that matter, between any other sections of these communities – Partition established communal conflict and chauvinism as normal political devices to thwart any real threat to the politico-economic system or the balance of class forces.

In the 1960s a tremendous growth in urban unemployment, especially of educated people, and an absence of any genuine attempt to unite unemployed youth on class lines, created a basis for a politics of right-wing reaction in which diverse and contradictory interests aligned against the pro-monopoly policies of Indira Gandhi. Besides this there was a clear conflict between the particularist interests of private capital and the state as the general protégé of the capitalist interest, a conflict which was resolved in the form of the Janata government of 1977-80, heralding the end of state-regulated capitalism. Subsequent governments were more and more inclined to take the path of liberalization.

The inability of the bourgeoisie to completely overthrow the old rural order, for fear of destabilizing their own position, meant that they had to wait for the gradual 'trickle-down' effects of macro-economic policy to open up the country's vast rural market for direct profit-making. They had to give the landlords an opportunity to transform themselves into capitalist farmers by the so-called green revolution. This, however, could work only in perennially irrigated areas; in other areas, the transformation of the country's political-economic system was an example of what Gramsci called a 'passive revolution', occurring through monetization, commercialization and the slow fragmentation of landholdings. The social elements left over from the old regime fed on the new one, but still the revolution occurred. Kulaks – rich peasants and rural entrepreneurs – did slowly evolve.

With the rise of new elites from the rural gentry in north India the 'Hindiwallahs' once more tried to claim places in the administration. Hindi again became a tool for mobilizing the masses: Lohia's Angrezi Hatao movement, and the Brahminical Hindi Sangharsh Samiti, comprising communals, Gandhians and intellectuals, were products of this period. State-regulated capitalist development had also seriously afflicted merchants, shopkeepers and moneylenders. The strengthening of the state sector through nationalized banks and the attempted state-monopolization of the grain trade created a large discontented element within the urban and rural bourgeoisie too. All these forces combined with the organizations of the old 'nobility' and mercantile capital, most of which had a communal-chauvinist orientation, like the RSS and the Jan Sangh, and rallied to the call of the Gandhian 'national' socialist Jayprakash Narayan for 'total revolution', which was already attracting a growing portion of the educated unemployed in north India. The national big industrial bourgeoisie, united under the banner of the Congress, were bewildered by this unprecedented combination and resorted to the declaration of an emergency and authoritarianism. The conflicts between these sections of the propertied class thus provided an opportunity to 'save' the country from any real radical transformation, such as was evolving in the late '60s and early '70s, with an increase in local class conflicts and social unrest due to unemployment.[13]

By the time Rajiv Gandhi came to power in 1984, liberalization was the only course of capitalist development the Indian ruling class wanted to pursue. Even when an alternative government was formed under the leadership of V.P.Singh in 1989, on a platform of social justice, the finance ministry continued with the policy of liberalization. The eventual toppling of the V.P. government was a clear indication that the ruling class would destabilize any government that faltered in satisfying its needs. But one thing was clear about this government: it included that section among the ruling elite which had struggled hard to over-throw the parasitic class of high-caste absentee-landlords in the rural sector. This new elite of newly-rich peasants was composed of former tenants who had acquired a somewhat independent status after the legal abolition of landlordism and the imposition of ceilings on landholdings, but who still did not have a defi-nite lobby at the heart of the government, at least in the northern belt. Hence, its spoils: a statutory quota of 27 per cent of the positions in the mandarin-like bureaucracy.[14]

The rise of the right

The re-communalization of politics in the 1980s and 1990s and an increasingly chauvinistic tendency reaffirmed the subtle link between politics and the ongoing economic transformation of the country. In 1991 the new Congress government of Narasimha Rao responded to the call of indigenous capital for the further liberalization it required for its expansion. In this process, an invitation to foreign capital and signing the GATT agreements were also important, as these concessions in turn gave national capital access to global markets.

In the wake of the new inflows of foreign capital indigenous industrial capital needed to check and control their all-round effects, and for this strong govern-ment was required – a 'magnetic' political formation with a disciplined rank and file, capable of uniting all the social forces in the country while remaining committed to the basic tenets of liberalization. The Congress had lost much of its credibility due to open corruption during its tenure of office, and had always been recognized as a rather 'polite' force whose loose-knit organizational struc-ture made it unsuitable for militant policy decisions. A 'third front' had emerged on the initiative of left forces, but after V.P. Singh's government of 1989 its relevance rapidly declined as it failed to propose any clear alternative socio-economic agenda, and merely bewailed the destruction of the secular and democratic fabric of the Republic. Initially, the third front played an important role in bringing to the fore the hitherto 'subaltern' voices of rural capital in north India, but it became a spent force, and power was soon transferred to a strong right-wing coalition government led by the BJP. The Hindu chauvinist and nationalistic slogan of 'Swadeshi' provided an appropriate ideological plank, which appealed to a broad range of politico-economic interests – even, as seen above, the industrial sector, whose ultimate aim was secure access to the global market. It also proved able to mesmerize even the educated unemployed youth who were becoming a potential threat to the status quo.

Along with these developments, a movement began against those aspects of the GATT agreements, and of the subsequent activities of the WTO, which were detrimental to indigenous capital, including agrarian capital. On the whole national industrial capital benefited from the GATT, but it found it could insert its own items into the Swadeshi agenda – such as opposition to the WTO's call to curb industries which employed child labour – and could also use the militancy of the Swadeshi movement as a weapon to hegemonize the domestic market. This dual face of industrial capital finally found perfect expression in the actions of the Vajpayee Government.

The first time Hindu nationalist militancy was used directly by industrial capital to curb militant trade unionism was right after independence in 1947. Industrialization and the gradual intrusion of capital in agriculture had created a vast population of urban have-nots who were becoming unionized. Trade unionism had already shown its militancy during the last few years of British rule, and industrialization threatened to increase its strength still further, especially around the city of Bombay. The rise of the fascistic regional party Shiv Sena, now one of the most important constituents of the Vajpayee government, was a product of this process.

Despite frequently successful attempts to play the chauvinist card, however, the representatives of industrial capital were themselves by and large secular, as they needed a smooth process for industrial expansion, and communal fascism was a force that could not be tamed for long. On the other hand they had to form coalitions with regionally-based agrarian interests, since in spite of the agrarian sector's declining share of the GDP the strength of the rural vote gave them a major political voice. And once these interests had secured a political and administrative lobby for themselves, their declining economic strength was bound to draw them towards the assertive communal politics of the Right, which captured their aspirations in the name of Swadeshi, and towards a nationalistic assertion in geo-politics; not with a compromise, but with a bang – a series of nuclear tests.

The Vajpayee government's nuclear tests, coming early in its term of office when it had not yet obtained the confidence of the parliament, represented everything that the critics said; but more than that, they expressed the dream of all the ruling economic interests. In fact, those who criticized the government were mostly competing to take credit for the tests. The explosions were intended to warn foreign capital that it should not take the Indian market for granted; in return foreign capital would have to recognize the strength of indigenous capital, and not merely recognize it but make concessions to it. This confidence arose from the fact that global capital could not afford to neglect the Indian market.

Indeed, after the USA imposed sanctions as a response to the tests a group of American industrialists immediately realized what their repercussions would be: on the one hand, other western capitals would enter India, and on the other hand

domestic capital would get a breathing-space and be able to consolidate its position while dealing with the problems caused by the sudden inflow of foreign
capital. Nuclear tests and the Swadeshi movement in India are in no way a negation of liberalization or of the process of global integration, but a political bid by
a section of Indian capital to set its own terms for India's participation in such
processes. The Vajpayee government's 'strong' policies express the logic of this
binary politico-economic exigency.

THE QUEST FOR AN ALTERNATIVE

Communal mobilization is an important tool for stabilizing the hegemonic
interests in society. It serves two purposes. First, it creates a social tie between
rulers and ruled, giving the former a potent language in which to communicate
with the latter, and fetishizing the real politics of production relations. Second, it
reduces the potency of counter-hegemonic forces by diverting their energy and
resources, by dividing them. It is not that in these apparent tensions the essential
conflict is un-represented – on the contrary, the ideological miasma is composed
of the fumes arising from that conflict, the mode in which the hegemony realizes
itself. The thickness of this miasma depends on the subjective preparedness of the
counter-hegemony at the moment of crisis, and how the radical forces have
prepared themselves – through day-to-day guerrilla battles, as Marx called the
struggle for political and economic reforms – for open class conflict.

For any alternative politics, the question is not how a particular community
can gain concessions from the existing system, or how its rights are defined and
secured, but rather how united action can be taken against the system which
breeds community conflicts. The problem for us is not how to handle community politics but how to transcend it. The former perspective is the ground on
which modern 'secular' politics in India stands – recognizing the hegemonic
voices in communities, while ignoring their internal conflicts, and ultimately
building bridges between hegemonic interests of different shapes and colours.
This is basically like the petty bourgeois utopia in which free and 'just' competition is accepted and even sanctified, without recognizing the necessary logic
inherent in it, its inevitable transformation into monopolies as a result of capitalist accumulation. 'Secularism' as professed in India is an abstraction made in
the capitalist polity to sublimate the different voices within the ruling class, and
secure its unity. It does not exclude 'communal politics for secular purposes'.

An alternative agenda will have to begin by exposing the real semantics of
status quo politics – secular and communal. To return, by way of example, to
the language question: the Hindi-Urdu debate resulted in a big minority everywhere being withdrawn from the political mainstream. These citizens were
insulated from participating democratically and freely in political movements,
especially counter-hegemonic movements, as they naturally looked on these with
suspicion and also lived in fear of being suspected of anti-'national' designs. Thus,
the scope for radical progressive politics within their 'communities' was mini-
mized. And the imputed homogeneity of those who were ghettoized and

excluded could be continually posed by the state and its allies as a potent threat
– thus creating a counter-ghetto of the 'majority'. Hence, any permanent solution to the problem of communal mobilizations will have to confront this politics
directly and aim at the de-ghettoization of the multitude. Strategy will have to
be built on reforms that expose and thwart the hegemonic model. We will have
to hit at the ideological assumptions that rationalize such politics. By implication,
in this particular case, for example, if Hindi-Urdu is really one language, why
cannot both scripts be taught compulsorily and to everybody, like Japanese?[15]
This will simply do away with all the communal schisms and sectarianism that
have been developed on this particular issue, while also partially dealing with the
real danger of the marginalization of the country's 'progressive literary heritage'.
Any other solutions are futile exercises, based on false assumptions.

NOTES

The author wishes to acknowledge Dr. Ather Farouqui not only for his inspiration, but also for his determination to make his collaborators and associates
deliver for a definite cause.

1   Under the category of militant Dalit struggles I include the rural
     mobilizations by Naxalite outfits. Though the mobilizers themselves would
     generally resist such categorization, because of their allegiance to Marxist
     ideology, the rural struggles in 1980s and 1990s reveal that the issues on
     which mobilizations took place were largely linked to notions of dignity, or
     issues relating to the sphere of circulation. They rarely centred on the system
     of production, but focused more on cultural and social vestiges of the *ancien
     regime* which in fact were regularly reproduced by the system of production.
2   'The "salariat" is an *"auxiliary class"* (a concept that must be distinguished
     from that of a "ruling class") whose class role can be fully understood only in
     terms of its relation to "fundamental classes" (from which the "ruling class"
     is drawn); i.e. the economically dominant classes viz. the economically
     dominant metropolitan and indigenous bourgeoisies and the land owning
     classes on the one hand and, and the subordinate classes, the proletariat and
     the peasantry on the other. Given a particular configuration of class forces in
     the state and society members of the salariat attach themselves to
     "fundamental classes" by virtue of their own personal "class origins" or
     through "class affiliation" by virtue of its need and willingness to serve an
     economically dominant class for career considerations regardless of their
     individual class origins. An example of such careerism can be seen in the
     willingness of the Indian and Pakistani salariat to serve anti-national purposes
     of foreign (metropolitan) bourgeoisies at the cost of the nation that they
     purport to serve' (Hamza Alavi, 'Pakistan and Islam: Ethnicity and Ideology',
     http://ourworld.compuserve.com/homepages/sangat/Pakislam.htm,
     originally published in Fred Halliday and Hamza Alavi, eds., *State and Ideology
     in the Middle East and Pakistan*, New York: Monthly Review Press, 1988.

3   Alavi, 'Pakistan and Islam'.

4   Ibid.

5   Sumit Sarkar, *Modern India (1885-1947),* Delhi: Macmillan, 1983, p. 63.

6   Sarkar, *Modern India,* p. 63.

7   Alavi, 'Pakistan and Islam'.

8   Alok Rai, *Hindi Nationalism,* Hyderabad: Orient Longman, , 2000, p. 19.

9   Alavi, 'Pakistan and Islam'.

10   Sarkar, *Modern India,* pp. 361-2.

11   K. Antanova, G. Bongard-Levin, G. Kotovsky, *A History of India (Book 2),* Moscow: Progress Publishers, 1979, pp. 272-3.

12   The Rashtriya Swayamsevak Sangh (literally the National Voluntary Organisation) is the biggest cadre-based Hindu organization based on fascist principles. Though declaring itself to be a cultural organization, it is the mother of all the major Hindu fundamentalist organizations in the country, including the Bharatiya Janata Party (BJP) which is leading the ruling coalition in India.

13   In this the propertied classes were helped by the homogenizing ideology of 'oppositional politics', which again dominates the scene today. Every real radical option was thwarted by rhetorical verbosity and sloganeering, such as the call for 'total revolution'.

14   The reservation policy or quota system reserves government jobs for members of specified castes. Earlier, 22 per cent of jobs were reserved for scheduled castes and tribes (SC&ST), which due to their prevailing lack of educational opportunities meant low-paid menial jobs such as sweepers and peons, or at most clerks. Initially, for these castes, government job reservation provided an opportunity to become part of the mainstream proletariat. But with the rise of a rural bourgeoisie coming mostly from middle-status castes, another 27 per cent reservation was demanded and conceded to these castes. In contrast to the SC&ST reservation, this demand was primarily aimed at securing a lobby in the All-India and regional state bureaucracies. It definitively broke the political power of the upper-caste leadership in rural India, and provided an opportunity for the new rural rich to articulate their interests in policy-making. In fact, caste-based reservation, by neglecting class divisions within castes, ensures that the benefits go to the new-rich sections within each caste. Castes in India, like other identities, express political-economic competition within the propertied interest.

15   Attempts have been made to make Urdu part of the secular curriculum. It is a welcome idea, as it would draw Urdu away from the obscurantist fold. But it should be remembered that as long as Hindi (the specific Brahminist Khari Boli) exists as a separate 'language', seeing Urdu in a secular light is implausible. Hindi's existence depends on the marginalization and ghettoization of Urdu. Urdu's inclusion as part of a 'three-language formula' would also evidently be dishonest in relation to non-Hindi/Urdu speakers.

MAKING SENSE OF POLITICAL VIOLENCE IN POST-COLONIAL AFRICA

Mahmood Mamdani

We have just ended a century replete with violence. The twentieth century was possibly more violent than any other in recorded history. Just think of world wars and revolutions, and of colonial conquests and anti-colonial resistance, and, indeed, of revolutions and counter-revolutions. Yet even if the expanse of this violence is staggering, it makes sense to us.

The modern political sensibility sees political violence as necessary to historical progress. Ever since the French Revolution, moderns have come to see violence as the midwife of history. The French Revolution gave us terror and it gave us a citizens' army. The real secret behind Napoleon's spectacular battlefield successes was that his army was not comprised of mercenaries but of patriots, who killed for a cause, who were animated by national sentiment, by what we have come to recognize as a civic religion, nationalism. Reflecting on the French revolution, Hegel thought of man – in the generic sense – as different from animals, in that he was willing to die for a cause higher than life. Hegel should have added: man is also willing to kill for a cause higher than life. This, I think, is truer of modern man and woman than it is true of humanity in general.

The modern political sensibility is not horrified by all violence. Just put millions in the wrong uniform: citizens and patriots will celebrate their death as the end of enemies. The world wars are proof enough of this. What horrifies modern political sensibility is not violence per se, but violence that does not make sense. It is violence that is neither revolutionary nor counter-revolutionary, violence that can not be illuminated by the story of progress, that appears senseless to us. Not illuminated paradigmatically, non-revolutionary violence appears pointless.

Unable to explain it, we turn our back on history. Two such endeavours are worth noting. The first turns to culture, the second to theology. The cultural turn distinguishes modern from pre-modern culture and then offers pre-modern culture as an explanation of political violence. If revolutionary or counter-revolutionary violence arises from market-based identities such as class, then non-revolutionary violence is said to be an outcome of cultural difference. On a world scale, it is called a clash of civilizations.[1] Locally – that is, when it does not cross the boundary between the West and the rest – it is called communal conflict, as in South Asia, or ethnic conflict, as in Africa.

Faced with political violence that arises in a modern context but will not fit the story of progress, theory has tended to take refuge in theology. The violence of the Holocaust is branded as evil that can only be understood outside historical time.[2] Rather than understand the Holocaust as a clue to the debased and grim side of humanity, this kind of thinking turns the horror into a question mark against the very humanity of its perpetrators. There is a huge resistance, moral and political, to thinking through this violence by locating it in a historical context.

THINKING THROUGH THE HOLOCAUST: THE VIOLENCE OF THE SETTLER

In the corpus of Holocaust-writing Hannah Arendt stands apart. Rather than talk of the uniqueness of the Holocaust, Arendt insisted on locating it in the history of genocide. The history she sketched was that of settler genocide of the native. It was the history of imperialism, specifically, of twin institutions – racism in South Africa, and bureaucracy in India and Algeria – forged in the course of an earlier European expansion into the non-European world.

> Of the two main political devices of imperialist rule, race was discovered in South Africa, and bureaucracy in Algeria, Egypt and India; the former was originally the barely conscious reaction to tribes of whose humanity European man was ashamed and frightened, whereas the latter was a consequence of that administration by which Europeans had tried to rule foreign peoples whom they felt to be hopelessly their inferiors and at the same time in need of their special protection. Race, in other words, was an escape into an irresponsibility where nothing human could any longer exist, and bureaucracy was the result of a responsibility that no man can bear for his fellow man and no people for another people.[3]

Not only did genocide have a history, but modern genocide was nurtured in the colonies: the 'elimination of Hottentot tribes, the wild murdering by Carl Peters in German Southwest Africa, the decimation of the peaceful Congo population – from 20 to 40 million reduced to 8 million people and ... worst of all ... the triumphant introduction of such means of pacification into ordinary, respectable foreign policies'.[4]

The idea that 'imperialism had served civilization by clearing inferior races off the earth' found widespread expression in nineteenth-century European thought, from natural sciences and philosophy to anthropology and politics.[5] When Lord

Salisbury, the British Prime Minister, claimed in his famous Albert Hall speech on May 4, 1898 that 'one can roughly divide the nations of the world into the living and the dying', Hitler was but nine years old, and the European air was 'soaked in the conviction that imperialism is a biologically necessary process, which, according to the laws of nature, leads to the inevitable destruction of lower races'. The paradigmatic example of the destruction of lower races was Tasmania, an island the size of Ireland where European colonists first arrived in 1803, the first massacre of natives occurred in 1804, and the last original inhabitant died in 1869. Similar fates awaited the Maoris of New Zealand, the Native Americans, the Hereros of Southwest Africa, and so on.[6]

By the time the twentieth century dawned it was a European habit to distinguish between civilized wars and colonial wars. Laws of war applied to wars among the civilized but laws of nature applied to colonial wars – biological necessity expressed in the extermination of the lower races. In the Second World War, Germany observed the laws of war against Western powers, but not against Russia. As opposed to 3.5 per cent of English and American prisoners of war who died in German captivity, 57 per cent of Soviet prisoners – 3.3 million in all – lost their lives. Gassings of Russians preceded the gassings at Auschwitz: the first mass gassings were of Russian prisoners of war in the southern Ukraine,[7] and the first to be gassed in Auschwitz were Russians, beginning with intellectuals and communists. The Nazi plan, writes Sven Lindquist, was to weed out some ten million Russians with the remainder kept alive as a slave labour force under German occupation. When the mass murder of European Jews began, the great Jewish populations were not in Germany, but in Poland and Russia, forming 10 per cent of the total population and up to 40 per cent of the urban population 'in just those areas Hitler was after'. The Holocaust was born at the meeting-point of two traditions that marked modern Western civilization: 'the anti-Semitic tradition and the tradition of genocide of colonized peoples'.[8] Here then was the difference in the fate of the Jewish people. They were to be exterminated as a whole. In that, their fate was unique – but only in Europe.

This historical fact was not lost on the postwar intellectuals from the colonies. In his Discours sur le Colonialisme (1951) Aime Césaire writes that a Hitler slumbers within 'the very distinguished, very humanistic and very Christian bourgeois of the twentieth century', and yet the European bourgeois cannot forgive Hitler for 'the fact that he applied to Europe the colonial practices that had previously been applied only to the Arabs of Algeria, the coolies of India and the Negroes of Africa'.[9] 'Not so long ago', recalled Fanon in The Wretched of the Earth (1961), 'Nazism turned the whole of Europe into a veritable colony'.[10]

The first genocide of the twentieth century was the German annihilation of the Herero people in southwest Africa.[11] The German geneticist, Eugene Fischer, did his first medical experiments on the 'science' of race-mixing in concentration camps for the Herero. His subjects were both Herero and mulatto off-springs of Herero women and German men. Fischer argued that the Herero 'mulattos' were physically and mentally inferior to their German parents. Hitler read Fischer's book, *The Principle of Human Heredity and Race Hygiene* (1921), while in prison. The Führer later made Fischer rector of the University of Berlin, where he taught medicine. One of Fischer's prominent students was Joseph Mengele, who would run the gas chambers at Auschwitz. The Holocaust was the imperial chickens coming home to roost.

The link between the genocide of the Herero and the Holocaust was race branding, whereby it is possible not only to set a group apart as an enemy, but also to annihilate it with an easy conscience. To understand the mindset that conceived the Holocaust, one would have to return to political identities crafted by modern imperialism, the settler and the native. Hannah Arendt, and more recently Sven Lindquist, focused on the agency of the settler, but not on the agency of the native. But it is not just the settler; the native too is a product of the imperial imagination. Framed by a common history, they define two sides of a relationship. Unless they are transcended together, they will be reproduced together.

The historians of genocide have sketched half a history for us: that of settler annihilation of the native. To glimpse how this could trigger a counter-tendency, the native annihilating the settler, one has to turn to Frantz Fanon.[12] Hailed as a humanist by most of those who came to pay him homage after his death, Fanon has ironically come to be regarded as a prophet of violence, following Hannah Arendt's claim that his influence was mainly responsible for the growing violence on American campuses in the 1960s.[13] Fanon was recognized as the prophet of decolonization on the publication of his monumental study, *The Wretched of the Earth*; and yet one needs to recognize that he was also the first critic of decolonization. To understand the central thesis in *The Wretched of the Earth* – summed up in a single sentence, 'The colonized man liberates himself in and through violence' – one needs to put it in a triple context: that of the history of Algerian colonization, of modernist thought on the historical necessity of violence, and of the postwar movement to decolonization. Put in context, Fanon's thesis was at the same time a description, a claim and a problematization. First, it was a *description* of the violence of the colonial system, of the fact that violence was key to producing and sustaining the relationship between the settler and the native. Second, it was a *claim* that anti-colonial violence is not an irrational manifestation but belongs to the script of modernity and progress, that it is indeed a midwife of history. And third – and most important for this essay – it was a *problematization*, of a derivative violence, of the violence of victims turned killers.

It is in Fanon that one finds the premonition of the native turned perpetrator, of the native who kills not just to extinguish the humanity of the other, but to defend his or her own, and of the moral ambivalence this must provoke in other human beings like us. Although the extermination of colonizers by natives never came to pass, there were enough uprisings that killed many for extermination to hover in the settler imagination as a historical possibility.[14] No one understood the genocidal impulse better than this Martiniquan-born psychiatrist and Algerian freedom fighter. Native violence, Fanon insisted, was the violence of yesterday's victims, the violence of those who had cast aside their victimhood to become masters of their own lives.

Listen to Fanon: 'He of whom they have never stopped saying that the only language he understands is that of force, decides to give utterance by force.... The argument the native chooses has been furnished by the settler, and by an ironic turning of the tables it is the native who now affirms that the colonialist understands nothing but force'. For Fanon, the proof of the native's humanity consisted not in the willingness to kill settlers, but in the willingness to risk his or her own life. 'The colonized man', he wrote, 'finds his freedom in and through violence'.[15] If the outcome was death, natives killing settlers, that was still a derivative outcome. The native who embraces violence to safeguard his and her freedom is the victim-turned-perpetrator.

LEGAL AND POLITICAL IDENTITIES

If we are to make political violence thinkable, we need to understand the process by which victims and perpetrators become polarized as *group identities*. Who do perpetrators of violence think they are? And who do they think they will eliminate through violence? Even if the identities propelled through violence are drawn from outside the domain of politics – such as race (from biology) or ethnicity or religion (from culture) – we need to denaturalize these identities by outlining their history and illuminating their links with organized forms of power.

Just as we need to locate identities such as class in the history of markets in order to understand them as the outcome of specific historical relations, so we need to turn to the history of state formation to understand the historical nature of political identities. This is particularly so with the modern state, which tries to naturalize political identities as anything but political. On the one hand, the modern state enforces particular group identities through its legal project; on the other, it gives depth to these same identities through a history-writing project. It is by giving group identities both a past and a future that the modern state tries to stand up to time.

Settler and native may be drawn from biological discourses on race, but they need to be understood as political identities enforced by a particular form of the state. If they became politically potent, it is because they were legally enforced by a state that made a distinction between those who were indigenous (natives) and those who were not (settlers) and turned it into grounds for political, social and civic discrimination. Where indegeneity was stigmatized as proof of lack of civilization and taken as sufficient reason to deny the rights of the conquered, and foreignness was valorized as a hallmark of civilization and turned into a guarantee of rights – indeed privileges – for immigrants, there 'settler' and 'native' were racialized as legal and political identities.

Contemporary colonial history of Africa lends itself to a distinction between two distinct modes of rule, each identified with a different form of the colonial state. In the literature on modern colonialism, these two modes are characterized as direct and indirect rule. The transition from direct to indirect rule is one from a modest to an ambitious project. Whereas *direct rule* was preoccupied with shaping elite preferences, *indirect rule* aimed to shape popular preferences. Indirect rule needs to be understood as a response to the crisis of direct rule. Direct rule focused on native elites. It aimed to create native clones of Western modernity through a discourse on civilization and assimilation. Direct rule generated a dual crisis. On the one hand, its civilizational project tended to divide society between an alien minority claiming to be civilized, and a native majority stigmatized as backward. On the other hand, the products of this civilizational project – native intellectuals and entrepreneurs – aspired to replace alien rule by self-rule as the basis of a native modernity. The demand for self-rule was the crisis of direct rule.

The colonial response was to subordinate the civilizational project to a law and order project. The big shift was in law: whereas direct rule aimed at introducing rule of law as a single project, indirect rule replaced the idea of a single rule of law with the construction of many sets of 'customary' laws. Thus, it bypassed modernizing native elites by championing alternative elites – said to be traditional – who would be allies in the enterprise to shape mass preferences through a discourse grounded in tradition. But indirect rule did not accept tradition benignly, as a historical given. It treated history as a raw material, putty from which to shape 'genuine' tradition. Whereas direct rule was dogmatic and dismissed native tradition as backward and superstitious, indirect rule was analytical. The political project called indirect rule aimed to unpack native tradition, to disentangle its different strands, to separate the authoritarian from the emancipatory, and thereby to repack tradition, as authoritarian and ethnic, and harness it to the colonial project. By repacking native passions and cultures selectively it aimed to pit these very passions and cultures against one another. I wrote of this in *Citizen and Subject*,[16] an argument I need not elaborate here.

Unlike those who seek to explain political violence by turning to the domain of culture, I intend to argue that even when political identities are drawn from the domain of culture, they need to be understood as distinct from cultural identities. Theoretically, the experience of indirect rule should alert us to the relationship between culture and politics. When the raw material of political identity is drawn from the domain of culture, as in ethnic or religious identity, it is the link between identity and power that allows us to understand how cultural identities are translated into political identities, and thus to distinguish between them. At the same time, to historicize political identity by linking it to political power is to acknowledge that all political identities are historically transitory and all require a form of the state to be reproduced.

Politically, indirect rule was an attempt to stabilize colonial rule by moving away from direct rule that created a volatile context in which the identity of both rulers and ruled was racialized, but the former as a minority and the latter as a majority. Indirect rule did this through a legal project that fractured the singular, racialized and majority identity, *native*, into several, plural, ethnicized, minority identities – called *tribes*.

To understand how political identities may be defined through the force of law, let us take an African example from any indirect rule colony in the first half of the twentieth century. Recall that the colonial census classified the population into two broad, overall groups. One group was called *races*, and the other *tribes*. This single distinction illuminates the technology of colonial rule. To elaborate this technology of rule, I would like to make five observations.

First, the census divides the population into two kinds of groups: some are tagged as races and others as tribes. Why? On examination, one can discern a clear pattern: non-natives are tagged as races, whereas natives are said to belong to tribes. Races – specifically Europeans, Asians, Arabs – were all those the colonial state defined as not indigenous to Africa. Tribes – called ethnic groups in the postcolonial period – were all those defined as indigenous in origin.

Second, this distinction had a direct legal significance. All races were governed under a single law, civil law. True, civil law was full of discriminations: racial discrimination distinguished the master race (Europeans) from subject races (Asians and Arabs). Subject races were excluded from the exercise of certain rights considered the prerogative only of members of the master race. But this discrimination needs to be understood as internal, for the domain of civil law included all races.

The situation was different with tribes and customary law. There was not a single customary law to govern all tribes defined as one racialized group – natives. Instead, each tribe was ruled under a separate set of laws, called customary laws. It was said that each tribe was governed by a law that reflected its own tradition. Yet most would agree that the cultural difference between races – such as Whites, Asians and Arabs – was greater than that between different tribes. To begin with, the different races spoke different languages, mutually unintelligible. Often, they practiced different religions. They also came from different parts of the world, each with its own historical archive. Different tribes, in contrast, spoke languages that were often mutually intelligible.

My point is simple: even if races were as different culturally as whites, Asians, and Arabs, they were ruled under a single law, imported European law, called civil law. Even if their languages were similar and mutually intelligible, ethnic groups were governed under separate laws, called 'customary' laws, which were in turn administered by ethnically distinct native authorities. With races, cultural difference was not translated into separate legal systems. Instead, it was contained, even negotiated, within a single legal system, and was enforced by a single administrative authority. But with ethnicities, the case was the opposite: cultural difference was reinforced, exaggerated, and built up into different legal systems and, indeed, separate administrative and political authorities. In a nutshell, different races were meant to have a common future; different ethnicities were not.

My *third* observation: the two legal systems were entirely different in orientation. We can understand the difference by contrasting English common law with colonial customary law. English common law was presumed to change with circumstances. It claimed to recognize different interests and interpretations. But customary law in the colonies assumed the opposite. It assumed that law must not change with changing circumstances. Rather, any change was considered prima facie evidence of corruption. Both the laws and the enforcing authorities were called 'traditional'. Indeed, Western colonial powers were far more concerned to establish the traditional credentials of their native allies than they were to define the content of tradition. Their preoccupation was with defining, locating, anointing the traditional authority. Most importantly, traditional authority in the colonial era was always defined in the singular. We need to remember that most African colonies had never before had an absolutist state. Instead of a single state authority whose writ was considered law in all social domains, the practice was for different authorities to define separate traditions in different domains of social life. The rule–defining authority thus differed from one social domain to another; besides chiefs, the definers of tradition could include women's groups, age groups, clans, religious groups, and so on.

The big change in the colonial period was that Western colonial powers exalted a single authority, called the chief, as *the* traditional authority. Marked by two characteristics, age and (male) gender, the authority of the chief was inevitably patriarchal. As David Laitin showed in his study of Yorubaland, the practice was to look for those local elites most in danger of being sidelined, local elites that had legitimacy but lacked authority, and then to sanctify their position and enforce their point of view as customary, and reinforce their authority in law as traditional.[17]

Colonial powers were the first fundamentalists of the modern period. They were the first to advance and put into practice two propositions: one, that every colonized group has an original and pure tradition, whether religious or ethnic; and two, that every colonized group must be made to return to that original condition, and that the return must be enforced by law. Put together, these two propositions constitute the basic platform of every religious or ethnic fundamentalism in the postcolonial world.

Fourth, this legal project needs to be understood as part of a political project. The political project was highlighted by the central claim of the indirect rule state, that natives are by nature tribal. Even though this claim was first fully implemented by Britain in those African lands it colonized in late nineteenth century, in the aftermath of the Berlin Conference, the claim had already been made by Sir Henry Maine, Law Member of the Viceroy's Commission in post-1857 India. To quote from Maine's *Ancient Law*: 'I repeat the definition of a primitive society given before. It has for its units, not individuals, but groups of men united by the reality or the fiction of blood–relationship'.[18] In time, this very claim, that natives are by nature tribal, would be advanced as reason why the African colonies have no majority, but only tribal minorities. This claim needs to be understood as political, not because it is not true but because this truth does not reflect an original fact but a fact created politically and enforced legally.

It is not that ethnicity did not exist in African societies prior to colonialism; it did. But I want to distinguish ethnicity as a cultural identity – an identity based on a shared culture – from ethnicity as a political identity. When the political authority and the law it enforces identify subjects ethnically and discriminate between them legally, then ethnicity turns into a legal and political identity. Ethnicity as a cultural identity is consensual, but when ethnicity becomes a political identity it is enforced by the legal and administrative organs of the state. These organs make a distinction between ethnic groups, between those considered indigenous and those not, the former given right of access to rights considered 'customary', such as the right to use land, but the latter denied these same rights.

This takes me to my *fifth* observation. When law imposes a cultural difference, the difference becomes reified. Prevented from changing, it becomes frozen. But as the basis of legal discrimination, between those who are said to belong – whether in terms of religion or ethnicity – and those said not to belong, between insiders entitled to customary rights and outsiders deprived of these rights, these culturally symbolic differences become political.

The distinction between cultural and political identities is important for my argument. Cultural identities are as a rule consensual and voluntary, and can be multiple.[19] All post-modernist talk of hybridity and multiple identities belongs to the domain of culture. Once enforced by law, however, identities cease to be all of these. A legal identity is not voluntary, nor is it multiple. The law recognizes you as one, and as none other. Once it is enforced legally, cultural identity is drawn into the domain of politics and becomes political. Such an identity cannot be considered a vestige of tradition because of its ancient history, nor can it be dismissed as just an invention of the colonial power because of its legal enforcement. Even if grounded in a genealogy that precedes colonialism, popular identities like religion and ethnicity need to be understood as the very creation of colonial modernity. To distinguish between cultural and legal/political identities is to distinguish between self-identification and state-identification.

RWANDA: A METAPHOR FOR POLITICAL VIOLENCE

Colonial Rwanda was different in one important respect from the picture I have just described. In colonial Rwanda, the census did not identify any tribes. It only identified races: Hutu as Bantu, and Tutsi as Hamites. The Bantu were presumed to be uncivilized, and the Hamites civilizing agents. We shall see that this difference between Rwanda and other African colonies – the fact that political identities in Rwanda were racialized, but not ethnicized – would turn out to be of great significance. Rwanda is today a metaphor for political violence, more particularly for senseless violence in politics. I recently wrote a book on Rwanda. Here, I would like to describe the intellectual and political journey that came to be the writing of the book.[20]

Rwanda had a revolution in 1959. On the face of it, the revolution pit Hutu, the indigenous majority, against Tutsi, the immigrant minority. The identities 'indigenous' and 'immigrant' came straight out of colonial history books and colonial law. Within the revolution, there was a debate as to who was the enemy, and thus, who were the people. Two tendencies contended for supremacy.

Those who lost maintained that the battle was not of Hutu against Tutsi, but of the majority against the minority, the poor against the rich, and the nation against the colonizers. This tendency lost, not because it lacked support but because its support eroded when the counter-revolution attempted a restoration of the Tutsi monarchy. With the defeat of the counter-revolution, the target of revolutionary violence broadened, from those who had symbolized the local manifestations of power (such as the chief) to all Tutsi. When the revolutionaries of 1959 talked of justice, they did not talk of justice for the poor or for Rwandans but of justice for the Hutu – at the expense of the Tutsi. To ensure that justice would indeed be done, they insisted that the revolutionary state continue the colonial practice of issuing cards that identified every individual as Hutu or Tutsi (or Twa, an insignificant minority). Henceforth, the Hutu would be the Rwandan nation and the Tutsi an alien minority.

One can today find two kinds of writings on Rwanda. The first is preponderant in the academy, the second in the world of journalism. Academic writing on Rwanda is dominated by authors whose intellectual perspective was shaped by sympathy with the Rwandan Revolution of 1959.[21] They saw the Revolution and the political violence that effected it as progressive, as ushering in a more popular political and social order. Unable to see the dark underbelly of the Revolution, and thus to grasp the link between the 1959 Revolution and the 1994 genocide, this kind of writing portrays the genocide as exclusively or mainly a state project of a narrow ruling elite. In doing so, it totally avoids the question of mass participation in the genocide. In portraying racism and racialized identities as exclusively state-defined and state-enforced, it fails to explain how these same identities got socially embedded and were reproduced socially. In portraying the genocide as exclusively a *state project*, its singular failing is an inability to come to terms with the genocide as a *social project*.

But this claim is not easy to make. Massacres in the Rwandan genocide were carried out in the open. Roughly 800,000 Tutsi were killed in a hundred days. The state organized the killings, but the killers were by and large ordinary people. The killing was done mainly by machete-wielding mobs. You were more than likely to be killed by your neighbours or your workmates, or by your teachers or doctors or priests, or even by human rights advocates or your own husband. A few months ago, four Rwandese civilians stood trial in Belgium for crimes against humanity. Among the four were two nuns and a physicist. How do we explain their participation – and the participation of other sectors in civil society – in the genocide?

In contrast, journalistic writing focuses precisely on this aspect of the genocide.[22] Its peculiar characteristic is to write a pornography of violence. As in pornography, the nakedness is of others, not us. The exposure of the other goes alongside the unstated claim that we are not like them. It is a pornography where senseless violence is a feature of other people's cultures: where they are violent, but we are pacific, and where a focus on their debasedness easily turns into another way of celebrating and confirming our exalted status. In the process, journalistic accounts also tend to reinforce larger claims: that the world is indeed divided into the modern and the pre-modern, whereby moderns *make* culture, but those pre-modern live by a timeless culture.

If the social science account is overly *instrumentalist*, accenting only the agency of the state and elites, journalists tend to lean heavily on a *primordialist* account that tends to explain contemporary conflicts as replays of timeless antagonisms.[23] If social science accounts tend to explain mass participation in the genocide as mass obedience to rulers (for ordinary Rwandans, goes the most widespread explanation, an order is as heavy as a stone), for journalists it explains the agency of masses gripped in ancient passions and antagonisms. In the final analysis, neither the instrumentalist nor the primordial account is able to give a plausible historical explanation of agency in the genocide.

Politically, journalistic writing has given us a simple moral world, where a group of perpetrators face a group of victims, but where neither history nor motivation are thinkable because both stand outside history and context. When journalists did address the genocide as a social project, I thought they failed to understand the forces that shaped the agency of the perpetrator. Instead, they looked for a clear and uncomplicated moral in the story. In a context where victims and perpetrators have traded places, they looked for victims distinguished from perpetrators for all times. Where yesterday's victims are today's perpetrators, where victims have turned perpetrators, this attempt to find an African Holocaust has not worked. Thus I called my book: *When Victims Become Killers.*

How many perpetrators were victims of yesteryear? What happens when yesterday's victims act out of a determination that they must never again be victimized, *never again*? What happens when yesterday's victims act out of a conviction that power is the only guarantee against victimhood, so the only dignified alternative to power is death? What happens when they are convinced that the taking of life is really noble because it signifies the willingness to risk one's own life and is thus, in the final analysis, proof of one's own humanity?

I thought it important to understand the humanity of the perpetrator, as it were, to get under the skin of the perpetrator – not to excuse the perpetrator, and the killing, but to make the act 'thinkable', so as to learn something about ourselves as humans. How do we understand the agency of the perpetrator? Framed by what history? Kept alive, reproduced, by which institutions? Who did the Hutu who killed think they were? And whom did they think they were killing in the persons of the Tutsi?

THE HISTORY OF VIOLENCE BETWEEN HUTU AND TUTSI

The significance of Fanon became clear to me as I tried to understand the history of political violence in Rwanda, specifically, of violence between Hutu and Tutsi. I was struck by one fact: I could not find any significant episode before 1959 where battle lines were drawn sharply between Hutu on one side, and Tutsi on the other. 1959 was the first significant episode where Hutu were pitted against Tutsi in a political struggle, so that Hutu and Tutsi became names identifying political adversaries.

I thought this contrasted sharply with earlier political struggles, such as Nyabingi at the outset of the colonial period. Nyabingi was the name of a spiritual cult, also a political movement, in what is today northern Rwanda, the region incorporated into the expanding Kingdom of Rwanda at the beginning of the twentieth century. I thought two facts striking about this movement. First, when the Bakiga of this region fought the alliance of German imperial power and the Tutsi aristocracy of the Rwandan kingdom, they did not fight as Hutu against Tutsi. They fought the Tutsi in power, but in alliance with the Tutsi out of power, first under the leadership of a former Tutsi queen, Muhumuza, and then under the leadership of her son, Ndungutse.

Second, these mountain people did not call themselves Hutu, but Bakiga (the people of the mountains). Only when they were defeated, and incorporated into the Rwanda Kingdom, did they cease to be Bakiga, and became Hutu. For Hutu was not the identity of a discrete ethnic group, but the political identity of all those subjugated to the power of the Rwandan state. In Rwanda before colonialism, prosperous Hutu became Tutsi, over generations. True, the numbers involved were too few to be statistically significant. Yet, this was a process of great social and ideological significance. This process of ritual ennoblement, whereby a Hutu shed his Hutuness, even had a name: *Kwihutura*. Its counterpart, whereby an impoverished Tutsi family lost its status, this too over generations, also had a name: *Gucupira*.

Belgian colonialism did not invent Tutsi privilege. There was Tutsi privilege before colonialism. So what was new about Belgian colonialism? Not Tutsi privilege, but the justification for it. For the first time in the history of Rwanda, the terms Hutu and Tutsi came to identify two groups, one branded indigenous, the other exalted as alien. For the first time, Tutsi privilege claimed to be the privilege of an alien group, a group identified as Hamitic, as racially alien. Only with Belgian colonialism did Hutu become indigenous and Tutsi alien, the degradation of the Hutu a native degradation and Tutsi privilege an alien privilege. As Belgian authorities issued identity cards to Hutu and Tutsi, Tutsi became sealed off from Hutu. Legally identified as two biologically distinct races, Tutsi as Hamites and Hutu as Bantu, Hutu and Tutsi became distinct legal and political identities. The language of race functioned to underline this difference between indigenous and alien.

The point will become clear if we return to the difference between race and ethnicity in twentieth century colonial thought. I have pointed out that only natives were classified as tribes in colonial Africa, and as 'ethnic groups' in post-colonial Africa. Non-natives, those not considered African, were tagged as races. Tribes were neighbours, not aliens. In this context, ethnic violence is different from racial violence. Ethnic violence is between neighbours. It is about borders. It is about transgression across borders, about excess. In the conflict between neighbours, what is at issue is not the legitimacy of the presence of others. At issue is an overflow, a transgression. It is only with a race that the very presence of a group can be considered illegitimate, and its claim for power an outright usurpation. This is why when political violence takes the form of a genocide, it is more likely between races, not between ethnic groups.

The racialization of the Tutsi, and of the difference between Hutu and Tutsi, is key to understanding the political violence between Hutu and Tutsi. This was for one reason. It is the language of race that defined insiders and outsiders, distinguishing those who were indigenous from those who were aliens. Ultimately, it set apart neighbours from outsiders, and friends from enemies.

POLITICAL IDENTITIES AND THE
NATIONALIST REVOLUTION

Colonialism is the genesis of Hutu-Tutsi violence in Rwanda. But colonialism does not explain why this violence continued after the Revolution. If colonialism is the site of the origin of the Hutu-Tutsi problem as one of racialized political identities, then nationalism reproduced that problem. Here is the dilemma we must confront: race-branding was not simply a state ideology, it also became a social ideology, reproduced by many of the same Hutu and Tutsi branded as native and alien. That reproduction took place through the nationalist political project which translated the colonial identity of Hutu as the indigenous Bantu race into the postcolonial Rwandan identity, thereby translating the colonial race-branding project into the postcolonial nation-building project. To problematize the nation-building project is simultaneously to critique the revolution of 1959 and the popular agency that it shaped.

The Rwandan Revolution of 1959 was heralded as the 'Hutu Revolution'. As the revolutionaries built Rwanda into a 'Hutu nation', they embarked on a program of justice: justice for Hutu, a reckoning for Tutsi. And in doing so, they confirmed Hutu and Tutsi as political identities: Hutu as native, Tutsi as alien. When does the pursuit of justice turn into revenge? The Revolutionaries turned the world upside down, but they failed to change it. The irony is that instead of transforming the political world created by colonialism, the world of natives and settlers, they confirmed it. Here then is the question for a post-colonial study of nationalism in Rwanda: Why did nationalism fail to transform the colonial political edifice?

Popular agency has been the subject of an ambitious project in history-writing in South Asia, called Subaltern Studies. Taken from Antonio Gramsci, the word subaltern signified popular strata as opposed to those who command. The great historical contribution of Subaltern Studies was to rescue the subaltern from the status of being a victim in world history by illuminating him and her as an agent in history, as one capable of changing things. The historical lesson of Rwanda suggests that we accept the limits of this contribution and recognize that subaltern agency too is undergirded by specific institutions. To accept the time-bound nature of subalternity – as did Fanon – is to begin to subvert it. To generate a perspective that can transform existing identities, we need to stand outside the institutions that reproduce our identities so as to understand group identities as institutionally produced and thus of limited historical significance.

Is not every perspective, no matter how popular, locked in the narrow parameters of the relations that generate and sustain it? Untransformed, a subaltern identity is likely to generate no more than an aspiration for trading places, for hegemonic aspirations. This is why a subaltern identity can neither be embraced nor rejected unconditionally. Unless we highlight its historical boundaries and limitations, the subaltern struggle will be locked in a dilemma, a Catch-22. Without a recognition and subversion of limits, without an institutional transformation leading to a transformation of identities, every pursuit of justice will tend towards revenge and every reconciliation will tend to turn into an embrace of institutional evil.

Lenin once chided Rosa Luxembourg with being so preoccupied with Polish nationalism that she could not see beyond it and so risked being locked in the world of the rat and the cat. The world of the rat and the cat is the political world of Hutu and Tutsi as produced by colonialism and reproduced by the 1959 Revolution. For the rat, there is no animal bigger in the presence of the cat: neither lion, nor tiger, nor elephant. For the cat, there is none more delicious than the rat. The political world set in motion by the modern state and modern colonialism too generates subaltern identities endlessly, in binary pairs. For every sergeant, there is a subaltern; for every settler, a native. In a world where cats are few and rats are many, one way for cats to stabilize rule is to tag rats by tapping their historicity through a discourse on origins, indigenous and non-indigenous, ethnic and racial. This is why in a world where rats have belled cats, it is entirely possible that rats may still carry on living in the world as defined by cats, fired by the very identities generated by institutions created in the era of cats.

My point is simple and yet fundamental: you can turn the world upside down, but still fail to change it. To change the world, you need to break out of the world view of not just the cat, but also the rat; not only the settler, but also the native. Unless we break out of the world view of the rat, postcolonialism will remain a purgatory punctuated by nonrevolutionary violence. More than any other contemporary event, the genocide in Rwanda poses this dilemma more sharply than ever before.

THE CIVIL WAR AND THE GENOCIDE

For a political analysis of the genocide in Rwanda, there are three pivotal moments. The first moment is that of colonization and the racialization of the state apparatus by Belgians in the 1920s. The second moment is that of nationalism and the Revolution of 1959, a turning of tables that entrenched colonial political identities in the name of justice. The third moment is that of the civil war of 1990. The civil war was not born of a strictly internal process; it was an outcome of a regional development, one that joined the crisis in Rwanda with that in Uganda.

The Tutsi exiles of 1959 found refuge in many countries, including Uganda. Living on the margins of society, many joined the guerrilla struggle against the oppressive Obote regime in 1981-85. When the victorious National Resistance Army entered Kampala in January 1986, roughly a quarter of the 16,000 guerrillas were Banyarwanda. Banyarwanda had emigrated to Uganda throughout the colonial period. In the Luwero Triangle – the theatre of the guerrilla struggle – migrants were nearly half the population. The largest group of migrants was from Rwanda.

Every time NRA guerrillas liberated a village and organized an assembly, they confronted a challenge: Who could participate in an assembly? Who could vote? Who could run for office? The dilemma sprang from the colonial political legacy, which linked rights to ancestry; by defining migrants as not indigenous, it deprived them of political rights. The NRA's answer was to redefine the basis of rights, from ancestry to residence. Simply put, every adult resident of a village was considered as having the right of participation in the village assembly. This new notion of rights was translated into a nationality law after 1986: anyone with a 10-year residence in the country had the right to be a citizen. The consequence was that the 1959 refugees of the Rwandan Revolution were now considered Ugandans.

This political inheritance was called into question with the NRA's first major political crisis in 1990, triggered by an attempt to honour one of the ten points in the guerrilla program: the pledge to redistribute absentee-owned land to pastoralist squatters. When it came to distributing the land among a population of mobile pastoralists, there arose the question: Who should get the land? Who was a citizen?

The opposition mobilized around this question, aiming to exclude Banyarwanda as non-citizens. The magnitude of the resulting crisis was signified by an extraordinary session of parliament, lasting three days. At the end of its deliberation, parliament changed the citizenship law from a ten-year residence criterion to a requirement that to be recognized as a citizen you must show an ancestral connection with the land, i.e., show that at least one of your grandparents were born in the territory later demarcated as Uganda. In another month, the Rwanda Patriotic Front crossed the Uganda-Rwanda border into Rwanda. My point is that this was not simply an armed return to Rwanda; it was also an armed expulsion from Uganda.

To understand the explosive impact of the civil war on Rwanda, we need to understand the changing political position of the Tutsi from the First Republic inaugurated by the 1959 Revolution to the Second Republic that began with the 1973 coup that brought Habyarimana to power. We have seen that the First Republic was a culmination of the struggle between two lines in the Revolution. The victorious line, associated with the new President, Kayibanda, defined Hutu and Tutsi as two different races, two different nations: Tutsi were to be treated as aliens in Rwanda, the home of the Hutu nation. In Habyarimana's Second Republic, Tutsi were redefined from a race to an ethnie. From resident aliens in the First Republic, Tutsi became a political minority in the Second Republic. Instead of the distinction between Hutu and Tutsi, the Second Republic highlighted the distinction between Tutsi in Rwanda and Tutsi exiles outside

Rwanda: whereas the former were politically elevated as a Rwandan minority that could legitimately expect minority representation in its political institutions, the latter were denationalized as perpetual aliens for whom there was no longer any room in Rwanda. During the Second Republic, the key political division inside Rwanda was not between Hutu and Tutsi, but within the Hutu elite, between those from the North and those from the South.

It was the military organization of the exile Tutsi as the Rwanda Patriotic Army (RPA), and their entry into Rwanda, which triggered the civil war. The civil war, in turn, had multiple political effects. To begin with, it allowed the Habyarimana regime to pose as the defender of the nation against what was said to be an attempt by exiled Tutsi to restore the colonial monarchy – a repeat of 1963 – at a time when the regime was under great pressure from the predominantly Hutu internal opposition to liberalize. Second, it allowed radical Hutu, hitherto marginalized under the Second Republic, to re-emerge in the political mainstream. Describing themselves as the defenders of 'Hutu Power', this tendency organized a variety of media, from radio and television to print media, which claimed that the gains of the Revolution were under threat from Tutsi who were indeed a race, not an ethnie; non-Rwandan aliens, not a Rwandan minority.

Third, the more the civil war grew and the RPA gained ground, the more the internal opposition was discredited as a political fifth column tied to the RPA, and its democratic program painted as an anti-national agenda. Fourth, everywhere the RPA gained military control, the local Hutu population either fled or was expelled through administrative pressure. Most observers estimate that by 1994 as many as 15 per cent of the Rwandan population had been so displaced, some of them as many as four times. Most now lived in camps in and around Kigali and the southern part of the country. Some of the most enthusiastic participants in the genocide came from the youthful population of these camps. Finally, against the backdrop of the victorious march of the RPA, the plight of the displaced spread fear among those who were yet to be engulfed in the civil war. The 'Hutu Power' media warned them of a fate that the sight of the displaced only confirmed: if the Tutsi returned to power, they would lose both their land and their freedom – in short, everything.

The civil war of 1990-94 thus hurled Rwanda back into the world of Hutu Power and Tutsi Power. Faced with a possible return of Tutsi power, it provided radical Hutu, a marginal tendency in the Second Republic, with their first opportunity to return to the political centre stage as defenders of the 1959 revolution. Without the civil war, there would have been no genocide.

The Rwandan genocide, then, needs to be located in a context shaped by three related moments: the global *imperial* moment defined by Belgian colonialism and its racialization of the state; the *national* moment, which was the 1959 Revolution, and which reinforced racialized identities in the name of justice; and the *postcolonial* regional moment born of a link between the citizenship crisis in post-Revolutionary Rwanda and its neighbours. True, the crisis of postcolonial citizenship was regional in scope and led to civil wars not only in Rwanda, but also in Uganda, and in Congo. But only in Rwanda did the civil war unfold in a context that could and did set alight a powder keg born of a distinctive colonial legacy, *race-branding*, that was reproduced as a revolutionary legacy of *race-as-nation*. Though not a necessary but a contingent outcome, it is imperative that we draw lessons from the Rwandan genocide.

POLITICAL POWER AND POLITICAL IDENTITY

My argument on the Rwandan genocide links the violence in the genocide to political identities that drove the violence, and the reproduction of these political identities in turn to a particular form of the state. Instead of taking group identities as a given, I have tried to historicize the process of group formation. By linking political identities to the process of state formation, it becomes possible to distinguish all pre-political identities – whether, cultural, economic, or biological – from political identities. In addition, it allows for an understanding of the dynamics whereby binary political identities, like Hutu and Tutsi, become polarized.

The Rwandan genocide raises three important issues for those who must live in its aftermath, as for those who study it. The *first* concerns the link between political identities and the process of state formation. To understand how Hutu became synonymous with indigenous and Tutsi with alien, I found it necessary to go beyond an analysis of the colonial state to a critique of the nationalist revolution of 1959 which embraced political identities created by colonial power in the name of justice. The *second* issue arises from the combined legacy of colonial rule and nationalist power. It is also the issue that represents the most troublesome legacy of the Rwandan genocide and has bitterly divided those who write on it. Was not the organization of genocidal violence from the summit of political power linked to mass participation on the ground? The evidence shows that this was indeed the case, which is why we need to understand the genocide as both a state project and a social project. The *third* issue highlights the citizenship crisis in the entire region. Just as the civil war that began in 1990 joined the citizenship crisis in Rwanda with that in Uganda, so the entry of Rwandan troops into eastern Congo in 1996 joined the citizenship crisis in Rwanda with that in Congo. If the 1959 Revolution and its aftermath underlined the difference between the colonial experience of Rwanda and that of its neighbours – that colonial rule in Rwanda created racialized, but not ethnicized, political identities – post-genocidal Rwanda underlines the similarities in the regional colonial experiences. I argued in my book that colonial Rwanda was like a half-way house between direct and indirect rule. Like direct rule, it generated exclusively racialized political identities; at the same time, like indirect rule, it legitimated the despotic power of local chiefs as a carryover of pre-colonial practices rather than a colonial reorganization of the state. The discourse on custom ties citizenship (and rights) to cultural identity and historical origins.

The proliferation of political minorities in the contemporary African context is not a necessary reflection of the cultural map of Africa. Rather, this proliferation is the outcome of a particular form of the state, the indirect rule state, whose genesis lies in the colonial period. The real distinction between race and ethnicity is not that between biology and culture, with race a false biological identity and ethnicity a true and historically created cultural identity. Rather, both race and ethnicity need to be understood as the politicization of identities drawn from other domains: race a political identity of those constructed as not indigenous (settlers), and ethnicity an identity of those constructed as indigenous (natives). Africa's real political challenge is to reform and thus transcend the form of the state that has continued to reproduce race and ethnicity as political identities, alongside a discourse on nativism and 'genuine' tradition.

Colonial power not only shaped the agency of popular strata. It was also stamped on the agency of the intellectual. Colonial power was etched not only on the boundaries of the public sphere, it was also imprinted in the table of contents of scholarly works. Just as colonial power set into motion, first the settler and then the native, in the public sphere, so it preoccupied the intellectual imagination with the question of *origins*. How origin was understood depended on the language of power, specifically, on how power framed agency through customary law.

In the African context, customary law framed agency – and 'custom' – as ethnic. In another context, such as India, that agency was framed as religious. Is it then mere coincidence that if the postcolonial African preoccupation is with who is a native and who is not, the postcolonial Indian preoccupation has been with who is a convert and who is not? Is it any less surprising that if the native imagination in postcolonial Africa tends to absorb the immigrant into a script of invasion, the native imagination in postcolonial India seems to view the agency of the convert as veritable treason, as a transgression so subversive that the convert is seen as forever lacking in authentic agency?

Why is it that when it comes to postcolonial political vocabulary, Hindu and Muslim in India, or for that matter Sinhala and Tamil in Sri Lanka, like Hutu and Tutsi in Rwanda, are political synonyms for native and settler? The challenge, I have argued, is neither to deny separate histories, nor to build on this separation. It is, rather, to distinguish our notion of political community from that of cultural community and, as a consequence, separate the discourse on political rights from that on cultural or historical origins. The point of difference between cultural identity and political communities is sharpest when we contrast diasporic with immigrant communities. Diasporic communities share a common history, but not necessarily a common future. Immigrant communities, in contrast, are dedicated to build a common future, but may not necessarily share a common past. To distinguish between cultural and political communities is to distinguish between the past – several pasts – and a single future. The single uniting feature of a political community is the commitment to build a common political future under a single political roof. This recognition should be an important step to creating a single political community and citizenship from diverse cultural and historical groups and identities.

NOTES

1   See, for example, Samuel Huntington, *The Clash of Civilizations and the Remaking of World Order*, New York: Simon and Schuster, 1996.
2   For a discussion of group violence as evil, see Ervin Staub, *The Roots of Evil: The Origins of Genocide and Other Group Violence*, Cambridge: Cambridge University Press, 1989. On the relationship between evil and historical time, see Paul Ricoeur, *The Symbolism of Evil*, New York: Harper & Row, 1967; Alain Badiou, *Ethics: An Essay on the Understanding of Evil*, London/New York: Verso, 2001; Georges Bataille, *Literature and Evil*, London: Calder & Boyars, 1973; Malcolm Bull, ed., *Apocalypse Theory and the Ends of the World*, Oxford/Cambride, Mass.: Blackwell, 1995; and Alenka Zupancic, *Ethics of the Real*, London/New York: Verso, 2000. I am thankful to Robert Meister of the University of California, Santa Cruz, for suggesting this latter set of readings.
3   Hannah Arendt, *The Origins of Totalitarianism*, New York: Harcourt Brace, 1975, p. 185.
4   Ibid.
5   Herbert Spencer wrote in *Social Statics* (1850): 'The forces which are working out the great scheme of perfect happiness, taking no account of incidental suffering, exterminate such sections of mankind as stand in their way'. Charles Lyall pursued this train of thought in *Principles of Geology*: If 'the most significant and diminutive of species ... have each slaughtered their thousands, why should not we, the lords of creation, do the same'? His student, Charles Darwin, confirmed in *The Descent of Man* (1871): 'At some future period not very distant as measured in centuries, the civilized races of man will almost certainly exterminate and replace throughout the world the savage races'. 'After Darwin', comments Sven Lidquist in his survey of European thought on genocide, 'it became accepted to shrug your shoulders at genocide. If you were upset, you were just showing your lack of education'. See Sven Lindqvist, *'Exterminate all the Brutes', One Man's Odyssey into the Heart of Darkness and the Origins of European Genocide*, New York: The New Press, 1996, pps. 8, 117, 107.
6   This paragraph is based on Sven Lindqvist, *'Exterminate all the Brutes'*, pp. 141, 119, 149-51.
7   Arno J. Mayer, *Why Did the Heavens not Darken? The Final Solution in History*, New York: Random House, 1988.
8   Except where indicated, this paragraph is based on Sven Lindqvist, *'Exterminate all the Brutes'*, pp. 158, 160.
9   Aime Césaire, *Discours sur le Colonialisme*, Paris and Dakar: Présence Africaine, 1995, p. 12.
10 Frantz Fanon, *The Wretched of the Earth*, London: Penguin, 1967, p. 75; for a discussion, see, David Macey, *Frantz Fanon, A Biography*, New York: Picador, 2000, pp. 471, 111.

11 For details, see Jan-Bart Gewald, *Herero Heroes: A Socio-Political History of the Herero of Namibia, 1890-1923*, Oxford: James Currey, 1999, pp. 141-230; Tilman Dedering, '"A Certain Rigorous Treatment of all parts of the Nation": The Annihilation of the Herero in German Southwest Africa, 1904', in Mark Levine and Penny Roberts, eds., *The Massacre in History*, New York: Berghahn Books, 1999; Regina Jere-Malanda, 'The Tribe Germany Wants to Forget', *New African*, London, no. 383, March 2000; Horst Dreschler, *'Let Us Die Fighting': The Struggle of the Herero and the Nama against German Imperialism, 1884-1915*, London: Zed Press, 1980.

12 Fanon, *The Wretched of the Earth*; also see David Macey, *Fanon*, p. 22.

13 Hanna Arendt, *On Violence*, New York: Harcourt, Brace and Company, 1970.

14 For a journalistic account of the spectre of genocide in the White South African imagination, read Rian Malan, *My Traitor's Heart: a South African Exile Returns to Face His Country, His Tribe, and His Conscience*, New York: Atlantic Monthly Press, 1990.

15 Fanon, *The Wretched of the Earth*, pp. 33, 66, 68, 73.

16 Mahmood Mamdani, *Citizen and Subject: Contemporary Africa and the Legacy of Late Colonialism*, Princeton: Princeton University Press, 1996.

17 David Laitin, *Hegemony and Culture: Politics and Religious Change among the Yoruba*, Chicago: Chicago University Press, 1986.

18 Sir Henry Maine, *Ancient Law*, Washington D.C.: Beard Books, 1861, p. 178.

19 I write this without any intent to romanticize the domain of consent or to detract from the existence of power relations in the domain of culture.

20 Mahmood Mamdani, *When Victims Become Killers: Colonialism, Nativism and Genocide in Rwanda*, Princeton: Princeton University Press, 2001.

21 See, for example, René Lemarchand, *Rwanda and Burundi*, New York: Praeger, 1970; Catharine Newbury, *The Cohesion of Oppression: Clientship and Ethnicity in Rwanda, 1860-1960*, New York: Columbia University Press, 1989.

22 The most compelling journalistic account is to be found in Philip Gourevitch, *We Wish to Inform You that Tomorrow We Will be Killed with our Families*, New York: Picador, 1999.

23 For a cross-over journalistic account that strongly criticizes journalistic voyeurism but gives an unabashed conspiratorial (instrumentalist) explanation, see Bill Berkeley, *The Graves Are Not Yet Full: Race, Tribe and Power in the Heart of Africa*, New York: Basic Books, 2001.

THE LEFT AND THE ALGERIAN
CATASTROPHE

Hugh Roberts

In explaining their sharply opposed positions following the attacks on the World Trade Center and the Pentagon on 11 September 2001, two prominent writers on the American Left, Christopher Hitchens and Noam Chomsky, both found it convenient to refer to the Algerian case. Since, for Hitchens, the attacks had been the work of an Islamic fundamentalism that was a kind of fascism, he naturally saw the Algerian drama in similar terms:

> Civil society in Algeria is barely breathing after the fundamentalist assault ...We let the Algerians fight the Islamic-fascist wave without saying a word or lending a hand.[1]

This comment was probably music to the ears of the Algerian government, which had moved promptly to get on board the US-led 'coalition' against terror, as Chomsky noted in articulating his very different view of things:

> Algeria, which is one of the most murderous states in the world, would love to have US support for its torture and massacres of people in Algeria.[2]

This reading of the current situation was later supplemented by an account of its genesis:

> The Algerian government is in office because it blocked the democratic election in which it would have lost to mainly Islamic-based groups. That set off the current fighting.[3]

The significance of these remarks is that they testify to the fact that the Western Left has not addressed the Algerian drama properly, so that Hitchens and Chomsky, neither of whom pretend to specialist knowledge of the country, have not had available to them a fund of reliable analysis on which they might draw. Outside France, the Left has accommodated this drama on the edge of its field of vision and entertained peremptory surrogates for an analysis of it.

That the Left, inside as well as outside Algeria, has been marginal to events there since the Algerian state went into flux in the riots of October 1988 may be thought to absolve it of responsibility for what has happened. The catastrophe which has overtaken the country, the undoing of the principal achievements of Algerian independence between 1962 and 1978, the brutalization of the state-society relationship, the colossal toll in human lives, the subversion of the national identity, the erosion of the fabric of national society, the liquidation of much of the country's enormous investment in human capital, the destruction of much of Algeria's already sparse forest cover in the course of the army's counter-insurgency operations, the surrender of the substance of sovereignty in the spheres of defence and foreign affairs as well as economic policy – all this and more can certainly be laid at the door of the policies which have been followed by the Algerian authorities, and these policies have been those of the Right at home and abroad. But the Left can derive no comfort from this fact unless it develops the capacity to challenge these policies with a progressive alternative. And it cannot begin to do this until it recognizes its complicity in the disastrous policies which have been followed.

The complacent attitude of the Western Left, and its abdication – by delegation to the French – of its responsibilities in this matter, have contributed to the fact that the Algerian drama remains unresolved and is still killing people. For the most part, external leftwing commentary on the Algerian drama has reflected, and so reflected back, the principal positions of the Algerian Left itself. Since the latter has been dependent on external sources for its own worldview, an entirely negative game of mirrors has been taking place, movement in the mind has been precluded, and the intellectual premises of a lethal impasse have been reproduced.

THE RISE OF IDENTITY POLITICS: THE PROBLEM STATED

Central to the conflict at one level has been the problem of identity politics. Far from permitting substantial democratic reform, the political 'opening' which occurred in the wake of the promulgation of a pluralist constitution in February 1989 facilitated a spectacular expansion of the Islamist movement, in the shape of the newly-formed Islamic Salvation Front (*Front Islamique du Salut*, FIS), on the one hand, and of militantly secularist and Berberist movements, based primarily on the largest of the Berber-speaking populations, that of Kabylia to the east of Algiers, on the other. While the development of identity politics in 1989-90 was not the only significant change to occur – for other important changes were simultaneously occurring in the internal structure of the regime (notably in the army and the intelligence services), its economic policy and its relations with foreign partners – it dominated the newly-established sphere of party politics and thus the foreground of the political stage, on which the Algerian Left itself was necessarily operating.

The rise of Islamism confronted the Left with a major challenge, since the FIS's landslide victory in the local and regional elections in June 1990 raised the possibility of a FIS victory in the eventual legislative elections and thus the prospect of the domination of a politics opposed to Western-inspired conceptions of democracy and implacably hostile to the Left in particular. While the army's intervention in January 1992, following the FIS's astonishing lead in the first round of the legislative elections on 26 December 1991, appeared to put paid to this scenario, the problem of identity politics and of Islamism in particular has continued to vitiate the prospects for a progressive outcome to the crisis. The violence which has been ravaging the country since the onset of the Islamist rebellion following the banning of the FIS in February 1992 has had devastating implications for the democratic cause, as we shall see. But the concomitant militarization of Algerian politics has not occurred at the expense of identity politics at all. On the contrary, not only have the regime's military decision-makers taken care to preserve the forms of political pluralism throughout the last decade, but they have also allowed a variety of 'constitutional' Islamist parties to remain in business and even to prosper, notably the Movement for an Islamic Society (HAMAS) and the Islamic Nahda Movement (MNI) – respectively renamed the Movement of Society for Peace (MSP) and the Nahda Movement (MN) in 1996 – while simultaneously indulging the Berberist movement and the militantly secularist party which developed out of this, the Rally for Culture and Democracy (RCD).

The rise and continuing salience of identity politics in Algeria should have been the object of the most searching interrogation by serious analysts and progressive activists. Virtually all Algerians are Muslims, about 99.7% of them are Sunni Muslims and virtually all of these are Sunni Muslims of the Maliki rite.[4] There has simply been no comparison with those states confronting a significant Sunni-Shi'i fault-line (Iran, Iraq, Pakistan, etc.) or Muslim-Christian fault-line (Egypt, Sudan), let alone Lebanon. And while the régime's refusal, until very recently, to recognise the claims to national status of *Tamazight* (the Berber language, spoken by 20–25 per cent of the population) has long furnished the basis for a Berberist movement, the widely acknowledged fact that most Algerians are descended from Berber ancestors, that Berberism has been an essentially Kabyle affair, that the other Berberophone populations (the Shawiyya, the Mzabis and the Tuareg) have been indifferent to the Berberist cause and that the Kabyles themselves, far from suffering from discrimination, have actually been over-represented in the Algerian state and prominent in the army command as well as in all the main political parties (including not only the various 'democratic' and leftwing parties but also the régime-sponsored FLN and even the FIS), furnish strong grounds for questioning the advent of Berber identity politics as well.[5]

Yet almost all commentary has taken an uncritical attitude towards the explosion of identity politics which has occurred in Algeria, accepting these forms of politics and their explanations of themselves at face value. In addition, the Left has tended to align itself with one or another position in the debate between rival brands of identity politics, instead of keeping a healthy distance from them all by taking a position on a different ground altogether. In particular, since the onset of the violence following the fateful turning point of early 1992, the various left-wing organizations have allowed themselves to be drawn into the dispute between the two main policy positions within the regime itself, the so-call 'eradicators', notionally intent on 'eradicating' the Islamist opposition, and the so-called 'conciliators', supposedly intent on striking a bargain with it. Thus the Left has been sucked into both the mêlée of identity politics and the mêlée of intra-regime factional manoeuvring, and has forfeited the possibility of exercising an independent influence on the situation.

LEFT ERADICATIONISM: THE EX-COMMUNISTS AND THE SECULARIST IDENTITY

The principal protagonist of the position of root and branch hostility to the Islamist movement on the Algerian Left has been the Socialist Vanguard Party (*Parti de l'Avant-Garde Socialiste*, PAGS) and its successors, *Ettahaddi* and the Democratic and Social Movement (*Mouvement Démocratique et Social*, MDS). The PAGS, an evolution of the old Algerian Communist Party, performed dismally in the 1990 elections which resulted in the FIS's first landslide; it then boycotted the first round of the legislative elections in December 1991 which were again swept by the FIS, and was among those forces calling for the second round to be cancelled and applauding the army's intervention in January 1992. At its congress in December 1992, a faction within the PAGS headed by its 'Coordinator', El Hachemi Cherif, secured the party's dissolution and immediately founded a new party, *Ettahaddi* ('Challenge' or 'Defiance') committed to supporting the army in the name of a 'they shall not pass' attitude towards the Islamists.

The change from PAGS to *Ettahaddi* involved the jettisoning of the PAGS's commitment to socialism and its orientation to the working class, and precipitated the eviction from political life of many of the PAGS's former leaders and militants. It also involved the adoption of an explicit commitment to a secular constitution. The substance of *Ettahaddi*'s positive vision was the embracing of an almost entirely vacuous 'modernity', in the name of which it rationalized its opposition to Islamism on the grounds that it was 'obscurantist' and 'reactionary'. The further metamorphosis of *Ettahaddi* into the MDS in 1999 was little more than a change of name, El Hachemi Cherif and his associates remaining firmly in control.

There has been nothing particularly left wing about the Ettahaddi-MDS position. Its opposition to Islamism – which has extended well beyond an understandable hostility to the armed Islamic movements, and has covered from the outset not only the FIS from the days when this was a legal party, but all other Islamist parties – has been shared by at least two other parties of note: Dr Saïd Sadi's RCD, formed in 1989 as a development out of the Berberist movement in Kabylia, and former prime minister Redha Malek's *Alliance Nationale Républicaine*, ANR, formed in 1995 as a splinter from the FLN.

The antipathy of these formations to Islamism has not been predicated upon a rejection of identity politics as such, but has articulated a rival brand of identity politics, namely secularism. Their invocations of the ideal of 'the modern Republican state' has expressed their acceptance of the French state as the universally valid model of political modernity. Given Algeria's colonial history, it is understandable that it should be the French experience which serves as the principal reference for Algerian 'modernists'. What has defined their outlook, however, is the way they have been fixated on one aspect of the French model, the secularist aspect, to the virtual exclusion of all other aspects.

It is a striking feature of political debate in Algeria that the weaknesses of this position have not been pointed out. The first weakness is inherent in the uncritical borrowing from the French secularist tradition. This tradition arose in opposition to a Church – indeed, an international Church; French democracy became anti-clerical and secularist in reaction to the absolute hostility of the Roman Catholic Church to the revolutionary advent of democracy in France. But there is no Church, or counterpart of a Church, still less an infallible Pope, in Sunni Islam. The model of the separation between Church and State cannot be simply transplanted into the Algerian context, for there is no organization comparable to the Church whose exploitation of its authority in the political sphere for counter-revolutionary and anti-democratic purposes might warrant a democratic ambition to challenge this authority and end it.

In so far as the leaders of Algerian Islam – the 'ulama – constituted themselves into an organized body in the course of the twentieth century, they did so with the founding of the Association of Muslim 'ulama of Algeria (Association des 'ulama musulmans d'Algérie, AUMA) under the leadership of Sheikh Abdelhamid Ben Badis in 1931. The AUMA did not take a counter-revolutionary position during the war of national liberation, but publicly rallied to the FLN in January 1956. And after independence, while the 'ulama certainly canvassed conservative positions, notably on the family and the position of women, they nonetheless served the independent nation-state and went along with its ambitious development project and even its socialist rhetoric throughout the Boumediène period, when the state was at its most progressive. In addition, although the anti-socialist wing of the 'ulama was in the ascendant by the end of the 1980s, by which time the Chadli regime had in any case abandoned Boumediène's socialism, it should be noted that the doyen of the Badisiyyan tradition, Sheikh Ahmed Sahnoun, not only did not oppose the advent of political pluralism in 1989 but also explicitly opposed the formation of an Islamist party, and his followers played no part in the initial leadership of the FIS.[6] The political rationale for the militantly secularist position which obtained in France from 1791 onwards simply did not obtain in Algeria in 1989 or thereafter.

Moreover, the secularist demand that Islam cease to be the official religion of the Algerian state, and be relegated to the private sphere as a matter of merely personal belief, has actually required the Algerian nation-state to relinquish its authority over the religious field, and thus to leave this field wide open to the various brands of radical Islamism and their external as well as internal supporters and sponsors, while furnishing fresh ammunition for the Islamists' challenge to the state by inducing the state to forfeit its own claim to religious legitimacy. It is a proposal to disarm the nation-state in the religious sphere while aggravating its vulnerability to the Islamists' critique.

Finally, far from facilitating the constitution of a broad front to resist the Islamist demand for *dawla islamiyya*, an Islamic state, the secularist position has played into the hands of Islamist propaganda by identifying resistance to the Islamist project with a conception of Islam – as a purely private matter – with which few Muslims would agree. It has therefore made it much easier for the Islamists to claim that their project is one which all Muslims should support.

The refusal of these parties to calculate the elementary realpolitik of the situation and to recognize that broadly-based resistance to the Islamist project could be developed only on the basis of the defence of the 1989 constitution, including its provision of official status for Islam – i.e. on the basis of a *non*-secularist position – has testified to the fact that the secularist position has been every bit as much a form of identity politics as its Islamist *bête noire*. The logic of this identity politics can be understood only in the context of the relationship of the secularist parties with both the Algerian army and the French political class.

All of these formations have functioned as sources of legitimation for the army's repression of the FIS and its endless war against the armed Islamic movements. But the harnessing of their support by the regime and its military 'decision-makers' has gone well beyond merely rhetorical legitimation. Both the RCD and Ettahaddi–MDS, for example, have been implicated in the development, since 1994, of civilian auxiliary forces, the so-called 'Patriot' militias, now known as *Groupes de Légitime Défense* (GLD), to which the army has delegated much of the business of resisting the Islamist insurgency on the ground, but their involvement has not given them any leverage or status in the military sphere. By licensing auxiliary forces the army commanders have induced civilians to bear some of the burden and brunt of the violence, without surrendering an iota of their entirely unaccountable control over security policy.

Ettahaddi–MDS has also allowed itself to be implicated by default in the regime's economic policies. In abandoning the PAGS's original socialist outlook and programme, Ettahaddi–MDS disarmed itself in the economic sphere, and its position evolved into a largely uncritical acceptance of the regime's surrender to 'globalization' in respect of economic policy.[7]

This support for the regime has been only formally qualified by the party's rhetorical rejection of the regime's most indefensible features. In the resolution passed at its founding congress in 1999, the MDS defined its 'strategic line' as 'the rejection of the bureaucratic, corrupt and mafia-like rentier system and of all forms of compromise with political Islam' – that is, in entirely negative terms.[8] At no point have Ettahaddi or the MDS outlined a positive programmatic vision beyond vague invocations of '*l'État républicain moderne*'.[9] Because their criticism of 'the rentier system' has been unaccompanied by any practical policy proposals or serious analysis, the regime and the army commanders – that is, the principal managers and beneficiaries of 'the mafia-like rentier system' – have been free to disregard this criticism altogether, and to take the operative element of the Ettahaddi-MDS position as being its opposition to any compromise with political Islam, and thus as legitimation for whatever repression of Islamists the regime has engaged in. And because this repression has never been total, but has always been tempered by selective indulgence towards and cooptation of tame varieties of Islamism (notably the MSP and the MN, both of which have been represented in the National Assembly, and even the government, since June 1997), the regime has been able to rebut the charge that it is the prisoner of the secularists, while leaving Ettahaddi-MDS and the other secularist parties constantly dissatisfied and demanding more sweeping repression.

In this way the secularist, modernist and, in their own estimation, 'democratic' parties in Algeria have connived at their own bankruptcy. They have allowed the Algerian army and its regime, and not merely the various Islamist parties, to stand between them and their notional constituency, the Algerian people. And their inclination to look to the French political class for external support, while the main aspect of their usefulness from the army commanders' point of view , has aggravated their isolation within Algeria.

The collapse of the Soviet Union and the Communist bloc deprived the PAGS of its international bearings and made obsolete its claim to be the representative in Algeria of the 'true' model of 'scientific socialism' by virtue of which it could presume to criticize, but also to orient, the unsatisfactorily empirical socialism which the state professed in the 1962-88 period. Its reaction was to reinvent itself, *qua* Ettahaddi and then MDS, as the representative in Algeria of the 'true' model of 'Republican' modernity *à la française*, a stance in which its connection to the French Communist Party assumed strategic significance, enabling it to canvass the radical anti-Islamist position with political opinion in France. By securing support for its position in *L'Humanité* and the other organs of the PCF, Ettahaddi-MDS has played an important role in determining leftwing intellectual opinion in France, while engaging in polemical opposition to those elements of French progressive opinion inclined to make an issue of the accumulating evidence of the Algerian army's involvement in massive human rights violations. In this way the last offshoots of the Communist tradition in Algeria have ended up acting as little more than a fan club for the Algerian army, performing increasingly desperate public relations services for it while helping to disable left-wing opinion in France and elsewhere from seeing the Algerian drama clearly.[10]

LEFT CONCILIATIONISM

The principal party with left-wing credentials advocating a 'conciliationist' policy towards the Islamists has been Hocine Aït Ahmed's Socialist Forces' Front (Front des Forces Socialistes, FFS). A smaller left-wing party which has taken a similar line is the Workers' Party (Parti des Travailleurs, PT), led by Louisa Hanoune, the first woman to lead a political party in the Arab world.

Structurally, the line-up of the 'Left conciliators' mirrors that of the 'Left eradicators'. As a party based primarily on the population of Kabylia (and its ramifications in Algiers and other large towns, as well as in the Algerian diaspora in France and elsewhere), the FFS is the opposite number of Saïd Sadi's RCD. But, as a party which originated in 1963 as a splinter from the historic FLN, of which Aït Ahmed was a founder-member in 1954, the FFS is also a counterpart of sorts to Redha Malek's ANR, another chip off the old FLN block. And the PT, an evolution of a Trotskyist group called the Workers' Socialist Organisation (Organisation Socialiste des Travailleurs, OST), is clearly the opposite number of Ettahaddi-MDS.

Neither the FFS nor the PT are really forms of identity politics. Although the FFS has sought electoral dividends from supporting the agitation over the Berber language and identity issue in Kabylia, it is not a product of the Berberist movement and has not taken its main political bearings from it. The principal rationale for its foundation in 1963 was opposition to the dictatorial style adopted by Algeria's first president, Ahmed Ben Bella, and while Aït Ahmed found his main support in the disaffected guerrilla forces of the National Liberation Army (Armée de Libération Nationale, ALN) in Kabylia, his efforts to 'de-kabylize' the FFS enabled its armed rebellion in 1963-65 to elicit a degree of support across the country, in the Algérois, the Nord-Constantinois and the Sud-Oranais. Having maintained the FFS networks in being during his years in exile from late 1966 onwards, Aït Ahmed returned to Algeria following the legalization of his party in late 1989. The FFS could claim to have pioneered the democratic opposition to the one-party system since long before the advent of the pluralist constitution in February 1989, and its democratic credentials have been widely accepted.

Its socialist credentials are perhaps another matter. It called itself 'socialist' in 1963 essentially because socialism was the fashion of the time and because, as Aït Ahmed, a shrewd tactician, undoubtedly recognized, Ben Bella could be effectively challenged only on his left flank. The party did not, however, have a class base at all, and there is no reason to think that the socialist element of its discourse reflected the outlook of the disgruntled guerrilla fighters who formed the core of its strength. Since its legalization in 1989, the FFS has had time to develop its programmatic thinking and expand its constituency in the townships of Kabylia and the cities of the Algerian littoral while sloughing off its association with the *maquisards* of yesteryear, but this has not enhanced its socialist character at all. While retaining the old name, Aït Ahmed and his associates have not canvassed recognizably socialist policies with respect to the economic and social problems which have beset the country. The FFS has actually had little to say about these problems and, apart from the Berber language question, the party's programme has concentrated almost exclusively on narrowly political issues. That it should have gained admission to the Socialist International (as a consultative member in 1992 and as a full member in 1996) says more about the condition of the latter than the outlook of the former.

As for the PT, it is, of all Algerian political formations, the one whose orientation to class, as opposed to identity, politics is most pronounced, although its small size, a consequence in part of its Trotskyist origins, has prevented it from living up more fully to the pretension proclaimed in its name.[11] While it has been committed to the secularist vision as a matter of principle, this commitment has not impeded it from taking other considerations into account in framing its attitude to the Islamist parties in general and the FIS in particular. In this, the PT has resembled the FFS, which has also espoused the secularist ideal, at least formally. Unlike the 'eradicationist' parties, the FFS and the PT have not canvassed secularism as a matter of identity and so have not interpreted it to imply the denial of democratic rights to Islamists.

Despite the FFS's credentials as a democratic party operating outside both the identity politics bazaar and the intra-regime factional scrum – credentials which have won it international respect and support – the party has actually allowed itself to be entangled in both the identity mêlée and the power-struggles within the regime in a way which has proved fatal to its stated objectives. It has been implicated in the competition between forms of identity politics both through the informal alliance it contracted with the FIS in January 1992, and which it sustained until at least 1995 (if not later), and, simultaneously, through its conflict with its Kabyle rival, the RCD, which has embroiled it in an endless struggle for leadership of the Berberist agitation in Kabylia. And since the factions within the regime have been constantly engaged in manipulating both Islamists and Berberists, the FFS's involvement in these matters has simultaneously implicated it in the factional conflict.

Having emerged from the first round of the legislative elections in December 1991 with 25 seats, in second place to the FIS with its 188 seats and ahead of the FLN (16 seats), the FFS had a natural interest in opposing both the army's intervention on 11 January 1992 and its further decision to cancel the second round of the elections and establish an unconstitutional directorate, the High State Committee (Haut Comité d'État, HCE), to run the country in lieu of the deposed President Chadli. It was also perfectly consistent of the FFS to criticize the HCE's subsequent banning of the FIS, and to call thereafter for its re-legalization on democratic and constitutional grounds. But what is striking about the FFS's behaviour is that it went much further than this, making the campaign to rehabilitate the FIS the crux of its strategy. This strategy appears to have taken the military aspect of the regime as its principal target. The FFS slogan: 'ni état islamique, ni état policier' ('neither an Islamic state nor a police state' – like the Ettahaddi-MDS slogan, a tale of two negatives) formally opposed the Islamist project of dawla islamiyya as much as the army's regime, but it was clear from early 1992 onwards that it was the latter which the FFS primarily had in its sights for as long as this attitude led the FFS into a tug-of-war which it was bound to lose.

For as long as the regime maintained a repressive policy towards the Islamist rebellion throughout 1992 and most of 1993, the FFS's championing of opposition to this policy was unproblematic. But when a 'conciliationist' tendency within the regime began to assert itself in late 1993 and 1994, the FFS's position became an increasingly tortuous affair. For, far from throwing its weight behind the 'conciliators', the FFS apparently regarded them as rivals and certainly did nothing to reinforce them.

The emergence of the conciliators within the regime occurred in conjunction with the return to office of retired General Liamine Zeroual, first as defence minister, from July 1993, and then, from 30 January 1994, as head of state.[12] On assuming the presidency, Zeroual immediately announced a 'dialogue open to all', which implicitly included the FIS, and released two FIS leaders to sound out the leaders of the armed rebellion about a possible negotiation. Although forced by opposition from the 'eradicator' faction to backtrack for a while, Zeroual returned to this policy in August 1994 when he invited eight political parties to talks on how a return to the electoral process might be arranged, talks which initially went so well that it became possible for Zeroual to bring the imprisoned leaders of the FIS into the dialogue via parallel discussions. Five parties accepted the invitation – the FLN, ex-President Ahmed Ben Bella's Movement for Democracy in Algeria (MDA), Mahfoud Nahnah's HAMAS, Abdallah Djaballah's MNI and Noureddine Boukrouh's Party of Algerian Renewal (PRA). The two secularist 'eradicator' parties, the RCD and Ettahaddi, predictably rejected the invitation, but so did the FFS, for reasons it never explained. That a breakthrough was in prospect was strongly suggested by reports of two letters from the imprisoned Abassi Madani (the FIS's principal leader) to President Zeroual announcing his acceptance of democratic principles and floating the possibility of a truce in the armed struggle, and Zeroual's decision in response to release three imprisoned FIS leaders completely and to move Abassi and his deputy, Ali Ben Hadj, from prison to house arrest, to enable them to consult those of their colleagues in the ex-FIS leadership who were at liberty.[13] While responsibility for the eventual failure of the talks can be attributed primarily to the 'eradicator' faction in the army, which engineered a dramatic escalation of the violence at this point in order to prevent the FIS leaders from consulting the leaders of the armed movements, the fact remains that the FFS did nothing to support Zeroual's initiative, and its refusal of support undoubtedly tilted the factional balance in favour of the 'eradicators'.

No sooner had Zeroual abandoned this attempt to broker a settlement than the FFS took the lead in organizing two meetings of various political parties, hosted by the Catholic Sant' Egidio community in Rome, in November 1994 and January 1995. The second meeting agreed on a *Platform for a Peaceful Political Solution of the Algerian Crisis*, signed by the FLN, the FFS, the MDA, the MNI, the PT and Abdennour Ali Yahia's Algerian League for the Defence of Human Rights (LADDH), as well as by Anwar Haddam and Rabah Kebir, the two leading representatives of the FIS at liberty outside Algeria. All signatories committed themselves to accepting the rules of the democratic political game, notably pluralism, '*l'alternance*' (the principle that a party voted into power will allow itself to be voted out again), and the renunciation of violence as a strategy for gaining or keeping power. In return, the platform proposed that the regime should revoke its ban on the FIS as the condition of securing its assistance and that of the other signatories in negotiating an end to the violence, and then permit the democratic process to resume.[14]

It was now the regime's turn to dismiss this initiative. It appeared by this stage that the 'conciliator' tendency within the regime and its counterparts within the party-political opposition considered each other to be rivals rather than allies, and there is no doubt that the Rome Platform became in effect a rival to the proposal, which President Zeroual had already announced on 31 October 1994, to hold presidential elections a year early to inaugurate a return to the electoral process interrupted in January 1992. That the FFS should have been in competition with Zeroual and his supporters can be understood. What is remarkable, however, is that, while posing as the architect of a rival project, the FFS should have refused to contest the presidential election when this was finally held in November 1995.

By boycotting this election, the FFS forfeited a major opportunity to canvass its own position with the Algerian electorate and demonstrated its inability to follow through in practice its pretension to incarnate a democratic opposition worthy of the name. Aït Ahmed thus allowed Zeroual to secure a monopoly of popular support for a political solution to the crisis, and simultaneously allowed the RCD's Saïd Sadi a free run in the election as the representative of Kabylia and the Berberist cause. By winning 1,115,796 votes (9.6 per cent of total votes cast) on a secularist-eradicationist platform, Sadi erased the memory of the RCD's paltry score of a mere 200,267 votes (2.9 per cent) in December 1991, and eroded the hegemony which the FFS had enjoyed in Kabylia since then. And within weeks of Zeroual's return to office as the constitutionally elected President of the Republic, Abdelhamid Mehri, the General Secretary of the FLN who had been allied with Aït Ahmed's FFS since January 1992, was replaced by Boualem Benhamouda, under whom the FLN returned to its traditional role since 1962 as the docile mouthpiece of the regime, and the 'Rome alliance' was in ruins. The FFS's campaign to instrumentalize the banning of the FIS and the ensuing armed rebellion, as a means of putting pressure on the regime to concede a measure of democratization, was strategically lost by November 1995.

Throughout 1996 and the first half of 1997, the FFS's position had no positive content. Bereft of allies, it proffered purely negative criticism of Zeroual's proposals for a revision of the constitution when these were published in May 1996, and won only twenty seats to the RCD's nineteen when National Assembly elections were finally held in June 1997. And when Zeroual's adversaries in the army took over the secret negotiations which had been taking place with the leaders of the main armed movement, the Islamic Salvation Army (Armée Islamique du Salut, AIS), in the summer of 1997, and concluded a cease-fire agreement with the AIS the following September, the FFS could only protest in vain that this deal between the military wing of the regime and the military wing of the FIS behind the backs of the Algerian people and the entire civilian political class was the opposite of what it had sought.[15]

The appalling massacres of civilians at Raïs, Beni Messous and Bentalha in August–September 1997, and further massacres in late December 1997 and January 1998, gave the FFS a new lease of life however, as Western concern grew and calls proliferated for an international commission of enquiry. The FFS repositioned itself in relation to these issues, and developed a new strategy based on a new alliance. In place of the old alliance with the FIS and Mehri's FLN, the FFS made itself the principal interlocutor of international concern about human rights violations in Algeria. This concern had long been pressed by leading elements of several European socialist parties, with which the FFS enjoyed privileged relations as a member of the Socialist International. In advocating international intervention from 1997 onwards, the FFS continued to act as the principal source of party-political opposition to the army-backed regime (and became the favourite of international human rights organizations), while tending to isolate itself further within the country and, in particular, forfeiting its alliance with the PT, which refused to endorse the violation of national sovereignty which international intervention would entail.

The extent to which the FFS had lost ground in the country became clear during the presidential elections held in April 1999 following Zeroual's decision, under pressure from the army commanders, to step down before the end of his five-year term. In addition to Abdelaziz Bouteflika, whose candidacy was sponsored by major military power brokers, six opposition candidates were allowed to stand. Aït Ahmed was among these, but was unable to capitalize on his earlier support for the FIS, since FIS supporters preferred Dr Ahmed Taleb Ibrahimi, whom they regarded as a more appropriate interlocutor,[16] while much of the 'democratic reform' vote went to former prime minister Mouloud Hamrouche,[17] and the old *maquisard* vote was spoken for by Khatib Youcef.[18] In the event, the six candidates announced their withdrawal from the election on the eve of the ballot, a decision taken at the FFS headquarters in Algiers on 13 April and explained the next day in a communiqué which claimed that the authorities had failed to ensure an honest election.[19] But this withdrawal may also have masked the prospect of a disappointing showing for Aït Ahmed's candidacy, while having the principal effect of delegitimating the entire proceedings and thus placing Bouteflika, the winner by default, at a massive disadvantage vis-à-vis his military sponsors, a position which he has struggled to escape from ever since.

The 'Left conciliationists' are not primarily to blame for Algeria's disastrous evolution since 1992, but the failure of their successive strategies has certainly contributed to the fact that the general crisis of the Algerian nation-state has eluded all efforts at a resolution. Eventually, moreover, Kabylia itself, which despite incursions by Islamist guerrillas had survived as something of a sanctuary of democratic pluralism throughout the 1990s, became the arena for the latest brutal manifestation of this crisis in the series of riots which followed the unexplained killing of an unarmed youth by a gendarme at Beni Douala in Greater Kabylia on 21 April 2001, riots which the gendarmes repeatedly re-ignited by their own violent responses.[20] The inability of the FFS to canalize and control the anger of Kabyle youth, or even defend its own party offices from the rioters,[21] and the extent to which it was marginalized by a new grassroots protest movement in the region,[22] testified to its failure to articulate effectively Kabyle – let alone wider Algerian – aspirations for democratic government. The party's response, its call for the convoking of a Constituent Assembly[23] as the precondition of a democratic departure from the impasse in which the Algerian polity has been trapped, fell on deaf ears, in part because this demand was entirely – and characteristically – unaccompanied by any suggestion of how the new constitution to be drawn up by such a Constituent Assembly might be a significant improvement on previous ones.

THE HEART OF THE MATTER

With the onset of the riots in Kabylia, Algeria's crisis came full circle. The Kabyle youths who have been braving the gendarmes' bullets since April 2001 have not been mobilized primarily by the traditional identity concerns of the Berberist movement, but have been protesting above all against what Algerians call *la hogra*, the brutal contempt with which they are treated by the Algerian state, the intolerable humiliations they suffer through endless abuses of authority and denials of rights – in short, against what they have in common with their fellow Algerians across the country. For this was actually what the rioters in Algeria's big cities were protesting against in October 1988, when the Algerian state first went into flux. The problem of *la hogra* is central to the crisis of the state-society relationship as a whole, and it has not been adequately addressed by the Left either inside Algeria or outside, because the explosion of identity politics has constituted both a perverted expression of this problem and a massive form of displacement activity, and the Left itself has been party to this continuous evasion of the issue.

In crystallizing into the FIS in 1989, the Islamist movement became the vector of a political project, the establishment of an Islamic state in place of the nation-state created by the FLN in 1962 and modified by the pluralist constitution of 1989. It is accordingly remarkable that the Chadli regime should have licensed and tolerated the FIS's activities in the 1989-91 period, since these clearly tended to subvert the constitution which this regime had just introduced. What is also remarkable, however, is that the Left should have taken this form of politics at face value, by taking its advertised political project as its principal if not sole *raison d'être*, and that the Left should have framed its responses (of resistance or cooptation) towards the FIS in terms of the latter's notional political project alone. For the FIS was a very complex and ambiguous affair, a mediation of several distinct things all at once, and the point of departure of an effective response to it had to be a clear recognition of this fact.

To put matters in a necessarily schematic manner, we can say that the FIS mediated:

1. the aspiration to leadership within Algerian Islam – and hence to influence in the political sphere – of a new generation of proselytizers disposed to

contest the 'national Islam' of the state and who validated their claim to authority by reference to the latest ideological fashions in the Middle East;

2. the growing hegemony over the Algerian religious field of the neo-Salafiyya movement, oriented primarily to the Wahhabi tradition of Saudi Arabia, and secondarily to radical Islamism elsewhere (notably Egypt);[24]

3. the ambitions of Algeria's frustrated *arabisants*, resentful of the privileged position of the *francis*ant elite, and disposed to invest in Islamist themes in order to validate their own claims to preferment and delegitimate the claims of their rivals;

4. the hostility of the commercial and entrepreneurial petty bourgeoisie towards the increasingly predatory as well as inefficient state bureaucracy;

5. the anger and despair of the urban poor and especially the popular demand for justice and good government, expressed in protests against *la hogra* and corruption.

In addition, however, the FIS mediated something else altogether. For the remarkable decision to legalize the FIS was motivated by the presidency's determination to 'play the Islamist card', that is, to play off the FIS against the FLN itself, because it was the FLN which was the bastion of nationalist resistance to Chadli's policies, especially his policy of rapprochement, at the expense of Algeria's national sovereignty, with Mitterrand's France.

In effect, Chadli and Co. were using the Islamists in 1989-90 as Sadat had used Egypt's Islamists against the Nasserists in the early 1970s and as Chadli and Co. themselves had used them in their campaign of 'de-Boumedienisation' in 1980-81.[25] Thus the FIS initially functioned as the cat's paw of the Chadli presidency against its critics in the FLN. But matters became more complicated during the crisis over Iraq from August 1990 onwards. For, in the context of popular mobilization across the Arab world against 'Operation Desert Shield' and especially 'Operation Desert Storm', the FIS leaders were forced to choose between their Saudi sponsors and their Algerian popular base, and opted decisively to stay abreast of the massively pro-Iraqi public opinion. This decision put them on a collision course with the Chadli presidency and enabled Chadli's adversaries within the power structure to turn the tables by converting the FIS into auxiliaries of their counter-moves, a development which precipitated a crisis within the FIS leadership and led inexorably to the regime's decision to suppress the party altogether. Thus a crucial aspect of the FIS was that it also mediated –

6. the incessant – and by now no-holds-barred – factional conflict within the regime.

Recognition of the complexity of the FIS's mediating functions has been entirely absent from the discourse of all formations on the Left both within Algeria and without, with the result, *inter alia*, that this discourse has had *zero* educational effect on either Algerian or international public opinion. The Left 'eradicators' have merely taken the notional project of *dawla islamiyya* as expressing the substance of the FIS and as justifying both the 'reactionary' (and even 'fascist') tag and a policy of absolute denial of democratic rights to the party.

Left 'conciliationism' as developed by the FFS, on the other hand, has essentially taken the FIS's hostility to the regime from January 1992 onwards as its significant aspect and, while inducing the FIS leaders to declare their acceptance of democratic principles, has sought to use the FIS as an auxiliary in its own strategies of opposition to the regime.

An effective Left politics would have taken a very different attitude. Its strategic aim from 1989 onwards would have been to deny the FIS the role of principal – let alone exclusive – political representative of the urban poor and especially the unemployed youth in Algeria's crowded cities, by offering itself as a credible alternative. To do this it would have needed to neutralize the religious issue by defending the constitutional status of Islam as the official religion of the state, while simultaneously depoliticizing the cultural-linguistic issue by canvassing thought-out proposals to promote access for *arabisants* to gainful employment. It would also have been intelligent to take account of the legitimate concerns of private entrepreneurs by proposing reforms aimed at cleaning up the administration and simplifying bureaucratic controls on entrepreneurial activity. But the main thing it would have needed to do is to address the problem of *la hogra* – the grievance of the masses – and the problem of the factional conflict within the regime – the problem of the elites, recognizing that these problems are connected and have a common solution.[26]

The immediate premise of *la hogra* is the arbitrary way in which Algeria is ruled, the fact that officials can treat ordinary Algerians with contempt by denying them their notional rights, and engage in myriad forms of corruption with impunity. The prevalence of arbitrary rule and abuse of authority at all levels of the administrative hierarchy is symptomatic of the fact that the Algerian state has not been a state bound by law. But it is also symptomatic of the fact that much of the behaviour of official power holders is determined by the ferocious rivalry between informal clienteles competing for control of state resources and, at the higher levels especially, by the incessant conflict between factions for control of the commanding heights of the state machine – the army command, the upper echelons of the bureaucracy and its ramifications in the public sector, and the government itself. The conflict between clienteles and factions within the state apparatus is the principal motor of arbitrary rule. Those not protected by a powerful patron or by membership of an influential coterie are permanently exposed to *la hogra*.

But the fundamental premise of this state of affairs is the massive predominance of the executive branch of the state – the armed forces, the presidency, the government, the police and the administration – over the two other branches, the legislature and the judiciary. The weakness of the legislature ensures that the principal social interests seek representation directly in the executive rather than in the legislature. The executive is accordingly where interests and viewpoints are effectively articulated and conflicts arbitrated, where the important political decisions are taken. But these decisions are inevitably taken informally, on the basis of the eternally shifting *rapports de force* between coteries and factions, and thus they rarely if ever conform to any rule other than the law of the jungle. And the weakness of the legislature means that it can never hold the executive to account and so can never curb its arbitrary power, and in these circumstances the judiciary is condemned to be the dependent appendage of the executive also, and is incapable of upholding the notional laws of the land against executive power-holders and incapable of guaranteeing the rights or redressing the grievances of the mass of the Algerian people.

It follows that the most important change which has needed to be made since the advent of formal pluralism in 1989 has been the empowerment of the legislature. Only if the balance of power between executive and legislative branches were altered to the advantage of the latter could the Algerian government and administration become accountable, their capacity for arbitrary behaviour be curbed, and the judiciary acquire the minimum of independence of the executive that is the precondition of its acting to uphold the law rather than debase it. Only if the legislature became the locus of serious decision-making and, in particular, the source of ministerial mandates, could major social interests acquire the incentive to insist on effective formal representation in the Algerian Parliament instead of contenting themselves with representation through occult networks in the executive. Only if this were to happen would the Algerian middle classes recognize their interest in insisting upon proper elections to the legislature and an end to the cynical electoral charades which the regime has been organizing since 1990. Only in these circumstances could the parties come into their own as organizations providing effective representation of public opinion, and the factional conflict within the executive be reduced to the phenomenon of secondary if not minor significance that it is in most modern states. Only if a reliable framework of law were thus established could Algeria's numerous millionaires be induced to invest in productive ventures in Algeria instead of abroad. Only in this way could Algerian men and women become citizens in reality as well as in name, and the blight of *la hogra* become a memory. And only if the resistance to the Islamists in Algeria had been oriented by a positive political project of this order could it have hoped to provide an effective counter to the FIS's utopian vision of *dawla islamiyya*, whose fundamental appeal to its popular constituency lay in the fact it promised a state ruled by the *Shari'a*, God's law, when no alternative conception of law-bound government was on offer.

The terrible thing is not that this was not obvious to the Algerian Left in the bewildering flow of events in 1989-92, but that it still has not dawned on the Algerian Left ten years later.

THE DEARTH OF CONSTRUCTIVE IDEAS

Nothing in the Algerian Left's traditions equipped it before 1989 to develop an adequate conception of the necessity of law-bound government or a realistic conception of how this might be established. The derivation of the PAGS-Ettahaddi-MDS, but also the PT, from the Leninist tradition oriented these parties in the very different direction of Jacobin, vanguardist, revolutionism. But the derivation of the FFS and the ANR from the historic FLN oriented them in the same direction as well, since the FLN, as an offshoot of the radical nationalist tradition launched by Algerian migrants in France in 1926, with the formation of the Étoile Nord-Africaine under the aegis of the French Communist Party and the Comintern, was also the heir to the Jacobin tradition which the Communist movement had reinvigorated, such that the FLN was a kind of radical nationalist variant of Leninist substitutionism, the Front substituting itself for the Nation and the People much as the Party substituted itself for the Proletariat. Algeria's colonial history, and especially its early amputation from the Ottoman Empire prior to the experience of the Ottoman reforms, account in part for this state of affairs. The resulting absence from Algeria of a tradition of constitutionalist politics,[27] such as has been a significant feature of the political history of Turkey and Tunisia but also Egypt and Iran, has meant that virtually all forms of politics in modern Algeria have been shaped by authoritarian doctrines and utopian visions of one kind or another, and none of them have been able to draw on a national tradition of political thought shaped to the problem of establishing constitutional government, let alone representative government, through the arduous processes of incremental political reform.

Rooted in this legacy of a tragic history, the crippling lacunae in Algeria's political traditions have made the Algerian Left, like every other element on the political spectrum, intensely reliant on external sources of ideas and political bearings. But when the crisis broke in 1989, not only had the unhelpful Communist tradition foundered, but there was scarcely a European Left to speak of any longer, and the traditions of constitutional and democratic reform which had been sustained by previous generations of European democratic socialists were suddenly no longer available for the Algerians to draw upon. What the West had to offer was something else altogether.

From 1988 onwards, the increasingly monolithic Western discourse on Algeria, as on all other ex-colonies, has relentlessly insisted on 'economic and political reform', while rarely specifying what it has meant by this beyond measures to abolish national economy combined with the introduction of formal pluralism by decree. In Algerian leftwing circles, proposals for reform have been much rarer, whereas calls, especially from Leftist intellectuals, for something called 'rupture' (but also undefined) have been frequent. In fact, the notion of 'rupture' has tended to dovetail with what the West has really meant by 'reform', namely the abrupt and painful breaking with and dismantling of the Algerian state system as this was constructed by the FLN. This has now been largely although not wholly achieved, and reportedly well over 100,000 Algerians have been killed in the process. The failure of the Western Left to do anything to prevent this hecatomb has been connected to the advent in Europe since the early 1980s of a general condition of mindlessness in the matter of reform, which has aggravated and reinforced the Algerians' inability to recognize that what the West has meant by 'reform' in the Algerian context is not at all what this word has historically meant in Britain or the US (or even France) in previous eras, but what it has meant when the West has been confronting older states which it aspires to destroy – the Ottoman empire and the USSR, for instance.

It is precisely the constructive concept of reform as reserved by the Western political classes for domestic use which has needed to be developed and applied in Algeria since 1989. The absence of a serious politics of constructive reform in the direction of a law-bound state has been a fundamental premise of the exaggerated salience of identity politics in the Algerian case. It follows that what is left of the Algerian Left will have to discover for itself what the Western tradition of political reform was all about, if it is to be able at last to chart a course out of the wasteland to which Algeria has been reduced.

As for the French Left, it might ask itself whether it should not rethink its view of Algeria as well as of France, and question, among other things, the policy of the French socialist government in 1988-89 of insisting on the rapid advent of formal pluralism in Algeria at a time when no true counterpart to the French Socialist Party so much as existed in Algeria, and when the Algerian Left was completely unprepared for the change in prospect, which could accordingly only benefit other political forces. And the rest of what remains of the Western Left might at last realize that it needs to take a serious interest in Algeria, if only in order to know what the devastating political implications of a wholly avoidable 'war against terrorism' may be.

NOTES

1   Christopher Hitchens, 'Against rationalization', *The Nation*, 8 October 2001.
2   Noam Chomsky, Interview on MSNBC Chatroom, 2 October 2001.
3   Noam Chomsky, 'The new war against terror': talk to the Technology Culture Forum, Massachusetts Institute of Technology, 18 October 2001.
4   Apart from the tiny Christian community, a legacy of the colonial era sustained by expatriates, the small Berber-speaking population (c. 100,000) of the Wadi Mzab in the northern Sahara are Ibadis, not Sunnis; a small element of the urban population belong to the Hanafi rite, a legacy of the Ottoman period.
5   I have discussed the Berberist movement in detail in *Co-opting identity: the manipulation of Berberism, the frustration of democratisation and the generation of violence in Algeria*, LSE, Development Research Centre, Working Paper No. 8, December 2001.
6   Abdelkader Harichane, *Le FIS et le pouvoir*, Algiers, Éditions Lalla Sakina, n.d. but c. 1999, pp. 26-8; Ahmed Merani, *La Fitna: témoignage d'un membre fondateur du Front Islamique du Salut*, Algiers, publisher not identified, n.d. but c. 1999, p. 37. For the significance of this, see my article 'From radical mission to equivocal ambition: the expansion and manipulation of Algerian Islamism, 1979-1992', in Martin E. Marty and R. Scott Appleby, eds., *Accounting for fundamentalisms: the dynamic character of movements*, American

Academy of Arts and Sciences, The Fundamentalism Project, Chicago: University of Chicago Press, 1994.

7   See notably the motion (especially clause 7) passed at the National Conference called by Ettahaddi to launch the MDS and held at Sidi Fredj near Algiers on 30 April – 1 May 1998.

8   *Congrès Constitutif du Mouvement Démocratique et Social*, Sidi Fredj, 7–8 October, 1999: *Résolution politique*, paragraph 2.

9   *Congrès Constitutif du MDS*, Sidi Fredj, 7–8 October, 1999: *Rapport politique et moral au congrès*, paragraph 4.

10   For an analysis of how the formal positions of Algerian parties have been relayed by different sectors of political opinion in France and elsewhere, and how this has disabled international opinion from understanding the Algerian drama, see my article, 'The international gallery and the extravasation of factional conflict in Algeria', *Cambridge Review of International Affairs*, XII(1) (Summer/Fall), 1998.

11   For the political positions of the PT, see the various issues of its publications, *Tribune Ouvrière* and *Fraternité*, and Louisa Hanoune, *Une autre voix pour l'Algérie: entretiens avec Ghania Mouffok*, Paris: La Découverte, 1996.

12   I have discussed the power struggle within the regime in 1993-94 in my article, 'Algeria between eradicators and conciliators', *Middle East Report*, No. 189 (24(4), July–August), 1994.

13   *Libération*, 1 September 1994; *El Watan*, 5 and 14 September 1994; BBC Summary of World Broadcasts: Middle East, 6 September 1994 (reporting Algiers Radio, 3 September); *Le Monde*, 8 and 14 September 1994.

14   For a fuller discussion of the Rome platform, see my article 'Algeria's ruinous impasse and the honourable way out', *International Affairs*, 71(2) (April), 1995.

15   Declaration by Hocine Aït Ahmed, Geneva, 3 September 1997, reported by AFP.

16   The son of Cheikh Bachir al-Ibrahimi (1889-1965) who succeeded Ben Badis as leader of the Association of the Muslim *'ulama* of Algeria from 1940 to 1951, Taleb held numerous ministerial portfolios between 1965 and 1988, culminating in that of foreign affairs.

17   The leader of the 'reformers' within the FLN, Hamrouche was widely credited with the introduction of liberal reforms during his premiership in 1989-91.

18   As commander of *wilaya* IV (Algérois) of the ALN in 1961-62, Khatib had led the resistance of the interior *maquis* to the seizure of power by Boumediène's 'army of the frontiers' in 1962; he was accordingly especially hostile to the candidacy of Bouteflika, Boumediène's close colleague at that time.

19   For the text of the communiqué, see the *Journal of Algerian Studies*, 4/5, 1999-2000, p. 171.

20   Hugh Roberts, 'Algeria: riots without end?', *Middle East International*, No. 651, 1 June 2001.

21 Seven FFS offices in Kabylia were destroyed between 23 April and 20 June 2001, as were seven RCD offices; see Roberts, *Co-opting identity*, p. 7.

22 Roberts, 'Algeria: riots without end?', p. 17.

23 FFS, *Memorandum: 'Pour une transition démocratique'*, Algiers, 12 May 2001.

24 The original Salafiyya movement, of which Ben Badis's AUMA was an extension, preached a return to the traditions of the venerable founding fathers (*as-salaf as-salih*) of Islam and thus privileged scripturalist Islam over later tendencies, notably Sufism, which they stigmatized as deviant or even heretical; in contemporary usage, the term 'Salafi' refers to Islamists oriented essentially by the extremely conservative interpretation of scripturalist orthodoxy pioneered by Wahhabism in Saudi Arabia. The influence of the Egyptian Islamist Sayyid Qutb (1906-66) has also been noticeable in Algerian Islamism, especially in the disposition to contest the state as 'impious' and to envisage its overthrow.

25 Roberts, 'From radical mission to equivocal ambition'; see also my article 'Doctrinaire economics and political opportunism in the strategy of Algerian Islamism', in John Ruedy, ed., *Islamism and Secularism in North Africa*, Georgetown University, Center for Contemporary Arab Studies, New York: St Martin's Press, 1994.

26 The PAGS in 1989 initially recognized the need to neutralize the religious issue, but entirely failed to address the other issues effectively.

27 For an elaboration of this point, see my article 'The struggle for constitutional rule in Algeria', *Journal of Algerian Studies*, 3, 1998, pp.19-30.

THE INTERNATIONAL POLITICS OF
FORCED MIGRATION

STEPHEN CASTLES

THE 'GLOBAL MIGRATION CRISIS'

Europeans, North Americans or Australians who rely on the tabloid press might well believe that their countries were being besieged by asylum seekers and illegal immigrants. Sensationalist journalists and right-wing politicians map out dire consequences like rocketing crime-rates, fundamentalist terrorism, collapsing welfare systems and mass unemployment. They call for strict border control, detention of asylum seekers and deportation of illegals. The public appeal of such polemics is obvious: recent right-wing electoral victories in countries as disparate as Denmark, Austria and Australia can be attributed to fears of mass influxes from the South and East. Even prominent academics ague that the world is in the throes of a 'global migration crisis'.[1]

The political potency of fears of immigration is nothing new. Historians recall campaigns against Jewish immigrants in Britain in the 1880s, and the US Nativist movement of the 1920s. The White Australia policy, designed to keep out Asians, was supported by the labour movement and all political parties up to the 1960s. With the end of the Cold War, migration again became a key issue, with fears of 'up to 50 million' East-West migrants,[2] as well as countless more from the South. Extreme right-wing parties mobilized public opinion, and racist violence escalated throughout Western Europe.[3] States strengthened border controls and tightened up refugee rules.

But the predicted mass influxes from the East never happened. Most migrants to the West were people returning to ancestral homelands: ethnic Germans to Germany, Albanians of Greek origin to Greece, and so on. Other migrants usually came only if they could link up with existing social networks of previous migrants, who helped them find work and housing. Migration stabilized and declined. By 2000, the International Organization for Migration (IOM) put the global migrant population (defined as people living outside their country of birth) at 150 million.[4] Even allowing for under-counting – especially of undocumented migrants – only 2-3 per cent of the world's population are migrants. Moreover, UN data shows that the number of international migrants has only grown slightly faster than overall world population since 1965.[5] Hardly a cause for panic, it seems.

Yet by the beginning of the new millennium, migration was again a hot topic. Britain experienced growing entries of asylum seekers and undocumented workers. Germany adopted measures to turn the descendants of the 'guest-workers' of the 1960s and 1970s into citizens. Southern European countries became aware of a sharp fall in fertility, while inflows across the Mediterranean from North Africa increased. Both Canadians and Americans were divided about the merits of their relatively open immigration policies.

Is this all a re-run of old themes, or is something new happening? It seems that population movements are taking on increased significance in the context of current global social transformations. First, forced migration is growing in volume and importance, as a result of endemic violence and human rights violations. Second, policy-makers are attempting to implement differentiated policies for various categories of migrant. There is global competition to attract highly skilled migrants, but refugees, unskilled migrants and their families are unwelcome. Third, there is growing understanding that migration – both economic and forced – is an integral part of processes of global and regional economic integration. Fourth, it has become clear that immigrants do not simply assimilate into receiving societies, but rather tend to form communities and retain their own languages, religions and cultures. Finally, migration has become highly politicized, and is now a pivotal issue in both national and international politics. These are the themes of this essay. The discussion will focus mainly on issues of forced migration. At the end I shall return to the question: is there a 'global migration crisis'?

THE MANY FACES OF FORCED MIGRATION

Forced (or involuntary) migration includes a number of legal or political categories. All involve people who have been forced to flee their homes and seek refuge elsewhere. Popular speech tends to call them all 'refugees', but this is quite a narrow legal category. The majority of forced migrants flee for reasons not recognized by the international refugee regime, and many of them are displaced within their own country of origin.

Refugees

According to the 1951 *United Nations Convention Relating to the Status of Refugees*, a refugee is a person residing outside his or her country of nationality, who is unable or unwilling to return because of a 'well-founded fear of persecution on account of race, religion, nationality, membership in a particular social group, or political opinion'. About 140 of the world's 190 states have signed the

1951 Convention.[6] Member states undertake to protect refugees and to respect the principle of *non-refoulement* (that is, not to return them to a country where they may be persecuted). This may require allowing refugees to enter and granting them temporary or permanent residence status. Officially recognized refugees are often better off than other forced migrants, as they have a clear legal status and enjoy the protection of a powerful institution: the United Nations High Commissioner for Refugees (UNHCR).

The global refugee population grew from 2.4 million in 1975 to 10.5 million in 1985 and 14.9 million in 1990. A peak was reached after the end of the Cold War with 18.2 million in 1993. By 2000, the global refugee population had declined to 12.1 million.[7]

Refugees came from countries hit by war, violence and chaos. The ten main places of origin were Afghanistan (with 2.6 million refugees in 1999), Iraq (572,000), Burundi (524,000), Sierra Leone (487,000), Sudan (468,000), Somalia (452,000), Bosnia (383,000), Angola (351,000), Eritrea (346,000) and Croatia (340,000).[8]

Table 1[9] shows the top ten refugee hosting countries in 2000 according to three different criteria. The first column shows the total refugee population. Pakistan and Iran have by far the largest refugee populations – mainly from Afghanistan. Africa figures prominently in the Table, but the USA is also in the list, together with two European countries: Germany and the Federal Republic of Yugoslavia. However, to understand the weight of the 'refugee burden', it is more useful to relate refugee population to overall population in host countries. This is shown in the second column of Table 1, which consists mainly of very poor countries, with the sole exceptions of Yugoslavia and Sweden. Even more instructive is to relate refugee populations to the wealth of the receiving country (third column). This list does not include a single developed country. Refugees are overwhelmingly concentrated in the poorest countries. This puts the frequent Northern claims of being unfairly burdened by refugees in perspective.

Asylum-seekers

These are people who move across international borders in search of protection, but whose claims for refugee status have not yet been decided. Annual asylum applications in Western Europe, Australia, Canada and the USA combined rose from 90,400 in 1983 to 323,050 in 1988, and then surged again with the end of the Cold War to peak at 828,645 in 1992.[10] Altogether, 5 million asylum seekers entered western countries from 1985 to 1995.[11] Applications fell sharply to 480,00 in 1995, but began creeping up again to 534,500 in 2000.[12] Nearly the whole of the decline can be explained by falls in asylum applications following changes in refugee law in Germany (438,200 applications in 1992, but only 127,900 in 1995) and Sweden (84,000 in 1992, 9000 in 1995). The UK had relatively few asylum seekers in the early 1990s, with 32,300 in 1992, but numbers increased at the end of the decade to 55,000 in 1998 and 97,900 in 2000.[13]

TABLE 1:
THE TOP TEN REFUGEE HOSTING COUNTRIES, 2000

Country	No of Refugees ('000s)	Country	No of Refugees per 1000 inhabitants	Country	No of Refugees per US$1m of GDP
Pakistan	2,002	Armenia	79.7	Armenia	172.4
Iran	1,868	Guinea	58.5	Guinea	119.9
Germany	906	Yugoslavia	45.7	Tanzania	86.0
Tanzania	681	Congo	42.5	Zambia	74.9
USA	507	Djibouti	36.3	Congo	62.9
Yugoslavia	484	Iran	27.6	Central African Republic	52.7
Guinea	433	Zambia	27.3		
Sudan	401	Liberia	21.7	Congo	47.7
Congo	333	Tanzania	20.3	Uganda	35.6
China	294	Sweden	17.7	Pakistan	31.3
				Ethiopia	30.1

Source: *UNHCR, Global Report 2000: Achievements and Impact*, UNHCR, Geneva, 2001, p. 28.

The media and politicians sometimes claim that asylum seekers are not real victims of persecution, but simply economic migrants in disguise. Yet in many conflict situations it is difficult to distinguish between flight because of persecution and departure caused by the destruction of the economic and social infrastructure needed for survival. Asylum seekers live in a drawn-out limbo situation, since determination procedures and appeals may take many years. In some countries, asylum seekers are not allowed to work, and have to exist on meagre welfare handouts. Up to 90 per cent of asylum applications are rejected – yet the majority of asylum seekers stay on. In many cases, they cannot be deported because the country of origin will not take them back, or because they have no passports. In fact asylum seeker are a useful source of labour which fuels western countries' burgeoning informal economies.

Internally displaced persons (IDPs)

IDPs are generally defined as 'persons who, as a result of persecution, armed conflict or violence, have been forced to abandon their homes and leave their usual place of residence, and who remain within the borders of their own country'.[14] It is estimated that the number of IDPs world-wide rose from 1.2 million in 1982 to 14 million by 1986, and to over 20 million by 1997.[15] The number of countries with IDP populations increased from five in 1970 to thirty-four in 1996.[16]

The increase is due to new types of wars which deliberately target civilian populations. Indeed mass displacement of the population may be a deliberate instrument of warfare, as in Bosnia, Kosovo, Chechnya, Rwanda or Myanmar. The long-lasting war in Sudan between the Muslim-Arab North and the African-Christian South has generated 4 million IDPs. Other major IDP populations in 1996 were in Turkey (0.5 - 1 million), Afghanistan (1.2 million). Angola (1.2 million), Bosnia (1 million), Myanmar (0.5 - 1 million), Liberia (1 million), Iraq (0.9 million), Sri Lanka (0.9 million) and Colombia (0.6 million).[17] In Sri Lanka, Angola and the Sudan, some people have lived as IDPs – often in great insecurity and poverty – for over twenty years.

IDPs are more numerous than refugees, yet are often without any effective protection or assistance. There is no international legal instrument specifically designed to protect them, although they are covered by general human rights conventions.[18] Nor is there any international agency like the UNHCR with responsibility for IDPs. The key problem is sovereignty: in international law, IDPs are the responsibility of their own government, since they have not crossed international borders, yet it is often this very government that has persecuted and displaced them.

Development displacees

These are people compelled to move by large-scale development projects, such as dams, airports, roads and urban housing. The World Bank – which funds many such projects – estimates that they displace an average of 10 million people per year. Growing awareness of the problem in the 1980s led the World Bank to impose conditions on its loans designed to ensure compensation and appropriate resettlement.[19] Millions of development displacees experience permanent impoverishment, and end up in a situation of social and political marginalization.[20] One reason for this is that dams are often built in remote areas, inhabited by indigenous people or ethnic minorities. Such groups often practice extensive forms of agriculture, and have deep bonds with their ancestral land. Displacement means losing these ties and being forced to adopt a completely new way of life.

Development displacees constitute another group larger than official refugee populations, for whom there is no protective regime. Many of them end up drifting into urban slums, or becoming a part of floating populations, which may spill over into international migration.

Environmental and disaster displacees

This category includes people displaced by environmental change (desertification, deforestation, land degradation, water pollution or inundation), by natural disasters (floods, volcanoes, landslides, earthquakes), and by man-made disasters (industrial accidents, radioactivity). A report by environmentalist Norman Myers in 1995 claimed that there were at least 25 million environmental refugees, that the number could double by 2010, and that as many as 200 million people could eventually be at risk of displacement.[21] Refugee experts reject such apocalyptic visions and argue that their main purpose is to shock western governments into taking action to protect the environment. A study by geographer Richard Black argues that there are no environmental refugees as such. While environmental factors do play a part in forced migration, displacements due to environmental factors are always closely linked to social and ethnic conflict, weak states and abuse of human rights. The emphasis on environmental factors is a distraction from central issues of development, inequality and conflict resolution.[22]

Similarly, it is impossible to distinguish clearly between natural and man-made disasters. A mudslide that buries a Brazilian favela (shantytown) appears to be a natural disaster, but on closer examination it may be seen to be a result of land speculation, unplanned urban growth and lack of government accountability. Thus we cannot clearly define who is an environmental or disaster displacee, nor quantify this category in any meaningful way.

People-trafficking and smuggling

A final form of forced migration is the trafficking of people across international boundaries. It is important to distinguish between people-trafficking and people-smuggling. To quote Ann Galagher:

> Smuggled migrants are moved illegally for profit; they are partners, however unequal, in a commercial transaction ... By contrast, the movement of trafficked persons is based on deception and coercion and is for the purpose of exploitation. The profit in trafficking comes not from the movement but from the sale of a trafficked person's sexual services or labour in the country of destination, Most smuggled migrants are men. Most trafficked persons are women and children.[23]

The trafficking of women and children for the sex industry occurs all over the world. Thai and Japanese gangsters collaborate to entice women into prostitution in Japan by claiming that they will get jobs as waitresses or entertainers. Victims of civil war and forced displacement in former Yugoslavia, Georgia or Azerbaijan are sold to brothels in Western Europe. Women in war zones are forced into sex-slavery by combatant forces, or sold to international gangs.

It is impossible to quantify the number of people affected by trafficking and smuggling, but both are widespread practices. They are a product of the increasingly restrictive immigration policies of rich countries. The high demand for labour in the North, combined with strong pressure to emigrate from the South, and strong barriers to mobility, have created business opportunities for a new 'migration industry'. This includes legal participants, such as travel agents, shipping companies and banks, as well as illegal operators.

THE EVOLUTION OF THE REFUGEE REGIME

Forced migration has become a major factor in global politics and in the relationship between the rich countries of the North and underdeveloped countries of the South and East. This growing importance is reflected in the changing nature of the international refugee regime as it has evolved since 1945. What started off as a relatively modest framework designed to cater for European refugees has developed into a much wider system of humanitarian action.

The refugee regime in the Cold War

The international refugee regime consists of a set of legal norms based on humanitarian and human rights law, as well as a number of institutions designed to protect and assist refugees. The core of the regime is the 1951 *United Nations Convention Relating to the Status of Refugees*. The regime defines who is officially a refugee – a definition which can make the difference between life and death – and what rights such persons should have. The most important institution is the UNHCR, but many other organizations play a part: intergovernmental agencies like the International Committee of the Red Cross (ICRC), the World Food Programme (WFP) and the United Nations Children's Fund (UNICEF); as well as hundreds of non-governmental organizations (NGOs) such as OXFAM, CARE International, Médecins sans Frontiers (MSF) and the International Rescue Committee (IRC).

The refugee regime was shaped by two major international issues. The first was the presence of over 40 million displaced persons in Europe at the end of World War II.[24] The preferred solution was to repatriate them to their countries of origin, but since many were unable or unwilling to return, large-scale resettlement programmes were introduced. Many Eastern Europeans were selected for permanent migration to Australia and Canada, where they met the demand for labour to fuel post-war expansion. That they were white and anti-communist was an added bonus. Others went to the USA, the UK and other European countries. This experience helped establish the principle of exile and permanent resettlement as a solution to refugee issues.[25]

The second major formative influence was the Cold War. Offering asylum to those who 'voted with their feet' against communism was a powerful source of propaganda for the West. The refugee regime was 'used with the intent of frustrating the consolidation of communist revolutions and hopefully destabilizing nascent communist governments'.[26] Since the 'non-departure regime' of the Iron Curtain kept the numbers low, the West could afford to offer a warm welcome to those few who made it. The numbers rose following events like the 1956 Hungarian Revolution or the 1968 Prague Spring, but were still manageable.

The refugee regime in the era of decolonization

The international regime was essentially a eurocentric model designed to provide protection to (mainly white) political refugees and to support Northern political aims. Yet very different refugee situations were developing in the South. The colonial legacy led to weak undemocratic states, underdeveloped economies and widespread poverty in Asia, Africa and Latin America. Northern countries sought to maintain their dominance by influencing new elites, while the Soviet Bloc encouraged revolutionary movements. Many local conflicts became proxy wars in the East–West struggle, with the superpowers providing modern weapons. Such factors gave rise to situations of generalized violence, leading to mass flight.[27] The escalation of struggles against white colonial or settler regimes in Africa from the 1960s, resistance against US-supported military regimes in Latin America in the 1970s and 1980s, and long-drawn-out political and ethnic struggles in the Middle East and Asia – all led to vast flows of refugees.

Northern countries and international agencies responded by claiming that such situations were qualitatively different from the individual persecution for which the 1951 Convention was designed.[28] The solution of permanent resettlement in developed countries was not seen as appropriate – except for Indo-Chinese and Cuban refugees who did fit the Cold War mould. In 1969, the Organization of African States (OAU) introduced its own Refugee Convention, which broadened the definition to include people forced to flee their country by war, human rights violations or generalized violence. A similar definition for Latin America was contained in the Cartagena Declaration of 1984. Many African countries provided a generous welcome to refugees from apartheid or civil war, while Pakistan and Iran practised 'Islamic solidarity' with Afghanis fleeing the Soviet invasion, with a peak of 6.3 million refugees in 1990.

The UNHCR began to take on new functions as a humanitarian relief organization. It helped run camps and provided food and medical care around the world. It became the 'focal point' for coordinating the activities of the various UN agencies in major emergencies.[29] This expanding role was reflected in UNHCR's budget, which tripled from US$145 million in 1978 to $510 million in 1980,[30] making it one of the most powerful UN agencies.

The 'asylum crisis' of the 1980s and 1990s

By the 1980s, increasing flows of asylum seekers were coming directly to Europe from conflict zones in Latin America, Africa and Asia. Politicians and the media began to claim that they were really economic migrants in disguise. Indeed, many asylum seekers had 'mixed motivations', for impoverishment and human rights abuses went hand-in-hand. This had been equally true of many of the Spanish, Portuguese and Greek 'guestworkers' of the 1960s, who were fleeing fascist regimes as well as unemployment. But following the 1973 'Oil Crisis', most Western European countries had introduced zero-immigration policies. Asylum was seen as a way of circumventing these.

The USA also experienced increasing inflows of asylum seekers entering illegally across land borders or by boat. Moreover, they were often on the wrong side in the Cold War, as victims of the very military regimes the USA was backing. The USA favoured supporters of the Contras who were fighting the left-wing Sandinista government of Nicaragua, but turned back most asylum seekers from Guatemala and El Salvador. Anti-Castro Cuban boat people were allowed in, while the US Coastguard stopped vessels carrying Haitians fleeing the Duvalier regime.

Asylum seeker numbers increased dramatically with the collapse of the Soviet Bloc. The most dramatic flows were from Albania to Italy in 1991 and again in 1997, and from Former Yugoslavia during the wars in Croatia, Bosnia and Kosovo. Many of the 1.3 million asylum applicants arriving in Germany between 1991-95 were members of ethnic minorities (such as Roma) from Romania, Bulgaria and elsewhere in Eastern Europe. At the same time, increasing numbers of asylum seekers were arriving in Europe from the South, especially from Afghanistan, Angola, Ghana, Iran, Iraq, Nigeria, Pakistan, Somalia, Sri Lanka, Vietnam and Zaire.[31] The situation was further complicated by ethnic minorities returning to ancestral homelands as well as undocumented workers from Poland, Ukraine and other post-Soviet states.

The early 1990s were thus a period of panic about migration. Extreme-right mobilization, arson attacks on asylum-seeker hostels and assaults on foreigners were threatening public order. European states reacted with a series of restrictions, which seemed to herald the construction of a 'Fortress Europe':[32]

- *Changes in national legislation* to restrict access to refugee status. This was particularly important in Germany, whose Basic Law had laid down an absolute right to asylum for persecuted persons. The Government's efforts to amend Paragraph 16 of the Basic Law were highly contentious, but were eventually accepted through the 'asylum compromise' of 1993. This made it much more difficult for asylum seekers to make a claim for protection in Germany, leading to a sharp fall in entries.
- *Temporary protection regimes* for people fleeing the wars in former Yugoslavia. Instead of permanent refugee status, they were to be given limited term permits to remain, and sent home once conditions allowed.
- *Non-arrival policies* designed to prevent people without adequate documentation from entering Western Europe. Citizens of certain states were required to obtain visas before departure. 'Carrier sanctions' were introduced, whereby airline personnel had to check documents before allowing people to embark. Such rules made it impossible for many genuine refugees to make asylum claims, forcing them to rely on people-smugglers.
- *Diversion policies*, designed to shift responsibility for processing claims and providing protection to other countries. By declaring Central European countries such as Poland, Hungary and the Czech Republic to be 'safe Third countries', Western European countries could return asylum-seekers to these states, if they had used them as transit routes.
- *Restrictive interpretations* of the 1951 UN Refugee Convention, for instance by excluding persecution by 'non-state actors', or by declaring certain countries to be safe. However, many people refused refugee status were allowed to remain under such labels as 'exceptional leave to remain' in the UK or *Duldung* (toleration) in Germany. Such inferior asylum status leads to insecurity and confusion for both refugees and the receiving populations.

- *European cooperation* on asylum and immigration rules, such as the 1990 Schengen Convention, designed to create a common migration space in Western Europe, and the 1990 Dublin Convention, which aimed to prevent 'asylum shopping', i.e. people making multiple applications for asylum in different European countries. The 1997 Treaty of Amsterdam laid down a commitment to introduce common EU policies on immigration and asylum by 2004. This would make the EU Council of Ministers responsible for this policy area, representing a considerable shift in sovereignty.

In the USA even Cubans began to be perceived as economic migrants, with 35,000 'rafters' attempting to reach Florida in 1994. President Clinton ordered them to be detained at the Guantanamo base, and made an agreement with Cuba to admit 20,000 migrants per year. In September 1994, a US–led military force arrived in Haiti, forcing the military junta to resign. The main aim of this operation was to stop mass flows of boat people to the USA. Two years later, in 1996, Congress passed a law designed to prevent illegal migration and abuse of the asylum process. Persons who had been convicted of a crime in their home country were excluded from asylum. The law introduced accelerated procedures for screening asylum seekers, and for deporting those not considered to have a strong case. The law also prescribed detention for asylum seekers during the screening process.

Such restrictive measures – rather than real improvements in human rights – are the main reason why the number of officially recognized refugees worldwide has fallen since 1995. The refugee regime of the rich countries of the North has been fundamentally transformed over the last twenty years. It has shifted from a system designed to welcome Cold War refugees from the East and to resettle them as permanent exiles in new homes, to a 'non–entrée regime', designed to exclude and control asylum seekers from the South.[33]

GLOBALIZATION AND THE POLITICS OF CONTAINMENT

Even at the height of the 'asylum crisis' in the early 1990s, refugee populations in the North were tiny compared with those in some Southern countries. For instance the ratio of refugees to host populations in 1992 was 1:10 in Malawi, compared with 1:869 in Germany and 1:3,860 for the UK.[34] The burden of caring for refugees falls overwhelmingly on the poorer countries of Asia and Africa. The 'non–entrée regime' is designed to keep things that way, but the experience of the last ten years has shown that border restrictions alone are not sufficient. Just as Europeans were willing to endure danger and hardship to seek a better future in the New World a century ago, today's poor and oppressed are prepared to take enormous risks to reach the North.

This desire for mobility can be seen as an integral part of global processes of social transformation. Globalization involves the proliferation of cross-border flows not only of capital and commodities, but also of cultural values, ideas and people.[35] Flows of people are managed through differentiation of rules and mechanisms to allow the movement of some groups – especially highly-skilled personnel and contract workers – while preventing or restricting the movement of others – especially forced migrants, low-skilled workers and dependants. However, globalization generates factors favouring mobility, which may be far more powerful than official control measures. The most obvious of these is the growth in inequality between North and South. A second factor is the political destabilization in many countries of the South resulting from unequal power relations. Often this is exacerbated by the structural adjustment policies of the World Bank and International Monetary Fund, which undermine social policy. A third factor is the cultural attraction of Northern lifestyles, beamed into every village by the mass media. As Zygmunt Baumann argues, 'mobility has become the most powerful and most coveted stratifying factor'.[36] The new global economic and political elites are able to cross borders at will, while the poor are meant to stay at home: 'the riches are global, the misery is local'.[37] The problem is that many of the poor also perceive that mobility brings the chance of wealth, and are desperate to migrate.

This is why entry restrictions in the North are not sufficient. The rich states and the international agencies (which style themselves 'the international community') are increasingly moving towards a politics of containment, designed to prevent unwanted migrants and asylum seekers from leaving their countries of origin. This is part of a much broader security agenda, in which the excluded South is perceived as a source of conflict, terrorism and instability.

'New wars', humanitarian action and military intervention

The trend towards containment led to the further growth of UNHCR. Its budget doubled between 1990 and 1993, from $564 million to $1.3 billion.[38] Other agencies also expanded their activities, and the UN made successive attempts to improve its coordination capacities, and to improve cooperation between major humanitarian agencies that tend to compete like feudal fiefdoms. However, traditional forms of humanitarian assistance often proved incapable of preventing mass displacement. In the 1990s the 'international community' undertook a series of military interventions designed specifically to prevent or stop mass exoduses from conflict zones.

The context for such attempts at global social policy and policing is the changing character of warfare. Mary Kaldor argues that the nineteenth century 'Clausewitzean' notion of modern war was that of conflict between states with the aim of achieving rational objectives. War involved a monopoly of the means of violence by the state, and conflict according to formal rules which limited violence against civilians. However, the inherent logic was towards 'total war': the increasing mobilization of whole societies and economies, as occurred in the two World Wars. In the Cold War, the doctrine of 'mutually assured destruction' ensured that actual fighting between the great powers was replaced by a militarized peace. At the same time, irregular or guerrilla wars broke out, which often became proxy wars between the two blocs. These were harbingers of what Kaldor calls the 'new wars', which became dominant as the Cold War drew to a close.[39]

The new wars are usually internal conflicts in less-developed countries, connected with identity struggles, ethnic divisions, problems of state formation and competition for economic assets. But they are simultaneously transnational as they involve diaspora populations, foreign volunteers and mercenaries, and international intervention forces. They also draw in international journalists, UN aid organizations, NGOs, and regional organizations like the OAU or the Organization of American States (OAS). International economic interests (such as the trade in oil, diamonds or small arms) also play a part in starting or prolonging local wars. New wars arise mainly in the context of weak or disintegrating states, which have lost (or never had) a monopoly of the means of violence. The means of warfare have also changed. The protagonists are not large standing armies but irregular forces. The aim is not control of territory, but political control of the population. Most important for understanding forced migration, Mary Kaldor argues, is that:

> ... the strategic goal of these wars is population expulsion through various means such as mass killing, forcible resettlement, as well as a range of political, psychological and economic techniques of intimidation. That is why, in all these wars, there has been a dramatic increase in the number of refugees and displaced persons, and why most violence is directed against civilians.[40]

The number of wars at any one time has increased, from an average of about nine in the 1950s to fifty in the late 1990s. Ninety per cent of those killed are civilians. Both government forces and insurgents use exemplary violence including torture and sexual assault as means of control. Genocide and ethnic cleansing are not, or not just, the 're-surfacing of age-old hatreds' as the media sometimes claim, but systemic elements of the new form of warfare.[41]

The implication is that attempts to contain refugees must involve intervention in conflicts. From the 1980s, UN-led relief operations grew in frequency and scope. Starting with Operation Lifeline Sudan (OLS) in 1989, such operations tried to assist both sides in civil wars, by working in both government and rebel-held areas. The principle of 'neutral humanitarianism' meant that aid agencies were supposed to take an impartial position, providing food, shelter, transport and medical assistance to both sides with the central objective of 'saving lives'. The problem with this approach was, as Mark Duffield comments, that humanitarian assistance 'inevitably became part of the local political economy'.[42] The aid goods were used by the combatants as a way of sustaining the conflict.

In any case, provision of aid did little to protect victims of war, or to stop mass exoduses. Increasingly, the 'international community' turned to direct military intervention. This also had the advantage of justifying the continued existence of Northern military establishments now that the threat of large-scale war had receded. In the course of the 1990s there were seven major military operations designed (at least in part) to prevent mass refugee flows. Six were under the auspices of the United Nations Security Council (in Northern Iraq, Bosnia and

Herzegovina, Somalia, Rwanda, Haiti and East Timor), while a seventh (in Kosovo) was carried out by NATO. It is impossible to discuss these cases fully here,[43] but a few comments are necessary.

The intervention in Northern Iraq at the end of the Gulf War in 1992 was mainly designed to prevent Iraqi Kurds entering Turkey – a NATO country engaged in a civil war against its own Kurdish population. US-led forces set up a 'safe haven', giving rise to an 'autonomous federated Kurdish state'. This still exists in 2002, but its existence has been marked by constant internal conflict as well as incursions by Turkish and Iraqi forces. The Bosnian operation from 1992-95 was one of the largest and most publicized UN peacekeeping operations. However, the limited mandate of the UN forces and their unwillingness to use force or risk casualties made the action ineffective. Ethnic cleansing, shelling of civilians, and outflows of refugees all continued. The Srebrenica massacre – before the eyes of Dutch peacekeeping troops – showed the problems of neutrality. This led to a NATO bombing campaign which finally forced a cease-fire, leading to the Dayton Agreement in 1995. However, formerly multicultural Bosnia remains divided into ethnic cantons today. The US-led intervention in Haiti in 1994 can be counted a success in terms of stopping a mass refugee flow, but has done little to improve political or economic conditions in the country.

In other cases, international military intervention has – at least initially – precipitated the very mass forced migrations it was designed to prevent. In Kosovo, the NATO bombing campaign of 1999 was the signal for Serb forces to carry out massive ethnic cleansing of the Kosovar population. The NATO strategy of high-level bombing and zero casualties for their own forces was important in gaining public support at home, but made the human costs higher for those who were supposed to be protected.[44] Similarly, the arrival of Australian-led forces in East Timor in October 1999 did not hinder the forced displacement of a large proportion of the population to West Timor. Both operations are officially considered to have achieved their objectives, since the displaced populations mainly returned home in the long run, but is not clear that the overall effects of military action have been beneficial.[45]

The 'international community' is much less willing to intervene in conflict situations that do not lead to mass influxes to the North. There has been no such intervention in Myanmar, Sri Lanka, Azerbaijan, Sudan, Ethiopia or Angola – to name just a few recent major conflicts. This selectivity indicates that intervention is not based on lofty moral interests, but on the security and political interests of the rich countries. The two international interventions in Africa illustrate this point. The US-led action in Somalia in 1992 was only undertaken after criticism by UN Secretary General Boutros Ghali of Western inaction in the face of a humanitarian disaster, compared with the willingness to intervene in Former Yugoslavia. Action in Somalia was also justified by the perceived threat to regional stability and peace resulting from the collapse of the state. This operation was a disastrous failure, ending in a precipitate withdrawal of the UN forces.[46]

In the other case, Rwanda, international forces were not sent to prevent the genocide of early 1994, even though UN observer forces in the country had called for reinforcements. Instead, these troops were withdrawn at the height of the slaughter. An international operation was only mounted months later, after the victory of Tutsi-led forces led to a mass exodus of one million people, especially Hutus who participated in the genocide. The UN forces were then faced by the dilemma of trying to separate armed militias from civilians in the camps in Zaire, Uganda and other bordering countries. Failure to do so – due to the unwillingness of Northern governments to commit forces to this dangerous task – set the scene for escalating violence in the Great Lakes region and civil war in Zaire (now the Democratic Republic of Congo).[47]

Conflict prevention as social transformation

By the end of the 1990s it was evident that the capacity of international humanitarian action to prevent mass exoduses was severely limited:

- The 'international community' lacked the political will, and the economic and military resources, to intervene effectively in most conflict situations causing mass displacement.
- The selectivity of intervention undermined the moral and political legitimacy of such action.
- Where intervention took place, it often failed to achieve its objectives, and sometimes exacerbated conflicts and precipitated mass displacement.
- The principle of neutral humanitarianism required aid organizations to help both sides in a conflict, thus often providing resources to sustain hostilities.
- Neutrality and limited mandates could mean looking on while atrocities were committed.

Such experiences questioned the principles of neutrality and altruism which are seen as crucial by humanitarian agencies such as the ICRC, Oxfam or MSF. Rather than being idealistic helpers, such organizations were becoming part of a transnational aid industry which included inter-governmental organizations, governments, the military and private companies. The idea of non-political, neutral assistance became unsustainable. Indeed, combatants in the internal wars of the South began increasingly to see international aid workers as protagonists in the conflict. This led to a disturbing upsurge in attacks on aid workers, including murders in Chechnya, Burundi and West Timor.

Duffield argues that this 'new humanitarianism' is linked to new forms of global governance.[48] He builds on Manuell Castell's analysis of the way globalization leads to selective inclusion and exclusion of certain societies and regions in the 'network society'.[49] The new global mode of economic and political regulation (which Duffield refers to as 'liberal peace') is marked by persistent underdevelopment in large parts of the South. This is not an economic problem for the North, because, apart from being the source of certain raw materials, many Southern countries are largely disconnected from the global economy. However, underdevelopment is increasingly seen as a threat to global security and stability. This is because the South connects with the North in ways unexpected and unwanted by the latter: through the proliferation of transnational informal networks, such as international crime, the drug trade, people smuggling and trafficking, and migrant networks which facilitate irregular mobility.[50] Such phenomena are partly a result of trends towards economic deregulation and privatization in the North, which open up the space for informal economies.

Underdevelopment has thus become a threat to the North – even though that very underdevelopment is a result of the hegemony of the North (and especially of the USA as the sole superpower). Duffield argues that the result is a funda-mental change in the objectives of both development policy and humanitarianism. Containment of forced migration through neutral humanitar-ianism has failed. Similarly, the 'Washington Consensus' – the neoliberal credo of the World Bank and the IMF – that underdevelopment could be countered by economic growth based on foreign investments and export-led growth has proved mistaken. Humanitarianism and development policy now have a new joint task: the transformation of whole societies in order to prevent conflict and to achieve social and economic change. The principle of transforming whole societies was contained in a remarkable lecture by the then Senior Vice-President of the World Bank, Joseph Stiglitz, in 1998.[51] He argued that development required fundamental shifts in cultural values and social relationships, and that it was the task of international agencies to help bring these about.

Development is now seen by Northern governments and international agen-cies as impossible without security and peace. This means that humanitarian action and military intervention (which Duffield calls 'liberal war') can no longer attempt to be neutral. Rather, such interventions seek to restore peace at the local level through imposing certain political and economic structures as part of a system of 'networked global liberal governance'. This system has 'a radical mission to transform societies as a whole, including the attitudes and beliefs of the people within them'.[52] The price of being connected to global economic and political networks is thus the adoption of Northern economic structures, polit-ical institutions and value systems.

It is possible to interpret recent international events in terms of this theory. After 11 September 2001, the US government identified Afghanistan as the source of the global terrorist network responsible for the attack. Rather than any attempt at containment, the USA immediately decided on a radical transforma-tion of Afghani society to deal with the root causes of the problem. The first step was military action to overthrow the Taliban regime (itself largely a result of past US support for anti-Soviet Islamic fundamentalism). It was anticipated that mili-tary action would lead to a mass outflow of refugees, as well as major IDP problems. The UNHCR and other UN agencies were thus included in the planned action, and were provided with substantial special funding. The next step was to help build a new political order in Afghanistan. Again, the UN is heavily involved in this effort. Return of refugees and IDPs to their homes is a central part of efforts at reconstruction. It is too early to say whether this second step will be successful.

It seems that such curtailment of state sovereignty through outside intervention is regarded as legitimate by majority public opinion in the North. Is Afghanistan an extreme, one-off case? Or has it set the pattern for future Northern-imposed social transformations in those states that President Bush considers to be 'the axis of evil'? The Israeli occupation of Palestine in March 2002 indicates that Afghanistan will not remain a unique case. So do US threats against Iraq. However, public opinion in the North is more divided in these cases.

How should we assess trends towards externally-imposed social transformation in countries of the South? Obviously, peace is better than chronic internal war. The regimes concerned are often notorious for corruption, economic rapaciousness, disregard for human rights and oppression of minorities and women. Many of the international civil servants and NGO personnel involved in processes of change are genuinely striving for greater equality, accountability and democracy. Yet is it really possible to believe that Northern powers want to help build political and economic systems that bring about higher living standards and better social conditions for the population of less-developed countries? The whole thrust of neoliberal politics and economics in both North and South for the last twenty-five years has been the removal of social safeguards and the reduction of controls over powerful corporations whose operations drive the inequalities and crises that fuel forced migration. It seems unlikely that the 'new humanitarianism' will do anything to reverse such trends.

Kaldor suggests that current trends in international cooperation could lead to a model of 'cosmopolitan governance' based on universalist humanist principles, in which transnational institutions, nation-states and local governments would work together to end war through 'cosmopolitan law-enforcement.[53] This project is worthy of support, but there are few signs that the world is moving in this direction. It seems much more probable that future humanitarian action and military intervention will follow the Afghanistan model of imposing a political and economic system that fits the interests of the North. This new form of Northern dominance is likely to reinforce resistance movements based on non-western identities and values.[54] Under these circumstances, local wars, terrorism, Northern intervention and forced migration seem destined to continue.

THE 'GLOBAL MIGRATION CRISIS' REVISITED

In August 2001, the Norwegian freighter MV Tampa picked up over 400 asylum seekers (mainly from Afghanistan) from a sinking boat off Northern Australia. The Australian Government refused the captain permission to land the asylum seekers, and the Tampa anchored near the Australian territory of Christmas Island. This was the start of a saga involving international diplomacy, heated public debates in Australia, and feverish political activity. A country previously noted for its openness to refugees rapidly adopted a set of draconian laws designed to exclude asylum seekers. Conditions in remote detention centres at places like Woomera and Port Hedland became so harsh that asylum seekers went on hunger strike or tried to kill themselves. Australia tried to export the asylum seekers to its neighbours New Zealand and Nauru – and was willing to spend vast sums of money to do so. Asylum became the central issue in the November Election, giving victory to Liberal-National Prime Minister Howard. Before the Tampa affair, a Labour victory had been predicted.

The Tampa case was in no way unique. Arrivals of asylum-seeker ships in the USA, Canada and France have evoked similar – if less extreme – responses. Attempts by asylum seekers housed in the Sangatte camp near Calais to board Channel Tunnel trains for the UK are a regular cause for tabloid headlines and angry notes from British ministers to their French counterparts. Entry by sea seems to evoke stronger fears of loss of sovereignty than the far larger numbers of asylum seekers and undocumented immigrants who enter Northern countries legally as 'tourists' and then stay on. Australia, for example, has mandatory detention rules for boat people, but not for over-stayers who come by air. In Italy, entries of Kurdish and Albanian asylum seekers have become a major focus for law and order campaigns by the right-wing coalition government.

To return to my initial question: is there a 'global migration crisis'? It seems misleading to speak of a migration crisis in isolation. Rather international migration is an integral part of relationships between societies. There is currently a crisis in North-South relationships, and migration is one facet of this crisis.

Migration does not present an economic or social crisis for the North. According to UN statistics, international migrants made up 4.5 per cent of the population of developed countries in 1990, compared with 1.6 per cent of the population of developing countries. The immigrant share was 8.6 per cent in North America, 3.2 per cent in Europe and the former USSR and 17.8 per cent in Oceania. Many of these migrants came from other developed countries.[55] But the main reason for the presence of economic migrants is that they are needed to fill jobs in industry and services. Undocumented entry of unskilled workers is seen as a problem, but is actually a result of Northern economic structures and immigration policies. Since there is a high demand for such workers in construction, manufacturing and services, the result is a burgeoning of undocumented work and the informal sector. Today, there is a growing realization that both demographic and economic factors make immigrant labour a necessity for countries of the North. Recent political initiatives, particularly in Germany and the UK, are opening up a debate on such topics.

Nor do refugees and asylum seekers present major economic and social problems for Northern countries. As pointed out above, the numbers are relatively small. Although entries fluctuate, they are currently lower than in the early 1990s. Most refugees stay in the South, and those that do come cannot be seen as a serious strain for rich Northern countries. Indeed, most refugees enter the labour market, and often provide valuable skills.

If there is a migration crisis in the North, it is an ideological and political one. Migration is symbolic of the erosion of nation-state sovereignty in the era of globalization. It is becoming increasingly difficult for states to control their borders, since flows of investment, trade and intellectual property are inextricably linked with movements of people. Elites generally benefit from transborder flows. It is the groups who feel threatened in their security by economic restructuring and social service cuts who generally oppose migration most vocally. The visible presence of migrants in Northern cities symbolizes wider changes in economy, culture and society. Polemics about the 'migration crisis' thus seem to have two sources. One is the manipulation of widespread popular fears about globalization to build right-wing parties and movements. This can be seen as a conservative-nationalist form of anti-migration mobilization.[56] The other source is the trend to 'securitization' of migration issues, which has gained new momentum in the aftermath of the events of 11 September 2001.[57] This can be seen as a neoliberal form of anti-migration mobilization, linked to US polemics against 'rogue states' and fundamentalism.

As for the crisis in the South, it has two main aspects. One is the massive increase in forced migration, due to the 'new wars' and the widespread abuse of human rights. The other aspect is the blocking of free mobility to the North, which forces would-be migrants to rely on informal networks or people-smugglers in their search for a better life.

Freedom of migration already virtually exists for middle-class citizens of Northern countries. It can be seen as a normal part of the relationships between societies with similar economic, social and legal levels. The so-called migration crisis arises because of the vast imbalances between North and South with regard to economic conditions, social well-being and human rights. Border restrictions, however draconian, will do nothing to eliminate unwanted migration flows as long as these fundamental disparities persist.

NOTES

I thank Matthew Gibney of the Refugee Studies Centre, University of Oxford, for comments and suggestions on an earlier draft of this essay.

1   This term forms the title of a book by MIT political scientist Myron Weiner, *The Global Migration Crisis: Challenges to States and Human Rights*, New York: Harper Collins, 1995. The cover shows a dilapidated ship overcrowded with poorly-dressed Asians.

2   Dietrich Thränhardt, 'European Migration from East to West: Present Patterns and Future Directions', *New Community*, 22(2), 1996.

3   Tone Björgo and Rob Witte, eds., *Racist Violence in Europe*, London: Macmillan, 1993.

4   IOM, *World Migration Report 2000*, Geneva: International Organization for Migration, 2000.

5   Hania Zlotnik, 'Trends of International Migration since 1965: What Existing Data Reveal', *International Migration*, 37(1), 1999.

6   None of the South Asian countries, which have some of the world's largest refugee populations, have signed the 1951 Convention.

7   UNHCR, *The State of the World's Refugees: In Search of Solutions*, Oxford: Oxford University Press, 1995; UNHCR, *Global Report 2000: Achievements and Impact*, Geneva: United Nations High Commissioner for Refugees, 2000. The broader category of 'people of concern to the UNHCR' (which includes refugees, some internally displaced persons and some returnees) peaked at 27.4 million in 1995, and was down to 21.1 million in 2000.

8   UNHCR, *The State of the World's Refugees: Fifty Years of Humanitarian Action*, Oxford: Oxford University Press, 2000, p. 315.

9   Table compiled by Margaret Hauser of the Refugee Studies Centre.

10   UNHCR, *The State of the World's Refugees: In Search of Solutions*.

11   UNHCR, *The State of the World's Refugees 1997-98: A Humanitarian Agenda*, Oxford: Oxford University Press for United Nations High Commissioner for Refugees, 1997.

12   Figures for selected OECD countries OECD, *Trends in International Migration*. Paris: OECD, 2001.

13   OECD, *Trends in International Migration*, p. 280.

14   UNHCR, *The State of the World's Refugees 1997-98: A Humanitarian Agenda*, p. 99.

15   Roberta Cohen and Francis M. Deng, *Masses in Flight: The Global Crisis of Internal Displacement*, Washington DC: Brookings Institution Press, 1998.

16   UNHCR, *The State of the World's Refugees 1997-98: A Humanitarian Agenda*, p. 120.

17   Cohen and Deng, *Masses in Flight*, p. 33. IDP figures are very inexact, due to the problems of data collection.

18   In an attempt to improve the plight of IDPs, the UN Secretary General has appointed a Special Representative, Professor Francis Deng. He has issued a set of 'Guiding Principles on Internal Displacement', which summarize the provisions of human rights and humanitarian law as they affect IDPs.

19   Christopher McDowell, ed., *Understanding Impoverishment: The Consequences of Development-Induced Displacement*, Providence/Oxford: Berghahn Books, 1996.

20   Michael M. Cernea and Christopher McDowell, eds., *Risks and Reconstruction: Experiences of Resettlers and Refugees*, Washington DC: World Bank, 2000.

21   Norman Myers and Jennifer Kent, *Environmental Exodus: An Emergent Crisis in the Global Arena*, Washington DC: Climate Institute, 1995; Norman Myers, 'Environmental Refugees', *Population and Environment*, 19(2), 1997.

22   Richard Black, *Refugees, Environment and Development*, London: Longman, 1998.

23   Ann Gallagher, 'Trafficking, Smuggling and Human Rights: Tricks and Treaties', *Forced Migration Review*, 12, 2002, p. 25.

24   UNHCR, *The State of the World's Refugees: Fifty Years of Humanitarian Action*, p. 13.

25 Jewish refugees sought resettlement in Palestine. This led to major conflicts at the time, with Britain (which controlled the territory under an international mandate) opposing Jewish entry. The establishment of the state of Israel and the displacement of many Palestinian Arabs led to the world's longest-standing refugee situation, which cannot be discussed in detail here. See Howard Adelman, 'From Refugees to Forced Migration: The UNHCR and Human Security', *International Migration Review*, 35(1), 2001.

26 Charles B. Keeley, 'The International Refugee Regime(s): The End of the Cold War Matters', *International Migration Review*, 35(1), 2001, p. 307.

27 Aristide R. Zolberg, Astri Suhrke and Sergio Aguayo, *Escape from Violence*, Oxford / New York: Oxford University Press, 1989.

28 B.S. Chimni, 'The Geo-Politics of Refugee Studies: A View from the South', *Journal of Refugee Studies*, 11(4), 1998.

29 Gil Loescher, 'The UNHCR and World Politics: State Interests Versus Institutional Autonomy', *International Migration Review*, 35(1), 2001.

30 UNHCR, *The State of the World's Refugees: Fifty Years of Humanitarian Action*, p. 166.

31 Ibid., p. 158.

32 The following points are partly based on UNHCR, *The State of the World's Refugees: Fifty Years of Humanitarian Action*, pp. 158–183. See also Keeley, 'The International Refugee Regime(s)', pp. 311–13.

33 See Keeley, 'The International Refugee Regime(s)'; and Chimni, 'The Geo-Politics of Refugee Studies'.

34 Chimni, 'The Geo-Politics of Refugee Studies'.

35 David Held, Anthony McGrew, David Goldblatt and Jonathan Perraton, *Global Transformations: Politics, Economics and Culture*, Cambridge: Polity, 1999.

36 Zygmunt Bauman, *Globalization: The Human Consequences*, Cambridge: Polity, 1998, p. 9.

37 Bauman, *Globalization*, p. 74.

38 By the end of the 1990s, as containment measures reduced the number of recognized refugees, the UNHCR's budget was cut to just under $1 billion, leading to major cuts in staffing.

39 Kaldor, *New and Old Wars: Organized Violence in a Global Era*, Cambridge: Polity, 2001, ch. 2.

40 Kaldor, *New and Old Wars*, p. 8.

41 Summerfield, 'Sociocultural Dimensions of War, Conflict and Displacement', in Alastair Ager, ed., *Refugees: Perspectives on the Experience of Forced Migration*, London/New York: Pinter, 1999.

42 Mark Duffield, *Global Governance and the New Wars: The Merging of Development and Security*, London/New York: Zed Books, 2001, p. 79.

43 For a discussion of all cases except Kosovo and East Timor, see Adam Roberts, 'More Refugees, Less Asylum: A Regime in Transformation',

Journal of Refugee Studies, 11(4), 1998.

44   Michael Ignatieff, *Virtual War: Kosovo and Beyond*, London: Chatto and Windus, 2000.

45   At the time of writing, a 'residual refugee population' remains in West Timor, apparently kept there against their will by pro-Indonesian militias. In the case of Kosovo, Kosovar refugees have returned home, but international forces have been unable to prevent the displacement of many Serbs.

46   Roberts, 'More Refugees, Less Asylum', pp. 385-6.

47   Ibid., pp. 386-7; Linda Melvern, *A People Betrayed: The Role of the West in Rwanda's Genocide*, London: Zed Books, 2000.

48   Duffield, *Global Governance and the New Wars*, especially ch. 4.

49   Manuel Castells, *The Rise of the Network Society*, Oxford: Blackwell, 1996.

50   Duffield, *Global Governance and the New Wars*, ch. 3.

51   Joseph E. Stiglitz, *Towards a New Paradigm for Development: Strategies, Policies and Processes*, 1998 Prebisch Lecture, UNCTAD, Geneva, 1998.

52   Duffield, *Global Governance and the New Wars*, p. 258.

53   Kaldor, *New and Old Wars*, pp. 147-52.

54   Manuel Castells, *The Power of Identity*, Oxford: Blackwell, 1997.

55   Zlotnik, 'Trends of International Migration since 1965'. These are the most recent global data. Numbers have increased since, but not dramatically.

56   Aristide R. Zolberg, 'Introduction: Beyond the Crisis', in Aristide R. Zolberg and Peter M. Benda, eds., *Global Migrants, Global Refugees: Problems and Solutions*, New York/Oxford: Berghahn, 2001, provides a valuable discussion of the political interests behind the notion of a migration crisis.

57   A recent development is the emergence of the new field of 'political demography': the study of migration and other demographic issues in relation to their effects on security and political stability. See: Myron Weiner and Sharon S Russell, eds., *Demography and National Security*, New York/Oxford: Berghahn, 2001.

XENOPHOBIA, IDENTITY POLITICS AND EXCLUSIONARY POPULISM IN WESTERN EUROPE

HANS-GEORG BETZ

In the most recent local election in Belgium, the *Vlaams Blok* gained more than 35 per cent of the vote in Antwerp, confirming its position as the largest party in one of Western Europe's most affluent cities. The result posed a fundamental challenge to the established parties, which for several years had pursued a policy of maintaining a cordon sanitaire with regard to the Vlaams Blok, essentially seeking to marginalize the party by treating it as an outcast. The established parties justified their strategy by arguing that the Vlaams Blok was 'an intolerant, xenophobic and racist party', which sought to promote hatred toward foreigners living in Belgium.[1] Given their growing support at the polls, the leaders of the Vlaams Blok grew increasingly frustrated with the strategy of the established parties to keep it out of power and started a campaign designed to counter the charges of racism. This in itself was hardly surprising. What is interesting is how they tried to justify their position. In a brochure entitled 'Prejudices' the party rejected the notion that it was racist. Defining racism as 'hatred of or disdain for another people or the bad treatment of somebody because of his race or ethnic origin', the party asserted that these feelings were 'completely alien' to them. Given the fact that the Vlaams Blok fought for 'the right of the Flemings to be themselves' why would the party 'refuse this right to others?'

Although acknowledging that they were nationalists, the party argued this meant that they regarded the 'world in its diversity (*meervoud*)' and that it regarded diversity as something that enriched the world. Nationalism, and particularly Flemish nationalism, however, should not be confused or equated with racism. Nationalism merely meant preferring one's own people to others. This

was as natural as 'the preference for the own family over outsiders, the preference for friends over people who one did not know personally, the preference
for one's own culture over foreign cultures'.[2] Filip Dewinter, the charismatic
leader of the Vlaams Blok, summarized his party's position, maintaining that it
only wanted 'to preserve our identity and our culture. After all, racism means a
belief that on the basis of racial features a group of people is superior or inferior
to another. This isn't what we believe; everyone is equal but not the same'.[3]

The Vlaams Blok is one of the most successful examples of a new type of
right-wing populist party, which during the 1990s emerged as one of the most
significant new political forces in Western Europe and other liberal capitalist
democracies.[4] Initially dismissed as a fleeting phenomenon, which would soon
fade away, the radical right has managed to establish itself firmly as a serious
contender for votes and, increasingly, for political offices (e.g., in Austria and
Italy).[5] The growing acceptance of radical right-wing parties as serious and legitimate contenders for political power raises important questions about the nature
and objectives of these parties. In recent years, there has been a great deal of
scholarship devoted to explaining their rise and electoral success.[6] Much of this
scholarship has focused on the search for structural factors and developments that
might help explain the remarkable surge in popular support for the radical right
in the 1990s. At the same time, there has been relatively little serious comparative analysis of the political doctrines espoused by these parties, their ideological
foundations and ideological justification.[7]

There are good reasons for the temptation to ignore or at least neglect the
question of ideology and doctrine when analyzing the contemporary radical
right. For one, these parties themselves, unlike earlier movements on the far
right, have generally made little effort to ground their political propositions and
demands in a larger ideological framework. Successful parties pursue a 'postmodern' populist strategy that consciously appeals to widespread anxieties,
prejudices, and resentments, and exploits them for political gain. Politically, the
radical right has generally derived legitimacy for its ideas directly from voter
sentiments and public opinion, e.g., on immigrants, foreigners, and refugees,
rather than a well-defined body of ideas. Concomitantly, the politics of the
contemporary radical right has often been seen as primarily issue-driven and
opportunistic. There has been a tendency to define it in terms of the major issue
associated with it – i.e. as anti-immigrant and/or anti-immigration parties.[8]

However, a closer look at the programmatic propositions, statements, and
utterances of contemporary right-wing radical parties and their leading proponents challenges this view. It suggests, as Roger Eatwell has argued, that the
radical right does have a 'common core doctrine', a distinct ideological platform,
which distinguishes it from other political parties and movements in contemporary liberal capitalist democracies.[9] The core of this ideological platform has
variously been described as 'reactionary tribalism', 'ethnocratic liberalism',
'holistic nationalism', 'exclusionary welfarism', or 'exclusionary populism'.[10] Its
main characteristic is a restrictive notion of citizenship, which holds that genuine

democracy is based on a culturally, if not ethnically, homogeneous community; that only long-standing citizens count as full members of civil society; and that society's benefits should be restricted to those members of society who, either as citizens or taxpayers, have made a substantial contribution to society.[11] Radical right-wing political marketing has deftly reduced the spirit of this doctrine to a single slogan – 'Our own people first' – and a single demand – 'national preference' – which, taken together, have had considerable electoral appeal.

In recent years, the radical right has increasingly gone beyond exclusionary populism to adopt a new form of cultural nativism, which, rather than promoting traditional right-wing extremist notions of ethnic and ethnocultural superiority, aims at the protection of the indigenous culture, customs and way of life. In the process, the radical right has increasingly shifted its focus to questions of national and cultural identity, and as a result their politics has become identity politics. Much of its language and most of its concepts are directly derived from the ethnopluralist conceptions developed by the French *nouvelle droite* in the late 1970s, which make up what Pierre-André Taguieff has called 'differentialist racism' or what might be more appropriately be referred to as differentialist nativism (where nativism stands for 'the xenophobic shadow of indigeneity', which 'values wholeness and separation, pure blood and autochthonous land').[12] Differentialist nativism is informed by the idea that political struggle in the contemporary world has to aim above all 'to preserve the diversity of the world', as Alain de Benoist, the intellectual leader of the *nouvelle droite*, once put it.[13] His position represented a significant identitarian and communitarian ideological turn on the far right, whose genealogy goes back to the romantic critique of modernity and the associated attempts to defend *Gemeinschaft* in the face of increasing social differentiation. The central characteristic of the resulting identitarian-communitarian position is an 'essentialist cultural justification for exclusionary policies', which the *nouvelle droite* adopted from Carl Schmitt.[14]

This is not to suggest that the radical right's electoral appeal can be narrowly reduced to its pronounced and vocal stance on immigration, multiculturalism, and other issues associated with the presence of foreigners in Western Europe. As has been repeatedly pointed out, the radical right's success in the 1990s was to a large extent also the result of widespread popular disaffection and disenchantment with the established political parties and elites, growing alienation from the political process and from the formal workings of liberal democracy in general. Radical right-wing parties have derived much of their electoral appeal from their ability to market themselves as the advocates of the common people, as spokespersons of the unarticulated opinions and sentiments of large parts of the population, who dared to say out loud what the 'silent majority' only dared to think, and who, to quote a memorable phrase coined by Jean-Marie Le Pen, in this way managed to 'return the word to the people' (*rendre la parole au peuple*).[15]

Whereas comparative studies of radical right parties have paid considerable attention to these aspects of their appeal, their adoption of a differentialist doctrine has largely gone unnoticed. Yet ideology has become increasingly important on the populist right. Starting from the claim that Europe's identity and cultural diversity are fundamentally threatened, the radical right promotes itself as the defender of difference and the fundamental right to cultural identity and *Heimat*. With this position the contemporary radical right has become a crucial actor in what Slavoj Zizek has identified as a central line of conflict in today's politics, between 'liberal democratic universalism' and a 'new "organic" populism-communitarianism'.[16] Seen from the perspective of the radical right, this political conflict pits the defenders of difference, diversity, particularity, and identity against the promoters of universalism, multiculturalism, and deracination, identified as an internationalized 'New Class' based in the multinational companies, the media, international organizations, and national administrations.[17]

The remainder of this essay explores to what degree differentialist and identitarian positions inform the political discourse of contemporary right-wing radical parties in Western Europe on issues central to the right-wing populist agenda. The analysis starts out with a brief discussion of the adoption and incorporation of differentialist racism in the *Front National*, for many years Western Europe's most important and most radical right-wing populist party. The focus of the rest of the analysis, however, is on what Kitschelt and others have defined as the 'milder', more moderate, and more pragmatist versions of the contemporary populist right, such as the Danish People's Party, the Italian Northern League, and the Swiss People's Party.[18] The point is to demonstrate that even these parties have begun to use differentialist and identitarian images and language to justify their political demands. A related, second point is to explore whether and to what degree differentialist ideology has been modified after getting integrated into populist right-wing discourse.

DEFENDING NATIONAL AND CULTURAL IDENTITY

The first party to adopt the doctrine of differentialist racism was Jean-Marie Le Pen's *Front National*. The party was quick to maintain that its French-nationalist position should not be construed as reflecting 'disdain for other peoples'. On the contrary, the goal was to protect French identity and 'to defend the fundamental values of our civilization'.[19] For this, the party proposed to accord absolute priority to a 'cultural politics designed to defend our roots' and reverse the process of deracination.[20] As early as 1988, Le Pen warned that the peoples of Europe were faced with a real danger of extinction. 'And we think that everything has to be done to try to save them'.[21] At the same time, the *Front National* addressed the question of racism, which it defined as a 'doctrine that denies the right of the peoples to be themselves', and which it declared to be among the main threats to the survival of the French people and the peoples of Europe in general.[22]

The *Front National* made it a point to charge the established political parties and the whole political class with having actively promoted the emergence and establishment of a 'multiracial and multicultural society' in France.[23] This had been 'justified in the name of abstract, universal human rights and based on a formalistic, juridical definition of French nationality in place of the bond of real, living community formed by shared historical legacies and shared memory of cae national past'.[24] Multiculturalism was part of a larger ideology, which the *Front National* called '*mondialisme*'. This was a new utopian ideology, which sought to destroy nations, mix peoples and cultures, do away with borders in an effort to erase all differences and, finally, destroy any sense of identity.[25]

For the *Front National*, multiculturalism was but an admission of the fact that the vast majority of the new immigrants entering France during the past decades could not be integrated into French society. As a major *Front National* exposition on the danger of immigration put it, France was a European nation whose population had been stable for more than two thousand years and whose culture derived 'from the three great European cultures – Celtic, Germanic, and Greco-Latin – and which was shaped by Roman Christianity'. In the past, immigrants coming to France had been able to assimilate because they had largely come from other European countries. By contrast, most new immigrants came from the Maghreb region, Turkey, South Asia, and sub-Saharan Africa and tended to form 'ethnic quarters and ghetto cities' – symptoms of a fundamental failure of integration, which would bring about disastrous consequences. By allowing entrance to people whose cultural background was completely different from that of the French, France risked importing 'the ethnic or religious conflicts of the rest of the world'.[26]

In response, the *Front National* advanced a whole catalogue of demands and 'concrete measures' designed not only to slow down the inflow of immigrants and eventually stop it altogether, but also to reverse the evolution of a multicultural society by 'repatriating' those immigrants the *Front National* deemed unable (or unwilling) to assimilate (*inassimilable*).[27] At the same time, the *Front National* promoted a policy of 'national preference'. The intent was to protect the 'fiscal and the national integrity of the welfare state' through a highly exclusionary immigration policy.[28]

Starting in the late 1990s, the party couched its demands increasingly in terms of a comprehensive assault on *mondialisme*, characterized as a 'monstrous totalitarian utopia, which exploited the economic phenomenon of the globalization of information and exchange' in order to 'attain a complete domination of the planet' via the destruction of the nations and their identity.[29] The party's strategy was to reconfigure political conflict in terms of a new cleavage between nationalism and *mondialisme* instead of the earlier dichotomy of rootedness versus *deracinement*.[30] Ideologically, the goal was to contextualize differentialist racism by making it part of a larger political strategy of comprehensive resistance to globalization, both within France and abroad.[31] In its own words, the party saw 'itself as the stronghold and bastion of national identity against cosmopolitan projects aimed at mixing peoples and cultures'.[32]

With this strategy, Le Pen not only re-emerged as a credible candidate for the 2002 presidential election, but even made it to the second round, having beaten Prime Minister Jospin in the first. The *Front National* thus recuperated much of the support the party had lost after the acrimonious split in 1998, which led to the establishment of the rival *Movement National Républicain* under Bruno Mégret. Despite the temporary turmoil in the French radical right, parts of the European populist right have continued to greatly admire Le Pen, with some going so far as to consciously model themselves after the *Front National*. This was most obviously the case with parties like the *Vlaams Blok* and the German *Republikaner*, which adopted much of *Front National* rhetoric and many of its demands and propositions.[33] But in recent years, elements of the *Front National*'s differentialist ideology have also been adopted by right-wing populist parties, which in the past had paid only minor attention to questions of immigration and multiculturalism.[34] In the process, these parties modified the ethnopluralist appeal to a significant degree, away from the original focus on the protection and preservation of national cultural identity and toward a growing concern with questions of European identity in the face of new socio-economic and socio-cultural challenges associated with globalization.

FROM NATIONAL IDENTITY TO EUROPEAN CIVILIZATION

In 1998, the Zurich branch of the *Schweizer Volkspartei* (Swiss People's Party, SVP), which in the 1990s made remarkable electoral gains in local and national elections, issued a position paper on immigration. In this paper, the party charged 'certain immigrant groups' with 'cultural intolerance', which made 'living together with them on a multicultural basis simply unthinkable'. The party was not loath to spell out precisely which groups it meant:

> Islam is increasingly becoming the main obstacle to integration. And yet, the proportion of immigrants from Islamic countries is continuously on the rise. In Europe, we fought for centuries for liberal and democratic values, for the separation of state and church, and gender equality. It is a particular irony of history that the same left-wing and liberal forces, who led this fight, are today the most eager to advocate generous immigration policies – policies that threaten the basic occidental values.[35]

The SVP is hardly an extremist party. Until the 1990s, it was the smallest of Switzerland's four major parties, a national-conservative party representing rural interests in the German-speaking parts of Switzerland. The party's fortunes changed dramatically with the rise to dominance of Christoph Blocher, a wealthy and influential businessman, in the party's Zurich branch. Under the charismatic Blocher, the SVP adopted a populist stance and strategy, which proved highly successful.[36] Within only a few years, the party more than doubled its support and became Switzerland's largest party. Blocher's major themes focused on the defense of Switzerland's political and cultural idiosyncrasies, particularly against the challenge of the process of European integration, as well as Switzerland's reputation as a neutral country, which had successfully withstood Nazi Germany during the Second World War against growing criticism from abroad.

In the process, the SVP tried to establish itself as the only true defender of Switzerland's values and cultural identity against the rise of multiculturalism promoted by the political Left and in response to the growing influx of foreigners and especially refugees. For the SVP, multiculturalism was a dangerous experiment that threatened to bring about nothing less than 'the demise of culture'.[37] Not surprisingly, the SVP in the canton Zurich, the city with the largest number of foreign residents in Switzerland, made the fight against multiculturalism the centre of its position on the future of immigration. Arguing that multiculturalism threatened Swiss culture with destruction while provoking hostility toward foreigners, the Zurich SPV demanded that foreigners intent on staying integrate themselves completely and unconditionally into Swiss society. The Zurich party's position was later adopted, albeit in somewhat modified form, by the SVP as the basis of its position on integration.[38]

The Zurich party's position on Islam has to be seen in this context. The argument was that Muslims were both incapable and unwilling to integrate themselves into Swiss society, i.e., to respect its laws, customs, and habits. At the same time, the party charged the political establishment with promoting a false culture of tolerance and understanding, which contributed to the destruction of Swiss culture. These latent fears are reflected in the title of a review of a book on Islam by the German orientalist Hans-Peter Raddatz, which appeared in *Schweizerzeit*, a weekly edited by the prominent SVP national councillor, Ulrich Schlüer: 'Islam in liberal Europe: Christian-Occidental Culture before its Self-Liquidation?'[39] Raddatz was once again given an opportunity to express his views on Islam in *Schweizerzeit* a few weeks after the attacks against the World Trade Center and the Pentagon. In the article, he charged the political and intellectual class with having created a type of 'dialogue fetishism', which 'prohibited under the threat of severe punishment' any kind of scepticism toward Islam, even if historically justified. Its proponents insisted that there was a difference between Islam and fundamentalism, which was largely the result of ignorance and 'fundamental incompetence'. Under the circumstances, the attacks against the United States on September 11 should hardly have come as a surprise.[40]

The case of the SVP offers a clear demonstration of the extent to which the preservation of European cultural identity, reflected in the strict rejection of multiculturalism and particularly Islam, has become central to differentialist nativism in contemporary Western Europe. To be sure, attacks against Islam had always been a staple of right-wing populist rhetoric. Already in the late 1980s, Mogens Glistrup, the leader of the Danish Progress Party, created quite a stir with his demand to make Denmark a 'Muslim Free Zone'. At about the same time, Carl Hagen, the leader of the Norwegian Progress Party sought publicity for his party by citing a letter sent to him, 'which later was shown to be a fake – saying that Norway was on the way to becoming a Muslim state unless the borders were closed'.[41] In Belgium and Germany, too, the radical right warned that the growing number of Muslim immigrants threatened to displace the native population. These early attempts to mobilize resentment against Muslim residents were rather sporadic and largely designed to take advantage of growing concern about the demographic development of Western Europe.

In recent years, however, the campaign against Islam has taken on a new dimension. In the context of differentialist nativism, Islam serves at least two purposes. For one, Islam generally serves as 'the other', against which the radical right constructs its notion of Western civilization and Western values. Second, given the all-encompassing, totalizing claim of Islamic fundamentalism, Islam fits perfectly well into the radical right's postmodern politics of difference. Islamophobia has therefore increasingly become a constituent element of radical right-wing populist ideology, both before and after September 11.

Again it has been some of the more moderate parties, such as the Danish People's Party (DPP) and the *Lega Nord* (LN), which have played a prominent role in propagating these ideas. A few months before the most recent national elections in Denmark, from which the DPP emerged as the third largest party, the party issued a 226-page pamphlet with lots of photos entitled *Denmark's Future: Your Country – Your Choice...*, solely dedicated to the question of foreigners and immigration in Denmark. Even before the election campaign, the DPP had made Islam the central issue of its political strategy. Among other things, the party resolutely objected to the building of mosques and the establishment of Muslim cemeteries and demanded that all members of Muslim families be deported if one member had committed a criminal offence. At the same time it started a billboard campaign asking whether one had to be a Muslim to get social housing in Denmark and placed a one-page ad in a national newspaper publishing the names of recent naturalized citizens, a majority of whom were from Muslim countries.

Although the party's pamphlet on immigration covered a range of issues and questions, a large number of the photos depicted Muslims, the vast majority of whom were dressed in traditional garb. The strategy clearly was to equate Islam with fundamentalism. This impression was supported by the way the party depicted Islam in the chapters devoted to it. The argument was that Islam was not a religion but a 'political program', which, because it left no scope for individual decisions, was fundamentally incompatible with democracy. Referring to the discrimination and oppression of women in Muslim countries, the party described Islam as promoting 'medieval practices', which were incompatible with a modern society. Finally, the pamphlet emphasized that Denmark was 'a Christian country' reflecting Christian values as they had evolved through history, such as tolerance, mutual understanding, and respect. Given its very nature, the 'Muslim way of life' is 'not compatible with the Danish Christian mentality'.[42]

Central to the DPP's line of argument is the notion of a fundamental cultural incompatibility between Islam and Danish values and the Danish way of life. There is no chance to integrate Muslim immigrants into Danish society, since by their very appearance the immigrants indicate that they do not want to adapt to the Danish way of life. Therefore, if Danes want to remain masters of their own country, they have no other choice than to expel all Muslim immigrants from Denmark and send them back to their countries of origin.[43]

Given the DPP's electoral success, this line of argument is likely to play an increasingly important role in radical right-wing populist strategy. Ideologically, it marks a significant departure from the simplistic xenophobia of the early years of right-wing mobilization. At the same time, as an examination of the *Lega Nord*'s ideological development in recent years shows, it is only a point of departure toward a comprehensive right-wing differentialist ideology.

Unlike the DPP, the *Lega Nord* experienced a substantial decline in electoral support in the past few years. A part of the current coalition government, it has largely come to depend on Berlusconi. At the same time, the party has increasingly radicalized its rhetoric, in the process adopting the language of differentialist nativism in order to launch a frontal assault on multiculturalism and globalization, which is distinct because of its internal consistency and comprehensiveness.

The party's differentialist turn started in the late 1990s. It was affirmed by the party's leader, Umberto Bossi, in 2000. According to Bossi, the party stood for 'the diversity of the peoples, starting from our own peoples, and from their right for freedom'.[44] Already two years earlier, a section of the party had produced a position paper on immigration, 'identity and multiracial society', which was later diffused via the party's web site (www.leganord.org). The authors claimed the 'sacrosanct right of our people to maintain and defend their ethnocultural and religious identity' and the right 'not to be reduced to a minority in their own home'.[45] For the authors, immigration and multiculturalism were part of a larger process of globalization (*mondialismo*) designed 'to destroy the peoples' in order to construct an 'Anglophone and totalitarian Global Village on the ruins of the peoples'.[46] This was not an anonymous development, but one propagated by two forces – the Americans and the Muslims, who used it to construct new global empires. Immigration threatened to transform the European countries into colonies by means of what the authors called 'a form of demographic imperialism' designed to turn 'our nations demographically, culturally, and politically into an appendix of countries that do not belong to the European continent'.[47] These trends could only be reversed if the people reaffirmed and defended their cultural identity and 'reappropriated' their own territory, presumably under the leadership of the *Lega Nord*, whose 'differentialist vision of the world' offered the most effective weapon against mondialismo and American and Muslim imperialism.[48]

In the next few years, Bossi himself not only adopted the pamphlet's differentialist vision but also its characterization of *mondialismo* as an American instrument to gain global hegemony. Starting in early 1999, Bossi warned on numerous occasions that the 'invasion' from outside Western Europe was intricately linked to the 'American ideology of *mondialismo*', an ideology 'which wants to impose on all of Europe a "multiracial society" in order to weaken the Old Continent and subordinate it even more to the American superpower'. Given the growing pressures from globalization, the *Lega* had to shift its strategic objective and concentrate on finding ways to get the people 'to revolt against this new authoritarian ideology, which seeks to annihilate all Europeans'.[49]

In this context it was hardly surprising that *Lega* increasingly focused on Islam.

Bossi had written as early as 1993 that 'Islam on the one side, and colonization by America on the other put the great European culture in danger .... (T)he battle for the cultural identity of the continent coincides today with the battle for the protection of the culture of the little people, ambushed by massification and by ideological or religious fanaticism'.[50] In the late 1990s, the *Lega*'s position on Islam turned into a comprehensive *Kulturkampf* inspired by Huntington's notion of the clash of civilizations.[51] Thus in a special issue in 1999 on Islam of the *Lega* journal, *Quaderni padani*, Islam was characterized as one of the 'three worst illnesses of history' (together with Roman imperialism and communism) – three 'great plagues', held together by 'the glue of *mondialismo*, the enemy of any difference (like communism), any autonomy (like Rome), any tolerance (like Islam) and any aspiration toward freedom (like all three)'.[52]

In the process, the *Lega* developed a comprehensive conspiracy theory built around an increasingly strident anti-Americanism. Thus the party maintained the Italians had a choice between a 'mondialist American multiracial society' and a 'Padanian (or Italian) and European society based on its peoples'. America meant an individualistic-type capitalism without guaranteed pensions and minimal health care, which would destroy the small enterprises and lead to mass unemployment while allowing America to regain its economic position which it had lost with the creation of the European Union in 1993.[53]

The *Lega*'s uncompromising anti-Americanism was once again evident in the party's vehement objection to NATO's campaign against Yugoslavia over the question of Kosovo. As far as the party was concerned, the war had nothing to do with humanitarian aims but was an American attempt to gain a foothold in the Balkans 'in order to prevent what Washington fears most, namely a commercial and geopolitical union between us Europeans and the Russian area'.[54] In Bossi's view, the conflict in Kosovo was a conflict between

> two different religious identities, on the one hand the Albanian immigrants – and, for future memory, I underline immigrants – who are Muslims and who are asking for the independence of Kosovo from Serbia and its annexation to their motherland, Albania; and on the other the Serbs who are Christians and for whom Kosovo represents a mythical place, the very root of their politics and history.

And, referring to the United States, Bossi continued that the Americans, 'men who only value money' and who want nothing more than to destroy all peoples, are fundamentally opposed to the values which the Serbs – 'a great people that keeps its word, solid and serious' as compared to the 'easy-going' and 'superficial Americans' – want to preserve, values such as family, children, and true beliefs.

In the course of the NATO intervention, the *Lega* adopted the ideas of an obscure French expert on Islam, Alexandre del Valle. Del Valle charged that the NATO war against Yugoslavia was essentially designed by the United States 'to compromise the construction of an independent and strong Europe' in order to prevent it from challenging the United States economically. US foreign policy aimed at bringing about a 'clash of civilizations' pitting the Europeans against the Muslim world.[55] At the same time, Islam itself presented a fundamental threat, hanging like a '"Damocles sword" over Europe'.[56] The *Lega*'s motives for opposing the NATO intervention in Kosovo were obvious: for Bossi and many in his party, in Kosovo, the Albanian minority had gradually reduced the Serb majority to a minority and pushed it out of the province, largely on a demographic basis. Kosovo thus was a prime illustration of what might happen if Europe failed to halt the 'Islamic invasion'.[57]

In line with these arguments, the *Lega*, in the late 1990s, started to promote itself with growing urgency as the defender of Western values, of a Christian Europe, and of the Catholic faith against the 'new colonialism' under the banner of Islam.[58] With this strategy, the *Lega* gained new visibility, especially after it had started to embark on a crusade against the construction of mosques in northern Italy. The most spectacular instance was a demonstration against the planned construction of a mosque in the town of Lodi in late 2000, which turned into a major anti-Islamic manifestation with slogans such as 'Europe is Christian and must remain so', and 'the shadow of the minaret will never darken our campanile'.[59] For the *Lega*, the aim was simple: to stop the 'Islamic invasion'. In the words of one of the *Lega* Nord's leaders, Islam was 'an intolerant religion'. The party was ready to call for 'new crusades in order to defend our culture, our identity, and our future'.[60]

By the time the *Lega* entered the second Berlusconi government, the party had made the question of illegal immigration and the defense of northern Italian cultural and religious identity the cornerstone of its political strategy. In the process, its position grew ever more extremist – a development recognized and applauded by Italy's re-emerging intellectual extreme right. Circles like *Rinascita* considered the *Lega* its most important ally in the campaign against 'the illegal immigrants invading our lands', a campaign provoked by 'the war against all men and all peoples waged by the City and Wall Street, by *mondialismo* and globalization, by the culture of homogenization'.[61]

SEPTEMBER 11

For the European populist right, the terror attacks of September 11 against the United States represented a strong vindication of their position on Islam. Bruno Mégret said as much when he charged that the attacks reflected the 'confrontation between two worlds, a genuine clash of civilizations', which pitted 'European and Christian civilization against the Arab-Muslim civilization'.[62] When the Americans had played the 'Arab and Muslim card in order to counter, contain and weaken Europe', they had played with fire. Now they reaped what they had sown.[63] The *Vlaams Blok* echoed the DPP's position that Islam represented a 'political-religious ideology, which with regard to essential aspects is incompatible with our European values'. The party proposed a list of measures both to control the activities of Islamic organizations in Belgium and to prevent the influx of new arrivals from Muslim countries.[64] Jean-Marie Le Pen, although more cautious in his references to Islam (in order not to antagonize Harki voters and their descendents), was also quick to evoke the memories of what he considered active American support for the 'reimplantation of Islam on the Balkans' by supporting the Bosnians and Albanians against the Serbs.[65] Undoubtedly, both men interpreted the events of September 11 as a historical turn, which presented an opportunity to revive their political fortunes. And in fact, by the end of October 2001, a survey by the renowned SOFRES institute showed a significant rise in support for Jean-Marie Le Pen's presidential candidacy.[66] As a result, by early 2002, Le Pen had once again become a serious political challenge commanding a steady 10 per cent support in opinion polls.

The *Lega Nord* saw in the attacks a declaration of war on the West on the part of a militant Islam, which it called the latest form of totalitarianism.[67] In the word's of del Valle, from an interview with *La Padania*, September 11 represented the beginning of the 'great war of the twenty-first century between post-colonial Islam and the rest of the non-Muslim world'. For Islam, the objective was to convert the whole world to Islam, to transform the whole world into one 'Islamic nation'. In order to reach this objective, any means was allowed, including violence and (holy) war, which Islam considered 'a collective duty'. And del Valle warned that, at least at the moment, Europe, which had allowed Islamic fundamentalists to settle in Europe without asking them to integrate into society, was too weak to face 'Islamic totalitarianism'.[68]

In order to overcome this weakness and to combat the new totalitarian threat to Europe, the *Lega* proposed both immediate and long-term measures. Within days of the attacks, leading representatives of the party called for strict controls of mosques and Islamic centres and even the closing of Italy's borders to foreigners from Islamic countries. Others proposed that Italy give preference to foreigners of Catholic faith, thus adopting an idea launched by Cardinal Biffi of Bolgona in late 2001, which at the time had caused a major uproar in the country.[69] At the same time, the *Lega* reaffirmed its position that only the recollection and reaffirmation of traditional Christian values would enable Europe to overcome the spiritual damage caused by Europe's adoption of globalization.[70]

DIFFERENTIALIST NATIVISM IN THE NEW EUROPE

This essay has tried to show that the contemporary Western European populist radical right has developed a comprehensive alternative ideology grounded in the notion of cultural difference. Among the core elements of this ideology are a strident Islamophobia and an increasingly pronounced hostility toward globalization. In the process, the populist right has sought to position and propagate itself as a resistance movement defending a conception of European identity that it sees as fundamentally threatened.

The populist right's challenge derives in large part from the fact that this ideology feeds directly into the 'politics of recognition', which Nancy Fraser has identified as the major area of political contestation in advanced liberal democracies. In her view, 'claims for recognition drive many of the world's most intense social conflicts – from battles around multiculturalism to struggles over gender and sexuality, from campaigns for national sovereignty and subnational autonomy to newly energized movements for international human rights. Theses struggles are heterogeneous, to be sure; they run the gamut from the patently emancipatory to the downright reprehensible'. Nevertheless, there is a 'widespread recourse to a common grammar', which, in Fraser's opinion, suggests 'an epochal shift in the political winds'.[71]

Although clearly on the reprehensible side, the claims advanced by the contemporary populist right are very much part of this new political configuration and derive their legitimacy, at least in part, from its common grammar. At the same time, the appeal of these claims has to be seen in the context of 'the culturally fragmenting, depoliticizing impacts of neoliberalism and postmodernization', and, one might add, globalization.[72] In significant ways, the populist right advances today one of the most trenchant critiques of these developments while problematizing their impact on society and the individual. Today it is more often than not the populist right (for example, in Denmark and Norway) which comes out most forcefully in defending the weakest and least well-off in society.[73]

This suggests that the success of the populist right's exclusionary appeal should also be seen in the larger context of the traditional left's retreat from central positions of the postwar social democratic agenda. As Douglas Holmes has forcefully argued, it was the 'unforeseen retreat of this wide ranging societal agenda' which 'opened the way for a tortuous resurgence of integralist politics and its tainted discrimination of human difference'.[74] In fact, during the past several years, the populist right has appropriated and, in the process, radically refashioned and redefined the two major projects associated with the left: on the one hand, the traditional left's focus on social justice and redistribution; on the other hand, the postmodern left's concern with identity and recognition.

The result is a coherent and internally consistent programmatic position of what one might characterize as a combination of differentialist nativism and comprehensive protectionism, which is arguably one of the main factors behind the populist right's success. It seeks to exploit the anxieties and feelings of insecurity provoked by the socio-economic turmoil and ruptures associated with globalization and neoliberalism as well as the widespread *ressentiments* in response to the socio-cultural transformation of Western European societies caused by the presence of a growing resident alien population. A second, equally important factor is the populist right's mobilization of resentment against political and intellectual elites, consciously designed to appeal to latent sentiments of political disenchantment, frustration and cynicism on the part of a large, and arguably growing, number of West European voters.

This suggests that the political success of the populist right in Western Europe is primarily a left-wing problem. As long as the left continues to fail to advance a convincing alternative vision to the prevailing neoliberal model while at the same time seeking to outdo the populist right on the question of immigration (as did, most infamously, the Danish Social Democrats), it will neither regain the constituencies that have defected to the radical right nor be in a position to reverse the resulting strategic gains of the political right. Given the disarray on the political left in Austria, Denmark and Italy, to name only the most prominent cases, the chances for a genuine revival of the left appear slim for the moment, which leaves the field wide open for the exclusionary nativist politics of the postmodern populist right.

NOTES

1   Nova Civitas, 'Het Cordon Sanitaire: een vloek of een zegen voor de democratie?', http://www.ping.be/novacivitas/cordonsanitaire.html.

2   Vlaams Blok, 'Vooroordelen', http://www.vlaams-blok.be/watzijnwe/vooroordelen.html.

3   'Our Nationality', BBC 2, May 13, 2001, http://news.bbc.co.uk/hi/english/static/audio_video/programmes/correspondent/transcripts/746195.txt.

4   For a discussion of why these parties should be categorized as right-wing populist rather than extreme right or neofascist see Hans-Georg Betz, 'Introduction', in Hans-Georg Betz and Stefan Immerfall, eds., *The New Politics of the Right*, New York: St. Martin's Press, 1998, pp. 2-6.

5   See Hans-Georg Betz, 'Exclusionary Populism in Austria, Italy, and Switzerland', *International Journal*, vol. 56, no. 3, 2001.

6   See, for example, Herbert Kitschelt, *The Radical Right in Western Europe*, Ann Arbor: University of Michigan Press, 1995.

7   Notable exceptions are the comparative work of Cas Mudde and Marc Swyngedouw. See, for example, Cas Mudde, *The Ideology of the Extreme Right*, Manchester: Manchester University Press, 2000; Marc Swyngedouw and Gilles Ivaldi, 'The Extreme Right Utopia in Belgium and France', *West European Politics*, vol. 24, no. 3, July 2001.

8   See, for example, Meindert Fennema, 'Some Conceptual Issues and Problems in the Comparisons of Anti-immigrant Parties in Western Europe', *Party Politics*, vol. 4, no. 4, 1997; Wouter van der Brug, Meindert Fennema and Jean Tillie, 'Anti-immigrant Parties in Europe: Ideological or Protest Vote?', *European Journal of Political Research*, vol. 37, no. 1, 2000; Rachel K. Gibson, 'Anti-Immigrant Parties: The Roots of Their Success', *International Issues*, vol. 38, no. 2, 1995.

9   Roger Eatwell, 'The Rebirth of the `Extreme Right' in Western Europe?', *Parliamentary Affairs*, vol. 53, no. 2000, p. 412.

10   Robert J. Antonio, 'After Postmodernism: Reactionary Tribalism', *American Journal of Sociology*, vol. 106, no. 2, 2000; Roger Griffin, 'Interregnum or Endgame? Radical Right Thought in the 'Post-fascist' Era', *Journal of Political Ideologies*, vol. 5, no. 2, 2000; Eastwell, 'The Rebirth', p. 413; Douglas Holmes, *Integral Europe: Fast-Capitalism,*

Multiculturalism, Neofascism, Princeton: Princeton University Press, 2000, pp. 121-124; Betz, 'Exclusionary Populism'.

11   Paul Hainsworth, 'Introduction: The Extreme Right', in Paul Hainsworth, ed., *The Politics of the Extreme Right*, London/New York: Pinter, 2000, p. 10.

12   Pierre-André Taguieff, 'From Race to Culture: The New Right's View of European Identity', *Telos*, no. 98-99, 1994, p. 101. The definition of nativism is from James Clifford, 'Indigenous Articulations', *The Contemporary Pacific*, vol. 13, Fall 2001, p. 483.

13   Alain de Benoist quoted in Taguieff, p. 103.

14   Antonio, 'After Postmodernism', p. 58, n. 18.

15   Pierre-André Taguieff, 'La doctrine du national-populisme en France, ' *Études*, no. 364, January 1986, p. 29.

16   Slavoj Zizek, 'The Spectre of Ideology', in Slavoj Zizek, ed., *Mapping Ideology*, London/New York: Verso, 1994, p. 3.

17   See the title of point 5 of the *Manifeste de la Nouvelle Droite*, 'Contre la Nouvelle Classe, pour l'autonomie à partir de la base'.

18   Kitschelt, *The Radical Right in Western Europe*. The *Lega Nord* is often not even considered to belong to the right-wing radical party family. The second edition of the Hainsworth volume has a chapter on the *Movimento Sociale Italiano / Alleanza Nazionale* (MSI/AN), but not on the *Lega Nord*. See Hainsworth, ed., *Politics of the Extreme Right*.

19   The quotations are from Le Pen's latest personal website created to promote his candidacy for the presidential elections 2002: http://www.lepen.tv.

20   Front National, *300 mesures pour la renaissance de la France*, Paris: Editions nationales, 1993, p. 23.

21   Jean-Marie Le Pen, *Passeport pour la Victoire*, Paris, 1988, p. 39.

22   Le Pen, *Passeport*, p. 96.

23   The term 'multiracial and multicultural society' can be found in Jean-Yves Le Gallou and Philippe Olivier, *Immigration: Le Front national fait le point*, Paris: Éditions nationals, 1992, p, 22.

24   Christopher Flood, 'The Cultural Struggle of the Extreme Right and the Case of Terre et Peuple', *Contemporary French Civilization*, vol. 24, no.2, 2000, p. 246.

25   Front National, *300 mesures*, pp. 15-16.

26   Gallou and Olivier, *Immigration*, pp. 19-22.

27   See, for example, 'Immigration: 50 mesures concretes', leaflet, 1991.

28   Douglas Holmes, *Integral Europe: Far-Capitalism, Multiculturalism, Neofascism*, Princeton: Princeton University Press, 2000, p. 69.

29   'Discours de Jean-Marie Le Pen – 1er Mai 2000', http://www.front-national.com/discours/2000/1mai2000htm.

30   Holmes, *Integral Europe*, p. 69.

31   As Le Pen put it as early as 1997, the *Front National* was the only political force in France to propose a complete break with *mondialisme*. See 'Discours

de Jean-Marie Le Pen – 17ème Fête des Bleu-Blanc-Rouge 1997',
http://www.front-national.com.

32 'The Front National – Real Politics', http://www.front-national.com.

33 See Mudde, *Ideology of the Extreme Right*.

34 See Betz, 'Exclusionary Populism'.

35 SPV Zürich, 'Das Konzept für eine Zürcher Ausländerpolitik',
http://www.svp-stadt-zuerich.ch/seiten/auslaenderkonzept.asp

36 See 'Von der Bauernpartei zur Blocher-Dominanz: Geschichte und Gesicht
der SVP', *Neue Züricher Zeitung*, 22 March 2000, p. 15.

37 Thomas Meier, 'Irrweg "Multikulturelle Gesellschaft"', *Schweizerzeit*,
March 3, 2000.

38 See 'Geld allein garantiert keine Integration. Positionspapier der SVP
Schweiz zur Integrationspolitik', January 2001.

39 Matthias von Eysz, 'Der Islam im liberalen Europa: Christlich-
abendländische Kultur vor der Selbsauflösung?', *Schweizerzeit*, 13 July 2001.

40 Hans-Peter Raddatz, 'Angriff gegen den Westen: Die Gefahr des
fundamentalistischen Islam', *Schweizerzeit*, 5 October 2001.

41 Jørgen Gould Andersen and Tor Bjørkland, 'Radical Right-Wing Populism
in Scandinavia: From Tax Revolt to Neo-Liberalism and Xenophobia', in
Hainsworth, ed., *Politics of the Extreme Right*, p. 205; Tor Bjørklund, 'The
1987 Norwegian Local Elections: A Protest Election with a Swing to the
Right', *Scandinavian Political Studies*, vol. 11, no. 3, 1988, p. 216.

42 *Danmarks fremtid – dit land, dit valg...*, Copenhagen, 2001, pp. 28, 190-191.

43 As Mogens Camre, the party's lone European Parliament deputy said after
September 11, 'Muslims are only waiting for the right moment to murder
us'. *Süddeutsche Zeitung*, 13 November 2001, p. 10.

44 Umberto Bossi, Pontida speech, 2000, http://www.prov-varese.
leganord.org/doc/bossipontida00.htm.

45 Enti Locali Padani Federali, 'Padania, identità, e società multirazziale', 1998,
http://www.leganord.org/documenti/elpf/padania_identità.pdf, p. 4.

46 Enti Locali Padani Federali, 'Padania, identità, e società multirazziale', p. 14.

47 Ibid., p. 22.

48 Ibid., p. 14.

49 Guido Colombo, 'In difesa dell' Europa', *La Padania*, 31 January 1999.

50 Umberto Bossi and Daniele Vimercati, *La Rivoluzione*, Milan: Sperling &
Kupfer, 1993, pp. 205-206. Here cited from the English translation
available at the party's website http://www.leganord.org/eng/rev_ch5.htm.

51 Renzo Guolo, 'I nuovi crociati: la Lega e l'islam', *Il Mulino*, vol. 49, no. 5,
2000, p. 890.

52 Brenno, 'Roma, il comunismo, l'islam: I tre peggiori morbi della storia',
Quaderni padani, no. 22/23, 1999, available at http://www.stellina.net/
users/padani/tremorbi.htm.

53 Lega Nord leaflet 'Anche Tu! Dal 20 Febbraio firma per il referendum
"Contro l'invasione di immigrati clandestini"', Milan, 1999.

54 Gianlucas Savoini, 'Non dobbiamo essere una colonia Usa', *La Padania*, 26 March 1999, internet version, http://www.lapadania.com/index.htm.

55 Alexandre del Valle, 'La stratégie américaine en Eurasie', http://utenti.tripod.it/ArchivEurasia/delvalle_sae.html; 'Genèse et actualité de la "stratégie" pro-islamiste des États-Unis', http://members.es. tripod.de/msrsobrarbe/valle.htm.

56 Alexandre del Valle, 'La poussée islamiste dans les Balkans: la responsabilité américaine et occidentale', http://www.geo-islam.org/content.php3? articleId=23.

57 Stefano Piazzo, 'No all'impero mondiale', *La Padania*, 29 April 1999.

58 'Siamo davanti a nuovo colonialismo: un tempo fa opera degli occidentali, ora sono i musulmani a farlo a casa nostra' ('We confront a new colonialism: in the past it was the work of the occidentals, now it is the Moslems who do it in our home'). Quoted in 'Sull'Islam le bugie della sinistra', *La Padania*, 17 October 2000.

59 Claudio Morgoglione, 'Lodi, la Lega all guerra santa', *La Repubblica*, 15 October 2000; Gianluca Savoini, 'Basta all'invasione islamica', *La Padania*, 15 October 2000.

60 Savoini, 'Basta all'invasione islamica'.

61 Ugo Gaudenzi, 'Con la Lega: La battaglia contro l'immigrazion', http://rinascita.net/analisi.htm.

62 Bruno Mégret, 'Discours de Salon de Provence', 16 September 2001, 'Discours de Poitiers' (1), 30 September 2001. http://www.m-n-r.com

63 Mégret, 'Discours de Salon de Provence'.

64 'Actieplan "Stop Islamterreur"', http://www.vlaams-blok.be/archief/ dossier/pdf/dossier_actieplan_terreur.PDF

65 'Discours integral de Jean-Marie LePen, Convention nationale BBR 2001 Devant plus de 11000 personnes', 23 September 2001, http://www.front-national.com/discours/2001/bbr2001.htm.

66 'Presidentielle: Jean-Marie Le Pen arriverait en troisième position', *Le Monde*, 29 October 2001.

67 See, '"Totalitarismo islamico" – La Lega s'interroga', *La Stampa*, 20 October 2001; Elena Maccanti, 'Torino si interroga sull'Islam', *La Padania*, 21 October 2001.

68 Elena Maccanti, 'Alexandre del Valle: Europa debole', *La Padania*, 21 October 2001.

69 See Padovani Gigi, 'Dopo I manifesti di Venezia a l'ordine del giorno in Piemonte si apre un altro fronte', *La Stampa*, 20 September 2001; Colonello Paolo, '"Torino e Milano, chiudete la moschea"', *La Stampa*, 16 October 2001; Guido Passalacqua, 'La crociata die Speroni: "Via tutti I musulmani"', *La Repubblica*, 17 October 2001; Poletti Fabio, 'Tensione e paura alla moschea di Milano', *La Stampa*, 20 October 2001. On Biffi, see Michele Smargiassi, 'Biffi: ninte moschee in Italia', *La Repubblica*, 1 October 2000.

70 'Il Senatur: "Recuperare I valori cristiani"', *La Padania*, 31 October 2001;

Maccanti, 'Torino si interroga sull'Islam'.

71 Nancy Fraser, 'Social Justice in the Knowledge Society: Redistribution, Recognition, and Participation', presented at conference 'Gut zu Wissen', Heinrich-Böll-Stiftung, May 2001, http://www.wissensgesellschaft.org/themen/orientierung/orientierung.html, p. 2.

72 Antonio, 'After Postmodernism', p. 56.

73 Nicholas Aylott, 'Paradoxes and Opportunism: The Danish Election of March 1998', Government and Opposition, vol. 34, no. 1, 1999, p. 70; Ketil Bujat, 'The 1997 Norwegian Parliamentary Election: A Swing towards Parliamentary Power', The Political Quarterly, vol. 69, no. 2, 1998, p. 179.

74 Holmes, Integral Europe, p. 16.

THE EUROPEAN RIGHT AND WORKING LIFE: FROM ORDINARY MISERIES TO POLITICAL DISASTERS

JÖRG FLECKER

INTRODUCTION

The scope and intensity of the recent political swing towards right-wing populism and authoritarianism in Europe has been rather frightening. Since 2000, xenophobic movements, some of which are hostile to representative democracy, have come into power and formed governments in Austria, Italy, Denmark and Portugal. In large parts of Europe right-wing extremism is on the rise. A frequently heard explanation of this phenomenon is that the populists have succeeded in winning over the 'modernization losers', i.e. those who have lost out in the process of socio-economic change. It is often assumed that people who have difficulty in coping with the dynamics of social change develop 'fundamentalist' reactions that make them more receptive to right-wing extremism or populism. However, the countries and regions where voting support for the extreme Right is particularly high are not among Europe's backward or declining areas nor do they have particularly high rates of unemployment. On the contrary, some of them, such as Denmark, Austria, Flanders and Northern Italy, are particularly well off by international standards.

Understanding the reasons for the rise of the extreme right, and strengthening political resistance to it, is clearly going to be a major challenge in the years to come. Among the crucial questions that need to be answered are: How have people reacted to socio-economic change and especially to the neoliberal restructuring of the economy and society in recent decades? Under what conditions do changes in working life make people more receptive to right-wing populist ideologies? And the answers are rather more complex than they might seem at first sight.

'Flexibility and Security' was a much quoted policy objective throughout the second half of the 1990s.[1] Yet while 'flexibility' has come to be taken for granted, 'security' remains problematic. In addition, the debate generally focuses rather narrowly on the statistical evidence concerning the transformation of employment and the connection between changes in work organization and changes in social security provision. The subjective element of these changes – i.e. the importance working people themselves attach to the security or insecurity of their jobs, and the injuries and despair experienced by those affected, or threatened, by drastic structural change – has so far received much less attention.

In fact, disadvantaged groups experiencing high levels of insecurity do seem to be receptive to nationalism and racism. Those with low levels of education, for example, are the most vulnerable and at the same time seem to be more likely to vote for right-wing populists. But similar attitudes can also be found among the well-off. Research has shown that it is not only the 'losers' who contribute to the success of right-wing populist or extremist politicians, but also members of the middle and upper-middle classes who are either afraid of losing their economic status or who face severe competition – and even people who expect to gain from neoliberal policies. One explanation is that intensifying competition makes ideologies propagating exclusion along national or ethnic lines more attractive. A psychoanalytic explanation suggests that pressures for ever intensified performance and productivity are likely to lead to hostility towards groups perceived or construed as unproductive, lazy or free-riding.

The danger right-wing populism poses for democracy can be seen in different ways. Optimists regard the electoral successes of right-wing populist parties as temporary phenomena. According to them, the host of promises such parties make, which have little chance of being kept, will more or less automatically lead to dissatisfaction with the actual performance of populists once they have been elected. A more pessimistic approach not only points to the way right-wing parties can weaken people's attachment to democratic principles through media influence and/or attacks on constitutional government; it also suggests that we could be confronted with self-prolonging radical right-wing populist rule, as the far right exploits growing dissatisfaction and anger provoked by the consequences of its own neoliberal policies to mobilize a xenophobic and anti-system vote. There is a danger that far-right politicians may benefit from the aggravation of problems they actively contribute to.

We will try to clarify some of the conceptual and empirical questions involved. We will first consider that working life may play an important role, in addition to that of the political system itself, the media, etc. Secondly, we will approach the problem from the opposite angle and ask why right-wing populism and extremism gain from the consequences of changes in working life. Why do adverse changes of working and living conditions lead to authoritarian and exclusionist protest rather than solidaristic and democratic opposition? Finally, in the conclusion, we will indicate some of the conditions that are particularly conducive to translating the negative effects of socio-economic change into support for the extreme right.

WHY WORKING LIFE?

Insecurity in working life is not a recent phenomenon nor can capitalist economies exist without it. Why should the conditions in working life have played a particularly important role in recent political changes? One line of argument points to the culmination of long-term trends often addressed as 'individualization'. On this view, the erosion of the institutions of bourgeois society in late capitalism, together with the consequences of globalization, are responsible for the widespread insecurity experienced today. As Beck puts it, a number of old securities have slowly disappeared, particularly in the second half of the twentieth century: '[m]uch like the family, the job has lost much of its former security and protective functions. With their jobs, people are losing an inner backbone that has given shape to their lives since the industrial revolution…'.[2]

This process of individualization decreases traditional forms of dependency and gives individuals new scope to design their lives according to their own ideas and wishes. Thus the loss of security is only the flip side of greater freedom. What, then, turns the loss of security that accompanies greater freedom into a problem? It is argued that individualization may lead to isolation, insecurity of orientation and action, and to feelings of powerlessness – anomic conditions that can be targeted by right-wing extremist ideology.[3]

Another attempt to explain such 'pathological' developments argues that we have lost a social character trait that would be needed in order to use this new-found freedom independently. For Sennett, this is a problem of late-twentieth-century 'flexible' capitalism, with its dedication to the 'short term'. Qualities such as trust and commitment are abandoned, which makes social relationships that rely on interdependence impossible, and in the end undermines self-respect. People begin to 'drift', characters corrode. The qualities of character and personality needed to 'design' one's life can no longer develop.[4]

Given that we are mainly interested in a political development that has emerged mainly since the 1980s, it seems preferable to focus on the most recent stage of capitalist development, rather than on the long-term evolution of industrial society. In the era of post-war prosperity, labour-market regulation promised more security for employees; since the 1970s employment insecurity has been on the rise again, while the neoliberal restructuring of labour-market regulation has weakened the protection of workers. From this vantage point, the recent rapid changes in socio-economic structures and the triumph of neoliberalism are the major reasons for the drop in employment security. There are two main aspects of this development: first, the peripheral labour market, providing precarious and informal work, is expanding in the core capitalist countries; and, second, insecurity is becoming ubiquitous through far-reaching changes in standard employment relationships within the 'core' labour market.

Precariousness and the informalization of work

There is no denying that mass unemployment and the threat of losing one's job remain crucial problems of contemporary societies. But overt unemployment has also been complemented by various forms of underemployment, which partially integrate unemployment into the employment system. It seems reasonable to assume that the resulting forms of insecure and precarious employment cause levels of subjective pressure no less high than those caused by unemployment.

Recent statistics do show a rise in non-standard employment, i.e. forms of employment, such as part-time work, that do not yield a living income, or which are not protected by labour or social law to the same extent as 'regular' jobs. The fact that part-time work accounts for a major part of 'atypical' employment reflects the fact that its growth has been at least partly due to the growing integration of women into the labour market, since in many countries women do not seek full-time employment. Moreover, atypical employment is increasing less in industries that rely on world markets than in the retail, health and catering industries, all of which rely heavily on women workers.[5]

The theory of the 'informalization of work'[6] offers an explanation for this phenomenon. If a country accepts the rules of international competitiveness, it will have to surrender country-specific forms of employment regulation and the social security provisions that go along with them. Its economy 'cannot bear the restrictions or "practical constraints" imposed by world markets in its entirety. Economic coherence and aspirations to become or remain attractive to foreign investors can only be achieved by pushing surplus labour into unemployment, and into informal, precarious and atypical work (exclusion)'.[7] The result is a 'fragmentation' of the economy and society brought about by companies or even entire business sectors which try to succeed by undercutting world-market labour standards.

According to this argument, globalization not only contributes to the spread of informal employment but also to 'tertiarization', i.e. the expansion of the service industry. In particular, in sectors based on labour-intensive personal services that cannot be relocated to low-wage countries one can witness an increase in jobs that fall below the standards of previously prevailing norms and laws:

> A ... small number of highly productive workers and competitive enterprises experience a strong increase in value, while other types of work – even if it is indispensable social reproduction work – are devalued, especially with respect to remuneration. As a consequence, there is an increase in the proportion of workers who are denied a complete and long-term integration into society – via household income, the stability of their working life and the working conditions they are subject to.[8]

This in turn widens the cleavages in society. 'The "meritocratic" gap in income, education and status between a "cosmopolitan elite" of the wealthy, who speculate on global markets, the highly-qualified specialists of the "information age", the strata of skilled workers and middle management, who fear losing their economic security, and a growing "functional underclass", is widening'.[9] These realities are partly reflected, though in a distorted way, in public discourse and political propaganda about flexibility, mobility and 'employability'. Insecurity is accepted as endemic: everyone for themselves!

But the assumption is maintained that in principle everyone can achieve a secure existence on the basis of wage labour. Gorz has shown, however, that a significant part of wage-based labour is being abolished by rationalization, leading to widespread insecurity among people, whose income, social affiliation and self-confidence nonetheless continue to depend on paid work. Conditions familiar in Third World contexts increasingly spread to the First World. The accumulation of capital is increasingly separated from production, but an individual's right to a suitable income and to a wide range of civil rights is still tied to the obligation to work.

The fact that these outdated ideas about a work-based society still shape people's hopes and expectations, and that these expectations must necessarily be disappointed, is clearly crucial for our enquiry into the connection between changes in working life and right-wing populism: as Gorz says, '[i]t is by reinforcing "public opinion" in its unrealistic expectations, in its adherence to outdated norms, in stereotyped interpretations wholly out of step with the realities they claim to decipher, that credence and sustenance are given to manichaean visions, scapegoat theories and proto-fascist ideologies and practices'.[10]

But hasn't public discourse since the 1980s abandoned promises of security, even if it still maintains the wage-based working society as a central element? Doesn't it instead assert that former job and employment standards are outdated and that everyone will have to get used to disrupted careers, frequent job changes, lifelong learning – in other words, to general insecurity? For Bourdieu, 'precariousness' is part of a new form of hegemony based on 'general insecurity that turned into a permanent state of affairs'. This insecurity is used as a strategy to ensure workers' compliance and submission: '[i]n a way, the flexible enterprise deliberately takes advantage of a situation which is marked by insecurity and which it further aggravates'.[11] Seen from this point of view, we are no longer talking about the side effects of socio-economic changes brought about and accelerated by globalization, which political attempts at 'flexicurity' seek to alleviate. If we see insecurity as a central element of capitalist hegemony, it becomes clear that corrective measures will not be achieved through social policy. Space for right-wing populism clearly exists here.

The new standard employment

Yet unemployment, the increase of precarious employment, and labour-market deregulation do not comprise the full extent of individual insecurity. Formal employment and long-term work contracts have also undergone dramatic changes over the past decade or so. In many countries, privatization, the growing significance of 'shareholder value' and new forms of control have created radically different conditions for employees. This can also be observed from the changes that have taken place in standard employment contracts, which nowadays tend to include a number of new elements like performance-related pay and flexible time-arrangements. At the same time, values of mutual understanding and trust between management and staff are increasingly abandoned in favour of a reorientation towards short-term profit. Of course, in continental Europe companies still have plenty of reason to rely on their long-term staff to help them adapt to difficult times; similarly, they often avoid a straightforward hire-and-fire policy in order not to generate fear and distrust among their staff, especially if the company depends on its employees' experience, cooperation and commitment.[12] But even the well-known Volkswagen model[13] offered employment security only in exchange for concessions on the part of the workers, including additional mobility, more flexible working hours and increased performance. Concession bargaining is more and more widespread, leading to 'pacts' whereby employers offer to keep employment levels in exchange for lower pay and increased flexibility.

Rising insecurity can thus be found at the heart of the social relations within a company. Long-term employees, temporary workers and freelancers increasingly work side by side. This puts pressure not only on those who hope to achieve better positions by working harder, but also on those whose social standing and security are at risk. In many enterprises, competition among employees is on the rise, and the risk of failure becomes ever-present. How rules of mutuality tend to be broken and expectations are disappointed can be seen from the decrease in the provision of 'niche' employment opportunities for older workers, or employees with health problems. The transformation of the social order within companies is felt especially dramatically in former state-owned industries or recently privatized institutions of the public sector: companies that used to operate on the basis of promises of long-term security are now listed on the stock exchange and rely on the creation of quasi-markets within the company. It is not hard to imagine how many implicit contracts have been broken and how many injuries employees have experienced. Social insecurity has returned to the core workforce and to the ranks of skilled workers, which is particularly distressing given expectations of continuously increasing living standards and reduced risk on the part of wage labour.[14] This is particularly true for blue-collar workers, who are not only most affected by international competition but also suffer from cultural and symbolic devaluation.

Recent moves towards new forms of work organization do not mitigate such developments although, at first sight, demanding a high degree of independence and self-organization from workers might seem to upgrade them. In areas where bureaucratic rules and orders from superiors used to determine the direction of work and assure a consistent work process, today what counts is individual achievement. Expectations of increased responsibility on the part of individuals or groups of workers are combined with tighter control of results. Such changes in working life make great demands on employees' personalities, but at the same time limit the opportunities for the formation of identity. Workers find that new work structures do not yield the promised work autonomy. Conflicts about reorganization are widespread and aspirations keep exceeding realities.[15]

In summary, we can say that rising insecurity represents one of the foremost aspects of socio-economic change and the transformation of working life. This conclusion is widely shared and often voiced in combination with the suggestion that insecurity triggers fears which may in turn lead to a rise in nationalism and racism. In the words of the 'Group of Lisbon', 'most people live with a permanent feeling of uncertainty. The promotion and defence of one's own identity is linked to the rejection and destruction of other identities. Growing uncertainty produces additional insecurity, growing insecurity produces more violence. Many people are caught in a logic of war and struggle of all against all, in the interest of their own survival'.[16]

WHY RIGHT-WING EXTREMISM AND POPULISM?

It is often implicitly assumed that increased insecurity in working life makes people more or less automatically receptive to right-wing populism. In fact, of course, these changes can and do provoke quite diverse reactions. Authoritarian-exclusivist protest is only one possible form these reactions can take. Another is denial of adverse effects and a retreat into isolation. One might also expect solidaristic-democratic protests against worsening living and working conditions. Why then should these socio-economic changes lead to increased receptiveness to extreme right-wing ideologies? In other words: What is 'on offer' from the extreme right today that makes it attractive? How can analysis grasp the interrelation between increasing insecurities and threats in working life and the readiness to adopt scapegoat theories and exclusionist ideologies? The success of radical right-wing populists in rich European countries and regions with comparatively low and even declining rates of unemployment reminds us that it is not enough to look only for obvious and absolute distress and misery.

With Bourdieu, we assume that in order to answer this question we have to look at the problem from the vantage point of those most affected by recent changes. It is from this perspective that we can assess the 'positional suffering' resulting from an inferior position and relative decline within the social order.

> This positional suffering, experienced from inside the microcosm, will appear, as the saying goes, 'entirely relative', meaning completely unreal, if we take the point of view of the macrocosm and compare it to the 'real' suffering of material poverty (la grande misère). This is invariably the point of reference for criticism ('You really don't have anything to complain about'), as for consolation ('You could be worse off you know'). But using material poverty as the sole measure of all suffering keeps us from seeing and understanding a whole side of the suffering characteristic of a social order which, although it has undoubtedly reduced poverty overall

(though less than often claimed) has also multiplied the social spaces (specialized fields and subfields) and set up the conditions for an unprecedented development of all kinds of ordinary suffering (la petite misère).[17]

In their study, *The Weight of the World*, Bourdieu and his colleagues deal with people's longing for social upward mobility, the investments they make to achieve it, and their sense of disappointment when these hopes are crushed by economic crisis or the hidden devaluation of what they have achieved. For many people, for instance, owning a house in a respectable area might be the object of such hopes. Seen from this point of view, conflicts with immigrant families and xenophobic reactions are much easier to understand:

> These conflicts are all the more significant because they have almost no objective basis. They must therefore be understood as the last manifestations of resistance put up by this fraction of the population – which has acquired only very late in life the longed-for single family house as well as the (geographical and social) space associated with it, that is, the space on which it has projected all its aspirations and hopes for social promotion, in which it has invested and in which it is invested – to contest the process of decline, devaluation and disqualification in which it fears being caught.[18]

Learning from this approach we can put into perspective our question as to whether the effects of the socio-economic change of recent years have prepared the ground for the extreme right. First, changes in forms of employment as well as changes within enterprises have resulted in increasingly insecure conditions for employees. These changes must be seen in the context of people's hopes and expectations if we want to understand individual strategies for coming to terms with potential disappointment and injury. Second, what matters most in this context is not the actual extent of negative effects on labour and employment conditions but the subjective perception of personal upward or downward mobility compared with other individuals or social groups whose position you aspire to, or want to leave behind. Third, the perceived changes and opportunities have to be seen in relation to the expectations and responsibilities produced and/or enhanced by the prevailing public discourse about work.

So what does the extreme right offer to people experiencing high levels of uncertainty? To answer this question let us first try to define more concretely what is meant by radical right-wing populism. The term populism goes back to the late nineteenth century, when North American farmers sought the government's protection against the excessive prices asked by the railway companies and the exorbitant rates of interest charged by the banks. Their movement was characterized by romantic anti-capitalism and a distrust of professional politicians and lawyers. According to Dubiel, '... in Anglo-Saxon sociology "populist" social movements are primarily characterised by reaction, passivity and victimisation in the face of economic, political and cultural modernisation processes ... Populist movements ... cannot be defined by means of a certain set of interests they represent (e.g. economic class interests). The image of "us" they project rather addresses ascriptive collective traits, such as regional or national affiliation, language community, gender, skin colour, ethnic origin, etc.'.[19] Today the expression 'right-wing populism' refers to 'neo-conservative strategies of symbolic integration', seen as an alternative to integration into the welfare state. 'A form of political mobilisation such as this always depends on the resentment, prejudice and fears automatically created by excluding the lower classes from power and education. The cultural features of class rule thus become the agents of their own prolongation'.[20]

Radical right-wing populism is further characterized by the perception of 'the people' as a passive political subject, a homogeneous collective opposed to the political elite. 'The subject assumed and created by populist politics', says Steinert, 'is passive, without strong, clearly defined interests, driven by feelings of resentment; it can be mobilised from above and is prepared to follow; it is a "mass" which must be seduced and won over, perhaps organised, instructed and guided – which needs a "leader"'.[21] The collective identity addressed by right-wing populists is usually defined in terms of ethnicity, race or nationality. Additional in-groups of, for instance, 'honest and hard working people' are often constructed through the exclusion of outcasts.

Coming back to the question as to what radical right-wing populism has to offer, we often find the following main aspects:

Orientation: In an increasingly complex world people have problems understanding the forces that impact on their lives. In face of contradictions and existential insecurities the adoption of certain strategies and interpretations, such as scapegoat theories or authoritarian views of society, can help individuals to create a subjective sense of consistency in their apprehension of social reality.[22] Views and concepts based on ethnicity, anti-elite sentiments or in-group/out-group distinctions provide simple explanations for complex problems and thus provide people with an orientation.

Supporting identity: Political messages can promote a sense of belonging to an (imaginary) ethnic or national community, which may compensate for lost certainties and therefore help to stabilize the self. A 'shadow identity'[23] can easily be borrowed if one's existing social identity is damaged. For Ottomayer, 'xenophobia is an easy-to-get self-esteem drug'[24], while Sennett speaks of the re-emergence of that 'dangerous pronoun "we"': 'One of the unintended consequences of modern capitalism is that it has strengthened the value of place, aroused a longing for community. (...) All these conditions impel people to look for some other scene of attachment and depth. Today in the new regime of time, that usage of "we" has become an act of self-protection. The desire for community is defensive, often expressed as rejection of immigrants or other outsiders...'.[25]

Displacement of problems: Problems in working life, especially the exploitation, devaluation etc. of labour, lead to imbalances and tensions. If their causes cannot be legitimately addressed they may be 'discharged' in objectively unrelated areas.[26] Thus xenophobic impulses may be a way of voicing frustration, even though the original problem has nothing to do with foreigners.

Projection: In psychoanalytical explanations aggressive exclusionist views stem from libidinous and aggressive impulses that are projected onto others. Those out-groups that allegedly realize one's suppressed wishes become the targets of aggression. The more people are forced to surrender to rules of ever intensified performance and productivity the more likely are attacks on groups perceived as unproductive, lazy or free-riding.[27] This is one of the reasons why people who are 'winners' from modernization may also be attracted to right-wing populist ideologies.

These concepts are valuable because they help us to understand how politicians succeed in seducing people without addressing the real sources of their problems – let alone offering viable solutions. It would be a mistake, however, to put the phenomenon as a whole down to 'false consciousness'. Part of radical right-wing populism is actually 'interest politics', and some people's support for it can be assumed to be quite rational – however difficult this is for some of us to accept. There are two aspects to this. First, there are real problems caused by immigration which are not being addressed by the established political forces. Second, it may be a rational strategy to use ethnicity, race or nationality in the struggle over the distribution of wealth.

In his explanation of right-wing extremism in Germany, Jaschke argues that people in disadvantaged suburbs who experience the seamy side of multicultural life are faced with an official ideology of an ethnically homogenous Germany. They do not feel represented by the main parties, nor does the public debate on immigration address their situation.

> 'While cosmopolitan intellectuals and service workers despise the poorly-educated and narrow-minded mob, the conservatives, protecting their possessions, tend to make use of the urban losers from modernisation. Their problems are acknowledged as legitimate, but eventually taken advantage of to justify policies of isolating themselves off, and avoiding the need to share. Despised by both groups, [for the 'mob'] it is only a small step to [fall into] political apathy or to [support] extreme right-wing parties'.[28]

Official ideologies of national ethnic homogeneity do not exist in all countries, yet even so members of the working class may still resort to 'defensive nationalism' if they feel their group interests are being violated or their social position and status threatened. They turn to exclusion on ethnic terms to protect what they have achieved and to keep their distance from the 'underclass'.[29] The internationalism of the workers' movement conceals the fact that in many countries the working class and workers' organizations are not opposed to nationalism.[30] This can take the form of socialist nationalism, linked to the national welfare state and based on the integration of the working class into the nation-state, but it can also take the form of conservative nationalism when, for example, anti-immigrant resentments are stirred up. In fact, these distinctions are much less clear-cut in real life, as Erich Fromm showed long ago in his research on blue- and white-collar workers at the advent of the Third Reich.[31] Even then, the political orientations of large parts of the working population were highly ambiguous. Now, after the dissolution of solid political camps and social milieus, the boundaries between interest politics and identity politics, between socialist and conservative nationalism, and between solidarity and authoritarian protest are much more likely to be blurred.

We should, however, also avoid attributing the phenomenon exclusively to the protest vote of modernization 'losers'. First of all, some nationalist reactions are in fact not opposed to, but rather well integrated into, the dominant ideology. Butterwegge, for example, calls the liberal and conservative view of national interests in a global capitalist world 'Standortnationalismus' ('business location nationalism'). This form of nationalism is based on the idea that in the face of a hostile world of international markets the economic superiority of one's own ethnic community can only be proven by ingenuity, hard work and the willingness to make sacrifices. This ideology can be easily adapted to the purposes of right-wing extremism. Because of its adoption of neoliberal ideologies, this is a strain of right-wing extremism that for the first time since 1945 offers a set of aims and objectives which 'does not only tie in with that of mainstream society, but also corresponds with the interests of influential groups and the strategic concepts of elites in the economy and administration'.[32]

Second, support for radical right-wing populism is not limited to particular disadvantaged groups in society. According to Kitschelt, the potential electorate of the extreme right is partly made up of the 'petit bourgeois', who support a free-market economy, ethnocentrism and the reduction of the welfare state – and probably count themselves among the 'winners of modernization'; and only partly by 'modernization losers', who are drawn towards 'welfare chauvinism', with its aim of excluding some groups, especially immigrants, from the benefits of the welfare system.[33] Research into social milieus and mentalities also shows that both authoritarian and democratic orientations can be found at all levels of society. All attempts to establish differences between 'authoritarian and democratic mind-sets on the vertical axis (of social inequality) have failed completely'.[34]

Even an increase in social insecurity can be dealt with in a democratic or authoritarian way, depending on mentality. Vester argues that authoritarianism and hostility towards immigrants do not depend on 'the intensity of social frustration but on its interpretation inherent in some mentalities'.[35] Researchers in Germany note that the socio-political camp of 'disappointed-authoritarians' accounts for 27% of the population where modernization losers are concentrated (elderly workers, unskilled workers and workers with outdated qualifications, young workers without career prospects). In terms of milieus the right (authoritarian) and the lower social classes are over-represented: the petty-bourgeoisie, 'traditionless' workers, and to some extent also the traditional and performance-oriented working-class.[36]

In Italy the right-wing populist party Lega Nord is largely supported by entrepreneurs and workers in successful small and medium enterprises in the north.

Owing to this social base the party articulates the resentments of the 'winners' of modernization.[37] Unfortunately available research findings do not allow for a clear judgement as to what extent the groups that are gaining most from current restructuring actually support right-wing populism. International comparative research shows that in general the unemployed, people with low levels of education and those perceiving deprivation are more likely to vote for the extreme right.[38] But voting statistics also show that the right-wing vote is not made up only of the unemployed and the low-skilled. In Austria, for example, according to one estimate 47 per cent of the blue-collar workers, but also 33 per cent of the self-employed and 22 per cent of the white-collar workers, voted for the *Freiheitliche Partei Österreichs* (FPÖ) in the 1999 general elections.[39] This also holds true for France: in the first round of the 2002 French presidential elections 25 per cent of Front National voters were unemployed, but 13 per cent were middle managers and 18 per cent salaried employees. Of course, further research is needed to understand the motives of different groups of people to support the extreme right. But it seems to be quite clear that general, simple explanations do not take us very far.

CONCLUSIONS

There is some indication of a connection between socio-economic change and, in particular, recent transformations of working life and political developments, such as the rise of radical right-wing populism. Though the analysis of the exact nature of their relationship is a difficult undertaking, we can draw several conclusions from what has been said so far.

Neoliberal politics, globalization and rapid technological change have given rise to, or intensified, feelings of insecurity among the broad mass of the population. These changes may bring about existential fears and multiply feelings of injury. Owing to socialization, hegemonic ideologies and societal power relations the resulting 'free-floating aggression' is turned against other vulnerable groups, in particular those widely seen as scapegoats. 'Also in this form aggression remains powerless but it may be expressed with impunity, and may even earn approval'.[40] Similarly, in a methodological note Bourdieu describes hostility towards immigrants among farmers and owners of small businesses who have no direct contact with 'foreigners' as problem displacement:

> One can only get beyond the appearance of denseness and absurdity which, by comparison with an understanding-based interpretation, seems to characterize that hostility, if we see that, by a form of displacement, it offers a solution to the contradictions specific to these small-time capitalists with proletarian incomes and to their experience of the governments which they see as responsible for an unacceptable redistribution of wealth. The real bases of the discontent and dissatisfaction expressed, in inappropriate forms, in this hostility can only be brought to consciousness – that is to explicit discourse – where an effort is made to bring to light these things buried deep within the people who experience them ...[41]

To some extent, right-wing populists and extremist politicians do take up factual problems. They primarily use them, however, to present 'scapegoat' theories and similar interpretations which are used to voice rage and discontent caused by experiences that are not actually related to 'immigrants', 'foreigners' or other constructions of 'the other'.

Disappointments, fears and injuries may trigger different reactions; they do not automatically result in particular interpretations and political reactions. The dramatically different political developments in countries subject to similar socio-economic transformations, as well as different reactions within the same socio-economic classes, lead us to assume that there must be a number of additional influences. Among the conditions frequently leading to a strengthening of right-wing extremism or radical populism, the following seem to be of particular importance:

- The traditions and political culture of a country as well as the range of right-wing populist or extremist interpretations 'on offer' at a certain time contribute to determining how individuals cope with these changes. De Witte and Verbeeck are convinced that it is not ethnocentrism or racism in society itself that is on the increase (and yields better election results for the *Vlaams Blok* in Flanders) but that it is right-wing populist and extremist parties that are making 'foreigners' or 'immigrants' a burning socio-political issue. The success of such parties adds to their media presence as well as that of the 'immigrants' issue itself.[42]

- Depending on their social milieu and their position within the total 'social space', individuals process similar experiences and interpret similar events in entirely different ways. As mentioned above, Vester shows that, depending on mentality and milieu, similar experiences of socio-economic disintegration can produce either authoritarian or democratic reactions.[43] In addition to the social milieu, the extent to which certain groups of the population are integrated into political organizations and traditions plays a significant role, as does the direction mobilization is currently taking.

- The release of 'potentials of political subjectivity'[44] which determine whether certain political attitudes are adopted or not seems to constitute a further important factor. Dubiel defines these potentials as 'hardly tangible … aspirations for happiness and justice, the need for recognition in society and cultural identity'[45]. According to the theory of the 'populist moment'[46], sudden phases of change and modernization release these potentials of political subjectivity, which are kept at bay in more stable times and in politically stable, culturally well-integrated societies. 'In such [suddenly changing] moments in social history, the collective experiences of injury, fear of losing one's status and thwarted hopes for happiness of some groups of the population are dropped, as it were, from established discourse and become "floating potentials", at odds with the traditional spectrum of political orientation'.[47]

In conclusion, I would like to formulate the following hypothesis. Recent socio-economic changes have exacerbated 'positional suffering', experiences of injury, insecurities and fear in large sections of the population. The simultaneous neoliberal reorientation of politics and the prevalent unrealistic discourse concerning labour and employment have undermined the integration of potentials of political subjectivity. On the basis of respective cultural traditions, right-wing populist and extremist movements and politicians take advantage of the resulting 'floating potentials'. The success of these movements in turn strengthens tendencies to transform latent discontent into racist, nationalist and authoritarian attitudes. To some commentators this is not so frightening after all, because populists do not pass the acid test of having to rule. Their empty promises and programmatic contradictions and ambiguities will ensure that they cannot stay in power very long.

But the injured 'loser' from modernization is not the whole explanation, nor is right-wing populism thriving on the protest vote alone. Three qualifications are needed. First, mainstream ideology, i.e. economic nationalism as part of globalism, addresses both losers and winners – and the well-off may have their own reasons to support right-wing populists. Second, an analysis of the problem should avoid the cosmopolitan prejudice that perceives anti-immigrant attitudes only as morally inappropriate and politically incorrect. Such attitudes are not all just triggered by identity politics but to some extent reflect economic interests and justified anxieties. Third, radical right-wing populism is not necessarily a temporary phenomenon: populists may well thrive on the problems they produce or exacerbate. Even if they do disappear from the political sphere here and there, not much is gained as long as mainstream parties continue to pursue the policies they adopted from the extreme right in order to contain its rise.

But what can the political and societal left learn from these experiences? Of course the complex and varied realities in the different countries do not allow sweeping generalizations or simple panaceas. But some points seem to be pertinent to most European countries or regions that have recently experienced a renaissance of the extreme and populist right. First and foremost, social problems such as precariousness, poverty, growing inequality and insecurity as well as worries caused by immigration need to be properly acknowledged and addressed. This seems to be a banality but it is sad enough that it is not. For instance, when we read in a Danish Association leaflet that 'There are 30,000 homeless Danes. WHEN will there be built asylum shelters for them?',[48] we should recognizethat what is really scandalous is not only how the weakest in society are played off against each other in this way, but also that one of the richest nations in the world does not provide housing for its desperate citizens. Ignoring factual problems and countering the ensuing protest with the demand for political correctness[49] is all too easy and, at least on the basis of the experience in Austria, proves to be the best support for right-wing populists. Second, providing orientation through ideology and a vision of a just society are badly needed. Not for the first time, aggression that is caused by humiliations stemming from the capital-labour relationship, the repressive state or welfare bureaucracies is displaced to unrelated areas and utilized for scapegoating. Intellectuals and politicians accepting or even contributing to the factual taboo on social domination and economic exploitation should at least not be shocked about the victims that blame the immigrants for taking away jobs or welfare benefits. Finally, and related to the previous points, the blurring of social-democratic, conservative and liberal political positions and practice led to a situation where, in some European countries, protest against the consequences of neoliberal restructuring of society can only be voiced through support for the populist right.[50] Growing insecurity and inequality need to be addressed directly and effectively instead of paying lip-service to abstract aims of an inclusive society. And those on the left who actually do that should not be reproached with being populist.

NOTES

The essay is based on work carried out in preparation for, and during the early stages of, the project SIREN (Socio-Economic Change, Individual Reactions and the Appeal of the Extreme Right) on eight European countries which is carried out by Gabrielle Balacz and Jean-Pierre Faguer at the Centre d'Etudes de l'Emploi (France), Hans de Witte, Guy van Gyes and Yves de Werdt at Hoger Institut voor de Arbeid (Belgium), Edvin Grinderslev and Eva Thoft at Center for Alternative Samfundsanalyse (Denmark), Gudrun Hentges and Malte Hennings at the University of Cologne (Germany), Francesca Poglia, Riccardo Tondolo and Franz Schultheis at the Univerity of Neuchatel (Switzerland), Andras Toth and Istvan Grajczjar at the Hungarian Academy of Sciences and coordinated by Jörg Flecker, Sabine Kirschenhofer, Ingrid Mairhuber, Ulrike Papouschek at Forschungs- und Beratungsstelle Arbeitswelt (Austria) with funding from the European Commission's 'Improving Human Potential' Programme. The translation and language checks were carried out with great care by Christine Wagner. I am particularly grateful to Sabine Kirschenhofer, the co-author of a joint discussion paper this essay draws on (J. Flecker and S. Kirschenhofer, 'Liaisons dangereuses' – neo-liberal capitalism and the appeal of the extreme right, SIREN discussion paper No. 1, FORBA, Vienna, 2001).

1   European Commission, *Modernising and Improving Social Protection in the European Union*, COM(97) 102 final, 12 March 1997.

2   U. Beck, *Risikogesellschaft*, Frankfurt / Main: Suhrkamp, 1986, p. 222.

3   W. Heitmeyer, *Rechtsextremistische Orientierungen bei Jugendlichen*, Weinheim / München: Juventa, 1992.

4   Richard Sennett, *The Corrosion of Character: the personal consequences of work in the new capitalism*, New York: Norton, 1998.

5   J. Flecker, '"Sachzwang Flexibilisierung"? Zum Zusammenhang zwischen betrieblichen Anpassungsstrategien und flexibelen Beschäftigungsformen', in H. Minssen, ed., *Begrenzte Entgrenzungen*, Berlin: Edition Sigma, 2000.

6   E. Altvater & B. Mahnkopf, *Grenzen der Globalisierung*, Münster: Westfälisches Dampfboot, 1999.

7   Altvater & Mahnkopf, *Grenzen der Globalisierung*, pp.336ff.

8   Ibid., p.339.

9   Ibid., p.357.

10 A. Gorz, *Reclaiming work: Beyond the Wage-based Society*, Cambridge: Polity Press, 1999, p.58.

11 P. Bourdieu, *Gegenfeuer. Wortmeldungen im Dienste des Widerstands gegen die neoliberale Invasion*, Konstanz: UVK, 1998, p.99.

12 M. Seifert and P. Pawlowsky, 'Innerbetriebliches Vertrauen als Verbreitungsgrenze atypischer Beschäftigungsformen', *Mitteilungen aus der Arbeitsmarkt- und Berufsforschung*, Vol. 3, 1998.

13 P. Hartz, *Das atmende Unternehmen. Jeder Arbeitsplatz hat einen Kunden – Beschäftigungssicherung bei Volkswagen*, Frankfurt / Main: Campus, 1996.

14 K. Dörre, 'Modernisierung der Ökonomie – Ethnisierung der Arbeit: Ein Versuch über Arbeitsteilung, Anomie, deren Bedeutung für interkulturelle Konflikte', in W. Heitmeyer, ed., *Was treibt die Gesellschaft auseinander?*, Frankfurt / Main: Edition Suhrkamp, 1997.

15 Dörre, 'Modernisierung der Ökonomie'; J. Flecker and J. Hofbauer, 'Capitalising on subjectivity: The "new model worker" and the importance of being useful', in P. Thompson and C. Warhurst, eds., *Workplaces of the future*, Houndsmill / London: Macmillan, 1998.

16 Group of Lisbon, *Grenzen des Wettbewerbs. Die Globalisierung der Wirtschaft und die Zukunft der Menschheit*, München: Luchterhand, 1997, p. 90.

17 P. Bourdieu, 'The Space of Point of View' in P. Bourdieu et al., *The Weight of the World: Social Suffering in Contemporary Society*, Cambridge: Polity Press, 1999, p. 4.

18 A. Sayad, 'A Displaced Family'; in Bourdieu, *The Weight of the World*.

19 H. Dubiel, *Ungewissheit und Politik*, Frankfurt / Main: Edition Suhrkamp, 1994, p. 190f.

20 Dubiel, *Ungewissheit und Politik*, p. 197.

21 H. Steinert, 'Kulturindustrielle Politik mit dem Großen & Ganzen: Populismus, Politik-Darsteller, ihr Publikum und seine Mobilisierung', *Politik und Gesellschaft Online. International Politics and Society*, 4, 1999, p. 8.

22 R. Zoll, ed., *'Hauptsache, ich habe meine Arbeit'*, Frankfurt / Main: Edition Suhrkamp, 1984.

23 K. Dörre, 'Reaktiver Nationalismus in der Arbeitswelt', *Widerspruch*, 41 (1), 2001.

24 K. Ottomeyer, 'Fremdenfeindlichkeit als Selbstwertdroge' in J. Berghold, K. Ottomeyer, E. Menasse, eds., *Trennlinien – Imagination des Fremden und Konstruktionen des Eigenen*, Klagenfurt / Celovec: Drava, 2000.

25 Sennett, *The Corrosion of Character*, New York: Norton, 1998, p. 138.

26 H. Bohle, W. Heitmeyer, W. Kühnel, U. Sander, 'Anomie in der modernen Gesellschaft: Bestandsaufnahme und Kritik eines klassischen

Ansatzes soziologischer Analyse', in Heitmeyer, ed., *Was treibt die Gesellschaft auseinander?*, p. 54.

27 Zoll, ed., *'Hauptsache, ich habe meine Arbeit'* , Dörre, 'Modernisierung der Ökonomie', p. 103.

28 H.-G. Jaschke, *Rechtsextremismus und Fremdenfeindlichkeit*, Wiesbaden: Westdeutscher Verlag, 2001, p. 93.

29 Dörre, 'Modernisierung der Ökonomie', p. 97.

30 P. Pasture, and J. Verberckmoes, 'Working class internationalism and the appeal of national identity: Historical dilemmas and current debates in western Europe', in P. Pasture, and J. Verberckmoes, eds., *Working class internationalism and the appeal of national identity*, Oxford, New York: Berg, 1998.

31 Erich Fromm, *The Working Class in Weimar Germany: a psychological and sociological study*, Leamington Spa: Berg Publishers, 1984.

32 C. H. Butterwegge, *Wohlfahrtsstaat im Wandel. Probleme und Perspektiven der Sozialpolitik*, Opladen: Leske-Budrich, 1999, p. 95.

33 H. Kitschelt, *The Radical Right in Western Europe. A Comparative Analysis*, Ann Arbor: University of Michigan Press, 1995, p. 259.

34 M. Vester, 'Wer sind heute die "gefährlichen Klassen"? Soziale Milieus und gesellschaftspolitische Lager im Wandel', in D. Loch and W. Heitmeyer, *Schattenseiten der Globalisierung*, Frankfurt / Main: Suhrkampf, 2001, p. 305.

35 Vester, 'Wer sind heute die "gefährlichen Klassen"?', p.323

36 M. Vester, P. Oertzen, P. Geiling, T. Hermann, D. Müller, *Soziale Milieus im gesellschaftlichen Strukturwandel*, Frankfurt / Main: Suhrkamp, 2001.

37 H.-G. Betz, 'Radikaler Rechtspopulismus im Spannungsfeld zwischen neoliberalen Wirtschaftskonzepten und antiliberaler autoritärer Ideologie', in D. Loch, W. Heitmeyer, eds., *Schattenseiten der Globalisierung*, Frankfurt / Main: Edition Suhrkamp, 2001.

38 M. Lubbers, *Exclusionist electorates. Extreme right-wing voting in Western Europe*, Nijmegen, 2001.

39 Peter A. Ulram, 'Sozialprofil und Wahlmotive der FPÖ-Wähler: Zur Modernität des Rechtspopulismus am Beispiel des Phänomens Haider', in Loch and Heitmeyer, eds., Schattenseiten der Globalisierung, pp. 215f.

40 B. Geissler, '"Vielleicht kann ich sogar sagen, dass ich ein fanatischer Gewerkschafter bin"', in Rainer Zoll, ed., *'Hauptsache, ich habe meine Arbeit'*, Frankfurt / Main: Suhrkamp, 1984, p. 183.

41 P. Bourdieu, 'Understanding', in P. Bourdieu et al., *The Weight of the World*, p.796.

42 H. De Witte, and G. Verbeeck, 'Belgium: Diversity in Unity', in L. Hagendoorn et al., eds., *European Nations and Nationalism: Theoretical and Historical Perspectives*, Ashgate: Aldershot, 2000.

43 Vester, 'Wer sind heute die "gefährlichen Klassen"?'.

44 Dubiel, *Ungewissheit und Politik*.
45 Ibid., p. 200.
46 Goodwynn, quoted in ibid.
47 Ibid., p. 203f.
48 René Karpantschof, *Populism and Right Wing Extremism in Denmark 1989-2001*, National Report, SIREN Literature review, 2002.
49 Hans-Georg Zilian, 'Der "Populismus" und das Ende der Gleichheit', in W. Eismann, ed., *Rechtspopulismus – Österreichische Krankheit oder europäische Normalität?*, Wien: Czernin, 2002.
50 Jean-Yves Camus, 'Die radikale Rechte in Westeuropa', in Eismann, ed., *Rechtspopulismus*.

COOL BRITANNIA OR CRUEL BRITANNIA?
RACISM AND NEW LABOUR

HUW BEYNON AND LOU KUSHNICK

Post-war British society has witnessed a very significant inward migration of people from the 'New Commonwealth', and the complex diaspora this immigration has created in many British cities is widely recognized as having fundamentally altered British society. Some observers have emphasized the positive aspects of the change, suggesting that the new kinds of identity and forms of living which it has produced have resulted in a transition towards an ethnically plural society. Others, while welcoming the changes, have drawn attention to the inequalities experienced by ethnic minorities and the persistence of racism in daily life, and in the major institutions of British society. The role of the state, and the ways in which 'the race card' has been played in British politics, have from the outset been the subject of extensive and often heated debate.

A key focus of this debate has been crime and policing. In 1979 the Institute of Race Relations raised policing as a central issue for ethnic minorities in Britain. It concluded that there was powerful evidence to suggest that arrest and police powers were being used to keep the black community in its place both physically and psychologically.[1] In 1983 the Policy Studies Institute extended this finding by examining the operation of the 'sus' law. This law (originally instituted to control the working class in the early nineteenth century) made it a criminal offence to be 'a suspicious person loitering with intent to commit a crime'. The PSI established that a disproportionate ratio (8:1) of young black men were being stopped, compared with young white men of the same 'crimeogenic' age.[2]

A central theme of the racialization of crime, and the criminalization of Afro-Caribbean youth in the 1970s and 1980s, was the construction of 'mugging' as a threat to British society, and as a crime committed by young black men. The media, the police, the courts and politicians succeeded in importing a racialized concept from the United States to 'explain' street crime. Street crime, well-known in British cities since the days of Dickens and Mayhew, was redefined as a feature of ethnic minority behaviour. As a result the campaign to reform the 'sus' law became a central component of Afro-Caribbean community politics and campaigns throughout the 1970s and early 1980s.

In the early 1990s the issues of 'immigration', 'race relations' and a 'threat to the British way of life' resurfaced with new force. There was now a shift of focus, from the 'threat' posed by 'black' culture to the 'threat' posed by 'Islam'. The Conservative MP Winston Churchill asserted that 'the population of many of our northern cities is now well over 50 per cent immigrant, and Moslems claim there are now more than two million of their co-religionists in Britain'. He developed a local campaign about this in the north-west of England, arguing that the time had come for the government 'to come clean on this issue and to crack down firmly on all illegal immigrants'.[3] The *Manchester Evening News* polled its readers with the question 'Is he right?' The paper received more responses to this question than on almost any other issue: 96 per cent of respondents said Yes.[4] In 1995 the erstwhile social democrat Paul Johnson reflected on results such as these and gave voice to the core theme of the cultural Right – the story of an 'island people' betrayed. In his opinion,

> The smouldering anger among the British people reflects the view that they believe that they have been lied to twice. The first time was in the late Forties and Fifties when a flood of Commonwealth immigrants arrived without anyone asking the British electorate if they were welcome. Within a generation, fundamental changes had taken place in the composition of the nation and we had become a multi-cultural, multi-racial society without any of us being give the smallest choice in the matter. The only prominent politician who told the truth about this invasion was Enoch Powell. Despite his gifts, his political career came to an abrupt end and never again did he hold office. His demise acted as an effective deterrent on anyone else speaking the truth.[5]

This kind of interpretation held considerable sway as New Labour reached office in 1997. Right-wing Conservative politicians, egged on by a significant section of the tabloid press, would be tempted in defeat to seek popularity by endorsing it. Tony Blair's New Labour party, in contrast, presented itself as differing radically from 'Old Labour' as well as from the Conservatives in laying a new emphasis on social inclusion, individual responsibility and incentives – defining features of the *Third Way*.[6] So how the new government responded to the anti-immigrant campaign would be a key test of its credentials as a progressive, anti-racist party.

BREAKING NEW GROUND: THE STEPHEN LAWRENCE INQUIRY AND POLICING

Rhetorically, New Labour embraced multiculturalism – especially in its exotic aspects. The doors of Number 10 were opened to rock stars and footballers and cultural practitioners of all colours. Multi-culturalism added an important cosmopolitan flavour to Blair's idea of 'a young country'. The conflictual field of 'race relations' thus presented the new government with some significant challenges if its claim to stand for a new, 'Cool Britannia' was to be justified.

A major focus for these challenges was a public inquiry established by the incoming Home Secretary, Jack Straw, into matters arising from the 1993 murder of a young black man, Stephen Lawrence, in south London. The injustice and police incompetence revealed in various accounts of the police investigation of the murder, and the way in which Stephen Lawrence's Afro–Caribbean parents had been treated, had given rise to a sustained demand for a public inquiry and became a key issue in the 1997 General Election. New Labour promised that if elected, it would ensure that an inquiry was held. The inquiry, chaired by Sir William Macpherson, reported in 1999 and reached the damning conclusion that the investigation had been 'marred by a combination of professional incompetence, institutional racism and a failure of leadership by senior officers'.[7] The report confirmed the view of David Muir, representing senior Black church leaders, that 'the experience of black people over the last thirty years has been that we have been over-policed and to a large extent under-protected'.[8] There was, it said, 'inescapable evidence' of a severe 'lack of trust ... between the police and the minority ethnic communities'.[9]

The Report's adoption of the idea of 'institutional racism' broke new ground. It cited extensively a statement submitted by the race relations expert Robin Oakley, who wrote that

> The term institutional racism should be understood to refer to the way institutions may systematically treat or tend to treat people differently in respect to race. The addition of the word 'institutional' therefore identifies the source of the differential treatment ...The production of differential treatment is institutionalized in the ways the organisation operates ... institutional racism in this sense is in fact pervasive throughout the culture and institutions of the whole of British society.[10]

The Inquiry itself advanced a somewhat narrower definition. In its view, institutional racism consisted of

> The collective failure of an organisation to provide an appropriate and professional service to people because of their colour, culture or ethnic origin. It can be seen or detected in processes, attitudes, and behaviour that amounts to discrimination through unwitting prejudice, ignorance, thoughtlessness, and racist stereotyping which disadvantage minority ethnic people.[11]

The sources of these deficiencies were not identified, but the condition was seen as pathological. Institutional racism was a 'disease' that 'infested' organizational life and culture.

The Macpherson Inquiry's conclusion that 'institutional racism' (however conceived) was a fact of life brought the question of racism into public debate in a new way. In flatly contradicting the opinion of Lord Scarman, in his report on the Brixton riots of 1981,[12] that 'institutional racism does not exist in Britain', the Macpherson report can be seen as progressive. But the scale of the problem it was acknowledging was vast.

In the first place, as of 1998 only two per cent of all officers in England and Wales were drawn from ethnic minorities, although the latter accounted for over five per cent of the population; in Scotland the figure was 0.2 per cent. Promotion to senior posts is consistently more limited for ethnic minority officers,[13] who also have a much higher incidence of resigning or being dismissed.[14] Internal inspections have drawn attention to a 'canteen culture' of sexist and racist banter, an antagonistic attitude towards equal opportunities, and outright harassment. In 1995, in a much-publicized case, Simon Holdaway resigned from the police having been an officer for eleven years. In his analysis of his experiences he focused on this 'canteen culture' and the difficulties it created for cooperative work between white and ethnic minority officers.[15]

The problems faced by ethnic minority police officers mirror those experienced by black and Asian people in their daily dealings with the police. Since April 1993 all police forces have been required to publish annual figures on the ethnic origin of all those stopped and searched. In its 1995 analysis of these data *Statewatch* found that black people were much more likely to be stopped and searched than white people. Its report concluded that:

> These figures confirm what black people have known for some time, i.e. that they are being targeted by the police. There is a concern that we are seeing the return of the old 'sus laws' which were repealed in the early eighties, and which led to the very serious distrust between the police and the black community. This concern is greater because of the enhanced Stop and Search Powers contained in the Criminal Justice Act.[16]

The Macpherson Inquiry also carried out a comprehensive analysis of the figures for 1996/97. Some of its findings were astonishing, including the fact that black people were 7.5 times more likely than white people to be stopped and searched, and 4 times more likely to be arrested. In some places (mainly London and the northern cities) the disparity in treatment was even more extreme. In fifteen selected areas, the police had arrested the equivalent of one in five of the total black population aged ten or over. A similar pattern related to sentencing policy in these areas, where the numbers of black people sent to prison following sentence was proportionally four to seven times greater than the corresponding numbers of white people.[17]

This pattern of mistreatment and 'over-policing' is also evident in the use of police violence. The first people to die as a result of the introduction of the long-handled baton and CS gas were black. Deaths in police custody show the same pattern too.[18] Police assaults against black people, or use of excessive force, have been so widespread that an increasing number of civil actions have been taken out against the police, and in particular against the Metropolitan Police. The annual amount of compensation paid out by the Met increased from £393,000 in 1986 to £1,560,000 in 1995. The damages awarded to one man in March 1996 were a record £220,000.[19]

When the Institute of Race Relations gave evidence to the Macpherson Inquiry, it was thus amply justified in speaking of a 'discriminatory pattern of policing', pointing out that the impact of current police practice was twofold. First, racial discrimination in policing stereotypes whole sections of the black community, especially young people, as involved, or *potentially* involved, in criminal activities, ranging from street robbery (so-called 'mugging') and drug-dealing through to violent public disorder. Second, because of its focus on supposed black criminality, policing in the black community tends to downplay the position of black people as victims of crime and the significance of those types of criminal activity (e.g., violent and racist assaults) which most adversely affect them.[20]

The conclusions of the Macpherson inquiry did not go quite so far. But they did go beyond identifying institutional racism as something confined to police investigations of crimes. Macpherson saw the 'stop and search' data as worrying, along with the failure of the police to investigate seriously a number of 'racial incidents'. More generally the report tackled the question of 'canteen culture' and the training of the police. In these ways, broader and more worrying trends were hinted at, and following the government's acceptance of the report significant changes have been introduced in police training, and in efforts to recruit and retain officers from ethnic minorities.

But with crime and immigration being kept at the top of the political agenda by right-wing politicians and newspapers, resistance to change has also been strong. Claims have been made that the recommendations of the Macpherson report are hampering police activity and that many police officers have become afraid of the consequences of arresting members of ethnic minorities. Yet when in May 2002 the Home Secretary announced new measures to deal with street crime he noted that while the use by the police of stop and search powers declined by 17 per cent in the year up to April 2001, the number of black people stopped increased by 4 per cent. As *The Guardian*'s Home Affairs correspondent Allan Travers commented: 'The new figures dispel the myth that the police have retreated from using powers to stop and search black people because of a fear of being branded racist'.[21] In this atmosphere, a weakening of political will was evident within the New Labour government. Blair's claim, in April 2000, that 'our record on race relations is exemplary and one we are extremely proud of' needs at least some qualification as far as the government's record on policing is concerned.[22]

DISCRIMINATION IN THE LABOUR MARKET

Since the 1960s a series of reports have documented racial discrimination within British society.[23] It was hoped that with the passage of time the labour and housing markets would adjust to accommodate the new immigrant minorities. It is not clear, however, that markets have operated in this way. While the first generation of workers established themselves within the labour forces of large factories and public corporations, they were unable to do so in ways that gave them economic security. A study undertaken for the New Labour government by the Cabinet Office described the employment experiences of these workers as 'a depressing story of continuing disadvantage'. Shamit Saggar, who led the research, described how after adjusting for age, language fluency, education and a range of other possible explanations for under-performance at work, the research team kept coming back to racial discrimination in the workplace as the key explanatory factor.[24]

Despite a generation of race relations legislation these patterns of wage inequality persist. The largest wage gap exists between the earnings of white men and those of Pakistani and Bangladeshi background and the narrowest is between white men and those of Indian background.[25] The *Financial Times* noted that by the autumn of 1994 the unemployment rate for ethnic minorities was almost two-and-a-half times as high as that for whites; in 1984 it had not been twice as high.[26] The Cabinet Office study even found the chances of ethnic minorities being jobless were higher in the tight labour markets of 2000 than they had been for whites a decade earlier, when the economy was in much worse shape. These patterns are reinforced by the fact that minority ethnic groups are concentrated in low paid and vulnerable sectors of the economy and so were particularly badly hit by the recession of the early nineties.

The patterns of discrimination discussed above have been replicated over time, leading people to talk of a 'cement roof' rather than a 'glass ceiling' above ethnic minority employees.[27] In no sector of enterprise did ethnic minorities constitute more that 0.5 per cent of employment in management occupations.[28] Historically, the expectation has been that the professions (especially those in the public sector) will provide a more even playing field for members of ethnic minorities. But even those with academic qualifications have found advancement in these fields difficult. Evidence consistently points to the operation of institutionalized racism in the health service, the legal profession, the civil service, higher education and local authorities.[29]

The 'Asian corner shop' and the 'Indian restaurant', on the other hand, have become an established part of British life, and the Indian and Pakistani immigrants who run them have been commonly supposed to be repeating the experiences of previous groups of migrants (notably Jews and East Europeans) who made a niche for themselves in retailing before extending their entrepreneurial activities into other branches of industry and commerce. But while some South Asian family firms are becoming established as successful medium-sized companies, most are small businesses, 42 per cent have no employees at all and have been described as an 'economic dead end'.[30] In explaining why people stay in such 'dead ends' the Policy Studies Institute concluded in 1996 that perceived and experienced patterns of discrimination in labour markets had been a strong influence.[31] This was particularly the case amongst businesses owned by people of Pakistani origin, 56 per cent of whom indicated that they were self-employed because they felt that discrimination in the job market limited their opportunities (compared with only 8 per cent of Indian origin). Over half the people contacted did not want their children to take over their business, and the fact that this was least true of people of Pakistani background suggested that they were most likely to perceive the next generation as suffering from a similar lack of opportunity as themselves.[32] In the nineties this issue became a source of inter-generational conflict as young people became increasingly dissatisfied with the options available to them, and with their parents' strategy of de facto ghettoization – a conflict exacerbated by the recent expansion of superstores offering 24-hour opening and Sunday trading, leading to an estimated decline of 25 per cent in the number of family-run Asian corner shops over the past decade.[33]

In assessing New Labour's record in grappling with discrimination in the labour market it thus unfortunately appears that its commitment to the free operation of markets has been greater than its political will to intervene as powerfully as it needed to against the forces of institutionalized racism. As a result, when commenting on the mounting evidence of discrimination, John Monks, the General Secretary of the TUC, declared with some justice 'that racism still blights the working lives of thousands of black and Asian people'.[34]

THE NEW RACISM

Similar patterns of discrimination exist in other aspects of social life, including public services such as housing, education, health care and so on. Taken together, the data go a long way towards supporting the thesis that a 'racist attitude permeates society on the individual and institutional level, covertly or overtly'.[35] However the data also reveal complex patterns of differentiation *between* ethnic minority groups.

For one thing, the ethnic minority population has changed over time. In many cases we are talking of individuals who were born in the UK and who speak with broad regional accents. While these people (and their parents and grandparents) have experienced racism in their daily lives, they have not been simply victims. They have adapted and developed social relationships in the context of UK society and in doing so they have changed it in a variety of ways. An obvious example is to be found in cuisine. British diet has been transformed over the past thirty years and the availability of a wide variety of ethnic foods has been a major influence. The overwhelming presence in the retail economy of people of Bangladeshi origins reflects their dominance of the 'Indian restaurant' trade, serving 2.5 million customers every week. To them is due the creation of 'chicken tikka masala' (a dish unknown in 'India'), described by Robin Cook in 2001 as 'Britain's national dish'. Marks and Spencer now sells 18 tonnes of this pre-packed meal every week. Similar innovative contributions to British culture have come from British 'Indians' – or 'Indian Britons' – in the media, from films like *Bhaji on the Beach* to popular television series like *Goodness Gracious Me*. It is ultimately in these ways that British multi-culturalism has really been created, and presented as an historical fact.

And as the society has changed so has the nature of racism. Here the shift has been from a coherent set of ideas that organizes people into a hierarchy of biologically defined races, to one that emphasizes and makes symbolic certain cultural features.[36] In this cultural form, racism operates under many guises. It becomes intertwined strongly with ideas of nation and national identity. Important here is the way in which the British Empire (strongly ordered on lines of biological racism[37]) ended, and the questions that this left about the 'place of Britain in the world'. As the 1990s progressed, this discourse was developed and brought to bear in complex ways on Muslims, economic migrants and 'asylum seekers' (always, it seems, with the prefix 'bogus'). These developments were based partly on a move from biological to cultural racism. Muslims were attacked not because of their 'race' or the colour of their skin but because of their religion, because of the practice of arranged marriages, and latterly because of the association made between Islam and terrorism.

This stretching of racism to include such cultural and political attributes developed alongside a growing xenophobia that was also brought to bear upon the thousands of white people arriving dispossessed on the shores of the UK in the late 1990s and early 2000s. In reflecting upon this phenomenon Sivanandan has written of 'xeno-racism':

> ... a xenophobia that bears all the marks of the old racism, except that it is not colour-coded. It is a racism that is not just directed at those with darker skins, from the former colonial countries, but at the newer categories of the displaced and dispossessed whites, who are beating at western Europe's doors, the Europe that displaced them in the first place. It is racism in substance but xeno in form – a racism that is meted out to impoverished strangers even if they are white.[38]

A racism that once flourished on the football terraces, with bananas being thrown at black players, now flourishes on the streets as Islamic women become fearful of wearing head-scarves and Croatians too become victims of wanton violence.[39]

If a week is a long time in Labour politics, three years is an epoch; and the years that followed the publication of the Macpherson Report were especially long ones in political time. Street crime, ever salient, became more and more a cause for concern for 'middle Britain', and this was played out in the tabloid press at a time when the issue of immigration came, once again, into the forefront of the public mind. New Labour responded with an increasingly tough stance that culminated in the 1999 Immigration and Asylum Act and its subsequent amendments. If the Macpherson Inquiry marked the high point of new Labour's policies, this was its low, the basis of Nick Cohen's depiction of *Cruel Britannia*.[40]

One of the features of the new world order that replaced the Cold War has been the large numbers of displaced peoples moving around the world in search of a better and safer life. These flows of people, packed into rusting ships and lorries, have moved northwards and westwards where they have been systematically repelled by the concerted armoury of 'Fortress Europe'. In ways that are difficult to contemplate, people still arrive and it is in its response to this crisis that New Labour has revealed its reactionary side. Seemingly driven by the violent rhetoric of the Tory right wing, New Labour attempted to put a stranglehold on migration by instructing its Embassies in key states not to issue visas, and by introducing severe penalties to punish any carrier of 'illegal immigrants' into the UK. Illegal immigrants and asylum seekers were to be dealt with summarily; sometimes held in special centres and provided not with money but with vouchers (asylos) that could be exchanged only for food in supermarkets, and for which they could receive no change. Deprived of cash and the legal status of a worker, many of these people turned to begging, others to crime, encouraging calls for even harsher treatment and demands for their expulsion.

The problem undoubtedly came to dominate the public mind in the late nineties. Bill Morris, the moderate black General Secretary of the Transport and General Workers Union, attacked the Home Secretary Jack Straw's policies as 'giving life to the racists', creating a climate where 'the mood music is playing a hostile tune for black Britons'.[41] He attacked the voucher system as 'utterly insane', and was supported by other black leaders. The black Labour MP Dianne Abbott, for example, told Tony Blair that 'as a child of economic migrants I took personal exception to ministers constantly talking about bogus asylum-seekers and economic migrants as if they are some sort of parasite'. In offering an explanation of these policies she maintained that

> Although Jack's [Straw's] personal commitment to race relations is quite strong, when the interests of good race relations clashes with the prejudices of middle England, middle England wins every time.[42]

Here we see a classic example of a 'moral panic', centred upon the middle classes but expressed most violently amongst the most dispossessed of white workers. Poor people, living in poor accommodation in the southern port towns (especially Dover), complained that the immigrants arriving there were being treated better than they were. Poor white communities, suffering from economic dislocation and political abandonment and appalling living conditions, saw asylum-seekers housed in privately-run, profit-making accommodation in their neighbourhoods. The asylum-seekers, barred from employment, were a daily embodiment of media and politician-inspired myths. When they went shopping local people encountered 'them' paying with asylos rather than money, an object of attention and further proof that 'they' were getting everything that 'we', the British, were denied.

Although the 'they' in these scenarios were at this point overwhelmingly white, the validation of an 'us' versus 'them' politics was clear. The previous politics had demonized the non-white 'them' as the undeserving usurpers who entered 'our country' to take our houses, jobs and benefits. These ideas and sentiments were refurbished, reinvigorated and applied to the new influx of 'illegal immigrants' and 'bogus' asylum seekers. In port towns like Dover radio phone-ins were dominated by a growing rhetoric of hatred. The Labour MP for Dover, Gwyn Prosser, explained how 'ninety per cent, if not all, of the 175 asylum seekers here are unaccompanied minors. I'm not saying that all these young men are criminals ... but I talk to people who have lived here all their lives and can now no longer walk down the streets'. These asylum seekers, he adds, 'do not live in accordance with local people's social habits'.[43]

The elements of the problem, and of the moral panic, are all revealed here. All recent estimates of net immigration indicate either a steady state or a decline. Nevertheless, immigration emerged as a major political issue, the shape of which seemed to be agreed by the major political parties. In its first attempts to defuse such tensions (others were to follow), the government opted for a policy of dispersal. Thus over a thousand migrants were, for example, moved into refurbished accommodation in the centre of one of the poorest parts of Glasgow. The local authority had accepted these people because they came with a 'financial package' from the central government. Local people viewed this development with intense resentment. Such were the feelings that one of the refugees was murdered in the street. Many of the others talked of being afraid to leave their apartments.

RIOTS, RACISM AND THE POLITICS OF POVERTY

Many facets of the race tragedy in Britain, and New Labour's role in it, came together in a number of northern cities in the summer of 2001. In the old textile towns of Oldham and Burnley (Lancashire) and Bradford (Yorkshire) riots took place in which young working class men ('Asians' and whites) fought each other. Here, and especially in Oldham, the National Front was directly involved in a provocative role, claiming to defend white workers and their families. As a result, in some of the most deprived locations in the UK, the cold reality of 'multi-culturalism' became clear. In these towns, in the context of the collapse of the clothing and textile industries and a depletion of the public housing stock due to continued privatization policies, multi-culturalism had come to border on separate development.

Among young men from the ethnic minorities in these towns there emerged a

> sense of grievance ... not far beneath the surface. Many ... believe that things are harder for them than for their parents, who came to Huddersfield in the fifties and sixties to work in the mills. There are no jobs now and young people are less likely to take any sort of low paid work.
>
> 'No one is going to do us any favours,' said Nicholas Modeste. 'The police have attitude, they are more likely to blame us. Politicians don't do anything for us.[44]

And in these same communities white working-class people also looked for an explanation for the dislocation and despair that overwhelmed them. Abandoned by their employers and the state, they increasingly turned to racialized explanations of their situation. These explanations had the validation of 'common sense' ('things were alright before *they* came'). The policies of local and national govern-ments, and the competitive rules that determined the distribution of inadequate levels of resources, served to reinforce these views ('*They* are getting everything around here'). This became the reality of life in the northern towns and cities mentioned above. In these places what one gained the other seemed to lose.

And there is more. Racially/ethnically segregated housing policies played a major role in the development of racially/ethnically segregated schooling in these places.[45] Local authority decisions about school boundaries, the sites of new schools and other decisions made along racial/ethnic lines, also contributed to the development of segregated schooling. We are thus left with the dramatic and sad conclusion of the Independent Review into the Oldham riots:

> Whether in school or out of school there are few opportunities for young people across the communal boundaries to mix within Oldham. Except where people have significant contact in the workplace this is the case for adults, too, and relationships between the communities at adult level are largely confined to business transactions (shops, restaurants, taxis). Pakistanis, Bangladeshis and whites simply do not meet one another to any significant degree, and this has led to ignorance, misunderstanding and fear.[46]

The review concluded that this separation had produced a climate of distrust, competition and conflict. This ignorance and misunderstanding was reinforced by government policies which failed to provide investment in physical and human infrastructure to prepare for the decline and later the collapse of the textile industry, or to counter institutional racism in the educational, housing, employ-ment and criminal justice areas. Such interventions as did occur were more often than not ineffective and, worse, involved making different groups, areas, and communities compete for limited funds.

The dominant motif was that of a zero-sum game. Each community saw the causes of their economic and social dislocation in the gains made by the other. In the 2001 General Election the far-right British National Party (BNP – the political and more respectable arm of the militant National Front) stood in many of these northern towns. Here it developed a radical right-wing politics that focused on and identified with the problems of poor white workers, the unem-ployed and the dispossessed. It voiced and amplified the anger of these neglected white communities. It pointed to the alleged dominance of 'the others' and the ways in which they were using legislation and the law to obtain special treatment; 'better treatment than we get in our own country'.

The BNP not only increased racial tensions in these communities, but provided a vehicle for mobilizing the alienation and betrayal felt by white workers in these areas. In a real way, the BNP is the other side on the New Labour coin. For while New Labour indulged in the rhetoric of multiculturalism and social inclusion, the BNP focused on and exploited the daily material circumstances of a de-industrialized society and its rotting former heartlands.

Here (and in the old coalfield areas too) white workers who once occupied key positions in unionized factories look upon the rubble of their lives in a flexible de-unionized world. With no one to speak up for them they come to hate the politicians. Feeling isolated and unrepresented, their anger can provide the dynamic for racially-constructed interpretations and violent solutions.

In May 2001 all these forces came to a head. Increasing levels of racist violence and fears of more violent National Front invasions of the Asian communities provided the torch to light the powder keg of rage, resentment and racism that characterized life in Oldham. In this context the BNP portrayed itself as the voice of reason, condemning violence but in sombre tones declaring that it merely proved that a multiracial society was not possible. The party gained its highest ever level of votes as a result.

In the 2002 local elections the BNP concentrated their efforts in this area. Nearly 10,000 voters in Burnley cast their ballots for them, and they won 3 seats. Although they did not win any seats in Oldham they contested only five wards and took an average of 28 per cent of the vote in each. In the St James ward the Liberal-Democratic candidate won by a margin of only 3 per cent. They also broke the 10 per cent barrier in 16 of the remaining 48 seats they contested.[47] In some Northern towns and cities these elections also involved votes for a new position of mayor. In Hartlepool and Middlesborough the established political candidates were defeated by populist independents, like the local football team's mascot in Hartlepool, campaigning in a monkey suit, and the former chief of police in Middlesborough, cashing in on his reputation for having pursued a policy of 'zero tolerance'. After these results (and the disaffection from Labour politics that they seem to imply) the Government shelved plans for similar mayoral elections in Bradford and Birmingham, fearing that the BNP might steal victories there. As a 'senior government figure close to the negotiations' put it: 'Giving the BNP a campaign platform in places like Bradford, which had race riots last summer, and Birmingham, cannot be a good idea'.[48]

CONCLUSIONS

These local elections in northern England followed the strong performance of Le Pen in the first round of the French Presidential elections. and were succeeded by the developments in the Dutch elections that led to the assassination of Pim Fortuyn. These defeats for the Left and Centre Left in Western Europe were widely seen as relating to the growing strength of feeling against immigration. Sometimes dubbed 'Fascist', the new right-wing populist parties which made these gains are in fact more akin to older forms of reactionary conservatism. Across Europe they share similar concerns. They are opposed to immigration and mostly justify this in terms of the *xenoracism* mentioned above. They are also militantly opposed to crime, linking it to immigration, and by extension to particular racially defined groups. They claim to speak for the poor and the dispossessed; they are opposed to the elites, the 'fat cats' and the 'spin' with which comfortable politicians surround themselves.

Anthony Giddens, one of the originators of Blair's Third Way, declared that New Labour provided the only feasible model for the European left. It needed, he said, to follow Blair's 'celebrated intention to be tough on crime and tough on the causes of crime', which he described as 'a major element of New Labour's rise to prominence'. In his view the slogan now needed to be extended to include 'policies … which are "tough on immigration, but tough on the causes of hostility to immigrants"'.[49] How the latter was to be achieved was unclear. Suggested policies here were all ones that stress assimilation rather than multiculturalism. On the former, however, it seems that New Labour needed little instruction from Professor Giddens. The British Home Secretary in the second New Labour government, David Blunkett, followed in the footsteps of his predecessor and focused on issues of crime and immigration almost to the exclusion of all others. On 23 April, 2002, following the first round of the French Presidential elections and before the May local elections in Britain, Blunkett's officials announced that his 'tough policies on street crime, immigration and asylum were vital if jaundiced voters were not to abandon the mainstream parties'.[50] Blunkett himself argued that 'the centre left must take this fight [against the far right] head on. We cannot face this challenge by ducking hard debate'.[51] In the elaboration of this 'hard debate', however, it becomes increasingly clear that in most instances the ground is conceded to the new populist parties of the right. Hence there is an immigration problem, asylum seekers are a problem, crime is a problem. 'But we can solve it'.

There is a considerable danger that these policies of toughness will legitimate rather than challenge the new populism. In France, Denmark and elsewhere policies have been developed that attack asylum seekers and refugees and attempt to build security around 'Fortress Europe'. While politics become increasingly concerned with these issues, the problems of dislocated communities, and complex patterns of racial segregation, racial hierarchy and racial tension go unchallenged. In April 2002 *The Guardian* quoted a white youth in Bradford as asking 'What is Bradford for? … We've got no industry, the place is falling apart and if you want anything worthwhile then you have to go to Leeds'.[52] The left needs to develop a politics capable of entering this world and dealing honestly and effectively with its problems.

NOTES

1   Institute of Race Relations, *Police Against Black People,* London: Institute of Race Relations, 1979 (reprinted in Institute of Race Relations, *Policing Against Black People,* London: Institute of Race Relations, 1987).

2   Stuart Hall, Chas Critcher, Tony Jefferson, John Clarke and Brian Roberts, *Policing the Crisis: Mugging, the State, and Law and Order,* London: Macmillan, 1978.

3   *Manchester Evening News,* 7 February 1995.

4   *Manchester Evening News,* 9 February 1995.

5   Paul Johnson, *Daily Mail*, 13 February 1995.
6   See for example Leo Panitch and Colin Leys, *The End of Parliamentary Socialism: From New Left to New Labour*, London: Verso, 1998.
7   W. Macpherson, T. Cook, J. Sentamu, and R. Stone, *The Stephen Lawrence Inquiry*, Presented to Parliament by the Secretary of State for the Home Department (Report), Stationery Office, London, 1999, 46.1, p. 317.
8   Macpherson et al., *The Stephen Lawrence Inquiry*, 45.7. p. 312.
9   Ibid., 45.6, p. 311.
10   Quoted in ibid., 1999, pp. 26-7.
11   Ibid., 6.34, p. 28.
12   Lord Scarman, *The Brixton Disorders, 10-12 April 1981, Report of an Inquiry*, London: HMSO, 1981, Cmnd 8427.
13   See for example, Commission for Racial Equality, *Race and Equal Opportunities in the Police Service: A Programme for Action*, London: Commission for Racial Equality, 1996; Robin Oakley, *Race and Equal Opportunities in the Police Service*, London: Commission for Racial Equality, 1996.
14   HM Inspectorate of Constabulary, *Winning the Race, Policing Plural Communities Revisited*, London, Home Office, 1998, p. 45.
15   Simon Holdaway, *The Racialisation of British Policing*, London: Macmillan, 1996, p. 166.
16   *Statewatch*, 'Policing the Streets: The Use and Abuse of Police Powers', *Statewatch*, 5 (4), 1995, p. 20. See also Louis Kushnick, '"Over Policed and Under Protected": Stephen Lawrence, Institutional and Police Practices', Sociological Research Online, 4(1), http://www.socresonline.org.uk/socresonline/4/1/kushnik.html.
17   For a discussion see *Statewatch*, 'The Cycle of UK Racism: Stop and Search, Arrest and Imprisonment', *Statewatch*, 9(1), 1999, p. 1.
18   The Institute of Race Relations identified a pattern of almost seventy deaths of black people in custody between 1987 and 1991. Inquest, a non-governmental organization working directly with the families of those who die in custody, identified thirty-seven Black custodial deaths between 1991 and February 1996 of which fourteen were in police custody. The Institute of Race Relations evidence to the Stephen Lawrence inquiry indicated that 67 per cent of people knew some one who had experienced physical abuse by a police officer; 40 per cent had personally experienced racial abuse from an officer; 78 per cent believed that police treated a crime in which the victim was white more seriously than one with a black victim; and 64 per cent of black inmates said they had witnessed an average of eight incidents over the same period. See Institute of Race Relations, *Deadly Silence: Black Deaths in Custody*, London: Institute of Race Relations, 1991; Inquest, *Racial Discrimination and Deaths in Custody: A Report to the United Nations Committee on the Elimination of Racial Discrimination*, London: Inquest, 1996, pp. 20-1; Institute of Race Relations, *Online Resources: Institute of Race*

Relations Evidence, Submitted for Part 2 of the Inquiry into Matters Arising from the Death of Stephen Lawrence, 1999, http://www.homebeats.co.uk/resources/lawrence.htm.

19 *Statewatch*, May–June 1996, p. 3.

20 Institute of Race Relations, *Stephen Lawrence*, p. 1.

21 *The Observer*, March 10 2002 .

22 *Daily Mail*, 15 April 2000.

23 W.W. Daniel, *Racial Discrimination in England*, Harmondsworth: Penguin Books, 1968; David Smith, *Racial Disadvantage in Britain: The PEP Report*, Harmondsworth:Penguin Books, 1977; David Smith, *Black & White Britain: The Third PSI Survey*, London: Heinemann Educational Books, 1984; T. Modood, R. Berthoud, J. Lakey, J. Nazroo, P. Smith, S. Virdee, and S. Beishon, *Ethnic Minorities in Britain: Diversity and Disadvantage*, The Fourth National Survey of Ethnic Minorities, London: Policy Studies Institute, 1997.

24 These matters are discussed further in David Walker, 'Study Reveals Job Plight of Muslims', *The Guardian*, 20 February 2002.

25 TUC, *Black and Underpaid: How black workers lose out on pay*, London, TUC, 12 April 2002.

26 *Financial Times*, 17 June 1996.

27 Wainwright Trust, *The Cement Roof: Afro-Caribbean People in Management*, Wane, Herts: Wainwright Trust, 1996.

28 African and Caribbean Finance Forum, *Foundation for Management Education, Windsor Fellowship*, 1996.

29 See for example Naaz Coker, *Racism in Medicine*, London: Kings Fund, 2001; MSF, *The Ethnic Status of NHS Staff: Damning New Statistics,* London: MSF, 1997; J. Carter, S. Fenton and T. Madood, *Ethnicity and Employment in Higher Education,* London, Policy Studies Institute, 1999.

30 H.E.Aldrich et.al. 'Business development and self-segregation: Asian enterprise in three British cities', in C. Peach, V. Robinson and S. Smith, eds., *Ethnic Segregation in Cities*, London: Croom Helm, 1981.

31 H. Metcalfe, T. Modood and S. Virdee, *Asian Self-Employment: The Interaction of Culture and Economics in England,* London: Policy Studies Institute, 1996.

32 Ibid., pp.125–6.

33 Paul Brown, 'Family-run Asian Shops Disappear', *The Guardian,* 5 January 2002

34 Quoted in *The Guardian*, 11 January 2001.

35 Stokely Carmichael and Charles V. Hamilton, *Black Power: The Politics of Liberation in America,* London: Penguin Books, 1967, pp. 20-1; quoted in Macpherson, 1999, 6.22, p. 23.

36 For an earlier account of this development see Martin Barker, *The New Racism and the Ideology of the Tribe*, London: Junction Books, 1981. For the ways in which these processes impact upon young people see Les Back,

New Ethnicities and Urban Culture: Racism and Multiculture in Young Lives, London: University College London Press, 1996.

37 For a recent powerful account see Amita V. Ghosh, *The Glass Palace,* London: Harper Collins, 2000.

38 A. Sivanandan, 'Poverty is the New Black', *Race & Class,* 43(2) (October–December), 2001, p. 2 .

39 See for example, P. Francis, and R. Matthews, eds., *Tackling Racial Attacks,* Leicester: University of Leicester Press, 1998; Ben Bowling, *Violent Racism,* Oxford: Oxford University Press, 1998.

40 Nick Cohen, *Cruel Britannia,* London: Verso, 1999. For a discussion of the earlier Tory variant see also Craig Young, 'Political Representations of Geography and Place in the United Kingdom Asylum and Immigration Bill', *Urban Geography,* 1997, 18(1).

41 *The Independent,* 14 April 2000.

42 *The Daily Telegraph,* 15 April 2000.

43 Quoted in Richard Woods, 'Asylum Isn't Working', *The Sunday Times,* 19 May 2002

44 *The Observer,* 28 July 1996, p. 16.

45 See for example Valerie Karn and D. Phillips, 'Race and ethnicity in housing: a diversity of experience', in T. Blackstone, B. Parekh & P. Sanders, eds., *Race Relations in Britain: a developing agenda,* London: Routledge, 1998.

46 Oldham Independent Review. *Report,* 2001, p. 8 Similar Reports were produced for Bradford and Burnley where similar riots had occurred and where similar processes were seen to be at work.

47 Alan Travis, 'The Devil is in the Detail', *The Guardian,* 9 May 2002.

48 *Sunday Times,* 5 May 2002.

49 Anthony Giddens, 'The Third Way can Beat the Far Right', *The Guardian,* 3 May 2002.

50 *The Guardian,* 23 April 2002.

51 Ibid.

52 Gary Younge, 'The Burnley Offensive', *The Guardian,* 15 April 2002.

THE POLITICS OF
LABOUR AND RACE IN THE USA

BILL FLETCHER, JR. AND FERNANDO GAPASIN

Understanding the question of race and labour in the USA can be helped by reference to a story. In the mid-1700s there was a slave conspiracy in the New York colony. Like many slave conspiracies this was uncovered before it could be hatched. What was unusual about this particular conspiracy was that the rebels were both Africans and Irish. Prior to their execution, the rebels were interviewed and asked about the objectives of the planned uprising. The Africans answered that they sought to kill all the white people. No surprise there. The Irish were interviewed as well. They answered, in turn, to kill all the white people – i.e. Irish people in the Americas had yet to become what we know as 'white'. The ironic contrast, of course, can be found one hundred years later in the New York 1863 Draft Riots, where Irish immigrants conducted a pogrom/mass lynching targeted at freed Africans, as a way of venting their anger about the Civil War and the unfair draft laws. By the mid-1860s, the Irish were well on their way to becoming 'white'.[1]

While the Irish, as Europeans, could become 'whites', what is fascinating is that they were not immediately assumed to be white.[2] In other words, a process had to unfold in order for the Irish to become white, at least in the manner in which we have come to understand that term. Thus, *whiteness*, like racial identity in general, must be understood as a socio-political construct rather than anything fundamentally rooted in biology. It is this kind of understanding that underlies the conception of US capitalism as a racialized capitalism. US capitalism does not exist in the abstract, to which race is then added on. Race as a socio-political construct, and racist oppression, are centre factors in comprehending the history and politics of the USA.[3]

Capitalism engenders competition within the working class. This competition is not a Machiavellian conspiracy, but exists at the heart of the system. The competition is one for limited resources. The resource may be employment, income, or, as much of the world is presently discovering, it may be water. In any case, the nature of the system is such as to promote competition. There are never enough resources – no matter what the form – to serve the existing population because of the manner in which resources are divided up. The surplus, whether the surplus value produced by the workers themselves, or the societal surplus, is not up for some sort of equitable distribution. All of this leaves aside intent. Intent is irrelevant. It is for that reason that capitalism is correctly described as an amoral system. There is no morality contained in it. The competition for limited resources places one section of the working class at odds with other sections. That internal contradiction within the working class is a source of delight for the capitalists. Crabs in the barrel, so to speak. In response to this competition, trade unions first developed, originally as guilds and later as the organizations that we recognize today.

This basic understanding is critical because the divide-and-conquer element of capitalism is not something that has to be introduced from outside the system. It is inherent to the system, and has served to undermine threats to the system. The tension that the original settlers faced when arriving in the North American colonies between the labouring population and the colonial ruling class was relieved to a great extent by the racial divide that was created by the ruling class within the labouring population. It was in this context that one could witness the fusion of what has come to be known as 'race' with the capitalist system. As Manning Marable has been fond of saying, US capitalism can never be understood as some sort of capitalism in the abstract, but must be understood as racial capitalism.

Race has been the trip-wire of progressive and radical movements in the USA. The central argument of this essay is that the failure by the bulk of organized labour, including many progressives and radicals, to address race and racism, has undermined efforts to develop a consistent class-consciousness within the US working class. US labour's historical tendency to define its constituency in exclusively 'white' terms, to match the racial nature of US capitalism, has been one of the greatest limitations on US trade unionism. But even *within* racially inclusive unionism there remains the problem of the resolution of real world contradictions. Even a trade unionism that is inclusive, i.e., that seeks to unite all who can be united, can still miss the fundamental nature of racial capitalism in the USA and its impact on the working class. This flaw, or blind spot, can lead even some of the best leaders to believe that it is possible to build a successful, class-conscious, or even a trade union-conscious movement without an anti-racist analysis and practice. The core of this view, which can be described as *pragmatic idealism*, is that building a movement around a set of issues which everyone shares in common can overcome any differences – real or perceived – which might exist. This idealism downplays the material basis for racism, which is white privilege and racial/national oppression, reinforced by the ideology of white supremacy. Despite repeated evidence that pragmatic idealism does not work, it remains a largely hegemonic view – albeit repeatedly challenged – within US trade unionism.

AMERICAN LABOUR AND RACE IN HISTORICAL PERSPECTIVE

'Organized labor, for the most part be it radical or conservative, thinks and acts, in the terms of the White Race'.[4] Thus did Ben Fletcher, a leading Black organizer for the Industrial Workers of the World in the early part of the twentieth century, put the issue of exclusivist American trade unionism. The USA, as objectively a settler state, has been relatively successful in absorbing into full citizenship successive waves of European immigrants, but it has found it more problematic to be inclusive of indigenous or pre-existing populations on land that was expropriated – e.g., Native Americans, Mexicans, and Puerto Ricans. And even more problematic for the USA, given that from its colonial origins it had to define itself in terms of the realities and the legacy of racial slavery, has been its population of African Americans. This dilemma had already made its way into the burgeoning US trade union movement in the 1800s. What could then be identified as a trade union movement was for all intents and purposes a movement of white men in the northern states. It immediately fractured on the question of slavery, some taking a position in favour of slavery, and others in opposition to it, while still others took the view that it was not something on which labour should take a position.[5]

While this debate was quite obviously about race, it was also at its core about competition within the working class for limited resources. The leadership of the growing trade union movement, both before and after the Civil War, was torn over how to resolve this very fundamental contradiction, always fearing that an inclusive strategy might have the effect of reducing the wages and benefits of the core workforce. The alternative view held that the exclusive approach needed to be challenged in its fundamentals. This debate never focused solely on African-Americans, although that was to be a major flashpoint during the nineteenth and most of the twentieth century. The mid to late 1800s saw the emergence of an Asian workforce in the USA that was actively excluded from the ranks of organized labour. One of the early efforts at independent 'working class' political action, for example, was the Workingmen's Party in California. The *raison d'être* of this party, however, was opposition to Asian labour.

But long before workers of colour played central roles in white-led labour formations (e.g., the Industrial Workers of the World), they consistently found means of self-organization. At that time, however, understanding labour in these terms meant defining the labour movement more broadly than was generally accepted. Lerone Bennett, Jr., in his insightful work, *The Shaping of Black America*, describes a Black worker insurgency that immediately followed the Civil War:

> Even before the Radical Reconstruction governments were installed, black workers sprang into action, staging sit-down demonstrations and strikes. In 1865 black washwomen organized a union in Jackson, Mississippi, and

demanded what a Southern newspaper called 'exorbitant' prices for laundry. The next year, in August, black Union veterans employed at the iron factories in Elyton (later known as Birmingham) struck for higher wages and were driven out of town. Three months later a New York Times correspondent reported from South Carolina that the freedmen were organizing unions to force concessions from the employers ... He said the movement 'is entirely spontaneous on the part of the freedmen' and has the 'symptoms of something very like a Northern "strike"'.[6]

This Southern movement, however, for all intents and purposes did not happen, at least from the standpoint of white labour. Organized labour during this same period was basically defined by the activities of (mainly) white men, many of whom were active in the development of the National Labor Union, an early attempt at a federation. Indeed, workers of colour – largely African-American – were also involved in the development of what came to be known as the Colored National Labor Union when they were excluded from membership in the all-white NLU. Progressive historians, such as the late Philip S. Foner, gave such formations respectful and legitimate attention, but most established labour history has placed them on the sidelines. Such a misunderstanding or misreading of history leads one to see the labour movement as limited to the official – i.e., white-dominated – unions.

The clash between a trade unionism representing a consistent inclusive democracy and a trade unionism representing exclusiveness did not always break down on strictly racial terms. Nevertheless, the often-racial character of this split was regularly quite graphic. In 1903, for example, a labour formation known as the Japanese-Mexican Labor Union (situated on the West Coast of the USA) applied for a charter from the American Federation of Labor. The legendary AFL President Samuel Gompers offered a charter on condition that the Japanese workers were excluded. The response by the union was poignant:

> I beg to say in reply that our Japanese brothers here were the first to recognize the importance of cooperating and uniting in demanding a fair wage scale ... In the past we have counseled, fought and lived on very short rations with our Japanese brothers, and toiled with them in the fields, and they have been uniformly kind and considerate. We would be false to them and to ourselves and to the cause of unionism if we now accepted privileges for ourselves which are not accorded to them. We are going to stand by men who stood with us in the long, hard fight which ended in victory over the enemy. We therefore respectfully petition the A.F. of L. to grant us a charter under which we can unite all sugar beet and field laborers of Oxnard without regard to their color or race.[7]

A myriad other examples in the late nineteenth and twentieth centuries can be used to demonstrate the actuality of self-organization among workers of colour, and the resistance of the mainstream labour movement to this. But the problem went beyond the labour establishment, as even militant trade unionists reflected an orientation shaped by the settler nature of the USA. Take, for example, the International Seamen's Union of the nineteenth century, whose orientation could have been described as militant, if not radical. It was highly critical of capitalism, but at the same time, it was white supremacist, not only in terms of internal segregation but also in terms of its stand toward Asian workers and Asia generally. For the ISU, in other words, there appeared to be no inconsistency between its militant critique of capitalism and its white supremacy.

Despite dramatic moments of fundamental restructuring of the union movement, such as the shift from a local (particularly municipal) to national focus, or when industrial unionism was created with the founding of what became the Congress of Industrial Organizations in 1935, the bulk of organized labour – including many 'inclusive' unions – has historically been unwilling to tackle this contradiction on the inclusionist side of the equation. The unfulfilled promise of the CIO, particularly with regard to matters of race, is documented in dramatic detail in Foner's classic work, *Organized Labor and the Black Worker*.[8]

In the 1930s several different ideological points of view pushed the US union movement from its narrow trades perspective to industrial unionism. The opposition within the union movement to industrial unionism (whole plant or sector organizing), in this case, came from those traditional union bureaucrats who believed that the maintenance of the trades orientation (organizing by trade skill) was the best way to preserve their own way of life and the well-being of those they conceived the trade union movement to be for, i.e., white, relatively well-paid workers. Change was brought about by an alliance between pragmatists and a broadly-defined Left, which advocated an inclusive unionism from a variety of socialist perspectives. The pragmatists addressed the practical needs of a union movement where the nature of work was shaped by Fordism and thus required a more practical way of organizing large groups of workers in order to build and maintain the union movement. The left viewed industrial unionism as potentially a more effective way to organize workers, providing them with the opportunity to improve their day-to-day lives while, at the same time, giving them an education about the need for class struggle and the overthrow of the capitalist system itself. Since the creation of the CIO, leftists have had most impact on the union movement when they were able to influence the direction of pragmatic trade unionists like John L. Lewis. One reason they were able to do this was the credibility that they brought to the table as a result of their leadership and influence in particular unions within the CIO.

The CIO, and to some extent the American Federation of Labor (from which the CIO split), led to the unionization of hundreds of thousands of African-Americans and their subsequent rise from often abject poverty. This said, it was also the case that the CIO, which had a significant left-wing presence until the late 1940s, had its own limitations. Fundamental to these was the fact that while the CIO unions made a commitment to organize workers of colour, they were uneven in challenging structural discrimination in the workplace.[9] This was especially clear in the way unions like the United Steelworkers of America reinforced traditional or de facto seniority arrangements, 'leading inevitably to unrealized expectations for many African American workers'.[10] While some of the left-led unions had a different practice, most notably the Packinghouse Workers, and the Food, Tobacco and Agricultural Workers, this was not the dominant reality of the CIO.[11] The way CIO collective bargaining agreements froze in place existing discriminatory employment practices through the modern era was exemplified by the case of the General Dynamics Quincy (Massachusetts) shipyard, which as late as the mid-1970s employed approximately 5000 workers, represented by Local 5 of the Industrial Union of Marine and Shipbuilding Workers of America. The employer traditionally had carried out little in the way of affirmative action in order to hire workers of colour, but after receiving some major contracts to build liquefied natural gas tankers, there was a significant increase in hiring of women and workers of colour. But workers of colour tended to be hired into the worst departments, e.g., welding, cleaning and sandblasting; and since seniority in the shipyard was by department, a worker in the welding department could accumulate years of seniority in that department, they would start at the bottom of the seniority ladder if he or she attempted to move to a more skilled department. The union leadership never challenged this sort of seniority system. In fact, when a reform movement in the local union attempted to raise the problems with it, the conservative leadership of the local united in its defence.

Many of these issues emerged in the late 1960s and early 1970s as flashpoints for rank and file rebellion on the part of workers of colour and the development of what has come to be known as the *caucus movement* of that period. By this time, the US labour movement had lost whatever dynamic potential for change industrial unionism had represented. In the post-war McCarthy era, the pragmatists moved deliberately towards the traditional union forces. The left's growing isolation in the CIO, and ultimately in the AFL-CIO, could be seen quite clearly in the isolation of leftists around their opposition to the Marshall Plan, and became still more acute when eleven 'red' unions were purged from the union central. Under the leadership of George Meany, the AFL-CIO institutionalized anti-communism within the union movement. By-laws were written to exclude communists and other leftists. Internationally, the AFL-CIO became known as the labour arm for the enforcement of US foreign policy. Domestically, during the Vietnam era, local Central Labor Councils were threatened with losing their charters if they officially opposed US policy in Vietnam. The fear of leftists infiltrating the AFL-CIO, the discriminatory policies of unions, and the AFL-CIO's pro-Viet Nam War stance all increased the distance between the union movement and other social movements that should have been close allies, e.g., the civil rights movement and the anti-war movement.

THE BACKLASH OF THE LATE TWENTIETH CENTURY

So long as the labour-capital social accord held through the post-war boom, the deep divisions within the working class based on race, gender, ethnicity and national origin, not to mention political and religious views, did not greatly disturb the US labour movement. But the breakdown of this 'deal' in the 1970s was accompanied by a right-wing backlash with regard to race and racism, which starkly reopened these divisions. The essence of the backlash came down to this: yes, there has been racial discrimination in the USA, but the various Civil Rights statutes have remedied this. No further action is necessary; indeed, any further action amounts to reverse racism, or reverse discrimination targeted at whites. In a nutshell, there were no longer issues of racial discrimination, let alone racist/national oppression in the USA. The argument was compelling and persuasive to many white people who were not prepared to accept the consequences of hundreds of years of slavery, colonialism, Jim Crow segregation and de facto segregation.

Even before the accord's breakdown, indeed almost simultaneously with the passage of the Civil Rights Act in 1964, a neo-conservative racial agenda or project emerged which transformed the issue of race from a group or societal issue to an individual 'problem'. It alleged that racism no longer existed; because the laws of the land had changed, the ability of an individual to achieve has become the only significant key to personal success. This concept of reverse discrimination and the right-wing neo-conservative agenda reached the national spotlight in the Bakke Supreme Court case of 1978.[12] This right-wing argument achieved the force of presidential power when Ronald Reagan embraced it.

But what was termed a conservative backlash turned out to actually be a more complex phenomenon integrally related to the economic restructuring of capitalism. This restructuring, in response to the stagnation of the economy, eventually produced what we have come to know as neoliberal globalization, which has had a direct impact on race and racism in the USA through its effect on the security and incomes of the white working class. The decline in average wages, which only started to bottom out around 1996, pushed down the real wages of US workers to around what they were in the late 1960s.[13] This wage decline was accompanied by a wealth polarization: whereas the upper 10 per cent of the US population owned approximately 49 per cent of the wealth in 1976, by 1999 it held no less than 73 per cent.[14] The response by workers has been, by and large, individual and familial. There are many reasons for this that go beyond the scope of this essay. One of the most important has been the crackdown on unions by employers and the government, as well as lethargy within the trade union movement. In any event, US workers have worked more hours, have had to depend on more members of their family going to work, and have had to go into deep personal debt in order to ward off a decline in their living standard.[15]

This has had a crushing psychological impact on the white working class. Brought up to believe that their living standard would increase over time and that the living standard for their children would always be greater than their own, they have found that none of these beliefs has turned out to be valid. As capitalism has restructured, and in particular, as manufacturing has reorganized and in many cases shifted offshore, their worlds have unravelled. While many people benefited from the economic expansion of the 1990s, many sectors of the working class continued to take major hits.

Significant numbers of white workers and sections of the petty bourgeoisie have responded to this assault by retreating into various forms of right-wing populism, protectionism and xenophobia. The changing complexion of the country with the entrance of new immigrants (overwhelmingly from Asia and Latin America, but also from Africa and parts of Europe) helped foster a siege mentality which, while not being unique to the USA, began to effect a recon-struction of race in the United States. This energized the political Right, bringing support for politicians like Pat Buchanan and others. One of the intriguing aspects of this right-wing populism is its racial message, encouraging, whether subtly or not so subtly, the notion that there has been a betrayal of white people by the multinational corporations. Right-wing populism argues, in essence, that it does not pay to be white any more. The deal, which these movements suggest existed between white people and capital, has been called off. Generally, right-wing populism puts the blame for this on Blacks and immigrants; capitalism as such is rarely the target.

The irony is that right-wing populism has part of the story correct (which is what makes their message so dangerous). The 'deal' between sections of capital and the more organized sector of the working class *has* been called off. For white workers, particularly in the USA, the expectation of a continued rise in living standards was tied directly to an implicit assumption that there would be a cushion beneath them – a cushion made up of workers of colour – to protect them from the ravages of capitalism. A combination of the struggles of people of colour as well as the threat to white living standards has undermined any sense of safety. A high level of stress and anxiety, even during the so-called boom period of the '90s, pervaded the working class.

The result has been that since the mid-1970s advances in the anti-racist struggle have been halted and, indeed, reversed. While this period of destabi-lization and decline ensued, it did not result in a levelling of conditions between whites and workers of colour. With regard to African-Americans, the period from 1979 till at least the mid-1990s saw a rise of inequality in wealth and income not only between African-Americans and whites, but also among African-Americans.[16] A similar tendency over the same period of time could be seen in the situation facing Latino workers.[17] For African-American men, the situation has become very stark. In 1979, for instance, Black men earned $0.77 for every $1.00 earned by white men. By 1991, this had dropped to $0.65 for every $1.00 earned by white men. The gap between the pay of Black women and white women showed a similar pattern until the late 1980s, but then started to move in the other direction, so that by 1992 Black women earned $0.89 for every $1.00 for white women.[18]

These racialized wage gaps are due to a number of factors. The most promi-nent relate to manufacturing employment and unionization. The wages of Black men have been hit hard by the contraction of heavy manufacturing and the decline in unionization. Research also suggests that workers in organizations with higher percentages of women are paid lower starting wages; and, especially in service industries, companies are hiring higher percentages of women.[19] This larger percentage of women on lower wages may be bringing down the overall average wages for all women, thus contributing to the decline in the wage differential between Black women and White women.

Blacks continue to experience more long-term unemployment than whites.[20] The period of industrial contraction also had a disproportionate impact on workers of colour in other ways. In the period 1982-97, African-American participation in jobs such as machine operators, assemblers, tenders, fabricators, handlers, helpers and labourers shrank by 5 per cent, compared with a 2 per cent drop for whites. At the same time, African-American participation in sales jobs increased by 3 per cent, compared with 0.5 per cent for whites.[21]

Much was made of falling poverty rates with the economic expansion of the 1990s. But in good times or bad, the racial differential continues to exist. In 1997, during a supposed boom, the poverty rate for African-Americans and Latinos was more than double that of whites (27 per cent compared with 11 per cent).[22] One important point to note about this is that the common assumption that being below the poverty line must mean being on unemployment is inaccurate. Working poverty has become a part of the landscape of the USA. Roughly a fifth of Latinos and African-Americans work at the low end of the employment ladder in low-paid service jobs. This compares with slightly more than 10 per cent of whites.[23] Statistics such as these demonstrate the continued reality of the racial differential, particularly when it comes to African-Americans, Latinos, Native Americans and many Asians. Whether in areas of employment or housing, or encounters with the police and incarceration, the racial differential runs through US society as real as any wall a society can build. Despite this, far too many white workers go on believing that either racial discrimination has ended entirely, or that it has minimal consequences on the workforce today.[24] For many whites, their own decline plus a racial blind spot made it difficult to grasp what has been happening to workers of colour.

CHANGING COMPLEXION

Much has been made of increased immigration over the last twenty years. This is a complicated picture. The number of immigrants relative to the existing population was higher in the first half of the 1990s than in the 1950s, but quite a bit lower than in the early part of the twentieth century.[25] What had changed were the countries of origin. While the early twentieth century witnessed immigrants from Europe, the most recent wave of immigration, as mentioned earlier, has been largely driven by migrants from Asia and Latin America. This must be seen in the context of global economic changes and migration. Global poverty, war and economic reorganization are driving a phenomenal wave of immigration, and few labour movements have a clue about how to address this sea change. It is hardly surprising, given its chequered past, that the US labour movement is no exception.

The US trade union movement has a long history of both resisting immigration as well as organizing new 'white' immigrants. This dichotomy reflects the exclusion/inclusion contradictions addressed earlier. Amidst the myriad challenges for the US union movement that this wave of immigration presents, is the way it has accompanied economic restructuring. As always, employers, as they have traditionally, have targeted those sectors of the workforce which they have determined to be the most vulnerable. In a fascinating study of the electronics industry in southern California, M. Patricia Fernandez-Kelly explored the hiring policies that led to very clear ethnic niches being established. One of the issues that she examined was the rationale for the low numbers of African-Americans in the workforce. Her findings are noteworthy:

> In addition to the connections established by workers with members of a common ethnic, immigrant, or gender group, we considered the preferences of employers. From that vantage point, the contrast between the level of incorporation of Blacks and Hispanics in the Southern California electronics industry is related to varying perceptions about the groups in question. Managers stated their preference for Hispanic workers, particularly the foreign-born. These groups are seen by employers as more 'diligent,' 'hard-working,' and 'loyal' than native-born Americans, especially those of African descent. The opinion emerged in several of our conversations that Asians are almost as desirable as Hispanics for assembly work. However, employers complained that Asians tended to be ruthlessly competitive and, therefore, less loyal to individual companies. Echoing a widespread feeling, a manager told us that '[i]n a flash, Asians will drop us for a 10 cent difference in wages'. As to Blacks, they are generally assumed to be less reliable, more likely to make demands, to claim rights, and to seek the backing of unions.[26]

Entire industries have been reshaped by the immigration patterns of the last twenty years. Two that stand out are building services (janitorial) and poultry. In both cases, employers have made a conscious decision to change hiring patterns in such a way as to seek out Latino immigrants and cut back on the African-Americans, a significant point in that African-Americans were often the major segment of the workforce.

In the Los Angeles janitorial industry, a conflict of interest emerged between Latinos and African-Americans in the mid-'90s. Down to the 1980s the janitorial workforce was largely African-American. In the 1980s, the janitorial industry restructured. Janitors were no longer employed by building-owners but instead by independent contractors. In a few short years, the janitorial workforce became low-paid Latino immigrants. This process destabilized the union representing this sector (the Service Employees International Union, Local 399), which had to reorganize the entire sector. Black workers, having been the core of this sector in earlier times, now felt excluded and ignored. While the new Latino workforce in commercial buildings came to be largely organized, the conflict of interest between the Latinos and African-Americans went unresolved.

When these exploded within Local 399 in 1995 – resulting in a trusteeship by SEIU – due to a political struggle between a dissident group (largely Latino) and the old-line leadership (which was largely Anglo), African-American workers, leaders and staff were largely on the side-lines. There was some feeling among African-American staff that they were on the verge of being displaced by Latinos and had lost any influence within the Local. The trustee of the local, Mike Garcia, paid close attention to these simmering contradictions and while fighting to increase Latino power in the Local, made significant overtures to the African-American staff, leaders and members as well.

In the poultry industry, tensions between African-Americans and Latinos have grown over the years as well. The poultry industry, located to a significant extent in the southern states of the USA, has largely employed African-Americans and poorer whites. Over the last fifteen or so years, this has changed dramatically. Latino immigrants have come to represent a significant section of the workforce, if not a majority in some places. This demographic change coincided with greater emphasis being placed on organizing by the official trade union movement. Thus, a response in some sections of Black America runs something like this: 'Why weren't the unions interested in organizing the poultry industry when the workforce was largely African-American? Now that it is majority or nearly majority Latino, the unions are talking about organizing. What's in it for us?'

The implications of this for the union movement have been profound. Not only have employer hiring policies created tensions between Latinos and African-Americans, the new immigration patterns have helped to redefine race in the USA, and for organized labour too. Until quite recently, racial relations in the USA were largely determined by the black/white dichotomy (though not so much in the West). This is no longer the case. The emergence of Latinos as the largest minority group (though themselves quite diverse),[27] and the rise in Asian and African immigration numbers, have changed this relationship. This does not mean that anti-Black racism is any less important, but that African-Americans feel increasingly marginalized, while a right-wing move is underway to incorporate segments of Latinos and Asians (and some African-Americans) into the dominant bloc. This was evidenced in the mid-1990s in California where a right-wing ballot initiative attacking illegal immigrants (Proposition 187) was approved by the voters. Clearly aimed at hitting Latino and Asian immigrants, and carrying with it subtle and not so subtle racist messages, the initiative was supported by a significant percentage – though not a majority – of African-American, Latino and Asian voters. Its appeal among African-Americans lay in the notion that Latino immigrants in particular were taking their jobs. These divisions gained national attention again in the 2001 Los Angeles mayoral election that pitted the local AFL-CIO unions and Latino-backed Antonio R. Villaraigosa against the African-American supported James Hahn, a white candidate and son of a 'legendary' white politician who had been favourably disposed towards African-Americans. Although both were liberal Democrats, the fear of growing immigrant power aligned conservative whites and African-

Americans in favour of Hahn, who won the election: 86 per cent of African-Americans voted for Hahn while 86 per cent of Latinos voted for Villaraigosa. The tensions around limited resources and the shifting terrain of defining who is 'white' in America's racialized capitalism squarely confronts organized labour as it attempts to find its own basis for growth and renewal.

In Los Angeles, at the same time, in an example of Black and Brown unity, the Labor Community Strategy Center and the Bus Riders Union waged an eight-year civil rights battle for the right of workers of colour, regardless of immigration status, to have environmentally safe and affordable public transportation. Charging racial discrimination against all people of colour, this community movement won a Consent Decree that required the Los Angeles Metropolitan Transportation Authority to buy hundreds of environmentally safe buses to meet the transportation needs of working-class communities of colour. Victory was finally realized when the Supreme Court of the United States refused to hear appeal from the Los Angeles Metropolitan Transportation Authority. In addition to organizing a multiracial and multi-ethnic constituency, members of the Labor Community Strategy Center and the Bus Riders Union were able to build international ties and support with their 'social justice' approach by developing and implementing an explicitly anti-racist, anti-neoliberal and anti-imperialist action plan.[28]

A 'social justice' approach that has been taken to the issue of racial workforce competition in North Carolina is also noteworthy. A state that until a decade ago was largely marked by a black/white dichotomy has witnessed a dramatic demographic change. An influx of Latino immigrants has altered the social and political complexion of the state including its workforce composition. This has been observed in various industrial sectors, including agriculture, poultry, hogs, hotels and restaurants. In the agricultural sector, there is now little racial and ethnic workforce competition given that the workforce is overwhelmingly Latino. The hog and poultry industries, however, are sites of intense struggle. The non-union hog industry has a legacy of racial stratification that has only been increased with the influx of Latinos. Thus, there are jobs reserved for African-Americans; for Native Americans; for Whites; and now for Latinos. The stratification is expressed in different ways, including but not limited to wages. North Carolina trade union leader Ajamu Dillahunt described a de facto 'oath of secrecy' that exists in the industry whereby workers are discouraged from revealing their actual wages, lest the racially determined wage differentials be revealed. In the poultry industry a similar pattern of racial stratification and ethnic replacement exists. An industry that until the 1990s was largely African-American has witnessed a dramatic decline of Black workers, replaced by Latino immigrants. The same is true of the North Carolina hotel and restaurant industries.

The historical irony of these patterns is that it appears that 'labor agents' (a term used at the turn of the twentieth century, which should actually be 'employer agents') are being used to recruit workers from Mexico for various jobs in the USA. These workers come to the USA with little understanding of its racial dynamics, and others lack any knowledge of its history – and legacy – of racial slavery.

There have been various progressive responses to the challenge of racial/ethnic workforce contradictions in North Carolina. One of the most interesting is the African-American/Latino Alliance forged between the Farm Labor Organizing Committee (FLOC) led by Baldemar Velasquez, and the Black Workers for Justice,[29] a labour/community organization dating back to the early 1980s. FLOC has been organizing agricultural workers in North Carolina who face horrendous conditions of employment. Though in the agricultural workforce, as noted above, there is little racial/ethnic workforce competition, the leaders of both of these organizations recognized that building Black/Brown unity was of strategic importance. For FLOC, winning support for their organizing particularly at the Mount Olive pickles company, necessitated broad outreach to the African-American community. African-American support would both help in addressing broader community tensions, as well as placing significant pressure on the employer to respect the right of workers to organize trade unions.[30]

Unfortunately few unions have had the visionary or 'social justice' approach of FLOC, or of the Black Workers for Justice or the Bus Riders Union (neither of the latter two organizations is a trade union). It is far more common for a trade union to attempt to conduct organizing efforts without reaching out to community-based organizations. It is also quite common for unions to attempt to ignore racial/ethnic/gender contradictions, hoping that with an emphasis on the common economic struggle such contradictions will disappear.

THE NEED FOR SOCIAL JUSTICE UNIONISM

The AFL-CIO's 'Union Cities' program – in an effort to reinvigorate the central labour councils – opened the door for new ideas to be discussed and contributed to such changes as the shift from an anti-immigrant stance to one that now calls for full amnesty for illegal immigrants. 'Union Cities', which emphasized the importance of union organizing, accountability of politicians, community partnerships and increasing the number of women union leaders and union leaders of colour, was an attempt by pragmatic and Leftist trade unionists to reorient the American union movement and redirect union resources to organizing the unorganized. Also contained in the 'Union Cities' program was recognition by some in the US union movement that if organizing were to occur on a large enough scale to make a difference, strategic ties had to be made with significant, progressive, social movements. The essence of this 'social movement unionism' approach is thus the rebuilding of a sense of being a movement within US trade unionism, and creating connections with progressive social movements. We agree on the importance of social movement unionism, but we believe that within a capitalist state social movement unionism is insufficient to change unions in the way that is needed. While there are often only semantic differences among those who use various terms for more progressive trade unionism (e.g., class struggle unionism, transformative unionism, social movement unionism), we want to make a distinctive case for what we call 'social justice unionism'.

What is meant by this? First, that there must be a break with idealism and a recognition of the extensive divisions within the US working class. Given this, a class-conscious unionism must strive for a practice aimed at uniting the working class on solid grounds. The dominant practice of the CIO, mentioned earlier, represented an advance over the backwardness of the AFL with respect to organizing workers of colour. At the same time, the failure to challenge racist hiring and employment practices set the stage for recurring tensions. A class-conscious practice needs to challenge such divisions as part of their organizing and bargaining strategies. This is not a tactical prescription: each situation will have to be judged according to the conditions it presents. Nevertheless, an anti-racist practice must be developed which gives priority to striking down such divisions.

In order for such challenges to be successfully made, a tremendous educational effort must be conducted among the union members. This speaks to one of several debilitating problems in current US trade unionism: the neglect of worker education. Given the history of white supremacy in the USA, taking on a direct challenge to racist employment practices will simply not succeed unless a base of support for this has been built within the membership. Thus, when we speak about social justice unionism, we are starting with the centrality of the struggle against racist oppression as part of the strategic and tactical approach necessary in order to build working-class unity.

Second, there is the related question of what happened to the post-war 'deal'. To the extent that white workers continue to hark back to the good old days, no trade unionism will be constructed which can successfully resist, let alone defeat, neoliberalism. The framework in which we need to operate must begin with the understanding that the dominant sectors of capital see no particular reason to accommodate the trade union movement, at least in the USA. Rather their intent is to eliminate or neutralize trade unionism as a force within the working class. This may happen with greater brutality, e.g., making use of current anti-terrorist measures in order to eliminate the Left and the more vibrant sectors of the trade union movement, or it may take place through mere continued corporate resistance and obstruction. There is little basis to believe that, at the present time, a significant section of capital is interested in reversing this direction. Even the more liberal elements in the Democratic Party display something approaching benign neglect of trade unionism.

Thus, social justice unionism must advance a program that challenges the state in new ways. The unions must take the lead, particularly in the absence of an independent political party, in building a progressive, alternative bloc which aims at power. Thinking in these terms means rethinking the relationship of organized labour to other progressive social movements, most especially the political movements of people of colour. Building such a bloc will necessitate moving the union movement in such a way that it confronts racist/national oppression outside of the workplace context as well as within it. This is a matter not simply of supporting progressive legislation, but also of offering concrete material assistance to projects in communities that advance a working-class agenda. The objective of this is not charity, but building a base for power.

Third, in addition to being more class-conscious, social justice unionism must focus strategically on the southern and southwest parts of the USA. This is critical both because of the high concentrations of workers of colour in this region and because of the way US and global capital has shifted facilities into it.[31] In order to alter the political balance in the USA, the southern and southwestern regions must be won by progressives. If successful in this, social justice unionism could act as a bridgehead for progressive politics.

Fourth, and despite the backlash that accompanied the terrorist attacks of September 11, 2001, the union movement must uphold a new movement around immigrant rights. Some unions, for example the Service Employees International Union, Hotel and Restaurant Employees, the Union of Needle Trades, the Industrial and Technical Employees, and the United Food and Commercial Workers have focused attention on immigrants. This work must be expanded. The Los Angeles area, for example, is the largest site for manufacturing in the USA. The core workforces are Latino and Asian immigrant workers. Nevertheless, little attention has been devoted to organizing this area. Admittedly a daunting task, in most unions the political will to tackle it is absent. When, several years ago, some progressives initiated a project called the Los Angeles Manufacturing Action Project (LAMAP), unions that had expressed some cautious interest dropped the ball, and the AFL-CIO itself did not follow through for lack of affiliate support. Tackling LA manufacturing means not only organizing immigrant workers in their workplaces around workplace issues, but also organizing them as individuals in their communities around broader issues that affect their communities. This approach goes beyond the current notion of trade unionism. In tackling the immigrant question, special attention must be given to building bridges between Asian and Latino immigrants on the one hand, and African-Americans on the other. We have already mentioned the African-American Latino Alliance in North Carolina and the Labor Community Strategy Center/Bus Riders Union in Los Angeles. Also in Los Angeles similar not-for-profit organizations like the Korean Immigrant Workers Advocates and the Coalition for Humane Immigrant Rights in Los Angeles has initiated an Asian/Latino/Black approach to organizing workers. These groups recognize that a multiracial multi-interethnic alliance is essential.

Another point about social justice unionism: a frame of reference must be fought for which acknowledges that there are working class organizations within communities of colour that need to be considered part of the labour movement. This is not a point limited to the tactics of organizing in immigrant communities. Rather it is a suggestion that a labour movement represents the sum total of organizations and activities within the working class that promote advancement, self-organization and power. Trade unions are one part of this larger tapestry.

HOW DO WE GET FROM HERE TO THERE?

There are three key questions that need to be addressed in this respect:

1. Who is the constituency of the labour movement?
2. Who are the friends, allies and enemies of the labour movement?
3. What is the geographic scope of our concern for the working class?

Today's 'traditionalist', 'pragmatic' and 'leftist' ideological orientations in the American labour movement, although each one contains a range of views, have distinctive ways of answering these questions. This wide variety of ideological perspectives ranges from some that favour collusion with neoliberalism and global capitalism to others that call for the destruction of the capitalist system and imperialism. By no means are we suggesting that the movement could or should become ideologically monolithic. But, if 'social justice unionism' is to become more than an abstract concept, the role of the Left will be crucial – and it too will have to change.

Leftists have never been the dominant force in the US union movement. Sometimes they have had more influence, for example, during the era when the Industrial Workers of the World (IWW or Wobblies) were a significant force, and within the CIO up to the purge of the eleven 'red' unions in 1949. One could argue that they had an effect on the 1995 change of leadership in the AFL-CIO, but certainly not as obvious an impact as the previous two examples. For nearly two decades after the social 'deal' was broken by US corporations in the early 1970s, pragmatic and traditional unionists tried to breathe life into the already dead accord. Only when union density radically dropped, when unions were forced to engage in wide scale concession bargaining, and when US industry engaged in dramatic and rapid restructuring, did pragmatists begin to look for a change in leadership within the union movement. In a less obvious, but not insignificant way, leftists also influenced the change in the union movement from business-as-usual, service unionism, to an emphasis on organizing to increase union density. The Left included some people who had remained in the union movement even after the 1949 purges, but they were now joined by many younger, college-educated leftists who entered the union movement during the 1960s and 1970s. Many of these new union leaders were influenced by the anti-war and civil rights movements, solidarity movements in Latin America and, more generally, by Marxism.

The social forces that have affected the nature of work in the last quarter century may be forcing the union movement to face the need for another dramatic restructuring. If such a restructuring is to occur, the three sometimes conflicting ideological strands in the history of the US labour movement must be tied together to lay the foundation for rebuilding the movement by lifting the standard of living for all workers in the USA, linking different sectors of the labour movement (AFL-CIO unions, independent labour organizations and community forces) around common economic and political demands, and building international institutions that can create coordinated worker solidarity movements internationally. As some of our above examples indicate, these strands must be tied together in four primary arenas: schools, legislatures, working-class communities, and work places.

Above all, from a left perspective, the future of the union movement lies in the ability of local unions to transform themselves. Not only are 70 per cent of the union movement's resources tied up in local unions, but also it is at the local union level that workers and communities interact every day with the union movement. The shift from business unionism to social justice unionism requires a dramatic cultural as well as structural shift in the movement. The dominant culture of the US union movement today remains the one largely framed during the McCarthy era, with the fear of leftist infiltration still very strong. The distance between unions and community groups is also an obstacle to moving beyond the unions' own white chauvinism and organizing minority and immigrant workers,[32] as well as to the community unionism that is being advocated by the national AFL-CIO in its 'Union Cities' program. Social justice unionism, as we have described it here, means narrowing this gap and thus improving the fighting and winning ability of the US labour movement and the working class as a whole.

The internal constraints that exist in the US union movement which make such a dramatic change difficult point directly to the challenges that must be met. The greatest constraint is the inability to overcome the effects of racial oppression on unions' own behaviour and structures. Social justice unionism will require more than inclusive unionism in the sense of finally recruiting individuals of all races. It must go beyond this to ally and actively collaborate with – become an organic part of – the community organizations fighting against the oppression inherent in America's racially structured capitalism.

At the same time it will require a very different orientation to the American state and its place in the world. Anti-immigrant views and practices, for instance, are common across the racial divide in the American working class. Rarely is there a discussion about why immigrants, particularly from the global South, come to the USA (or for that matter, to the global North generally). The US trade union movement has done a great disservice in not taking up this question, and it will remain unable to do so unless it is prepared to tackle the implications of US foreign policy and the implications of empire. We are not dealing with everyone wanting to come to the US to live out their dreams, but rather we are living with the implications of colonialism and imperialism and the destruction of economies and ecologies. As a British immigrant rights group says: '*We are here because you were there*'.

The reconstruction of class and class–consciousness in the USA cannot be accomplished without addressing the reality of racial capitalism. Class-consciousness, let alone class unity, will not be built by simply understanding that there are masses of people who have similar relations to the means of production, distribution and exchange and thus have a common basis for unity. Unless the racial trip–wire is defused, if not destroyed, the closest we may ever come to working-class consciousness is the kind of tactical unity on economic issues that will fail to counter the appeal of right-wing populism within a significant segment of white workers.

NOTES

1   The story was related by Professor Michael Merrill to one of the authors
    (Bill Fletcher, Jr.) in the early 1990s. Professor Merrill was then attached to
    Rutgers University in New Jersey.
2   Lou Kushnick offered the following insight: 'Furthermore, acceptance and
    opportunity are of crucial importance in the construction of "whiteness."
    Although the Irish suffered discrimination at the hands of the "white,
    Anglo-Saxon Protestant" (WASP) elites, they had the basis of gaining
    acceptance in US society as whites rather than as Catholic Celts'. (Lou
    Kushnick, *Race, Class & Struggle*, London / New York: Rivers Oram Press,
    1998, p. 207).
3   This approach to the understanding of 'race' in the USA has its roots among
    many theorists, including, but not limited to W.E.B. Dubois, Theodore
    Allen, Anne Braden, Lerone Bennett, Jr., David Roediger and Michael
    Omi and Howard Winant. While there are significant differences among
    them, they share an understanding of 'race' as a socio-political construct and
    as a central factor in comprehending the history and politics of the USA.
4   Quoted in Robin D. G. Kelley, 'Building Bridges: The Challenge of
    Organized Labor in Communities of Color', *New Labor Forum,* 5
    (Fall/Winter), 1999, p. 48.
5   In Dubois's classic *Black Reconstruction in America*, there is a description of
    some of these debates that took place within what was then understood to
    be organized labor.
6   Lerone Bennett, Jr., *The Shaping of Black America*, Chicago: Johnson
    Publishing Company, Inc., 1975, pp. 246-7. The reference to Union
    veterans did not mean trade union, but rather veterans of the Union (or
    Federal) government who fought against the southern secessionists known
    as the Confederate States of America.
7   Statement quoted in Hector L. Delgado, 'Immigrant Nation: Organizing
    America's Newest Workers', *New Labor Forum,* Fall/Winter 2000, p. 33.
8   New York: Praeger Publishers, 1974.
9   For the role of Black workers in the formation of the CIO, Foner is the
    premier work. We would also refer the reader to the pictorial booklet: Bill
    Fletcher, Jr. and Peter Agard, *The Indispensable Ally: Black Workers and the
    Formation of the Congress of Industrial Organizations, 1934-1941*, Boston:
    William Monroe Trotter Institute, 1987.
10 James B. Stewart, 'The Pursuit of Equality in the Steel Industry: The
    Committee on Civil Rights and Civil Rights Department of the United
    Steelworkers of America, 1948-1970', in Patrick L. Mason, ed., *African
    Americans, Labor and Society,* Detroit: Wayne State University Press, 2001, p.
    179.
11 On the Packinghouse Workers and matters of race, see Rick Halpern and
    Roger Horowitz, *Meatpackers: An Oral History of Black Packinghouse Workers*

and Their Struggle for Racial and Economic Equality, New York: Monthly Review Press, 1999.

12　Michael Omi and Howard Winant, *Racial Formation in the United States.* New York: Routledge, 1994.

13　Given the onset of the recession in 2001, it is not clear what will ultimately happen to these wage levels.

14　Chuck Collins and Felice Yeskel, *Economic Apartheid in America,* New York: The New Press, 2000, p. 55.

15　Collins and Yeskel, *Economic Apartheid in America,* pp. 15-19.

16　Patrick L. Mason, 'African Americans, Labor and Society – Current challenges and Twenty-first Century Aspirations', in Patrick L. Mason, ed., *African Americans, Labor and Society,* p.13.

17　James Heintz, Nancy Folbre, et.al., *The Ultimate Field Guide to the U.S. Economy,* New York: The New Press, 2000, p. 76.

18　Patrick L. Mason and Michael Yates, 'Organized Labor and African-Americans: Contemporary Challenges and Opportunities', in Mason, ed., *African Americans, Labor and Society,* pp. 25-6.

19　P. England, L.L.Reid, and B.S. Kilbourne, 'The Effect of the Sex Composition of Jobs on Starting Wages in an Organization – Findings From the NLSY', *Demography,* 33(4) (November), 1996; H.J. Holzer, 'Employer Skill Demands and Labor Market Outcomes of Blacks and Women', *Industrial & Labor Relations Review,* 52(1) (October), 1998; L. McCall, 'Sources of Racial Wage Inequality in Metropolitan Labor Markets: Racial, Ethnic, and Gender Differences', *American Sociological Review,* 66(4), 2001.

20　Mason and Yates, 'Organized Labor and African-Americans', p. 45.

21　AFL-CIO, *The Continuance of Racial Disparity,* Washington, DC: AFL-CIO, 1998, chart 7.

22　Heintz, Folbre, et. al., *The Ultimate Field Guide to the U.S. Economy,* p.77.

23　Ibid., p. 75.

24　Opinion polls regularly demonstrate a differential in the way in which whites and African-Americans, for instance, see the reality of racial discrimination. One of the most interesting tangents in this whole debate revolves around the case of O.J. Simpson. Simpson's case (where he was charged with murdering his ex-wife and a friend of hers) became a racial time bomb in the USA. In recent opinion polls whites continue to be inflamed by this not guilty verdict. This case, more than any in recent times, speaks to the very different experiences blacks and whites have with the police.

25　Heintz, Folbre, et. al., *The Ultimate Field Guide to the U.S. Economy,* p.70.

26　M. Patricia Fernandez-Kelly, 'Labor Force Recomposition and Industrial Restructuring in Electronics: Implications for Free Trade', *Hofstra Labor Law Journal,* Spring 1993, pp. 648-9. A similar point of view is expressed about agricultural workers in California in: Don Mitchell, *The Lie of the*

Land: Migrant Workers and the California Landscape. Minneapolis, MN: University of Minnesota Press, 1996.

27 See the demographic summary in Heintz, Folbre, et. al., *The Ultimate Field Guide to the U.S. Economy*, p. 69.

28 Eric Man, "'A Race Struggle, a Class Struggle, a Women's Struggle all at once": Organizing on the Buses of L.A.', in Leo Panitch and Colin Leys, eds, *Socialist Register 2001: Working Classes, Global Realities*, London: Merlin Press, 2000.

29 United Electrical Workers 150 and the North Carolina Latino Workers Alliance are also part of the alliance.

30 Information based on an interview with Ajamu Dillahunt, President of Local 1078 of the American Postal Workers Union, and a steering committee member of the Black Workers for Justice.

31 The Interstate 85 Corridor, for example, which goes through North Carolina, South Carolina and Georgia has become a major site for foreign investment. Major manufacturing facilities have relocated to this area in search of cheap labor.

32 Fernando Gapasin and Edna Bonacich, 'The Strategic Challenge of Organizing Manufacturing Workers in Global/Flexible Capitalism', in Bruce Nissan, ed., *U.S. Unions in a Globalized Environment: Shifting Borders, Organizational Boundaries and Social Roles*. N.Y.: M.E. Sharpe, Publishers, 2002.

IS THE NORTH AMERICAN ANTI-GLOBALIZATION MOVEMENT RACIST? CRITICAL REFLECTIONS

AMORY STARR

A number of criticisms about racism have been levelled at the North American anti-globalization movement. They include: The movement is disproportionately white. When confronted with the lack of diversity in the movement, whites tend to claim that their groups are already open and accessible, or propose to solve the problem by doing 'outreach'. White-dominated organizations have exclusionary practices and when challenged refuse to respond, calling concerns about racism, sexism, etc., 'distractions' from more 'urgent' work. Activists who can afford time and money to travel to mass events must be affluent and they protest at low risk because they know their 'white skin privilege' will protect them from police brutality. White activists position themselves as the experts and are the visible spokespeople and de facto leadership. Cultural modes (lifestyles, intellectual styles, meeting styles, and protest tactics) preferred by anti-globalization activists are alienating to people of colour. Local communities of colour are put at risk by mass protests operating out of their neighbourhoods. Anti-globalization activists do not seem to care about domestic problems faced by people of colour within the US and Canada, continuing a tradition of organizing which ultimately perpetuates white supremacy. Activism around issues in third world countries is psychologically remote and therefore easier than activism around issues of race at home. Privileged activism on behalf of oppressed others is paternalistic and salvific.

Activists with these concerns have developed a set of proposals which include: Anti-globalization organizations should prioritize 'anti-oppression' training and organizing techniques. Challenging white supremacy must be the primary work of movements which seek to challenge globalization. Instead of 'outreach' and 'recruiting' people of colour, activists should go find out what people of colour in their town are already working on. Activists should be equally or more committed to working on local struggles being waged by people of colour as they are to international actions. People of colour have been fighting globalization for 510 years and therefore are experts who should be looked to for leadership in fighting the current phase of globalization. These criticisms and proposals draw on three anti-racist theories – Black Power, multiculturalism, and Racism Awareness Training (RAT) – which were hegemonic in progressive political circles in the US and Canada before Seattle.[1]

Saddened, concerned, and surprised that people were finding the movement in North America[2] to be racist, I started studying this phenomenon in August 2000. This analysis of the discourse on racism and anti-racism within the North American anti-globalization movement draws primarily on texts published in alternative press and on the Internet and secondarily from participant-observation at local actions and the following mass mobilizations: Seattle/World Trade Organization (WTO), November 1999; Washington, D.C./IMF-World Bank, April 2000; Los Angeles/Democratic National Convention (DNC), August 2000; Cincinnati/Trans Atlantic Business Dialogue (TABD), November 2000; Québec City/Free Trade Area of the Americas (FTAA), April 2001; Washington, D.C./anti-war, September 2001; and New York City/World Economic Forum (WEF), February 2002. My perspective is from what could be called a 'rank and file' affinity group which is not privy to the internal workings of the Direct Action Network (DAN), the Colours of Resistance network, or any of the host city coordinating committees.

I'll start with a timeline of the data I was able to collect. An article by Elizabeth Martinez on the 30 November 1999 Seattle WTO protests (commonly referred to among the activists as 'N30') is constantly cited by anti-oppression advocates. Martinez claimed that only 5 per cent of the N30 protesters were people of colour. She then explored a number of reasons: spokespeople included in media coverage leading up to the event were all white, activists of colour were 'unfamiliar' with the WTO, feared being accused of abandoning community issues to protest the WTO, and were alienated by the culture at the activists' Convergence Center. Her coverage of these issues is exploratory and even-handed, including quotes by activists of colour who said they realized they could have learned a lot more if they hadn't let themselves be alienated by (white) protest culture.[3] In the hour-long IndyMedia film on Seattle, first released in January 2000, the vast majority of the talking heads were people of colour and the presentation of the WTO focused on the impacts for third world peoples (rather than on deregulation, environment, or sovereignty issues). The film included segments on the prison industrial complex and on media portrayals of youth of colour which go beyond the immediate project of portraying what happened in Seattle. This emphasis was consistent in the second, September 2000, edition of the film, *This is What Democracy Looks Like.*[4]

Colin Rajah's review of race in the Washington D.C. 16 April 2000 mobilizations ('A16') quoted activists complaining of 'a sea of white' and that 'Black and Latino leaders were not even asked to speak at the main events, let alone to really help lead the actions'.[5] On the other hand, a detailed report on those events by Robin Hahnel claimed that those involved in A16 organizing made connections with local communities of colour not only by creating 'special materials linking corporate sponsored globalization and IMF and World Bank policies to local economic problems like gentrification, job loss, and bank redlining' but also by working in solidarity on a tenants' rights campaign.[6] A key event was the creation of a squat by A16 activists in an African American neighbourhood. Folks from the neighbourhood were angry about the squat because of the increased police presence it brought. Fellow activists critiqued the squatters for setting up a squat without being well-informed about the community. Whether the squat folks were typically or peculiarly 'clueless' was debated.

At the Los Angeles Direct Action Network (DAN-LA) Convergence Center for the Democratic National Convention in August 2000, I sought evidence of the need for 'principles of anti-oppression organizing' and 'anti-oppression trainings for white folks'. Very little specific evidence was available. Two earlier incidents were cited repeatedly: in Seattle some activists had made comments such as 'Black people just want to shop' and 'people of color aren't interested in direct action'; in New York, the Direct Action Network (DAN-NY) had 'refused to translate materials into Spanish'. Chris Crass' uncontested report on the LA DNC actions described the use of 'anti-oppression organizing' as a 'major jump forward' despite anti-democratic organizing, the alienation of many anarchists, and such timid protests that the media felt no need to cover them at all.[7] At the Québec City FTAA protests in April 2001, elaborate systems of gender and ethnic equity were used at the bilingual spokescouncils and the protests were trilingual. Issues of class came to the forefront as neighbourhood residents who had not agreed to any 'action guidelines' joined the protest, some throwing beer and wine bottles across the fence at the occupying forces.

Since L.A. the language about racism in the movement has become steadily more intense. This could reflect an increase in racist events or increasing awareness of them. While it is unreasonable to expect activists to compile a comprehensive, systematic empirical study, the many articles written on the topic provide little documentation of the nature and extent of racist events. Two articles provide some data.

Gabriel Sayegh describes his involvement in DAN organizing in Seattle, claiming that although '[c]ommunity organizations of color were very active in anti-WTO organizing ... We made no effort to work with these groups ...'. In LA, he describes outside white organizers trying to take over the DAN-LA organizing on the basis that local people didn't know how to organize a mass action. He concludes that 'while the white Left has not been entirely successful in replicating another Seattle, it has found great success in perpetuating racism and upholding white supremacy ... Were we to listen, we'd discover our real successes: not in our attempts to shut down the institutions of global capital, but in alienating people of color in these efforts ... our vision of "what democracy looks like" successfully excluded most people of color'.[8]

Sonja Sivesind wrote an article based on a year of interviewing US and Canadian 'grassroots groups doing radical political work'. She concludes that, both before and after N30, the leadership of Seattle DAN was 'unwilling to recognize, address, and struggle with the issue of white privilege and racism'. People who kept bringing up these issues and who wanted to have an 'anti-racism training' suffered hostility and an incident of physical intimidation. A street theatre piece invoked slavery in a questionable way and organizers refused to deal with challenges from people of colour about the piece.[9] The Sonoran Justice Alliance in Tucson AZ was resistant to criticisms of the exclusionary effects of their meeting location and style, misrepresented statement signatories as a 'coalition', and took credit for an alliance built by other groups. At the Boston October 2000 presidential debate protests, the Freedom Rising affinity group 'disregarded ... ongoing local work by people of color' and a group distributed a spoof newspaper which used radical people of colour in disrespectful ways. Sivesind doesn't quantify her data, but summarizes it qualitatively as follows: 'white supremacist ways of organizing have been perpetuated across the country in the name of Seattle'; 'all across the country racism is tearing apart social justice work'; 'examples of racism being perpetuated like this are endless'; and 'in most all cities ... seasoned organizers ... were wary of the "know it all" attitude that came with the boom in participation' after Seattle.[10]

Colours of Resistance (hereafter 'Colours') was founded around November 2000[11] and has become the most prominent vehicle for anti-oppression orga-nizing in the North American movement. Colours has gathered documents written from the anti-oppression perspective, some of which are published only on the Internet but many of which were circulated prior to Colours posting. Colours hosted a conference in March 2001 in preparation for the Québec City protests. Some Colours affiliates were involved in an invitation-only conference on anti-oppression organizing held in Los Angeles in August 2001. Reports have not been circulated from either of these conferences. Approaching the June 2002 G8 meetings in Kananaskis, some 'anti-oppression' organizers were saying '[t]his time we should encourage people NOT to come at all, unless they are from the region' and instead 'make principled connections with those people and move-ments who are already fighting against their oppression, in our own communities'.[12]

This essay does not attempt to adjudicate the generalizability of documented claims about interpersonal and organizational racism. Given the shortage of data, for the time being I think it is safe to conclude that enough of this is happening to take it seriously. Any organization which people of colour in particular are quitting or where complaints about oppression-related group dynamics are repeatedly raised clearly has a problem. Racism Awareness Training (RAT) materials, such as *Teach Me to Thunder*[13] or *Challenging White Supremacy*[14] (which was developed specifically for anti-globalization activists) should be used in organizations where complaints about oppressive group dynamics are raised.

Having said this, I want to make three cautionary notes. First, activists of colour are not the only ones who feel left out or locked out of insider activist circles. Vanguardism needs to be disentangled from the issue of white privilege. The second cautionary note is that youth tend to be arrogant, righteous, self-important, and insufficiently respectful to elders. These tendencies are inextricable from youths' courage, vision, and determination which make important contributions to social movements. Young activists holding many different views in the movement (including 'anti-oppression') show these qualities.

The rest of this essay elaborates a third cautionary note. Marginal rigid ideological approaches are easily recognizable as sectarianism. But when rigid ideological approaches are hegemonic, they just appear as correct. A particular 'anti-racist' framework has become hegemonic in progressive and radical North American circles. This framework has become self-enforcing. Any challenge to it or dissent from it is immediately described as defensive or apologist and it's a short trip from there to 'white supremacist'. Since nobody wants to be labelled this way, people are reluctant to dissent, which gives a false impression of consensus, but, more importantly, allows for increasingly extreme statements from the hegemonic 'anti-racist' position to stand uncontested. Most unfortunately, the fear of being perceived as pro-oppression effectively stifles any critical discourse.

In hope of breaking open some space for dialogue, I want to challenge several logics currently circulating unchallenged. I distinguish between these logics and the facticity of interpersonal racist events and organizational dynamics which I believe do occur and must be addressed as described above.

1. The movement is 'too white'

1.1 *The identity politics of white anti-racism.* Something is at stake for white anti-racists in working on a project that people of colour are not hugely interested in. White anti-racists have come to know and evaluate their radicalism in part by the multicultural vision of racially diverse organizations and movements. Likewise, the RAT perspective conceptualizes white spaces as inherently spaces of privilege. Any suggestion that they might be doing something that people of colour do not like or want to be part of is annihilating to white activists' sense of anti-racist self. Maybe white activists need to feel OK about working on projects that people of colour don't want to work on. The fact that people of colour are working on something that seems more important to them doesn't mean whites shouldn't do what they are doing. A richer conception of multiculturalism acknowledges diverse efforts to achieve liberation according to different communities' visions while expressing solidarity by showing up and supporting each other when asked.

1.2 *Multicultural vs. Black Power work.* While multiculturalism teaches whites to measure anti-racism by how multicultural their space is, Black Power sends them off to work with white constituencies on their privilege. Fair trade, anti-sweatshop work, and debt relief are projects within the anti–globalization movement in which whites are working with other whites to deal with global racism. These projects teach privileged whites about the ways they benefit from the global exploitation of people of colour and challenge them to take action on a number of levels to disrupt the international systems that deliver the goods to them.

1.3 *Leadership*. Black Power exhorts white activists to listen to and follow the leadership of people of colour and to refrain from asserting expertise. The most significant moment of 'leadership' for the North American movements was the Zapatista uprising. The most familiar scholar to the North American movement is Vandana Shiva. Ken Saro-Wiwa was perhaps the first hero of the current wave of anti-corporate consciousness. So white activists are surprised to be accused by North Americans of not following activists of colour. How should white anti-racists deal with different calls to action coming from first world activists of colour, third world/postcolonial activists, and fourth world/indigenous activists?

1.4 *Goals*. 'The fact is that if the movement against corporate sponsored glob-alization remains this white in the U.S. it will fail to achieve its goals'.[15] This statement cries out for an explanation of why race trumps age, consumption status, class, and urban/suburban/rural as the strategic axis for organizing a partic-ular movement. Robin Hahnel's prediction of failure is echoed by Chris Crass and Sharon Martinas' 'Challenging White Supremacy' approach, which asserts that 'the major barrier to creating these mass movements is racism or white supremacy'.[16] Martinas' political work was strongly influenced by a RAT-style organization, the People's Institute for Survival and Beyond, whose principles start with '[r]acism is the single most critical barrier to building effective coali-tions for social change'.[17] Crass, Martinas, et al. don't talk about being part of a particular anti-racist group, citing an academic work, Robert and Paula Allen's 1974 book *Reluctant Reformers*, as proof that US movements which fail to work effectively with people of colour will themselves ultimately fail. The Allens are consistent with other scholars who find that white working-class movements in the US have repeatedly chosen 'the wages of whiteness' at moments when inter-racial organizing could have won more material gains.[18]

But Hahnel takes a slightly different tack, arguing that while racialized organi-zational dynamics should be addressed, he is 'not as discouraged by the lack of quick success' in 'creat[ing] a multiracial movement against globalization'. He argues that local activists of colour will continue doing community work. 'The movement against corporate sponsored globalization, much less the Mobilization for Global Justice/A16, is not the whole movement for progressive social change in this country. Nor should we make the mistake of thinking we should be'. Recognizing that activists of colour are busy dealing with urgent local and national issues, we can also hope they will find the time and energy – and every opportu-nity – to participate in the anti-globalization movement, and be provided with every opportunity to make their mark on that movement at every level.

The North American movement against globalization is also not the whole movement against globalization. The preponderance of globalization direct action occurs in the Global South and is waged by people of colour. Most activist scholars cited within the North American movement represent concerns of the Global South. The most powerful proposals for addressing globalization have been generated from the South: 'Monsanto Quit India', Jubilee South's 'Don't Owe Won't Pay', incessant 'IMF Riots', the Like Minded Group's 'no patents on life', Zapatismo, Sem Terra's land occupations, the Declaration of Food Sovereignty, the Korean Confederation of Trade Unions' alliance with farmers, and the proposal for a debtors' cartel.

If we take the lessons emphasized by the Allens and others to an international level, challenging white supremacy means finally overcoming postcolonial paternalism. North America is a small part of the international movement; 'anti-globalization' is not 'ours' to decide what to do with. Our job is to do what we can from here to support third and fourth world struggles to destroy the sanctity and legitimacy of exploitative international organizations (multinational corporations and institutions like IMF, World Bank, and WTO). Of course we will continue to work on local and national issues that we were working on before and some of us who are activated through the movement will be available to work on these issues as well.

2. White anti-globalization activists don't care about issues that affect people of colour

2.1 *Anti-imperialist analysis.* 'September 11 threw many young white activists … into a tailspin … Meanwhile, young activists of color jumped into action and created mass antiwar-anti-racist movements protesting the bombing of Afghanistan, supporting Muslims against racist attacks, and bringing a critique of global capital into peace work'.[19] One of the painful lessons of identity politics is that identity is a bad predictor of folks' politics, so such simplistic delineations are rarely true. The largest US anti-war/anti-racism mobilization is ANSWER, organized by the white-led International Action Center whose largest previous campaign was to free Mumia Abu-Jamal. Two of the major US student activist groups, the 180° Movement for Democracy and Education and STARC (Students Transforming and Resisting Corporations) took anti-imperialist positions immediately after 9/11. The US anti-globalization movement's initial faltering was due to wavering on the part of radical NGOs worried about alienating their funders, not to any lack of anti-imperialist sentiment on the part of grassroots activists.

2.2 *Making the connections.* Chris Dixon writes '[w]hether it's global capitalism … or state authority … connections to everyday lives are frequently lost. What about privatization of city services as neoliberalism on the home front? … The connections are all there … yet many white, middle-class radicals simply aren't seeing them'.[20] The 'white' sectors of the anti-globalization movement include activism coming out of organizations like the American Friends Service Committee, which has been 'bringing a critique of global capital into peace work' for decades and the Jubilee USA Network (formerly Jubilee 2000), which decided at its 2001 meeting to endorse the South-South Summit Declaration (Gauteng, South Africa November 1999) even though they knew that some of the US constituency would leave Jubilee, finding the Declaration's demands for total debt cancellation too radical.

If it is true that white anti-globalization activists are 'college kids', what kind of perspective might they have on domestic race issues? The biggest movements on US campuses the last few years have been Free Mumia, the defence of affirmative action and ethnic studies programs, anti-sweatshop, World Bank Bonds boycotts, and student worker organizing (many campaigning jointly with service-sector workers). Such students are likely be more familiar with Zapatismo than Chicanismo, the Ogoni than the Black Panthers, and the environmental justice movement than the feminist movement.

Asked by a South African radio programme to explain why US youth, internationally reputed for insularity, are involved in this movement, I interviewed a group of young anarchists. Bemused at the question, they consulted together and then patiently explained: 'We know that what's happening to third world people can happen to us. We're really angry that we are benefiting every day from the exploitation of third world people and that we have no choices about it. And we believe in the liberation of all people'. One said 'because I have a heart and it bothers me that people are in chains'. I cannot find a single piece of data from the anti-globalization movement that suggests anybody is not interested in making connections between international injustices and domestic ones. People know that Plan Colombia and structural adjustment are intimately linked with immigrant issues in the North. They know that the FTAA's privatization policies, under the guise of allegedly unfair 'appropriations of investor assets', threaten the possibilities for progressive transportation policies of the kind that the LA Bus Riders Union is struggling for, as well as the possibilities for affordable housing programs being struggled for in communities across North America. And they know that domestic anti-terrorism legislation undermines the possibilities for achieving accountable policing policies.

2.3 *Working on third world issues is easy/escapist.* The best data I have to address this issue is my experience as a teacher introducing undergraduate students to both domestic and international issues affecting people of colour. The legacies of colonialism are much more complex to teach than domestic issues of continuing discrimination, cultural appropriation, and debates over the relationships between race, class, and criminality. It is also much harder to help students respond meaningfully to their concerns about what is happening to the third world because neocolonial 'participatory development' projects are a paralyzing activist minefield – it's hard even to figure out where to send money! According to Anti-Slavery International, there are over twenty million people living in forms of modern slavery, including bonded labour and trafficking. But there seems to be an implication that if it's happening far away, activists who prioritize concern with it are avoiding the hard issues. If anti-globalization activists respect people who work exclusively on local domestic issues – and it may be that not all respect this as much as they should – those people working on global issues ought be respected as well.

2.4 *The need for local campaigns.* Exhorting people to give up 'summit hopping' or 'protest tourism' and work solely on local actions presumes a false dichotomy. There are individuals and affinity groups who do 'summit hop'. I estimate that there are about fifty activists each in the US and Canada who spend months setting up legal support and other logistics for each mass action; the rest of us show up for a day to a week and then return home to ongoing local work. The proposal to do only local organizing not only abandons international solidarity but also gives up the empowerment, radicalizing experiences, and sense of critical mass of national actions. (Mass direct action is an initiation into community and courage which could be understood as part of the second Black Power project, organizing a 'white power bloc dedicated to the goals of a free, open society'.) It should also be noted that when groups take advantage of other groups' organizing to try to talk people into abandoning that action and doing something different (like going home and just supporting existing local struggles), we usually call it 'sectarianism'.

3. Protest culture is white culture

3.1 *Whites don't like it either.* One of Martinez's interviewees at Seattle is quoted as saying: 'When we walked in, the room was filled with young whites calling themselves anarchists. There was a pungent smell, many had not showered. We just couldn't relate to the scene'.[21] Savegh put the problem more generally: 'the Convergence Center was a space created exclusively by, and thus for, white people .... Predictably, the very center where activists were meant to learn skills to shut down the WTO was thus largely inaccessible to people of color'.[22] Yet people of colour were not the only people alienated by the culture in the Convergence Center and other spaces. A minority of whites, and a minority of people of colour, are attracted to hippy and punk cultures. Few of us are comfortable living in public spaces for days on end.

In Seattle, the first scouts from my affinity group came back from the Convergence saying 'that place is crazy!' But we knew that it had not been designed with our comfort in mind. It seemed obvious that people were sleeping there who had no other place, people were dirty because they had no opportunity to get clean, and the atmosphere was intense because people were trying to organize something big quickly, somewhat clandestinely, and with improvised resources. Now our orientation packets for first-timers say 'the Convergence is not a pleasant or comfortable place. Nevertheless you must spend a great deal of time there in order to help out and learn what's happening'.

3.2 *On the cheap.* Convergence spaces tend to be dirty and unappealing in large part because very little money is spent making them nice. Likewise, in order to make participation in actions affordable, activists don't stay in hotels or travel by airplane. Often our generous hosts and campsites cannot accommodate daily showers for everyone. Long days of action and meetings also limit the time spent on the appearance and cleanliness of activists and our spaces. Most of us smell better when we're at home.

3.3 *Consumption.* This focus also avoids serious conversation about first world consumption and global injustice. One letter to the editor in Colorlines contended: 'Seattle DAN folks romanticize the wholesale abandonment of main-stream culture. They boast of dumpster-diving and television-smashing, dream of self-sufficiency … But of course, dropping out of society has a different appeal for those who have always–already been invited to participate fully than it does for those whose invitation is eternally lost in the mail'.[23] No one could deny that having access to consumers' goods brings comfort, and even a sense of dignity, to those so long denied them. But why would people of colour be exempt from dealing with the destructive effects of first world consumerism? The ameliora-tion of inequality in the first world through widening the base of mass consumption relies considerably on the resources of the third and fourth worlds. Reducing first world consumption is certainly not a sufficient strategy for confronting globalization, but it will be part of any plan for global justice, the real cost of which is not the risks we take in the streets but allowing third and fourth world peoples to keep their resources for their own uses. Some people have worked on creating alternative forms of identity and celebration ('Look what I found in the dumpster!') to go along with their attempt to take responsibility for the racist effects of first world consumption.

4. Direct action is a privileged form of activism

4.1 *Safety*. It is claimed that as part of the benefits of white supremacy package white people get to choose when to interact with police, while people of colour are always already subject to excessive police attention and harsher sentencing. Thus choosing to do direct action or civil disobedience is an expression of white privilege. But every anti–globalization mass action has included 'safe', permitted options. The protests at the Democratic National Convention in Los Angeles included 27 legal/'safe' activities. In New York at the February 2002 World Economic Forum protests, although a legal permitted rally was already organized by ANSWER, the direct action organizers put all their energy into a second, simultaneous legal/'safe' march.

4.2 *Direct action*. According to Emcee Lynx, an Organizer of the Hip Hop Congress, 'direct action has a long and proud tradition in movements of oppressed peoples for self-determination and autonomy (and the anarchist movement in particular) as action that directly accomplishes participants' goals instead of demanding that someone else fix the problem for them'. According to this definition, 'permitted marches and rallies are never direct action and – unless the purpose of the march is to assert the right to gather and march without a permit – unpermitted marches are not either'. Direct action can be distinguished from civil disobedience on the basis that 'civil disobedience is indi-rect; it is based on the idea – advanced by Tolstoy (an anarchist!) – of a soul-force that changes people's hearts and minds by acting nonviolently with pure intent'. Whereas '[d]irect action is the act of taking direct control over one's own life and destiny and doing what needs to be done without taking orders from anyone or attempting to influence anyone'. Lynx asserts that both are necessary.[24]

DAN-LA organizers, focused on the goal of 'bringing a diverse and radical movement to the streets',[25] chose to organize only permitted marches (and no direct action) in an attempt to make the protests 'safe' for 'unarrestable' undocumented people, already 'over-arrested' people of colour, and people who could be facing 'three strikes' life sentences. What is confusing is the insistence that by associating non-radical tactics ('safety') with a radical ideology ('anti-oppression') they could appropriate the name for radical tactics ('direct action'). We need to consistently distinguish between radical ideology and radical tactics; they are not synonymous.

4.3 *Affluence & privilege.* Traveling to protests, risking direct action, and being willing to spend time in jail have been interpreted as privileges and proofs of affluence. People who have chosen the security of regular jobs and the joys of children have been positioned as unable to 'afford' mass actions. Should people stay home because other people cannot afford to go? If we accept the logic being proposed here, we would also have to insist that people who have time, transportation resources, and surplus energy to organize local activism should refrain from doing so because they are relatively privileged compared with other people in their town.

More importantly, these one-dimensional characterizations betray impoverished conceptions of agency, diversity, and organizing. There are people in every social position who are unwilling to take risks. The burden is on organizers to design actions with a wide variety of roles and risks so that everyone who is interested can be involved and empowered. As one LA organizer interviewed by Sayegh put it: 'The actions against the DNC would have happened whether white people showed up from out of town or not. We were just worried about what to do with them once they got here'.[26] If we are interested in winning this struggle, we need every available resource. Do we deal with privilege by berating individuals for having it or by mobilizing their affluence, flexibility, and peculiar tolerances in a strategy designed to win this struggle?

4.4 *Who wants to be safe?* What is the relationship between privilege, willingness to take risks, and preference for radical tactics? It is paternalistic to suggest that marginalized people are not interested in and should not be invited to take risks. For instance, the gays who first fought back against police raids leading to the 1969 Stonewall riots (which inspired a new wave of gay liberation in the US) were not, in fact, the most privileged, with the least to 'lose'. They were crossdressers of colour, the most marginalized and unsafe group. Also people's ideas about risk evolve in particular situations. In Seattle, plenty of union members thought they couldn't risk much and then their perspective changed in the situation.

Suggestions

It is my hope that this analysis will assist anti-globalization activists to move toward more careful dialogue about our theories of action and participation. General prescriptions seem trite here, but a few may be in order. First, we must be vigilant about rumour control as the spreading of rumours is a very inexpensive way to create divisions between us. Before repeating that 'DAN-NY refused to translate materials into Spanish' too many times, send an email and check out what actually happened.

Second, whenever people are in pain or feeling marginalized, even if the articulation of that pain makes others uncomfortable, we must respond seriously and meaningfully within our organizations. We must deal with specific incidents of racism, sexism, homophobia, etc. that arise in our organizing.

Third, we must be consistent in thinking critically about the development of hegemonic ideas within our own circles and always create space for dissent and diversity. Indeed, the more sure we may be about a particular approach, the more we must push ourselves to protect spaces for dissent, just in case we are wrong. (This is painfully clear in the context of 'US patriotism' right now.) Respecting dissent means refraining from trivializing, bullying, stigmatizing with the use of words like 'apologist', or psychologizing dissent as 'defensiveness' or 'resistance'.

Fourth, stereotyping and wholesale accusations are not going to advance solidarity around political projects. Rather than promulgating logics describing international work as escapist, domestic work as short-sighted, or making suppositions like 'Black people just want to shop', or 'white activists went into a tailspin', we should challenge specific instances of failure to show solidarity.

Fifth, we need to initiate a slow, careful, and respectful dialogue about the question of organizing. Political organizing, like 'anti-racism', has a hegemonic form in which an 'organizer' makes one-on-one contacts with people, building a movement in a slow process of 'empowering' them to organize to deal with their issues. Some critics find this approach elitist, condescending, or even 'missionary'. Alternative approaches range from using 'fun', cultural rupture, or militancy to get people excited about participating. Acknowledging these and other alternative approaches to organizing enables us to understand that direct action types do not disdain organizing, they just have a different idea about what might empower people. Spontaneously taking and holding space, witnessing the cops back down, building a barricade with strangers who speak different languages, creatively disrupting elite procedures or messages – these experiences empower and organize people too. Even breaking corporate retail stores' windows can be understood as a 'small winnable issue' in the classic community organizing conception of slowly developing empowerment. Clearly, different kinds of organizing and activities appeal to different people. Having acknowledged this, we also need to remember that people who favour direct action may also be involved in the hegemonic form of organizing at some time.

Sixth, we must continue the already vigorous dialogue on 'diversity of tactics'. This concept has been developed to provide equal respect to candlelight vigils, property crime, permitted marches, and everything in between. It is an approach which has yet to be perfected. Within a 'diversity of tactics' framework in Québec City, direct actions had the effect of tactical totalizing. Once the police started attacking, only two forms of protest were possible: throwing things at the cops or breathing in the gas (at various distances from the perimeter) in a valiant (and, for some, empowering) effort simply to be present. Scott Weinstein wrote '[a]s some of us predicted, when you mix tactics the most provocative tactic against property or the police absorbs all others'.[27] Mark Engler argued that the lack of 'non-violence guidelines' and 'discipline' led to an 'uncontrolled melee' and 'made spectators of those who might have had a supporting role', limiting 'the real diversity of protest'.[28] Of course it's not clear that 'red' actions as opposed to green (safe) or yellow (non-violent) ones[29] are entirely to blame for the police attack. In Seattle it was effective non-violent civil disobedience which brought on the police attack – the broken windows were blocks away and hours later. In New York for World Economic Forum there was an increased awareness of the relationships between areas and actions. We used the phrases 'yellowish-green' and 'greenish-yellow', and talked at length about how to effect a transition from a 'green day' to a 'yellow night' while making sure to inform people fully. At the last minute, a spontaneous spokescouncil halted this transition entirely due to the presence of children and other 'unarrestables' who were trapped in the area that was supposed to 'turn yellow'.

Awareness and responsiveness to protesters' needs for safety must continue to develop. The Zapatistas provided the theory of 'one no, many yeses'. Recently, other Southern Cone activists have developed the concept of 'specifismo' to encourage fluid shifting of tactics appropriate to the situation.[30] Let's work to collaborate respectfully in our diversity of approaches to anti-globalization and anti-oppression.

NOTES

This essay depends heavily on two years of dialogue with Brian Cairns. It is written with great trepidation.

1   In 1967, Stokely Carmichael & Charles V. Hamilton argued that if liberation was to go beyond integration, Black Power needed to be developed entirely independent of even the most sympathetic White Power. Whites could contribute to building Black Power in three ways: 1) 'go into their own communities – which is where racism exists – and work to get rid of it'; 2) use their access to poor white communities to 'creat[e] a poor-white power block dedicated to the goals of a free, open society'; 3) when called upon for support, follow Black leadership and respect Black wisdom, skills, and self-determination (*Black Power: The Politics of Liberation in America,* New York: Random House, 1967).

As part of the development of the Power perspective, 1960s movements rejected assimilation and positioned culture as an important part of empowerment. 'Multiculturalism' has come to signify a variety of at times acrimoniously competing activities in cultural curation, education, anti-racist activism, and government policy. Its most radical interpretations of self-determination have proposed anarchist-type theories of decentralized control and mutual aid between communities in order to enable 'all cultures to survive and thrive' (Mel King, *Chain of Change: Struggles for Black Community Development*, Boston: South End Press, 1981). At its most common, white progressive activists and organizations now are judged (and shape their identity) in part by the diversity visible in their political and social lives.

In 1978, responding to a US military crisis involving interracial tension among enlisted men, Judith Katz developed 'Racism Awareness Training' (RAT). This program aimed to train whites to be better community members by helping them to 'take responsibility' for their power, privilege, and unconscious racism (*White awareness: Handbook for anti-racism training*. Norman OK: University of Oklahoma Press, 1978). More radical subsequent versions have used this awareness as the starting point for eliciting commitments to anti-racist political practices. Ambalavander Sivanandan critiques the RAT approach for separating race from class and is concerned that the emphasis on personalistic relationships to oppression permits capitalism to carry on its racist projects ('RAT and the Degradation of Black Struggle', *Race & Class*, 25(4), 1985, reprinted in *Communities of Resistance*, London: Verso, 1990).

2   The Canadian and US anti-globalization movements share practices but are distinct, as are the two nations' histories of and discourses on racism. Specific forms of 'anti-racism' have traveled between the US, Britain, and Canada.

3   Elizabeth Martinez, 'Where was the Color in Seattle?: 'Looking for reasons why the Great Battle was so white', circulated on the Internet shortly after N30 and eventually published in *Colorlines*, 3.1, Spring 2000.

4   Independent Media Center Seattle and Big Noise Films, *This Is What Democracy Looks Like*, September 2000, http://www.thisisdemocracy.org.

5   Colin Rajah, 'Globalization and Race at A16 in D.C.', *Colorlines*, 3.3, Fall 2000.

6   Robin Hahnel, 'Speaking Truth to Power: Speaking Truth to Ourselves', *Z Magazine,* June 2000.

7   Chris Crass, 'Thoughts and reflections on Los Angeles and taking on global capitalism' circulated widely on the Internet and was eventually published as 'Confronting the Democratic National Convention and Working to Build a People's Movement for Justice', *Socialist Review*, 28(3+4), 2001.

8   Gabriel Sayegh, 'Redefining Success: White Contradictions in the Anti-Globalization Movement', posted on Colours of Resistance website http://www.tao.ca/~colours, n.d.

9   Sivesind does not specify when, where, or by which group this street theatre was proposed and/or performed.

10   Sonja Sivesind, 'Combating white supremacy in the anti-globalization movement', posted on Colours of Resistance website http://www.tao.ca/~colours, n.d.

11   Colours' website does not provide a founding date. Infoshop.org, a

reputable source for such information, lists the Colours website as 'new on the web' in November 2000. Colours is housed in Montréal.

12 Yutaka Dirks, 'Doing things differently this time: Kananaskis G8 meeting and movement building', posted on Colours of Resistance website http://www.tao.ca/~colours, n.d..

13 Alma Estable, Mechthild Meyer and Gordon Pon, *Teach Me To Thunder: A Training Manual for Anti-racism Trainers*, Ottawa: From the Margin Publishing & Canadian Labour Congress, 1997.

14 Chris Crass and Sharon Martinez, 'Challenging White Supremacy' workshop, materials available at http://www.prisonactivist.org/cws/.

15 Hahnel, 'Speaking truth to power'.

16 Sharon Martinas, 'Political Perspectives of the Challenging White Supremacy Workshops', revised Summer 2000, http://prisonactivist. org/cws.

17 http://www.thepeoplesinstitute.org. Interestingly, the Institute ran a workshop in Seattle *during* N30 and took no interest in the WTO protests.

18 Robert L. Allen and Paula P. Allen, *Reluctant Reformers: Racism and Social Reform Movements in the United States,* Washington DC: Howard University Press, 1983 (1974). David R. Roediger, *The Wages of Whiteness: Race and the Making of the American Working Class,* London: Verso, 1991. Another competing approach to anti-racism proposes that 'the white race' is an artificial construct which must not be reified in attempts to stop racism (see http://www.racetraitor.org). How these arguments map to Canada is an important question that can not be dealt with here.

19 Mike Prokosch, United for a Fair Economy, 'Three Tasks for the US globalization movement', http://globalroots.net/themoment/, 2002.

20 Chris Dixon, 'Finding Hope After Seattle: Rethinking Radical Activism and Building a Movement', posted on Colours of Resistance website http://www.tao.ca/~colours, n.d.

21 Martinez, 'Where was the Color?'

22 Sayegh, 'Redefining'.

23 Sage Wilson, letter to the editor, *Colorlines* 3.2, Summer 2000.

24 See http://www.hiphopcongress.org and http://www.circlealpha.com.

25 Crass, 'Thoughts and reflections'.

26 Sayegh, 'Redefining'.

27 Scott Weinstein, 'Québec's Intifada', email, 24 April 2001.

28 Mark Engler, 'Conflict in Québec: Eyewitness Report and Analysis', posted on http://www.zmag.org, n.d.

29 'Green' means 'safe' activities which are supposed to run no risk of arrest or police attack either because they are strictly legal or because they have state permits. 'Yellow' is classic civil disobedience and non–violent direct action which, depending on the situation, could result in arrest or police attack, but which also could end up being safe. 'Red' are tactics expected to attract police aggression (this could include property crime, trying to cross police

lines, or non-violent direct actions such as a lock-down in a particularly sensitive area). Since planned 'red' actions are more secretive and might be organized with a small affinity group, participants might also be more vulnerable simply because fewer people will be around.

30 Jason Adams, 'WSF2002: Hopes for a True International', http://www.zmag.org, 13 February 2002.

IS THIS WHAT DEMOCRACY LOOKS LIKE? THE POLITICS OF THE ANTI-GLOBALIZATION MOVEMENT IN NORTH AMERICA

STEPHANIE ROSS

In multiple ways, the anti-globalization movement invokes the democratic imaginary. A central element of the movement's critique of contemporary capitalism is that corporate power organized on a global scale undermines the capacity of citizens and national communities to make independent decisions about social, economic and political priorities. Anti-globalization activists challenge governments that enact international trade and investment agreements which enshrine the interests of multinational capital, arguing that both the means – the restriction of dissent and meaningful participation in decision-making – and the ends – the ordering of society according to the interests of the few – violate even minimal norms of democratic practice, such as majoritarianism and representativeness. Although by no means characterized by a coherent ideological approach, especially to the question of alternatives, the anti-globalization movement can be said to be united in its appeal to citizens' democratic sensibilities.

Given the central ideological role of democracy in the movement, we clearly need to ask: how democratic is the anti-globalization movement itself? The decision-making processes developed by activists – most notably the use of 'affinity groups' and 'spokes councils' – are said to be more democratic than those of previous left-wing or working-class organizations, such as trade unions or political parties. Two key ideas in this decentralized notion of democracy are autonomy from central leaders or structures, and the commitment to a diversity of tactics. I will argue that the democratic character of such autonomy needs to be interrogated, particularly in terms of its negative impact on the creation of a space for sustained debate about strategies, tactics and visions. In the absence of a common, legitimate and widely accepted forum for decision-making, groups of activists are able to act as vanguards by default, thereby 'leading' or directing the movement without any accountability. Through an analysis of the anarchist and post-modern roots of a significant section of the movement, I will argue that organizational practices not only fail to live up to the movement's democratic ideals, but also limit its effectiveness and inclusiveness.

POLITICAL IDEAS IN THE ANTI-GLOBALIZATION MOVEMENT

The issue of democracy is central to the anti-globalization movement, both in its critique of the current political-economic configuration, and in the principles guiding internal organization. The diversity of groups and issues encompassed by the movement has made it all but impossible for mainstream commentators to see these common key themes; as Naomi Klein has put it, observers have been 'missing the forest for the people dressed as trees'.[1] Even some participants in the demonstrations held in Seattle and U.S. cities throughout the year 2000 emphasized how this diversity might impede the effectiveness of the movement, as 'perhaps energies were excessively scattered'.[2]

However, as the website of Stop the FTAA, a clearing house of information on anti-FTAA organizing throughout the Western hemisphere, makes clear, it is precisely the negative impact of 'corporate globalization' or neoliberalism on 'nearly every sector of society' which provides the basis of unity, 'the possibility of uniting broad sectors into a mass movement'.[3] Furthermore, not only are people harmed in concrete material terms, they are harmed by processes over which they have no democratic control. The movement is therefore about changing both the content of global social practices and relations and the processes by which communities make decisions about how they are to be organized. David Graeber, a Yale University anthropologist, self-described anarchist and active participant in the direct action elements of the anti-globalization movement, makes this point forcefully in his rejection of the dominant media's interpretation of the movement as structureless and lacking ideological coherence. He characterizes the movement's ideology as particularly evident in its *approach to organization*: 'this is a movement about reinventing democracy. It is not opposed to organization. It is about creating new forms of organization. It is not lacking in ideology. Those new forms of organization *are* its ideology'.[4]

To some extent, this claim sidesteps the important differences over analysis and strategy – whether to be anti-capitalist, whether to reform international institutions or to create wholly new ones, whether to engage positively with the state or to reject it as irredeemably capitalist and authoritarian, or whether to accept violence as a legitimate tactic – differences which pervade the movement and give rise to a significant element of disunity. There is, however, something important in what Graeber says: a significant portion of the movement is organizing around coherent ideological commitments that are reflected in the decision-making practices governing and linking groups of activists. If it is indeed the generation of new organizational forms that constitutes the anti-globalization movement's core contribution to contemporary Left politics, it is incumbent upon the entire Left to engage with these practices and their underlying ideas, in a way which appreciates and yet does not romanticize them.

An important section[5] of the anti-globalization movement is based on one central value: running throughout the analysis of a variety of groups is *a critique and rejection of hierarchy*. Although the source and nature of hierarchical organization is defined variously, as rooted in capitalism, patriarchy, racism, homophobia, imperialism, bureaucracy, and/or human domination over nature, common to all is a rejection of any authority that imposes decisions on individuals and communities. This anti-authoritarianism takes as its main inspiration the tradition of anarchist thought, which includes but is not limited to Kropotkin, Bakunin, Goldman, Chomsky and Bookchin, as well as the concrete political experiments of the anarcho-syndicalists of the Spanish Civil War and the North American Industrial Workers of the World (the IWW, or 'Wobblies'). Anarchism is centrally concerned with the conditions that impede the exercise of 'maximum individual liberty for all'.[6] Although one may distinguish between libertarian and socialist forms of anarchism, which differ on the issue of what conditions will actually achieve such liberty, at the centre of both is the idea that 'there is no legitimate authority outside the individual'.[7] It is fair to say that it is the anti-capitalist variant of anarchism which is attracting a significant number of activists and which has been prominent in the large demonstrations of recent memory. As such, the emphasis is placed on the way social inequality – as embodied in private property, the institution of the state, and even organizations seeking the liberation of the working class – reproduces hierarchy and domination.

Anarchists reject the state for both the content and the purpose of its power, as well as its form. Following Proudhon, socialist anarchists disavow state power as it is 'synonymous with the power of capital' and therefore an irremediably corrupt institution through which human emancipation could never come.[8] Goldman, for instance, insisted that organized state authority 'is necessary *only* to maintain or protect property and monopoly'.[9] State regulation of human behaviour does not promote 'human liberty, human well-being and social harmony' in that it has not 'induced man [sic] to do anything he could and would not do by virtue of his intellect or temperament, nor prevented anything that man was impelled to do by the same dictates'.[10] In the same vein Ammon Hennacy, U.S. anarchist organizer with the Catholic Worker Movement, was fond of saying, when charged with civil disobedience: 'Ah judge, your damn laws, the good people don't need 'em and the bad people don't obey 'em, so what use are they?'[11] Outside regulation of any kind, in whatever form, and from whatever source, is seen as inherently invasive and ultimately counterproductive. According to this analysis, the state can never be made to work for progressive ends. Furthermore, the form of popular participation in state power adopted by capitalist democracies – institutionalized representative democracy – is viewed with profound suspicion.

Other forms of hierarchy, produced by those also seeking the liberation of the working classes, like a party or bureaucratic and centrally directed trade unions, are also equally repugnant to anarchists. Both Proudhon and Bakunin held that all political parties were 'varieties of absolutism' and thus were not the vehicle through which the working classes should be organized.[12] This is particularly because, in seeking to capture the state through revolutionary or electoral means, socialists become embroiled in the very oppressive relations they once sought to eliminate. They become caught in a political trap, deceived by the illusion of minor reforms and corrupted by holding state power.[13] For anarchists, the ultimate outcome of the Bolshevik Revolution is a vindication of this position. Noam Chomsky summarizes the rejection of all forms of hierarchy quite well: 'democracy is largely a sham when the industrial system is controlled by any form of autocratic elite, whether of owners, managers, and technocrats, a "vanguard" party, or a state bureaucracy'.[14]

The ideal of socialist anarchism is thus the reconciliation of individual(ism) with social(ism). In Goldman's formulation, the goal is to discover how to be one's self and at the same time live in oneness with others.[15] Whereas hierarchy prevents this reconciliation, direct action leading to forms of direct self-governance will lead to its realization. Order, for anarchists, comes not from authority, but from 'freely undertaken cooperation, mutual aid, and improvisation'.[16] In other words, for anarchists, organization must have as its central governing principle the fostering and protection of people's ability to govern themselves. In practical terms, self-governance usually involves forms of direct democracy.

This anti-authoritarianism has led to the development of three concrete organizational principles in the anti-globalization movement: (1) an adoption of decentralized, autonomous structures; (2) a rejection of leadership; and (3) a respect for diversity, especially in the realm of tactics. Each of these principles is aimed at fostering maximum human freedom and the creativity that flows from such freedom.

Commentators like Rick Salutin, keen to cut through the fog of misperceptions about anarchism that accompanied the fog of tear gas, have rightly emphasized that anarchism is about neither chaos nor structurelessness. Rather, as pointed out previously, anarchists reject particular *kinds* of structures: centralized, hierarchical structures that impose authority from above.[17] Therefore, significant elements of the anti-globalization movement have developed a variety of decentralized decision-making structures, which tend to be fluid in terms of membership and loose in terms of the extent to which participants are bound by the decisions made. The most popular organizational form composing the backbone of post-Seattle demonstrations is the affinity group, a small group of people united by friendship, a history of political work together, a common issue or identity, or a shared adoption of a particular tactic.[18] The affinity group transforms the traditional demonstration, characterized by passive marching, contained by parade marshals, on a pre-planned route to and from a raft of speeches, and permits individuals to be active participants in the construction of a diverse mass action. According to Stop the FTAA, '[a]ffinity groups challenge top-down decision-making and organizing, and empower those involved to take creative direct action. Affinity groups allow people to "be" the action they want to see by giving complete freedom and decision-making power to the affinity group'.[19] The affinity group is a concrete challenge to the type of disempowering, centralized decision-making often prevalent in the labour movement.

Coordination of mass action is of course still necessary, but the structures used to accomplish this are also decentralized. Autonomous 'affinity groups' send representatives to meet in 'spokes councils', in which information is shared, tactical, strategic or organizational issues are discussed, and decisions are made. A spokes council, like the affinity groups which are its constituent units, attempts to use consensus decision-making processes rather than voting and majoritarian rule so as to ensure that 'all affinity groups have agreed and are committed to the mass direct action'.[20] Ultimately, however, unlike in traditional forms of representative democracy, the decisions of the spokes council are not binding on the affinity groups, which 'function as discrete units, with the power to make their own strategic decisions'.[21] Spokes councils therefore attempt to combine the organization of common actions with small group autonomy from central control.

Affinity groups are also encouraged to employ consensus decision-making processes as a way to achieve agreement in which all participants have 'equal voice and power' but also have some chance of having their concerns integrated into outcomes. This method is held to be superior to majority rule, which produces outcomes not everyone is able to live with or which fail to meet everyone's needs and interests. Instead of a majority making a decision for and imposing it on the group, minority or divergent views are integrated into a consensus decision. Group members register varying levels of dissent rather than voting 'yes' or 'no', so that proposals may be revised and refined rather than stopped outright. Only in instances where a decision is held to be antithetical to the goals and principles of the group can a 'block' or veto be registered. In such instances, rather than the majority carrying the day, the group must find a new way to proceed.[22] According to Stop the FTAA, consensus

> allows people to collectively explore solutions until the best one for the group emerges. Consensus assures that everyone has a voice in the decision making process, synthesizing all ideas into one plan that all participants agree to implement. Since all participants agree to the decision, people are more invested in carrying out what has been decided. The process promotes commitment to carry out decisions ... It attempts to minimize domination and empowers the community in the process of making a decision.[23]

Avoiding the tyranny of the majority, consensus is held to be more democratic and more effective at building solidarity. While Graeber admits that such processes can be difficult, this is so because of the way in which liberal democratic society actually provides so few opportunities for democratic deliberation.[24]

These methods and the structures in which they exist can be said to contribute to the building of democratic capacities which, under capitalism, the vast majority surrender to others to shape, and in ways that serve the interests of the few.[25]

Decentralization in general is also credited with being not merely democratic, but also effective in the context of increasing attempts by security forces to control and undermine the anti-globalization movement. Decentralized, leaderless 'coalitions of coalitions' are less vulnerable to state intervention and repression; as Klein argues,

> there is no doubt that one of [the model's] great strengths is that it has proven extraordinarily difficult to control, largely because it is so different from the organizing principles of the institutions and corporations it targets. It responds to corporate concentration with a maze of fragmentation, to centralization with its own kind of localization, to power consolidation with radical power dispersal.[26]

As the Rand Corporation has conceded, without a 'central leadership or command structure', the movement is 'multiheaded, impossible to decapitate'.[27]

The rejection of hierarchy also had led to a suspicion and rejection of leadership. Again, there is a rational strategic basis to a leaderless movement in the context of the 'hyper-organized security response' to the anti-globalization movement.[28] As Klein points out, having easily identifiable leaders is dangerous, and '[t]he systematic police targeting of protest "leaders" goes a long way towards explaining the deep suspicion of traditional hierarchies'.[29] However, the rejection of leadership is more profoundly rooted in a philosophical commitment to egalitarianism. In keeping with the emphasis on self-activity, anarchists seek to create conditions in which 'people [are] exercising political power themselves' rather than via elected representatives.[30]

If there is a role for leadership, it is of a completely different sort from that of 'representatives' or 'spokespersons' who become ensconced in their positions of power. The role of professional anarchist revolutionaries was not, for Bakunin, one of mobilizing the working classes through political party organization, but of 'arousing and encouraging the oppressed classes ... to overthrow the existing order by their own direct action'.[31] Such inspirational activity could come in a variety of forms, from propaganda of the deed to civil disobedience, and these distinguish the violent and non-violent traditions that co-exist within anarchism.

There is today perhaps no more vital expression of the rejection of leaders in favour of egalitarian participation than that of the Zapatistas. Sub-Commandante Marcos symbolizes this new form of political 'leadership', which merely communicates what is decided by the group, rather than acts in its place. In the statement read by Marcos which emerged out of the 1996 Encuentro, the Zapatistas emphasized that what was being created was not an 'organization' but 'a network of voices that resist the war Power wages on them ... that not only speak, but also struggle and resist for humanity and against neoliberalism ... that covers the five continents and helps to resist the death that Power promises us'.

This network 'has no central head or decision maker; it has no central command or hierarchies. We are the network, all of us who resist'.[32]

Decentralized, leaderless structures are believed to allow for the maximization of diversity in the movement. Rather than being made to receive 'from above' a set analysis or appropriate strategy, individuals and small groups are to be supported in the choices they make about how to understand and express their opposition. This commitment to multiplicity and individual choice must be seen in a broader context of anarchist spontaneism – in which Bakunin envisaged 'spontaneous uprisings of the oppressed classes, peasants as well as industrial workers, in widespread insurrections in the course of which the state would be abolished'.[33] For the creative energy of the people to be fully expressed via direct action, it is antithetical to place a priori limits or constraints on the forms of political expression and activity. In fact, to engage in practices of self-policing like parade marshalling or non-violence agreements is seen as authoritarian, a means of controlling difference and dissent within the Left, of maintaining the legitimacy of leaders in the eyes of the state and capital, and ultimately of 'cooperation in [the Left's] own disempowerment'.[34] This ethos is nowhere more evident than in the acceptance of a diversity of tactics by an enormous array of groups, some of which have been central organizers of demonstrations.

Diversity of tactics, like the association of anarchism with structurelessness, has also been widely misunderstood. Emphatically not a pro-active advocacy of violent tactics, it instead involves two important elements: the acceptance of tactics ranging from popular education to direct action, and the refusal to condemn or stop others who opt to employ violent or confrontational tactics. Cindy Milford, an anarchist academic and faculty member at the Institute for Social Ecology in Vermont, argues that the adoption of the 'diversity of tactics' principle is not only inclusive, but broadens the definition of 'radicalism':

> By embracing on an equal footing 'education' and 'action,' thereby also breaking down the supposed theory versus practice divide, the conflation of 'militancy' with 'radicalism' was shattered. One wasn't a revolutionary because one was a priori a militant; and this indirectly affirmed that not all revolutionaries can afford to take the same risks – just compare a healthy eighteen year old to a wheelchair-bound octogenarian.[35]

Diversity of tactics is also held to reflect the real diversity which exists amongst those in the movement, and which is needed to construct a democratic, broadly representative and majoritarian movement. However, it fosters a heterogeneous movement that is radical in content as well, seeming to address what has been a central and problematic tendency in Left politics, that of compromising radical analysis and goals in order to attract and keep a mass membership.[36] As Milford argues regarding the use of this principle in Quebec City,

> rather than an assertion of difference for difference's sake – potentially implying a diverse movement emptied of content – what emerged in practice was an explicitly radical movement that was diverse. One could argue

that the convergence of anti-capitalists in Quebec City wasn't diverse enough, of course. Yet it provided the first real guide of how to go about nurturing inclusiveness and unity in a way that is at once qualitative and sincere, and moreover, that allows the particular and universal to complement rather than crush each other as part of a social movement.[37]

Diversity of tactics is also consistent with the anarchist commitment to spontaneism: the people, as an untapped well-spring of creativity, must not be hindered in their search for effective tactics. Moreover, it is argued that the very dynamics of protest, the tactical fluidity on 'the street', requires certain tactics that may become necessary not be ruled out of bounds in advance. As one anarchist contributor to the debate on tactics has put it, '[d]iscussions about tactics don't translate easily into well-defined actions on the streets'.[38] Maximum freedom for people to respond to rapidly changing situations must be preserved.

The commitment to diversity is not merely an outgrowth of classical anarchist ideas, and the anti-globalization movement is not a direct and unmediated descendant of Bakunin and Goldman. It is also profoundly influenced by the intervening historical development of postmodernism and post-Marxism which has had an enormous influence on progressive political thought over the past two decades, especially in the universities. Post-Marxists attempt to account for radical transformations occurring *vis à vis* the international political economy, political actors and emancipatory strategies, primarily in the form of what have been called the 'new social movements'. For example, Laclau and Mouffe point to the 'structural transformations of capitalism' as the source of new forms of domination, new agents and new political spaces, which Marxist theory is deemed unable to account for. For them, advanced industrial countries have moved into a post-industrial period in which there has been a 'decline of the classical working class' due to processes of deindustrialization, 'increasingly profound penetration of capitalist relations of production in areas of social life' resulting in commodification and massification, and a rise in 'forms of bureaucratization which have characterized the Welfare State'.[39] Combined with this was the impact of the experiences of state socialism, the domination of popular struggles by vanguardist Party elites in both the North and the South, and the institutionalization of social-democratic parties and trade unions and their absorption into the operation of the Keynesian welfare state. For post-Marxists, these Left practices resulted in a rigidification of theory and acceptable political practice, and widespread disillusionment stemming from the perception that the major Left institutions have failed to pursue radical social change while clinging to the old rhetoric.[40]

These processes, according to Carl Boggs, have 'undermin[ed] traditional social and political forces' while spawning 'newly emergent forms of opposition'.[41] Emerging from these conditions is a 'more diversified, complex and contradictory horizon of experiences', making it impossible to believe in unified and class-based identities.[42] Instead, in the post-Marxist view, individuals occupy a multiplicity of subject positions, and there is no way to determine a priori how they come to understand themselves in relation to others and the world. Identities cannot be read off structures; instead, identity formation is a fluid, conflictual and constantly changing process. Similarly, occupants of these subject positions cannot be assumed to participate in any particular mode of collective action or struggle. Instead, resistance and emancipation, in keeping with the diffuse and multifarious forms of oppression, can occur in a variety of spaces, especially in the realm of culture and the symbolic in which identities themselves are constructed.

It is the very 'new social movements' whose emergence and politics post-Marxists attempted to explain – feminism, environmentalism, post-colonialism, student activism, and pacifism to mention but a few – which now form important elements of the anti-globalization movement; their multiplicity defines the movement and its politics. Indeed, the anti-globalization movement is not one movement, but rather, as Klein says,

> thousands of movements intricately linked to one another, much as 'hotlinks' connect their websites on the Internet ... Thanks to the Net, mobilizations are able to unfold with sparse bureaucracy and minimal hierarchy; forced consensus and laboured manifestos are fading into the background, replaced instead by a culture of constant, loosely structured and sometimes compulsive information-swapping.[43]

In their multiplicity, these movements insist on the generation of diverse, if mutually supporting and interconnected, forms of political and cultural expression and organizing; to do otherwise would be to return to the failed institutions of the Left. Instead, what is being created resembles what Mouffe terms an 'expansive hegemony', characterized by a 'chain of equivalences between all the democratic demands to produce the collective will of all those people struggling against subordination'.[44] It is, in the language of post-Marxism, a 'decentred' politics of protest in which there is no overarching coalition or leadership to speak on behalf of protesters, and which signifies for some a political maturation that goes beyond the 'narrow sectarianism' of earlier Left formations.[45]

ANTI-GLOBALIZATION ANARCHISM IN ACTION: SOME CRITICAL REFLECTIONS

There is little doubt that the practices described above have generated an extraordinary amount of energy and creativity in protests, to an extent unseen even in the massive labour-organized Ontario Days of Action and other political strikes that swept the globe in the late 1990s.[46] Perhaps most importantly, the demonstrations kicked off by Seattle have elicited a longed-for sense of possibility, of the potential to actually change the decisions of the powerful. On the ground, thousands of (especially young) people have become activists, and have developed a sense of ownership over the movement due to their ability to participate in decision-making in a way not possible in established Left institutions.

That said, there are reasons to think that the expectations generated by the anti-globalization movement will remain unfulfilled. This is not only because of the robustness of structures of economic and political power, which are more flexible and responsive than movement theorists like Klein give them credit for. It is also because the democratic potentials claimed by the movement for decentralization, leaderlessness and diversity are limited by important theoretical and practical contradictions.

a) Decentralized decision-making: consensus or morass?

The elevation of decentralized decision-making to an absolute virtue derives from both the anarchist-inspired commitment to the individual's liberty and direct control over events that affect her, as well as the postmodern acceptance of the existence of multiple identities that require direct, unmediated representation. Both anarchism and postmodern identity politics reject the unitary class subject which socialists are said to posit, as well as the assumption of common interests accompanying this idea. From this standpoint, decentralization is merely a reflection of the diversity of actually existing interests and identities, and it is the form of organization that allows for both a direct and radically plural form of democracy. Thus Klein argues that decentralization in the anti-globalization movement is 'not a source of incoherence and fragmentation. Rather, it is a reasonable, even ingenious adaptation both to pre-existing fragmentation within progressive networks and to changes in the broader culture'.[47]

But this begs the question of whether such fragmentation – of identities, issues, organizations, loyalties, and ideologies – is something to be celebrated uncritically and internalized into the structures of the Left. Decentralization may indeed represent a creative accommodation to the current fragmented state of the Left and of society more generally, but this accommodation often implicitly accepts the fragmentation as natural, positive, even to be embraced as the height of democratic individualism. But the fragmentation of identities can be seen not only as an expression of 'liberated individuals', but also of the fragmented consciousness which capital actively and diligently works to foster, so as to break down forms of collective action which posit a universal interest. Seen in this light, the differences which exist amongst workers are not inherent or primordial, but the outcome, in terms of real material experience and consciousness, of capital's structuring of the labour process and the economy more generally in stratified ways.[48] While not wanting to rehabilitate the 'unitary class subject', one must still ask whether an effective Left alternative to capitalism can be built by an organizational form which exhorts people to congregate on the basis of identities which emphasize differences over commonalities.[49]

Structural decentralization itself expresses a form of fragmentation that has not always facilitated the development of broader forms of solidarity. Local unionism in North America, for instance, though grounded in the immediate material reality of people's lived experience of work, long constituted a serious barrier to the development of bonds of identification beyond the level of the workplace, bonds which could fuel a workers' movement capable of contesting the ravages of early industrial capitalism.[50] Yet the autonomy to make local decisions has often been treated as sacrosanct, even where such decisions may conflict with the needs and interests of others. This powerful though limited definition of community is reproduced in the affinity group model, a unit that retains a kind of sovereignty regardless of the implications of its decisions for other affinity groups. Insistence on absolute freedom from higher levels of legitimate authority and decision-making can have serious negative consequences, both for effectiveness and for the democratic capacities of others.

It is therefore not clear whether the decentralized model is able to process and manage differences effectively, or to actually reach consensus on a variety of important questions, many of them rather fundamental ones facing the contemporary Left. The affinity group structure is an important form of grassroots participation, but it can also function as an evasion of the problems which have always plagued mass organizations, and which do not disappear with radical decentralization. These problems involve questions of the relationship between different levels of organization, the role of leaders and their relationship to the mass base, the process by which decisions are made democratically, and most importantly, what 'democratic process' actually means. These issues – in addition to the substantive questions of analysis, goals and strategy – have always been a source of conflict within the Left, and have resulted in the tendency towards splintering into factions and 'sectlets', and the affinity group structure makes it possible to circumvent these admittedly often tiresome debates: as Klein points out, although with a positive tone, '[i]f somebody doesn't feel like they quite fit in to one of the 30,000 or so NGOs or thousands of affinity groups out there, they can just start one of their own and link up'.[51] The affinity group model can thus be seen as reproducing a debilitating sectarian tradition: smaller and smaller groups are formed by those who already agree with one another, who can't stand such and such a group's philosophy or so-and-so's leadership, sidestepping the fundamental issue of learning how to work together in the midst of such differences. While affinity groups offer an opportunity to develop democratic capacities, the tendency towards radical individualism can limit these skills and can lead to an easy retreat to those with whom one already agrees. While allowing for the ultimate in diverse expression, the proliferation of affinity groups fails to address the need for building genuine agreement on a wide variety of issues, whether tactical, strategic or ideological.

In important ways, the autonomy of affinity groups can also lead to incoherent and ultimately ineffective strategic interventions. While Klein emphasizes the ingenuity and flexibility of autonomous affinity groups, she also illustrates precisely how such decentralization can undermine the groups' goals in her recounting of events from the April 2000 Washington D.C protests against the IMF and World Bank. Affinity groups blockading street intersections were informed that delegates had bested them and entered the IMF/World Bank headquarters at least an hour before they set up. The subsequent decision made in the face of this intelligence was both 'impeccably fair and democratic' and completely nonsensical: as each intersection had autonomy, each was empowered to decide whether to continue their blockade or to join the main march at the Ellipse. As Klein says, '[s]ealing off the access points had been a coordinated action. If some intersections now opened up and other, rebel-camp intersections stayed occupied, delegates on their way out of the meeting could just hang a right instead of a left, and they would be home free. Which, of course, is exactly what happened'.[52] In other words, strategic and structural decentralization can be profoundly contradictory, allowing for both the autonomous expression of democratic will and the undermining of the achievement of the goals of that will.

Klein's illustration of incoherence at least involved some decision being taken, ineffective though that decision was. However, the affinity group structure and the consensus decision-making model often used can and do lead to strategic paralysis in the midst of circumstances requiring rapid responses. Ellie Kirzner provides a dramatic demonstration of 'the vulnerability of the affinity-group structure' in her account of attempts to organize a blockade of the Grande Allée entrance to the Summit of the Americas zone in Quebec City. The gate was able to let Summit participants in and out of the cordoned-off area unhindered for most of Friday, mere blocks away from the confrontations between police and demonstrators marching with the anarchist groups Convergences des Luttes Anti-Capitalistes (CLAC) and the Comité d'Acqueil du Sommet des Amériques (CASA). In the absence of a central body collecting, coordinating and distributing information, it was already midnight when

> a cluster of affinity groups – about 400 people in all – discover the oversight. They march to within two blocks of the gate and sit down in the road for a meeting. One speaker establishes the essential: 'We need to keep this action yellow. No throwing things,' he says pointedly to the Black Bloc'ers on the periphery. Some sweet soul announces he's spent all day with his wire cutters making a hole in the isolated Plains of Abraham perimeter, but he says he's getting nervous and could anyone come and help him? One francophone speaks passionately in favour of a silent sit-in – 'Everyone just shut your mouths,' he proclaims, though it's evident no one can do it. They can't decide whether to block this route or some other; they can't agree on whether there are enough escape routes or how close to the fence to sit. In fact, they are so busy deciding what their consensus is that cars are inching around the supposed blockade. 'There's a car coming,' yells one frustrated protestor. 'Can't we just block this one fucking car?' By 1 am, after a valiant struggle against the centrifugal pressures to party, the group throws in the towel and becomes just one more clutch of people dancing to the drums and pipes on Boulevarde René Lévesque.[53]

What is centrally important to understand here is that affinity groups and especially consensus decision-making require particular conditions to be fully effective, conditions that are rarely present in contexts where time is of the essence.

Decentralization itself is also not inherently democratic, as its democratic character depends greatly on the specific nature of relationships between people and groups. While such structures may indeed enhance participation, they do not inherently guarantee that relationships of mutual accountability between affinity groups, and between central coordinating bodies and affinity groups, are developed, sustained and robust. Without this kind of mediation, how can broader bonds of solidarity, trust and mutual obligation be created? Without mutual accountability, one's allegiance can remain primarily local, vested in the affinity group, and without regard for the effects of one group's actions on others.

Moreover, it is not entirely clear that the structures of decentralized coordination are sufficient to ensure equal and effective participation. Consensus produces its own tyranny, that of *endurance*, in which 'the last ones left at the table get to make the decision'.[54] The conditions and resources required to engage in consensus decision-making – especially time and energy – are themselves not equally distributed. While it is possible to compensate for such maldistributions, as often as not they are seen not as structural inequalities but as manifestations of the various levels of commitment of the participants.

It appears that consensus is not always consistently used by groups committed to its practice, implicitly indicating the limits of the process. The CLAC, for instance, in their 'Consulta' around organizing for the recent G8 Summit in Kananaskis, reverted in one important decision to majority rule. In their report on the parallel protests being planned for Ottawa, the organizers indicated that the decision to operate the days of action on the basis of respect for diversity of tactics, and to insist that these actions embody 'a clear anti-capitalist and anti-imperialist analysis', was 'accepted by more than 75 per cent of the delegates present'.[55] On such questions as tactics, strategy and analysis, it is clear that compromise positions cannot always be reached. So decisions with which some do not agree, and yet which will affect them fundamentally, will and must be made. And yet, decision-making processes like majoritarian rule contradict the anarchist spirit which infuses groups like the CLAC, which insist that no-one should be made to submit to decisions with which they fundamentally disagree. It is clear that it is not always possible for a movement such as this to adopt such libertarian notions of democracy; what is risky, however, is the inculcation of a cultural commitment to democracy defined as consensus, even when it is clear that such a model will not always be possible. The implications of the contradiction between the ideal of consensus and the reality of the need for majoritarian forms of decision-making will foster splits, disunity, and demobilization of some sectors, as readily as will the kinds of top-down decision-making that are under critique.

b) Leaders who aren't leaders, or vanguardism through the back door

The commitment to a leaderless movement, to a movement where everyone is a leader, is often more slogan than reality: despite decentralization and broader forms of participation, leaders always emerge in movements for a variety of practical reasons. Not least of these reasons is the fact that, given the reality of wage labour under capitalism, the vast majority must work at jobs that are poorly remunerated, intense, stressful and alienating. While this is a major reason why resistance to globalization has emerged, it also explains why so many are unable to engage in the ongoing activity of political work. And while it should certainly be the goal of the Left to carve out more time and space for workers to develop their capacities to engage in such activity, the current realities are such that leaders who are committed to full-time political work are needed and have indeed emerged.

What is then problematic in the politics of the anarchist-inspired elements of the anti-globalization movement is not that leaders exist, but that they are denied. Such denial, twinned with an uncompromising ideological rejection of leadership *tout court*, results in leadership unbound by structures of accountability, and/or the castigation of those who take on necessary leadership functions. As Barbara Epstein argues,

> Anti-leadership ideology cannot eliminate leaders, but it can lead a movement to deny that it has leaders, thus undermining democratic constraints on those who assume the roles of leadership, and also preventing the formation of vehicles for recruiting new leaders when the existing ones become too tired to continue. Within radical feminism a view of all hierarchies as oppressive led to attacks on those who took on the responsibilities of leadership. This led to considerable internal conflict, and created a reluctance to take on leadership roles, which weakened the movement. Movements dominated by an anarchist mindset are prone to burning out early.[56]

Such dynamics not only drive people away from political activism; they also make it difficult to answer some rather important questions about leadership – what should its precise role be? What should be the relationship between leaders and other movement participants? Such questions are evaded if 'leaderlessness' is posited as both ideal and reality.

CLAC and other anarchist organizations that have been central in preparing anti-globalization demonstrations in fact have leaders who are involved in defining what the movement should be about and what concrete actions should be taken. Take, for instance, this account of the way that information was distributed amongst affinity groups in Quebec City:

> In the name of 'security concerns,' the place of the spokes council was not to be announced until the last minute. It seemed one had to already be privy to the organizers' communications network to find out where the meeting was. This prevented many out-of-town people, and probably even local people, from finding the meeting where the action plan was to be discussed. The next day many people were not aware that if they did not want to be in a militant 'red' zone, they should not be in the non-violent direct-action oriented 'yellow' zone. It was an amazing, spontaneous, wonderful, and perhaps even historical moment when the red zone emerged out of the yellow zone to tear down the fence! The only problem was some people were not prepared to be in the thick of the police violence that followed. There were people who didn't realize what they were getting themselves into by being in the yellow zone.[57]

In other words, decisions were made which not only affected who could participate in spokes councils, but also shaped people's decisions about how to intervene in the demonstration. However, there was no effective mechanism providing feedback or for holding decision-makers accountable. Other decisions are made to define the terms of a particular discussion or debate; for instance, in CLAC's call to participants wanting to organize around G8 they state that '[t]he Consulta is explicitly aiming to build on the above basis of unity, and not to fundamentally alter the main political and organizing principles'.[58] These principles have already been decided, but by whom? With what recourse?

Such ideas and practices also lead to some contradictory positions. Take, for instance, Cindy Milford, who writes admiringly of the 'libertarian anti-capitalists' who 'took a leadership role to bring down' the widely despised Quebec City fence. For her, that act of 'taking leadership' was valuable as it both 'gained the respect and admiration of other demonstrators, much of the local populace, and a healthy cross section of the broader Canadian public' and allowed 'the anti-authoritarian contingent … to come into its own as a strong and visible force, rather than a marginal, marginalized, or even feared element'.[59] Such an assessment is entirely consistent with the anarchist tradition of both spontaneism and of professional revolutionaries ascribing to themselves the role of inspiring the masses to act. In other words, there are some actions which, by their very nature, put individuals into leadership roles – calling a meeting, defining the parameters of a debate, deciding which information to distribute, attempting to pull down a fence. Even anarchists find it difficult to repudiate such actions, as they are often undeniably useful. From this it is clear that even anarchists will 'lead', and that, implicitly, leadership is necessary. However, when individuals or groups 'take a leadership role' in a context that denies that leaders exist or are necessary, such acts are a form of vanguardism. While not Leninist in the sense of actively organizing the exploited masses and instructing them in revolutionary theory, such interventions imply that some understand better the current conditions of struggle and seek to catalyze the people to act in particular if not in exactly predetermined ways.

Such 'leaderless leadership' removes any possibility of holding people accountable for their actions. The community is left to express preferences rather than having agreed-upon evaluative mechanisms or processes. However, leadership per se cannot be deemed acceptable merely because it engages in actions that one likes or agrees with – what can be done when they engage in less agreeable actions? Leadership acting on its own cannot be judged acceptable post facto just because it happens to represent the (in this case rather vaguely defined) 'will of the people'; in other contexts this might be called 'virtual representation' (à la Edmund Burke) or *caudillismo* (à la Latin American authoritarianism). Heroism on the part of a self-selected few, though perhaps admirable and inspirational, does not help to develop the capacities of the many to make decisions about their activism or the social structures in which they live. This is why leadership as a function must be openly acknowledged rather than fantasized away – so that forms of leadership accountability can develop.

c) A diversity or a hierarchy of tactics?

The refusal to make decisions that have some binding force on the whole community or to have forms of legitimate leadership thus results in a vanguardism by default. This is most readily seen when it is combined with a commitment to diversity of tactics. Not only do some groups emerge as a self-selected avant garde, they do so by deploying tactics which are not only defined as the 'radical' leading edge but which, by their very nature, make the practice of other tactics next to impossible. Yet the deployment of such tactics is not only justified in democratic terms ('we should not decide for people what they can and cannot do in a demo'), but also in moral terms. Whether intentional or not, the morality of radical, often physical confrontation, comes to be used as a form of covert coercion of those who would argue for a collectively agreed-upon set of tactics and more visible forms of discipline.

Debates about the 'diversity of tactics' within the coalition of groups organizing the Quebec City demonstrations, depicted in the recent National Film Board of Canada documentary *View from the Summit*, are particularly instructive here. While representatives from Operation SalAMI argued for a non-violence agreement, Jaggi Singh of CLAC countered that such an imposition would be undemocratic and exclusionary. He went further in his justification, claiming that activists have an obligation to be 'in solidarity with those who are on the front line, who are willing to take the risks'.[60] However, important and rather undemocratic things are implied here. First, as *Guardian* journalist Andy Beckett points out, a *hierarchy* rather than a diversity of tactics is being formed: 'People who are prepared to take risks, or who possess useful skills, can come to dominate, or even have contempt for, the more cautious and amateurish participants'.[61] There is in fact a narrowing of the definition of what constitutes radicalism or even resistance, an implicit moral argument which privileges risk-taking, regardless of whether the majority believes such risks are worthwhile, effective, or justified. It is those who 'take risks', and by extension 'take leadership', who define the leading edge and make a claim to the support of others unwilling or unable to engage in such actions. As L.A. Kauffman warns, a growing 'mystique of insurrection' defines and celebrates 'militant acts on the front lines', independent of connections to more grounded, concrete political struggles and communities.[62]

The practical result of the diversity of tactics position is inevitably to involve those who had chosen other tactics – classic civil disobedience, satirical street theatre and self-expression of alternative values – in the confrontational relationship between police and the anarchist vanguard hoping to demonstrate 'the violence inherent in the system'. As opposed to Milford's claim that the diversity of tactics expands what it means to be anti-authoritarian and anti-capitalist, Judy Rebick argues that the reality is more exclusionary, and actually narrows the scope of tactics for all: 'The problem with the "diversity of tactics" argument is that a tiny group who wants to throw stones at cops can put thousands of people into danger who have not chosen to be in danger. In Quebec City and Genoa, organizers created a safe or Green zone ... but when police violence escalated no one was safe'.[63] André Drainville's account of the result of the attack on the wall in Quebec City amply demonstrates the elimination of the tactical middle ground and of the possibility for forms of resistance that did not involve physical confrontation:

> Carnivalesque happenings – the most fragile indicators of a sense of place and event – were swept away: the *Funk Fighting Unaccountable Naughty Korporations* were gassed out of their efforts to reclaim the streets, the *Lanarkists* were not given much time to catapult stuffed toy-animals into the security perimeter, the Ilôt Fleuri was charged by police and the Saint-Jean Baptiste neighbourhood – a green zone no more, as of Saturday – was inundated with tear-gas. The only puppets seen were on the People's march as it walked away from the security perimeter.[64]

In part a result of the security apparatus' ultimately reductionist view of protesters as all posing the same threat, in part the outcome of choices made by a small minority of demonstrators, 'diversity' of tactics quickly becomes narrowed to a bipolar choice between 'genuine radicalism' and cowardly retreat to spaces which are said to pose no challenge to power. For the sake of including some, diversity of tactics means that 'a much larger group is de facto excluded because they can't afford to risk arrest, violence or a backlash in their member-ship'.[65] In this view, the flow of solidarity is unidirectional and radicalism is narrowly defined by a self-selected vanguard.[66]

Indeed, with the focus on physical forms of confrontation, the intended diver-sity in demonstrations has in fact become, as David Moberg characterizes it, a repetitive 'monotony of tactics':

> Police [in Quebec City] began firing tear gas both at the rock throwers and into the surrounding crowd. While most people fled the stinging gas, a few militants picked up canisters and threw them back at the police. For the rest of the day on Friday, then for most of Saturday afternoon and evening, there was a give and take of protesters advancing on police, usually with a few people throwing things, then the police firing tear gas – as well as water cannons and rubber and plastic bullets – and then moving out to disperse the crowd.[67]

The possibilities for sorting through the question of tactics, let alone strategy and vision, are ultimately seriously limited by the decentralized structure of the movement. It is not so much that a particular set of values must be adopted, but that, as Epstein argues, some ethical guidelines are needed and must be adopted. Even Milford agrees that such relations of accountability are required, both for democratic and strategic reasons: 'Without a bit more definition to the diversity principle, and a way to make people accountable to any parameters decided on, the anti-capitalist movement is wide open to stupidity or sabotage – or at least more than it needs to be'.[68] But this of course begs the central question: how does a movement of autonomous affinity groups, who reject both the legitimacy and practicability of forms of authority, set, not to mention enforce, ethical guidelines? Without a willingness to accept that more regularized and centralized structures are needed, that forms of legitimate authority are possible and not inherently opposed to democracy, that some forms of leadership need to be developed, such principles will remain mere exhortations, not norms upon which a community can be built.

CONCLUSIONS

The movement's commitment to diversity of tactics – and to bracketing off discussion of the relative merits of such tactics – promotes a disconnection between tactics and broader strategic goals. Because tactics are off-limits, to be chosen by individuals or small groups, there is little opportunity to engage in discussion about what actions will be most likely to achieve goals, or even to define what those goals are. An unnamed anarchist writing in the Ireland-based *Red and Black Revolution* wonders about the extent to which confrontational tactics are carefully considered: 'The decision about which tactic to use isn't based on what's best for advancing anarchism, it's about how exciting it is to mask up and break things, against how boring it is to try to persuade people. If the Black Blocs continue at summit protests, will it be because people have weighed up their pros and cons and decided they are the most effective tactic, or because people like to dress up in gas masks and bandanas?'[69] Rather harsh words, perhaps, but the question is important – how, in the absence of a discussion over tactics, can such evaluations be made?

Ultimately, the 'diversity of tactics' principle obviates the need to engage in political debate and struggle within the Left. The work of persuading, of convincing, of arguing over key issues amongst an ever-broadening group of people is made unnecessary by agreeing to disagree. While this may have allowed a temporary coalition of disparate groups to gather together, it is unlikely to form the basis for a more lasting and durable coalition between the more institutionalized elements of the Left and those who are inspired by direct action and anarchist political ideas. The vaunted Teamster-Turtle alliance, formed in the electric days of Seattle, will not endure if methods to bridge these gaps are not developed. In many ways, such an alliance is not an option – but it is central to the ultimate success of the anti-globalization movement, for as Kim Moody points out, it is only the pulling together of 'the mobility and audacity of the movement in the streets with the social weight and numbers of the organized working class' that will lead to fundamental change, to 'dismantl[ing] the mechanisms of capitalist globalization'.[70] Rebick also believes that an alliance between the two wings of the movement is absolutely necessary, and that a permanent split is simply a dead end:

> Neither wing of the movement can be effective without the other. The radical wing has created the energy, dynamism and attracted the youth that has put the anti-corporate movement back on the map after the failure of the old left. The institutional wing provides resources, continuity, credibility, establishment contacts and a broader base. Each group thinks they are justified in their disagreements with the other. But the cost of allowing disagreements to turn into permanent splits is too high.[71]

Understanding the ways in which this coalition is now hindered is thus central to the future of the movement.

The nature of the tensions that exist between organized labour and the anarchist-inspired elements of the anti-globalization movement merit examination in a separate essay. However, several things can be said about the way that the anarchist approach to democratic decision-making, the critique of leadership, and the unwillingness to make collective and binding decisions about tactics (and other issues), make coalition-building with the labour movement quite difficult.

Kim Moody is right to point to the conservatism of the labour leadership itself as one important barrier to such a coalition. Moody contends that it is not because organized labour shies away from confrontation with the state – the many strikes involving engagement with the police are a testament to such willingness. For him, it is the dominance of business unionism in the North American labour movement that prevents a coalition from solidifying. In other words, the union leaders fear confrontational tactics they cannot control; if left to their own devices, union members would engage in a more radical politics. This analysis may indeed be true to some extent; certainly, the development of flying squads in many union locals in Ontario is evidence of a willingness of union members to engage in more radical forms of direct action. It would also explain why the Quebec union leadership and their marshals at the Saturday parade in Quebec City were unwilling to let members choose whether to march left to the wall or right to the parade grounds and away from confrontations (even though many union members did just that and marched to the wall to get gassed). There is no question that, as Epstein argues, major political shifts within the labour movement are required for such a coalition to gel.

However, there are also hindrances that emerge from the anarchist wing. A complete rejection of labour movement institutions, leadership and desire for immediate reforms will make it difficult to find middle ground, with both union leaders and members. Some 'relaxation of anti-bureaucratic and anti-hierarchical principles on the part of activists in the anti-globalization movement' will also be necessary, if a permanent split is to be avoided.[72] This is vital if the movement is to move beyond demonstrations and expressions of opposition and onto building a movement not only capable of 'transforming structures of power' but of discussing how that transformation might be carried out. In a situation of radical autonomy, however, there will always be limits on the bonds of solidarity that will be built. By failing to acknowledge the existence and need for leaders, mechanisms of accountability will remain undeveloped. By accepting diversity of tactics a priori, the evaluation of such tactics and their relationship to strategy is short-circuited. As Michael Albert argues, 'without stable and lasting institutions that have well-conceived and lasting norms and roles, advanced relations among disparate populations and even among individuals are quite impossible'[73] – which is equally true for any alternative social structure capable of replacing 'corporate globalization'.

NOTES

1   Naomi Klein, 'Farewell to the "End of History": Organization and Vision in Anti-Corporate Movements', in L. Panitch and C. Leys, eds., *Socialist Register 2002: A World of Contradictions*, London: Merlin Press, 2001, p. 6.

2   Alexander Cockburn, Jeffrey St. Clair and Alan Sekula, *Five Days That Shook the World: Seattle and Beyond*, London: Verso, 2000, pp. 2-3. In an interview with *New Left Review*, John Sellers, director of the Ruckus Society, a U.S.-based organization that trains activists in non-violent direct action and other methods of political campaigning, discusses how fragmentation was exhibited at the demonstration at the Democratic National Convention in Los Angeles in 2000. When asked if there had been 'too many messages' in LA, he responded that '[w]e were driven into a false competition between messages, between campaigns, with far too little time to talk about a people's platform which has lots of diverse planks to it. They were all based on social justice, but they were different and there was no chance to talk properly about any of them' (John Sellers, 'Raising a Ruckus', *New Left Review*, 10 (July-August), 2001, pp. 75-6).

3   Stop the FTAA homepage, www.stopftaa.org.

4   David Graeber, 'The New Anarchists', *New Left Review*, 13 (January-February), 2002, p. 70; emphasis in original.

5   It is important to clarify what I take to be the various sections of the anti-globalization movement. For the most part, I am discussing the element of the movement, engaged in direct action tactics of various kinds, that rejects the possibility of transforming institutions, as opposed to the more institutionalized opponents of globalization – labour movements, political parties, and non-governmental organizations which have engaged in both demonstrations and attempts at reforming and participating in the structures which are authoring globalization (be they national states or international organizations). As well, my focus tends to be on the dynamics within the North American section of the movement.

6   Geoffrey Ostergaard, 'Anarchism', in T. Bottomore, et.al., eds., *A Dictionary of Marxist Thought*, 2nd ed., London: Blackwell, 1991, p. 21.

7   Ostergaard, 'Anarchism', p. 21; Alix Kates Shulman, 'Preface to Part One: Organization of Society', of Emma Goldman, *Red Emma Speaks: Selected Writings and Speeches by Emma Goldman*, A.K. Shulman, ed., New York: Vintage, 1972, p. 32.

8   Ostergaard, 'Anarchism', p. 21-2.

9   Emma Goldman, 'What I Believe', in Shulman, ed., *Red Emma Speaks*, p. 37; emphasis in original.

10   Goldman, 'What I Believe', p. 37.

11   Utah Phillips and Ani Difranco, 'Anarchy', on *The Past Didn't Go Anywhere* (compact disc), Righteous Babe Records, 1996.

12   Geoffrey Ostergaard, 'Michael Bakunin', in T. Bottomore, et.al., eds., *A*

Dictionary of Marxist Thought, 2nd ed., London: Blackwell, 1991, p. 44.

13   Emma Goldman, 'Socialism: Caught in the Political Trap', in Shulman, ed., *Red Emma Speaks*, pp. 79-80.

14   Noam Chomsky, 'Notes on Anarchism', *New York Review of Books*, 14 (10), May 21, 1970, pp. 31-5.

15   Rick Salutin, 'Anarchism: Its Time Has Come Again', *The Globe and Mail*, 10 August 2001, in Canadian Periodical Index, http://web6. infotrac. galegroup.com.

16   Shulman, 'Preface to Part One', p. 29.

17   Salutin, 'Anarchism'. It is worth mentioning that not all anarchists agree with this position. In an interesting debate on Znet, the website of the U.S.-based anarchist-leaning *Z Magazine*, Michael Albert engages a number of anarchist interlocutors who challenge his advocacy of 'different kinds of structures' as authoritarian and Leninist. In this exchange, Albert's critics express their belief that no forms of authority, in which individuals are made to abide by decisions with which they do not agree or which constrain them from exercising their individual will, can be legitimate; Albert, claiming the anarchist tradition as his own as well, attempts to differentiate between forms of authority which are based on power hierarchies, and those which are not. He maintains that the critique of hierarchy does not obviate the need for regularized decision-making forms and norms, in which legitimate and authoritative decisions can be made. It is difficult to ascertain which view is more widely espoused in the anti-globalization movement. See Michael Albert, et. al., 'Albert Replies to Critics of His Anarchism Essay' on ZNet, http://zmag.org/anardebate.htm.

18   Stop the FTAA, 'Affinity Group Information and Resources', http://www. stopftaa.org/activist/act_ags.html.

19   Stop the FTAA, 'Affinity Group'.

20   Ibid.

21   Klein, 'Farewell', p. 5.

22   Graeber, 'The New Anarchists', p. 71.

23   Stop the FTAA homepage.

24   Graeber, 'The New Anarchists, p. 72.

25   Sam Gindin, 'Socialism with Sober Senses: Developing Workers' Capacities', in L. Panitch and C. Leys, eds., *Socialist Register 1998: The Communist Manifesto Now*, London: Merlin Press, 1998, pp. 78-9.

26   Klein, 'Farewell', p. 7.

27   Quoted in Klein, 'Farewell', p. 8.

28   See Lyle Stewart, 'Getting spooked: the anti-globalization movement is gaining momentum, but law enforcers are quickly catching up', *This Magazine*, 34 (5) (March-April), 2001, pp. 24-8, for an analysis of the impact that the criminalization of anti-globalization activism is having on the politics of the movement.

29   Klein, 'Farewell', p. 3.

30   Salutin, 'Anarchism'.

31   Ostergaard, 'Bakunin', p. 44-5.

32   Quoted in Graeber, 'The New Anarchists', pp. 63-4.

33   Ostergaard, 'Anarchism', p. 22.

34   Chuck Munson, 'Against Generalization, For Diversity of Tactics' on Tactical Media Crew website, 28 November 2001, http://squat.net/tmc/msg02339.html.

35   Cindy Milford, 'Something Did Start in Quebec City: North America's Revolutionary Anti-Capitalist Movement', Institute for Social Ecology website, http://www.social-ecology.org/learn/library/ milstein/qc.html.

36   For the classic statement of such arguments, see Adam Przeworski, *Capitalism and Social Democracy*, Cambridge: Cambridge University Press, 1985.

37   Milford, 'Something Did Start'.

38   Munson, 'Against Generalization'.

39   Ernesto Laclau and Chantal Mouffe, *Hegemony and Socialist Strategy: Towards a Radical Democratic Politics*, London: Verso, 1985, p. 80.

40   Carl Boggs, *Social Movements and Political Power: Emerging Forms of Radicalism in the West*, Philadelphia: Temple University Press, 1986, pp. 7-8.

41   Boggs, *Social Movements*, p. 4, p. 5.

42   Laclau and Mouffe, *Hegemony*, p. 80.

43   Klein, 'Farewell', p. 4.

44   Chantal Mouffe, 'Hegemony and New Social Subjects: Towards a New Concept of Democracy', in C. Nelson and L. Grossberg, eds., *Marxism and the Interpretation of Culture*, Urbana: University of Illinois Press, 1988, p. 99.

45   Roger Burbach, 'North America', in E. Bircham and J. Charlton, eds., *Anti-Capitalism: A Guide to the Movement*, rev. ed., London: Bookmarks Publications, 2001, p.159, p. 168.

46   Kim Moody, *Workers in a Lean World*, London/New York: Verso, 1997. pp. 9-23.

47   Klein, 'Farewell', p. 7.

48   Mike Davis, *Prisoners of the American Dream*, London/New York: Verso, 1986, pp. 40-5.

49   There is evidence that sections of the movement are attempting to deal with its overly fragmented nature. The World Social Forum is perhaps the most large-scale manifestation of an attempt to foster analyses and identifications which bridge nationalities, issues and particular interests. Other less dramatic indications are also there: the Ottawa Coalition to Stop the FTAA, for instance, has renamed itself Global Democracy Ottawa in the process of organizing protests against the IMF/World Bank and G20 meetings in November 2001, expressing a broader vision and set of goals. See the Global Democracy Ottawa homepage, http://www.gdo.ca.

50   Bryan Palmer, *Working Class Experience: Rethinking the History of Canadian Labour, 1800-1991*, Toronto: McLelland and Stewart, 1996, pp. 106-8.

51 Klein, 'Farewell', p. 7.

52 Ibid.

53 Ellie Kirzner, 'They've Grown Up: Anti-globalization movement now too big for on-the-spot decision-making', *NOW Magazine* (online edition), 25 April - 2 May 2001, http://www.nowtoronto.com/issues/2001-04-25/news_story.html.

54 Sellers, 'Raising a Ruckus', p. 76.

55 Convergences des Luttes Anti-Capitalistes (CLAC), 'Ottawa Anti-G8 Consulta Report', 15-17 February 2002, online at http://www.quebec2001.net/english/consulta_report.html

56 Barbara Epstein, 'Anarchism and the Anti-Globalization Movement', *Monthly Review*, 53 (4), September 2001, http://www.monthly review.org/0901epstein.htm.

57 Ben Grosscup and Doyle, 'An Open Letter to the Anti-Authoritarian Anti-Capitalist Movement' on Protest.net, March 2nd, 2002, http://www.protest.net/view.cgi?view=2383.

58 *Convergences des Luttes Anti-Capitalistes* (CLAC), 'Regional Consulta and Assembly on Anti-G8 Organizing', http://www.quebec2001 .net/english/consulta.html.

59 Milford, 'Something Did Start'.

60 Magnus Isacsson, dir., *View from the Summit*, National Film Board of Canada, 2002. Other justifications for such tactics are also used. Maude Barlow, when asked by the media to comment on the confrontations in Quebec City, argued that they were the expression of anger of a generation of disenfranchised youth; as their anger was socially created, society therefore bears responsibility for its results. Roger Burbach also subscribes to this interpretation: he argues that 'the anarchists and the anti-globalization protests provide an outlet for the pent-up frustrations and sense of alienation of a new generation'; see Burbach, 'North America', p.168; Rachel Neumann, 'A Place for Rage', *Dissent*, Spring 2000. Others rightly put the 'violence' entailed in anti-globalization protests in the context of the organized violence of the state at these protests and the structural violence of inequality under capitalism, to which the former simply does not compare. See opinion ranging from the ACME Collective, 'N30 Black Bloc Communiqué', and Barbara Ehrenreich, 'Anarkids and Hypocrites', both in E. Yuen, et.al., *The Battle of Seattle: The New Challenge to Capitalist Globalization*, New York: Soft Skull Press, 2001, to Leo Panitch, 'Violence: A Tool of Order and Change', *Monthly Review*, 54(2) (June), 2002. While these positions are valid, they also sidestep the question of whether the movement's tactics should ultimately be determined by anger.

61 Andy Beckett, 'When Capitalism Calls', review of John Lloyd, *The Protest Ethic: How the Anti-Globalization Movement Challenges Social Democracy*, *London Review of Books*, 24 (7), 4 April 2002, p. 22.

62 L.A Kauffman, 'Turning Point', *Free Radical*, 16, May 2001,

http://www.free-radical.org/issue16.shtml.

63   Judy Rebick, 'Qatar reveals impact of Sept 11 on trade battle' in ZNet, November 17 2001, http://www.zmag.org/sustainers/content/2001-11/17 rebick.cfm.

64   André Drainville, 'Quebec City 2001 and the Making of Transnational Subjects', in L. Panitch and C. Leys, eds., *Socialist Register 2002: A World of Contradictions*, London: Merlin Press, 2001, p. 32.

65   Rebick, 'Qatar'.

66   Such an analysis in part underpins Operation SalAMI's call for a commitment to 'strategic non-violence'. They argued in their statement on the Quebec City demonstration that '[n]onviolent direct action through the use of affinity groups also allows for genuine *diversity of tactics*, a real *plurality in political views*, and a *spirit of respect* for each other. To build participatory democracy we need trust, we need assurances that nobody simply because he/she 'feels like it' or wants to 'show us the way' will take it upon themselves to hurt other people or put our lives at risk through some irresponsible act of destruction or violence' (Operation SalAMI, 'FTAA 2001: The Quebec Odyssey', http://www.alternatives.ca/salami/HTML_an/ftaa_2001.html, emphasis in original).

67   David Moberg, 'Tear Down the Walls: The movement is becoming more global', *In These Times.com*, 28 May, 2001, http://www.inthesetimes.com/issue/25/13/moberg2513.html.

68   Milford, 'Something Did Start'.

69   Unknown Author, 'Bashing the Black Bloc?', *Red and Black Revolution*, 6, Winter 2001, http://flag.blackened.net/revolt/rbr/rbr6/black.html.

70   Kim Moody, 'Unions', in E. Bircham and J. Charlton, eds., *Anti-Capitalism: A Guide to the Movement*, rev. ed., London: Bookmarks Publications, 2001, p. 293.

71   Rebick, 'Qatar'.

72   Epstein, 'Anarchism'.

73   Albert, 'Albert Replies to Critics'.

THE PORTO ALEGRE THERMIDOR?
BRAZIL'S 'PARTICIPATORY BUDGET'
AT THE CROSSROADS

Sérgio Baierle

In the formation of leaders, one premiss is fundamental: is it the intention that there should always be rulers and ruled, or is the objective to create the conditions in which this division is no longer necessary? – Gramsci[1]

The 'Participatory Budget' experience in Brazil, directly associated with the rise of the Workers Party (PT) over the past two decades, has become a focus of world-wide attention for the Left. This is especially the case with Porto Alegre, the city which has hosted the World Social Forum meetings where anti-globalization activists from every continent have come together to declare that 'another world is possible'. In this essay, I intend to present an array of problems for discussion – all based on the hypothesis that the Participatory Budget (PB) experience in Porto Alegre faces a thermidorian[2] phase: a situation in which the PB's transformative process will be dramatically challenged by internal and external constraints. Radical republicanism of the Tocquevillean type, the notion of a 'non-state public sphere',[3] where the state at the local level is open to the participation of all members of society, runs the risk of being side-tracked by an old impulse: to put the plebeians back 'in their place' – despite the local PT-led Popular Front government's efforts to increase the number of participants. I believe that by studying the current limits of the experience of Porto Alegre it is possible to shed some light on the potential directions of democratic radical-ization for the popular classes.

The PB is understood here as the emergence of a plebeian public space in local politics. It involves a structure and process through which popular sectors can prioritize public works and services in a municipal investment plan. Structurally, the PB consists of a system of co-management between representatives of popular sectors and local government. It is organized through an annual cycle of activities that combines direct participation with the election of representatives (delegates and councillors), as well as governmental commitment to the processing of the demands that emerge through previously approved criteria. With regard to process, PB signifies the emergence of a plebeian public; one with its origin in a long history of popular struggles for access to the city, beginning in the 1950s with the first *malocas*[4] in Porto Alegre. PB represents the creation of space for popular organization in community-based deliberative arenas.[5]

In this space, the management of social and physical problems within neighbourhoods is based on public debate. The public consists of local citizens, community and religious groups, and social and professional movements involved in such areas as education, health care, social assistance, law and culture. In some regions of the city these spaces have been named Popular Councils (Conselhos Populares), in some, Neighbourhood Associations (Uniões de Vilas), and in others they are not differentiated from the Participatory Budget Regional Forum (FROP), the co-management organ of the PB at the regional level. Autonomous and/or co-managed, meetings in these spaces are open and have a public agenda, while the way in which deliberations are constructed varies, reflecting the degree of autonomy among the organized popular sectors (independent or co-managed) and the nature of their organizational structure (open or corporative). This fluctuation is not arbitrary, but rather expressive of a permanent tension between forces that are as plural as they are unequal.

Table 1 demonstrates the remarkable character of PB participation in Porto Alegre, involving a public that includes far more women than men (female participation growing from 46.7 per cent in 1993 to 51.4 per cent in 1998 and to 57.3% in 2000), and a great majority of unskilled workers (manual or not), with only a primary level of education. And even above the plenary level, where anyone can attend, the PB has permitted the emergence of leaders among directors of neighbourhood associations and delegates and councillors at higher levels of decision making from women and the less-educated in a proportion far greater than is traditionally the case. Moreover, no less than 54 per cent of those attending the plenary assemblies in 2000 were poor people (with average monthly family incomes below US$281, when the city average is US$420), and even 42 per cent of delegates and 32 per cent of councillors were poor according to this measure. The PB has also become a venue for strategic action for blacks and indigenous peoples – segments of the popular classes previously excluded from participation and political representation. It is very significant in the Brazilian context that one fourth of PB councillors in Porto Alegre represent blacks or indigenous peoples. This is unprecedented in a city where, until recently, true segregation existed; black people were not accepted in the principal supermarkets, and were excluded from industrial work.

Today, there are black movements linked to the samba schools and other

Table 1

Gender of Participatory Budget Participants – annual first meeting 2000 (per cent)

Sex	Plenary 2000	Dir. AMs	Delegates	Counsellors
Female	57.3	58.9	54.7	27.3
Male	41.5	41.1	44.8	72.7
NR	1.3	-	0.5	-

Ethnicity of Participatory Budget Participants – annual first meeting 2000 (per cent)

Ethnic Group	Plenary	Dir. AMs	Delegates	Counsellors
Black	21.1	15.9	21.7	22.7
White	61.9	63.6	59.9	52.3
Indigenous	3.6	5.6	4.7	4.5
Other	4.9	5.6	6.1	9.1
NR	8.4	9.3	7.5	11.4

Education Level of Participatory Budget Participants – annual first meeting 2000 (per cent)

Level	Plenary	Dir. AMs	Delegates	Counsellors
Primary or less	52.4	46.7	39.2	36.4
High School (complete or not)	23.9	38.3	34.9	34.1
Post-Secondary (complete or not)	19.9	12.2	23.1	29.5
NR	3.7	2.8	2.8	-

Age of Participatory Budget Participants – annual first meeting 2000 (per cent)

Years	Plenary	Dir. AMs	Delegates	Counsellors
16 - 25	17.8	5.6	8.1	2.3
26 - 33	16.5	13.1	9.6	6.8
34 - 41	20.6	13.1	16.7	20.5
42 - 49	18.8	26.2	27.8	18.2
50 - 80	26.2	42.1	37.8	52.3

Source:	CIDADE/PMPA, Participatory Budget Research, 2000.
Plenary:	Participants interviewed at the annual first meeting of the Participatory Budget process.
Dir. AMs:	Directors of Neighbourhood Associations (AM) interviewed at the annual first meeting in 2000,
Delegates:	Delegates in the Participatory Budget (or those who have been delegates in previous years).
Counsellors:	Counsellors in the Participatory Budget process (or those who have been counsellors in previous years).
NR:	No response

cultural activities that are working to identify strategies to change this situation. Similar work has been done by groups of the disabled as well as retired workers. The work of the church has also been facilitated by the existence of the PB process in popular communities. Access to communities has increased, as well as access to financing from the municipality and individual donations, allowing the church to enhance programs ranging from popular education, inspired by Paulo Freire, to traditional social assistance programs.

Three issues will be examined here to gain a better understanding of current challenges to the Participatory Budget process: (1) the need to politicize those experiences of direct community management that make use of municipal resources (financial or material); (2) the need for improved articulation of link-ages between the public budget and city planning, so as to foster deeper analyses of municipal finances and public policies; and (3) the need for further discussion of the political aspects of the PB experience. The latter include the challenges associated with democratic radicalization that is limited to the level of a city, the drawbacks associated with government staff recruitment among community leaders, and the effects of the increasingly mass character of the PB experience, which underscores a widening gap between a body of specialized leaders and participants at the base.

To begin with, I will provide an overview of the political conjuncture, one in which neoliberal forces are striving for hegemony in the so-called 'third sector' via a privatized, decentralized 'community' model for social policy, focused on the poor. With regard to local party-politics, my objective is not to provide an exhaustive study of partisan life, but to reveal some consequences of the electoral impact of the Participatory Budget. I will examine the extent to which ordinary citizens involved in PB interact with the government sector and with the party structure that underlies it, as well as the consequences of this interaction for participatory practices.

PORTO ALEGRE IS NOT AN OASIS IN THE NEOLIBERAL DESERT

There are some apparent paradoxes in the conjuncture of the 1990s that bear on the arguments considered in this essay. The first of these consists of the fact that, for the first time in history, Brazil has experienced the re-establishment of formal democracy combined with social deterioration. 'Inequality increased in Brazil between 1992 and 1998, and the proportion of wages to national revenue, which was 44 per cent of GDP in 1993, fell to 36 per cent of GDP by the decade's end ....'[6] Shrinking wages have been accompanied by the deterioration of labour rights and a change in the social base of economic power.

> Foreign capital, privatization and mergers created a new bourgeoisie in the country, and have destabilized political forces. In the six years under FHC [President Fernando Henrique Cardoso], there has been a transference of property and patrimony which the political regime does not resist. About 30 per cent of the GDP has changed hands. It is an earthquake. With the privatizations, the government lost a good deal of its capacity within the state to distribute benefits among its allies. At the same time, the new regu-lating agencies represent little more than a simulacrum. They have little or no capacity to impose criteria and public rules on a heavily competitive system that now works on an international scale.[7]

At other moments in history (e.g. the 'New State' after 1937, or the period of authoritarian/military rule after 1964), it was necessary to break with democ-racy in order to impose limits on working-class demands and promote rearrangement among the ruling classes. In the 1990s, not only did this social crisis coexist with formal democracy, but the federal government was legitimized without the need for hegemonic measures (such as income redistribution) to secure active consent, and thus without the establishment of a more direct relationship with the popular classes. Apart from the patrimonial and patriarchal ties of a significant part of the government alliance (the traditional Brazilian *coronelismo*), it mostly relied on an indirectly articulated process of domination, with government actions hyped by the mass media, substituting virtual political space for any real one, so that citizens became mere spectators.

Thus the democratization of the 1980s was replaced by the 'governance' of the 1990s. Placing blame for the country's crisis on the state bureaucracy made it possible to convince the public that privatization and the dismissal of public servants would allow the country to 'rescue' the public debt. The mystique of a stable currency, the Real (and what it represented in terms of the break from the inflationary spiral that had severely affected the popular classes), was fundamental for the consolidation of the neoliberal order in Brazil. So long as the government's dollar reserves lasted, it was possible to maintain the illusion that the invisible hand of the global market would place Brazil directly in the 'First World'. But following a ten-fold increase in the public debt (despite the revenue generated by the privatizations), and due to foolishly high interest rates amidst a highly restrictive monetary policy, the time soon came to pay the bill. As before, the only policy anchor they could come up with was lower wages – both individual and social.

Experiences such as the Participatory Budget in Porto Alegre – reproduced today in more than one hundred Brazilian cities (in form if not always in substance) – go against the tide of this process. Rather than diminishing the state's role and submitting the public budget to an endless logic of fiscal adjustment, the Popular Front government in Porto Alegre invested in the recovery of public capacity to meet the demands of the popular sector. A new public community emerged on the municipal scene through the Participatory Budget's well-attended public meetings; through the inversion of priorities and the effort to put proposals for fiscal justice into practice; through the opening of channels for participation in practically all areas of municipal administration; and above all, through investment and services in poor neighbourhoods. Boycotted for years by major newspapers, radio stations and television networks, the PB itself has become a form of popular media.

However, Porto Alegre is not an oasis in a neoliberal desert. It is impossible to avoid the consequences of macro-politics of adjustment imposed at the federal level. No matter how fiercely the deconstruction of the public sector[8] is fought at the local level (such as by implementing anticyclical politics, increasing municipal property and service taxes, and generally taking advantage of the margin of resources available through the limited decentralization process brought about by the Constitution of 1988) cities still control only a thin slice of the national public budget (down from approximately 17 per cent in the beginning of the 1990s, to the current level of 14 per cent, owing to the reconcentration of tax revenues at the federal level[9] that are not redistributed to states or cities).

Moreover, the Municipal Government cannot overlook the new neoliberal common sense: the increasingly community-centred nature of social policies and the categorization of urban deterioration as merely a problem of management. Areas of poverty and absolute exclusion exist that are impossible to reach by participatory policies; direct social action is necessary to reach these sectors. Social assistance policies always have a Sisyphus-like character, although while the rock is being pushed up the mountain, thousands of people may be aware of the vital difference such assistance makes to holding their footing. In a country such as Brazil, with the fourth worst income distribution on the planet, any public or private actions intended to fight poverty are to be welcomed, but they are not a substitute for the legal, constituent and transforming dimension of politics. In the Metropolitan Region of Porto Alegre, with a population of just under 3.4 million, there were approximately 280,000 unemployed people in the year 2000 (16.6 per cent of the economically active population).[10] A March 2001 study comparing the periods of 1981-85 and 1995-99 shows a deterioration in the indices of employment and income, despite advances in the areas of education and health. The percentage of working ten to fourteen year-olds increased by 11 per cent; the rate of employment in the formal sector of the economy fell by 31.1 per cent; the rate of employment in industry fell by 14.7 per cent. In addition, the unemployment rate went up by 78.4 per cent, increasing the percentage of poor persons in the population of Porto Alegre by 19.8 per cent, and the inequality of income by 16.4 per cent. Overall, there was a 100 per cent increase in the poverty index.[11] However good local policies of social assistance and job creation may be, there exist harsh limits in the economic system which constantly intensify social exclusion.

Compensatory actions demand additional effort in order to achieve a mini-mally significant result, since cities not only have insufficient resources to deal with the situation, but their public services also consume more resources than those provided by non-profit and community organizations. This is illustrated by the example of community day-care centres in Porto Alegre.[12] The cost of a day-care centre constructed and maintained by the municipal government is enough to maintain several, perhaps more than ten, day-care centres run by community associations, where labour costs are much lower. The result is that today Porto Alegre has 118 day-care centres run by community associations with funds from City Hall. The same applies in other areas, from Carnival to cooperatives for waste recycling. An immense network of community-managed activities has resulted from the financial and material support provided by the municipality.

This poses a strategic challenge for the PB that is hardly ever mentioned either by the Popular Front government in Porto Alegre, or by the popular move-ments. To what point can the political learning the PB has provided be extended to other social relations? Is it reasonable to assume, considering the PB process as a 'school for citizenry', that citizens will begin to incorporate democratic methods and concepts in their autonomous organizations? While agreements between City Hall and community organizations have a public character and are processed on the basis of suggestions from society itself, a significant number of management issues tend to be left out of public discussion. Let us reconsider the example of the day-care centres. How can it be guaranteed that the professionals who are hired are not relatives of the leader of the community organization? How do we approach the fact that parents often still pay for the service? In that case, what is a fair price? Why must some parents pay and others not, since in the few municipal day-care centres no monthly fee is charged? How can it be guaranteed that the criteria for registration and length of stay of the children are equitable and unbiased? How can it be ensured that public money is managed in a transparent fashion and with the agreement of parents and the community, and that those involved can participate in the proper pedagogical management of the centre (as is the case in the public schools where councils bring together parents, students and educational professionals)?

I do not mean to suggest that the state is the only arena of democratic public administration. State management does not per se guarantee the public interest. The challenge I wish to recognize here is the democratic transformation of society. Democracy is not just about controlling the state; society also must democratize itself. No one would suggest ending agreements such as the community day-cares initiative, yet without a democratic revolution in their management, there can be no progress vis-à-vis neoliberal 'common sense'. This is defined and defended across the national and international political spectrum in terms of responsibility for social problems being placed back on communities – with the state offering help but not guaranteeing rights. Challenging this consensus, Boaventura de Souza Santos argues that 'democratization of citizenship space is emancipating only as far as it is united with the democratization of all remaining structural spaces, and citizenship alone is sustainable only to the extent that it spreads beyond the citizenship space'.[13] Otherwise, there is a risk of weakening the Participatory Budget process, understood here as a new form of power building which redistributes power away from the executive and the parliament.[14] There is a real danger that PB may be transformed into 'yet another' organ of public administration in the 'third (community) sector'. Autonomy is a basic principle of citizenship and popular sovereignty, yet it is not a given character of popular organizations; to acquire and keep it is a permanent task.

This is especially important because the new 'common sense' envisages the transference of social policy management to the community level. This reflects both the strengths and the weaknesses of neoliberalism. On the one hand, there is a recognition that the new model of 'flexible accumulation' is increasingly exclusionary, and cannot coexist, in the medium and long term, with democratic legitimacy. On the other hand, there is an effort to create hegemonic actions that socially consolidate 'market fundamentalism' through the extension of 'total quality' principles to the social actions of large companies, in a kind of results-based social policy. This has been characterized as a process of social fascism,[15] where 'society' (those with socio-economic power and status) turns against the 'social' (the excluded).[16] I prefer to label this an initial situation of 'hegemonic absence', disclosing, with growing transparency, the permanent crisis of legitimacy in which it operates, and making the monetary mysticism of its conceptual scheme more difficult to decipher with each electoral cycle. A lack of socially constructed hegemony does not signify the absence of social domination: neoliberal activity seems to be moving forward assertively in the field of social action, a field hitherto somewhat abandoned to old *caudilhos*, churches and talk show hosts – and the left.[17]

It was in the context of the dimming of the lights of the Cardoso government and the lack of new tricks in the hats of IMF and World Bank economists (the real managers of economic policy) that the need for hegemonic measures acquired a fresh appeal among the ruling classes. Governmental propaganda at the federal level promised Hayekian social policies (e.g. a guaranteed annual income) and the business sector invested in the concept of social responsibility through the creation of non-profit foundations. This is the new consensus of late neoliberalism: free market, fiscal responsibility and community management of social policy. What is interesting is that among those who do not like social movements there is now a desire to fortify civil society. Seeing that it is now impossible to conceal the disastrous results of a decade of destruction of social rights,[18] it is the private sector itself that is seeking – what a contradiction! – to reconstruct the state outside the state.

Nevertheless, we should not allow ourselves to have any false impressions. With the public character, universality and uniformity of social rights shattered (through privatization, decentralization and the focused bias of social policies),[19] the ruling classes are working hard to reconstruct direct relations with a clientele in the popular classes. And this is done through diverse mechanisms: the creation of new organizations, the financing of NGOs, the construction of new corporate concepts of social action – reproducing in each locus of action the logic of fiscal responsibility and pragmatic administration. Clearly, the precarious nature of work relations has been amplified through the new concept of a 'voluntary sector'. We are reminded of the philanthropic management of poverty in Victorian Britain whereby, it was imagined, class struggle could be averted.

Within companies neoliberal ideology is dubbed the 'absolute quality program'. In a nutshell, this represents the placement of responsibility for business challenges directly on the worker ('productivity or death').[20] It strives for the utopia of complete alienation of the working class. Its main focus is on the final result, and the purification of productivity – removing anything that does not add value to the product. This implies the negation of the subjectivity of the workers, including their collective identity as expressed in trade unions. In the case of community organizations, the 'subjectivity' that corporate logic intends to eliminate is precisely their political character – their capacity to organize class actions that place pressure on governments, their capacity for social revolt. These postmodern management techniques might make us regard companies not only as productive units, but also as vehicles of a new 'market ideology'. Corporations do not only sell goods, they sell a model of society in which their goals can be achieved. Similarly, major television networks not only expect to win a public for their televised products, they desperately need to transform this public into a product, or run the risk of a system failure. Fear of unemployment is not enough to dominate the working class. It is necessary that the capitalist universe (the empire of private property) be confused with nature itself.

The formulation of the 'third sector' concept, therefore, is not a secondary element in the legitimization of capitalism by neoliberals; it fits into the same central axis of systematic expropriation of the working class. The small world of great oligopolies perceived, sooner than many intellectuals, that the increasingly financial character of economies allowed them to destroy or marginalize working-class organizations, while still paying attention to social reproduction, precisely by transforming all of society into a corporation, all people into winners or losers, all social activities into market relations. It is only in this way that the control of so few over so many becomes possible and is reproduced. It is not by chance that those agencies financing third sector activities are accustomed to counting on voluntary work as a fundamental element in their projects (so-called 'leverage capacity'). Thus, solidarity is transformed into merchandise, and civil society into a third sector,[21] notwithstanding the sincere good will of its protagonists.

The success of the Participatory Budget has had to do with its ability to locate the eye of the needle. That is, its capacity to create a realm that, headed by the logic of popular sovereignty, is opposed to the logic of the market (regulated by the law of private property and contract with a public sphere reduced to infra-structure, coercion and legitimacy) as well as the intrinsic legal-bureaucratic logic of the modern state (regulated by criteria of hierarchy and competence and char-acterized by technocratic authority and lack of transparency – as in the term 'state secrets'). Today, the PB is the backbone of the participatory system in Porto Alegre, where more than thirty-five sectoral councils exist, where periodic conferences evaluate and define the direction of municipal public policy, and where there are popular 'City Congresses' debating proposals for the future of the city. It is at this point of expansion, both internal and external, due to esca-lating support for direct community management, that PB runs the risk of a thermidorian reaction; as much due to market logic, through the mechanisms described above, as to bureaucratic logic, which is discussed below.

THE POLITICAL SIGNIFICANCE AND CONTRADICTIONS OF THE PB PROCESS

A second paradox of the Brazilian political scene in the nineties was the rela-tive electoral success of left-wing parties in large urban centres; particularly the Workers Party (PT), despite the erosion of its original base of sustenance, the unionism of the CUT (*Central Única dos Trabalhadores*), the radical new union central founded in 1983. As in Thatcher's Britain with the miners' strike, it took an emblematic repression of the state oil company Petrobras workers (in which even the use of the Armed Forces was not ruled out) to break trade union mili-tancy in Brazil. The Collor and Cardoso governments had insisted on asserting themselves against organized workers, using a discourse of opposition to the '*descamisados*' (shirtless) and the unions in their strategy of deconstructing formal sector workers' rights. By the beginning of the 1990s, the CUT moved away from its earlier principal demands (cancellation of the external debt; nationalization of the financial system; expansion of public health, education and transport services; agrarian reform under workers' control; a halt to privatization) and adopted a much more defensive line, defined in terms of the unity of civil society against the government rather than in terms of the class struggle essence of militant trade unionism.[22] However, CUT's hope that this shift would result in tripartite agreements among government, business and labour to ease the neoliberal offensive against labour laws was eventually dashed by the federal government and, to a degree, by entrepreneurs themselves. The extreme difficulty CUT encountered in attempting to open public space for negotiation in working relations made way for the advance of conservative unionism, particularly the *Força Sindical*.[23]

In Porto Alegre, CUT unionism has comprised mainly middle-class sectors – bank clerks, professors, architects, journalists. It was only at the end of the 1980s that sectors such as the steelworkers in the city adhered to the CUT. The major strikes in Porto Alegre were undertaken primarily by public sector workers (public banks, schools and companies) – i.e. those most sensitive to fiscal adjustment. One of the few unions that still maintains a certain fighting capacity is the CPERS-Sindicato (the public sector teachers' union). However, successive strikes by teachers not only failed to restore their real wages, but were used against them (due to the disruption they caused) and led to the isolation of teachers from public opinion.

How does this relate to our analysis of the Participatory Budget? It helps explain why it is that the public involved in the process are not primarily members of the Workers Party, much less of the CUT. During the first annual meeting of the PB for the year 2000, only 2.8 per cent of the leaders of Neighbourhood Associations (AMs) were also members of unions, and only 9.5 per cent of elected delegates and 13.5 per cent of elected PB council members were union members. Only 13.8 per cent, 21.6 per cent and 31.8 per cent, respectively, were affiliated with political parties.[24]

There were strong links between union and popular movements during the early 1980s when the struggle against military rule led to the building of a mass movement, through which the PT gained hegemony over the process of building the Urban Union of Neighbourhood Organizations (UAMPA). The work of the Artisans Union and Architects Union was fundamental in drafting the Municipal Organic Law of Porto Alegre, approved in 1990. This process opened up space for discussion among community militants, trade unionists and liberal professionals, which eventually led to the formation of a new NGO, Cidade – Centro de Assessoria e Estudos Urbanos (Advisory Centre for Urban Studies). Important links between unionists and community movements still existed during the first two years of the Olívio Dutra mayoralty in 1989-90.

Some municipal government staff came from this joint movement, since architects, engineers, lawyers, economists and sociologists with community experience were recruited into the new municipal government. Gradually, however, ruling members of unions shifted away from counter-hegemonic alliances and mobilizations, moving towards the construction of a more 'professional' (i.e. techno-corporative) unionism.[25]

After 1989, social movement leaders in Porto Alegre gradually moved from CUT unionism and from the Workers Party to the Popular Front government. It seemed natural that in the early days of this transition many of them would experience a certain identity crisis: between being a union member, a party leader or a government official. Some government staff members acted as if the government was part of the social movements, others turned against the social movements in order to confirm their accountability to city hall departments, and still others became critical of the government while working in it. The first years of the Popular Front government were marked by tension between the Workers Party and the government. There was an extremely positive element in this process that invigorated these relations, and this was the absence of absolute predominance of a single tendency within the Party. Although the group linked to Mayor Olívio Dutra (Articulação) was the most significant at that time, both at the local and national level, it quickly became understood that coalitions between party factions were needed for competent governance.

It was a time of very rich debate regarding the character of the government; whether it would be a government of the workers for the workers, or a government for all the citizens. The notion of a government of the workers for all the citizens prevailed. This allowed for the establishment of some standards. First, the government would not direct social movements, but it would open itself to the participation of social movements in the management of municipal public policy. Second, the government would not be directly controlled by the Workers Party, but there would be space for the party to participate in the government. Thus, for example, government officials would be selected from the names appearing on a list previously approved by the Municipal Directory of the Workers Party (although the mayor would have the right of veto and he could, in the last instance, submit the names he preferred). In the same way, the views of city hall departments chiefs and of party cells would be considered in the making of municipal policies.

Although not without problems, the government's relative autonomy gradually liberated it for action directed at the city as a whole. It was in this context that PB gained centrality, as it gave substance to the concept of a government of the workers for all the citizens. That is, through PB it became possible to acknowledge not just the voices of social movements, but of all community organizations, based on a non-clientelistic processing of demands that affirmed the principle of popular sovereignty.

The hegemony of the Workers Party (PT) in Porto Alegre was not established in a traditional populist manner (the old trade-off between patronage and

Table 2

Party preferences – annual first PB meeting, 2000 (per cent)

Party	Plenary	Dir. AMs	Delegates	Counsellors
PT	38.9	43.0	47.6	50.0
All 12 Others	6.2	9.1	15.4	13.7
No Response	14.2	12.4	13.7	11.3
No Preference	40.7	35.5	28.3	25.0

Source: CIDADE/PMPA, Participatory Budget Research, 2000.
Plenary: Participants interviewed at the annual first meeting of the Participatory Budget process.
Dir. AMs: Directors of Neighbourhood Associations (AM) interviewed at the annual first meeting in 2000.
Delegates: Delegates in the Participatory Budget (or those who have been delegates in previous years), inter viewed at the annual first meeting in 2000.
Counsellors: Counsellors in the Participatory Budget process (or those who have been counsellors in previous years), interviewed at the annual first meeting in 2000.

paternalism), but by affirming the possibility of radical citizenship, where rights were not only assured, but became the outcome of purposeful action by orga- nized sectors of society. Through this process, the Popular Front government freed movements from narrow political clientelism, gaining the affection of thou- sands for the PT. Research conducted by JB-Vox Populi[26] in August–September of 1996 verified a spectacular turn in party preferences of the city: 46 per cent of the population identified itself with the PT, followed by 6 per cent with the PDT, and only 34 per cent had no party identification (compared to 56 per cent and 58 per cent in Rio de Janeiro and Sao Paulo, respectively). Ten years earlier, in 1986, the situation was entirely different: 27.7 per cent had identified them- selves with the PDT, 20.9 per cent with the PMDB and only 6.4 per cent with the PT.[27] The growth in PT membership was also impressive. In 1990, the PT in Porto Alegre had 8817 members; by May of 2001, it had 24033.[28] Among those directly involved in the PB process, the overwhelming majority were favourable to the PT, as Table 2 indicates.

When it opened space for direct participation in PB assemblies, the Popular Front achieved what was already a target for some community movements: the end of the monopoly of regional representation held by Neighbourhood Associations. In 1989, in at least three regions of the city, Norte, Cruzeiro and Glória, a new organizational format already existed: the Popular Councils or Unions of *Vilas* (a local term referring to poor neighbourhoods). Essentially open to the participation of all people and entities in the regions, these spaces already possessed a certain plenary character, where decisions were made following collective debate. It was this movement that would force the popular govern- ment, then in its first year, to review proposals for the regionalization of the city, extending it from five to sixteen regions in order to respect the territorial tradi- tion of community organization.

The PB not only attracted existing community organizations, but also stimulated the creation of new entities and the participation of people who had not previously

Table 3

Participants in PB Meetings by Affiliation (or Described Situation) (per cent)

AFFILIATION/YEARS	1993	1995	1998	2000
Neighbourhood Associations	71.3	50.5	40.9	37.2
Popular Councils or Unions of Vilas	n.d.	8.7	4.0	3.7
Cultural or religious groups	n.d.	10.6	9.1	14.8
Political parties	n.d.	4.5	6.0	7.7
Unions	n.d.	4.2	4.9	4.2
Organizations in general (including those listed above)	n.d.	75.9	66.9	60.9
First time participating in the PB	n.d	48.5	38.5	49.5

Source: PMPA-1993, FASE/CIDADE/PMPA-1995, CIDADE/PMPA-1998 e CIDADE/PMPA-2000.
Note: 1995 research was done in the Second Round of PB assemblies, the others during the First Round.

been organized.[29] In this way, the Popular Front government went beyond the limits of community movements. Thus, in publicizing PB assemblies – regardless of the central role taken by Neighbourhood Associations – the Government has gradually increased its own role as a source of information for participants. In 1995, 48.2 per cent of those polled said they had been informed of PB meetings through Neighbourhood Associations. In 1998, this percentage fell to 41.8 per cent, and in 2000, to 31.2 per cent. During this period, people informed through government-sponsored publicity (radio and television) went up from 1.6 per cent in 1995, to 7.8 per cent and 7.3 per cent, in 1998 and 2000 respectively.[30] About 20 per cent of participants said they consistently got their information from other forms of publicity used by city hall (posters, loudspeakers etc.). Another significant observation is the gradual fall in the number of participants affiliated with Neighbourhood Associations and Popular Councils, as Table 3 indicates.

These data show that the Participatory Budget functioned as a stimulus to participation, initially rooted in community movements and subsequently acquiring a dynamic of its own, beyond the mobilizing capacity of community organizations themselves. The implementation of the Regional and Thematic sections of the PB in 1992 was an indication of effort to reach a new public. The numbers of first-time participants (fluctuating between 38 per cent and 48 per cent) demonstrate the enormous attraction of the experience among the population. Thus there was a high degree of turnover among the participants even while the number of participants went on rising (as we see in Table 4).

The fact is that for thousands of the people who have participated in the PB, the process of getting involved was a result of the way in which the PB itself functioned. Initially, neither the Workers Party nor the community movements coming out of the eighties had organized this new public that was generated by the PB. The absence of career politicians in this new public has favoured the development of a civic-republican culture (active participation, respect for plurality, decision-making through debate). It has also favoured a certain *comu-*

Table 4

Annual Participation in the First Round of PB Assemblies

YEAR	1990	1994	1997	2000	2001
Participants	628	8011	11075	14408	16612

Source: CRC-PMPA, 2001.

nitarismo de resultados (results-based community action), fostered by the expanding possibilities brought about by the Popular Front government. Differences in ethnicity, education, and income, while respected, were eventually overridden by the 'general interest' of the community.

Until 1992, participants' choices of budget priorities predominantly involved paving streets and sanitation, reflecting a strong consensual community identity. The urban reform movement (especially for land regularization) in 1991-92 was the first thing to shake up this supposed common identity. As a result of the tax reform carried out by the Popular Front government in 1990-91, as well as the improved fiscal distribution between local, state and federal levels afforded by the 1988 Constitution (where cities obtained the right to a 17 per cent share of total public funds), the municipal government acquired the capacity to make significant investments on a regular basis. A cycle was initiated that allowed the municipality to invest annually between 10 per cent and 20 per cent of the budget during the remainder of the decade. However this process soon encountered structural limits to investments in urban areas of extreme need. Most of these areas were located in the 'informal city' where poor people had 'illegally' occupied unused private land, and the situation of 'irregular property' made it impossible to invest in street paving and sanitation under existing law. It would become necessary to regularize these areas, linking the process to their effective urbanization; but since land regularization involves a long process with uncertain results, the initial solution adopted by city hall was to carry out all the improvements that were legally possible in those areas. This included providing public equipment in schools, day care and health centres, fixing or building water supply pipes, providing garbage collection and lengthening the distances served by public transport (especially by paving the main access roads to *vilas*), as well as arranging, together with other actors (private or public), the supply of electricity and telephone service. In the most critical situations, where proprietors sought to eject 'illegal' tenants, the government opened space for negotiation, and in extreme cases, settled homeless families in other areas (although often distant from the downtown area and job opportunities).[31]

Initially, the popular government did not feel comfortable assuming responsibility for land regularization. It tried to transfer responsibility to the occupants themselves, inviting NGOs and law students to advise them. However, as pressure from tenants increased, articulated in part by their legal advisors,[32] the government yielded and assumed responsibility for regularizing approximately 100 areas. A decade later, however, the regularization process had been completed in only ten of these areas. Moreover, following the processing of these

100 areas, the possibility of regularization of new areas was virtually nil (only one new area per year is accepted).[33]

The Organic Law of Porto Alegre is considered one of the most progressive in Brazil. Approved in 1990, it establishes a series of legal instruments that could facilitate the urbanization and regularization of those irregular and/or slum areas that shelter around 25 per cent of the population of the city. Nevertheless, these mechanisms are dependent on additional legislation, and they involve the municipalization of housing policy, compelling the popular government to use its own resources for housing (whereas the tradition was to use financing from the federal government while concentrating local investment on improving occupied areas unsuitable for habitation: riverbanks, hillsides, and areas of environmental preservation). Only by the end of 1999, with the approval of the new Master Plan of Porto Alegre, did it become possible to use these legal urban instruments as the basis of a new policy for urban planning and housing.[34] And this effort still confronts the challenge of getting several city hall departments to work together, as well as the absence of a clearly defined relationship among related sectoral councils and among various social actors, including business and professional organizations.

Curiously, it is the organized popular sectors that have been pressing for precisely this sort of coordination. In the regions of Lomba and Partenon, for example, it is already common to hear PB participants calling for the formulation of Integrated Plans for their regions, involving the new possibilities of the Master Plan and the PB. In the same way, new methods of organizing regional demands are being discerned in many regions, within a broader framework that involves income generation, culture, social services and so on, as interrelated components of overall regional needs. It is community action that presses for dialogue among governmental sectors (often blocked by internal disputes inside the Workers Party), but this clearly only has limited potential for linking PB with city planning and for converting the rhetoric of City Congresses into coordinated and effective local policy.

The difficulties that the popular government has experienced in coping with continuous outbreaks of violence in settlement areas (Cavalhada and Mário Quintana) are a concrete expression of the need for coordinated planning. Mass removal of families had been undertaken without sufficient attention to economic needs and social networks; regulations in new settlements ruled out the possibility of raising animals (such as horses, pigs and hens) or having domestic vegetable plots; social services (schools, health and day-care centres) became overloaded. These conditions resulted in the formation of gangs which used children for drug dealing, and engaged in violence against people and institutions. In addition, the relationship between possession and ownership had not been adequately discussed, with inhabitants of these areas paying for a symbolic lease, but never obtaining property title. This has made room for a populist discourse on the part of some conservative political parties who have promised property titles in the event that they win office.

Another example of this disarticulation between PB and urban planning can be seen in the unforeseen consequences of uncoordinated street paving projects in popular neighbourhoods.[35] While street paving was one of the main demands of the city's inhabitants (and a street drainage system was installed before paving), the fact that it was not approached in a coordinated fashion throughout the city resulted in increased erosion and flooding (not to mention the dangerous increase in traffic speed on residential streets). Another example was the expansion of the sewage network, which now covers more than 80 per cent of the city. This work was not accompanied by an investment in water treatment, which has resulted in a considerable increase of untreated sewage flowing into the city's main water source, Lake Guaíba.

It is as if 'city planning' has been chasing reality without ever attaining it. It is understandable that PB participants have difficulty contemplating urban questions in a global sense, since for this public an inclusive vision of society must be learned and constructed (because it is a new development not yet written into their praxis). The same cannot be said about the Popular Front government. It is incomprehensible that today, after more than a decade of PB, the government still has no map detailing, region by region, subject by subject, the failures and conquests of the PB experience – a tool that would facilitate both evaluation and planning for future possibilities in collectively-determined municipal public investment. The existence of participatory space does not itself eliminate the social division of labour, nor the split between technical knowledge and social and practical knowledge, even if the experience does point to ways these divisions may be overcome. Despite contrary claims by the government, it is only by focusing on these challenges that PB will take citizens beyond the attainment of their most basic demands.

It is futile to open additional sectoral participatory spaces, as was done in the areas of housing, planning, health, education, social assistance and income generation, without the availability of coordinated, strategic information. This is crucial for the enrichment of public debate and the quality of PB's effect on public policy development. Today, Porto Alegre has more than thirty-five municipal councils with highly varied participatory arrangements, permitting discourse between the government and neighbourhood residents, professionals of diverse areas, other governmental agencies and the most diverse institutions of civil society. City congresses have accomplished much in terms of the elaboration of differences and the reaching of consensus among these diverse fields. There is undeniable willingness to proceed with problem-solving within government sectors, yet there is still no mechanism for evaluation – no means of measuring results. It is perhaps for this reason that ad hoc changes in the political orientation of city hall departments are still easily made, constrained only by the internal balance of forces within the PT and among the parties of the Popular Front government.

A profound comprehension of the concept of public space is crucial. It is not simply a matter of political will: political strategies are necessary. Part of the solution to the challenges of city planning and community management involves giving more power, visibility and representation to the spaces that already constitute PB, such as the tripartite sectoral commissions that involve the PB Council, members of the government and third parties such as the civil servants' union, other city departments or even other city councils. If they could establish dialogue among the PB regions and the various tripartite commissions dealing with public servants, community day-care centres, social assistance, and even the Master Plan and housing policy, this could serve to expose existing participatory processes to greater debate and reach new levels of accountability on the part of leaders and managers at all levels. The public interest can only emerge out of such a democratic construction of public space.[36]

THE WORKERS PARTY IN GOVERNMENT: DEMOCRATIC HEGEMONY EVAPORATES?

At the same time that the fight for urban land regularization changed the scope of governmental action, another challenge surfaced for the main party of the Popular Front government, the Workers Party (PT). This was the impact that governing had on the party (the first challenge being the debate on the character of the government that occurred when the Popular Front took office). This is the third paradox of the conjuncture: the fact that, at its conception, the main critics of PB were PT affiliates or sympathizers. While community activists affiliated with other parties were fascinated by the degree of openness created by the PB (the respect for pluralism and the link between socially constructed demands and the budget), many long-standing PT activists within popular movements criticized the lack of openness in the government and its supposed reformism.

The PT experienced an internal rearrangement of forces between 1991 and 1993. Some currents divided, others changed their positions in light of the national situation. In Porto Alegre, a new PT tendency appeared that sought the inclusion of some of the community activists who had previously criticized the party and the government. Several activists of this tendency, the so-called *Chapinha*, were recruited by the popular government as community advisors in various city hall departments, yet none of them gained the status of secretary or department chief. There was never complete opposition between community and trade union activists – because the major party currents also had their community sections – but the dispute did modify internal party life. Perhaps the increasing absence of the party as a force in the social movements after it was elected was the reason for the radical criticisms put forward by many PT activists. Soon, the axis of the dispute shifted, and particularly in light of the enormous popular and international success of the PB, all groups focused their attention on PB as a privileged space for recruiting new members. And as the Popular Front government and PT members of the city council took on more and more militants as advisors, and at the same time increased the financing for community management of public projects (day-care centres, cooperatives etc.), this expansion of job opportunities for activists made participation in community movements more attractive both economically and politically. This has brought about the emergence of the 'professional citizen',[37] a kind of amateur politician acting individually but always available to represent the community or mediate relations between community and government. On the one hand, it is normal that some community leaders become professional and take on a political career; on the other, participatory processes can only last if a permanent renewal of leaders takes place. NGOs often work as institutional brokers, but they are socially constructed groups whose goal should not be to substitute for people's participation but to empower people to participate on their own.

In this argument there is a variable that requires greater investigation: is it the case that from the moment of its election the party started to lose part of its traditional importance as an agent in the social construction of movements, and an instrument in their political articulation? Our hypothesis is that with the mass movement of party staff to positions in government, the axis of debate on policy and party strategies shifted to government departments. The city of Porto Alegre has 600 government-appointed positions, and this means that about 10 per cent of the local membership of the PT in 1990 came to be employed by the municipality. As a result, policy for diverse sectors (finance, education, health, social assistance, etc.) tended to be made inside city hall departments. While departments must maintain respect for the general orientation of the Popular Front parties, they have an immense margin for manoeuvre.

Why is this a problem for the PB experience? Is it not normal to recruit elites among party activists? First, there is the risk of hollowing out the autonomous organizing spaces of the popular sectors. If it is true that the PB contributed to the development of new community organizations and increasing the number of participants in these organizations, it is also correct to say that most of those organizations and participants find themselves shaped by the opportunities of social action provided by the Popular Front government. This trade-off can be positive and empower people, but there is, at the same time, a great risk of recreating populist relations. One can argue that this is not the only reason for the urban popular movements' failure to organize more significant actions at the state and federal levels. Nevertheless, how can popular movements act at a global level – how can they pressure state and federal levels of government, if the forces that could push them in this direction find themselves drained? In June of 2001, for example, the National Congress approved an important law: the so-called City Statute, expanding the legal possibility of using the instruments foreseen in the Porto Alegre Master Plan. However, the organized community sectors of Porto Alegre got involved in this only as spectators, as the power of previously existing spaces, such as the municipal and state fora for urban reform, had become diluted inside the government.

With the exception of electoral campaigns, the PT in Porto Alegre is being reduced to a kind of 'parliament of tendencies', with internal party agencies for affiliation, planning and social articulation transformed into 'partisan collectives' constituted around government departments or parliamentary representatives. As rivalries among party tendencies took the form of measuring how many departments, positions and elected parliamentarians each one controlled, a new logic of internal party life was created, one quite different from the programmatic nature of previous intra-party debate. In the last municipal election, even the consensual rule of proportionality between the forces that compose the 'party parliament' (the municipal party directorate) was broken. In this context, instrumental agreements and ad hoc majorities have tended to grow up and to compromise the political performance of the Popular Front. These internal cleavages increased the difficulty for left-wing forces in Brazil to constitute themselves as a consensual alternative to neoliberal governments at the national level, exactly at the moment when the Cardoso government showed signs of exhausting the political arrangements that supported it.

CONCLUSION

The above considerations suggest that that are three grounds for accepting my hypothesis that the participatory spaces fortified by the PB in Porto Alegre are facing a thermidorian phase. First of all, the proliferation of funding to community organizations for management of local social services has not been accompanied by guarantees for the democratization of these services. Nor has public debate in the city even identified this as a problem. This runs a serious risk of simply fortifying the neoliberal consensus on the 'community management of social policies', accepting the mainstream path of decentralization, privatization and focus on the poor, while losing the dimension of political action. The creation of public guidelines is urgent, not only for the establishment of agreements between city hall and neighbourhood organizations for the provision of services, which already exist, but also for control over the management of these services. It is also crucial to approach community management with the overall goal of creating a solidarity-based popular economy.

Secondly, even if the Popular Front government has coexisted very well with PB demands for infrastructure, it has had difficulty in assuming a role in the construction of the PB as a formulator of policy. This could be due to the fact that it assumes a very defensive position in relation to its sectoral councils, or perhaps to its underestimation of the learning capacity of PB participants. Two other explanations could be that the Popular Front government itself feels pressured by the corporate forces inside municipal departments and by outside business forces (operating in relation to the Master Plan, for example); or that it has not succeeded in establishing a practical program out of the generic formulations of sectoral conferences and city congresses. These problems could be tolerated during the initial stages of the Participatory Budget, yet it will become increasingly difficult for the government to justify the existence of spaces supposedly created for participatory policy-making that lack strategic information, and whose deliberations and accords do not influence the creation and collection of result indicators.

Finally, the interplay of the forces that make up the Popular Front can generate a perverse effect on the Participatory Budget process, either as a result of disputes within and outside the left at the national and state level, as a result of the exponential growth in the number of PT members and sympathizers; or, finally, as a result of the rupture and degradation of collegiality within the party and of the programmatic level of debates. Civic-republican participation risks being crushed by the cooptation efforts of the 'partisan collectives' around both government departments and city council. Without re-negotiation of party life, the democratic hegemony of PT and PB erodes. Without the autonomy of popular movements, there is no popular sovereignty.

Until now the preferred solution to these problems has been to increase the number of participants in the PB, and to re-establish, with each new year, a connection between participation and the accomplishment of demands. The result has been, on the one hand, the preservation of the 'demand-making' aspect of PB, and on the other, the formation of a more specialized leadership within the PB. Today, this expresses a dramatic tension between community militancy and 'public service' defined in terms of the third-sector commodification of social rights, as discussed in the first part of this essay. This appears in the form of a conflict between pragmatic demands and the strategic management of public policy-making, and between autonomy and participation in government. What is clear is that plenary participation seems to have hit a glass ceiling, which in turn has raised other possibilities for participation, such as using the internet, or implementing referenda to define priorities – i.e. generally extending the plebeian character of the experience, even at the risk of partially breaking with the assembly system (if referenda or electronic 'chat rooms', for example, become substitutes for meetings).

The Popular Front governments in Porto Alegre opened the gates for an explosive combination of plebeian and civic participation (popular classes and active participation).[38] The international success of the Participatory Budget has also generated a certain pride. The common people – active citizens – decide the future of the city. A utopian participatory city was projected: the mystique of a third-world city with a first-world quality of life. But what happens when the plebeian public brought together by PB has more than pragmatic demands? What happens when they are dissatisfied with participatory spaces that multiply indefinitely without reaching decisions, with the absence of real power, with always sending issues to a third arena? What happens when the plebeians, after awakening, refuse to delegate their sovereignty? A *riscossa*, or counter-wave, of organized popular movements, urging an extension of the civic dimension of their participation, is now testing the transformative potential of the PB. Conflict-management has always been one of the constitutive elements of the Participatory Budget experience, but we have yet to discover to what point this rope can be stretched, and where the breaking point is.

NOTES

1 Antonio Gramsci, *Selections from the Prison Notebooks*, London: Lawrence and Wishart, 1971, p. 144.

2 Thermidor is one of the republican calendar months created by the Convention during the French Revolution. In July, 1794 (Thermidor 9), the Jacobins dropped out of power and a bourgeois reaction took place (the thermidorian reaction), obliterating popular conquests like the universal suffrage and price controls (Maximum Law), opening space for the incarnation of the hero myth and the end of the Republic: Napoleon Bonaparte.

3 According to Tarso Genro, 'Reforma do Estado e democratização do poder local', in: Renata Villas Boas e Vera S. Telles, eds., *Poder local, participação popular e construção da cidadania. Revista do Fórum Nacional de Participação Popular*, 1(1), 1995.

4 *Vilas de Malocas* is a local (Porto Alegre) word for favela.

5 The plebeian character of the PB in Porto Alegre is not guaranteed by the PB structure (the institutional engineering), but by the historical process of popular struggle in the city. The reproduction of the experience at the state level indicates differences, such as the growing weight of middle sectors and of business participation. In 2001, it is estimated that 320,000 people participated in the state level PB.

6 José Luís Fiori, 'Entrevista: Fiori manda era tucana para o espaço', *Folha de São Paulo*, 13 May 2001.

7 Francisco de Oliveira, 'Entrevista da 2a: Novo poder econômico gera crise política', *Folha de São Paulo*, 7 May 2001.

8 A study by José Serra and José Roberto Rodrigues Afonso ('Federalismo fiscal à brasileira: algumas reflexões', *Revista do BNDES*, Rio, 6(12), 1999) shows that municipalities absorb 50 per cent of gross fixed capital formation.

9 Apart from increased social security contributions (initially presented as a temporary solution to the lack of resources in the health sector, but in fact used as a permanent means of augmenting general federal revenues), the other key measure was the *Contribuição Provisória sobre a Movimentação Financeira*, a tax paid on each pay check or money transfer – in fact, a kind of distorted Tobin Tax paid by common people, since big investors or big corporations can use compensatory mechanisms to avoid paying it or are simply exempted as regards some of their transactions.

10 According to *Informe PED, FEE*, year 9, special number, January 2001.

11 PMPA-SGM, *Desenvolvimento humano e condições de vida em Porto Alegre*, Porto Alegre, PMPA, May, 2001 (mimeo).

12 Mayor Tarso Genro signed the Crèches Agreement in 1993, following pressure from a movement of community crèches managers (including a demonstration, replete with the banging of pots in front of the city hall)

after federal support for community crèches disappeared.

13   Boaventura de Souza Santos, *A crítica da razão indolente: contra o desperdício da experiência*, São Paulo: Cortez, 2000, p. 340.

14   See Márcia Dias, *Na encruzilhada da teoria democrática: efeitos do Orçamento Participativo sobre a Câmara Municipal de Porto Alegre*, Rio, IUPERJ (Tese de Doutorado), 2000. Ex-mayor Raul Pont sees PB as potentially transformative of the traditional parliamentary structure (marked by personalism, absence of party links and relative autonomy vis-à-vis the electors). See: Raul Pont, 'Porto Alegre e a luta pela democracia, igualdade e qualidade de vida', in Adair Barcelos e Raul Pont, eds., *Porto Alegre, uma cidade que conquista*, Porto Alegre, Artes e Ofícios, 2000.

15   Boaventura de Souza Santos, 'Entrevista da 2a: Democracia convive com fascismo social', *Folha de São Paulo*, 21 May 2001.

16   Renato Janine Ribeiro, *A sociedade contra o social: o alto custo da vida pública no Brasil*, São Paulo: Cia. das Letras, 2000.

17   The Census of the Third Sector, organized by the GIFE (*Grupo de Institutos, Fundações e Empresas*), embracing fifty-nine foundations and institutions linked to large private corporations, shows an investment of R$ 593 million for the year 2000; an amount higher than the social budget of the State of Sao Paulo or of the City of Sao Paulo (both around R$ 400 millions each). See Gabriela Athias, 'Empresas aplicam R$ 593 milhões na área social', *Folha de São Paulo*, 22 May 2001.

18   According to IBGE data, the Gini index in Brazil has changed little, from 0.571 in 1992, to 0.567 in 1999, revealing one more lost decade on the fight against inequality. In 1999, as in 1992, the 50 per cent poorest of the population received only 14 per cent of the country's income, while the 1 per cent richest received 13 per cent. In absolute terms, the gap between the average income of the poor and the rich has increased.

19   See Marta Arretche, 'Políticas sociais no Brasil: descentralização em um Estado federativo', *Revista Brasileira de Ciências Sociais*, 14(40) (June), 1999; and Ivete Simionatto, *Reforma do Estado ou modernização conservadora? O retrocesso das políticas sociais públicas nos países do Mercosul*, at http://www.artnet.com.br/gramsci/arquiv150.htm

20   For a critique of the 'absolute quality program', a psychological tyranny based on 'fear of death' (submission or unemployment), see Maria Luiza Gava Schmidt, 'Qualidade Total e Certificação ISO 9000: História, Imagem e Poder', *Revista Psicologia*, n.d., (www.pol.org.br).

21   For an analysis of the concepts of civil society and third sector, see Grupo de Estudos sobre a Construção Democrática, 'Sociedade civil e democracia: reflexões sobre a realidade brasileira', *Revista Idéias* (IFCH-UNICAMP), 5(2)/6(1), 1998-99.

22   See Armando Boito Jr., *Política neoliberal e sindicalismo no Brasil*, São Paulo: Xamã, 1999.

23   A measure of its opportunism was provided by the participation of the *Força*

Sindical in the May 1 commemorations in São Paulo, 2001 – they raffled apartments and cars, and hosted a concert with national music stars.

24 Research conducted during the first round of PB meetings in 2000, *Cidade-PMPA*, 2001.

25 The pro-impeachment movement against Collor's tenure as Brazilian president between 1990 and 1993 was perhaps the last militant act of the broad coalition of unions and community organizations, in which the unions clearly were just one sector among many, and most attention was won by face-painted youth.

26 Dias, *Na encruzilhada da teoria democrática*, p. 14.

27 See Marcello Baquero, 'Novos Padrões de Comportamento Eleitoral: pragmatismo nas eleições municipais de 1996 em Porto Alegre', in Marcello Baquero, ed., *A Lógica do Processo Eleitoral em Tempos Modernos*, Porto Alegre: Editora da Universidade-UFRGS, 1997.

28 Data obtained from the Workers Party of Porto Alegre.

29 According to research conducted by Leonardo Avritzer, 37.5 per cent of the 2440 community organizations that have participated in the PB of Porto Alegre emerged after 1989; 17.7 per cent emerged during the seventies or before, and 44.8 per cent emerged during the eighties. See: Leonardo Avritzer, *Sociedade Civil, Espaço Público e Poder Local: uma análise do OP em Belo Horizonte e Porto Alegre* (Final Report of the research project 'Civil Society and Democratic Governance', promoted by the Ford Foundation), Belo Horizonte, mimeo, 2000.

30 Cidade – Centro de Assessoria e Estudos Urbanos; Prefeitura Municipal de Porto Alegre, *Quem é o público do OP – 2000*, Porto Alegre: PMPA, 2002.

31 In areas of irregular habitation occupied before 1989 where the municipality itself was the proprietor, it was possible to apply the concession of the *direito real de uso* (right to possession based on monthly payments to the municipality).

32 The SAJU, Serviço de Assessoria Jurídica (law assessorship service) of the Federal University of Rio Grande do Sul State, was established by law students sympathizing with community movements. The first time outside observers were not allowed to speak in the PB Council was to stop the pressure SAJU exercised on the PB councilors and on government members.

33 An area that belongs to the state, situated in the Partenon region, provides an example of the administrative and legal ineffectiveness of the process. Even in the absence of litigation between the state and the occupants, the basic legal process through official channels of justice and city hall bureaucracies will take at least six years.

34 For a deeper analysis of the possibilities of the new Master Plan of Porto Alegre, see: Letícia Marques Osório, 'La ciudad informal y el nuevo Plan Director de Porto Alegre, Brasil', in E. Fernandes, ed., *Derecho, Espacio Urbano y Medio Ambiente*, Madrid: Dykinson, 2000.

35 Giovanni Allegretti, 'Porto Alegre tra democratizzazione e ricerca della sostenibiltà'. In A. Magnachi et al., *Democrazia fai-da-te*, Roma: Coop. Carta Arl (supplemento al mensile 'Carta'), 1999, p. 60.

36 See Vera da S. Telles and Maria Célia Paoli, 'Direitos sociais: conflitos e negociações no Brasil contemporâneo', in S. Alvarez, E. Dagnino e A. Escobar, eds., *Cultura e política nos movimentos sociais latino-americanos*, Belo Horizonte: UFMG, 2000, p. 123.

37 I borrow this expression from Daniel Schugurensky of the Ontario Institute for the Study of Education, University of Toronto.

38 Cícero Araújo identifies three normative ideals of democratic citizenship: civism, plebeanism and pluralism. Civism refers to the capacity to integrate into the community of citizens, the political community. Plebeianism refers to the extension of citizenship. Pluralism implies an ideal of tolerance with differences. In the modern world, '[t]he State is an artificial person set in the place of the political community. It is its representative, and it can only exist while the political community is seen as its author behind the scenes'. See Cícero Araújo, 'República e democracia', *Lua Nova*, 51, 2000, p. 28.

SCIENCE AND RACE: BEFORE AND AFTER THE HUMAN GENOME PROJECT

NANCY LEYS STEPAN

INTRODUCTION

In 2001, the Human Genome Project (HGP) and Celera Genomics (the venture capital organization led at the time by the scientist, Dr. J. Craig Venter) jointly published the first working draft of the human genome. The race for fame and fortune in sequencing the three billion nucleotide bases making up the 30-40 thousand human genes now known to exist ended in a deliberately orchestrated tie.[1]

Race is also at stake in quite another way in the HGP. On the one hand are those scientists who point out that their long-standing assertion that 99.9 per cent of genes are shared by all human beings is fully confirmed by the HGP; the human genome project thus proves that, scientifically speaking, human races do not exist. But others equally involved with the genome project argue that the 0.01 per cent difference makes all the difference – in how individuals and groups look and behave; they maintain that the variations in sequences of nucleotide bases that constitute our genes have significant effects. The Stanford University-based molecular geneticist, L.L. Cavalli-Sforza, for instance, foresees the employment in the future of new genetic definitions of human groups, because such definitions will be very useful from a practical point of view.[2] For example, knowledge of the variations in the nucleotide base sequences associated with disease in various ethnic groups would allow medical scientists to produce diagnostic tests and therapies targeted to those groups, in a new 'pharmacogenomics'.[3]

So is the message of the HGP that it supports anti-racism, or racism?

Understandably, given the entanglement of the HGP with such a socially sensitive issue as race, ethnic minorities are divided in their response. Some support the HGP because they want to be sure that their distinctive genetic variations are not left out of the potential benefits of the new genomic medicine. They worry that if their DNA is left out, the supposedly universal template of the human genome will be defined by the genetics of only a small, largely European, segment of humankind.[4] Other minority activists, on the contrary, oppose the HGP on the grounds that it overstates the genetic determinants of identity and health in human populations at the expense of environmental, social and economic factors, and because they believe the HGP could result in new genetic definitions of groups that would, advertently or inadvertently, give biological validity to racism.[5]

As Donna Haraway says, in debates such as the ones surrounding the HGP, race seems to be 'at once an uncanny unreality and an inescapable presence', something 'whose referent wobbles from being considered real and rooted in the natural, physical body, to being considered illusory and utterly socially constructed'.[6] Like the return of the repressed, 'race' is something that, however much we try to dispense with it as a concept, keeps pushing its way back into science and politics.

The purpose of this essay is not to describe in detail all the ramifications of the HGP for racial politics, but to reflect rather more generally on the science and politics of race before and after the human genome. I want to place the HGP in the context of a long-standing, Western discourse on the 'same and the different' in nature, in order to make the case that a science of similarity and difference can never be a reliable basis for assigning civil and political rights. This is true even when, as is the case in the general consensus that has emerged since World War II, science seems to support an anti-racist view of human variation – to show that 'races don't exist' in any biologically meaningful sense.

POLITICAL LIBERALISM, THE SAME AND THE DIFFERENT

My point of departure concerns not race but the difficulties women have in achieving full citizenship rights.[7] The reason I start with gender is that it points economically to the repetition and intractability of 'the same' and 'the different' in modern Western political philosophy. No sooner do women deny they are different from men because of their sex, and protest against their political and other exclusions, than they find themselves calling upon the very difference of sex (claiming they are not the same as men and therefore have special needs or interests) that they want to deny.[8]

This tension between sameness and difference is not a transcendental phenomenon, produced by the timeless features of womanhood, but the result of a *specific history, or more correctly, two or three or more histories*, of the modern period. One of these specific histories is about liberalism and democratic theory, and it is this history that has drawn most attention from feminist scholars. Starting in the seventeenth century, and culminating in the writings of the social contract theorists of the eighteenth century, a new concept of the political individual was formulated – an abstract and innovative concept, an apparent oxymoron – the imagined universal individual who was the bearer of equal political rights. The genius of this concept was to define, theoretically at least, a human individual who was stripped of all individual substantiation and specification; unmarked by the myriad particularities (e.g. of wealth, rank, education, age, sex) that make each person unique, this abstract, non-specific individual provided the theoretical basis for articulating the concept of universal political rights.

But as many scholars have argued, the universal individual, the bearer of rights, who seemed to be everyone and no particular one, turned out on closer inspection to be male, European, and property-owning. The seemingly transcendental emptiness of rights discourse was a logical possibility, but an historical illusion. The individual of liberal theory was (and still largely is) actually masculine, a sexual identity disguised by the language of universalism. Since the male is understood implicitly to be the norm of the universal individual, women's difference from men presents itself as a problem, a deviation, and a challenge to the neutrality of rights. Against the theoretical universality of individual rights, affirmative action on behalf of (some) women (or ethnic groups) then looks suspect, because it seems to privilege the difference of sex. On the other hand, to claim to be the same as men often backfires against women, because some women – not all, not all the time – are different in some respects from (some) men.

Feminists, then, argue that the difficulties women have faced in achieving full citizenship, the feeling that women are stuck circling around the dilemmas of the same/different/equality/inequality, without surcease, are not of women's own making, but a symptom of something else, namely a tension within the heart of liberal theory itself. The abstract citizen of liberal theory has been tacitly conceived of as male, and it is this that forces women either to make the case for being the same as men, thereby suppressing their particular needs, or to insist they are not-men, thereby emphasizing their special or different needs.

The value of recalling this now long-standing argument about liberalism and gender is to point out its relevance to arguments about racial difference. The universal liberal theory was also defined, historically, in racial and ethnic terms, as well as sexual; the universal subject of rights was Western, European, civilized, as opposed to non-Western, non-European, barbaric. These norms of ethnicity were disguised, like the male norm, by the language of universality (until recently whiteness was effaced as a race, it was the universal). Those making the argument for racial equality have often been trapped in the same disputes concerning the same/different/equality/inequality that have marked the history of feminism and the demand for women's rights.

RIGHTS AND THE NATURALIZED BODY

As we will see later, despite the limitations of the liberal concept of citizenship, it remains a powerful political and intellectual framework for making demands for political rights. There is a case to be made for the universalism of rights, for making liberal universalism live up to its name. Yet this has proven extremely difficult to do. The question is why? Are sexism and racism basic to the very creation of liberalism and the identity of Western political subject?

At this point in my argument, I want to go beyond the story of political liberalism to look at another critical history (or set of critical histories) connected to the paradoxes of modern citizenship. This is the history of the naturalized body – the construction of race and gender as natural, biologically grounded entities, entities which apparently render their members 'lesser' or even 'non' individuals, as defined by abstract political theory. It is my argument that the historical counterpart to the *disembodiment* of the individual citizen of modernity – an individual imagined stripped of all substantiation – has been the *ontologizing via embodiment* of sex and racial difference, thereby separating groups biologically from an implicit white, male norm.

As I have said, the conception of the individual imagined stripped of all specific substantiation was critical to the formulation of our modern, abstract idea of political democracy. But not all individuals, it turned out, could free themselves from the specificities of the body; instead, they were considered a substantiated representative of a larger group, race, or gender. And it was the characteristics of the group – the very features of its natural difference from the norm – that disbarred them from the right to full citizenship. Thus some differences (within the white, male population) could theoretically be stripped away and discounted in relation to rights; but other differences could not be so discounted. If, the argument went, bodily similarity to an implicit or explicit norm of the body was found, then political similarity in rights followed; if bodily difference was found, then political difference in rights (or political inequality) also followed.

The search for embodied differences in the human species turned a political/ethical argument about equality of rights into an argument about the inequality of bodies – a move made repeatedly throughout the nineteenth and twentieth centuries.[9]

My point, then, is that the history of race and embodiment must be seen to be intertwined with the story of citizenship and its limits; and that it is no accident that 'race' and 'sexual difference', in their modern, primarily naturalized or biological meanings of the terms, emerged most clearly in the nineteenth century, when the new political principle of equality and rights was extended (e.g. in suffrage laws). Racism was of course not new to the eighteenth or nineteenth centuries; but the principle of political equality altered the meaning of race (and gender) by exposing the contradiction between the abstract universal and the reality of the particular – the particular, that is, of social inequality.

It was here, of course, that science and medicine came into the story. The search for measurable signs of human difference was the work of anatomists, physiologists, anthropologists and physicians. Starting with the founders of modern biology and physical anthropology, such as Linnaeus, Blumenbach, and Buffon, scientists began to apply to human beings a zoological concept of species and varieties. The 'human' (or *humaine*) became transformed through scientific investigation into the 'the human species' and its zoological variations. By the mid-nineteenth century, a dense web of practices and measurements was employed to give empirical precision to race – to establish the 'natural facts' of human variation, facts increasingly understood not as a continuum of traits linking all members in a common human family, but in terms of categorical distinctions between groups or races (and the two genders). Physical anthropology, clinical medicine, the new bacteriology, social statistics and evolutionary biology were all at different historical periods drawn into the task of separating human populations into racial and sexual types, and weighing the meaning of such differences for social reform and social policies.[10]

Science did not, of course, simply step in to explain political, social or economic inequalities in terms of inherent or inherited bodily differences from a European, male norm; the relations of science and medicine to social, political and economic life are surely more complicated. We should think, rather, in terms of the many histories that were linked to the shifts we see in the scientific study of human variation, especially in the crucial period of transition to industrialization and modern colonialism between roughly 1770 and 1900. These histories would include the history of work, and the new division of labour; the history of slavery and abolition; the history of the emergence of new definitions of the public and private; the history of religion and secularization; the histories of class politics and changes in political economy; the history of women and their demand for equality and the suffrage. The history of nature itself is another; eighteenth-century meanings of nature, signifying plenitude, harmony, and perfection, gave way to a sense of nature as limit, facticity, necessity; appeal to *this* nature, as Lorraine Daston says, was often to remind people of the impossibility of change in the places assigned to them in society, or to suggest that human variations were independent of society, or human will.[11] Taken together, these histories did not cause the new sexualized (and racialized) body to come into existence; rather, as Laqueur suggests, the remaking of the human body was implicated in all these developments.[12]

I do not intend to review here the long histories of racial and sexual sciences, and their intersections.[13] I only wish to make the following two points. First, the sciences of human differences cannot be easily dismissed as something belonging to the past; evolutionary biology, modern genetics, bacteriology, and tropical medicine still provide the framework of our biology and medicine today; the race concept was thus critical to the development of modern science. Moreover, it is arguable that race is still critical to the contemporary *social* (and cultural) sciences that supposedly replaced the outworn biology of race after the Second World War (a point to which I will come back).

Second, the assumptions made by scientists about races – that they formed distinct types whose bodily and mental differences were the main sources of their social inequalities – were extremely widely shared. They were normative. Critics of the claims made in the racial/sexual sciences (often the people most stigmatized by the sciences of their day) found themselves stuck in the terms of 'the same and the different' with which we started, as though accurate facts of difference and similarity would answer questions about rights.

Minority social groups confronting a supposedly 'purely factual' science, whose message was apparently ever more negative about themselves, tried to resist the process of naturalization associated with the sciences. They tried, that is, to keep to the fore the political (and/or religious or humanitarian) principles that earlier had governed discussions of rights (and which scientists now dismissed as a 'sentimentality' that had no place in an empirical, objective science), and to make the case that no facts in themselves had inevitable or simple social meanings, but were always part of an *already* political argument. But over time, the authority of science and its professionalization made this line of argument less and less effective. Resistance to racial science and racial inequality had to be carried out in the languages and terms of science to which the challengers often stood in problematic and marginalized positions (the construction of racial and gender difference being one of the ways in which groups were marginalized and made objects, not authors, of science).[14]

THE POST-WAR LIBERAL ANTI-RACIST CONSENSUS IN SCIENCE

But if the science of racial/sexual difference is part of the story of liberal individualism and its limitations from the late eighteenth century until well into the twentieth century, it is also true that scientific racism was eventually contested from within that same liberal framework. The pendulum swung back to universalism (to the unity of the human species, to a shared humanity, to universal rights). After the Second World War a new consensus emerged in science that 'races don't exist'; an effort was made to substitute for race other terms, such as 'ethnic group', the 'population', the 'cline', and most recently, the 'genome'. The word 'race' lost its legitimacy in science, and an effort was made to sever it from its basis in biology. The idea that human races formed closed, static, biological units that determined human behaviours or entire cultures was given up; biology gave way to sociology, to the new field of 'race relations'. New definitions of what was to count as 'human' in the 'human species' emerged, in a liberal, anti-racist moment.[15]

Why did the old paradigm of racial science break down? In part, the very scientific methods that produced races led to an undermining of the concept of race. As more and more measurements of human skulls, noses, hair types, and brain parts were made, scientists found it more and more difficult to agree on what the basic racial units of human societies were. The epistemological weakness of 'race' as a biological category was apparent in the inconsistencies of, and disagreements about, racial classifications. Within physical anthropology, indeed, there was by the early twentieth century a 'hopeless mistrust of anthropological measurement'.[16]

But if science helped destabilize racial science, the larger world of politics in which science and medicine operates played the decisive role. *The political made the natural, and the political undid the natural.* We can date the collapse of the morphological, anatomical, and genetic (eugenic) sciences of race to the Second World War, and to the crime of the systematic extermination of the Jews (and Gypsies) carried out at least in part in the name of racial science. In the circumstances, racial science became morally repugnant and politically unacceptable.

Though there is not space here to sketch the slow, hesitant, piecemeal and very incomplete ways in which the biological concept of race was undermined in science itself, it is worth remarking that much of the change was fuelled by the entry into science (especially in the UK and the USA where the chief critiques were made) of individuals belonging to those social groups who were themselves stereotyped as inferior in the racial sciences (e.g. Jewish scientists, such as Franz Boas, who became the most vocal opponent of scientific racism in the USA).[17] On the relation of the political to science, it is also important to note that assumptions about race were very often challenged or reversed without any new scientific information being added to the pool of knowledge. So, for example, Mendelian genetics, which before the war had been used to support eugenics (the movement for racial improvement based on genetics), was after the war employed to dismantle racial science; the supposedly evil effects of racial hybridization were also challenged by scientists, without the addition of any new scientific data.[18] The political valence of racial science changed, for political reasons.

The most public expression of these shifts in the politics and science of the human species were the well-known UNESCO *Statements on Race*, the first of which was published in 1950. By this time, as Donna Haraway notes, the Cold War struggles and colonial independence movements gave further urgency to the racial issue:

> Perched on the cusp between the Allied victory over the Axis powers, the ideological contest for defining human nature waged by socialism and capitalism in the Cold War, and the struggles for third world decolonisation that sharpened after World War II, the U.S.-sponsored documents were intended to break the bio-scientific tie of race, blood, and culture that had fed the genocidal policies of fascism and still threatened doctrines of human unity in the emerging international scene.[19]

Ashley Montagu, a British-born Jewish anthropologist who had been Boas' student and was a committed anti-racist, organized the first statement. Based on a draft prepared by a group of twelve scientific experts, with emendations by several others, the *Statement* opened with a ringing endorsement of human universalism. The human species, it said, was one; there was mental equality between all human groups; and all humans were bound to each other by a fundamental instinct for cooperation. 'Equality as an ethical principle', it added, 'in no way depends on the assertion that human beings are in fact equal in endowment'. Finally, the *Statement* declared that 'for all practical purposes, "race" was not so much a biological phenomenon as a social myth'; as a consequence, it was proposed that scientists replace the word 'race' by the more neutral 'ethnic group'.[20]

To many more conservative physical anthropologists and geneticists, however, this was going far too far; they believed that the first *Statement* was too socio-logical and cultural. They were dubious about the evidence for racial mental equality, rejected any notion of an instinct of cooperation, and believed 'race' was a valid term in science. These views were reflected in the second *UNESCO Statement on Race* (1952), which advanced only the negative argument that no evidence existed for inherited mental inequality between races. Despite this caution, the second statement, signed by ninety-six prominent scientists, is usually taken to represent a considerable public move away from the old certain-ties of racial science, and a reassertion of the claims of human unity.

In the 1950s and 1960s, as the civil rights movement gained ground in the United States, the new population genetics that emerged from the old eugenics was put to use in support of the non-essentialist position in science. Many popu-lation geneticists, for example, claimed, as Ashley Montagu had argued, that the word 'race' was unnecessary in science, since everything that needed to be said about human variation could be said without reference to a word and a concept so weighed down with negative connotations. The genes distributed differen-tially in different human populations were viewed not as marking out 'races', but as characterizing assemblages of individuals showing successful, evolutionary, genetic adaptations to specific environments.

A good example of the change in emphasis was the interpretation of the excruciating, and usually fatal, genetic blood disease, sickle cell anaemia. The sickling of blood cells was a phenomenon identified by physicians before the Second World War. Labelled a 'black' condition because it was found mainly in African-Americans, so strong was the racial identity of the disease that when on occasion physicians found white individuals with the condition, their 'whiteness' was questioned, rather than the racial view of disease.[21] After the war, however, sickling of the blood was recast as an example of the new genetics; the molec-ular geneticist, A.C. Allison, showed that sickling was a result of a gene causing variant haemoglobin which, when present in the heterozygous condition, was associated with increased resistance to malaria (though in the homozygous condi-tion the gene causes an illness that can be fatal). Sickling was therefore re-conceptualized in terms of an adaptive mutation found in populations subjected over evolutionary time to malarial environments. Since the sickle cell gene is selected in populations where malaria is intense, it is found in people in quite different parts of the world (West Africa, the Mediterranean) where malaria has been historically prevalent; though recessive diseases like sickle cell disease occur more frequently in certain populations, it is not exclusive to a defined population, and is not a racial disease in the old sense of the word.[22]

SCIENTIFIC POPULATIONS AND EVERYDAY RACES

Of course, racism did not disappear because scientists apparently no longer provided the biological-ontological grounding for racial thinking (post Second World War South African apartheid is an obvious case in point).[23] With race and ethnicity we are dealing, after all, with political and historical definitions of 'the self' and 'the other' that derive from social relations of inequality and inequalities in power, not scientific argument, for their continued currency. Even if the majority of scientists claim to prefer to avoid the term race, race was (and is) commonly used to designate groups of people in politics and the law; it undergirds, explicitly or implicitly, contemporary debates on citizenship, nationality, immigration and naturalization; in the U.S. it is used regularly in affirmative action policies. The U.S. Census is another example of the political relevance, inconsistency and power of race categories; today, Cambodians and Laotians are lobbying the government to change their classification from Pacific American to Asian. Some African-Americans wish to claim a new mixed race identity for the offspring of black and white parents; the difficulty of deciding who will qualify for this racial designation brings us back to the extraordinary debates about fractions of 'colouredness' that preoccupied the census-makers early in the twentieth century, when four out of the eight categories employed in the Census referred to fractions of blackness. [24] Any examination of contemporary usages of the term 'race' usually shows it to be mired in these kinds of confusions.

The undercutting of the old certainties of racial science turned the issue of human inequality back to the realm where it started – the realm of the political, the economic, and the social. The factors that create group identities and social inequalities, that increase hostilities between groups, or that make people divide the world into 'us' and 'them', are extremely varied, and our new terminologies do not always add clarification. 'Ethnicity' is not the same kind of thing everywhere, and the term 'ethnic' is often only a convenient, and in my view not always useful, shorthand for extremely diverse political, social, religious and economic groups and/or phenomena. Generally speaking, it is used to escape from a biological definition of race, in keeping with the anti-racist consensus in science; but the inconsistencies in its usage parallel the inconsistencies of the term race itself. The same might be said of many uses of 'cultural difference', a term which like 'ethnic difference' is also used to escape from the biological connotations of race. Yet again, much of what is meant when culture is used to explain differences between groups or communities of people was in the past expressed by the term 'race'. Indeed, the literary critic Walter Benn Michaels maintains that every effort to come up with an anti-essentialist account of cultural identity fails – it is either banal (because a cultural identity simply defines what people are presently doing), or relies ultimately on a genealogical (descent or racial) definition.[25]

At the same time, of course (and most importantly), the scientific denial of the reality of race – the claim that 'races don't exist' – flies in the face of everyday political experience, and can cause anger on the part of groups who know the weight of racial discrimination in their own lives. As an example, we might take the National Sickle Cell Anemia Control Act of 1972 in the United States. Legislated during the new post-war anti-racist era, with an apparently non-racial definition of the disease, the reaction to the programme revealed the gap between scientists' understanding of genetics and that of politicians and minorities. The screening of blacks in schools and the workplace was received with hostility by many African-Americans because they believed that its main purpose was to target genetically an already disenfranchised and discriminated group, causing an ethnic profiling that resulted in loss of jobs and insurance. The case for screening was not helped when politicians and administrators persisted in calling sickle cell a 'black disease', confused the sickle cell trait (which does not cause illness) with the sickle cell disease (the homozygous condition which does), often mandated screening in the workplace and in schools without adequate attention to individual consent, and in general did not consult adequately with the African-American communities involved.[26] In the circumstances, the *meaning* of a genetic screening programme was determined not by science, but by the larger social realities in which race was lived and experienced.

In other circumstances, of course, as an oppositional strategy, claiming a racial identity for a disease will often make sense (e.g. when British blacks pushed for screening programmes for themselves in the UK and protested against the neglect of sickle cell disease by the National Health Service). People thus find themselves positioned within the framework of the same/different, equality/inequality with which this essay began.

THE UNRAVELLING OF THE POST SECOND WORLD WAR CONSENSUS ON RACE? FROM THE 1970S TO THE HUMAN GENOME

A further word of caution is in order here. For if there is a lesson to be drawn from this history of science, race and liberalism, it is that the human – all too human – sciences of ourselves are social products and tend to reflect in general terms the political and social values of the times. Racial science came into being as a systematic, scientific endeavour in the late eighteenth century, and came into prominence in the nineteenth century, in a period of nation-building and nationalism, conflict and differentiation, and reflected the values of national homogeneity, social differentiation (ethnic, class), and exclusion. It was challenged in mid-twentieth century only after a murderous world war of destruction against selected human populations made racial science politically and ethically unacceptable.

Today, however, the period of the Cold War has ended. Is it possible that the post-war scientific anti-racist consensus will end also?[27] One certainly does not have to look hard to find evidence of growing political illiberalism in nearly all the European countries and the United States. A racial backlash was already evident in the anti-immigrant (anti-coloured) legislation passed in the UK in the 1970s; similar changes in attitudes to minorities and immigrants occurred in France.[28] And even at the *height* of the anti-racist consensus in the 1980s, surveys showed that 50 per cent of the biological anthropologists working in graduate departments in U.S. universities claimed that race was a meaningful concept in human biology (in this regard, going against the anti-racial view in science).[29]

In the thermidorian climate in which we now live, is it conceivable that new scientific knowledge will be given political interpretations that are harmful to groups? If so, the comfort that science offers the anti-racists may be short-lived. The huge attention given in the United States to Herrnstein and Murray's book, *The Bell Curve: Intelligence and Class Structure in American Life* (1994), which argued that class inequalities (and by implication race inequalities) are due to inherited differences in intelligence, suggests a move in this direction. The success of this book (it sold over 400,000 copies) indicates the appeal such arguments have in a period of white backlash and growing neo-conservatism.[30]

Of even greater importance is the HGP, in part because of the enormous excitement the project arouses. The genome promises to be our 'book of life', telling us what we 'really' are. Indeed, scientists, politicians, doctors, and the media seem to have adopted an almost completely genetic view of human beings, attributing behaviours, sports ability, group identities and diseases to our genes, leaving the environment with little explaining to do. Nevertheless, like all human sciences, the HGP is open to multiple interpretations, a racial one being balanced by a non-racial one, as the opening pages of this essay indicated. The most commonly used metaphor of the genome, for example, is of a 'genetic data bank'; this suggests not so much the categorical distinctions of race, as a picture of humans made up of endlessly computable 'bits' of information (literally bankable assets for the scientific and medical industry).

On the other hand, though, because scientists and physicians tend to use 'race' as crude shorthand in scientific discourse, the new genomic research sets traps for the unwary. This was especially evident in the controversy that erupted around the Human Genome Diversity Project (HGDP). Set up in 1991 by the molecular geneticist, L. Luigi Cavalli-Sforza, the aim of the proponents of the HGDP was to focus on diversity within the genome, something they believed the much larger HGP was neglecting.[31] They proposed to collect DNA (e.g. from blood, or hair) from as many ethnic groups as possible, perhaps some six or seven hundred, with special attention to be paid to small, isolated, or 'indigenous' groups that they feared might disappear before scientists had a chance to study their interesting genetic characteristics.[32]

Cavalli-Sforza himself was aware of the dangers of confusing notions of genetic diversity with race, but he believed that the results of the HGDP would give support to scientific anti-racism, not provide the racists with ammunition; his approach was that of a liberal who was convinced that science was a social good, and that HGDP would demonstrate that the important genetic traits in human beings vary less between groups than within them.

Nevertheless, the HGDP was vehemently resisted, especially by the indigenous peoples from whom the DNA samples were to be taken, precisely because it raised the possibility of distinguishing groups by genetic traits, in ways that could turn out to be to the group's disadvantage.[33] At stake were issues of who owned the genes collected, whose consent was needed to take bodily tissues, and who was going to profit from the commercialization of genetic information. The

Rural Advancement Foundation International (RAFI), a Canadian organization that monitored agricultural and pharmaceutical research by multinational corporations in developing countries, picked up news of the project. RAFI proceeded to use the Internet to alert indigenous groups to the project. They accused the HGDP of racism, colonialism, the theft of genetic information, and the commercialization of human genetic data without people's proper consent. By a piece of good timing (or bad, depending on one's viewpoint), in 1993 RAFI learned that the U.S. Secretary of Commerce was trying to patent a cell line taken from a Panamanian Guaymi woman with leukaemia; the publicity given the case by RAFI led the Guaymi to defend their rights to their own tissues, and the patent application was eventually withdrawn.[34] Since then, the HGDP has been more or less stalled through lack of public funding.[35]

Human genetics will always be a terrain of struggles over its social meaning; this is especially the case when genes are used to provide answers to what are essentially questions of social and/or political identities. A good example provided by Sheldon and Marks are the tests for ethnic identity offered commercially. One such test has been developed to identify certain Native American stocks on the basis of genetic markers indicating ancestry. The problem is, however, that the test sometimes 'proves' that some members of the Native American stock in question lack the genetic marker; they are not, the test indicates, who they think they are; they don't have the 'right' genes. At the same time, some individuals who have never been members of a Native American community are identified as having the genes. The trouble with such tests is that they usually rely on a highly selective sample of genetic information (e.g. reflecting only the maternal line); the genes in question are also found in non-Native American groups; and the tests are associated with high rates of false positive and false negative answers.[36] More importantly, they are problematic because a genetic definition of a population is not the same thing as a social definition; being a Native American is a matter of social history and politics, not biology.[37]

Just as complicated and potentially divisive are genetic-racial definitions of disease.[38] As we have already seen in the case of a disease of known genetic causation, such as sickle cell anaemia, doctors often use the term 'race' as a rough and ready guide to refer to disease in a particular population. Another example would be Tay-Sachs disease, a hereditary metabolic disorder causing retardation and death in children that is often described as a 'Jewish' disease because of its high rates in the offspring of people of Ashkenazi Jewish descent. But in employing 'race' as a guide to medical genetics, doctors may overlook the disease altogether in individuals that do not fit the racial profile (e.g. non-Jews with Tay-Sachs). Similarly with 'black diseases'; as a basis for medical and social policies, using race as a diagnostic guide may be quite misleading, especially given the crude rule used to define blackness in the US (i.e. the 'one drop' rule by which a person with the slightest appearance of 'blackness', or with any 'black' ancestry, is classified as 'black').[39]

So should we follow a racial/ethnic strategy, or not? The answer will surely depend on the political circumstances, especially the relative political standing and rights enjoyed by the groups involved. Ashkenazi Jews in the USA, for instance, have supported their own genetic screening (using genetic testing and counselling to reduce the numbers of children with Tay-Sachs disease), because on the whole they are able, as a well-educated and politically powerful group of citizens, to control the process and meanings attached to medical and genetic interventions.[40]

The issue may be quite different with more politically vulnerable communities. In the UK, for instance, there is at present only 'targeted' screening for sickle cell anaemia, meaning that screening is focused on people identified as black. Such targeted screening can be a quick way of getting answers about specific social groups; it is also cheaper than universal screening. But in multi-ethnic places where universal screening of newborns is the norm (as in many of the states in the US today), thousands of 'non-white' children are identified each year as carriers of the sickle cell trait or the disease. So we have to ask whether a race-based approach does not risk missing such children, while at the same time giving Afro-British citizens a genetic profile that may be disadvantageous to them.

RIGHTS AND HUMAN VARIATION IN THE NEW MILLENNIUM

So will the Human Genome Project ultimately support the idea of human similarity and equality, or human difference and inequality? Or is this the wrong question?

For what this brief history of the rise and (perhaps temporary) decline of racial science suggests is that science is not a reliable guide to issues of human morality and politics. This point was made over a hundred years ago, and brilliantly, by the black abolitionist Frederick Douglass in a little known address on anthropology. In an argument that could hardly be bettered today, Douglass first reviewed for an audience of young African-American college students what was known at the time of the facts of human racial differences, according to science. He attacked the claims of the race scientists of his day, by questioning their logic, the quality or accuracy of their data, and their conclusions concerning the supposed gulf separating white and black races. He argued that anatomically and craniologically the similarities between African-Americans and the white race far outweighed the differences, that the human species was one, and that the African-American could therefore claim full membership in the human family.

But at the end of his address Douglass made a crucial move from the discourse of anatomy to the discourse of ethics, politics and rights. 'What', he asked, 'if the case [of anatomical similarity] is not made out? Does it follow, that the Negro should be held in contempt?'. He answered his own question with a resounding 'No', because the title to freedom, liberty and knowledge was not a question of 'natural' difference or similarity, but a matter of rights and morality.[41] Douglass here asked a question that would virtually disappear from science and politics from that time to this: What difference does difference make to human rights?

His answer was that it made no difference, because equality and rights are moral, religious and political issues. The silence on this matter within most scientific work, then and now, suggests the power of science to occupy the terrain of political and/or moral discourse, while disguising the political projects that help constitute the scientific field.

This is not an argument that science has nothing to offer our understanding of the human body, or to deny the positive gains we have made in our understanding of human variation. Science is a productive form of knowledge that allows us to manipulate the material world in which we live for good and ill. It is to argue, however, that the social meanings or conclusions we derive from nature are not the predictable outcomes of the inherent content or logic of science; that nature, or the science that as a human practice produces it, does not escape the value conflicts existing in its social surroundings. Inferences from nature are therefore not merely extrapolated, but are themselves always a matter of values and interpretation – are, that is, socially constructed. At issue here is the complicated circle of meanings that tie the natural human body to the political.[42]

This is not – I emphasize not – to argue that scientific knowledge is irrelevant to human experience, or without consequences in men and women's lives. Nor is it to mire us in pure scientific relativism. No one would deny that we can, and do, know more about the human body today than in the past, or that science has contributed much knowledge that is useful to men and women.

My project in this regard would be two-fold – to demonstrate the lack of coherence in many representations of racial groups' supposed 'nature', *and* to use science to get an accurate picture of actual, specific individuals and/or populations' biological realities. A particular group of people may, for example, share certain biological characteristics (e.g. an increased risk of genetic disease) that *could* provide an appropriate basis for devising social policies (e.g. genetic screening). The aim of the analysis here is different – it is to avoid reducing complex populations to simple dichotomous groupings or seeing the world only by or through such groupings; and above all, it is to separate arguments about rights (or social policies concerning citizenship more broadly) from any simple view of the 'natural'. Recognizing the interlaced histories of politics and biology, recognizing that there is never going to be a nature of ourselves out there that can arbitrate among the political meanings of our human variations, recognizing that this is the wrong question to ask, we can ask different questions: how have political meanings already been written into race and sex, so that we cannot go to a neutral ground of 'natural facts' to answer questions of meaning? Why have we been so preoccupied by small biological variations amongst ourselves? Why have these small variations been translated into notions of inequality? And why cannot real biological variation, in disease, in height, in strength, be accommodated in the notion of political rights and equality? Asking these kinds of historical questions will perhaps allow us to acquire a deeper understanding of the significance of embodiment in our political histories, and in the long run, to construct a more adequate model of citizenship, equality and rights.

NOTES

ACKNOWLEDGEMENTS: This is a somewhat different and expanded version of the argument I developed in 'Race, Gender, Science and Citizenship', *Gender and History*, 10(1), 1998, pp. 26-52. Here I have concentrated more specifically on race and science.

1   The Human Genome Working Draft Sequence was published simultaneously in *Science* (16 February 2001) and *Nature* (15 February 2001).
2   Luigi Luca Cavalli-Sforza, *Genes, Peoples and Languages*, Berkeley: University of Los Angeles Press, 2000, p. 31. Genetic variations in groups are also relevant to the paleo-anthropology of the human species; see Douglas Steinberg, 'Genetic Variations Illuminate Murky Human History', *The Scientist*, 14(15), 24 July 2000, p. 10.
3   On the commercialization of contemporary genetics, see Lori Andrews and Dorothy Nelkin, *Body Bazaar: The Market for Human Tissue in the Biotechnology Age*, New York: Crown Publishers, 2001.
4   *The Challenges and Impact of Human Genome Research for Minority Communities*, Conference Presented by Zeta Phi Beta Sorority National Educational Foundation, 7-8 July 2000, Philadelphia, Pa.
5   Svante Pääbo, 'The Human Genome and Our View of Ourselves', *Science*, 291(5507), 16 Feb 2001, pp. 1219-20; 'For Genome Mappers, The Tricky Terrain of Race Requires Some Careful Navigating', *New York Times*, 20 July 2001, late edition (East Coast), p. A17.
6   Donna J. Haraway, *Modest_Witness@Second_Millenium. FemaleMan©_ Meets_ OncoMouse™*, New York: Routledge, 1997, p. 213.
7   Post-1989 Eastern Europe is especially important to our understanding of women's citizenship; there, the opening of the spaces of civil and political society almost paradoxically created new *kinds* of gender inequalities. The persistence of women's inequality of citizenship in democracy is confirmed when we look to Western Europe and North America (where women have long had the vote and other political rights), but where they are significantly under-represented in national legislatures, earn less than men even when in the same line of work, and in general do not enjoy the same degree of autonomy of the self (e.g. bodily autonomy) as men. On Eastern Europe, see Peggy Watson, 'The Rise of Masculinism in Eastern Europe', *New Left Review*, I/198, 1993.
8   The references for this and the next sections are found in the original article cited above in the acknowledgements. It draws on the work of several well-known feminist scholars.
9   On this point see Kenan Malik, *The Meaning of Race: Race, History and Culture in Western Society*, London: Macmillan, 1996, p. 71.
10   See Nancy Stepan, *The Idea of Race in Science: Great Britain, 1800-1960*, Oxford/London: Macmillan, 1982, for an overview.

11   Lorraine Daston, 'The Naturalized Female Intellect', *Science in Context*, 5, 1992.

12   Thomas Laqueur, *Making Sex: Body and Gender from the Greeks to Freud*, Cambridge, Mass.: Harvard University Press, 1990.

13   Stepan, *The Idea of Race in Science*; Alan Chase, *The Legacy of Malthus: The Social Costs of the New Scientific Racism*, New York: Knopf, 1977; Cynthia E. Russett, *Sexual Science: The Victorian Construction of Womanhood*, Cambridge, Mass.: Harvard University Press, 1989.

14   For an analysis of the strategies of resistance to scientific racism used by different minorities, see Nancy Leys Stepan and Sander L. Gilman, 'Appropriating the Idioms of Science: The Rejection of Scientific Racism', in Dominick LaCapra, ed., *The Bounds of Race: Perspectives on Hegemony and Resistance*, Ithaca/New York: Cornell University Press, 1991.

15   Stepan, *The Idea of Race in Science*, chs. 6-7; Haraway, *Modest_Witness @Second_Millenium*, pp. 232-244.

16   Charles Myers, 'The Future of Anthropometry', *Journal of the Royal Anthropological Institute*, 33, 1903, pp. 36-40.

17   Racial inequality and discrimination towards African Americans in the United States did *not* produce a similar critique until after the war.

18   William B. Provine, 'Genetics and the Biology of Race Crossing', *Science*, 182, 23 Nov. 1973.

19   Haraway, *Modest_Witness@Second_Millenium*, p. 239.

20   Ashley Montagu, *Statement on Race,* Oxford: Oxford University Press, 1972, pp. 9-10.

21   Melbourne Tapper, 'Interrogating Bodies: Medico-Racial Knowledge, Politics and the Study of a Disease', *Comparative Studies in Society and History*, 37(1), 1995, pp. 76-93; Keith Wailoo, *Drawing Blood: Technology and Disease Identity in Twentieth-Century America*, Baltimore, Maryland: The Johns Hopkins University Press, 1997, pp. 134-49.

22   See Stepan, *The Idea of Race in Science*, pp. 172-82 for details.

23   Saul Dubow, *Scientific Racism in Modern South Africa*, Cambridge: Cambridge University Press, 1995.

24   Lawrence Wright, 'Annals of Politics: One Drop of Blood', *New Yorker*, 25 July 1994; Sharon M. Lee, 'Racial Classification and the U.S. Census: 1890-1990', *Ethnic and Racial Studies*, 16 January 1993. For a critique of the biracial category favoured by some groups in the U.S., see Lewis R. Gordon, 'Specificities: Cultures of American Identity: Critical "Mixed Race"?', *Social Identities*, 1, 1995.

25   Walter Benn Michaels, 'Race Into Culture: A Critical Genealogy of Cultural Identity', *Critical Inquiry*, 18, 1992, and 'Critical Response: The No-Drop Rule', *Critical Inquiry*, 20, 1994.

26   Wailoo, *Drawing Blood,* pp. 184-86; Inez Smith Reid, 'Science, Politics, and Race', in Sandra Harding and Jean F. O'Barr, eds., *Sex and Scientific Inquiry*, Chicago: Chicago University Press, 1987.

27   This is the theme of Marek Kohn's, *The Race Gallery: The Return of Racial Science*, London: Jonathan Cape, 1995.

28   Malik, *Meaning of Race*, pp. 11–38.

29   Leonard Lieberman, Blaine W. Stevenson, and Larry T. Reynolds, 'Race and Anthropology: A Core Concept without Consensus', *Anthropology and Education Quarterly*, 20, 1989. Their study shows that the greatest support for race in biology came from physical anthropologists in the private universities; they suggest that in state universities, where students and faculty tended to be drawn from a wider range of social classes and ethnic (often immigrant) groups, the concept of biologically-based differences had less appeal.

30   Richard J. Hernstein and Charles Murray, *The Bell Curve: Intelligence and Class Structure in American Life*, New York: Free Press, 1994. For critiques, see Steven Fraser, ed., *The Bell Curve Wars: Race, Intelligence and the Future of America*, New York: Basic Books, 1995.

31   The well-known anti-racist and Marxist population geneticist, Richard C. Lewontin, points out in his book, *Biology as Ideology: The Doctrine of DNA*, New York: Harper, 1991, p. 68, that the sequence of DNA will be a mosaic of some hypothetical, average person that may correspond to no one; given polymorphism, every human genome is unique, and ideally we should sequence the same part of the genome from many different individuals for an adequate picture.

32   Cavalli-Sforza et al., 'Call for a Worldwide Survey of Human Genetic Diversity: A Vanishing Opportunity for the Human Genome Project', *Genomics,* 11, 1991, pp. 490–1.

33   Troy Duster, 'Buried Alive: The Concept of Race in Science', *Chronicle of Higher Education*, 48(03), 14 September 2000, pp. B11–12.

34   See Andrews and Nelkin, *Body Bazaar*, pp. 66–81; Haraway, *Modest_Witness@Second_Millenium,* pp. 248–53. The *Declaration of Indigenous Peoples of the Western Hemisphere Regarding the Human Genome Diversity Project*, Phoenix, Arizona, 1993, rejected all forms of genetic technology.

35   Karen Young Kreeger, 'Proposed Human Genome Diversity Project Still Plagued by Controversy and Questions', *The Scientist*, 10(20), 14 October 1996; David B. Resnik, 'The Human Genome Diversity Project: Ethnical Problems and Solutions', *Politics and the Life Sciences*, 18(1), March 1999. A similar project to the HGDP, called the 'Biological History of European Populations', which aims to study European genetic diversity and paleo-anthropological history, has been funded by the European Union; apparently, this project is proceeding without controversy.

36   Brett Lee Sheldon and Jonathan Marks, 'Genetic Markers Not a Valid Test of Native Identity', http://www.gene-watch.org/magazine/vol14/14-5nativeidentity.html

37   The paper by A. Arnaiz-Villena et al., 'The Origin of Palestinians and their

Genetic Relatedness with other Mediterranean Populations', *Human Immunology*, 62(9) 2001, pp. 889-900, showing that Jews and Palestinians in the Middle East are genetically indistinguishable, was 'deleted from the scientific literature', in the words of the editors of the journal ('Editorial', 62(10), October 2001, p. 1063), not for its scientific conclusions about the historic, genetic similarity between the two populations divided sharply by politics and religion, but for the pro-Palestinian and anti-Israeli political views expressed by the authors. One wonders.... This is obviously sensitive stuff.

38   On disease differentials between African-Americans and whites in the United States, such as the much higher morbidity and mortality rates in African-Americans in cancer and heart disease, the dangers of implying genetic causes, and overlooking social and economic causes (such as low rates of medical insurance, second-rate medical care), are very clear; see on this point Joseph L. Graves, Jr., 'Race and the Disease Fallacy', in his *The Emperor's New Clothes: Biological Theories of Race at the Millenium*, New Brunswick/New Jersey: Rutgers University Press, 2001, ch. 11; and Tom Reynolds, 'Panel Grapples with the Legacy of "Race Medicine" in Research', *J. of the National Cancer Institute*, 89(11), June 4, 1997, pp. 758-61.

39   See the interview with Dr. Joseph L. Graves Jr., 'Beyond Black and White in Biology and Medicine', *New York Times, Science Times,* January 1, 2002, p. F5; also the article, 'For Genome Mappers, the Tricky Terrain of Race Requires some Careful Navigating', *New York Times*, 20 July 2001, p. A17.

40   In fact, carrier screening and genetic counselling have reduced the incidence in the high risk population to such an extent that a high percentage of the babies born today with Tay-Sachs disease are the offspring of couples who have not previously been considered at high risk (i.e. are not self-defined as Ashkenazi Jews); genes for Tay-Sachs, that is, do not map in their distribution the group we call 'Ashkanezi Jews'.

41   The speech was a commencement address before the literary societies of Western Reserve College (Rochester, New York, 1964); reprinted in P. S. Foner, ed., *The Life and Writings of Frederick Douglass,* New York: International Publishers, vol. 2.

42   This argument also extends to gender difference and its meanings in contemporary society.

IDENTIFYING CLASS,
CLASSIFYING DIFFERENCE

JOHN S. SAUL

There are more things between heaven and earth than are dreamt of in your philosophy, Ms. Marxist and Mr. Socialist. It's a critique we hear often these days from the principled spokespersons of anarchism, identity politics, oppositional post-modernism and 'radical democracy', and of course there's something in it. The unduly heroic claims that some Marxists have sometimes made for the ontologically prior determinacy of 'the material', for the centrality of the realm of the 'economic' and the priority of class-based exploitation in explaining the oppressive workings of 'capitalist society' and the unnuanced manner in which some socialists have argued the privileged role of 'the working class' (or, perhaps, 'the workers and peasants') in resistance have rendered the Marxist/socialist tradition[1] vulnerable to criticism – if also to quite a bit of caricature – in recent years. In such an intellectual environment, it behoves Marxists and socialists who do prioritize political economy, the centrality of class struggle, and the realization of socialism, and who choose in one way or another to wrap themselves in the mantle of the Grand Narratives of Emancipation, Universalism and quasi-Enlightenment values (even when abjuring anything that smacks of 'Essentialism', 'Economism', and 'Eurocentrism') to think ever more clearly and carefully about the premises of our work, both analytical and practical.

To begin with, it is by now impossible to ignore the fact that gender is more central to how society functions – its oppressions and its resistances – than most Marxists acknowledged not so very long ago. But even as regards race, nationalism and religion we know – more graphically than ever in the wake of September 11 – that there are religions that move some people to sacrifice their own lives (and those of others) in the name of social claims said to be rooted in the imperatives of those religions; that there are nationalisms, supra- and sub-, that can drive some people even to genocide and ethnic-cleansings in their name, or feed the orgy of national self-righteousness that currently underpins U.S. claims to determine which regimes will survive and which are to be overthrown throughout the world; and that there are racist imaginings that, as in South Africa or indeed in the global capitalist economy more generally, can so interpenetrate with class structures of oppression as to make it often difficult to say with any great confidence which variable is driving which.

Moreover, anyone who has spent his life, as I have, studying – while also trying to help build – a political project around southern Africa and its liberation is aware of the possible flip-side of these variables, when the consciousness of racial identity and racial oppression can interact positively with the mobilizing and framing of class consciousness and class struggle; when, as in Mozambique, the emotive force of national liberation can provide the seed-bed for radicalization and ultimately, in however flawed and transitory a form, socialist endeavour; and when, as in South Africa itself, a religious/theological impulse towards liberation can be a key force behind radical undertakings. Of course, each of these realities is, up to a point, subject to a 'material explanation'. Nonetheless, there is also something here that can fall below the radar of the too easy reductionism of some kinds of Marxist/socialist endeavour. It is this something else, these provocative 'disturbances to the field' of Marxism/socialism, that forces us to scan carefully the work of those who argue for the claims to our attention of the variables just mentioned – as well as the additional claims to our attention to be made in the name of gender, diverse sexual orientations, and even environmental concerns.

The aim of this essay is to register claims rooted in the lived saliency of 'identity' and 'difference' and, in doing so, contribute to striking a more useful analytical balance between political economy (focused principally on the structures of capitalist exploitation that frame our world) and the parallel examination of other structures and other discourses that help define the realities of oppression. The essay will also suggest the circumstances under which class struggle can intersect more positively and self-consciously with those racial (read, at least in part, 'anti-racist'), national and religious impulses that, in some circumstances, speak to our common humanity and our common struggle.

I MARXISM: 'MORALIZING SCIENCE', 'POINT OF VIEW', 'ENTRY-POINT'

Let's begin at the beginning. Why would anybody want to identify themselves as a Marxist or a socialist in the first place? The simple answer is that we see capitalism as an inhuman and inegalitarian system of exploitation that needs to be overthrown. And what if we privilege this entry-point into social analysis in order to place at the centre of our concerns both the nature of the capitalist economic structure itself and the struggle of exploited classes to challenge that system? Need we apologize for the fact that this represents at least as much an 'arbitrary' value judgment as a strictly 'scientific' procedure? For we don't need post-modernists to remind us that there are limits to the scientificity of the social science that we practice and apply. In fact, we don't need to dig very deep beneath the surface of 'common sense' to realize that the most efficacious social science doesn't merely drive itself but is framed by the questions that social scientists *choose* to ask. Recall, for example, that primary text of hard-headed procedural common sense, E. H. Carr's *What is History?*: 'Study the historian before you begin to study the facts', he counsels, for

> ... the necessity to establish these basic facts rests not on any quality of the facts themselves, but on an a priori decision of the historian .... It used to be said that the facts speak for themselves. This is, of course, untrue. The facts speak only when the historian calls on them: it is he who decides to which facts to give the floor, and in what order or context .... By and large the historian will get the kind of facts he wants. History means interpretation.[2]

And where do such choices come from? Not primarily, I would suggest, from some evolving and shifting consensus as to what is pertinent to the best 'scientific' explanations emerging within social science disciplines (even if that can have a certain weight). In another fine old book of clear-sighted common sense, Hugh Stretton canvasses diverse approaches to the question of what caused late nineteenth century imperialism, concluding that even if his wide range of authors had

> all agreed to explain the same events and had made no mistakes of fact ... it should still be clear that they would have continued to differ from each other. It should also be clear that their diverse purposes – to reform or conserve societies, to condemn or justify past policies, to reinforce theoretical structures – might well have been served by a stricter regard for truth, but could scarcely be *replaced* by it .... However desirable as qualities of observation, 'objectivity' and its last-ditch rearguard 'intersubjectivity' still seem unable to organize an explanation or to bring men of different faith to agree about the parts or the shape, the length or breadth or depth or pattern, that an explanation should have.[3]

Indeed, Stretton concludes that 'neutral scientific rules' cannot 'replace valuation as selectors' and that the 'scientistic' dream of developing an internally coherent, self-sustaining and (potentially) exhaustive model of society is not only misguided but dangerous – dangerous in the sense of encouraging a blunting of debate about the 'political and moral valuations' that necessarily help shape both the questions posed of society and the explanations that contest for our attention regarding social phenomena. Hence his argument for the self-conscious embrace of what he terms a (necessarily) 'moralizing [social] science'. We might wish to add that, once the questions themselves have been posed, the social scientist can still be judged by his or her peers in terms of the evidence discovered and adduced in the attempt to answer them, and in terms of the logic and coherence of the arguments presented. There are scientific canons of evidence and argument in terms of which explanations can, up to a point, be judged 'intersubjectively'. But the questions themselves quite simply do not emerge unprompted from such concerns.

Although not always acknowledged, this seems straightforward enough. But even if some social scientists are uncomfortable with this notion of an inevitably 'moralizing social science', the Marxist/socialist social scientist has no reason not to embrace it. After all, is this not what the unity of theory and practice is all about? This is the argument of Gavin Kitching, for example, who writes (affirmatively) that Marxism is much less a science than a 'point of view', and, more specifically, a point of view 'on or about the form of society that it calls capitalism'.[4] For Kitching, 'the Marxist point of view (which Kitching himself adopts) turns out to be a *rationally motivated willingness to act to transform capitalism*'. It has been, Kitching argues, 'the "objectively best" point of view to take on capitalism ... *in order to change it into a better form of society*'[5] – and hence also the basis for the kind of politics of persuasion and mobilization of interests that could alone make the struggle for socialism viable.

I find this convincing – even though Kitching himself seems to take his own argument much too far when he suggests that, whatever may be its positive moral–cum–political value, the Marxist point of view does not provide any 'privileged means' of understanding the workings of capitalist society and its contradictions. The truth is, of course, that Marxists and socialists seek not only to change the world but also to interpret it – and their central concerns have indeed given them tools with which to do so. Still, it is appropriate to ask just what, more broadly, is the kind of knowledge these concerns can produce. One well-known answer to this was articulated by Lucio Colletti in his widely-read essay 'Marxism: Science or Revolution?'[6] Colletti focused on the wage relationship within capitalism and conceded that 'bourgeois social science' (as viewed from 'the point of view of the capitalist', as Colletti put it) offers an understanding of that relationship as a free exchange that is quite plausible (and, we might add, fits neatly into the 'scientific' undertakings of neoclassical economics). But, Colletti insisted, equally plausible (and even more pertinent to the cause of socialist revolution) is an understanding of this relationship – 'from the viewpoint of the working class' – as one of exploitation, and this angle of vision can also offer a revealing (but very different) analysis of the workings of capitalism.[7]

'The worker's point of view'? It is tempting to put it like this, (not least for purposes of political mobilization) but we can actually advance the case for the prioritizing of a class analysis grounded in Marxist/socialist premises somewhat more modestly, albeit with equal effect. Indeed, Resnick and Wolff have done so convincingly in their volume, *Knowledge and Class*, rejecting both 'empiricist' and 'rationalist' epistemologies while announcing, unapologetically, that, as Marxists, they choose class analysis as their preferred 'entry point' into social enquiry.[8] Interestingly, they make no claim that this is the only useful approach to society for purposes of theory or practice but assert merely that it is the one they find most illuminating to build out from, both analytically and politically:

'Class then is [the] one process among the many different processes of life chosen by Marxists to their theoretical entry point so as to make a particular sense of and a particular change in this life'. But 'why choose class as an entry-point rather than, say, racial or sexual oppression?':

> Our answer may serve to clarify our relations both to Marx and to those people today (including friends) whose entry points and hence theories differ more or less from ours. What Marx sought and we continue to seek to contribute to struggles for social change are not only our practical energies but also certain distinctive theoretical insights. The most important of these for us concerns class. Marx discovered, we think, a specific social process that his allies in social struggle had missed. The process in question is the production and distribution of surplus labour in society. Marx's contribution lay in defining, locating and connecting the class process to all other processes comprising the social totality they all sought to change. Marx's presumption was that programs for social change had less chance of success to the degree that their grasp of social structure was deficient.[9]

Note, in addition, that Resnick and Wolff see this way of expressing things as avoiding any kind of reductionism and instead as defining a Marxism that is open, precisely, to 'the mutual overdetermination of both class and nonclass' dimensions, and thus to 'the complex interdependencies of class and nonclass aspects of social life ... that neither Marx nor we reduce to cause-effect or determining-determined essentialisms'.[10] This latter point is crucial and we will return to it in the next section. But what, first, of the core argument I have presented regarding Marxism's scientific-cum-political standing – as 'moralizing science', as 'point of view', as 'entry-point'– to our analytical understandings? No doubt philosophers, including Marxist philosophers, may wish to go further than this, but I'm not sure that the rest of us can't get on with our own work while they're doing so. Isn't this approach, in any case, the best way to stake our claim to be heard, to mobilize and expand our constituency for class analysis and class struggle, while also listening carefully to what others struggling alongside us have to say?

As for the post-Marxist and post-modernist sages, can we not safely leave them to recycling such assertions as that of Ernesto Laclau to the effect that 'class struggle is just one species of identity politics, and one which is becoming less and less important in the world in which we live'. No doubt Laclau's attendant claim that class struggle is hopelessly 'old fashioned' will be good news to the transnational corporations and the international financial institutions and the US State Department that drive the global economy – although they might be inclined to see this more as a whimper of defeat than a theoretical breakthrough. For Laclau's statement is linked in his text to a broader approach that characterizes 'anti-capitalism' as 'mere empty talk', the goal of socializing the means of production as a 'rather peculiar aim', and the height of left aspiration as just enough reform of the economy so that 'the worst effects of globalization are avoided'.[11] As Slavoj Zizek suggests (in critiquing Laclau), such a refusal to 'even imagine a viable alternative to global capitalism' inevitably produces the conclusion that 'the only option for the Left is … palliative measures which, while resigning themselves to the course of events, restrict themselves to limiting the damaging effects of the inevitable'.[12]

But let us be generous and also say to the 'posties': go ahead, 'deconstruct' us to your heart's content, expose our premises (our Eurocentrisms, essentialisms and the like) and we're prepared to learn from you just where we may have occluded things, thereby bettering both our science (our 'moralizing science') and our politics. At the end of the day, however, Marxists and socialists will also continue to insist that capitalism be taken seriously in its fundamentally oppressive reality – and to insist as well that, like all human constructs, it is not destined to last forever but can and must be replaced as soon as possible. And to assert that mobilizing people who are victims of that system around anti-capitalist themes and projects is essential to liberation. And to ask of others why they would want, in all conscience, to blunt that 'point-of-view'.

II MARXISM: ANTI-REDUCTIONIST AND NON-ESSENTIALIST

This, then, is our entry-point: we begin as Marxists with capitalism itself because we consider an understanding of its logic to be the crucial first step in our understanding of the world and we begin as socialists with the struggle to overthrow capitalism because we consider that overthrow to be a necessary (if not sufficient) condition of human emancipation. From this affirmation we can now return to the issues raised in our introductory paragraphs: following Resnick and Wolff, I will argue that there is simply no need, either theoretically or politically, for Marxists/socialists to downplay the importance of other kinds of oppression or other kinds of meaningful resistance to such oppressions.

For despite all the huffing and puffing over the past couple of decades by so many post-Marxists, post-structuralists and post-modernists, Marxism has the resources to deal with a complete plate-full of 'differences' and to keep its honour bright. Once again, Kitching has effectively phrased the point:

> Marx simply was *not* an economic reductionist. He did not believe that all forms of politics, or culture, or social conflict were simply expressions of underlying economic or class interests, and it would be extremely difficult to find any evidence in his writing that he did …. Marx was often concerned with those aspects of politics, or culture, or social conflict that had class or economic dimensions. But he certainly would not have thought that, for example, all classical Greek culture (which he loved) or all the politics of the French Second Empire (by which he was fascinated) could be explained by or reduced to economic or class factors.[13]

Of course, there are tensions within Marx's work (and also within the tradition he spawned): he did want to say that the production process – and the capitalist production process in particular – was a (sometimes, 'the') crucial variable for framing both social analysis and political practice. And there are those who will continue to argue, albeit in subtle ways, the case for the *primacy* of the 'economic' and of class struggle. Take, for example, the position asserted some years ago by Erik Olin Wright. He sought to sustain such a claim on the grounds that a tendency towards transformation of the class struggle is inherent in the very process of economic development (in the development of the productive forces), providing class relations with an 'internal logic of development' denied to other forms of domination: 'the apparent symmetry in the relationship between class and gender or class and race, therefore, is disrupted by the developmental tendencies of class relations. No such developmental trajectory has been persuasively argued for other forms of domination', Wright asserted.[14] Suggestive, but even then probably more reductionist than it need be. Not that 'suggestive' is a bad thing: the pull towards economic-cum-class reductionism within Marxism can be illuminating, even if also dangerous.

But dangerous? This need prove to be the case only if we fail to hold onto the expansive implications of the simultaneous pull towards 'agency' within Marxism.[15] 'Man [sic] makes his own history but he does not do so under conditions of his own choosing': a phrase from Marx that is often quoted but perhaps too easily forgotten. For if we take this (usefully contradictory) phrase seriously, we are acknowledging that there do exist tensions within our approach: tensions between structure and agency, tensions between the attractions of economic-cum-class reductionism (in both analysis and politics) on the one hand and the legitimate claims of a multi-variate analysis and a politically inclusive approach to struggle on the other. What we are then claiming is that it is precisely on the cusp of these tensions that the Marxist chooses, as creatively and self-consciously as possible, to think and to act.

In fact, we need only build on the possibilities (tensions) inherent in one of Marx's own most tantalizing formulations:

> It is always the direct relationship of the owners of the conditions of production to the direct producers – a relationship always naturally corresponding to the development of the methods of labour and thereby its social productivity – which reveals the innermost secret, the hidden basis of the entire social structure, and with it the political form of the relation of sovereignty and dependence, in short, the corresponding specific form of the state. *This does not prevent the same economic basis – the same from the standpoint of its main conditions – due to innumerable different empirical circumstances, natural environment, race relations, external historical influences, etc., from showing infinite variations and gradations in appearance, which can be ascertained only by analysis of the empirically given circumstances.*[16]

The absence of any mention of gender on Marx's list (or, one might add, of sexual orientation, religion or ethno-nationalism) is troubling, to be sure, and there is the word 'appearance' to be dealt with. And yet, merely expand the content of that 'etc.' and of those phrases 'empirical circumstances' and 'external historical influences', while also interpreting 'appearance' in the strongest possible sense (as capable of housing pertinent effects in its own right), and you have pretty much all that Marxists require: the ability to emphasize the production process as our chosen entry-point into social analysis and political practice while also taking seriously the concerns of those who wish to highlight, alternatively or simultaneously, the claims to our attention of other nodes of oppression and resistance. This done, all that Marxists need ask of those who speak out analytically and politically from the vantage-point of concern about these is that, whatever else they do, they take seriously the goal of overthrowing, sooner or later (but preferably sooner rather than later), the capitalist system.

Although their efforts are not the immediate focus of this essay, it bears emphasizing that it has been those engaged in gender-sensitive analysis and feminist struggles who have had most to contribute to the development of Marxist analysis along these expansive lines. This can be seen firstly with reference to the very notion of class itself. Himani Bannerji has underscored the 'absurdity' of attempting to see 'identity and difference as historical forms of consciousness unconnected to class formation, development of capital and class politics'. But in doing so she also emphasizes the impossibility of considering class itself outside the gendering (and 'race-ing') that so often significantly characterize it in the concrete.[17] Not that there need be anything so very startling in this. Katha Pollitt makes the relevant point about the United States (but the point is true more generally) in answering her own question: 'Are race and gender and sexual orientation distractions from basic issues of economic inequality and social class?'

> All you have to do is look squarely at the world you live in and it is perfectly obvious that ... race and gender are crucial means through which class is structured. These are not side issues that can be resolved by raising the minimum wage, although that is important, or even by unionizing more workplaces, although that is important too. Inequality in America is too solidly based on racism and sexism for it be altered without acknowledging race, and sex and sexuality.[18]

But this point can also be turned around, underscoring the extent to which gender oppression is also classed and the extent to which feminist assertions must interpenetrate with socialist ones in order to be pertinent to the life-conditions of most women. As Lynn Segal argued a decade ago, 'at a time when the advances made by some women are so clearly overshadowed by the increasing poverty experienced so acutely by others (alongside the unemployment of men of their class and group) it seems perverse to pose women's specific interests against rather than alongside more traditional socialist goals'.[19] Consider, too, Nancy Fraser's twin framing of the conditions of women's oppression (and a number of other oppressions as well) within the spheres of both distribution *and* difference: 'Demands for "recognition of difference" fuel struggles of groups mobilized under the banners of nationality, ethnicity, "race," gender, and sexuality. In these "post-socialist" conflicts, group identity supplants class interest as the chief medium of political mobilization. And cultural recognition displaces socioeconomic redistribution as the remedy for injustice and the goal of polit-ical struggle'.[20] And yet, she then argues, it seems extremely unlikely that tensions rooted in struggles for 'recognition' can be resolved, in the long-term, in any very effective and healing manner unless tensions rooted in struggles for 'redis-tribution' (broadly defined) are also being addressed. Her own aim, she suggests, is precisely 'to connect two political problematics that are currently dissociated from one another'.

True, Fraser casts her concern for the economic in narrowly redistributional terms rather than in terms of overcoming capitalism's class oppressions more radi-cally. Nonetheless, her refusal to let feminist scholarship and practice merely disappear into the morass of 'difference' and discourse theory is a bracing one. Moreover, other, more Marxist feminists have been prepared to take the point much further in viewing 'feminist struggle' as 'fundamentally a class war over resources, knowledge and power' and in seeking to 'reclaim anticapitalist femi-nism'. Thus Hennessy and Ingraham bemoan the fact that 'debate among first-world socialist and marxist feminists has drifted so far into theorizing women's oppression in terms of culture, consciousness and ideology that concerns over how to explain the connection between patriarchy and capitalism, or the links between women's domestic labour and ideology, have been all but abandoned'.[21] In contrast, as they and their co-authors have demonstrated in their work, a preoc-cupation with the mode of production and with the realities of wage labour, commodity production and consumption is crucial both to 'the scientific under-standing of sexual inequality' and to feminists gaining 'a sound basis for the evaluation of short- and long-term political and economic objectives'.[22]

Such a position is, of course, not seen as pre-empting the claims of anti-patri-archal struggle as carried out 'in its own right'. It is a commonplace, albeit a crucial one, that a 'mere' overthrow of capitalism will not, in and of itself, resolve the issues of oppressive sexism and gender emancipation (issues that have continued to haunt all previous experiments in socialist construction). As Hennessy and Ingraham are quick to acknowledge, 'violations of women's needs and rights as human beings by patriarchal practices like rape, battering, clitoridectomy and other forms of sexual violence, as well as the neglect and infanticide of girls, are not exclusively bound by or peculiar to capitalism'. But they do assert that 'the historical forms these practices take and their use against many women in the world are not independent of capitalism either', concluding that 'because marxist feminists see the continuous historical connections between women's oppression and capitalism, theirs is a politics of social trans-formation that ultimately looks to the elimination of class'.[23] Indeed as Hennessy – in articulating her own commitment, as socialist, feminist and lesbian activist, to Marxist analysis and politics – concludes another recent study: 'Full democracy [deemed by her to be essential to, amongst many other things, sexual emancipation of all kinds] cannot be achieved within capitalism'.[24] The inextricable links between capitalism and patriarchy, between class and feminist struggles, that Hennessy and others identify: we can learn from this model (and also from certain recent writings on ecological politics[25]) as we turn to an examination of other forms of identity politics.

There is one final preliminary point to be made, however. This concerns the complexity of grounding morally the resistance to oppression that might link feminist and other movements for equality and justice closely to socialist ones. Just what are we 'moralizing' about in our science, after all? Those on the Left have sometimes shown unease with any such question, preferring instead the assumption of an (at best) tacitly shared hunch as to what positive values might ultimately find expression if 'the workers of the world' really were to unite to build a new society. The challenge of post-modernist deconstruction has made it more difficult to let the matter rest there, however. Significantly, some feminist thinkers – Sabina Lovibond, writing against the grain of post-modernist feminism, for example – have confronted the issue head-on. Advocating the 'global' agenda of an 'abolition of the sex class system, and the forms of inner life that belong to it', she defined this programme as being global 'not just in the sense that it addresses itself to every corner of the planet, but also in the sense that it aims eventually to converge with those of all other egalitarian or liberationist movements'. And the basis of such 'convergence'? 'The movement should persist in seeing itself as a component or offshoot of Enlightenment modernism, rather than one more "exciting" feature (or cluster of features) in a postmodern social landscape'.[26]

Whether, in seeking to resist both relativism on the one hand and liberal/neoliberal universalism on the other, 'the Enlightenment' is the best point of reference for the Left may be open to question, of course. Nonetheless, as Lovibond senses, the problem will not simply disappear. We may find it easier to know what we are against (capitalism and its multiple alienations and oppressions, for example) than to clearly state just what it is that we are for and just what 'spaces of hope' we divine – even if concepts like emancipation from oppression and the freedom for self-expression and self-realization, community and equality can be expected to help us define our counter-hegemonic universalism more specifically as we proceed. Perhaps, too, we can affirm that any such 'universalism' as we may come to embrace will have to be global in its referent and democratic in the modalities of its emergence. These are, in any case, issues to which we will have to return.

III MARXISM: CLASS AND IDENTITY

We can now turn to a brief survey of issues raised for Marxists and socialists by the 'identities' highlighted in this volume of the *Register*. In doing so, we find ourselves confronted by variables even more difficult to pin down than are those of class and gender, although they are variables with a wide and undeniable range of pertinent effects. We will suggest that none of them can be reduced to mere reflexes of the economic, the material or the class-determined, either for purposes of analyzing oppression or for mobilizing resistance. However, we will see, once again, that Marxists and non-Marxist socialists have every reason to argue that these variables are best treated in close relation to an analysis and a politics of anti-capitalist class struggle. Finally, since the questions broached here are so far-reaching, I will approach them principally on the terrain of global develop-ment theory and 'third world' struggles that I know best.

(1) Race ... and (post-)colonialism

If it is indeed 'absurd', as we have seen Bannerji to argue, to ignore the inter-section of class not only with gender hierarchies but also with racial discriminations in advanced capitalist settings, then it would be even more foolish to do so when we focus on capitalism as a global system. As Oliver Cox and others have demonstrated, many of the central features we think of as consti-tuting modern racism in the cultural sphere were, in the first instance, shaped in close interaction with the expansion of global capitalism.[27] For this 'cultural vari-able' served both as rationale and booster rocket for 'the European consumption of tribal society' which 'when viewed as a single process ... could be said to represent the greatest, most persistent act of human destructiveness ever recorded'.[28] Such a meshing of 'race and class' had numerous faces: in driving American imperialism, for example, the vigorous seed of racism planted by the slave trade was complemented fatefully by what Drinnon calls the ideology of 'Indian-hating'. This, he continues,

> ... reduced native peoples to the level of the rest of the fauna and flora to be 'rooted out.' It reduced all the diverse Native American peoples to a single despised nonwhite group and, where they did survive, into an hereditary caste. In its more inclusive form, Western racism is another name for native-hating – in North America, of 'niggers,' 'Chinks,' 'Japs,' 'greasers,' 'dagoes,' etc.; in the Philippines of 'goo-goos'; and in Indochina of 'gooks.' ... Racism defined natives as non-persons within the settlement culture and was in a real sense the enabling experience of the rising American empire.[29]

Drinnon goes so far as to argue that 'in the [American] experience race has always been of greater importance than class, the corner-stone of European prop-erty based politics'. We may think the dialectic of class and race is rather more complicated than that, but of the impact of 'race' per se we can have no doubt. Thus, even when the most overtly racist canons of imperial ideology have been self-consciously modified by the Western powers (in order to rationalize the decolonization process of the post-war years, for example), that ideology's central premise of (racial) superiority has tended to be only lightly recast in 'moral' terms for both elite and popular consumption. As Furedi notes:

> Increasingly the vocabulary that is applied to the South is morally different from that which is used in relation to the North. Many societies in the South, especially those in Africa, are treated in pathological terms. Africans are routinely represented as devoid of moral qualities .... The new moral equation between a superior North and an inferior South helps

legitimize a two-tiered international system .... Race no longer has a formal role to play since the new global hierarchy is represented through a two-tier moral system. Gradually, the old silent race war has been replaced by moral crusades and by 'clashes of civilization'.[30]

The latter is, of course, the nether-world of ideology-making inhabited by the Samuel Huntingtons and the Bernard Lewises of the academy. But its public credibility in Western circles can be best gauged by the extraordinary success of Robert Kaplan's recent writings, in which the grimmest possible evocation – a crypto-racist tone, substituting for any real analysis of the structures of global inequality, is central to his work – of Africa's problems ('criminal anarchy', 'nature unchecked') is said to capture the essence of today's 'bifurcated world'.[31]

The sordid reality of global inequality has certainly reshaped the advanced capitalist centres themselves, the impoverished empire having 'struck back' (through migration to the metropole) to produce general populations of diverse ethnic and racial composition.[32] Writers like Bonacich and others more recently have explored the split labour markets that this process has produced, and their implications for divided working-class responses to capital.[33] And Stuart Hall and his colleagues have presented, in rich detail, an understanding of some of the cultural/ideological and political effects of such 'racial' diversity and the complexity of developing counter-hegemonic strategies in advanced capitalist countries that acknowledge this diversity while seeking to encompass and transcend it.[34] My own work, both scholarly and political, on South Africa has also schooled me here. The semi-autonomous but always tightly linked (and shifting) imperatives of class exploitation and racial oppression that have produced both apartheid and a distinctive form of 'racial capitalism' there have proven challenging to disentangle analytically. Similarly, consciousness of nation, race and citizenship has often been even more crucial than class consciousness in driving South African resistance. Perhaps the fact that, ultimately, the pull towards (somewhat) colour-blind class relations has produced a grim post-apartheid 'false decolonization' along neoliberal lines may seem like a retrospective vindication of class analysis. But the situation has never been that simple, nor has the politics it demands.[35] In fact, once taken seriously, the irreducible simultaneity of class and race can be seen everywhere to warrant 'the forging of alliances between the democratic movement and the labour and socialist movements for multi-racial organization and solidarity rather than sectarianism and chauvinism, and finally ... a strategy that links the struggle for reforms within capitalism with the struggle for its transformation'.[36]

However, for the purposes of the present essay let us narrow the focus here (while simultaneously expanding it!) by returning to the wider world and the intersection of class and race in the relationship between the capitalist centre and its periphery. As Biel has argued, 'Dependency theory uncovered part of this relationship, essentially the racial capitalism that exists between the North and the South'.[37] Of course, we know that the geography of global exploitation has become ever more complicated, the 'Third World' now to be found within the

First and the First within the Third such that Hoogevelt can even suggest that 'the familiar pyramid of the core-periphery hierarchy is no longer a geographical but a social division of the world economy'.[38] And yet things are not yet quite as simple as that either. As Giovanni Arrighi pointed out some years ago (and has reaffirmed in more recent work), the global hierarchy of national economies remains remarkably stable, whatever may be happening to class relationships within those economies: '… the nations of the world', he writes, 'are not all walking along the same road to high mass consumption. Rather they are differentially situated in a rigid hierarchy of wealth in which the occasional ascent of a nation or two leaves all the others more firmly entrenched than ever they were before'.[39] There is, in short, plenty of evidence for the existence of a global imperial hierarchy, both geographically and socially-defined, that is also 'raced' – a kind of 'global apartheid', as the point has recently been put.[40]

It is this phenomenon that lies at the heart of recent work carried out under the rubric of 'post-colonialism', much of it done in the name of cultural recovery as part of a challenge to the Eurocentric premises of both mainstream and Marxist studies of development and literature. The post-colonial school aims not merely to expose such Eurocentric biases within the global centres of cultural production, but also to listen afresh to those diverse voices of the South that otherwise would be squeezed out of 'the canon' and out of global public discourse. Nor is this done principally in the name of 'tradition'. Acknowledging the impact that Western imperialism and colonialism have had on peoples on the receiving end of that system – whether currently resident in the South or now in one or another diaspora – they speak in terms of 'hybridities' and 'syncreticisms' that articulate their presence around the world in voices that are complex and multilayered, local yet global, and that must be heard.

There have also, however, been numerous critics of such preoccupations who attack the tendency of this work to merely celebrate diversity (of 'identity' or of literary and artistic production) at the expense of saying nearly enough about how the world actually works for the vast majority of those who live at capitalism's periphery (whether in the North or the South). Amongst the most perceptive of such critics has been Ella Shohat:

> The circulation of 'post-colonial' as a theoretical framework tends to suggest a supercession of neo-colonialism and the Third World and Fourth World as unfashionable, even irrelevant categories. Yet, with all its problems, the term 'Third World' does still retain heuristic value as a convenient label for the imperialized formations, including those within the First World …. At this point in time, replacing the term 'Third World' with the 'post-colonial' is a liability. Despite differences and contradictions among and within Third World countries, the term 'Third World' contains a common project of (linked) resistances to neo-colonialisms [and] implies a belief that the shared history of neo-colonialism and internal racism form sufficient common ground for alliances among such diverse peoples.[41]

While she acknowledges that the use of the term 'Third World' risks blurring 'the differently modulated politics in the realm of culture, the overlapping spaces of inter-mingling identities' in diverse settings around the world, she nonetheless affirms that 'the cultural inquiry generated by the hybridity/syncreticism discourse needs re-linking to geopolitical macro-level analysis'.[42]

Shohat thus seeks to bring the cultural realities of global diversity into a strong interface with the realities of global capitalism and the need to resist it. More recently, Robert Young has attempted to defend post-colonial theory against such criticisms by asserting that 'many of the problems raised can be resolved if the postcolonial is defined as coming after colonialism and imperialism, in their original meaning of direct-rule domination, but still positioned within imperialism in its later sense of the global system of hegemonic economic power'.[43] This may be somewhat disingenuous, however. As Arif Dirlik argues, 'post-colonial critics have been largely silent on the relationship of the idea of post-colonialism to its context in contemporary capitalism; indeed, they have suppressed the necessity of considering such a possible relationship by repudiating a possible "foundational" role for capitalism in history'.[44] Moreover, even Young himself professes unease with the term 'post-colonial', suggesting his actual preference for the notion of 'tricontinentalism' to capture even more directly 'a theoretical and political position which embodies an active concept of intervention within such oppressive circumstances'. Nonetheless, he claims that 'post-colonialism' (as he defines it) can still serve the purposes he has in mind, capturing the 'tricontinental' nature of Southern resistance to imperialism while remaining sensitive to the sheer diversity of the settings in which such resistance occurs. Indeed this latter sensitivity is presented as being amongst 'the fundamental lessons of the Marxism of the liberation movements': 'The foundational concept here is the critique of eurocentrism and unreflective eurocentric assumptions, and the need to radicalize any politics or economics through constructive dialogue to accommodate the particularities of local cultural conditions'.

Are we not here, with Shohat, Young and others, gaining some ground, finding the terms in which we can acknowledge global cultural diversity and the quasi-racial structuring of the present global system (and of resistance to it), while also focusing on the simultaneous centrality of capitalism in driving the latter system's inequities and contradictions? There are two potential problems, however. One is the danger that both Shohat's retrieval of 'neo-colonialism' and Young's 'tricontinentalism' can produce a too simplistic 'Third-Worldism', blurring, in the interests of an anti-imperialist focus, the manner in which class divisions within the Third World must themselves be challenged by progressive forces. Such certainly is the fear of another critic of post-colonial theory, Aijaz Ahmad, who has challenged, in the name of a 'One World' anti-capitalist focus, the very concept of a Third World and who might well be equally uneasy about 'tricontinentalism'.[45] But this is merely to suggest that the task is an unfinished one: to develop a sensitivity to the realities of 'difference' and of race within the global system that can be linked creatively with a class-defined analysis of the capitalist workings of that system.

There is a second ambiguity. Young's formulations tend to paper over a tension amongst the various 'tricontinental' theorists he evokes, between those who resist the 'modernity' that the global system seems to thrust upon them and others who wish to seize hold of that very modernity, albeit on their own terms, in order to transform their material condition. There is a wide gap in this respect between a Gandhi and an Amilcar Cabral, although from a reading of Young you might not know it. What, then, would be the nature of the one world we might seek to build? Surely Marxists (of both Third and First Worlds) would not wish to dismiss altogether the promise of 'modernity', even though much of the currently fashionable postmodernist/post-colonial anti-developmental literature invites them to do so. As Sutcliffe – who finds real value in the analytical turn towards 'culture' and diversity[46] – nonetheless argues: 'The criticism of the standard development model seems at times too total. Because the old destination, which in the West we experience every day, seems so unsatisfactory, all aspects of it are often rejected as a whole. Along with consumerism out goes science, technology, urbanization, modern medicine and so on. And in sometimes comes a nostalgic, conservative postdevelopmentalism'.

> In all projects, there is a danger of losing the baby when we throw out the old bath water. In this case the baby is the material, economic, productive basis of whatever satisfactory utopia can be, to echo Vincent Tucker's suggestive words, imagined and democratically negotiated among the inhabitants of earth .... One way of rephrasing all these concerns would be to say that development and globalization are experienced in practice in conditions of profound inequality of wealth and power between nations (imperialism) as well as between classes and sexes (capitalist class exploitation and patriarchy). It is necessary to distinguish which of the rejected aspects of development and globalization are inherent in these concepts and which come about because of the unequal circumstances in which we experience them. If we reject them completely because of the form in which they arrive we will always be struggling against the wrong enemy.[47]

One world out of two, three or four, and not the world of capitalist globalization: here we are clearly being drawn back to the question of universalism that was posed in the previous section. Can there be any doubt that the 'race-ing' of the actually-existing world presents a reality autonomous enough in its workings (if also one rooted in material realities) to be a focus of political work in its own right? From this point of view, 'anti-racist' consciousness-raising must surely complement anti-capitalist mobilization. But, beyond that, what is to be said about the mobilization of 'positive' racial consciousness as part and parcel of a progressive movement?

This is clearly delicate ground, and it is to the credit of writers like Paul Gilroy that they have sought to negotiate it. Gilroy is well aware of the liberatory potential of some degree of racial self-identification in helping overcome the psychological and material scars inflicted upon 'people of colour' by the malignant workings of racism.[48] He is also a fierce critic of any too easy evocation of universalism – as his crisp exposé of the racist stereotypes underlying Kant's own 'Enlightenment values' eloquently demonstrates.[49] And yet Gilroy also identifies the dangers of a black 'raciology' that, in the name of identity and 'the disabling assumption of automatic solidarity based on either blood or land', risks merely a narrow inversion of white and racist definitions of 'difference' by black 'victims' that liberates no one. Instead he urges, in the name of a 'resolutely nonracial humanism', a 'fundamental change of mood upon what used to be called "anti-racism"' by asking it 'in an explicitly utopian spirit to terminate its ambivalent relationship to the idea of "race" in the interest of a heterocultural, postanthropological and cosmopolitan yet-to-come'.[50]

Not all militants, black or white, will agree with this way of posing things. Many Marxists, for example, will wish to ground their pursuit of 'utopian' goals more firmly in terms of class struggle than Gilroy's brand of 'humanistic voluntarism' seems to promise.[51] Following Sutcliffe's distinctions, they may also want to qualify Gilroy's premise that, for victims of capitalism, 'corrective or compensatory inclusion in modernity should no longer supply the dominant theme'.[52] And yet, at the same time, race does matter: Marxists must seek to avoid all traces of smugness as we accept the assistance of Gilroy and others across the racial divide. For his attempt to 'imagine political culture beyond the colour line' does help stake out terrain upon which the continuing effort to synthesize diverse resistances to oppression can occur.

(2) Ethno-nationalism and religion

Another challenging front for Marxists is that of 'ethno-nationalism'. Attempts to define precisely the attributes, shared and distinctive, of nation/nationalism, ethnic group/ethnicity, tribe/tribalism, and other related terms have filled hundreds of combative volumes. For present analytical purposes, the term 'ethnie' may help us to link all these notions: as defined by Anthony Smith, 'ethnie' refers to a community 'which unites an emphasis upon cultural difference with the sense of an historical community. It is this sense of history and the perception of cultural uniqueness and individuality which differentiates populations from each other and which endows a given population with a definite identity, both in their eyes and in those of outsiders'.[53] It has become a commonplace to recognize that such 'communities' are imagined, and even willed into active existence by class-defined protagonists and political actors, but that does not make the often long-lived histories and cultural attributes thus evoked entirely arbitrary. Nor does it make irrelevant the variable circumstances under which a sense of difference cast in such terms can become politicized, nor make less real the effects of actions taken by people (often in large numbers) in terms of such identities, as the last several centuries of history have made perfectly apparent. Marxists have been understandably troubled by this phenomenon, as ethno-national claims have cut across class identities and consciousnesses in wildly varying ways, so much so that Tom Nairn once famously argued that 'the theory of nationalism represents Marxism's great historical failure'.[54]

Not that Marxists need apologize for their profound suspicions of ethnonationalism: an emphasis on 'internationalism as the expression of a revolutionary humanist viewpoint' and on 'socialist, democratic and emancipatory alternatives to national exclusivism, chauvinism and xenophobia' is at the core of their perspective.[55] We have, in recent months, supped full of the United States' Great Power chauvinism and Israel's own brutally self-righteous project (both being defined at the grisly intersection of racism, nationalism and religious pomposity, as these things so often are); and we have scarcely recovered from the 'ethnic cleansings' of ex-Yugoslavia and Rwanda (to cite only two of the grimmest recent cases). But, as Ronaldo Munck has asked, is this pull towards 'the tribe' always and everywhere to be interpreted by Marxists as a mere 'problem', or should it not instead be treated as 'an integral element of the human condition'[56] – as being, quintessentially, one of those 'different empirical circumstances/historical influences' referred to by Marx that affect 'the economic basis' in ways that can be 'ascertained only by analysis of the empirically given circumstances'? Thus even Lowy, citing the range of manifestations of nationalism, from Nazism to the Vietnamese revolution, is prepared to emphasize 'the contradictory role of nationalism'; to define it as being, in fact, 'one of the great paradoxes in the history of the twentieth century'.[57]

Something similar can also be said of religious identities. Perhaps most Marxists may be atheists, comfortable enough with a materialist perspective on the transcendental and the 'last things'; this is certainly true of the present writer. They may even edge towards what Bryan Turner has termed 'reductionist' approaches to understanding the realm of the religious – tending to see religion 'as an epiphenomenon, a reflection or expression of more basic and permanent features of human behaviour and society', with the further implication that 'religious beliefs are false by reference to certain scientific or positivistic criteria and that the holding of religious beliefs is irrational by reference to criteria of rational thought'.[58] But is there any need for Marxists to be so reductionist? Our very silences regarding issues of death, evil and enchantment will seem to many quite one-dimensional. Surely people can be encouraged to find their own workable 'truths', spiritual or otherwise, regarding such issues. In sum, there seems no reason for Marxists to feel they must advocate 'existential materialism' to others, and, quite apart from the unlikelihood of succeeding in doing so,[59] there are many reasons not to even attempt it.[60]

Once again, then, it is not religious belief, but the way in which religion is institutionalized, politicized or 'classed', that should concern Marxists. And here there are good reasons to be suspicious. Once again, Michael Lowy asks the most pertinent of questions: 'Is religion still, as Marx and Engels saw it in the nineteenth century, a bulwark of reaction, obscurantism and conservatism? Is it a sort of narcotic, intoxicating the masses and preventing them from clear-sighted thought and action in their own interests?' To which he replies: 'To a large extent, the answer is yes'.[61] And yet Lowy, in the very book in which he writes these words, is primarily concerned to evoke the reality of 'liberation theology' (which he terms 'liberationist Christianity') and the positive ways in which it has come to frame certain contestations for radical space in Latin America, including, most recently, in Chiapas. This reality, too, suggests that there is work to be done by Marxists and socialists in better comprehending and acting upon the world's complexities.

Note that Lowy then proceeds to document the extent to which a significant tradition within Marxist theory has actually been alert to such issues. Both Marx and Engels, he argues, acknowledged the role that religion could play both in defining political hegemony and in inspiring political protest.[62] And Lowy also praises the efforts of Rosa Luxemburg 'to rescue the social dimension of the Christian tradition for the labour movement ... [i]nstead of waging a philo-sophical battle in the name of materialism'. True, 'Luxemburg's insight, that one could fight for socialism in the name of the true values of original Christianity, was lost in [the] rather crude and somewhat intolerant "materialist" perspective'[63] prevalent in the Marxist circles of the time. But he can also cite Gramsci, Bloch and Goldmann as Marxist writers who countenanced the possibility of a creative (if contested) interface between the utopianism and faith principles in both Marxism and religious belief.[64] For Lowy, the Peruvian Marxist José Carlos Mariategui is particularly central in this respect[65] – not least in influencing directly the work of his fellow Peruvian, the founder of liberation theology, Gustavo Gutiérrez. For, as noted above, it is in the emergence of liberation theology that Lowy identifies most clearly 'the appearance of religious thinking using Marxist concepts and inspiring struggles for social liberation [and] the creation of a new religious culture, expressing the specific conditions of Latin America: dependent capitalism, massive poverty, institutionalized violence, popular religiosity'.[66]

Of course, Lowy is well aware that this is contested terrain in Latin America as elsewhere; his analysis of the virulent reaction against liberation theology by the established Catholic church in Latin America (and in Rome) and the inter-ests clustered behind it, as well as the American-sponsored offensive of evangelical Protestant missionaries on that continent, is usefully sobering, as is his discussion of tensions within the camp of the liberationists themselves (with some, not surprisingly, being much more Romantic and/or populist than Marxist). Still, it is the possibility of a progressive articulation between religion and popular-cum-class struggle that bears primary emphasis here. As Dwight Hopkins also concludes, 'religions embodied in disparate human cultures have served as the foundations for national differences, racial conflicts, class exploita-tion, and gender discrimination, on the one hand, as well as for the resolution of hostility and the achievement of full humanity for those at the bottom of all societies, on the other'.[67]

Cannot something similar be said for 'ethno-nationalism'? The initial prog-nosis is not promising, as noted above: ethno-nationalist perspectives easily lend themselves to the purposes of great power chauvinism and the rationalization of bourgeois interests for popular consumption in wealthy countries. Moreover, 'the pitfalls of national consciousness' (in Fanon's phrase[68]) are familiar in poorer countries where they often mask petty-bourgeois in-fighting over power and serve to 'divide and rule' popular forces in the interests of elites, warlords and their sponsors. But even as we move to re-pose the next obvious question – why do large numbers of ordinary people, especially in impoverished circumstances, become available for the narrowest, most combative kind of mobilization in such terms? – we must pause. For, as Munck writes, 'the critique of nationalist discourse should not blind us to the popular struggles it has [also] fostered and animated .... The struggles of the subaltern may take many forms – nationalist, ethnic, regional and religious amongst others – and a marxism that seeks to have global influence needs to understand these and not just struggle to "demystify" them and reassert a "true" class struggle'.[69]

For the Marxist there will be two key foci here, the claims of universalism/internationalism on the one hand and the diverse modalities of 'articulation' between ethnie and class (just as between religion and class) on the other. Once again, the Marxist tradition does have helpful contributions to draw on, an internationalism that has been open to a diversity of struggles (including those cast in national terms) while also emphasizing their 'indivisible interdependence', in Trotsky's phrase.[70] Munck, like Lowy, cites Otto Bauer for his rich and subtle 'conception of the nation as historical process', and they acknowledge the contributions of Gramsci as well in this regard.[71] In my own work I have found the early formulations of Laclau – written before his post-Marxist turn – to be particularly helpful.[72] For here one finds a non-reductionist model that rejects the notion that nationalism belongs to any class and insists instead (through the deployment of case-studies of 1930s' Germany and Peron's Argentina) that it can be articulated with quite diverse class projects. More work certainly needs to be done along these lines – not least in light of the argument of Ahmad, Panitch and others that, despite globalization, the nation-state will remain crucial to the struggle for radical outcomes. For if the latter point is true, the challenge to the left of imagining a nationalism that is at once inclusive (with reference to difference), expansive (with reference to internationalism) and progressive (with reference to class) will persist.

It should be apparent from our earlier argument that a similar approach can also illuminate the political economy of religion. As noted, some Marxists may wish merely to challenge religion's 'irrational' claims root and branch (as the Frelimo leadership chose to do in Mozambique) or, faced with religion's often negative articulation with class and power, merely to urge an assertive commitment to secularism and to 'tolerance' as being the Left's optimal programme. And yet even this latter approach, if pushed too smugly, can easily overlook the kind of potentially positive articulations between religion and class that many situations may actually demand and that 'liberation theology' exemplifies.[73] Certainly, making links with those who are moved by the universally humane themes in the world's religious traditions must often be the correct approach by the Left to such a powerful, virtually inevitable, form of identity. In short, religion must not be abandoned to the Right. Here we can take our lead from Dussel's sense that liberation theology 'will be practiced in other parts of the Christian world, such as Africa and Asia [beyond Latin America], and by theologians of other world religions ... This theological perspective emerges from a commitment to the poor of the South, that is, those who have been excluded from the present globalization modernizing process'.[74] It is in this spirit, too, that Radhika Coomaraswamy, writing on recent developments in Sri Lanka, refuses to elide the distinction between Buddhist humanism and Buddhist chauvinism and then argues more generally (she comments on Hinduism, Islam and Christianity in addition to Buddhism) that 'all religions have this contradiction between orthodox doctrine and the humane heterodox traditions'. Herself a secularist, she nonetheless suggests that 'to collapse humanism and orthodoxy at this historical juncture would be a major setback'.[75]

And yet we must also face the fact that it will be uphill work to claim the high ground here. Recent studies have recognized not merely the vested interests that can benefit from stoking the fires of various fundamentalisms (cf. the political economy of contemporary Iran) but also the morbid global conditions that can make ordinary people see such identities as weapons in their hands. In this sense, Dussel's phrase 'globalization modernizing process' as a touchstone for progress suggests problems. For many students of the religious Right have found the latter's main roots to lie not so much in exclusion from modernity as in resistance to it. Thus, Karen Armstrong, a particularly subtle and sensitive writer on world religions, can underscore the extent to which the fundamentalist version of religious activism is an unsurprising effect of the disruptions that 'modernity' brings, and of the fact that 'in the developing world ... modern Western culture [is experienced as] invasive, imperialistic and alien'.[76] Similarly, Mark Jurgensmeyer writes that 'in many cases, especially in the areas of the world where modernization is a synonym for Westernization, movements of religious nationalism have served as liberation struggles against what their supporters perceive to be alien ideologies and foreign powers'.[77] Faith and fundamentalism, humanism and secularism, universalism and modernity: self-evidently, the complexities evoked by engaging such expansive terms out-run the limits of these pages. What can be insisted upon here, however, is that 'modernity' must not be identified as readily with capitalism as Armstrong and Jurgensmeyer (however tacitly) both seem prone to do. Contemporary socialists must insist (once again, with Sutcliffe) that the promise of the modern can be blended with the integrity of the local and the sacred in much more meaningful and efficacious ways than the 'universalism' of capitalist modernity (Benjamin Barber's 'McWorld'[78]) can ever hope to allow.[79]

The question therefore returns: is not *socialist* advance a key piece of the puzzle of building a different, more positive kind of universalism? I would suggest that this is the way the issue should now be framed, with Marxists forced to see the fever so often attendant upon rabid ethno-nationalisms and religions-turned-fundamentalist as a reflection not merely of the victory of capitalism but also the failure, at least for the moment, of 'progressive nationalism and revolutionary socialism throughout the globe'. As Panitch elaborates the latter point, 'Opposition to capitalism and imperialism is inevitable, but the atavistic form it took on 11 September can only be understood in terms of what, on that day, tragically filled the vacuum of the 20th century Left's historic defeat'.[80] And what, in addition, can be said of the nature of capitalism's 'victory'? As Arrighi reminds us, it has primarily been a victory for the continuing hegemony of capitalism's vicious irrationality – a victory scarred by inequality and the dramatic failure to realize the 'developmentalism' that that system has so often promised.

Indeed, it is the latter failure that has sown so many of the seeds of contemporary decay, producing 'a crisis which is most clearly visible in the rise of Islamic fundamentalism in the Middle East and North Africa but is apparent in one form or another throughout the South'.[81] For capitalism's grossly uneven development across the world has produced, as Ralph Miliband once put it, 'extremely fertile terrain' for the kind of 'pathological deformations' – predatory authoritarianisms and those 'demagogues and charlatans peddling their poisonous wares ... of ethnic and religious exclusion and hatred' – that now scar the global landscape.[82] Losing confidence in socialist and other humanely modern, humanly cooperative, projects, people turn for social meaning to more ready-to-hand identities, often with fundamentalist fervour.[83] Despite this, progressives committed to class struggle should continue to view the identities we have been exploring as contingent in their socio-political implications and, in many cases, as not being in contradiction with socialist purposes. And we should continue, when possible, to invite the bearers of such identities to be partners – alongside feminists, environmentalists, anti-racists, activists around issues of sexual orientation, and the like – within a broader community-in-the-making and within a universalizing democratic project of global, anti-capitalist transformation.

★   ★   ★

This remains the bottom-line. Yes, Marxists and other socialists are themselves ensnared in discourse; but it is a discourse – a 'moralizing science', a 'point of view', an 'entry-point' – of class analysis and class struggle that is user-friendly, meaningful and important to us, and one that, politically, can be rendered important to many others. And not, I would suggest, as folded into the melting pot of diverse oppressions, diverse resistances, diverse movements, under such rubrics as 'radical democracy', but as articulated – non-reductively, non-economistically, non-Eurocentrically, but centrally – with them. For Marxist and other socialist discourses imply a crucial demand, a demand to transcend the structural and cultural limits of capitalism that is too easily lost to view, not only by postmodernists but also within the commonsensical hegemonies and glib universalisms that currently haunt us. It is a discourse that is both central to human emancipation and essentially non-cooptable by either liberalism or reformism. Of course, the demands Marxist/socialist discourse encompasses are corruptible, as history has demonstrated, but that is another, if by no means irrelevant, story. Here let us merely affirm that, at bottom, class-based politics and anti-capitalism are too central to the cause of human emancipation to be drowned in 'difference', however sensitive we must be to the latter's claims. Struggle along such lines – at once methodological and practical – must continue.

NOTES

1   For ease of argument in the present essay I have tended to elide the terms 'Marxist' and 'socialist' throughout; however, I am aware that not all socialists will consider themselves to be Marxists, even if it is likely that all Marxists will (like myself) consider themselves to be socialists.

2   E. H. Carr, *What is History?*, New York: Alfred A. Knopf, 1962, pp. 9, 26.

3   Hugh Stretton, *The Political Sciences: General principles of selection in social science and history*, London: Routledge and Kegan Paul, 1969, p. 141.

4   Gavin Kitching, *Marxism and Science: Analysis of an Obsession*, University Park: Pennsylvania State University Press, 1994, p. 168.

5   Kitching, *Marxism and Science*, pp. 169-70.

6   Lucio Colletti, 'Marxism: Science or Revolution', in Robin Blackburn, ed., *Ideology in Social Science: Readings in critical social theory*, Glasgow: Fontana/Collins, 1972.

7   'I would say', Colletti ('Marxism: Science or Revolution', p. 375) argues in this respect, 'that there are two *realities* in capitalism: the reality expressed by Marx and the reality expressed by the authors he criticizes'.

8   Stephen A. Resnick and Richard D. Wolff, *Knowledge and Class: A Marxian Critique of Political Economy*, Chicago: University of Chicago Press, 1987: 'By entry point we mean that particular concept a theory uses to enter into its formulation, its particular construction of the entities and relations that comprise the social totality'(p. 25).

9   Resnick and Wolff, *Knowledge and Class*, p. 99.

10   Ibid., p. 281. That this approach can also lead to very soft definitions of capitalism and of anti-capitalist struggle – see J. K. Gibson-Graham, *The End of Capitalism (as we knew it)*, Cambridge: Blackwell, 1996 – is worth noting but does not undermine its merits.

11   The quotations are from Laclau's contribution 'Structure, History and the Political' in Judith Butler, Ernesto Laclau and Slavoj Zizek, *Contingency, Hegemony, Universality: Contemporary Dialogues on the Left*, London: Verso, 2000, pp. 203, 206.

12   Equally important to our purposes here is Zizek's further elaboration of this point (in Butler, Laclau and Zizek, *Contingency, Hegemony, Universality*, p. 321): 'The much-praised postmodern "proliferation of new political subjectivities," the demise of every "essentialist" fixation, the assertion of full contingency, occur against the background of a certain silent

renunciation and acceptance: the renunciation of the idea of a global change in the fundamental relations in our society (who still seriously questions capitalism, state and political democracy?) and, consequently, the acceptance of the liberal democratic capitalist framework which remains the same, the unquestioned background, in all the dynamic proliferation of the multitude of new subjectivities'.

13 Kitching, *Marxism and Science*, p. 68. As Kitching further explains, "The reason is that Marx was, if nothing else, an extremely intelligent man, and economic reductionism is an extremely silly, not to say incoherent, idea in which to believe."

14 Eric Olin Wright, 'Giddens' Critique of Marxism', *New Left Review*, 138 (March-April), 1983, p. 24.

15 See, for example, Nicos Mouzelis ('Sociology of Development: Reflections on the Present Crisis', *Sociology*, 22(1) (February), 1988) who argues that 'the neglect of the political ... is the Achilles heel of all development theory', including Marxist theories of development, but also finds in Marxism's potential openness to embracing the tension between 'systemic and agency terms' the key to its ability to overcome any collapse into economistic reductionism (pp. 39-40).

16 Karl Marx, *Capital, vol. 3: The Process of Capitalist Production as a Whole*, New York: International Publishers, 1964, pp. 790-1.

17 Himani Bannerji, *Thinking Through: Essays on Feminism, Marxism and Anti-Racism*, Toronto: Women's Press, 1995, pp. 30-1. In a related manner, Joan Acker seeks a 'fluid view of class as an ongoing production of gender and racially formed economic relations, rooted in family and communities as well as in the global organization of capital', thereby helping to overcome the way in which 'women's movements and anticolonialism and antislavery struggles' have often been 'divorced from class struggle'. See her 'Rewriting Class, Race and Gender: Problems in Feminist Rethinking', in Myra Marx Ferree, Judith Lorberg and Beth B. Hass, eds., *Revisioning Gender*, Thousand Oaks, Calif.: Sage Publishers, 1999, pp. 62-3.

18 Katha Pollitt, 'Race and Gender and Class, Oh My!' in her *Subject to Debate: Sense and Dissents on Women. Politics and Culture*, New York: Random House, 2001, pp. 218-19. As she continues: 'Everybody sees that now – even John Sweeney talks about gay partnership benefits as a working-class issue – except for a handful of old New Leftists, journalists and mini-pundits who practice the identity politics that dare not speak its name'.

19 Lynne Segal, 'Whose Left? Socialism, Feminism and the Future', *New Left Review*, 185 (January-February), 1991, pp. 87, 90. Segal is here critiquing, in particular, those former socialist-feminists like Zillah Eisenstein who had begun to abandon the link between socialism and feminism in favour (in Segal's summary) of a feminist politics that seeks to 'unite all women ... in their specific identity as women'.

20 Nancy Fraser, 'From Redistribution to Recognition? Dilemmas of Justice

in a "Post-Socialist" Age', *New Left Review*, 212 (July–August), 1995, p. 68.

21 Rosemary Hennessy and Chrys Ingraham, 'Introduction: Reclaiming Anticapitalist Feminism' in their edited volume *Materialist Feminism*, New York and London: Routledge, 1997; such authors regret that crucial concepts like 'social structure, production, patriarchy and class ... have been dismissed by post-modernist feminists [and by 'a flourishing postmodern cultural politics'] in favour of analyses that ... focus almost exclusively on ideological, state, or cultural practices, anchor meaning in the body and its pleasures, or understand social primarily in terms of the struggle over representation' (p. 5).

22 See, for example, Carol A. Stabile, 'Feminism and the Ends of Postmodernism' and Martha Gimenez, 'The Oppression of Women: A Structuralist Marxist View' (p. 82), in Hennessy and Ingraham, eds., *Materialist Feminism*.

23 Hennessy and Ingraham, eds., *Materialist Feminism*, p. 11.

24 Rosemary Hennessy, *Profit and Pleasure: Sexual Identities in Late Capitalism*, New York and London: Routledge, 2000, p. 232.

25 Thus Bob Sutcliffe ('Development after Ecology', in V. Bhaskar and A. Glyn, eds., *The North, the South and the Environment: Ecological Constraints and the Global Economy*, London: St. Martin's Press, 1995) demonstrates the necessity of developing a progressive politics that is sensitive simultaneously to ecology and to the imperatives of global redistribution: 'The only hope for a radical redistribution towards the future is a radical redistribution away from the rich in the present. If greater equality in the present is one of the traditional concerns of red politics, greater equality between generations is an essential characteristic of the new green politics. But not all reds are yet green; nor do all greens look as if they will become reds. The future of sustainable human development depends on a more thorough mixing of the colours' (p. 255).

26 Sabina Lovibond, 'Feminism and Postmodernism', *New Left Review*, 178 (November–December), 1989, p. 28.

27 Oliver Cox, *Caste, Class and Race*, New York: Monthly Review, 1948.

28 Mark Cocker, *Rivers of Blood, Rivers of Gold: Europe's Conquest of Indigenous Peoples*, New York: Grove Press, 1998, p. xiii. See also Sven Lindqvist, *'Exterminate All the Brutes': One Man's Odyssey into the Heart of Darkness and the Origins of European Genocide*, New York: The New Press, 1996.

29 Richard Drinnon, *Facing West: The Metaphysics of Indian-Hating and Empire Building*, New York: New American Library, 1980, p. xvi–xviii.

30 Frank Furedi, *The Silent War: Imperialism and the Changing Perception of Race*, New Brunswick: Rutgers University Press, 1998, p. 240.

31 Robert D. Kaplan, 'The Coming Anarchy', *The Atlantic Monthly*, February, 1994. This seems another paradigmatic example of the 'Western Us' being juxtaposed to 'The Others' that Howard Zinn has critiqued so effectively in a recent commentary on the bombing of Afghanistan. See his 'The Others',

The Nation, 11 February 2002.

32 Note, too, the link made by Hannah Arendt (in her *The Origins of Totalitarianism*, New York: Harcourt Brace, 1951) between the racisms of imperial expansion and that of genocidal anti-semitism (the latter being a racism with a unique historicity of its own, of course) in the German case.

33 Edna Bonacich, 'Class Approaches to Ethnicity and Race', *The Insurgent Sociologist* (Special Issue on 'Race and Class in Twentieth Century Capitalist Development'), 10(2) (Fall), 1980.

34 David Morley and Kuan-Hsing Chen, eds., *Stuart Hall: Critical Dialogues in Cultural Studies*, London/New York: Routledge, 1996, and Paul Gilroy, Lawrence Grossberg and Angela McRobbie, eds., *Without Guarantees: In Honour of Stuart Hall*, London: Verso, 2000.

35 See my 'Introduction: The Revolutionary Prospect', to John S. Saul and Stephen Gelb, *The Crisis in South Africa*, Revised Edition, New York and London: Monthly Review Press and Zed, 1986; Harold Wolpe, *Race, Class and the Apartheid State*, London: James Currey, 1988; and John S. Saul, 'Cry for the Beloved Country: The Post-Apartheid Denouement', *Monthly Review*, 52(8) (January), 2001.

36 John Gabriel and Gideon Ben-Tovim, 'Marxism and the concept of racism', *Economy and Society*, 7(2) (May), 1978, p. 147.

37 Robert Biel, *The New Imperialism: Crisis and Contradiction in North/South Relations*, London: Zed Books, 2000, pp. 131-2.

38 Ankie Hoogevelt, *Globalization and the Postcolonial World: The New Political Economy of Development*, Second Edition, Houndmills: Palgrave, 2001, p. xiv.

39 Giovanni Arrighi, 'World Income Inequalities and the Future of Socialism', *New Left Review*, 189 (September/October), 1991, and Arrighi and Beverley Silver, 'Industrial Convergence, Globalization and the Persistence of the North-South Divide', paper presented at the American Sociological Association Meetings, Anaheim, CA, 18-21 August 2001.

40 Salih Booker and William Minter, 'Global Apartheid', *The Nation*, 9 July 2001.

41 Ella Shohat, 'Notes on the "Post-Colonial"', *Social Text*, 31/32, 1992, p. 111. See also, in the same issue of *Social Text*, Anne McClintock, 'The Angel of Progress: Pitfalls of the Term "Post-Colonial"'.

42 Shohat, 'Notes on the "Post-Colonial"', p. 110.

43 Robert Young, *Postcolonialism: An Historical Introduction*, Oxford: Blackwell, 2001, p. 57.

44 Arif Dirlik, 'The Postcolonial Aura: Third World Criticism in the Age of Global Capitalism', in Anne McClintock, Aamir Mufti and Ella Shohat, eds., *Dangerous Liaisons: Gender, Nation and Postcolonial Perspectives*, Minneapolis: University of Minnesota Press, 1997, p. 502.

45 Aijaz Ahmad, *In Theory: Classes, Nations, Literatures*, London: Verso, 1992, esp. ch. 8, 'Three Worlds Theory: End of a Debate'.

46 Sutcliffe seeks, however, to incorporate these variables 'in a way that allows imperialism once again to become an important theoretical concept'. See his 'The Place of Development in Theories of Imperialism and Globalization', in Ronaldo Munck and Denis O'Hearn, eds., *Critical Development Theory: contributions to a new paradigm*, London and New York: Zed, 1999, p. 144.

47 Sutcliffe, The Place of Development', pp. 150-2.

48 See also on this subject Mahmoud Dhaouadi, 'Capitalism, Global Humane Development and the Other Underdevelopment', in Leslie Sklair, ed., *Capitalism and Development*, London: Routledge, 1994.

49 Paul Gilroy, *Against Race: Imagining Political Culture Beyond the Colour Line*, Cambridge, Mass.: The Belknap Press of Harvard University Press, 2000, pp. 58-61.

50 Gilroy, *Against Race*, p. 334.

51 On the pitfalls of "humanistic voluntarism," see Gabriel and Ben-Tovim, 'Marxism and the concept of racism'.

52 Gilroy, *Against Race*, p. 335.

53 As cited in Liz Fawcett, *Religion, Ethnicity and Social Change*, Houndmills: MacMillan Press, 2000, p. 3.

54 Tom Nairn, 'The Modern Janus', *New Left Review*, 94 (November-December), 1975, p. 3.

55 Michael Lowy, *Fatherland or Mother Earth? Essays on the National Question*, London: Pluto Press, 1998, pp. 2, 4.

56 Ronaldo Munck, *Marxism @ 2000: Late Marxist Perspectives*, Houndmills: MacMillan Press, 2000, esp. ch. 7, 'Difficult Dialogue: Marxism and Nation', p. 133.

57 Michael Lowy, *Fatherland or Mother Earth*

58 Bryan Turner, *Religion and Social Theory: A Materialist Perspective*, London: Heinemann Educational Books, 1983, p. 282.

59 As Hopkins writes (in the introduction to Dwight N. Hopkins, et. al., eds., *Religions/Globalizations: Theories and Cases*, Durham: Duke University Press, 2001), 'For the majority of cultures around the world, religion thoroughly permeates and decisively affects the everyday rituals of survival and hope. Reflected in diverse spiritual customs, sacred symbols and indigenous worship styles, global religions are permanent constituents of human life'.

60 I say this with some feeling in light of my own experience living and working in Mozambique in the 1970s and 1980s when the ruling liberation movement, Frelimo, paid what seems in retrospect to have been an unnecessarily heavy price in terms of popular legitimacy for eliding a struggle against the overbearing institutional presence of the Catholic Church with an attack on religious sensibility per se.

61 Michael Lowy, *The War of Gods: Religion and Politics in Latin America*, London: Verso, 1996, p. 4.

62 Lowy (*The War of Gods*, pp. 6-10) reminds us, for example, of Marx's pithy